AQUATIC TOXICOLOGY

Volume

13

in the Wiley Series in

Advances in Environmental Science and Technology

JEROME O. NRIAGU, Series Editor

AQUATIC TOXICOLOGY

Edited by

Jerome O. Nriagu

National Water Research Institute
Burlington, Ontario, Canada

A WILEY-INTERSCIENCE PUBLICATION

JOHN WILEY & SONS

New York • Chichester • Brisbane • Toronto • Singapore

Library of Congress Cataloging in Publication Data:

Main entry under title:

Aquatic toxicology.

   (Advances in environmental science and technology;
v. 13)
   "A Wiley-Interscience publication."
   Includes index.
   1. Water—Pollution—Environmental aspects.
2. Water—Pollution—Toxicology.   I. Nriagu, Jerome O.
II. Series.

TD180.A38 vol. 13   [QH545.W3]   628s [574.5′263]   83-5823
ISBN 0-471-88901-6

Printed in the United States of America

10 9 8 7 6 5 4 3 2 1

CONTRIBUTORS

BABICH, H., Laboratory of Microbial Ecology, Department of Biology, New York University, New York

BEST, JAY BOYD, Department of Physiology and Biophysics, Colorado State University, Fort Collins

BORGMANN, UWE, Canada Centre for Inland Waters, Burlington, Ontario

BOUDOU, A., Animal Ecology and Ecophysiology Laboratory, Bordeaux 1 University, Talence, France

BROWN, S. B., Freshwater Institute, Winnipeg, Manitoba

CHAU, Y. K., Canada Centre for Inland Waters, Burlington, Ontario

COUTURE, P., Institut National de la Recherche Scientifique, Université du Québec, Sainte-Foy, Quebec

DESMAZES, J. P., Research Center Paul Pascal-CNRS, Bordeaux 1 University, Talence, France

EVANS, R. E., Freshwater Institute, Winnipeg, Manitoba

GEORGESCAULD, D., Research Center Paul Pascal-CNRS, Bordeaux 1 University, Talence, France

GREENHALGH, ROY, Chemistry and Biology Research Institute, Agriculture Canada, Ottawa, Ontario

HARA, TOSHIAKI J., Freshwater Institute, Winnipeg, Manitoba

HAYA, K., Fisheries and Environmental Sciences, Department of Fisheries and Oceans, Biological Station, St. Andrews, New Brunswick

HECKMAN, CHARLES W., Institut fur Hydrobiologie und Fischereiwissenschaft, Universitat Hamburg, Hamburg, Federal Republic of Germany

JOUBERT, GERALD, Environnement Quebec, Complexe Scientifique, Sainte-Foy, Quebec

KICENIUK, J. W., Research and Resources Services, Department of Fisheries and Oceans, St. John's, Newfoundland

KHAN, R. A., Department of Biology and Marine Sciences Research Laboratory, Memorial University of Newfoundland, St. John's

KOCAN, RICHARD M., School of Fisheries, University of Washington, Seattle

v

LANDOLT, MARSHA L., School of Fisheries, University of Washington, Seattle

LEE, KENNETH, Ocean Chemistry Division, Institute of Ocean Sciences, Sidney, British Columbia

MOODY, R. P., Department of Biology, University of Ottawa, Ontario

MORITA, MICHIO, Department of Physiology and Biophysics, Colorado State University, Fort Collins

NIIMI, A. J., Canada Centre for Inland Waters, Burlington, Ontario

PATEL, D., Canada Centre for Inland Waters, Burlington, Ontario

RIBEYRE, F., Animal Ecology and Ecophysiology Laboratory, Bordeaux 1 University, Talence, France

SCHULTZ, T. WAYNE, Department of Animal Science, College of Veterinary Medicine, University of Tennessee, Knoxville

STOTZKY, G., Laboratory of Microbial Ecology, Department of Biology, New York University, New York

VAN COILLIE, R., Eco-Research Inc., Pointe Claire, Quebec

VISSER, S. A., Département des Sols, Université Laval, Cite Universitaire, Quebec

WAIWOOD, B. A., Fisheries and Environmental Sciences, Department of Fisheries and Oceans, Biological Station, St. Andrews, New Brunswick

WEINBERGER, PEARL, Department of Biology, University of Ottawa, Ottawa, Ontario

WEIS, JUDITH S., Department of Zoology and Physiology, Rutgers University, Newark, New Jersey

WEIS, PEDDRICK, Department of Anatomy, UMDNJ-New Jersey Medical School, Newark, New Jersey

WONG, P. T. S., Canada Centre for Inland Waters, Burlington, Ontario

INTRODUCTION TO THE SERIES

The deterioration of environmental quality, which began when humankind first congregated into villages, has existed as a serious problem since the industrial revolution. In the second half of the twentieth century, under the ever-increasing impacts of exponentially growing population and of industrializing society, environmental contamination of the air, water, soil, and food has become a threat to the continued existence of many plant and animal communities of various ecosystems and may ultimately threaten the very survival of the human race. Understandably, many scientific, industrial, and governmental communities have recently committed large resources of money and humanpower to the problems of environmental pollution and pollution abatement by effective control measures.

Advances in Environmental Sciences and Technology deals with creative reviews and critical assessments of all studies pertaining to the quality of the environment and to the technology of its conservation. The volumes published in the series are expected to serve several objectives: (1) stimulate interdisciplinary cooperation and understanding among the environmental scientists; (2) provide scientists with a periodic overview of environmental developments that are of general concern or of relevance to their own work or interests; (3) provide the graduate student with a critical assessment of past accomplishment that may help stimulate interest in career opportunities in this vital area; and (4) provide the research manager and the legislative or administrative official with an assured awareness of newly developing research work on the critical pollutants and with the background information important to their responsibility.

As the skills and techniques of many scientific disciplines are brought to bear on the fundamental and applied aspects of the environmental issues, there is a heightened need to draw together the numerous threads and to present a coherent picture of the various research endeavors. This need and the recent tremendous growth in the field of environmental studies have clearly made some editorial adjustments necessary. Apart from the changes in style and format, each future volume in the series will focus on one particular theme or timely topic, starting with Volume 12. The author(s) of each pertinent section will be expected to critically review the literature and the most important recent developments in the particular field; to critically evaluate new concepts, methods, and data; and to focus attention on important unresolved or controversial questions and on probable future trends. Monographs embodying the results of unusually extensive and well-rounded investigations will also be published in the series. The net result of the new editorial policy should be more integrative and comprehensive volumes on key environmental issues and pollutants. Indeed, the development of realistic standards of environmental quality for many pollutants often entails such a holistic treatment.

JEROME O. NRIAGU, Series Editor

PREFACE

Environmental Toxicology has become a full-fledged scientific discipline. Research devoted to aquatic toxicology has certainly kept pace with the mushrooming activity in the other fields in the new discipline. The rapid development necessitates a periodic review of the knowledge that has been gained on particular topics with emphasis on areas that need further research. This is an objective of the present volume.

This volume deals with the toxicity of many inorganic and organic contaminants to the aquatic biota. It assesses the response at community, species, tissue, cellular, and subcellular levels to particular toxicants and covers the mechanisms of uptake, metabolism, and excretion of many toxic pollutants. Changes induced by toxicants in the biochemical and physiological systems of organisms receive special attention. Recent developments in the methodology used in detecting perturbations in life processes of the aquatic biota are also covered.

The volume should be of interest to professionals and graduate students in marine biology, limnology, ecology and systematics, chemical oceanography, water management, and toxicology.

Any success of this volume reflects the combined efforts of our distinguished group of contributors. We thank the editorial staff at Wiley for invaluable editorial assistance.

JEROME O. NRIAGU

Burlington, Ontario, Canada
1983

CONTENTS

    Water Environment   437

    Pearl Weinberger and Roy Greenhalgh

16. The Use of Algal Batch and Continuous Culture
    Techniques in Metal Toxicity Study   449

    P. T. S. Wong, Y. K. Chau, and D. Patel

17. Detailed Method for Quantitative Toxicity Measurements
    Using the Green Algae *Selenastrum capricornutum*   467

    Gerald Joubert

18. Use of Algae in Aquatic Ecotoxicology   487

    R. Van Coillie, P. Couture, and S. A. Visser

19. Algal Fluorometric Determination of the Potential
    Phytotoxicity of Environmental Pollutants   503

    R. P. Moody, P. Weinberger, and R. Greenhalgh

    Index   513

AQUATIC TOXICOLOGY

1

INFLUENCE OF CHEMICAL SPECIATION ON THE TOXICITY OF HEAVY METALS TO THE MICROBIOTA

H. Babich and G. Stotzky

Laboratory of Microbial Ecology
Department of Biology
New York University
New York, New York

1

1. INTRODUCTION

Microbes, both in aquatic and terrestrial ecosystems, are the key components in the biogeochemical cycling of elements, serve as the basis for all food chains and food webs, are involved in the incorporation of energy by chemo- and photosynthesis, and are the main agents of waste reduction and of maintaining the fertility of aquatic and terrestrial ecosystems. Elimination of a specific metabolic group, such as cellulose decomposers, denitrifiers, nitrogen fixers, or chemoautotrophs, may adversely influence the overall ecology of the affected ecosystem. Consequently, clarifying the responses of the microbiota to pollutants and defining the biotic and abiotic physicochemical factors of the environment that determine microbial response to pollutant stress is of the utmost importance (Babich and Stotzky, 1974, 1980a,b; Stotzky and Babich, 1980).

Increased industrialization and domestic activities have accelerated the biogeochemical cycling of many elements, including heavy metals, causing increased deposition of elevated amounts of these metals into natural ecosystems, both aquatic and terrestrial. This chapter discusses the influence of cadmium (Cd), chromium (Cr), copper (Cu), lead (Pb), manganese (Mn), mercury (Hg), nickel (Ni), and zinc (Zn) on the microbiota, primarily from an environmental perspective rather than from a toxicological or biochemical viewpoint. Specifically, this chapter focuses on the influence of abiotic environmental factors that potentiate or attenuate the toxicity of heavy metals to the microbiota.

2. EVALUATING METAL–MICROBE INTERACTIONS

The microbiota, as has been extensively demonstrated with the macrobiota, is sensitive to metal pollutants. This sensitivity to metals has been demonstrated at various levels of physiological and experimental complexity:

2.1. Effects on Growth and Survival

A concentration of 4×10^{-4} M Ni extended the lag phase of growth of the marine bacterium *Arthrobacter marinus* from 3 to 70 hr (Cobet et al., 1970); 100 ppm (i.e., mg/liter) Ni reduced the growth rates of the estuarine/marine fungi, *Pleospora vagens, Dreschlera halodes, Asteromyces cruciatus,* and *Dendryphiella salina,* in nutrient-enriched seawater (Babich and Stotzky, 1983a); growth of the diatoms, *Skeletonema costatus, Thalassiosira pseudonana,* and *Phaeodactylum tricornutum,* were reduced initially in seawater amended with 50, 250, and 25,000 ppb (i.e., µg/liter) Zn, respectively (Jensen et al., 1974); 0.15–0.20 ppm Hg completely inhibited growth of the marine diatom, *Nitzschia acicularis* (Mora and Fabregas, 1980); 1.6 ppm Cr(VI) reduced growth of the alga, *Chlorella variegatus,* and completely inhibited that of the alga *Lepocinclis steinii* (Hervey, 1949); and 1 ppm Ni inhibited sporulation, but not mycelial proliferation, of the terrestrial fungi, *Aspergillus niger, Aspergillus giganteus, Penicillium vermiculatum,* and *Gliocladium* sp. (Babich et al., 1982a).

2.2. Effects on Morphology

The freshwater diatom, *Tabellaria flocculosa,* which normally forms zigzag chains of cells, formed a straight configuration when exposed to 0.001 ppm Cd (Adshead-Simonsen et al., 1981); the green alga, *Ankistrodesmus braunii,* produced multinucleate giant cells with thickened walls when grown in the presence of 10^{-4} M Cu (Massalski et al., 1981); and 50 ppm Zn inhibited trap formation by the nematode-trapping fungus, *Monacrosporium eudermatum* (Rosenzweig and Pramer, 1980).

2.3. Effects on Biochemical Activities

2.3.1. Pure Culture Studies

One ppm Cd inhibited photosynthesis and 2 ppm Cd inhibited nitrogen fixation by the cyanobacterium, *Anabaena cylindrica* (Delmotte, 1980); 0.05 M Ni reduced the rate of photosynthesis by the alga, *Chlorella vulgaris* (Greenfield, 1942); 0.005 ppm Zn inhibited nitrogen fixation by the cyanobacterium, *Anabaena spiroides* (Kostyaev, 1980); 15–18 ppm Pb reduced photosynthesis by the alga, *Chlamydomonas reinhardtii* (Malanchuk and Gruendling, 1973); and 5 ppb Cu decreased photosynthesis by the marine dinoflagellate, *Scrippsiella faeroense* (Saifullah, 1978).

2.3.2. Mixed Population Studies

Copper, at 1–2.5 ppb, or Zn, at 15 ppb, inhibited photosynthesis of a coastal marine phytoplankton community (Davies and Sleep, 1979, 1980); photosynthesis of a brackish water phytoplankton community was reduced by 0.1 ppm Cd or 1 ppm Pb (Pietilainen, 1975); addition of 5 ppb Cu to lake water reduced nitrogen fixation by the cyanobacterium populations (Horne and Goldman, 1974); 10 ppm Hg inhibited nitrification in surface waters from the Chesapeake Bay (Mills and Colwell, 1977); carbon mineralization of glucose by a heterotrophic freshwater microbiota was reduced by 0.1 ppm Cd, Cr(III), Hg, Pb, or Zn (Albright et al., 1972); and microbial decomposition of leaf litter was reduced in a freshwater stream amended with 5 or 10 ppb Cd (Giesy, 1978).

2.4.   Effects on Population Dynamics

Addition of Cu to a freshwater reservoir to treat a bloom of *Ceratium hirundinella* reduced the populations of the diatoms, which were replaced as the dominant population by the green algae, *Nannochloris* sp. and *Ourococcus* sp. (McKnight, 1981); addition of 0.002–1 ppm Ni to a freshwater stream decreased the diversity and abundance of the indigenous diatoms but increased that of cyanobacteria and green algae (Patrick et al., 1975); addition of 5–20 ppm Cu to a marine phytoplankton community reduced the species diversity and numbers of centric diatoms and resulted in a predominance of dinoflagellates (Sanders et al., 1981); and reductions in bacterial diversity occurred in freshwaters and brackish waters amended with either 2 ppm Cu or 0.04 ppm Hg or with a combination of both metals (Singleton and Guthrie, 1977).

2.5.   Effects on Food Chains and Food Webs

Because microbes serve as the bases of all food chains and food webs, accumulation of heavy metals by the microbiota may adversely affect the entire ecosystem (Trollope and Evans, 1976; Canterford et al., 1978). A marked reduction in the viability of the freshwater shrimp, *Gammarus pulex*, occurred when fed *Pythium* sp., an aquatic fungus, contaminated with Cd (Duddridge and Wainwright, 1980); poor growth and high mortalities were noted with larvae of the marine oyster, *Crassostrea virginica*, when fed *Isochrysis galbana*, an alga, that was contaminated with Cu or Cd (Wikfors and Ukeles, 1982); and elevated levels of metals were noted in tubificids fed freshwater bacteria contaminated with metals (Patrick and Loutit, 1976).

2.6.   Metal Speciation

Another aspect of heavy metal toxicity to the microbiota, as well as to the macrobiota, is the influence of abiotic environmental factors on metal speci-

Table 1. Chemical Forms (i.e., Speciation) of Zinc in the Environment[a]

Chemical Form	Examples	Approximate Diameter (nm)
Simple hydrated metal ion	$Zn(H_2O)_6^{2+}$	0.8
Simple inorganic complexes	$Zn(H_2O)_5Cl^+$; $Zn(H_2O)_5OH^+$	1
Stable inorganic complexes	ZnS; $ZnCO_3$; Zn_2SiO_4	1–2
Simple organic complexes	Zn citrate; Zn glycinate	1–2
Stable organic complexes	Zn humate; Zn cysteinate	2–4
Adsorbed on inorganic colloids	Zn^{2+}–Fe_2O_3; Zn^{2+}–SiO_2; Zn^{2+}–clay	10–500
Adsorbed on organic colloids	Zn^{2+}–humic acid; Zn^{2+}–organic detritus	10–500
Particulate matter	Retained by 0.45-μm filter	>450

[a]Adapted from Florence, 1980.

5

ation. The term "metal speciation" is used herein in its broadest sense to refer to all possible chemical forms of a metal that may occur in different environments. The variety of possible speciation forms of a representative metal (i.e., Zn) is presented in Table 1. The specific speciation form of a metal that is present in an environment is extremely important because the toxicity of different speciation forms varies (Babich and Stotzky, 1980a and b; Stotzky and Babich, 1980; Babich et al., 1981). For example, in hard freshwater at pH 8, Cd occurs predominantly as a precipitate of $CdCO_3$ that is unavailable for uptake by the microbiota, whereas in seawater at pH 8, Cd is almost totally dissolved and occurs as Cd–Cl complexes (Sibley and Morgan, 1975) that are available for uptake by the microbiota.

This chapter discusses primarily the influence of abiotic factors and metal–metal interactions on the toxicity of heavy metals to the microbiota. The abiotic factors that are discussed include pH, E_h, inorganic ionic composition, clay minerals, hydrous metal oxides, organics, temperature, and hydrostatic pressure.

3. ENVIRONMENTAL FACTORS

3.1. pH

Numerous studies have demonstrated that pH influences the toxicity of heavy metals to the microbiota (i.e., metal toxicity to the microbiota either increases or decreases as the pH is altered). However, many of the data are contradictory and mechanisms for this effect have not been clearly defined, because the pH affects several aspects of the cell–metal system. (a) pH affects the metabolic state of the cell, and a specific biotic response to a pH–metal interaction may simply reflect the altered physiology of the cell. (b) pH affects the chemical speciation of some metals. For example, in seawater of pH 8.5, Pb occurs as $PbOH^+$, Zn as $Zn(OH)_2$ (Hahne and Kroontje, 1973), Cu as $Cu(OH)_2$ (Zirino and Yamamoto, 1972), and Ni as Ni^{2+} (Richter and Theis, 1980); whereas in acidic lake waters, all these metals may occur as divalent cations. The different inorganic speciation forms of the same metal exert differing toxicities. (c) pH affects the extent of complexing of metals to the organic constituents of the medium, and metals complexed with organics are, in general, less toxic than the free forms of the same metals (Babich and Stotzky, 1980b).

Studies on pH–Cd interactions have yielded a variety of biotic responses. The toxicity of Cd to the bacteria, *Alcaligenes faecalis* and *Bacillus cereus*, and to the fungi, *Trichoderma viride* and *Aspergillus niger*, was potentiated when the pH of the medium was increased from 7 to 8 and 9. With the bacterium, *Agrobacterium tumefaciens*, the actinomycete, *Nocardia paraffinae*, and the fungus, *Rhizopus stolonifer*, this potentiation of Cd toxicity was initially evident when the pH of the medium was increased from 8 to 9. However, the toxicity of Cd to the actinomycete, *Streptomyces olivaceus*,was independent of changes in pH over the range from 5 to 9 (Babich and Stotzky, 1977a). Similarly, the toxicity of Cd to growth of *Aspergillus niger* was increased when a naturally acidic soil (pH 5.0) was adjusted to pH 7.2 (Babich and Stotzky, 1977b). This potentiation of Cd toxicity in alkaline media was attributed either to the formation of $CdOH^+$, which as a monovalent cation would presumably penetrate biological membranes more readily than divalent Cd^{2+}, or to the reduced competition between protons (H^+) and Cd^{2+} or $CdOH^+$ for sites on the cell, because when the pH is increased, less H^+ are available to compete successfully with Cd^{2+} or $CdOH^+$ for adsorption sites on the cell surfaces (Babich and Stotzky, 1980b). Similarly, increasing the pH from 6 to 8 increased the toxicity of Cd to the bacteria, *Micrococcus luteus, Staphylococcus aureus, Clostridium perfringens, Escherichia coli*, and *Pseudomonas aeruginosa*; however, there was no distinctive effect of pH on the toxicity of Cd to the bacteria, *Streptococcus bovis* and *Bacillus subtilis* (Korkeala and Pekkanen, 1978). Cadmium was more toxic to growth of the alga, *Chlorella pyrenoidosa*, at pH 8.3 than at pH 7.3 or 6.6, with enhanced toxicity at pH 8.3 being correlated with increased uptake of Cd (Gipps and Coller, 1980). Increasing the pH from 3 to 7 increased the uptake of Cd by living or heat-killed cells of the alga, *Chlorella regularis* (Sakaguchi et al., 1979).

Conversely, Cd toxicity has also been shown to decrease as the pH is increased. Cadmium was more toxic to growth of *Chlorella pyrenoidosa* at pH 7 than at pH 8, with enhanced toxicity being correlated with the greater uptake of Cd at pH 7 than at pH 8 (Hart and Scaife, 1977). Similarly, the toxicity of Cd to growth of the cyanobacterium, *Nostoc calcicola*, decreased as the pH was increased from 6 to 9 (Singh and Pandey, 1981).

This lack of uniformity in the biotic response to Cd as affected by changes in pH may be related, in part, to the composition of the different media. The various organic constituents commonly incorporated into microbiological media exhibit differential affinities for Cd (e.g., the order of the binding of Cd to organic substrates followed the sequence: casamino acids>proteose peptone>tryptone≫yeast extract, with peptone not binding any Cd), as well as for other metals (Ramamoorthy and Kushner, 1975); and the binding of metals to organics is pH dependent (Farrah and Pickering, 1978). Furthermore, recent studies have shown that the toxicity of Cd as affected by pH is influenced by the composition of the test medium. The freshwater fungi, *Saprolegnia* sp. and *Achyla* sp., were exposed to 25 ppm Cd in a medium containing either 2.0% glucose and 1.0% neopeptone (medium 1) or 1.0% glucose, 0.25% peptone, 0.1% NH_4NO_3, 0.05% $MgSO_4 \cdot 7H_2O$, 0.02% $CaCl_2 \cdot 2H_2O$, and 0.02% yeast extract (medium 2). For the *Saprolegnia* sp., increasing the pH from 5.5 to 7.5 did not affect the toxicity of Cd in either medium; however, from pH 7.5 to 9.5, Cd toxicity was reduced in medium 1 but was potentiated in medium 2. Similarly, for the *Achyla* sp., no differences in Cd toxicity occurred in either medium over the pH range from 5.5 to

8.5, but from pH 8.5 to 9.5, the toxicity of Cd was decreased in medium 1 and enhanced in medium 2 (Fig. 1) (Babich and Stotzky, unpublished).

The toxicity of Zn to *Saprolegnia* sp. and to *Achyla* sp. increased as the pH was increased from 5.5 to 7.5, but thereafter, further increasing the pH to 9.5 produced no additional potentiation of Zn toxicity (Fig. 2) (Babich and Stotzky, unpublished). Similarly, increasing the pH from 4 to 8 increased the toxicity of Zn to Zn-resistant and Zn-sensitive populations of the freshwater alga, *Hormidium rivulare* (Hargreaves and Whitton, 1977; Say and Whitton, 1977). Increasing the pH from 6.5 to 8 increased the toxicity of Zn to Zn-tolerant strains of the cyanobacterium, *Anacystis nidulans*, but decreased the toxicity of Zn to Zn-sensitive strains (Shehata and Whitton, 1982). Progressively increasing the pH from 4 to 8 decreased the toxicity of Zn to growth of *Chlorella vulgaris* (Rai et al., 1981). Increasing the pH from 7.1 to 7.6 decreased the toxicity of Zn to populations of the alga, *Stigeoclonium tenue*, isolated from a stream carrying a low level (i.e., 0.012 mg/liter) of Zn but had no effect on the toxicity of Zn to similar populations isolated from a stream with a high level (i.e., 2.39 mg/liter) of Zn (Harding and Whitton, 1977).

Increasing the pH of the medium from acidic to alkaline levels reduced the toxicity of Pb to the alga, *Selenastrum capricornutum* (Monahan, 1976), and to *Aspergillus niger, Trichoderma viride* (Babich and Stotzky, 1979a), *Achyla* sp., and *Saprolegnia* sp. (Fig. 2) (Babich and Stotzky, unpublished).

Although increasing the pH from acidic to alkaline levels had no effect on the toxicity of Hg to *Achyla* sp. and *Saprolegnia* sp. (Fig. 2) (Babich and Stotzky, unpublished), the toxicity of Hg to spores and mycelia of *Fusarium lycopersici* (Horsfall, 1956) and to *Chlorella vulgaris* (Rai et al., 1981) was enhanced as the medium was made more alkaline. The toxicity of methyl Hg$^+$ to growth of *Chlorella vulgaris* was reduced as the pH was increased from 4 to 8 (Rai et al., 1981).

There was no common relationship between increasing the pH from 5.5 to 8.5 and the toxicity of Mn to fungi. For example, increasing the pH increased the toxicity of Mn to *Rhizopus stolonifer* and *Trichoderma viride*, decreased that to *Scopulariopsis brevicaulis*, and had no effect on that to *Gliocladium* sp. (Fig. 3) (Babich and Stotzky, 1981a).

The acidophilic fungus, *Penicillium nigricans*, which exhibited maximum growth in a medium at pH 2.8, was more tolerant of Ni at pH 2.6 than at pH 3.5 or 5.9 (Singh, 1977). The greater tolerance to Ni at the lower pH may have reflected the enhanced physiologic state of the organism at this unusually low pH level. Other studies, with a variety of microorganisms, showed that Ni toxicity decreased as the pH was increased. Increasing the pH from 5.5 to 9.5 reduced the toxicity of Ni to *Achyla* sp. and *Saprolegnia* sp. (Fig. 4) (Babich and Stotzky, 1982f), and increasing the pH from 5.5 to 8.5 reduced the toxicity of Ni to the fungi, *Arthrobotrys conoides, Trichoderma viride*, and *Rhizopus stolonifer* (Fig. 5), *Scopulariopsis brevicaulis, Aspergillus giganteus, Aspergillus niger*, and *Oospora* sp., to

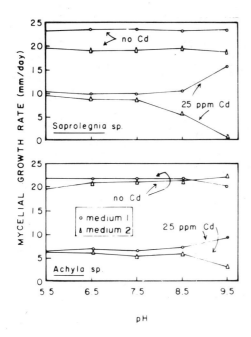

Figure 1. Effect of the composition of the test medium on the toxicity of cadmium as a function of pH. See the text for a description of medium 1 and medium 2 (Babich and Stotzky, unpublished).

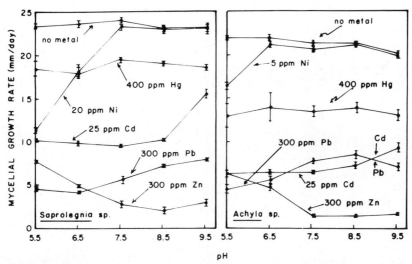

Figure 2. Effect of pH on the toxicity of cadmium, nickel, mercury, lead, and zinc to mycelial growth rates of a *Saprolegnia* sp. and an *Achyla* sp. Fungi were grown on medium 1; see text for a description of this medium (Babich and Stotzky, unpublished).

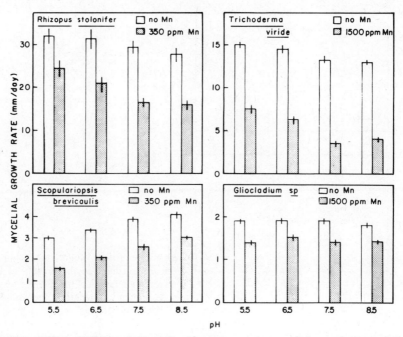

Figure 3. Effect of pH on the toxicity of manganese to mycelial growth rates of fungi. (Adapted from Babich and Stotzky, 1981a.)

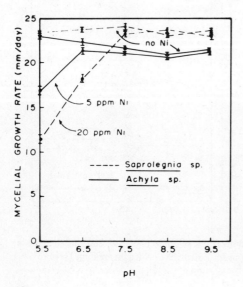

Figure 4. Effect of pH on the toxicity of nickel to mycelial growth rates of the freshwater fungi, *Saprolegnia* sp. and *Achyla* sp. (Babich and Stotzky, 1982a).

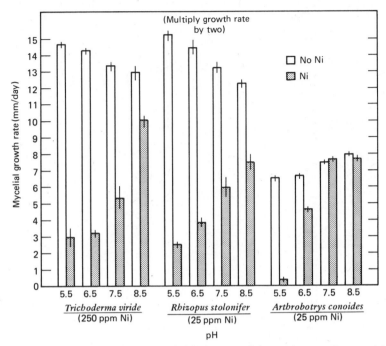

Figure 5. Effect of pH on the toxicity of nickel to mycelial growth rates of terrestrial fungi. (Adapted from Babich and Stotzky, 1982b.)

the yeast, *Cryptococcus terreus*, to the bacteria, *Bacillus brevis, Pseudomonas aeruginosa, Caulobacter leidyi*, and a marine species of *Acinetobacter*, and to the actinomycete, *Nocardia rhodochrous* (Figs. 6 and 7) (Babich and Stotzky, 1982b). Furthermore, mycelial growth rates of *Gliocladium* sp., *Trichoderma viride, Penicillium vermiculatum*, and *Aspergillus niger* were reduced to a greater extent by amendments of 1000 ppm Ni in a naturally acidic soil (pH 4.9) than in the same soil adjusted to pH 7.1 (Babich and Stotzky, 1982e), and survival of the bacterium, *Serratia marcescens*, and of the actinomycete, *Nocardia corallina*, in the presence of 75 ppm Ni was greater in a natural lake water of pH 6.8 than in the same water adjusted to pH 5.3 (Babich and Stotzky, 1983b).

The toxicity of Cu to spores of *Fusarium lycopersici* increased as the pH was increased (Horsfall, 1956), and increasing the pH from 5 to 8 increased the toxicity of Cu to growth (Steemann Nielsen and Kamp-Nielsen, 1970) and photosynthesis (Steeman Nielsen et al., 1969) of *Chlorella pyrenoidosa*. Increasing the pH from 3.5 to 4.7 increased the toxicity of Cu to the fungus, *Aureobasidium pullulans*, with increased toxicity paralleling increased uptake of Cu (Gadd and Griffiths, 1980). Acid-tolerant strains of *Scytalidium* sp. (Starkey, 1973) and *Penicillium nigricans* (Singh, 1977) tolerated Cu better in very acidic media, that is, pH 2.6 and 2.0, respectively, than in media at pH 4.6 and 6.8, respectively.

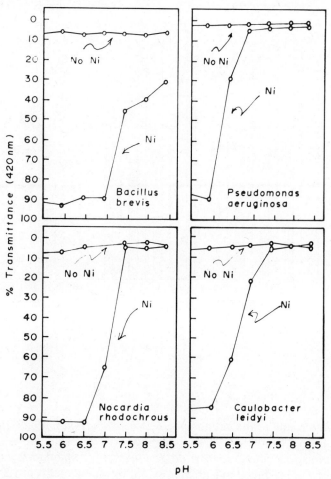

Figure 6. Effect of pH on the toxicity of nickel to the bacteria, *Bacillus brevis, Pseudomonas aeruginosa,* and *Caulobacter leidyi,* and to the actinomycete, *Nocardia rhodochrous* (Babich and Stotzky, 1982b).

3.2. E_h

The E_h (oxidation-reduction, or redox, potential), which is a measure of the availability of electrons, with negative E_h values being indicative of a reducing environment and positive values indicative of an oxidizing environment, is an important factor in determining the bioavailability of metals in the environment. Reducing conditions, such as those encountered in anaerobic ecosystems, may lead to the microbial conversion of sulfate (SO_4^{2-}) to sulfide (S^{2-}), with the subsequent precipitation of the sulfide salts of metals (e.g., NiS, HgS, CdS). The formation of insoluble sulfides greatly reduces the bioavailability of metals, thereby also reducing their potential uptake by, and toxicity to, the microbiota. For example, the toxicity of Hg to fermenta-

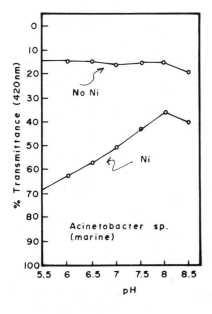

Figure 7. Effect of pH on the toxicity of nickel to a marine species of *Acinetobacter* (Babich and Stotzky, 1982b).

tion by a mixed rumen microbiota (Forsberg, 1978) and of Zn to photosynthesis of *Selenastrum capricornutum* (Hendricks, 1978) was eliminated by the addition of sufficient levels of S^{2-} to precipitate out the metals.

The E_h of the environment also determines the valency of some metals. For example, in the oxygenated part of the fjord of Saanich Inlet, British Columbia, Cr occurs as Cr(VI), whereas in the anoxic zone it occurs as Cr(III) (Cranston and Murray, 1978). Differentially charged forms of the same element may exert different toxicities to the microbiota. For example, Cr(VI) was more toxic than Cr(III) to mycelial proliferation of *Rhizopus stolonifer, Oospora* sp., *Trichoderma viride*, and *Penicillium vermiculatum* (Fig. 8); to spore germination (Fig. 9) and sporulation of *Penicillium vermiculatum* and *Aspergillus giganteus* (Babich et al., 1982b); to growth and survival of the bacterium, *Klebsiella pneumoniae* (Baldry et al., 1977); and to fermentation by a mixed rumen microbiota (Forsberg, 1978). Moreover, Cr(VI) exhibited much greater mutagenicity than did Cr(III) as determined with the *Salmonella typhimurium* assay (Lofroth and Ames, 1978; Tso and Fung, 1981) and the *Bacillus subtilis* rec-assay (Nishioka, 1975; Nakamuro et al., 1978).

3.3. Inorganic Ionic Composition

3.3.1. Inorganic Cations

The cationic composition (i.e., both the type and the amount of inorganic cations) in the environment may reduce the toxicity of metals to the microbiota. This reduction in toxicity is particularly significant for those metals

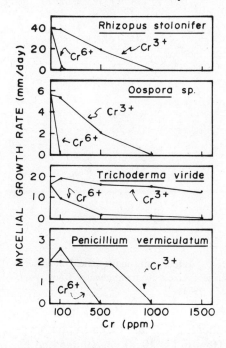

Figure 8. Comparative toxicity of tri- and hexavalent chromium to mycelial growth of terrestrial fungi. (Adapted from Babich et al., 1982b.)

that retain their cationic form (e.g., Hg^{2+} rather than $HgCl_3^-$), because competition for sites on cell surfaces between those cations normally present in an environment and the cationic speciation form of the heavy metals determines the extent of uptake of the metals by the microbiota. For example, iron (Fe) reduced the uptake of Cd by *Chlorella pyrenoidosa* (Hart et al., 1979).

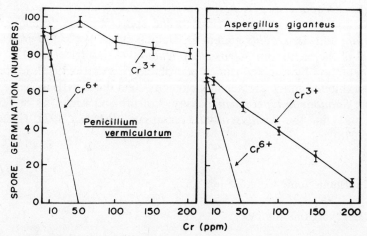

Figure 9. Comparative toxicity of tri- and hexavalent chromium to germination of fungal spores. (Adapted from Babich et al., 1982b.)

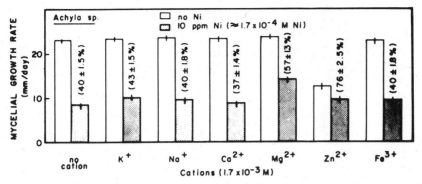

Figure 10. Influence of potassium, sodium, calcium, magnesium, zinc, and iron ions on the toxicity of nickel to mycelial growth of an *Achyla* sp. (Babich and Stotzky, 1982a).

Magnesium (Mg), in particular, influences the toxicity of many heavy metals. Increasing the level of Mg decreased the toxicity of Cu to photosynthesis (Overnell, 1976) and of Zn to growth (Braek et al., 1976) of *Phaeodactylum tricornutum;* of Cd to growth of *Escherichia coli* (Abelson and Aldous, 1950) and *Aspergillus niger* (Laborey and Lavollay, 1973); of Zn to growth of *Hormidium rivulare* (Say and Whitton, 1977), *Anacystis nidulans* (Shehata and Whitton, 1982), *Klebsiella pneumoniae* (Ainsworth et al., 1980), *Escherichia coli* (Abelson and Aldous, 1950), and the fungus, *Neurospora crassa* (Sastry et al., 1962); and of Ni to growth of the bacteria, *Bacillus licheniformis* (Haavik, 1976), *Bacillus megaterium, Bacillus subtilis* (Webb, 1970a and b), *Escherichia coli* (Abelson and Aldous, 1950), and *Klebsiella pneumoniae* (Webb, 1970a; Ainsworth et al., 1980), of an unidentified Gram-negative bacterium isolated from a deep-sea sediment (Yang and Ehrlich, 1976), of the yeast, *Torulopsis utilis* (Abelson and Aldous, 1950), and of the fungi, *Penicillium vermiculatum, Arthrobotrys conoides, Oospora* sp., *Trichoderma viride, Rhizopus stolonifer* (Babich and Stotzky, 1982d), *Achyla* sp. (Fig. 10) (Babich and Stotzky, 1982a), *Dendryphiella salina, Asteromyces cruciatus,* and *Dreschlera halodes* (Babich and Stotzky, 1983a). Furthermore, the ameliorating effects of seawater or salinity (as a solution of sea salts) on Ni toxicity to *Dendryphiella salina* (Fig. 11), *Asteromyces cruciatus,* and *Dreschlera halodes* was related to the Mg, rather than to the sodium (Na) or chloride (Cl), ions in the marine systems (Babich and Stotzky, 1983a).

Calcium (Ca) also affects heavy metal toxicity to microbes. Increasing the level of Ca decreased the toxicity of Cd to *Aspergillus niger* (Laborey and Lavollay, 1977), of Zn to *Hormidium rivulare* (Say and Whitton, 1977) and *Anacystis nidulans* (Shehata and Whitton, 1982), of Cu to *Phaeodactylum tricornutum* (Overnell, 1976), and of Zn and Hg to *Chlorella vulgaris* (Rai et al., 1981). Zinc, although a heavy metal pollutant when occurring in elevated levels in the environment, is also a micronutrient and has been shown to affect the toxicity of other metals. Increasing the level of Zn reduced the

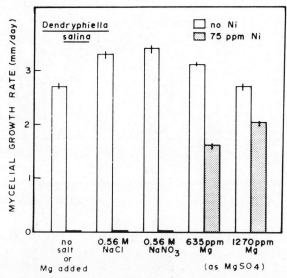

Figure 11. Influence of magnesium, sodium, and chloride ions on the toxicity of nickel to mycelial growth of *Dendryphiella salina*. The average concentration in seawater of magnesium is 1270 ppm and of chloride is 0.56 M; NaNO$_3$ was used as an internal control. (Adapted from Babich and Stotzky, 1982a.)

toxicity of Ni to *Achyla* sp. (Fig. 10) (Babich and Stotzky, 1982a), of Cu to *Phaeodactylum tricornutum* (Braek et al., 1976), and of Cd to freshwater species of *Chlorella* (Upitis et al., 1973; Gipps and Biro, 1978), to *Aspergillus niger* (Laborey and Lavollay, 1973), and to the freshwater protozoan, *Tetrahymena pyriformis* (Dunlop and Chapman, 1981).

3.3.2. Inorganic Anions

The type and amount of inorganic anions in an environment exert an influence on the speciation of metals and, hence, on their toxicities to the microbiota. Heavy metal cations form coordination complexes not only with hydroxyl (OH$^-$) ions (*see* Section 3.1), but also with other inorganic ligands, such as Cl$^-$, the dominant inorganic anion in seawater, where it occurs at an average level of 20,000 ppm. The various coordination complexes have different stabilities, and in seawater, Cd occurs as a mixture of CdCl$^+$/CdCl$_2$/CdCl$_3^-$ and Hg as a mixture of HgCl$_3^-$/HgCl$_4^{2-}$. However, in freshwater systems, depending on the pH, these metals may occur as Cd^{2+}, CdOH$^+$, Hg^{2+}, HgOH$^+$, Hg(OH)$_2$, and so on (Hahne and Kroontje, 1973). These different speciation forms of the same metal exert different toxicities to the microbiota. For example, the marine bacteria, *Aeromonas* sp. and *Acinetobacter* sp., the terrestrial bacteria, *Erwinia herbicola* (Fig. 12) and *Agrobacterium tumefaciens,* and the bacteriophages, φ11M15 of *Staphylococcus aureus* (Fig. 12) and P1 of *Escherichia coli*, tolerated Hg better as mixtures of HgCl$_3^-$/HgCl$_4^{2-}$ than as mixtures of Hg^{2+}/HgOH$^+$/Hg(OH)$_2$. These differ-

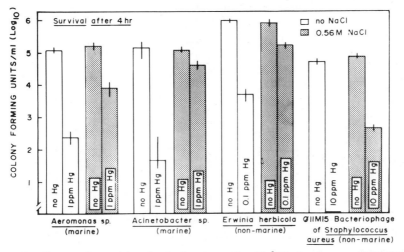

Figure 12. Comparative toxicity of cationic mercury (i.e., Hg^{2+} in the absence of $0.56\,M\,Cl^-$, as NaCl) and of $HgCl_3^-/HgCl_4^{2-}$ mixtures (i.e., mercury in the presence of $0.56\,M\,Cl^-$, the average chlorinity in seawater) to survival of bacteria and a bacteriophage. (Adapted from Babich and Stotzky, 1979b.)

ences in tolerance to Hg were evident also in natural ecosystems; *Aeromonas* sp., *Agrobacterium tumefaciens*, and the ϕ11M15 phage tolerated Hg better in seawater than in lake water (Fig. 13) (Babich and Stotzky, 1979b).

Salinity, or more specifically, chlorinity, also affected the toxicity of Cd to the microbiota. Increasing the salinity from 5 to 15‰ decreased the uptake by and toxicity of Cd to the estuarine alga, *Chlorella salina* (Wong et al., 1979), and increasing the salinity from 13.5 to 45‰ reduced the uptake by and toxicity of Cd to an unidentified marine bacterium (Gauthier and Flatau, 1980). Although seawater is a harsh environment for terrestrial fungi, increasing the concentration of seawater in a synthetic medium decreased the toxicity of Cd to *Rhizopus stolonifer, Trichoderma viride, Aspergillus niger*, and *Arthrobotrys conoides*. The ameliorating effect of seawater on the toxicity of Cd to these nonmarine fungi was correlated to its chlorinity component; progressively increasing the level of Cl (even to concentrations that themselves were inhibitory) decreased the relative toxicity of Cd to *Oospora* sp., *Trichoderma viride, Arthrobotrys conoides* (Fig. 14), *Sepedonium* sp., *Aspergillus niger, Rhizopus stolonifer*, and *Scopulariopsis brevicaulis* (Babich and Stotzky, 1982c). The lower toxicity of negatively charged Cd complexes than of Cd^{2+} was also noted in the growth response of a mixed microbiota from activated sludge exposed to $Cd(CN)_4^{2-}$ and Cd^{2+}; that is, at equivalent concentrations of Cd, $Cd(CN)_4^{2-}$ had a lower toxicity than did Cd^{2+} (Cenci and Morozzi, 1977). Conversely, $ZnCl_3^-/ZnCl_4^{2-}$ mixtures were highly toxic to T1, T7, P1, and ϕ/80 coliphages, whereas an

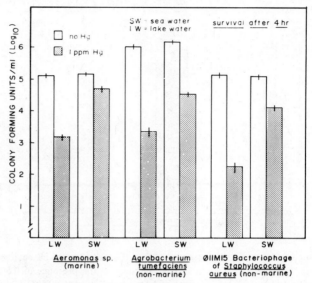

Figure 13.   Survival of bacteria and a bacteriophage in lake water an in seawater amended with mercury. (Adapted from Babich and Stotzky, 1979b.)

equivalent concentration of Zn as Zn^{2+} was slightly toxic or nontoxic (Babich and Stotzky, 1978a).

Metals whose speciation is not affected by the levels of chlorinity that occur in seawater do not exhibit differences in their toxicities as a function of increasing concentrations of Cl^- ions. For example, Ni occurs as Ni^{2+} in both seawater and lake water (Richter and Theis, 1980), and chlorinity, at a level occurring in seawater, did not affect the toxicity of Ni to *Dendryphiella salina* (Fig. 11), *Asteromyces cruciatus,* and *Dreschlera halodes* (Babich and Stotzky, 1983a).

Other inorganic anions also affect metal speciation and, in turn, the toxicity of metals to the microbiota. As already noted (see Section 3.2), S^{2-} forms insoluble salts with metals, thereby reducing the bioavailability of the metals. Similarly, as will be discussed later in greater detail (see Section 3.3.3), carbonate (CO_3^{2-}) ions influence metal toxicity. For example, CO_3^{2-} decreased the toxicity of Pb to growth of *Aspergillus giganteus* and *Fusarium solani*, presumably as the result of the formation of insoluble $PbCO_3$ (Babich and Stotzky, 1979a). Phosphate (PO_4^{3-}) also reduces the toxicity of metals, again probably by the precipitation of the metals as phosphate-containing salts. The addition of PO_4^{3-} decreased the toxicity of Pb to *Aspergillus giganteus, Fusarium solani* (Babich and Stotzky, 1979a), and *Chlamydomonas reinhardtii* (Schulze and Brand, 1978), and of Zn to *Chlorella vulgaris* (Rana and Kumar, 1974; Rai et al., 1981), *Hormidium rivulare* (Say and Whitton, 1977), and the cyanobacteria, *Plectonema boryanum* (Rana and Kumar, 1974) and *Anacystis nidulans* (Shehata and Whitton, 1982).

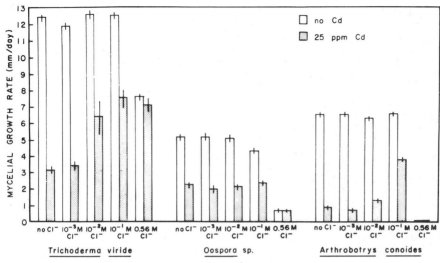

Figure 14. Effect of increasing concentrations of chloride ions (as NaCl) on the toxicity of cadmium to mycelial growth rates of terrestrial fungi. Seawater contains an average chloride concentration of 0.56 M. (Adapted from Babich and Stotzky, 1982c.)

3.3.3. Water Hardness

Although there has been much research on the effect of the degree of hardness on the response of the macrobiota to heavy metals, few studies have evaluated the response of the microbiota. Water hardness is caused by the metallic ions dissolved in water, which in fresh waters are primarily Ca and Mg. Hard waters are usually alkaline and contain substantial amounts of bicarbonate (HCO_3^-) and carbonate (CO_3^{2-}) rather than free carbon dioxide (CO_2), which occurs primarily in soft and/or acidified waters. The major components of water hardness, that is, Ca^{2+}, Mg^{2+}, and CO_3^{2-}, have been shown to reduce the toxicity of heavy metals to the microbiota (see Sections 3.3.1 and 3.3.2). Hardness is commonly reported as an equivalent concentration of $CaCO_3$, with waters containing from 0 to 75 mg/liter $CaCO_3$ being classified as "soft", from 75 to 150 mg/liter as being "moderately hard", from 150 to 300 mg/liter as being "hard", and greater than 300 mg/liter as being "very hard" (EPA, 1976).

The toxicities of Pb (Carter and Cameron, 1973), Cd, and Zn (Chapman and Dunlop, 1981) to *Tetrahymena pyriformis*; of Cd to the fungi, *Beauvaria* sp., *Aspergillus niger*, *Aspergillus giganteus*, *Penicillium vermiculatum*, and *Trichoderma viride*; of Ni to *Rhizopus stolonifer*, *Arthrobotrys conoides*, *Oospora* sp. (Fig. 15), *Cephalosporium* sp., and *Trichoderma viride*; of Pb to *Rhizopus stolonifer* and *Oospora* sp. (Babich and Stotzky, 1981b); and of Zn and cobalt (Co) to *Chlorella pyrenoidosa* (Wong, 1980) were reduced in hard, as compared to soft, water. Uptake of Cd by the alga, *Nitella flexilis*, was lower in hard than in soft water (Kinkade and Erdman, 1975).

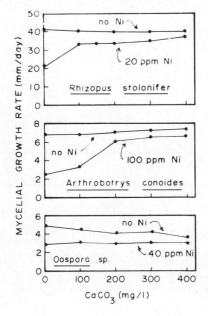

Figure 15. Influence of increasing levels of calcium carbonate on the toxicity of nickel to mycelial growth of fungi. (Adapted from Babich and Stotzky, 1982d.)

However, the toxicity of Hg to *Tetrahymena pyriformis* was twice as great in hard than in soft water (Carter and Cameron, 1973), and hardness did not affect the toxicity of Mn to fungi (Babich and Stotzky, 1981b).

Survival of the yeast, *Rhodotorula rubra,* after 35 days of exposure to 10 ppm Ni was greater in lake water amended with 200 or 400 mg/liter $CaCO_3$ than in the same lake water with a natural background of only 34 mg/liter $CaCO_3$ (Babich and Stotzky, 1983b). The toxicity of Ni to mycelial growth of *Rhizopus stolonifer, Arthrobotrys conoides, Trichoderma viride, Oospora* sp., and *Penicillium vermiculatum* was less in nutrient-enriched lake water amended with 400 mg/liter $CaCO_3$ than in lake water with a background of only 34 mg/liter $CaCO_3$ (Fig. 16). The ameliorating effect of $CaCO_3$ on the toxicity of Ni to fungi was correlated with the CO_3^{2-} rather than with the Ca^{2+} component of hardness (Babich and Stotzky, 1982d). In these latter studies, hardness was achieved with amendments of $CaCO_3$. However, if hardness had been studied as a mixture of Ca and Mg salts (as has been done in other studies, e.g., Kinkade and Erdman, 1975; Chapman and Dunlop, 1981), Mg also would have most probably been a major determinant in reducing the toxicity of Ni (see Section 3.3.1).

3.4. Clay Minerals

At the pH of most natural ecosystems, clay minerals possess surfaces that are predominantly negative and to which charge-compensating cations (e.g., H^+, K^+, Na^+, NH_4^+, Ca^{2+}, Mg^{2+}) are adsorbed. These cations are not

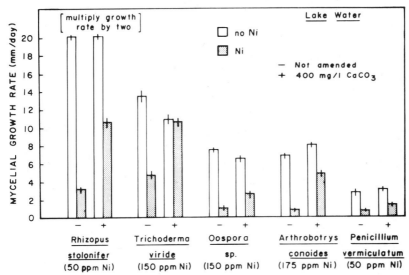

Figure 16. Comparative toxicity of nickel to mycelial growth of fungi in nutrient-enriched soft (i.e., not amended with CaCO₃ and with a background level of 34 mg/liter CaCO₃) and hard (i.e., amended with 400 mg/liter CaCO₃) lake water. (Adapted from Babich and Stotzky, 1982d.)

permanently bound to the clays and are constantly being exchanged by other cations. The total number of cations that can be exchanged by clays is expressed in milliequivalents (meq) per 100 g of oven-dried clay and is termed the cation exchange capacity (CEC). The CEC of some of the more common clay minerals is 3–5 meq/100 g for kaolinite, 5–30 for attapulgite, 10–30 for illite, 100–150 for vermiculite, and 80–150 for montmorillonite (Baver et al., 1972). The sorption of heavy metals to clay minerals is influenced by various abiotic factors, including pH [e.g., increasing the pH from 3.5 to 6.5 increased the amount of Cu, Pb, and Cd adsorbed to illite and kaolinite but had no effect on adsorption of metals to montmorillonite (Farrah and Pickering, 1977)]; concentration of competing cations [e.g., increasing the concentration of Ca or Mg reduced the adsorption of Cu to kaolinite (Gupta and Harrison, 1981)]; and the concentration and nature of any ligands that are present [e.g., increasing the concentration of Cl^- reduced the ability of Cd to adsorb to montmorillonite, presumably as a result of the conversion of divalent Cd^{2+} to negatively charged Cd–Cl complexes, which have a lower affinity for the negatively charged clay particles (Egozy, 1980)]. Consequently, the nature of the specific environment will determine the ability of metal pollutants to adsorb to clay particles.

Most of the studies that have evaluated the influence of clay minerals on metal toxicity to microbes have been performed with nonaquatic microbes and/or have used soil, rather than aquatic model systems. These studies, however, will be mentioned, because the principles involved probably apply to all ecosystems, and therefore, they have applicability to the influence of

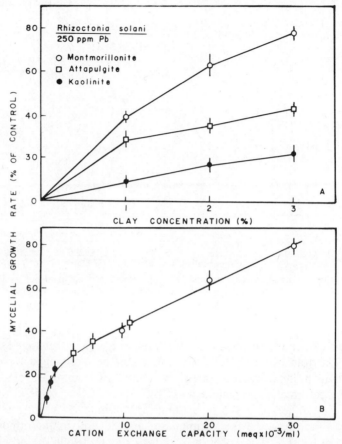

Figure 17. (A) effect of kaolinite, attapulgite, and montmorillonite on the toxicity of lead to mycelial growth of *Rhizoctonia solani*. (B) influence of the cation exchange capacity of the medium on the toxicity of lead to the mycelial growth of *Rhizoctonia solani* (Babich and Stotzky, 1979a).

sediment or suspended clay particulates on metal toxicity to microbes in aquatic ecosystems. Montmorillonite and, to a lesser extent, kaolinite protected *Bacillus megaterium, Agrobacterium tumefaciens, Nocardia corrallina, Trichoderma viride, Scopulariopsis brevicaulis, Aspergillus niger, Phycomyces blakesleeanus, Botrytis cinerea, Pholiota marginata, Thielaviopsis paradoxa, Chaetomium* sp., and *Schizophyllum* sp. against concentrations of Cd that were inhibitory or lethal to growth in a synthetic medium. The protective ability of the clays increased as their concentration increased, and the greater protection afforded by montmorillonite than by kaolinite was correlated with the higher CEC of montmorillonite (Babich and Stotzky, 1977c, 1978b). When an acidic soil was amended with montmorillonite, *Aspergillus niger, Penicillium vermiculatum, Penicillium brefeldianum,* and

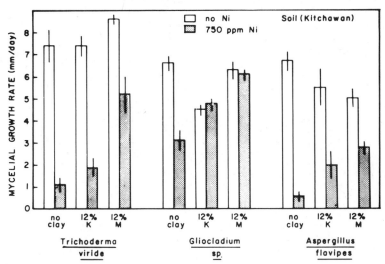

Figure 18.   Effect of kaolinite (K) and montmorillonite (M) on the toxicity of nickel to mycelial growth of fungi in soil. (Adapted from Babich and Stotzky, 1982e.)

Trichoderma viride were protected against Cd. Amendments with kaolinite provided only limited protection (Babich and Stotzky, 1977b). Clays may also protect against Cd toxicity in fresh waters, but the high level of competing cations (e.g., Na^+, Mg^{2+}) and of Cl^- [causing the formation of negatively charged Cd–Cl complexes which have lesser affinities than Cd^{2+} for clays (Garcia-Miragaya and Page, 1976)] may limit a similar protective effect in marine ecosystems.

Montmorillonite, attapulgite, and kaolinite protected *Fusarium solani, Rhizoctonia solani, Cunninghamella echinulata, Aspergillus niger,* and *Trichoderma viride* against inhibitory or lethal levels of Pb. The sequence of this protective ability (i.e., montmorillonite > attapulgite > kaolinite) followed the order of the magnitude of the CEC of the clays (Fig. 17) (Babich and Stotzky, 1979a). In contrast to Cd, the level of Cl^- present in seawater does not appreciably affect the speciation of Pb, as pH exerts the dominating influence and Pb occurs primarily as $PbOH^+$ (Hahne and Kroontje, 1973). As Pb maintains a cationic charge both in lake and seawater, clay minerals in these two diverse ecosystems may exert a protective effect against Pb toxicity.

Gliocladium sp., *Aspergillus flavipes, Trichoderma viride* (Fig. 18), *Aspergillus clavatus, Penicillium vermiculatum,* and *Rhizopus stolonifer* were protected against 750 ppm Ni in an acidic soil amended with montmorillonite; amendments with kaolinite provided less protection (Babich and Stotzky, 1982e). Survival in lake water of *Serratia marcescens* and, to a lesser extent, *Bacillus cereus* in the presence of 50 ppm Ni was enhanced when the water was amended with montmorillonite (Fig. 19) (Babich and

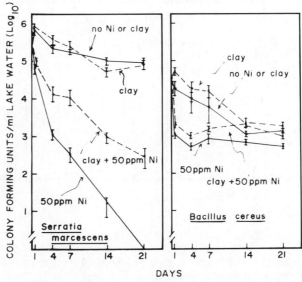

Figure 19. Effect of clay (as 1 mg/l montmorillonite) on the survival of bacteria in lake water amended with nickel. (Adapted from Babich and Stotzky, 1983b.)

Stotzky, 1983b). Similarly, incorporation of freshwater sediment, composed primarily of clays, into a synthetic medium reduced the toxicity of Hg to photosynthesis of a phytoplankton community consisting primarily of diatoms (Hongve et al., 1980).

3.5. Hydrous Metal Oxides

Amorphous hydrous ferric oxides ($Fe_2O_3 \cdot nH_2O$), aluminum oxides ($Al_2O_3 \cdot nH_2O$), and manganese oxides ($MnO_2 \cdot nH_2O$) are also capable, but to a lesser extent than are clays, of exchanging heavy metals (Hildebrand and Blum, 1974; Swallow et al., 1980) and, thereby, of decreasing their potential uptake by the microbiota. As with crystalline clays, adsorption of heavy metals to these amorphous metal oxides is dependent on several abiotic factors, including pH [e.g., increasing the pH from 4 to 8 increased the sorption of Pb to hydrous ferric oxide (Gadde and Laitinen, 1974)] and ligands [e.g., citrate, acting as a chelator, depressed the adsorption of Cd to hydrous aluminum and iron oxides (Chubin and Street, 1981)]. The mediating influence of hydrous metal oxides on metal toxicity to either terrestrial or aquatic microbes has received a minimum of attention. The protection against Cu toxicity towards photosynthesis of *Chlorella pyrenoidosa* by the addition of $FeCl_3$ to an alkaline medium was attributed to the adsorption of Cu to negatively charged $Fe(OH)_3$ colloids that were generated under the alkaline conditions (Steemann Nielsen and Kamp-Nielsen, 1970; Steemann Nielsen and Wium-Andersen, 1970).

3.6. Organics

The organic matter, both in soluble and particulate forms, in an ecosystem greatly influences the mobility, bioavailability, and toxicity of heavy metals to the microbiota. The humic acids present in freshwater (Wilson, 1978) and marine (Rashid, 1971) sediments and in the aqueous phases are capable of complexing variable amounts of metals (Stevenson et al., 1973; Gardiner, 1974a,b; Stevenson, 1976, 1977; Beveridge and Pickering, 1980). Interactions between organic matter and heavy metals are dependent on various abiotic factors of the environment. Those abiotic factors that reduce or eliminate the cationic valency of the metals will also reduce the ability of the metals to complex with organic matter. For example, the synthetic chelators, ethylenediaminetetraacetic acid (EDTA) and nitrilotriacetic acid (NTA), reduced the uptake of Cu, Pb, Zn, and Cd by humic acid (Riffaldi and Levi-Minzi, 1975; Beveridge and Pickering, 1980). Similarly, EDTA and the natural chelators, oxalate, citrate, and cysteine, reduced the adsorption of Cu, Pb, Zn, and Cd to cellulose (Farrah and Pickering, 1978), and EDTA reduced the adsorption of Cd to river mud (Gardiner, 1974b). The pH also affects organic–metal interactions. For example, increasing the pH increased the uptake of Cu, Pb, Zn, and Cd by humic acid (Riffaldi and Levi-Minzi, 1975; Beveridge and Pickering, 1980) and cellulose (Farrah and Pickering, 1978), and of Cd by river sediment (Reid and McDuffie, 1981).

Complexation of heavy metals with humus reduces their toxicities to the microbiota. For example, soluble humus obtained from marsh water decreased the toxicity of Cd to *Selenastrum capricornutum* (Gjessing, 1981), and of Zn, Pb, Cu, and Hg to a freshwater phytoplankton population (Hongve et al., 1980). Incorporation of particulate humic acids into a synthetic medium protected *Fusarium solani, Rhizoctonia solani* (Fig. 20), *Aspergillus giganteus, Aspergillus niger, Trichoderma viride, Cunninghamella echinulata,* and *Penicillium brefeldianum* against inhibitory or lethal levels of Pb (Babich and Stotzky, 1979a, 1980a) and *Saprolegnia* sp., *Cunninghamella blakesleeana,* and *Aspergillus flavus* from inhibitory concentrations of Ni (Babich and Stotzky, 1982a). The toxicity of Hg to an anaerobic bacterium of the genus, *Bacteroides,* and which was isolated from a freshwater sediment was reduced in the presence of sediment. This protective effect of sediment on the toxicity of Hg was apparently related to its organic matter content, because ashed sediment (i.e., sediment without the organic fraction) afforded no protection against Hg (Hamdy and Wheeler, 1978).

Copper was less toxic to growth of *Thalassiosira pseudonana* in "aged" seawater (i.e., seawater that contained natural detritus and phytoplankton communities which were allowed to decompose and release their cell contents prior to filtration and autoclaving) than in "fresh" seawater (i.e., seawater from which the natural phytoplankton and other particulates were removed immediately after collection) (Erickson, 1972). The influence of natural organics on Cu toxicity to the aquatic microbiota is well documented: for example, non-ultrafilterable organic macromolecules in lake wa-

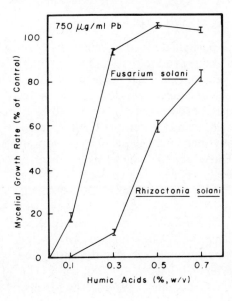

Figure 20. Effect of humic acid on the toxicity of lead to mycelial growth of fungi (Babich and Stotzky, 1980a).

ter reduced the toxicity of Cu to phytoplankton communities (Gachter et al., 1978), and treatment of seawater with UV radiation to destroy (i.e., photo-oxidize) the soluble organics increased the toxicity of Cu to the diatoms, *Asterionella japonica, Skeletonema costatum* (Fisher and Frood, 1980), and *Thalassiosira pseudonana* (Sunda and Guillard, 1976), the green alga, *Nannochloris atomus* (Sunda and Guillard, 1976), and to glucose mineralization by a heterotrophic microbiota (Gillespie and Vaccaro, 1978).

Organic exudates from aquatic microbes may be involved in regulating the bioavailability (i.e., reducing the toxicity) of metals in natural ecosystems. For example, the freshwater cyanobacteria, *Anabaena cylindrica* (Fogg and Westlake, 1955), *Anabaena flos-aquae, Anacystis nidulans, Microcystis aeruginosa, Nostoc muscorum, Gloeocapsa alpicola*, and *Coccomyxa chodatii* (McKnight and Morel, 1979), the freshwater algae, *Tribonema aequale, Synura petersenii, Chlamydomonas* sp., *Chlorella autotrophica* (McKnight and Morel, 1979), and *Cyclotella gigas* (Swallow et al., 1978), and the marine algae, *Thalassiosira weissflogii, Thalassiosira pseudonana* (McKnight and Morel, 1979), and *Cricosphaera elongata* (Gnassia-Barelli et al., 1978) released organic materials that complexed with and detoxified Cu. *Anabaena cylindrica, Navicula pelliculosa*, and *Scenedesmus quadricauda* released organic exudates that reduced the toxicity of Cu to photosynthesis of *Chlorella vulgaris* (Van den Berg et al., 1979). The toxicity of 0.5–2 ppm Zn to *Phaeodactylum tricornutum* was reduced by the addition of 100–2,000 ppb of polymeric polyphenols released from the marine brown algae, *Ascophyllum nodosum* and *Fucus vesiculosus* (Ragan et al., 1980). Chlorophyll reduced the toxicity of Ni to *Saprolegnia* sp., *Cunninghamella blakesleeana* (Fig. 21), and *Aspergillus clavatus*, and of Cd

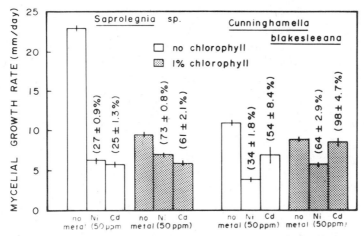

Figure 21. Effect of chlorophyll on the toxicity of nickel or cadmium to mycelial growth of a *Saprolegnia* sp. and *Cunninghamella blakesleeana* (Babich and Stotzky, 1982a).

to *Saprolegnia* sp. and *Cunninghamella blakesleeana* (Fig. 21). However, it has not been determined whether the effect of chlorophyll on the toxicity of Ni and Cd was related to the chelating ability of chlorophyll or to the release of Mg^{2+} from the chlorophyll, which antagonizes the toxicity of Ni and Cd (Babich and Stotzky, 1982a).

Natural soluble organics (e.g., dicarboxylic and amino acids) and synthetic soluble organics (e.g., EDTA, NTA), both types acting as chelators, reduce the toxicity of heavy metals, because chelated forms of the metals are less toxic than their free, noncomplexed forms. Chelation has been suggested to be the single most important abiotic factor in the reduction of Cu toxicity in aquatic ecosystems (Hodson et al., 1979). The amino acids arginine, glutamine, aspartic, and cysteine reduced the toxicity of Cd to *Nostoc calcicola* (Singh and Pandey, 1981); aspartic acid reduced the toxicity of Ni to *Klebsiella pneumoniae* (Ainsworth et al., 1980); histidine reduced the toxicity of Cu to *Thalassiosira pseudonana* (Davey et al., 1973) and *Chaetoceros socialis*, a marine alga (Jackson and Morgan, 1978); and cysteine reduced the toxicity of Hg to the marine bacterium, *Aeromonas* sp., the terrestrial bacterium, *Agrobacterium tumefaciens*, and the bacteriophage, ϕ11M15 of *Staphylococcus aureus* (Babich and Stotzky, 1980b), and of Pb to *Fusarium solani* and *Aspergillus giganteus* (Babich and Stotzky, 1979a). Citrate reduced the toxicity of Ni (Ainsworth et al., 1980), Cd, and Zn (Pickett and Dean, 1976) to *Klebsiella pneumoniae* and of Cu to *Chlorella pyrenoidosa* (Steemann Nielsen and Kamp-Nielsen, 1970); oxydisuccinate reduced the toxicity of Zn to *Microcystis aeruginosa* (Allen et al., 1980); and succinate reduced the toxicity of Pb to *Rhizoctonia solani*, *Fusarium solani*, *Aspergillus giganteus*, and *Cunninghamella echinulata* (Babich and Stotzky, 1979a).

EDTA reduced the toxicity of Cu to freshwater species of *Chlorella* and *Scenedesmus* (Stokes et al., 1973), to the marine algae, *Ditylum brightwellii* (Canterford and Canterford, 1980), *Thalassiosira pseudonana* (Davey et al., 1973), and *Phaeodactylum tricornutum* (Schulz-Baldes and Lewin, 1976), to the marine dinoflagellate, *Gonyaulax tamarensis* (Anderson and Morel, 1978), to glucose mineralization by a heterotrophic marine microbiota (Gillespie and Vaccaro, 1978), to the cyanobacteria, *Aphanizomenon* sp. (Horne and Goldman, 1974), *Nostoc calcicola* (Singh and Pandey, 1981), and *Anabaena cylindrica* (Fogg and Westlake, 1955), and to the bacterium, *Nitrosomonas europaea* (Loveless and Pointer, 1968); of Zn to *Microcystis aeruginosa* (Allen et al., 1980), *Ditylum brightwellii* (Canterford and Canterford, 1980), and *Klebsiella pneumoniae* (Pickett and Dean, 1976); of Cd to *Ditylum brightwellii* (Canterford and Canterford, 1980) and *Klebsiella pneumoniae* (Pickett and Dean, 1976); and of Pb to *Ditylum brightwellii* (Canterford and Canterford, 1980). EDTA reduced the mutagenicity of Cr(VI) to *Bacillus subtilis* (rec-assay) (Gentile et al., 1981). The rapid death of *Escherichia coli* in filter-sterilized seawater was eliminated by the addition of cysteine or the synthetic chelators, EDTA, 8-hydroxyquinoline, thioglycolic acid, and o-phenanthroline (Scarpino and Pramer, 1962; Jones, 1964; Jones and Cobet, 1975). NTA reduced the toxicity of Zn to *Microcystis aeruginosa* (Allen et al., 1980), of Pb to *Chlamydomonas reinhardtii* (Schulze and Brand, 1978), of Cu to an estuarine phytoplankton community (Erickson et al., 1970), and of Cu, Cd, Zn, and Pb to a freshwater phytoplankton community (Hongve et al., 1980).

More complex soluble organics also bind and detoxify metals, and these organics vary in their abilities to bind metals: for Hg, the sequence of binding capacity was casamino acids $\gg$ proteose peptone $>$ yeast extract $\gg$ tryptone $>$ peptone; for Pb, it was casamino acids $\gg$ yeast extract $>$ tryptone $>$ peptone $>$ proteose peptone; and for Cu, it was casamino acids $\gg$ yeast extract $>$ tryptone $>$ proteose peptone $>$ peptone (Ramamoorthy and Kushner, 1975). Increasing concentrations of peptone progressively reduced the toxicity of Cd to an unidentified marine bacterium (Gauthier and Flatau, 1980); yeast extract and increasing levels of neopeptone progressively reduced the toxicity of Pb to *Aspergillus giganteus* and *Cunninghamella echinulata* (Babich and Stotzky, 1979a); tryptone reduced the toxicity of Hg to the anaerobic bacteria, *Clostridium* sp. and *Bacteroides* sp. (Hamdy and Wheeler, 1978); increasing levels of peptone reduced the toxicity of Ni to a Gram-negative, marine bacterium isolated from a ferromanganese nodule (Yang and Ehrlich, 1976); and proteose peptone reduced the toxicity of methyl Hg^+ to *Tetrahymena pyriformis* (Hartig, 1971).

3.7.   Temperature

Temperature, similar to hydrostatic pressure, is an environmental factor that does not influence metal speciation but, instead, affects microbial sensitivity to metals. The data available on metal–temperature interactions are contradictory, with microbial sensitivity either increasing or decreasing as the temperature is altered. The main difficulty in interpreting these studies is that the optimal temperature for the specific process (e.g., growth, photosynthesis) being studied is seldom provided. The growth rates of *Scenedesmus* sp. and *Chlorella* sp. decreased less in the presence of Cu when exposed at 23°C (i.e., the optimal temperature for growth) than at 18, 29, or 35°C (Klotz, 1981). The toxicity of Zn^{2+} to growth of *Aspergillus niger* was unaffected by increasing the temperature from 25 to 37°C, but a $ZnCl^{+}/ZnCl_2/ZnCl_3^{-}$ mixture was more toxic at 25 than at 37°C. The greater tolerance of *Aspergillus niger* at 37°C may have reflected the enhanced physiological state of the organism, because in the absence of Zn, mycelial growth and production of conidia were greater at 37 than at 25°C (Babich and Stotzky, 1978a). Similarly, *Aspergillus flavus* was more resistant to Ni at 33 than at 23° C, which was correlated with the enhanced metabolic state of the fungus at the higher temperature (Babich and Stotzky, 1982a).

Euglena gracilis was more tolerant to Cr(VI) when exposed at 20°C than at the sublethal temperature of 31.5°C (Yongue et al., 1979). The toxicity of Cu to *Paramecium tetraurelia* (Szeto and Nyberg, 1979), of Hg to *Scenedesmus acutis* (Huisman et al., 1980), and of Zn to *Nitzschia linearis* and *Nitzschia seminulum* (Cairns et al., 1978) increased as the temperature was increased. However, the toxicity of Zn to *Chilomonas paramecium* decreased as the temperature was increased, and there were no definitive temperature–toxicity relationships for Cu and Cr(VI) (Honig et al., 1980). Growth of a Gram-negative, marine bacterium isolated from a ferromanganese nodule was stimulated in the presence of 5 ppm Ni at 18°C, whereas at 5°C, a similar concentration of Ni was neither stimulatory nor inhibitory. Growth of a Gram-negative bacterium isolated from a deep-sea sediment was reduced in the presence of 1 and 5 ppm Ni at 5°C but not at 18°C (Yang and Ehrlich, 1976).

3.8. Hydrostatic Pressure

There has been, apparently, only one study (Arcuri and Ehrlich, 1977) of the influence of hydrostatic pressure on the toxicity of heavy metals to marine microorganisms. Metal toxicity as a function of increasing hydrostatic pressure was studied on cell yields of three Gram-negative deep-sea bacteria: strain BIII 39, isolated from a ferromanganese nodule and characterized as a Mn^{2+}-oxidizer; strain BIII 32, also isolated from a ferromanganese nodule but characterized as a Mn^{4+}-reducer; and strain BIII 88, isolated from an ocean sediment and characterized as a Mn^{4+}-reducer.

Increasing the hydrostatic pressure from 1 to 272, 340, and 408 atm progressively increased the toxicity of Ni (e.g., at 1 ppm) to cell yields of strain BIII 39. Similarly, Ni had a greater toxicity to BIII 88 and BIII 32 at 340 than at 1 atm.

Progressively increasing the hydrostatic pressure from 1 to 408 atm did not affect the toxicity of Mn (0.1–10 ppm) to strain BIII 39, and no difference in the toxicity of Mn was noted for strain BIII 88 when exposed at 1 or 340 atm. However, at 340 atm, but not at 1 atm, 0.1–10 ppm Mn stimulated the growth of strain BIII 32.

Strain BIII 39 exhibited a varied response to Cu as the hydrostatic pressure was increased. At 1 atm, 0.1–1 ppm Cu caused a progressively increasing reduction in cell yields, but at 272 atm, the toxicity of 0.1 and 1 ppm Cu was eliminated. However, increasing the hydrostatic pressure to 340 atm caused the toxicity of 0.1 and 1 ppm Cu to be again apparent, but raising the pressure to 408 atm again eliminated the toxicity of Cu. With strain BIII 88, 1, but not 0.1, ppm Cu had a slight toxic effect at 1 atm; but at 340 atm, 0.1 ppm Cu had a slight stimulatory effect on cell yield and 1 ppm Cu had no effect. Increasing the hydrostatic pressure from 1 to 340 atm eliminated the toxic effect of 0.1 ppm Cu on cell yields of strain BIII 32.

4.   METAL–METAL INTERACTIONS

Pollutant emissions seldom, if ever, consist only of one toxicant. Such emissions usually contain multiple metals and, consequently, deposition into a common environment will simultaneously expose the indigenous microbiota to several metals. The microbial response to individual metals may differ from the response to stress from multiple metals, as indicated by several studies that have evaluated the potential antagonistic, synergistic, or additive interactions between multiple metals. Antagonistic interactions refer to the protective effect of one metal on the toxicity of a second metal and is probably a reflection of competition between the two metals for sites on the cell surfaces, with a reduction in the subsequent uptake and accumulation of both metals. Synergistic interactions refer to the enhanced toxicity of one metal in the presence of another metal and may reflect the increased permeability of the plasma membrane when stressed by several toxicants. Additive interactions are neither antagonistic nor synergistic, and the final toxicity is simply a sum of the individual toxicities.

Table 2, which is a compilation of some reported antagonistic, synergistic, and additive interactions between metals, clearly indicates that a specific metal–metal combination may produce a variety of interactions. For example, the combination of Cu + Zn was synergistic towards growth of the marine algae, *Amphidinum carteri, Skeletonema costatum,* and *Thalassiosira pseudonana,* but was antagonistic towards growth of *Phaeodactylum tricornutum* (Braek et al., 1976). The specific metal–metal interaction is also dependent on (a) the relative concentrations of the toxicants and (b) the sequence of exposure to the toxicants. For example, the effects of a combination of Cd + Pb on photosynthesis of a brackish water phytoplankton community were antagonistic when the concentration of Pb was greater than

Table 2. Interactions between Heavy Metals and Their Toxicities to the Microbiota

Metal Combination	Effect	Biotic System	Microbial Assay[a] — Specific Microbe and Reference
Cu + Zn	Synergism	Alga	*Skeletonema costatum, Amphidinum carteri, Thalassiosira pseudonana* (Braek et al., 1976)
		Bacterium	*Klebsiella pneumoniae* (Baldry et al., 1977)
	Antagonism	Alga	*Phaeodactylum tricornutum* (Braek et al., 1976)
	Additive	Cyanobacterium	*Anacystis nidulans* (Shehata and Whitton, 1982)
Cu + Mn	Synergism	Alga	*Selenastrum capricornutum, Chlorella stigmatophora* (Christensen et al., 1979)
Cu + Cd	Synergism	Bacterium	*Klebsiella pneumoniae* (Baldry et al., 1977)
	Antagonism	Alga	*Selenastrum capricornutum* (Bartlett et al., 1974)
Cu + Ni	Synergism	Alga	*Haematococcus capensis, Chlorella vulgaris* (Hutchinson, 1973)
Cu + Pb	Antagonism	Alga	*Selenastrum capricornutum, Chlorella stigmatophora* (Christensen et al., 1979)
Cu + Cr(VI)	Additive	Bacterium	*Klebsiella pneumoniae* (Baldry et al., 1977)

Table 2. (*Continued*)

Metal Combination	Effect	Biotic System	Microbial Assay[a] — Specific Microbe and Reference
Cd + Zn	Synergism	Alga	*Hormidium rivulare* (Say and Whitton, 1977)
		Bacterium	*Klebsiella pneumoniae* (Pickett and Dean, 1976)
		Fungus	*Physarum polycephalum* (Chin et al., 1978)
	Antagonism	Alga	*Chlorella vulgaris* (Gipps and Biro, 1978)
			Ankistrodesmus falcatus (Prasad and Prasad, 1982)
		Protozoan	*Tetrahymena pyriformis* (Dunlop and Chapman, 1981)
Cd + Mn	Antagonism	Alga	*Chlorella* sp. (Upitis et al., 1973)
Cd + Cr(VI)	Antagonism	Bacterium	*Klebsiella pneumoniae* (Baldry et al., 1977)
Cd + Ni	Synergism	Bacterium	*Klebsiella pneumoniae* (Ainsworth et al., 1980)
	Antagonism	Alga	*Ankistrodesmus falcatus* (Prasad and Prasad, 1982)
		Fungus	*Physarum polycephalum* (Chin et al., 1978)

32

Ni + Zn	Synergism	Bacterium	*Klebsiella pneumoniae* (Ainsworth et al., 1980)
	Antagonism	Fungus	*Achyla* sp. (Babich and Stotzky, 1982a)
	Additive	Cyanobacterium	*Anacystis nidulans* (Shehata and Whitton, 1982)
Ni + Pb	Antagonism	Fungus	*Achyla* sp. (Babich and Stotzky, 1982a)
	Additive	Alga	*Ankistrodesmus falcatus* (Prasad and Prasad, 1982)
Pb + Hg	Synergism	Protozoan	*Cristigera* sp. (Gray and Ventilla, 1973)
Pb + Mn	Antagonism	Alga	*Selenastrum capricornutum, Chlorella stigmatophora* (Christensen et al., 1979)
Pb + Zn	Additive	Cyanobacterium	*Anacystis nidulans* (Shehata and Whitton, 1982)
Zn + Cr(VI)	Synergism	Bacterium	*Klebsiella pneumoniae* (Baldry et al., 1977)
Zn + MN	Antagonism	Cyanobacterium	*Anacystis nidulans* (Shehata and Whitton, 1982)
Fe(III) + Cd	Antagonism	Alga	*Chlorella* sp. (Upitis et al., 1973)

[a]The microbial response most usually studied was growth/survival.

that of Cd, whereas they were synergistic when the concentration of Cd was greater than that of Pb (Pietilainen, 1975). The effect of a combination of Hg + Ni on the growth rate of the cyanobacterium, *Anabaena inequalis*, was synergistic when both Hg and Ni were added simultaneously or when Hg was added first, but it was antagonistic when Ni was added before Hg (Stratton and Corke, 1979). The apparent importance of the relative concentrations of the toxicants and the sequence of exposure to them may explain the variety of responses reported for specific combinations of metals.

5. BIOTIC FACTORS

Abiotic characteristics of the environment are not the only factors that influence the toxicity of heavy metals. Some biotic factors (i.e., characteristics of the organisms themselves) also influence the sensitivity of microbes to metals. Cell size may be a factor influencing microbial sensitivity to toxicants; for example, the concentration of Pb that caused a 50% reduction in photosynthesis was 15–18 ppm for *Chlamydomonas reinhardtii, Navicula pelliculosa,* and *Anabaena* sp. but only 5 ppm for the desmid, *Cosmarium botrytis,* which has a higher surface:volume ratio than the other algae and which may have accounted for its enhanced sensitivity to Pb (Malanchuk and Gruendling, 1973). Capsulated strains of *Klebsiella pneumoniae* were more resistant to Cu and Cd than were noncapsulated strains, presumably because the polysaccharide capsule bound the metals and prevented their intracellular accumulation (Bitton and Freihofer, 1978). Extracellular polypeptide chelators produced by *Anabaena cylindrica* (Fogg and Westlake, 1955) and by the marine alga, *Cricosphaera elongata* (Gnassia-Barelli et al., 1978), protected the cells against the toxicity of Cu.

The nutritional status of the organism also determines its response to stress by metals. For example, Mg^{2+}-, ammonium (NH_4^+)-, PO_4^{3-}-, and glucose-limited cells of *Klebsiella pneumoniae* were highly sensitive to Cd, and Mg^{2+}-, potassium (K^+)-, and glucose-limited cells were highly sensitive to Zn, when compared to cells grown in a medium containing an excess of these nutrients (Pickett and Dean, 1976). Although Mg^{2+}-limited cells of *Klebsiella pneumoniae* were more sensitive to Ni, K^+-limited cells were more resistant to Ni than were comparable cells harvested from a nutrient-sufficient medium (Ainsworth et al., 1980). The uptake of Ni was reduced in PO_4^{3-}-starved cells of *Phaeodactylum tricornutum* (Skaar et al., 1974) and of the yeast, *Saccharomyces cerevisiae* (Fuhrmann and Rothstein, 1968).

Microbial strains resistant to elevated levels of heavy metals are easily isolated from contaminated environments. For example, lake waters in the Sudbury smelting area in Canada contain elevated levels of Ni, and species of *Chlorella* and *Scenedesmus* isolated from these contaminated lakes also exhibited enhanced tolerance to Ni when compared to laboratory strains (Stokes et al., 1973). Gram-negative bacteria (e.g., *Pseudomonas aerugi-*

nosa, Escherichia coli, and *Salmonella* sp.) isolated from a river polluted with Cr were found to be resistant to Cr(VI) (Simon-Pujol et al., 1979). The increased tolerance of microbes to metals probably represents, in most instances, physiological rather than genetic adaptation. For example, the estuarine algae, *Isochrysis galbana* and *Phaeodactylum tricornutum*, could be trained (i.e., exposed for many passages to metals at concentrations that partially inhibited growth of the original inoculants) to tolerate elevated levels of Cu, and the estuarine alga, *Dunaliella echlora*, could be trained to tolerate elevated levels of Cd (Wikfors and Ukeles, 1982). Similarly, *Klebsiella pneumoniae* (Ainsworth et al., 1980) and the yeast, *Saccharomyces ellipsoideus* (Nakamura, 1962) could be trained to tolerate elevated levels of Ni.

Nevertheless, although most cases of increased resistance of microbes to elevated levels of metals in the environment probably reflect some sort of physiological adaptation, genetic mechanisms for resistance to heavy metals also may be involved. Strains of various bacteria have been shown to contain plasmids for resistance to various metals. For example, some *Escherichia coli* carry plasmids for resistance to Hg, Ni, and Co (Smith, 1967); some *Pseudomonas aeruginosa* carry plasmids conferring resistance to Hg, organomercurials (Clark et al., 1977), and Cr(VI) (Summers and Jacoby, 1978); and some *Staphylococcus aureus* carry plasmids conferring resistance to Cd, Hg, Zn, Pb, and arsenic (As) (Novick and Roth, 1968) (see Summers and Silver, 1978).

6. REGULATORY ASPECTS

The influence of environmental factors on the toxicity of pollutants, such as heavy metals, creates an added burden on the regulatory agencies to establish standards for toxicants that are applicable to *all* environments. As the authors are sufficiently familiar only with the regulatory decision-making processes in the United States, attention will focus on the methodologies used by the U.S. Environmental Protection Agency (EPA), the regulatory agency charged with protecting the health and welfare of human beings and of the environment from harmful exposures to toxic agents. In 1979, EPA set new criteria for pollutants occurring in aquatic ecosystems. These "Water Quality Criteria" for 65 classes of chemicals (and which were later defined in terms of 129 priority pollutants) that were considered toxic under the 1977 Amendments to the Clean Water Act were set at levels considered safe for human health and for various components of the aquatic biota (EPA, 1979a,b,c; 1980). In formulating these criteria, EPA noted that "the toxicity of certain compounds may be less in some water, because of differences in acidity, temperature, water hardness, and other factors. Conversely, some natural water characteristics may increase the impact of certain pollutants" (EPA, 1979a). Consequently, distinct criteria were formulated for fresh and marine ecosystems. Furthermore, as the toxicity of heavy metals to the macrobiota appeared to be directly related to the degree of hardness in fresh waters, the criteria for beryllium (Be), Cd, Cr, Cu, Ni, Pb, and Zn were formulated on a sliding scale, recognizing that as hardness increases, the level of each metal that can be tolerated without evoking a deleterious biological response also increases. The focus by EPA on only water hardness reflected the lack of significant amounts of data to establish relationships between other abiotic factors and pollutant toxicity: "Although EPA recognizes that other water characteristics such as pH, temperature, or degree of salinity (as in estuaries) may affect the toxicity of some pollutants, the data base at this time is not detailed enough for further specificity" (EPA, 1979a). However, as this chapter has emphasized, the toxicity of heavy metals to the aquatic, as well as to the terrestrial, microbiota (and, although not discussed, to the macrobiota) is greatly influenced by the physicochemical factors of the specific recipient environment. A criterion or standard for a toxicant that is based on only one set of environmental variables will be overprotective for one type of environment and underprotective for another environment having different physicochemical properties (Babich and Stotzky, 1980a,b; Babich et al., 1981).

It is the lack of such data on the influence of environmental factors on the toxicity of a pollutant (of which heavy metals are only one example) that has hindered EPA in setting criteria that are reflective of the different types of ecosystems in the United States. This dilemma is compounded when the number of chemicals that require toxicological evaluations is considered: 129 just for the Water Quality Criteria and an estimated 63,000 chemicals already in commerce and with 1000 new ones predicted each year (Maugh, 1978). There is little information for most of these chemicals about their toxicities to human beings.

This massive volume of chemicals that needs evaluation has prompted the suggestion (Babich and Stotzky, 1981c) of using microbes as rapid and inexpensive assay systems for initially identifying those abiotic factors that most significantly influence the toxicity of specific pollutants. After this initial screening, additional studies using plants and animals can focus on specific abiotic factor–pollutant interactions, so that more meaningful criteria and standards can be formulated. A compilation of data on the responses to Cd (the most extensively studied heavy metal and, thus, with the most data available) by representatives of the aquatic macrobiota, the terrestrial macrobiota; and the microbiota indicated many common biologic responses among these three distinct biologic groups and their sensitivities to Cd as influenced by abiotic factors (e.g., salinity, pH, inorganic cations and anions, chelating agents, clay mineralogy, organics) (Babich and Stotzky, 1981c). This similarity in responses strengthened the concept that microbes can serve as realistic indicators to predict the effects of abiotic factors on the response of the microbiota to heavy metals and other toxicants.

7. CONCLUDING REMARKS

The effects of heavy metals on the microbiota, in both aquatic and terrestrial ecosystems, are influenced to a large extent by the physicochemical characteristics of the specific environment. Physicochemical environmental factors, such as pH, E_h, inorganic cations and anions, organic materials, clay minerals, and hydrous metal oxides, influence the speciation of heavy metals and, hence, their bioavailability and, ultimately, their toxicity to the microbiota. In addition, other abiotic factors, such as temperature and hydrostatic pressure, as well as interactions between multiple heavy metals, influence the response of the microbiota to stress by heavy metals. As the response of the microbiota, as well as of the macrobiota, to heavy metals and to other pollutants is influenced by these abiotic factors, environmental quality criteria for toxicants that are based on only one set of environmental factors will be underprotective for some environments and overprotective for others.

ACKNOWLEDGMENTS

Some of the research mentioned in this chapter was supported in part by grant R808329 from the United States Environmental Protection Agency. The views expressed in this chapter are not necessarily those of the agency.

REFERENCES

Abelson, P. H. and Aldous, E. (1950). Ion antagonisms in microorganisms: interference of normal magnesium metabolism by nickel, cobalt, cadmium, zinc, and manganese. *J. Bacteriol.* **60**, 401–413.

Adiga, P. R., Sastry, K. S., and Sarma, P. S. (1962). The influence of iron and magnesium on the uptake of heavy metals in metal toxicities in *Aspergillus niger. Biochim. Biophys. Acta* **64**, 546–548.

Adshead-Simonsen, P. C., Murray, G. E., and Kushner, D. J. (1981). Morphological changes in the diatom, *Tabellaria flocculosa,* induced by very low concentrations of cadmium. *Bull. Environ. Contam. Toxicol.* **26**, 745–748.

Ainsworth, M. A., Tompsett, C. P., and Dean, A. C. R. (1980). Cobalt and nickel sensitivity and tolerance in *Klebsiella pneumoniae. Microbios* **27**, 175–184.

Albright, L. J., Wentworth, J. W., and Wilson, E. M. (1972). Technique for measuring metallic salt effects upon the indigenous heterotrophic microflora of a natural water. *Water Res.* **6**, 1589–1596.

Allen, H. E., Hall, R. H., and Brisbin, T. D. (1980). Metal speciation. Effects on aquatic toxicity. *Environ. Sci. Technol.* **14**, 441–443.

Anderson, A. C. and Abdelghani, A. A. (1980). Toxicity of selected arsenical compounds in short term bacterial bioassays. *Bull. Environ. Contam. Toxicol.* **24**, 124–127.

Anderson, D. M. and Morel, F. M. M. (1978). Copper sensitivity of *Gonyaulax tamarensis*. *Limnol. Oceanogr.* **23**, 283–295.

Arcuri, E. J. and Ehrlich, H. L. (1977). Influence of hydrostatic pressure on the effects of the heavy metal cations of manganese, copper, cobalt, and nickel on the growth of three deep-sea bacterial isolates. *Appl. Environ. Microbiol.* **33**, 282–288.

Babich, H. and Stotzky, G. (1974). Air pollution and microbial ecology. *Crit. Rev. Environ. Contr.* **4**, 353–421.

Babich, H. and Stotzky, G. (1977a). Sensitivity of various bacteria, including actinomycetes, and fungi to cadmium and the influence of pH on sensitivity. *Appl. Environ. Microbiol.* **33**, 681–695.

Babich, H. and Stotzky, G. (1977b). Effect of cadmium on fungi and on interactions between fungi and bacteria in soil: influence of clay minerals and pH. *Appl. Environ. Microbiol.* **33**, 1059–1066.

Babich, H. and Stotzky, G. (1977c). Reductions in the toxicity of cadmium to icroorganisms by clay minerals. *Appl. Environ. Microbiol.* **33**, 696–705.

Babich, H. and Stotzky, G. (1978a). Toxicity of zinc to fungi, bacteria, and coliphages: influence of chloride ions. *Appl. Environ. Microbiol.* **36**, 904–913.

Babich, H. and Stotzky, G. (1978b). Effects of cadmium on the biota: influence of environmental factors. *Adv. Appl. Microbiol.* **23**, 55–117.

Babich, H. and Stotzky, G. (1979a). Abiotic factors affecting the toxicity of lead to fungi. *Appl. Environ. Microbiol.* **38**, 506–514.

Babich. H. and Stotzky, G. (1979b). Differential toxicities of mercury to bacteria and bacteriophages in sea and in lake water. *Can. J. Microbiol.* **25**, 1252–1257.

Babich, H. and Stotzky, G. (1980a). Physicochemical factors that affect the toxicity of heavy metals to microbes in aquatic habitats. In: R. R. Colwell and J. Foster, Eds., *Proceedings of the ASM conference, aquatic microbial ecology*. University of Maryland Sea Grant Publication, College Park, Maryland, pp. 181–203.

Babich, H. and Stotzky, G. (1980b). Environmental factors that influence the toxicity of heavy metals and gaseous pollutants to microorganisms. *Crit. Rev. Microbiol.* **8**, 99–145.

Babich, H. and Stotzky, G. (1981a). Manganese toxicity to fungi: influence of pH. *Bull. Environ. Contam. Toxicol.* **27**, 474–480.

Babich, H. and Stotzky G. (1981b). Influence of water hardness on the toxicity of heavy metals to fungi. *Microbios Lett.* **16**, 79–84.

Babich, H. and Stotzky, G. (1981c). *Developing standards for environmental toxicants: the need to consider abiotic environmental factors and microbe-mediated ecologic processes*. Presented at the Ecotoxicology Workshop, Ecosystems Research Center, Ithaca, N.Y., Nov. 2–5.

Babich, H. and Stotzky, G. (1982a). Nickel toxicity to fungi: influence of some environmental factors. *Ecotoxicol. Environ. Safety* **6**, 577–589.

Babich, H. and Stotzky, G. (1982b). Nickel toxicity to microbes: effect of pH and implications for acid rain. *Environ. Res.* **29**, 335–350.

Babich, H. and Stotzky, G. (1982c). Influence of chloride ions on the toxicity of cadmium to fungi. *Zentral. Bakteriol. Mikrobiol. Hyg. Ser. C3*, 421–426.

Babich, H. and Stotzky, G., (1982d). Components of water hardness that reduce the toxicity of nickel to fungi. *Microbios Lett.* **18**, 17–24.

Babich, H. and Stotzky, G. (1982e). Toxicity of nickel to microorganisms in soil: influence of some physicochemical characteristics. *Environ. Pollut. Ser. A*, **29**, 303–315.

Babich, H. and Stotzky, G. (1983a). Nickel toxicity to estuarine/marine fungi and its amelioration by magnesium in sea water. *Water, Air, Soil, Pollut.* **19**, 193–202.

Babich, H. and Stotzky, G. (1983b). Temperature, pH, salinity, hardness, and particulates mediate nickel toxicity to eubacteria, an actinomycete, and yeasts in lake, simulated estuarine, and sea waters. *Aquat. Toxicol.,* in press.

Babich, H., Davis, D. L., and Trauberman, J. (1981). Environmental quality criteria: some considerations. *Environ. Management* **5,** 191–205.

Babich, H., Gamba-Vitalo, C., and Stotzky, G. (1982a). Comparative toxicity of nickel to mycelial proliferation and spore formation of fungi. *Arch. Environ. Contam. Toxicol.* **11,** 465–468.

Babich, H., Schiffenbauer, M., and Stotzky, G. (1982b). Comparative toxicity of trivalent and hexavalent chromium to fungi. *Bull. Environ. Contam. Toxicol.* **28,** 452–459.

Baldry, M. G. C., Hogarth, D. S., and Dean, A. C. R. (1977). Chromium and copper sensitivity and tolerance in *Klebsiella (Aerobacter) aerogenes. Microbios Lett.* **4,** 7–16.

Bartlett, L., Rabe, F. W., and Funk, W. H. (1974). Effects of copper, zinc, and cadmium on *Selenastrum capricornutum. Water Res.* **8,** 179–185.

Baver, L. D., Gardner, W. H., and Gardner, W. R. (1972). *Soil physics.* John Wiley & Sons, New York.

Beveridge, A. and Pickering, W. F. (1980). Influence of humate–solute interactions on aqueous heavy metal ion levels. *Water, Air, Soil Pollut.* **14,** 171–185.

Bitton, G. and Freihofer, V. (1978). Influence of extracellular polysaccharides on the toxicity of copper and cadmium towards *Klebsiella aerogenes. Microb. Ecol.* **4,** 119–125.

Bottino, N. R., Newman, R. D., Cox, E. R., Stockton, R. Hoban, M., Zingaro, R. A., and Irgolic, K. J. (1978). The effects of arsenate and arsenite on the growth and morphology of the marine unicellular algae *Tetraselmis chui* (Chlorophyta) and *Hymenomonas carterae* (Chrysophyta). *J. Exp. Mar. Biol. Ecol.* **33,** 153–163.

Braek, G. S., Jensen, A., and Mohus, A. (1976). Heavy metal tolerance of marine phytoplankton. III. Combined effects of copper and zinc ions on cultures of four common species. *J. Exp. Mar. Biol. Ecol.* **25,** 37–50.

Cairns, J., Jr., Buikema, A. L., Jr., Heath, A. G., and Parker, B. C. (1978). *Effects of temperature on aquatic organism sensitivity to selected chemicals.* Virginia Water Resources Center Bulletin 106, Virginia Polytechnic Institute, Blacksburg, Virginia.

Cairns, J., Jr., Lanza, G. R., and Parker, B. C. (1972). Pollution-related structural and functional changes in aquatic communities with emphasis on freshwater algae and protozoa. *Proc. Acad. Nat. Sci. Phila.* **124,** 79–127.

Canterford, G. S., Buchanan, A. S., and Ducker, S. C. (1978). Accumulation of heavy metals by the marine diatom *Ditylum brightwellii* (West) Grunow. *Aust. J. Mar. Freshwater Res.* **29,** 613–622.

Canterford, G. S. and Canterford, D. R. (1980). Toxicity of heavy metals to the marine diatom *Ditylum brightwellii* (West) Grunow: correlation between toxicity and metal speciation. *J. Mar. Biol. Assoc. U.K.* **60,** 227–242.

Carter, J. W. and Cameron, I. L. (1973). Toxicity bioassay of heavy metals in water using *Tetrahymena pyriformis. Water Res.* **7,** 951–961.

Cenci, G. and Morozzi, G. (1977). Evaluation of the toxic effect of Cd^{2+} and $Cd(CN)_4^{2-}$ ions on the growth of mixed microbial population of activated sludges. *Sci. Total Environ.* **7,** 131–143.

Chapman, G. and Dunlop, S. (1981). Detoxication of zinc and cadmium by the freshwater protozoan *Tetrahymena pyriformis.* I. The effect of water hardness. *Environ. Res.* **26,** 81–86.

Chin, B., Lesowitz, G. S., and Bernstein, I. A. (1978). A cellular model for studying accommodation to environmental stressors: protection and potentiation by cadmium and other metals. *Environ. Res.* **16,** 432–442.

Christensen, E. R., Scherfig, J., and Dixon, P. S. (1979). Effects of manganese, copper, and lead on *Selenastrum capricornutum* and *Chlorella stigmatophora*. *Water Res.* **13**, 79–92.

Chubin, R. G. and Street, J. J. (1981). Adsorption of cadmium on soil constituents in the presence of complexing ligands. *J. Environ. Qual.* **10**, 225–228.

Clark, D. L., Weiss, A. A., and Silver, S. (1977). Mercury and organomercurial resistances determined by plasmids in *Pseudomonas*. *J. Bacteriol.* **132**, 186–196.

Cobet, A. B., Wirsen, C., and Jones, G. E. (1970). The effect of nickel on a marine bacterium, *Arthrobacter marinus* sp. nov. *J. Gen. Microbiol.* **62**, 159–169.

Cranston, R. E. and Murray, J. W. (1978). The determination of chromium species in natural waters. *Anal. Chim. Acta* **99**, 275–282.

Davey, E. W., Morgan, M. J., and Erickson, S. J. (1973). A biological measurement of the copper complexation capacity of seawater. *Limnol. Oceanogr.* **18**, 993–997.

Davies, A. G. and Sleep, J. A. (1979). Photosynthesis in some British coastal waters may be inhibited by zinc pollution. *Nature* **277**, 292–293.

Davies, A. G. and Sleep, J. A. (1980). Copper inhibition of carbon fixation in coastal phytoplankton assemblages. *J. Mar. Biol. Assoc. U.K.* **60**, 841–850.

Delmotte, A. (1980). Influence of cadmium on growth and nitrogen metabolism of *Anabaena cylindrica* Lemm. *J. Exp. Bot.* **31**, 1107–1118.

Duddridge, J. E. and Wainwright, M. (1980). Heavy metal accumulation by aquatic fungi and reduction in viability of *Gammarus pulex* fed Cd^{2+} contaminated mycelium. *Water Res.* **14**, 1605–1611.

Dunlop, S. and Chapman, G. (1981). Detoxication of zinc and cadmium by the freshwater protozoan *Tetrahymena pyriformis*. II. Growth experiments and ultrastructural studies on sequestration of heavy metals. *Environ. Res.* **24**, 264–274.

Egozy, Y. (1980). Adsorption of cadmium and cobalt on montmorillonite as a function of solution composition. *Clays Clay Min.* **28**, 311–318.

Environmental Protection Agency (1976). *Quality criteria for water*. Washington, D.C.

Environmental Protection Agency (1979a). Water quality criteria. *Fed. Regist.* **44**, 15926–15981.

Environmental Protection Agency (1979b). Water quality criteria, availability. *Fed. Regist.* **44**, 43660–43697.

Environmental Protection Agency (1979c). Water quality criteria, availability. *Fed. Regist.* **44**, 56628–56657.

Environmental Protection Agency (1980). Water quality criteria documents, availability. *Fed. Regist.* **45**, 79318–79379.

Erickson, S. J. (1972). Toxicity of copper to *Thalassiosira pseudonana* in unenriched inshore water. *J. Phycol.* **8**, 318–323.

Erickson, S. J., Lackie, N., and Maloney, T. E. (1970). A screening technique for estimating copper toxicity to estuarine phytoplankton. *J. Water Pollut. Contr. Fed.* **42**, 270–278.

Farrah, H. and Pickering, W. F. (1977). Influence of clay–solute interactions on aqueous heavy metal ion levels. *Water, Air, Soil Pollut.* **8**, 189–197.

Farrah, H. and Pickering, W. F. (1978). The effect of pH and ligands on the sorption of heavy metal ions by cellulose. *Aust. J. Chem.* **31**, 1501–1509.

Fisher, N. S. and Frood, D. (1980). Heavy metals and marine diatoms: influence of dissolved organic compounds on toxicity and selection for metal tolerance among four species. *Mar. Biol.* **59**, 85–93.

Florence, T. M. (1980). Speciation of zinc in natural waters. In: J. O. Nriagu, Ed., *Zinc in the environment*, Part 1, *Ecological cycling*. John Wiley & Sons, New York, pp. 199–227.

Fogg, G. E. and Westlake, D. F. (1955). The importance of extracellular products of algae in freshwater. *Verh. Int. Verein. Limnol.* **12**, 219–232.

Forsberg, C. W. (1978). Effects of heavy metals and other trace elements on the fermentative activity of the rumen microbiota and growth of functionally important rumen bacteria. *Can. J. Microbiol.* **24**, 298–306.

Fuhrmann, G.-F. and Rothstein, A. (1968). The transport of Zn^{2+}, Co^{2+}, and Ni^{2+} into yeast cells. *Biochim. Biophys. Acta* **163**, 325–330.

Gachter, R., Davis, J. S., and Mares, A. (1978). Regulation of copper availability to phytoplankton by macromolecules in lake water. *Environ. Sci. Technol.* **12**, 1416–1421.

Gadd, G. M. and Griffiths, A. J. (1980). Influence of pH on toxicity and uptake of copper in *Aureobasidium pullulans*. *Trans. Br. Mycol. Soc.* **75**, 91–96.

Gadde, R. R. and Laitinen, H. A. (1974). Studies of heavy metal adsorption by hydrous iron and manganese oxides. *Anal. Chem.* **46**, 2022–2026.

Garcia-Miragaya, J. and Page, A. L. (1976). Influence of ionic strength and inorganic complex formation on the sorption of trace amounts of Cd by montmorillonite. *Soil Sci. Soc. Am. J.* **40**, 658–663.

Gardiner, J. (1974a). The chemistry of cadmium in natural water. I. A study of cadmium complex formation using the cadmium specific ion electrode. *Water Res.* **8**, 23–30.

Gardiner, J. (1974b). The chemistry of cadmium in natural water. II. The adsorption of cadmium on river muds and naturally occurring solids. *Water Res.* **8**, 157–164.

Gauthier, M. J. and Flatau, G. N. (1980). Etude de l'accumulation du cadmium par une bacterie marine en fonction des conditions de cultures. *Chemosphere* **9**, 713–718.

Gentile, J. M., Hyde, K., and Schubert, J. (1981). Chromium genotoxicity as influenced by complexation and rate effects. *Toxicol. Lett.* **7**, 439–448.

Giesy, J. P. (1978). Cadmium inhibition of leaf decomposition in an aquatic microcosm. *Chemosphere* **7**, 467–475.

Gillespie, P. A. and Vaccaro, R. F. (1978). A bacterial bioassay for measuring the copper-chelation capacity of seawater. *Limnol. Oceanogr.* **23**, 543–548.

Gipps, J. F. and Biro, P. (1978). The use of *Chlorella vulgaris* in a simple demonstration of heavy metal toxicity. *J. Biol. Ed.* **12**, 207–214.

Gipps, J. F. and Coller, B. A. W. (1980). Effect of physical and culture conditions on uptake of cadmium by *Chlorella pyrenoidosa*. *Aust. J. Mar. Freshwater Res.* **31**, 747–755.

Gjessing, E. T. (1981). The effect of aquatic humus on the biological availability of cadmium. *Arch. Hydrobiol.* **91**, 144–149.

Gnassia-Barelli, W., Romeo, M., Laumond, F., and Pesando, D. (1978). Experimental studies on the relationship between natural copper complexes and their toxicity to phytoplankton. *Mar. Biol.* **47**, 15–19.

Gray, J. S. and Ventilla, R. J. (1973). Growth rates of sediment living marine protozoan as a toxicity indicator for heavy metals. *Ambio* **2**, 118–121.

Greenfield, S. S. (1942). Inhibitory effects of inorganic compounds on photosynthesis in *Chlorella*. *Am. J. Bot.* **29**, 121–131.

Gupta, G. C. and Harrison, F. L. (1981). Effect of cations on copper adsorption by kaolin. *Water, Air, Soil Pollut.* **15**, 323–327.

Haavik, H. I. (1976). On the role of bacitracin peptides in trace metal transport by *Bacillus licheniformis*. *J. Gen. Microbiol.* **96**, 393–399.

Hahne, H. C. H. and Kroontje, W. (1973). Significance of pH and chloride concentration on behavior of heavy metal pollutants: mercury(II), cadmium(II), zinc(II), and lead(II). *J. Environ. Qual.* **2**, 444–450.

Hamdy, M. K. and Wheeler, S. R. (1978). Inhibition of bacterial growth by mercury and the effects of protective agents. *Bull. Environ. Contam. Toxicol.* **20**, 378–386.

Harding, J. P. C. and Whitton, B. A. (1977). Environmental factors reducing the toxicity of zinc to *Stigeoclonium tenue. Br. Phycol. J.* **12**, 17–21.

Hargreaves, J. W. and Whitton, B. A. (1977). Effect of pH on tolerance of *Hormidium rivulare* to zinc and copper. *Oecologia* **26**, 235–243.

Hart, B. A., Bertram, P. E., and Scaife, B. D. (1979). Cadmium transport by *Chlorella pyrenoidosa. Environ. Res.* **18**, 327–335.

Hart, B. A. and Scaife, B. D. (1977). Toxicity and bioaccumulation of cadmium in *Chlorella pyrenoidosa. Environ. Res.* **14**, 401–413.

Hartig, W. J. (1971). Studies on mercury toxicity in *Tetrahymena pyriformis. J. Protozool.* **18**, 26 (Abstr.).

Havlik, B., Stary, J., Prasilova, J., Kratzer, K., and Hanusova, J. (1979). Mercury circulation in aquatic bioconeses. Part 1: Mercury(II)–metabolism in phytoplankton. *Acta Hydrochim. Hydrobiol.* **7**, 215–227.

Hendricks, A. C. (1978). Response of *Selenastrum capricornutum* to zinc sulfides. *J. Water Pollut. Contr. Fed.* **50**, 163–168.

Hervey, R. J. (1949). Effect of chromium on the growth of unicellular Chlorophyceae diatoms. *Bot. Gaz.* **111**, 1–11.

Hildebrand, E. E. and Blum, W. E. (1974). Lead fixation by iron oxides. *Naturwissenschaften* **61**, 169–170.

Hodson, P. V., Borgmann, U., and Shear, H. (1979). Toxicity of copper to aquatic biota. In: J. O. Nriagu, Ed., *Copper in the Environment,* Part II: *Health effects.* John Wiley & Sons, New York, pp. 307–372.

Hongve, D., Skogheim, O. K., Hindar, A., and Abrahamsen, H. (1980). Effects of heavy metals in combination with NTA, humic acid, and suspended sediment on natural phytoplankton photosynthesis. *Bull. Environ. Contam. Toxicol.* **25**, 594–600.

Honig, R. A., McGinniss, M. J., Buikema, A. L., Jr., and Cairns, J., Jr. (1980). Toxicity tests of aquatic pollutants using *Chilomonas paramecium* Ehrenberg (Flagellata) populations. *Bull. Environ. Contam. Toxicol.* **25**, 169–175.

Horne, A. J. and Goldman, C. R. (1974). Suppression of nitrogen fixation by blue-green algae in a eutrophic lake with trace additions of copper. *Science* **183**, 409–411.

Horsfall, J. G. (1956). *Principles of fungicidal action.* Chronica Botanica Co., Waltham, Massachusetts.

Huisman, J., Ten Hoopen, H. J. G., and Fuchs, A. (1980). The effect of temperature upon the toxicity of mercuric chloride in *Scenedesmus acutus. Environ. Pollut.* **22A**, 133–148.

Hutchinson, T. C. (1973). Comparative studies of the toxicity of heavy metals to phytoplankton and their synergistic interactions. *Water Pollut. Res. Can.* **8**, 68–90.

Jackson, G. A. and Morgan, J. L. (1978). Trace metal–chelator interactions and phytoplankton growth in seawater media: theoretical analysis and comparison with reported observations. *Limnol. Oceanogr.* **23**, 268–282.

Jensen, A., Rystad, B., and Melsom, S. (1974). Heavy metal tolerance of marine phytoplankton. I. The tolerance of three algal species to zinc in coastal sea water. *J. Exp. Mar. Biol. Ecol.* **15**, 145–157.

Jones, G. E. (1964). Effect of chelating agents on the growth of *Escherichia coli* in seawater. *J. Bacteriol.* **87**, 483–499.

Jones, G. E. and Cobet, A. B. (1975). Heavy metal ions as the principal bactericidal agent in Caribbean sea water. In: A. L. H. Gameson, Ed., *International symposium on discharge of sewage from sea outfalls.* Pergamon Press, London, pp. 199–208.

Kinkade, M. L. and Erdman, H. E. (1975). The influence of hardness components (Ca^{2+} and Mg^{2+}) in water on the uptake and concentration of cadmium in a simulated freshwater ecosystem. *Environ. Res.* **10**, 308–313.

Klotz, R. L. (1981). Algal response to copper under riverine conditions. *Environ. Pollut.* **24A**, 1–19.

Korkeala, H. and Pekkanen, T. J. (1978). The effect of pH and potassium phosphate buffer on the toxicity of cadmium for bacteria. *Acta Vet. Scand.* **19**, 93–101.

Kostyaev, V. Ya. (1980). Effects of some heavy metals on cyanobacteria. *Microbiology* **49**, 665–667.

Laborey, F. and Lavollay, J. (1973). Sur la nature des antagonismes responsables de l'interaction des ions Mg^{++}, Cd^{++}, et Zn^{++} dans la croissance d'*Aspergillus niger*. *C. R. Acad. Sci. (Paris)* **276D**, 529–532.

Laborey, F. and Lavollay, J. (1977) Sur l'antitoxicite du calcium et du magnesium a l'egard du cadmium, dans la croissance d'*Aspergillus niger*. *C. R. Acad. Sci. (Paris)* **284D**, 639–642.

Liu, D. (1981). A rapid biochemical test for measuring chemical toxicity. *Bull. Environ. Contam. Toxicol.* **26**, 145–149.

Lofroth, G. and Ames, B. N. (1978). Mutagenicity of inorganic compounds in *Salmonella typhimurium:* arsenic, chromium, and selenium. *Mutat. Res.* **53**, 65–66 (Abstr.).

Loveless, J. E. and Pointer, H. A. (1968). The influence of metal ion concentrations and pH value on the growth of a *Nitrosomonas* strain isolated from activated sludge. *J. Gen. Microbiol.* **52**, 1–14.

Malanchuk, J. L. and Gruendling, G. K. (1973). Toxicity of lead nitrate to algae. *Water, Air, Soil Pollut.* **2**, 181–190.

Massalski, A., Laube, V. M., and Kushner, D. J. (1981). Effects of cadmium and copper on the ultrastructure of *Ankistrodesmus braunii* and *Anabaena* 7120. *Microb. Ecol.* **7**, 183–193.

Maugh, T. H. (1978). Chemicals: how many are there? *Science* **199**, 162.

McKnight, D. M. (1981). Chemical and biological processes controlling the response of a freshwater ecosystem to copper stress: a field study of the $CuSO_4$ treatment of Mill Pond Reservoir, Burlington, Massachusetts. *Limnol. Oceanogr.* **26**, 518–531.

McKnight, D. M. and Morel, F. M. M. (1979). Release of weak and strong copper-complexing agents by algae. *Limnol. Oceanogr.* **21**, 823–837.

Mills, A. L. and Colwell, R. R. (1977). Microbiological effects of metal ions in Chesapeake Bay water and sediment. *Bull. Environ. Contam. Toxicol.* **18**, 99–103.

Monahan, T. J. (1976). Lead inhibition of chlorophycean microalgae. *J. Phycol.* **12**, 358–362.

Mora, B. and Fabregas, J. (1980). The effect of inorganic and organic mercury on growth kinetics of *Nitzschia acicularis* W. Sm. and *Tetraselmis suecica* Butch. *Can. J. Microbiol.* **26**, 930–937.

Nakamura, H. (1962). Adaptation of yeast to cadmium. V. Characteristics of RNA and nitrogen metabolism in the resistance. *Mem. Konan Univ., Sci. Ser.* **6**, 19–31.

Nakamuro, K., Yoshikawa, K., Sayato, Y., and Kurata, H. (1978). Comparative studies of chromosomal aberration and mutagenicity of trivalent and hexavalent chromium. *Mutat. Res.* **58**, 175–181.

Nishioka, H. (1975). Mutagenic activities of metal compounds in bacteria. *Mutat. Res.* **31**, 185–189.

Novick, R. P. and Roth, C. (1968). Plasmid-linked resistance to inorganic salts in *Staphylococcus aureus*. *J. Bacteriol.* **95**, 1335–1340.

Oscarson, D. W., Huang, P. M. and Liaw, W. K. (1980). The oxidation of arsenite by aquatic sediments. *J. Environ. Qual.* **9**, 700–703.

Overnell, J. (1976). Inhibition of marine algal photosynthesis by heavy metals. *Mar. Biol.* **38,** 335–342.

Patrick, F. M. and Loutit, M. (1976). Passage of metals in effluents, through bacteria to higher organisms. *Water Res.* **10,** 333–335.

Patrick, R., Bott, T., and Larson, R. (1975). The role of trace elements in management of nuisance growths. United States Environmental Protection Agency, Corvallis, Oregon [cited in: Spencer, D. F. and Greence, R. W. (1981). Effects of nickel on seven species of freshwater algae. *Environ. Pollut.* **25A,** 241–247].

Pickett, A. W. and Dean, A. C. R. (1976). Cadmium and zinc sensitivity and tolerance in *Klebsiella (Aerobacter) aerogenes. Microbios* **15,** 79–91.

Pietilainen, K. (1975). Synergistic and antagonistic effects of lead and cadmium on aquatic primary production. In: *International conference on heavy metals in the environment, symposium proceedings,* Vol. II, Toronto, Ontario, Canada, October 27–31, pp. 861–873.

Prasad, P. V. D. and Prasad, P. S. D. (1982). Effect of cadmium, lead, and nickel on three freshwater green algae. *Water, Air, Soil Pollut.* **17,** 263–268.

Ragan, M. A., Ragan, C. M., and Jensen, A. (1980). Natural chelators in sea water: detoxification of Zn^{2+} by brown algal polyphenols. *J. Exp. Mar. Biol. Ecol.* **44,** 261–267.

Rai, L. C., Gaur, J. P., and Kumar, H. D. (1981). Protective effects of certain environmental factors on the toxicity of zinc, mercury, and methylmercury to *Chlorella vulgaris. Environ. Res.* **25,** 250–259.

Ramamoorthy, S. and Kushner, D. J. (1975). Binding of mercuric and other heavy metal ions by microbial growth media. *Microb. Ecol.* **2,** 162–176.

Rana, B. C. and Kumar, H. D. (1974). The toxicity of zinc to *Chlorella vulgaris* and *Plectonema boryanum* and its protection by phosphate. *Phykos* **13,** 60–66.

Rashid, M. A. (1971). Role of humic acids of marine origin and their different molecular weight fractions in complexing di- and tri-valent metals. *Soil Sci.* **111,** 298–306.

Reid, J. D. and McDuffie, B. (1981). Sorption of trace cadmium on clay minerals and river sediments: effect of pH and Cd(II) concentrations in a synthetic river water medium. *Water, Air, Soil Pollut.* **15,** 375–386.

Richter, R. O. and Theis, T. L. (1980). Nickel speciation in a soil/water system. In: J. O. Nriagu, Ed., *Nickel in the environment.* John Wiley & Sons, New York, pp. 189–202.

Riffaldi, R. and Levi-Minzi, R. (1975). Adsorption and desorption of Cd on humic acid fraction of soils. *Water, Air, Soil Pollut.* **5,** 179–184.

Rosenzweig, W. D. and Pramer, D. (1980). Influence of cadmium, zinc, and lead on growth, trap formation, and collagenase activity of nematode-trapping fungi. *Appl. Environ. Microbiol.* **40,** 694–696.

Saifullah, S. M. (1978). Inhibitory effects of copper on marine dinoflagellates. *Mar. Biol.* **44,**299–308.

Sakaguchi, T., Tsuji, T., Nakajima, A., and Horikoshi, T. (1979). Accumulation of cadmium by green microalgae. *Eur. J. Appl. Microbiol. Biotechnol.* **8,** 207–215.

Sanders, J. G., Ryther, J. H., and Batchelder, J. H. (1981). Effects of copper, chlorine, and thermal addition on the species composition of marine phytoplankton. *J. Exp. Mar. Biol. Ecol.* **49,** 81–102.

Sastry, K. S., Adiga, P. R., Venkatasubramanyam, V., and Sarma, P. S. (1962). Interrelationships in trace-element metabolism in metal toxicities in *Neurospora crassa. Biochem. J.* **85,** 486–491.

Say, P. J. and Whitton, B. A. (1977). Influence of zinc on lotic plants. II. Environmental effects on toxicity of zinc to *Hormidium rivulare. Freshwater Biol.* **7,** 377–384.

Scarpino, P. V. and Pramer, D. (1962). Evaluation of factors affecting the survival of *Escherichia coli* in seawater. VI. Cysteine. *Appl. Microbiol.* **10,** 436–440.

Schulz-Baldes, M. and Lewin, R. A. (1976). Lead uptake in two marine phytoplankton organisms. *Biol. Bull.* **150,** 118–127.

Schulze, H. and Brand, J. J. (1978). Lead toxicity and phosphate deficiency in *Chlamydomonas*. *Plant Physiol.* **62,** 727–730.

Shehata, F. H. A. and Whitton, B. A. (1982). Zinc tolerance in strains of the blue-green alga *Anacystis nidulans*. *Br. Phycol. J.* **17,** 5–12.

Sibley, T. H. and Morgan, J. J. (1975). Equilibrium speciation of trace metals in freshwater: seawater mixtures. In: *National conference on heavy metals in the environment, symposium proceedings,* Vol. 1. Toronto, Ontario, Canada, October 27–31, pp. 319–338.

Simon-Pujol, M. D., Marques, A. M., Ribera, M., and Congregado, F. (1979). Drug resistance of chromium tolerant Gram-negative bacteria isolated from a river. *Microbios Lett.* **7,** 139–144.

Singh, N. (1977). Effect of pH on the tolerance of *Penicillium nigricans* to copper and other heavy metals. *Mycologia* **69,** 750–755.

Singh, S. P. and Pandey, A. K. (1981). Cadmium toxicity in a cyanobacterium: effect of modifying factors. *Environ. Exp. Bot.* **21,** 257–265.

Singleton, F. L. and Guthrie, R. K. (1977). Aquatic bacterial populations and heavy metals. I. Composition of aquatic bacteria in the presence of copper and mercury salts. *Water Res.* **11** 639–642.

Skaar, H., Rystad, B., and Jensen, A. (1974). The uptake of ^{63}Ni by the diatom *Phaeodactylum tricornutum*. *Physiol. Plant.* **32,** 353–358.

Smith, D. H. (1967). R factors mediate resistance to mercury, nickel, and cobalt. *Science* **156,** 1114–1116.

Starkey, R. L. (1973). Effect of pH on toxicity of copper to *Scytaldium* sp., a copper-tolerant fungus, and some other fungi. *J. Gen. Microbiol.* **78,** 217–225.

Steemann Nielsen, E. and Kamp-Nielsen, L. (1970). Influence of deleterious concentrations of copper on the growth of *Chlorella pyrenoidosa*. *Physiol. Plant.* **23,** 828–840.

Steemann Nielsen, E., Kamp-Nielsen, L., and Wium-Andersen, S. (1969). The effect of deleterious concentrations of copper on the photosynthesis of *Chlorella pyrenoidosa*. *Physiol. Plant.* **22,** 1121–1133.

Steemann Nielsen, E. and Wium-Andersen, S. (1970). Copper ions as poison in the sea and in freshwater. *Mar. Biol.* **6,** 93–97.

Stevenson, F. J. (1976). Binding of metal ions by humic acids. In: J. O. Nriagu, Ed., *Environmental biogeochemistry,* Vol. 2, *Metals transfer and ecological mass balances.* Ann Arbor Scientific Publishers, Ann Arbor, Michigan, pp. 519–540.

Stevenson, F. J. (1977). Nature of divalent transition metal complexes of humic acids as revealed by a modified potentiometric titration method. *Soil Sci.* **123,** 10–17.

Stevenson, F. J., Krastanov, S. A., and Ardakani, M. S. (1973). Formation constants of Cu^{2+} complexes with humic and fulvic acids. *Geoderma* **9,** 129–141.

Stokes, P. M., Hutchinson, T. C., and Krauter, K. (1973). Heavy-metal tolerance in algae isolated from contaminated lakes near Sudbury, Ontario. *Can. J. Bot.* **51,** 2155–2168.

Stotzky, G. and Babich, H. (1980). Mediation of the toxicity of pollutants to microbes by the physicochemical composition of the recipient environment. In: D. Schlessinger, Ed., *Microbiology—1980,* American Society for Microbiology, Washington, D. C., pp. 352–354.

Stratton, G. W. and Corke, C. T. (1979). The effect of mercuric, cadmium, and nickel ion combinations on a blue-green alga. *Chemosphere* **8,** 731–740.

Summers, A. O. and Jacoby, G. A. (1978). Plasmid-determined resistance to boron and chromium compounds in *Pseudomonas aeruginosa*. *Antimicrob. Agts. Chemother.* **13**, 637–641.

Summers, A. O. and Silver, S. (1978), Microbial transformation of metals. *Ann. Rev. Microbiol.* **32**, 637–672.

Sunda, W. and Guillard, R. R. L. (1976). The relationship between cupric ion activity and the toxicity of copper to phytoplankton. *J. Mar. Res.* **34**, 511–529.

Swallow, K. C., Hume, D. N., and Morel, F. M. M. (1980). Sorption of copper and lead by hydrous ferric oxide. *Environ. Sci. Technol.* **14**, 1326–1331.

Swallow, K. C., Westall, J. C., McKnight, D. M., Morel, N. M. L., and Morel, F. M. M. (1978). Potentiometric determination of copper complexation by phytoplankton exudates. *Limnol. Oceanogr.* **23**, 538–542.

Szeto, C. and Nyberg, D. (1979). The effect of temperature on copper tolerance of *Paramecium*. *Bull. Environ. Contam. Toxicol.* **21**, 131–135.

Trollope, D. R. and Evans, B. (1976). Concentrations of copper, iron, lead, nickel, and zinc in freshwater algal blooms. *Environ. Pollut.* **11**, 109–116.

Tso, W.-W. and Fung, W.-P. (1981). Mutagenicity of metallic cations. *Toxicol. Lett.* **8**, 195–200.

Upitis, V. V., Pakalne, D. S., and Nollendorf, A. F. (1973). The dosage of trace elements in the nutrient medium as a factor in increasing the resistance of *Chlorella* to unfavorable conditions of culturing. *Microbiology* **42**, 758–762.

Van den Berg, C. M. G., Wong, P. T. S., and Chau, Y. K. (1979). Measurement of complexing materials excreted from algae and their ability to ameliorate copper toxicity. *J. Fish. Res. Board Can.* **36**, 901–905.

Webb, M. (1970a). Interrelationships between the utilization of magnesium and the uptake of other bivalent cations by bacteria. *Biochim. Biophys. Acta* **222**, 428–439.

Webb. M. (1970b). The mechanism of acquired resistance to Co^{2+} and Ni^{2+} in Gram-positive and Gram-negative bacteria. *Biochim. Biophys. Acta* **222**, 440–446.

Wikfors, G. H. and Ukeles, R. (1982). Growth and adaptation of estuarine unicellular algae in media with excess copper, cadmium, or zinc, and effects of metal-contaminated algal food on *Crassostrea virginica* larvae. *Mar. Ecol. Prog.* Ser. 7, 191–206.

Wilson, D. E. (1978). An equilibrium model describing the influence of humic materials on the speciation of Cu^{2+}, Zn^{2+}, and Mn^{2+} in freshwaters. *Limnol. Oceanogr.* **23**, 499–507.

Wong, K. H., Chan, K. Y., and Ng, S. L. (1979). Cadmium uptake by the unicellular green alga *Chlorella salina* Cu-1 from culture media with high salinity. *Chemosphere* **8**, 887–891.

Wong, M. H. (1980). Toxic effects of cobalt and zinc to *Chlorella pyrenoidosa* (26) in soft and hard water. *Microbios* **28**, 19–25.

Yang, S. H. and Ehrlich, H. L. (1976). Effect of four heavy metals (Mn, Ni, Cu, and Co) on some bacteria from the deep sea. In: J. M. Miles and A. M. Kaplan, Eds., *Proceedings of the third international biodegradation symposium*. Applied Science Publishers, London, pp. 867–874.

Yongue, W. H., Jr., Berrent, B. L., and Cairns, J., Jr. (1979). Survival of *Euglena gracilis* exposed to sublethal temperature and hexavalent chromium. *J. Protozool.* **26**, 122–125.

Zirino, A. and Yamamoto, S. (1972). A pH-dependent model for the chemical speciation of copper, zinc, cadmium, and lead in seawater. *Limnol. Oceanogr.* **17**, 661–671.

2

METAL SPECIATION AND TOXICITY OF FREE METAL IONS TO AQUATIC BIOTA

Uwe Borgmann

Great Lakes Fisheries Research Branch
Department of Fisheries and Oceans
Canada Centre for Inland Waters
Burlington, Ontario

1. INTRODUCTION

The toxicity of metals to aquatic biota has been studied extensively and has often been observed to vary considerably. The importance of metal speciation, and the concentration of the free metal ion in controlling metal toxicity has only recently been recognized. Published attempts at actually determining free metal ion concentrations in bioassays date from about the mid-1970s. Many reports claim that only the free metal ion is toxic, while others have suggested that metal complexes of hydroxide, carbonate, or some organic molecules are also toxic. This review covers some of the literature on the toxicity of various dissolved metal species (especially free metal ions), and wherever possible, examines discrepancies and explains these with the help of more recent data. No attempt is made to review the vast majority of published data on metal toxicity which does not contain information on free metal concentrations. Considerably more is known about the toxicity of the free copper ion than any other metal. Furthermore, most studies on copper toxicity and complexation by organic substances have been conducted using algae, whereas inorganic complexation has been studied primarily with fish bioassays. Consequently, various aspects of the following discussion are biased by results obtained from only one group of aquatic organisms, and considerable gaps remain in our knowledge of metal toxicity and speciation, especially for metals other than copper. Nevertheless, some interesting patterns have emerged, and these should provide clues and inspiration for future research.

2. COMPLEXATION BY ORGANIC SUBSTANCES

There is a considerable amount of literature indicating that the presence of organic substances reduces metal toxicity. The review by Rai et al. (1981) summarizes some of the evidence which shows that complexation by natural (e.g., amino acids, algal extracellular products, humic acids) and synthetic (e.g., EDTA and NTA) complexing agents reduces copper toxicity to algae. It has been believed for some time that natural organic complexing agents play an important role in phytoplankton ecology (Barber and Ryther, 1969; Steemann Nielsen and Wium-Andersen, 1970). This conclusion appears reasonable considering the ability of materials such as decomposed plankton and detritus to reduce copper toxicity (Erickson, 1972). The synthetic chelators EDTA (ethylenediaminetetraacetic acid) and NTA (nitrilotiacetic acid) also reduce metal toxicity to aquatic invertebrates (Biesinger et al., 1974; Stephenson and Taylor, 1975; Knezovich et al., 1981) and fish (Sprague, 1968; Shaw and Brown, 1974). Other organic materials such as sewage effluent, humic acids, amino acids, and sediment extracts have all been shown to reduce metal toxicity to both invertebrates (Lewis et al., 1972, 1974; Whitfield and Lewis, 1976; Knezovich et al., 1981) and fish

(Wildish et al., 1971; Brown et al., 1974). Even some industrial effluents such as pulp mill effluent (Wilson, 1972) and photoprocessing effluents (Bard et al., 1976) can reduce metal toxicity.

Although the evidence demonstrating reduced toxicity in the presence of organic complexing agents is substantial, most reports do not provide estimates of free metal ion concentrations. Consequently it cannot be determined conclusively whether reduced toxicity results from (a) a reduction in concentration of free metal with only the free metal ion being toxic, or (b) toxicity caused by the complexed metal but with the complexed metal having a lower toxicity than the free metal. To answer this question, both total and free metal ion concentrations causing toxicity must be determined in the presence of varying amounts of complexing agents. Examples of such studies are presented in the following sections.

2.1. Algae and Bacteria

Most studies on the relationship between free metal ion concentrations and toxicity to aquatic life in the presence of varying concentrations of organic complexing agents have been conducted using algae or bacteria (Tables 1 to 3). Tables 1 and 2 include data on copper toxicity in fresh and saltwater, respectively, and Table 3 is a summary of the data of Canterford and Canterford (1980) on metals other than copper. Most of these reports indicate that varying the concentration of a single complexing agent causes a variation in the total copper concentration found to be toxic, while the toxic free copper ion concentrations (or activities) are relatively constant (Sunda and Guillard, 1976; Jackson and Morgan, 1978; Sunda and Lewis, 1978; Sunda and Gillespie, 1979; Canterford and Canterford, 1980). Complexing agents used include EDTA, NTA, Tris [Tris(hydroxymethyl)aminomethane], histidine, humic acids, and natural organic substances found in river water. Anderson and Morel (1978) used two different complexing agents but still obtained similar estimates of free copper concentrations toxic to algae at different total copper concentrations. Even the free copper concentrations inhibiting bacterial glucose uptake in relatively fresh water (salinity 1.8 ppt) with humic acids and natural organic matter were found to be fairly close to those inhibiting the same organism in sea water with or without added NTA (Sunda and Gillespie, 1979; Tables 1 and 2). These studies all demonstrate a relatively constant copper toxicity if copper concentration is expressed on a free ion basis.

This approach was extended to other metals by Canterford and Canterford (1980) who obtained similar results for zinc, cadmium, and lead (Table 3). Mercury, silver, and thallium free ion concentrations toxic to algae were also constant at varying concentrations of EDTA, but this is to be expected since EDTA did not appreciably alter speciation of these metals. Anderson et al. (1978) also studied zinc complexation by EDTA and its effect on the

Table 1. Toxicity of Copper to Algae and Bacteria in Fresh and Low Salinity (≤1.8 ppt) Water[a]

Organism	pH	Organic Complexing Agents Present	Test Parameter	Inhibition (%)	-log Total Copper (moles/liter)	pCu[b]	Method of pCu Determination	Reference
Natural phytoplankton	8.1	Natural organics	Inhibition of photosynthesis	—	7.3	10.26	Calculated	Gächter et al., 1978
Bacteria	7.8–8.1	Humic acids and natural organics	Glucose uptake	0	—	10.1	Measured with electrode	Sunda and Gillespie, 1979
				50	5.5–7.0*	9.4		
				100		8.5		
Monochrysis lutheri	6.7–7.2	Natural organics ± 10^{-3} M Tris	Cell growth	0	—	9.3	Measured	Sunda and Lewis, 1978
				50	5.7–6.2*	8.4		
				100	—	7.0		
Selenastrum capricornutum	7.8	6.6×10^{-6} M EDTA	Cell growth via fluorescence)	100	5.2	8.0	Calculated	Guy and Kean, 1980
		5×10^{-6} M Bicine HMDA, NTA or TRIEN	Cell growth (via fluorescence)	100	—	8.0		
		2.5×10^{-6} M ethylenediamine	Cell growth (via fluorescence)	100	—	8.5		
		5×10^{-6} M ethylenediamine	Cell growth (via fluorescence)	100	5.5	8.7		
		10×10^{-6} M ehtylenediamine	Cell growth (via fluorescence)	100	—	9.1		
		5×10^{-6} M citrate	Cell growth (via fluorescence	100	—	9.8		
		10×10^{-6} M citrate	Cell growth (via fluorescence	100	—	9.9		
		10^{-3} M Tris	Cell growth (via fluorescence	100	—	9.0		
Nannochloris sp.	6.8	Natural organics ± 10^{-3} M Tris	Cell growth	50	—	6.7	Measured	McNight, 1981
Ourococcus sp.	6.8	Natural organics	Cell growth	50	<5.7	< 6.5	Measured	McNight, 1981
Ceratium hirundinella	6.8	Natural organics	Immobilization	100	—	9.5	Measured	McNight, 1981

[a]Values extrapolated off figures and tables are indicated by an asterisk.

[b]pCu = − log free copper.

Table 2. Toxicity of Copper to Algae and Bacteria in Seawater[a]

Organism	pH	Organic Complexing Agents Present	Test Parameter	Inhibition (%)	− log Total Copper	pCu[b]	Reference
Gonyaulax tamarensis	8.4	5×10^{-5} M EDTA	Immobilization	0	~-4.7*	~11.0	Anderson and Morel, 1978
				50	4.45*	10.4	
				100	4.32*	9.8	
		10^{-3} M Tris	Immobilization	0	6.4*	11.0	
				50	5.9*	10.4	
				100	5.3*	9.7	
Bacteria	8.1	$0-10^{-5}$ M NTA	Glucose uptake	0	—	~10	Sunda and Gillespie, 1979
				50	5.4–7.3*	9.1	
				100	—	8.3	
Thalassiosira pseudonana	8.1–8.2 (pH 7.7 + 8.7 also included)	$0-10^{-2}$ M Tris	Cell growth	0	—	10.6	Sunda and Guillard, 1976
				50	~3.2–5.0*	~ 8.7*	
				100	—	8.3	
Nannochloris atomus	8.1–8.2	$\pm\ 10^{-2}$ M Tris	Cell growth	0	—	10.4	Sunda and Guillard, 1976
				50	—	~ 9.4*	
				100	—	8.7	
Thalassiosira pseudonana	—	$0-4.9 \times 10^{-7}$ M EDTA	Cell growth	50	6.28–7.64	8.28–8.72	Jackson and Morgan, 1978 (data of Davey et al., 1973)
	—	$0-5.5 \times 10^{-7}$ M histidine	Cell growth	50	6.23–7.20	7.89–8.08	
Ditylum brightwellii	8.0	6.7×10^{-7} M to 10^{-5} M EDTA	Cell growth	50	5.04–6.63	7.99–8.44	Canterford and Canterford, 1980
11 Phytoplankton species	8.1	10^{-2} M Tris	Cell growth (via fluorescence)	50	—	< 8.5–10.5	Gavis et al., 1981

[a] Values extrapolated off figures and tables are indicated by an asterisk.

[b] All pCu values were calculated.

51

Table 3. Toxicity of Metals other than Copper to *Ditylum brightwellii* at EDTA Concentrations from 6.7 $\times$ 10^{-7} to 1 $\times$ 10^{-5} M in Seawater at pH 8.0^a

Metal	$-$ log Total Metal Concentration	$-$ log Free Metal
Zinc	4.91–5.82	6.34–6.61
Cadmium	4.97–6.27	7.12–7.71
Lead	5.71–6.71	8.20–8.32
Mercury	7.26–7.35	21.19
Silver	6.80–7.13	11.63–11.95
Thallium	5.77–5.79	6.08–6.12

^{a}Data from Canterford and Canterford, 1980.

diatom *Thalassiosira weissfloggii,* but they examined concentrations resulting in reduced growth due to zinc limitation by excessive complexation. Again, free zinc levels affecting growth were found to be relatively constant (Zn $\leq$ 10^{-11} mole/liter), even though total zinc levels varied widely with varying EDTA concentrations.

Tables 1 and 2 also include data demonstrating the wide range of free metal ion concentrations observed to be toxic to different species of phytoplankton. McNight (1981), for example, found an approximately 1000-fold difference in free copper concentrations toxic to the sensitive *Ceratium hirundinella* as compared to two copper resistant green algae. Free copper ions are toxic to algae at concentrations as low as 10$^{-10.26}$ molar in freshwater and 10$^{-10.5}$ molar in seawater (Tables 1 and 2), and some thresholds (i.e., less than 50% inhibition) occur at still lower concentrations (Gavis et al., 1981). On the other hand, maximum concentrations tolerated by some algae are as high as the solubility of copper in water (Gavis et al., 1981; McNight, 1981). Hence, although free copper exhibits a fairly uniform toxicity to single species, variability between species is extremely large.

The evidence indicating that toxicity to single species is related to free copper alone is sufficiently extensive to prompt some researchers to study toxicity only in highly buffered (with respect to free copper) solutions, without attempting to verify results in media with no complexing agents added (Gavis et al., 1981). However, not all the published data support the concept of uniform free metal concentrations at equivalent toxicities. For example, Van den Berg et al. (1979) were not able to show that primary production in the presence of different algal exudates and copper was related entirely to free copper ion concentrations. Guy and Kean (1980) observed that 100% growth inhibition in the presence of several chelating agents, including EDTA and NTA, occurred at pCu = 8.0 [pCu = $-$log(Cu^{2+} concentration)]. However, inhibition in the presence of ethylenediamine, citrate, and Tris occurred at lower free copper concentrations (Table 1). They concluded that the copper citrate and copper ethylenediamine complexes were toxic. Their results, especially noting the different pCu values calculated with EDTA and Tris, are at variance with the majority of the literature on algae (Anderson and Morel, 1978). It must be remembered that many of these experiments are interpreted using calculated, and not measured, free metal ion concentrations. Consequently, the accuracy of the results is subject to the accuracy of the metal ligand stability constants chosen to calculate metal speciation. Perhaps some of these discrepancies will be explained when better techniques for measuring free metal ion concentrations are more readily available.

2.2. Invertebrates and Fish

Free metal ion toxicity and complexation by organic substances have been studied less extensively in invertebrates and fish than in algae, although some data exists which conforms with most of the algal observations. Young et al. (1979) studied copper toxicity to shrimp larvae and found that toxicity was related to labile copper, as measured by anodic stripping voltametry. Unfortunately, this cannot be compared directly to free copper. If labile copper were predominantly composed of free and inorganically bound copper, then labile copper would be approximately proportional to free copper at constant pH and salinity. Sunda et al. (1978) calculated that after addition of various concentrations of NTA up to $10^{-4} M$, 96 hr LC50s for cadmium toxicity to grass shrimp were relatively constant at about $4 \times 10^{-7} M$ for free cadmium; total cadmium concentrations varied over tenfold during their study. Zitko et al. (1973) used the cupric ion electrode to predict the toxicity of copper to juvenile Atlantic salmon in waters with varying amounts of humic acids. A reasonable prediction of copper toxicity was possible, although a significant interference by water hardness was observed. Although they did not calculate free copper ion concentrations, electrode readings were a function of free metal, indicating a relationship between free copper and copper toxicity.

In contrast to these studies, Giesy et al. (1977) were not able to show any relationship between cadmium toxicity to a cladoceran and a fish and the complexing capacity of water as measured using a metal ion electrode. However, they did not take into account the stability constants of the various organic fractions analysed nor did they attempt to calculate free cadmium at toxic concentrations. Consequently, these results are not directly comparable with the studies discussed earlier.

We have attempted to verify the principle of a constant free metal ion concentration causing toxicity in our own laboratory using the cladocera *Daphnia magna*. Unpublished results indicate that additions of amino acids increase 48 hr LC50s for total copper but decrease the free copper LC50 values. For example, LC50s based on total copper were $0.50 \times 10^{-6} M$

without glycine and $10.3 \times 10^{-6} M$ with $2 \times 10^{-4}M$ glycine, at pH 8.4 in reconstituted water with hardness and alkalinity of 100 mg/liter. Free copper concentrations, determined by means of a cupric ion electrode, were 7.0 and $0.18 \times 10^{-9} M,$ respectively. Consequently, our data do not support the view that free metal concentrations are always constant in equally toxic solutions with and without organic complexing agents. Further research with invertebrates and fish is needed before results with algae are extrapolated to higher animals.

2.3. Summary

The majority of observations suggest that toxicity in the presence of organic complexing agents is primarily related to free metal concentrations. However, most of the evidence comes from work with algae, and hence the universality of this principle is not yet established. It is also important to remember that some complexing agents, called ionophores, not only bind metals, but are also readily absorbed by animal cells, thereby increasing the rate of metal uptake (Levinson et al., 1979). [EDTA does not appear to be an ionophore (Jackson and Morgan, 1978; Levinson et al., 1979) and hence reduces metal toxicity.] Therefore, it cannot be assumed a priori that all complexing agents which aquatic organisms encounter will reduce metal uptake and toxicity, and hence some exceptions to the common observation of constant free metal concentrations toxic to aquatic life are to be expected.

3. COMPLEXATION BY INORGANIC LIGANDS

Complexation studies in which only the concentration of organic ligands is varied may demonstrate that toxicity is proportional to free metal, but they cannot, by themselves, prove that only the free metal ion is toxic. This is because at constant pH and alkalinity (or salinity), free metal concentrations are proportional to the concentration of various inorganic complexes, any of which may also be toxic. Some examples of studies investigating toxicity and inorganic complexation are given in the following sections; other instances are cited by Babich and Stotsky (this volume).

3.1. Chloride Ions

The presence of chloride ions may affect the toxicity of those metals, such as cadmium and mercury, readily complexed by this ion. Of particular interest is the study by Sunda et al. (1978) on the toxicity of cadmium to grass shrimp. By varying the salinity from 5 to 29 ppt, the 96 hr LC50 increased from around 2 to $8 \times 10^{-6} M$ total cadmium, but the free cadmium LC50 did not vary appreciably (from approximately $4 \times 10^{-7} M$). Results were similar to those observed after addition of various concentrations of NTA, except that cadmium speciation and toxicity were now controlled by chloride ions. The authors suggested that other examples of reduced cadmium toxicity at higher salinity may also be due to increased complexation by chloride ions. Babich and Stotzky (1978, 1979, 1980) also observed decreased toxicity after addition of chloride ions in studies on the effect of mercury on microorganisms, although results with zinc were somewhat more complex. Unfortunately, they did not calculate the free metal concentrations.

3.2. Carbonate Ions

Several studies suggest that metal carbonate complexes, like metal chloride complexes, are generally not toxic. Most of the work has been done on copper toxicity to fish at various alkalinities. Stiff (1971) proposed that the difference in copper toxicity to fish in hard versus soft water was due to the difference in the degree of complexation by carbonate. This view was supported by the calculations of Pagenkopf et al. (1974), who showed that free copper LC50s varied much less than total copper LC50s from several published reports. However, they did not take into account the possible effect of water hardness (i.e., calcium and magnesium concentrations) on copper toxicity (see Section 4.1). Nevertheless, the ability of carbonate ions to reduce copper toxicity is demonstrated in several studies where alkalinity is varied independently of hardness and pH. Lethal concentrations of copper to cutthroat (Chakoumakos et al., 1979) and rainbow trout (Miller and Mackay, 1980) increase with increasing alkalinity, although water hardness also affects toxicity. Similarly, swimming performance and growth of rainbow trout appears to be related to free copper, but not to copper carbonate complexes (Waiwood and Beamish, 1978a,b). Lethal toxicity to fathead minnows and *Daphnia magna* also appears to be related to free copper but not to the concentration of copper carbonate or phosphate complexes (Andrew, 1976; Andrew et al., 1977). In contrast, Shaw and Brown (1974) felt that toxicity was a function of both free copper and copper carbonate complexes. However, they varied the degree of carbonate complexation by varying pH, and ignored possible effects of pH on copper toxicity through mechanisms other than complexation (see Section 4.1).

Most of the data therefore suggests that the copper carbonate complex is not toxic. In natural waters, however, increased alkalinity, and hence carbonate complexation, is usually associated with increased hardness and increased pH. To qualitatively evaluate much of the literature on copper toxicity at different alkalinities requires that all three factors, hardness, pH, and complexation, be taken into account simultaneously. This is attempted in Section 4.1.

3.3. Hydroxide Ions

It is very difficult to determine if metal hydroxide complexes are toxic to aquatic organisms. This is largely because hydroxide concentrations, and consequently the degree of complexation by hydroxide, cannot be varied independently of pH. If pH is held constant, the concentration of metal hydroxides will be proportional to the concentration of free metal. Furthermore, a change in pH could have a direct effect on metal toxicity to the organism, other than through complexation. Hence, Pagenkopf et al. (1974) and Andrew et al. (1977) could not prove that copper hydroxides were not toxic to fish and *Daphnia*. Waiwood and Beamish (1978a,b) found that both free copper and $CuOH^+$ were related to swimming performance and growth, whereas Howarth and Sprague (1978) obtained best correlations between lethal toxicity and free copper plus the ionic species $CuOH^+$ and $Cu_2(OH)_2^{2+}$. Chakoumakos et al. (1979) believed that free copper, $CuOH^+$, $Cu(OH)_2^0$, and $Cu_2(OH)_2^{2+}$ were toxic to cutthroat trout. Wagemann and Barica (1979) felt that the algicidal properties of copper were due to $CuOH^+$ and $Cu(OH)_2^0$ in addition to free copper, because of the toxicity of copper at high pH, but they provided no clear data to prove this point. Because of the cross correlation between free copper and copper hydroxide concentrations, none of the foregoing papers provide clear proof of the toxicity of the hydroxide complex.

In view of this dilemma, it may be best to ignore the metal hydroxide complex and describe toxicity as a function of free metal but specifying the pH. The relationship between free metal ion toxicity and pH is discussed next.

4. INFLUENCE OF pH AND HARDNESS

The majority of data examined so far suggests that toxicity is a function of the concentration of the free metal ions, with both inorganic and organic complexes being relatively nontoxic. A possible exception, the hydroxide complexes, can be ignored if the pH is taken into account. The influence of hardness (i.e., calcium and magnesium) and pH on the toxicity of the free metal ion will now be examined. Since most of the available data concerns copper toxicity, this metal will be considered first.

4.1. Copper Toxicity to Fish

The influence of water hardness, used in the general sense to include alkalinity, on the toxicity of metals is well known (e.g., Pickering and Henderson, 1966; Zitko, 1976). Pagenkopf et al. (1974) attributed this effect to the change in alkalinity. Andrew (1976) and Zitko and Carson (1976) also felt copper

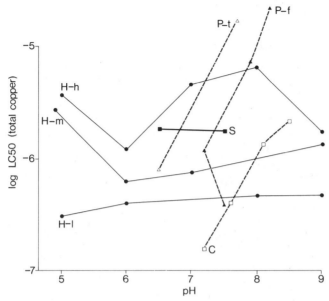

Figure 1. Lethal concentration of copper to fish as a function of pH. Copper concentration expressed as total copper (moles/liter). Solid lines connect points of equal hardness. Dashed lines connect points when hardness increased with pH (points connected in order of increasing hardness). P–f: Pagenkopf et al., 1974, 96 hr LC50, fathead minnows; hardness increases in order 31.4, 20, 198, and 360 mg/liter with increasing pH. P–t: Pagenkopf et al., 1974, 72 hr LC50, rainbow trout; hardness 17.5 and 320 mg/liter, increasing with pH. S: Shaw and Brown, 1974, 48 hr LC50, rainbow trout; alkalinity 100 mg/liter. C: Chapman and McCrady, 1977, 96 hr LC50 (extrapolated off their Fig. 8), chinook salmon; hardness 13, 46, 182, and 359 mg/liter, increasing with pH. H: Howarth and Sprague, 1978, 96 hr LC50, rainbow trout; hardness approximately 30 (l), 100 (m), and 370 (h) mg/liter.

toxicity was primarily related to alkalinity, although recent studies in which hardness was varied independently of alkalinity indicate that hardness itself significantly influences copper toxicity (Chakoumakos et al., 1979; Miller and Mackay, 1980). Hence, in the analysis of free copper ion toxicity, water hardness (i.e., calcium and magnesium concentrations) has to be taken into account. The effect of the alkalinity component of hardness is eliminated by expressing toxicity as a function of free copper, because alkalinity is believed to affect toxicity through complexation by carbonate and other ions.

The effect of pH on the lethal toxicity of copper, expressed both as total and as free copper, is summarized in Figs. 1 to 3. It is apparent that toxicity on a total copper basis is a complex function of pH, either increasing, decreasing, or even showing several inflection points as pH increases. The relationship between free copper toxicity and pH, on the other hand, is much more uniform. For example, the 96 hr LC50s for rainbow trout, *Salmo gairdneri* (Howarth and Sprague, 1978), compare favorably with those for cutthroat trout, *S. clarki* (Chakoumakos et al., 1979), if expressed on a free

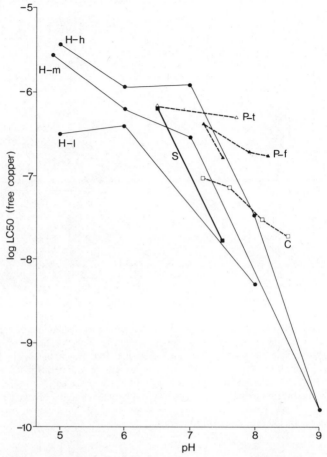

Figure 2. Lethal concentration of copper to fish as a function of pH. Copper concentration expressed as free copper ion (moles/liter). Symbols as in Fig. 1. Free copper LC50s for data of Shaw and Brown (S) calculated from regression of their free copper versus total copper data. S and C are measured concentrations, others are calculated from speciation models.

copper basis. Free copper LC50s decrease with increasing pH and decreasing hardness in both cases and the two sets of data overlap considerably, necessitating the use of separate figures for clarity (Figs. 2 and 3b). The total copper LC50s (Figs. 1 and 3a) however, bear little resemblance. The effect of pH on the free copper toxicity data of Shaw and Brown (1974) for rainbow trout (Fig. 2) agrees with the data of the other authors who conducted experiments at constant hardness. Comparison of their free and total copper toxicity values (Figs. 1 and 2) suggest that the increased toxicity of free copper ions at higher pH is offset almost completely by the increased complexation of copper by carbonate ions, resulting in almost no change in the total copper LC50 over their pH range. Consequently, these authors con-

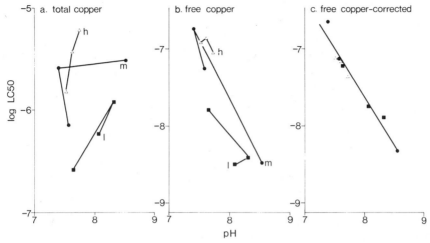

Figure 3. Lethal concentration of copper (96 hr LC50) to cutthroat trout as a function of pH. Data from Chakoumakos et al., 1979. Copper concentration expressed as *a*) total copper, *b*) free copper ion, and *c*) free copper X 100 X (1/hardness) to correct to a hardness of 100 mg/liter. Hardness approximately equal to 25 (l), 75 (m), and 200 (h) mg/liter. Data points joined in order of increasing alkalinity. For total copper, lowest point for each hardness indicates lowest alkalinity. For free copper, lowest point indicates highest alkalinity. Free copper was calculated from a speciation model.

cluded that copper carbonate complexes were toxic, a view disputed by most subsequent workers (e.g., Andrew et al., 1977; Howarth and Sprague, 1978; Waiwood and Beamish, 1978a,b; Chakoumakos et al., 1979). Considering the more recent publications, it appears that the conclusions of Shaw and Brown (1974) were erroneous, and resulted because two different factors cancelled one another out.

In a similar fashion, the decreased toxicity of free copper ions resulting from increased hardness can be influenced by the pH effect, and, in some cases, cause misinterpretation. Chapman and McCrady (1977) studied copper toxicity to chinook salmon (*Oncorhynchus tshawytscha*) in waters in which pH, hardness, and alkalinity all increased simultaneously, a situation similar to that expected in natural waters. Their estimates of total copper LC50s show a much steeper relationship between toxicity and pH than do the studies at constant hardness (Fig. 1), whereas the relationship between free copper LC50s and pH is flatter than in the other studies (Fig. 2). This is likely due to the hardness effect. In the absence of detailed data on the effect of hardness on free copper toxicity at any given pH, an initial attempt at correcting for the hardness effect could be made by assuming that free copper LC50s are directly proportional to hardness at constant pH. Free copper LC50s, corrected to a standard hardness of 100 mg/liter (by dividing the LC50 by the hardness and multiplying by 100) are shown in Figs. 3c and 4. The correction seems to remove much of the remaining variation in Fig.

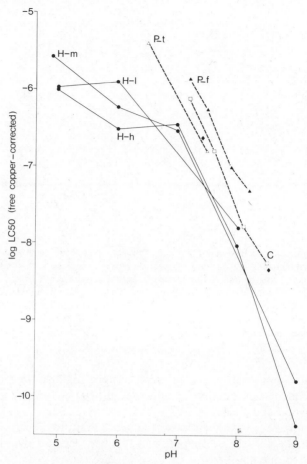

Figure 4. Lethal concentration of copper to fish as a function of pH. Copper concentration expressed as free copper ion X 100 X (1/hardness), to correct all values to a hardness of 100 mg/liter. Symbols as in Fig. 1. The cutthroat trout data at the highest and lowest pH values (from Fig. 3) are included for comparison (♦).

3*b,* even improving the observed relationship for free copper within data sets at one hardness (especially the low hardness plot). The corrected values for the three hardnesses studied by Howarth and Sprague (1978) also overlap, further supporting the validity of the corrected values (Fig. 4). It should therefore be possible to use hardness-corrected LC50s to compare data from experiments at constant hardness with those where hardness varies with pH. The slope of the corrected free copper LC50 plots for the different studies are all fairly close, including rainbow trout data from several authors, cutthroat trout, chinook salmon, and fathead minnows (*Pimephales promelas*) (Fig. 4). Not only is the slope more consistent with that of other studies but the corrected fathead minnow LC50s give a straighter line that those of the uncorrected free copper LC50s (Figs. 2 and 4).

Consequently, it appears that hardness plays an important role in toxicity of free copper ions, and this effect can counteract the increased toxicity observed at higher pH values. This explains why Pagenkopf et al. (1974) concluded that toxicity was only a function of free metal concentration, and not significantly influenced by pH or hardness (other than through complexation by increased alkalinity normally accompanying increased hardness). Hence, several discrepancies in the literature can readily be explained through the cancelling effect of one relationship on another (i.e., pH versus complexation, and pH versus hardness).

Analysis of the data on copper toxicity to fish indicates, therefore, that lethal toxicity of the free metal ion is relatively constant in water of equivalent hardness and pH. Toxicity ranges from about 1 to 3×10^{-8} M at pH 8, to 3 to 10×10^{-7} M at pH 7 for salmonids, with slightly higher LC50s for fathead minnows (corrected to a standard hardness to 100 mg/liter; Fig. 4). Increasing pH or decreasing hardness increases toxicity of free copper, and increasing pH increases complexation thereby decreasing toxicity on a total metal basis. These relationships, however, can easily be obscured in any single study if toxicity is not expressed on a free copper basis, and if pH and hardness are not varied independently of one another. It should also be noted that these relationships are expected to hold only if the proton concentration itself is not toxic. For example, Miller and Mackay (1980) observed the usual increase in rainbow trout LC50s from pH 5.4 to 4.7. However, below pH 4.7 where the hydrogen ion concentration was toxic by itself, further reductions in pH caused a reduction in LC50 values. Although their data are based on total copper, most of the copper would be expected to be free in this low pH range.

The data in Figs. 1 to 4 indicate that although toxicity expressed on a free metal basis is more consistent than when expressed on a total metal basis, the range in free copper concentrations found to be toxic is quite large, due to the rapid drop in free copper LC50s at high pH. At first glance this might suggest that the toxicity of copper may be partly due to copper hydroxide species, which would occur at these pH values. However, increased toxicity at higher pH values can be explained without consideration of hydroxide complexes. Organisms are composed of organic molecules, many of which are acids and would therefore exist in a more ionized state at higher pH, thereby facilitating copper complexation and uptake. Assume, for example, that copper uptake and toxicity is a function of copper complexing ligands on the animal's surface. The equilibrium between these ligands and hydrogen and copper ions can be written as

$$\frac{CuL_n}{Cu \cdot L^n} = \beta \tag{1}$$

$$\frac{HL}{H \cdot L} = K \tag{2}$$

L is a ligand responsible for copper toxicity, β and K are the stability con-

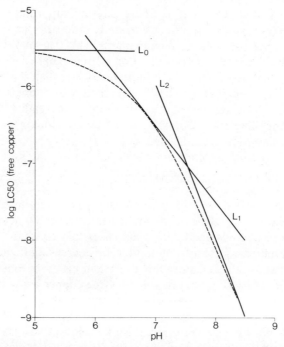

Figure 5. Free copper ion concentration giving equal degrees of complexation of three different ligands (L_0, L_1, and L_2), and resultant LC50 curve assuming mortality occurs when the given degree of complexation by any of the ligands is reached. See text for further explanation.

stants for the copper ligand and protonated complexes respectively, and n is an integer; charges, which may vary between ligands, are omitted for simplicity. If the ligand is mostly protonated at normal pH values (as glycine is, for example), then the total ligand concentration, which is constant, is approximately equal to HL. If we assume that equal toxicity occurs when complexation is constant, then CuL_n is constant. Rearrangement of Eqs. (1) and (2) gives

$$Cu = \frac{CuL_n K^n}{\beta (HL)^n} (H)^n \qquad (3)$$

$$\log Cu = -n(pH) + \log \frac{CuL_n K^n}{\beta (HL)^n} \qquad (4)$$

Hence, if only a single copper complexing ligand is involved, a linear relationship should occur between free copper LC50s and pH with a negative slope equal to n. Some ligands (e.g., acetic acid), however, do not have appreciably different degrees of ionization over the normal physiological range tolerated by aquatic animals, and consequently little effect of pH on degree of complexation is expected. If several copper ligands on the animal's surface are involved in controlling toxicity, some with different values of n and some with no change in complexation with pH, copper toxicity would be a function of uptake by the most heavily complexed ligand. If, for example, three ligands are involved, one with no pH effect (L_0), one with $n = 1$ (L_1), and one with $n = 2$ (L_2), as shown in Fig. 5, the LC50 would follow the lower of the three lines, and the steeper portion of the toxicity versus pH curve would be expected to occur at the higher pH range. The curve in Fig. 5 is close to the observed relationship between free copper toxicity and pH (Figs. 2, 3, and 4). This argument cannot be proven with the data available, but nevertheless demonstrates that the observed results can be rationalized without the necessity of assuming that copper hydroxide species are toxic. The observation that hardness influences free copper toxicity further supports this line of reasoning, since if copper toxicity is reduced by calcium and magnesium ion competition, it seems reasonable to assume hydrogen ion competition can also occur. Hence, copper toxicity can be explained by considering only the concentrations of free copper ion and their interaction with pH and hardness.

4.2. Copper Toxicity to Invertebrates and Algae

The relationship between pH and free copper toxicity has rarely been studied using invertebrates. Andrew et al. (1977), though not studying the pH effects directly, observed differences in toxicity of free copper ions to *Daphnia magna* in separate experiments. These were run at slightly different pH values, suggesting that increased pH resulted in an increase in free copper toxicity. They also suggested that a similar mechanism may be responsible for the observations of Shaw and Brown (1974), a conclusion already noted in the previous section. We have obtained some 24 hr LC50 values for *Daphnia magna* in reconstituted water with constant hardness and ionic strength (U. Borgmann and K. Ralph, unpublished data). Only the high-pH medium contained $2 \times 10^{-6} M$ NaHCO$_3$, which resulted in a pH of about 8.4, after equilibration with the atmosphere in our laboratory. Speciation was measured using an Orion 94-29 cupric ion electrode. The results, summarized in Table 4, agree well with the data on fish in Figs. 1 and 2. On a total copper basis, toxicity is greatest at intermediate pH values. Free copper becomes more toxic at higher pH values and this effect is more pronounced above pH 7. At pH values above 7, the increased toxicity of the free copper ion is counteracted by the increased degree of copper complexation.

The literature on the effect of pH on free copper ion toxicity to algae and microorganisms is not extensive. Sunda and Guillard (1976) calculated that a pH change from 7.7 to 8.7 did not affect the relationship between algal growth and free copper. Most of their experiments, however, were conducted at pH 8.1 to 8.2, with the pH 8.7 experiment showing no toxicity. Some data indicate that algae respond similarly to fish and *Daphnia*. For

Table 4.   24 hr LC50 Values for 12 $\pm$ 12 hr old *Daphnia magna* at Several pH Values in Reconstituted Water at 20°C. pH 6 and 7: 10^{-3} M CaCl$_2$ Plus 7 $\times$ 10^{-3} M NaCl. pH 8.4: 10^{-3} M CaCl$_2$, 2 $\times$ 10^{-3} M NaHCO$_3$ Plus 5 $\times$ 10^{-3} M NaCl.[a]

pH (range)	LC50 Total Copper 10^{-6} M (95% confidence limits)	LC50 Free Copper 10^{-6} M
5.93 (5.70–6.04)	0.37 (0.22–0.63)	0.37
6.95 (6.85–7.17)	0.24 (0.18–0.33)	0.23
8.41 (8.38–8.47)	0.92 (0.63–1.34)	0.014

[a] Free Metal Complexation Determined using Orion 94-29 Cupric Ion Electrode.

example, copper toxicity to *Chlorella pyrenoidosa* is lower at pH 5 than at pH 8, presumably because of competition between cupric and hydrogen ions (Steemann Nielsen et al., 1969; Steemann Nielsen and Kamp-Nielsen, 1970). Further examples of competition with hydrogen ions, and reduced toxicity due to complexation and precipitation at high pH are given in the reviews by Babich and Stotzky (1980, and this volume) and Rai et al. (1981). Unfortunately, most of the literature does not provide estimates of free copper concentrations, and hence it is difficult to interpret and will not be discussed here.

4.3.   Cadmium Toxicity

Some of the problems in understanding cadmium toxicity in seawater are analogous to those encountered with copper in freshwater. Numerous references indicate that cadmium toxicity to invertebrates drops with increasing salinity (e.g., O'Hara, 1973; Jones, 1975; Vernberg et al., 1977; Frank and Robertson, 1979) just as total copper toxicity drops with increasing water hardness. Uptake and toxicity of cadmium to fish also appears to decrease with increasing salinity and this has been attributed to the increased hardness accompanying increased salinity (von Westerhagen and Dethlefsen, 1975; Michibata, 1981). However, Zitko and Carson (1976) found no effect of calcium or magnesium on cadmium toxicity to Atlantic salmon, and Sunda et al. (1978) found no effect of salinity on toxicity of free cadmium to grass shrimp, although increased complexation by chloride ions caused an increased resistance to total cadmium with increasing salinity. Michibata (1981) using fish, and Wright and Frain (1981) using freshwater amphipods, concluded that increased water hardness reduced cadmium toxicity. Unfortunately, in both studies chloride concentrations were increased simultaneously with hardness, and the possible role of chloride complexation was not studied. However, cadmium uptake by shore crabs does appear to be related to calcium concentrations, because uptake is increased in artificial seawater with reduced calcium (Wright, 1977). In this study, the chloride concentrations were consistently high, and hence addition of $CaCl_2$ caused little change in total chloride levels. Hence, the reduced toxicity of cadmium at higher salinities could result from the combined effect of increased cadmium complexation and increased competition with calcium and/or magnesium. This is analogous to the reduced toxicity of copper in hard water, where copper complexation (in this case by carbonate rather than chloride ions) is higher and calcium and/or magnesium competition with copper ions is increased. Demonstration of a clear effect of water hardness or chloride complexation on cadmium toxicity requires, therefore, that care be taken to maintain the other variable constant, a point often overlooked in past studies.

Data on the influence of pH on free cadmium toxicity is scarce. Cadmium toxicity to microorganisms appears to increase with pH, and this has been attributed to competition between cadmium and hydrogen ions (Babich and Stotzky, 1977, 1980), a situation analogous to that for free copper (Figs. 2 and 3). Cadmium toxicity to *Chlorella,* on the other hand, was observed to decrease slightly with increasing pH from 7 to 8 (Hart and Scaife, 1977). The lack of data on the free metal ion in these studies makes interpretation difficult. It appears however that at least some of the data follows the pattern for copper, since if toxicity for total metal increases with pH, toxicity of free metal must also increase at higher pH values where complexation, if present, would be greater.

4.4. Zinc Toxicity

Patterns of zinc toxicity appear to parallel those of copper and cadmium. The toxicity of zinc to fish is lower in hard than in soft water (Mount, 1966; Pickering and Henderson, 1966). Studies in which hardness or calcium and magnesium concentrations are varied independently of alkalinity suggest that much of this effect stems directly from hardness (i.e., calcium and magnesium) (Zitko and Carson, 1976; Bradley and Sprague, 1983). The same response has been observed with lotic plants (Say and Whitton, 1977). At pH values of about 7 and below, most of the zinc is free and zinc toxicity increases with increasing pH (Pagenkopf, 1976; Bradley and Sprague, 1983). Increasing pH above 7 either increases (Pagenkopf, 1976) or decreases zinc toxicity (Bradley and Sprague, 1983). If toxicity decreases, this is generally attributed to the formation of less toxic zinc precipitates (Bradley and Sprague, 1983). Consequently, toxicity of free zinc ions appears to increase with increasing pH and decrease with increasing hardness, in much the same way as free copper and cadmium.

4.5. Summary

It is apparent that both pH and water hardness (i.e., calcium and magnesium concentrations) can affect the toxicity of free metal ions. Consequently, examination of the effect of complexation, pH or hardness on metal toxicity must be done under conditions in which the other two variables are held constant, or at least corrected for in some way. Failure to do so can result in misinterpretation due to several factors cancelling (e.g., pH and complexation or pH and hardness) or reinforcing (e.g., hardness and complexation) one another. If all three factors are taken into account, toxicity appears to be closely related to free metal concentration, at least for copper (Figs. 3 and 4). For metals other than copper, cadmium, and zinc, insufficient data on free metal toxicity could be found to permit critical analysis of pH and hardness effects.

5. FREE METAL DETERMINATION FROM BIOASSAY DATA

The frequent observation that free metal ion concentrations toxic to aquatic life are relatively constant at constant pH and hardness suggests the possible application of bioassay data to determine free metal ion concentrations, especially under conditions where chemical techniques for studying metal speciation cannot be used. However, initial attempts at employing bioassays for studying metal toxicity were designed to estimate the complexing capacity of waters, rather than free metal ion concentrations (Davey et al., 1973; Gillespie and Vaccaro, 1978). These assays compared the shift of the toxicity curve towards higher metal concentrations with the amounts of strong chelating agents present. The increase in the amount of copper required to reduce algal growth (Davey et al., 1973) or bacterial glucose uptake (Gillespie and Vaccaro, 1978) correlated well with the amount of EDTA or histidine added, and it was therefore assumed that differences in copper toxicity in natural waters represented differences in complexing capacity. However, weak complexing agents, such as most amino acids (which are generally weaker complexing agents than histidine) reduce copper toxicity by less than their total concentration (Borgmann, 1981; Knezovich et al., 1981). Consequently, if weak complexing agents are present in varying amounts, relative to strong complexing agents, no relationship between complexing capacity (in terms of total concentration of complexing agents) and metal toxicity need occur. It is not surprising therefore, that Giesy et al. (1977) found no relation between complexing capacity and toxicity of cadmium to cladocera or fish. The importance of considering free metal ion concentrations, and not just the complexing capacity, is now recognized, and both the data of Davey et al. (1973) and that of Gillespie and Vaccaro (1978) have been reanalyzed and free metal concentrations calculated (Jackson and Morgan, 1978; Sunda and Gillespie, 1979).

Sunda and Gillespie (1979) used copper inhibition of glucose uptake in bacteria as a bioassay for estimating free copper ion concentrations in natural seawater. They used seawater treated with ultraviolet radiation (to destroy naturally occurring organic complexing agents) with various added concentrations of NTA to produce a standard curve of bacterial response as a function of free copper concentrations. Free copper concentrations were calculated from speciation models in inorganic seawater with or without NTA. Results were compared with bioassays in untreated coastal seawater assuming equal response at equal free metal concentrations. This permitted determination of the relationship between free and total copper and the degree of organically bound copper in natural water, which ranged from 75% (at 6.4×10^{-8} M total copper) to 24% (at 2.1×10^{-7} M total copper).

Gächter et al. (1978) used a similar technique to estimate the concentration and strength of complexing agents in natural waters. They used ultrafiltration to remove natural organic complexing agents, and then compared the reduction in photosynthesis of phytoplankton in filtered water before and after addition of EDTA, and after enrichment with the residue obtained from the filters. By assuming that equal inhibition occurred at equal free copper concentrations, and by correcting for inorganic complexation (the only complexation assumed to occur in the filtered water), they estimated free copper concentrations in equilibrium with various concentrations of organically bound copper. From this, the concentration and stability constants of the natural ligands were estimated, and copper complexation in natural water was predicted. This procedure therefore, was similar to that of Sunda and Gillespie (1979), except that organic complexation was initially removed by ultrafiltration rather than ultraviolet radiation, and the natural organic complexing agents were concentrated above natural levels in the bioassay.

A slightly different approach was used to estimate free copper concentrations which inhibited growth of freshwater copepods (Borgmann, 1981). Instead of calibrating the bioassay using a medium of known complexing ability, toxicity curves were obtained in natural water before and after addition of weak complexing agents (i.e., metal ion buffers, in this case amino acids). Free metal ion concentrations were then calculated assuming that the difference in toxicity before and after addition of the ligand was due entirely to complexation by the added ligand. This technique is particularly useful for bioassays where unknown complexing agents cannot be removed, as for example, in tests with animals which must feed on fine particulate matter. Furthermore, complexation by inorganic ligands need not be estimated, as is normally the case with conventional calibration curves. Consequently, the mathematics involved is relatively simple; it involves consideration of only one ligand, and eliminates the need for complex computer programs for calculating speciation.

It must be remembered that all of these bioassays rely on the assumption that the toxicity of the free metal ion does not change as the degree of complexation and toxicity of total metal changes. Most of the data on algae suggests this is the case; however, little work has been done on invertebrates or fish to clearly show that at constant pH and water hardness and under widely varying degrees of complexation, toxicity of free ions is constant (the study by Sunda et al., 1978 is an exception). The general applicability of this approach for aquatic animals remains to be verified.

6. SUMMARY

Most of the literature indicates that data on toxicity of metals to aquatic biota present a much more coherent pattern if toxicity is described on the basis of free rather than total metal. Metal complexation by natural or synthetic organic agents generally reduces toxicity of metals on a total metal concentration basis, but usually has much less effect on free metal concentrations under equivalently toxic conditions. Most of the evidence comes from work on copper toxicity to algae (Tables 1 and 2). Complexation by inorganic ligands (e.g., Cl^-, CO_3^{2-}) also appears to result in nontoxic complexes. Most of the data here comes from studies on copper complexation by carbonate ions and the toxicity of copper to fish. The pH has a considerable effect on toxicity of copper, and apparently also on the toxicity of cadmium and zinc. This effect is not eliminated by describing toxicity on a free metal ion basis, but it becomes much more consistent, largely because of elimination of the compounding influence of pH on the degree of complexation. The dependence of free ion toxicity on pH could imply that metal hydroxide complexes are toxic. However, there is no concrete evidence to support this view. Increased toxicity at higher pH values can be explained equally well by the assumption that metal complexation, and consequently uptake, by organisms increases with pH through reduced competition of metal ions with hydrogen ions. Water hardness (i.e., calcium and magnesium) also frequently affect free metal ion toxicity, and this can obscure the pH effect if toxicity is studied in waters where hardness increases simultaneously with pH. Accurate comparison of the results of toxicity experiments from different laboratories is therefore facilitated by describing toxicity on a free metal ion basis and by taking both pH and hardness changes into account.

The reduced effect of complexing agents on free metal ion toxicity as compared to total metal, observed in many algal experiments, indicates the possibility of determining free metal concentrations toxic to aquatic organisms from bioassay data. This has already been attempted for algae and zooplankton (Sunda and Gillespie, 1979; Borgmann, 1981). However, the general scarcity of experimental evidence suggesting that toxicity for animals is constant on a free metal basis necessitates some caution until further research at constant pH, water hardness, and widely varying degrees of complexation is completed.

More information on the effects of organic complexation on invertebrates and fish is needed not just as background for application of free metal bio-assays, but also because of the likely importance of organic complexation in affecting sublethal toxicity to animals. Organic complexing agents are generally in lower abundance than inorganic ligands (e.g., bicarbonate) but have a stronger affinity for metals, especially copper. Consequently, the fraction of the total copper present as organic complexes even at lower copper concentrations is quite high (e.g., 70% or more). This decreases as the total copper concentration increases (Gächter et al., 1978; Sunda and Gillespie, 1979) and the adsorption sites on organic ligands become saturated. It is appropriate, therefore, that lethal toxicity to fish be studied with respect to the influence of inorganic complexation. However, sublethal toxicity, occurring at lower total metal concentrations, may be related more to organic complexation in natural waters.

ACKNOWLEDGMENT

I thank P. V. Hodson for reviewing the manuscript.

REFERENCES

Anderson, D. M. and Morel, F. M. M. (1978). Copper sensitivity of *Gonyaulax tamarensis*. *Limnol. Oceanogr.* **23**, 283–295.

Anderson, M. A., Morel, F. M. M., and Guillard, R. R. L. (1978). Growth limitation of a coastal diatom by low zinc ion activity. *Nature* **276**, 70–71.

Andrew, R. W. (1976). Toxicity relationships to copper forms in natural waters. In: R. W. Andrew, P. V. Hodson, and D. E. Konasewich, Eds., *Workshop on toxicity to biota of metal forms in natural water,* International Joint Commission, Windsor, Canada, pp. 127–143.

Andrew, R. W., Biesinger, K. E., and Glass, G. E. (1977). Effects of inorganic complexing on the toxicity of copper to *Daphnia magna. Water Res.* **11**, 309–315.

Babich, H. and Stotzky, G. (1977). Sensitivity of various bacteria, including actinomycetes, and fungi to cadmium and the influence of pH on sensitivity. *Appl. Environ. Microbiol.* **33**, 681–695.

Babich, H. and Stotzky, G. (1978). Toxicity of zinc to fungi, bacteria and coliphages: Influence of chloride ions. *Appl. Environ. Microbiol.* **36**, 906–914.

Babich, H. and Stotzky, G. (1979). Differential toxicities of mercury to bacteria and bacteriophages in sea and in lake water. *Can. J. Microbiol.* **25**, 1252–1257.

Babich, H. and Stotzky, G. (1980). Environmental factors that influence the toxicity of heavy metals and gaseous pollutants to microorganisms. *CRC Crit. Rev. Microbiol.* **8**, 99–145.

Barber, R. T. and Ryther, J. H. (1969). Organic chelators: Factors affecting primary production in the Cromwell current upwelling. *J. Exp. Mar. Biol. Ecol.* **3**, 191–199.

Bard, C. C., Murphy, J. J., Stone, D. L., and Terhaar, C. J. (1976). Silver in photoprocessing effluents. *J. Water Poll. Control Fed.* **48**, 389–394.

Biesinger, K. E., Andrew, R. W., and Arthur, J. W. (1974). Chronic toxicity of NTA (nitrilotriacetate) and metal-NTA complexes to *Daphnia magna. J. Fish. Res. Board Can.* **31**, 486–490.

Borgmann, U. (1981) Determination of free metal ion concentrations using bioassays. *Can. J. Fish. Aquat. Sci.* **38**, 999–1002.

Bradley, R. W. and Sprague, J. B. (1983). The influence of pH, hardness, and alkalinity on the acute toxicity of zinc to rainbow trout. Proc. at 8th Annual Aquatic Toxicity Workshop, Guelph, Nov. 1981 Can. Tech. Rep. Fish. Aquat. Sci. No. 1151, 172–179.

Brown, V. M., Shaw, T. L., and Shurben, D. G. (1974). Aspects of water quality and the toxicity of copper to rainbow trout. *Water Res.* **8**, 797–803.

Canterford, G. S. and Canterford, D. R. (1980). Toxicity of heavy metals to the marine diatom *Ditylum brightwellii* (West) Grunow: Correlation between toxicity and metal speciation. *J. Mar. Biol. Ass. U.K.* **60**, 227–242.

Chakoumakos, C., Russo, R. C., and Thurston, R. V. (1979). Toxicity of copper to cutthroat trout (*Salmo clarki*) under different conditions of alkalinity, pH and hardness. *Environ. Sci. Technol.* **13**, 213–219.

Chapman, G. A. and McCrady, J. K. (1977). Copper toxicity: A question of form. In: R. A. Tubb, Ed., *Recent advances in fish toxicology*, U.S. Environmental Protection Agency, Rep. No. EPA-600/3-77-085.

Davey, E. W., Morgan, M. J., and Erickson, S. J. (1973). A biological measurement of the copper complexation capacity of seawater. *Limnol. Oceanogr.* **18**, 993–997.

Erickson, S. J. (1972). Toxicity of copper to *Thalassiosira pseudonana* in unenriched inshore seawater. *J. Phycol.* **8**, 318–323.

Frank, P. M. and Robertson, P. B. (1979). The influence of salinity on toxicity of cadmium and chromium to the blue crab, *Callinectes sapidus*. *Bull. Environ. Contam. Toxicol.* **21**, 74–78.

Gächter, R., Davis, J. S., and Marès, A. (1978). Regulation of copper availability to phytoplankton by macromolecules in lake water. *Environ. Sci. Technol.* **12**, 1416–1421.

Gavis, J., Guillard, R. R. L., and Woodward, B. L. (1981). Cupric ion activity and the growth of phytoplankton clones isolated from different marine environments. *J. Mar. Res.* **39**, 315–333.

Giesy, J. P., Jr., Leersee, G. J., and Williams, D. R. (1977). Effects of naturally occurring aquatic organic fractions on cadmium toxicity to *Simocephalus serrulatus* (Daphnidae) and *Gambusia affinis* (Poeciliidae). *Water Res.* **11**, 1013–1020.

Gillespie, P. A. and Vaccaro, R. F. (1978). A bacterial bioassay for measuring the copper-chelation capacity of seawater. *Limnol. Oceanogr.* **23**, 543–548.

Guy, R. D. and Kean, A. R. (1980). Algae as a chemical speciation monitor—I, A comparison of algal growth and computer calculated speciation. *Water Res.* **14**, 891–899.

Hart, B. A. and Scaife, B. D. (1977). Toxicity and bioaccumulation of cadmium in *Chlorella pyrenoidosa*. *Environ. Res.* **14**, 401–413.

Howarth, R. S. and Sprague, J. B. (1978). Copper lethality to rainbow trout in waters of various hardness and pH. *Water Res.* **12**, 455–462.

Jackson, G. A. and Morgan, J. J. (1978). Trace metal–chelator interactions and phytoplankton growth in seawater media: Theoretical analysis and comparison with reported observations. *Limnol. Oceanogr.* **23**, 268–282.

Jones, M. B. (1975). Synergistic effects of salinity, temperature and heavy metals on mortality and osmoregulation in marine and estuarine isopods (Crustacea). *Mar. Biol.* **30**, 13–20.

Knezovich, J. P., Harrison, F. L., and Tucker, J. S. (1981). The influence of organic chelators on the toxicity of copper to embryos of the pacific oyster, *Crassostrea gigas*. *Arch. Environ. Contam. Toxicol.* **10**, 241–249.

Levinson, W., Idriss, J., and Jackson, J. (1979). Metal binding drugs induce synthesis of four proteins in normal cells. *Biol. Trace Element Res.* **1**, 15–23.

Lewis, A. G., Whitfield, P. H., and Ramnarine, A. (1972). Some particulate and soluble agents affecting the relationship between metal toxicity and organism survival in the calanoid copepod *Euchaeta japonica. Mar. Biol.* **17,** 215–221.

Lewis, A. G., Whitfield, P. H., and Ramnarine, A. (1974). The reduction of copper toxicity in a marine copepod by sediment extract. *Limnol. Oceanogr.* **18,** 324–327.

McKnight, D. (1981). Chemical and biological processes controlling the response of a freshwater ecosystem to copper stress: A field study of the $CuSO_4$ treatment of Mill Pond reservoir, Burlington, Massachusetts. *Limnol. Oceanogr.* **26,** 518–531.

Michibata, H. (1981). Effect of water hardness on the toxicity of cadmium to the egg of the teleost *Oryzias latipes. Bull. Environ. Contam. Toxicol.* **27,** 187–192.

Miller, T. G. and Mackay, W. C. (1980). The effects of hardness, alkalinity and pH of test water on the toxicity of copper to rainbow trout (*Salmo gairdneri*). *Water. Res.* **14,** 129–133.

Mount, D. I. (1966). The effect of total hardness and pH on acute toxicity of zinc to fish. *Air Water Pollut. Int. J.* **10,** 49–56.

O'Hara, J. (1973). The influence of temperature and salinity on the toxicity of cadmium to the fiddler crab, *Uca pugilator. Fish. Bull.* **71,** 149–153.

Pagenkopf, G. K. (1976). Zinc speciation and toxicity to fishes. In: R. W. Andrew, P. V. Hodson, and D. E. Konasewich, Eds., *Workshop on toxicity to biota of metal forms in natural water,* International Joint Commission, Windsor, Canada, pp. 77–91.

Pagenkopf, G. K., R. C. Russo, and Thurston, R. V. (1974). Effect of complexation on toxicity of copper to fishes. *J. Fish. Res. Board Can.* **31,** 462–465.

Pickering, Q. H. and Henderson, C. (1966). The acute toxicity of some heavy metals to different species of warmwater fishes. *Air Water Pollut. Int. J.* **10,** 453–463.

Rai, L. C., Gaur, J. P., and Kumar, H. D. (1981). Phycology and heavy-metal pollution. *Biol. Rev.* **56,** 99–151.

Say, P. J. and Whitton, B. A. (1977). Influence of zinc on lotic plants. II. Environmental effects on toxicity of zinc to *Hormidium rivulare. Freshwater Biol.* **7,** 377–384.

Shaw, T. L. and Brown, V. M. (1974). The toxicity of some forms of copper to rainbow trout. *Water Res.* **8,** 377–382.

Sprague, J. B. (1968). Promising anti-pollutant: Chelating agent NTA protects fish from copper and zinc. *Nature* **220,** 1345–1346.

Steeman Nielsen, E. and Wium-Andersen, S. (1970). Copper ions as poison in the sea and in freshwater. *Mar. Biol.* **6,** 93–97.

Steeman Nielsen, E. and Kamp-Nielsen, L. (1970). Influence of deleterious concentrations of copper on the growth of *Chlorella pyrenoidosa. Physiol. Plant.* **23,** 828–840.

Steeman Nielsen, E., Kamp-Nielsen, L., and Wium-Andersen, S. (1969). The effect of deleterious concentrations of copper on the photosynthesis of *Chlorella pyrenoidosa. Physiol. Plant.* **22,** 1121–1133.

Stephenson, R. R. and Taylor, D. (1975). The influence on EDTA on the mortality and burrowing activity of the clam (*Venerupis decussata*) exposed to sub lethal concentrations of copper. *Bull. Environ. Contam. Toxicol.* **14,** 304–308.

Stiff, M. J. (1971). Copper/bicarbonate equilibria in solutions of bicarbonate ion at concentrations similar to those found in natural water. *Water Res.* **5,** 171–176.

Sunda, W. G. and Gillespie, P. A. (1979). The response of a marine bacterium to cupric ion and its use to estimate cupric ion activity in seawater. *J. Mar. Res.* **37,** 761–777.

Sunda, W. G. and Guillard, R. R. L. (1976). The relationship between cupric ion activity and the toxicity of copper to phytoplankton. *J. Mar. Res.* **34,** 511–529.

Sunda, W. G. and Lewis, J. M. (1978). Effect of complexation by natural organic ligands on the toxicity of copper to a unicellular alga, *Monochrysis lutheri. Limnol. Oceanogr.* **23,** 870–876.

Sunda, W. G., Engel, D. W., and Thuotte, R. M. (1978). Effect of chemical speciation on toxicity of cadmium to grass shrimp, *Palaemonetes pugio:* Importance of free cadmium ion. *Environ. Sci. Technol.* **12,** 409–413.

Van den Berg, C. M. G., Wong, P. T. S., and Chau, Y. K. (1979). Measurement of complexing materials excreted from algae and their ability to ameliorate copper toxicity. *J. Fish. Res. Board Can.* **36,** 901–905.

Vernberg, W. G., DeCoursey, P. J., Kelly, M., and Johns, D. M. (1977). Effects of sublethal concentrations of cadmium on adult *Palaemonetes pugio* under static and flow-through conditions. *Bull. Environ. Contam. Toxicol.* **17,** 16–23.

von Westerhagen, H. and Dethlefsen, V. (1975). Combined effect of cadmium and salinity on development and survival of flounder eggs. *J. Mar. Biol. Assoc. U.K.* **55,** 945–957.

Wagemann, R. and Barica, J. (1979). Speciation and rate of loss of copper from lakewater with implications to toxicity. *Water Res.* **13,** 515–523.

Waiwood, K. G. and Beamish, F. W. H. (1978a). The effect of copper, hardness and pH on growth of rainbow trout, *Salmo gairdneri. J. Fish. Biol.* **13,** 591–598.

Waiwood, K. G. and Beamish, F. W. H. (1978b). Effects of copper, pH and hardness on the critical swimming performance of rainbow trout (*Salmo gairdneri* Richardson). *Water Res.* **12,** 611–619.

Whitfield, P. H. and Lewis, A. G. (1976). Control of the biological availability of trace metals to a calanoid copepod in a coastal fjord. *Est. Coast. Mar. Sci.* **4,** 255–266.

Wildish, D. J., Carson, W. G., and Carson, W. V. (1971). The effect of humic substances on copper and zinc toxicity to salmon, *S. salar* L. *Fish. Res. Board Can.* MS Rep. No. 1160.

Wilson, R. C. H. (1972). Prediction of copper toxicity in receiving waters. *J. Fish. Res. Board Can.* **29,** 1500–1502.

Wright, D. A. (1977). The effect of calcium on cadmium uptake by the shore crab *Carcinus maenas. J. Exp. Biol.* **67,** 163–173.

Wright, D. A. and Frain, J. W. (1981). The effect of calcium on cadmium toxicity in the freshwater amphipod, *Gammarus pulex* (L.). *Arch. Environ. Contam. Toxicol.* **10,** 321–328.

Young, J. S., Gurtisen, J. M., Apts, C. W. and Creselius, E. A. (1979). The relationship between the copper complexing capacity of sea water and copper toxicity in shrimp zoeae. *Mar. Environ. Res.* **2,** 265–273.

Zitko, V. (1976). Structure–activity relations and the toxicity of trace elements to aquatic biota. In: R. W. Andrew, P. V. Hodson, and D. E. Konasewich, Eds., *Workshop on toxicity to biota of metal forms in natural water,* International Joint Commission, Windsor, Canada, pp. 9–32.

Zitko, V. and Carson, W. G. (1976). A mechanism of the effects of water hardness on the lethality of heavy metals to fish. *Chemosphere* **5,** 299–303.

Zitko, P., Carson, W. V., and Carson, W. G. (1973). Prediction of incipient lethal levels of copper to juvenile Atlantic salmon in the presence of humic acid by cupric electrode. *Bull. Environ. Contam. Toxicol.* **10,** 265–271.

3

CONTAMINATION OF
AQUATIC BIOCENOSES BY
MERCURY COMPOUNDS:
AN EXPERIMENTAL
ECOTOXICOLOGICAL
APPROACH

A. Boudou and F. Ribeyre

Animal Ecology and Ecophysiology Laboratory
Bordeaux I University
Talence, France

1. INTRODUCTION

An ecological approach to the living world is based on a synthetic analysis of the functioning of natural systems. Biologically speaking, a natural system is a succession of organization levels, each of which is more complex than the preceding one, beginning with the cell, the basic functional unit, and culminating in the community or biocenosis, which is a group of populations living in a specific environment.

Because of the multitude of interrelations of abiotic and biotic factors which can occur, and the variability of these factors according to time and space, ecosystems can be extremely complex. Some natural evolutionary processes—the eutrophication of lakes, for example—lead to a fragmentation and a progressive disorganization of the homeostatic mechanisms that ensure the equilibrium of ecosystems. Most disruptions in the functioning of an ecosystem, however, are anthropic in origin. Because of the rapid development of civilization and the enormous population increase, the pressure that man is exerting on the biosphere is becoming more and more pronounced. Pollution is currently the primary factor in the disfunction of natural systems.

Ecotoxicology can be defined as the study of the contamination of the environment, and has very close connections with ecology and its concepts. Research carried out in the field, on the ecosystem as a whole, gives an accurate picture of ecotoxicological processes, but the great complexity of the structures involved and the limited investigation techniques that are available can often create problems in this kind of work. It is difficult, if not impossible in many cases, to advance beyond the basic stage of observing contamination levels in the main compartments of the system. In the same way, experimental research carried out in laboratory must be based on ecological structures that have been simplified. This kind of research does not pretend to be a perfect simulation of natural processes, but chiefly provides an aid to the understanding of the processes concerned, and complements research carried out *in situ,* to improve the knowledge of ecotoxicological phenomena.

The contamination of continental aquatic systems by mercury compounds is a good illustration of the complexity of the different research methods involved, and the way in which these methods can complement one another. Since 1977 our laboratory has developed an experimental approach to the processes involved in the bioaccumulation and transfer of mercury within aquatic biocenoses. The biogeochemistry of this metal has recently been examined in detail (Nriagu, 1979) and we shall therefore give only a brief summary of the ecotoxicological characteristics of the contamination of natural environments by mercury compounds, in order to concentrate on presenting our own research work.

2. STUDY OF MERCURY CONTAMINATION IN AQUATIC SYSTEMS

Mercury is a natural element and is therefore present in the main compartments of the biosphere. Exchanges which occur within a complex biogeochemical cycle originate in the metal's very varied residence times: 11 days in the atmosphere; 1000 years in soils; 2100 years in the oceans, and 2500 million years in sediments (Andren and Nriagu, 1979).

The direct use of mercury in human activity [world production: 10,000 to 15,000 tons/year (Nriagu, 1979)] combined with its indirect discharge into the ecosystems (e.g., from combustible fossils; WHO, 1976) has led to an important modification in the natural cycle of this element: a greater number of exchanges, localized discharges, chemical transformations, and so on. Accidents which have occurred throughout the world, in Japan, Iraq, Pakistan, Canada, and so on (Bakir et al., 1973; Charlebois, 1978; Takisawa, 1979), and the progressive increase in the number of contaminated biotopes are directly related to human activity.

From an ecotoxicological point of view several conclusions can be drawn from the current mass of research on the contamination of aquatic systems by mercury compounds:

1.   In an aquatic environment, the concentration of this metal in its free state is usually fairly low (order of ppb); organic and inorganic matter in suspension and also, though to a lesser degree, pelagic organisms are responsible for fixing the contaminant in this compartment. The respective importance of the processes of adsorption and absorption, however, are still not very well understood (Kudo et al., 1977, 1978).

2.   Organic and inorganic compounds in an aqueous solution are chemically very complex. Depending on the physico-chemical parameters of the environment (e.g., pH, salinity, oxidation-reduction potential), a wide variety of chemical species are liable to be formed, especially with different electrical charges and different solubilities. Mercuric chloride ($HgCl_2$) in solution, for instance, can speciate into $HgCl_2$, $Hg(OH)_2$, Hg^{2+}, $HgCl^+$, $Hg(OH)^+$, and $HgCl_3^-$, $HgCl_4^{2-}$, with anionic forms predominating in a marine environment. This chemical speciation is probably the most important of the parameters influencing the different ecotoxicological processes, but it is a very difficult factor to study, especially in a natural environment (Hahne and Kroontje, 1973; Shin and Krenkel, 1976; Rabenstein, 1978; Benes and Havlik, 1979; Burton, 1979; Astruc et al., 1981).

3. Sediments are of primary importance in mercury accumulation in an aquatic environment. They are vast reservoirs for the storage of this element, and they are the seat of the chemical transformations of the compounds [methylation, demethylation (Beijer and Jernelov, 1979; Craig, 1981)], but it is very difficult to estimate quantitatively the importance of these processes. The synthesis of methylmercury by bacteria from inorganic compounds present in the water or in the sediments is the major source of this molecule in aquatic environments. When we take into account the toxic properties of this compound and the fact that organisms have the ability to accumulate large amounts of the CH_3Hg form, then it is evident that biological methylation has a primary role in mercury's biogeochemical cycle.

Is the metal accumulated in the sediments stored definitively in this compartment, or are there risks of its spreading into the higher aquatic phase and the food chains? From an ecotoxicological point of view this question is of fundamental importance. Several in situ studies and laboratory studies too suggest that there are numerous parameters which have a considerable influence on these mechanisms, such as temperature, pH, endogenous fauna, and mechanical mixing (Frenet, 1979; Kudo et al., 1981).

4. Contamination of the biocenoses is due to the varying capacities for mercury accumulation exhibited by the different species and trophic levels being studied. In the case of consumer organisms, bioaccumulation is due to contamination by the direct route (where mercury is present in the environment) and by the trophic route (where the food supply is contaminated). In a natural environment, the relative importance of these two contamination routes is very difficult, if not impossible, to specify. There are also several parameters which can affect these mechanisms, such as the chemical nature of the contaminant, the species being studied, or the diversity of prey consumed.

Many in situ studies have shown an increase in mercury concentrations up the food chains (Potter et al., 1974; Bryan, 1980; Phillips et al., 1980). This process, called bioamplification or biomagnification by some authors, is believed to be an inevitable mechanism, specific to residual molecules which have a great ability to penetrate biological barriers and which are easily stored in organisms (the organo-chlorinated insecticides are a well-known example of this). A bioamplification of mercury such as we find within the aquatic biocenoses can only be explained by a conjunction of several phenomena, such as the chemical nature of the contaminant, the structure of the trophic chains, the efficacy of the transfers, and the average life span of the species.

In the organisms at the end of a trophic chain (the carnivorous fish, in particular) almost all the bioaccumulated mercury present is in the methylated form (Bishop and Neary, 1974; Windom and Kendall, 1979). This phenomenon has still not been satisfactorily explained, for although there are some methylation processes that occur at organism level (mucus, intestinal bacteria, enzymatic processes), these are of little quantitative importance (Van Coillie and Thellen, 1982), and concentrations of free methylmercury in the environment are much lower than concentrations of the inorganic compounds (Gardner, 1978).

A great number of toxicological studies have been carried out on mercury, but we still have only a very basic knowledge of many ecotoxicological processes, and in some cases no knowledge at all. The chemical complexity of the mercury compounds, which is closely related to the abiotic and the biotic factors of the aquatic environment, enables us to consider these contaminants as reference molecules in relation to mechanisms to be analyzed or methodologies to be established.

In parallel with studies carried out in the field on natural contaminated systems, the experimental approach has two main aims: to improve our basic knowledge of the processes concerned, and to try to establish standard (applied) methodologies, for future studies.

The tests are very widely used for controls or for estimating risk factors; there are a great number of tests to carry out, since the experiments involve many different species, and there are numerous analytic criteria and experimental conditions (Cabridenc and Chouroulinkov, 1977; Spehar et al., 1979). Their main interest lies in the fact that they allow rapid comparisons to be made between the degrees of toxicity of the contaminants in relation to a particular biological reagent. The tests have a limited use in that they are highly specific, and are being used in relation to artificial conditions. They become more complex according to the objectives sought. Initially they were concerned with a quantification of acute toxic effects (mortality tests, LD_{50}) but they are currently concerned more with the analysis of risks linked with contamination of a chronic nature, such as medium or long-term direct bioaccumulation effects on the biotic potential of species, and so on (Stern and Walker, 1978).

Laboratory experiments have attempted to study a greater number of abiotic and biotic parameters, by setting up ecotoxicological models. These correspond approximately to two types of biological structure:

1.   Experimental trophic chains: by choosing species which were representative of various trophic levels (primary producers, herbivores, carnivores) and by using very strictly controlled contamination methods, the bioaccumulation of a contaminant and transfers between species were analyzed. Depending on the complexity of the model, it is possible to differentiate the effects of the two contamination routes, the rates of interlevel trophic transfer, the role of certain parameters, and so on. The work done by Aubert, 1972; Reinert, 1972; Lillelund, 1974; Canton, 1975; Petrocelli, 1975; Parrish and Carr, 1976; Terhaar, 1977; Amiard-Triquet and Foulquier, 1978; and Tarifeno-Silva et al., 1982, is relevant here. The basis of these models are the

food chain links which unite the various species and the fact that the transfer of material occurs in one direction only, that is, from the producer toward the terminal consumer.

2. Microecosystems or microcosms: these models are of a slightly higher degree of complexity than the trophic chains. In this case the selected representative species are introduced simultaneously or progressively into a defined biotope. By taking samples from the environment and from the organisms at intervals after the introduction of the contaminant, the distribution of the molecule can be established over a period of time. A synthesis of work done in this field was published in 1979 in *International Journal of Environmental Studies*, and we shall mention in particular the models suggested by Metcalf et al., 1971; Caballa et al., 1978; Isensee et al., 1978; Luckinbill, 1979; Steele, 1979; and Nunney, 1980. Interspecies competition poses many problems: the growth of populations within the system; maintenance of alimentary autonomy, and so on. From an experimental point of view, the systemic approach of this model provides the most complete methodology when one considers the number of parameters taken into account, though it should not be thought of as a perfect simulation of natural conditions. Any experimental approach should be designed as an aid to analysis. It may have its own specific advantages and limitations, but it should also enable processes to be more easily understood, because complex biological structures and environmental characteristics have been simplified.

Several teams are currently working on an intermediate approach which falls between "natural ecosystems" and "laboratory models" (Davies and Gamble, 1979; Gächter, 1979). These correspond to enclosed areas (in a lake, for example), where an aquatic system of considerable volume has been isolated, and where only part of the natural biocenosis is present (mainly bacteria, phytoplankton, and zooplankton). It is possible to analyze contamination processes within the system using radioactive tracers.

Our laboratory work is based on an ecotoxicological approach to the contamination of continental aquatic systems by mercury compounds, and we have concentrated on analyzing bioaccumulation and transfer processes within trophic chains. With our experimental approach, we are attempting to gain a better knowledge and understanding of these processes, which are undoubtedly of considerable ecotoxicological importance. There were two main reasons for our decision to create an experimental trophic chain:

1. By using this model, many parameters can be compartmentalized, especially the contamination routes at each trophic level. It should thus be possible to estimate individually the roles of the different factors under consideration.
2. This model can also be the first stage in an experimental approach and be useful later as a basic aid and frame of reference in a more complex systemic analysis.

Four species were selected to represent the different levels in the experimental trophic chain: primary producer, *Chlorella vulgaris*; first level consumer, *Daphnia magna*; second level consumer, *Gambusia affinis* and *Salmo gairdneri* alevins; third level consumer, *Salmo gairdneri* (Boudou et al., 1977; Ribeyre et al., 1979; Ribeyre and Boudou, 1981b).

This was the basic biological framework, and the model became gradually more complex as further parameters were taken into account:

1. *Nature of compound.* Mercuric chloride ($HgCl_2$) and methylmercury chloride (CH_3HgCl) were selected for their ecotoxicological importance and their physico-chemical specificities.

2. *Concentration of mercury in the water.* This was set at 1 µg/liter (1 ppb), a level similar to that found in natural contaminated environments, and one which was compatible with the dosage techniques used.

3. *Contamination routes.* For each consumer level the respective amounts of contamination due to each of the routes was analyzed. Bioaccumulation was always studied from a dynamic point of view; the exposure period varied according to the trophic level being studied.

4. *Decontamination.* An analysis of this factor enables us to measure the rate at which the two compounds are eliminated from both the organism as a whole and from the main organs, and also the rate of elimination according to whether the original contamination was by the direct or the trophic route.

5. *Temperature.* Experiments involving the primary producer level were carried out at 10, 18, and 26°C, and other species at 10 and 18°C. This parameter is a very important one in an aquatic environment because it can affect several abiotic factors. It also enables us to analyze, in relation to the heterothermality of the organisms, the ecotoxicological effect of the adaptive processes which occur beyond the thermal preferendum range for each species.

6. *pH.* This parameter affects simultaneously the chemical speciation of the mercury compounds in the environment and the physiology and properties of the environment–organism interfaces. In order to study this factor, buffer systems were set up to maintain a constant pH value. As well as normal experimental conditions (pH 7.5 approximately) we also set up conditions with pH values of 5.0 and 10.0.

Figure 1 shows a summary of the structure of the ecotoxicological model set up, and the parameters studied to date.

Mercury dosage was established by means of atomic absorption without a flame (VARIAN AA 175 and 475 spectrophotometers); before dosage, the plant and animal samples (organisms and organs) underwent mineralization at 90°C in a pressurized acid environment.

An analysis of the data was produced by calculating for each set of parameters the averages and their confidence intervals ($P = 0.05$), adjusted curves

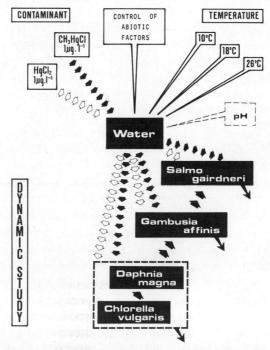

Figure 1. Structure of the ecotoxicological model showing main parameters considered.

(polynomial regression), interparameter relationships (multiple correlations) and the interrelations to be found within the data itself (factorial analysis of relationships).

Two basic themes have been highlighted to give a clearer overall picture of our experiments and the most important results obtained:

1. The alimentary chain as a whole: the bioaccumulation of mercury at each trophic level, in relation to the parameters presented.

2. The terminal consumer (*Salmo gairdneri*): a study of the processes of contamination by direct or trophic routes in the organism as a whole and in the main organs and the process of decontamination.

3. EXPERIMENTAL APPROACH TO THE BIOACCUMULATION AND TRANSFER OF MERCURY WITHIN AN EXPERIMENTAL TROPHIC CHAIN

3.1. Primary Producer: *Chlorella vulgaris*

Chlorella is an unicellular alga typical of the phytoplankton to be found in a lacustrine environment. It is an autotrophic organism, and with its high biotic potential (vegetative reproduction) and rapid turnover of only a few hours it is a very efficient primary producer, and is also a regular diet for the herbivorous organisms (mainly zooplankton).

Several studies of the capacity of unicellular algae to fix mercury compounds indicate a very high accumulation potential (Glooschenko, 1969; Shieh and Barber, 1973; Fillipis de and Pallaghy, 1976; Davies, 1978; Havlik et al., 1979; Cain and Allen, 1980). This is generally thought to be related to the organism's large surface area, where exchanges of ions can occur, but the respective roles of adsorption and absorption and the degree of intervention of passive and active mechanisms is still very much debated.

The dynamics of bioaccumulation of the two mercury compounds $HgCl_2$ and CH_3HgCl by *Chlorella vulgaris* in our experimental conditions and according to environment temperatures of 10, 18, and 26°C, was examined.

The results we obtained (Fig. 2) confirm that mercury fixation by this alga is very rapid, and that considerable quantities of mercury are involved; after 24 hr exposure, almost all of the metal had been accumulated, and this was the case for each of the experimental conditions, though the phenomenon occurred more rapidly with the organic form and at high temperatures.

When the pH of the environment was modified (pH 5.0 and 10.0) there was a very great difference in the amounts of mercury bioaccumulated in the case of the inorganic compound, while the amounts for CH_3HgCl remained the same (Table 1). The mechanisms which are responsible for this important difference are related to the chemical speciation of the mercury and the modifications which can occur in the algal walls (especially electrical charges) (Ribeyre and Boudou, 1982a).

It is difficult to locate with any great precision the mercury within the cell structures, and in the case of *Chlorella vulgaris* the pecto-cellulose wall makes it difficult to separate the membrane and cytoplasmic components (Northcote and Goulding, 1958). Is the metal fixed only on the external face of the alga, or does it penetrate into the adjacent structures? Tests to locate the mercury quantitatively using an electron microscope (Camebax microprobe) seem to indicate, in our experimental contamination conditions, that there is a preferential accumulation in the cytoplasm rather than at membrane level (Boudou, 1982).

While phytoplanktonic algae have a great capacity to fix mercury compounds, freshwater macrophytes also accumulate these contaminants very rapidly, especially when the leaves are submerged. Preliminary experiments conducted on *Elodea densa* have shown that after 10 days exposure to 1 ppb CH_3HgCl the average concentration in the leaves was 15 ppm. An increase in the temperature of the environment increased the occurrence of this phenomenon (Engrand, 1982).

3.2. Primary Consumer: *Daphnia magna*

Daphnia is a microphagic crustacean which occurs in many limnic food chains. It is fairly easy to grow in the laboratory; homogeneous populations

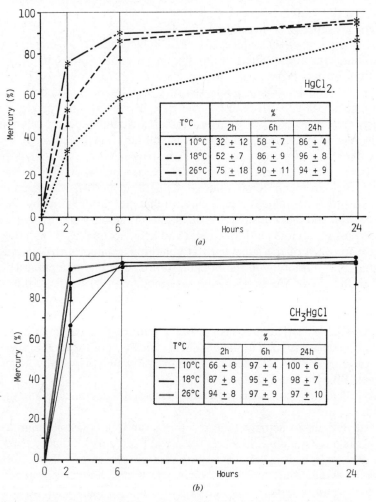

Figure 2. Accumulation of the two mercury compounds HgCl$_2$ and Ch$_3$HgCl by *Chlorella vulgaris* according to time and temperature of the environment (Confidence intervals: $P = 0.05$) (Ribeyre and Boudou, 1982a).

(sex, age, size) are thus easy to obtain and for this reason they are frequently used in ecotoxicological experiments.

The accumulation of the two mercury compounds was studied after direct contamination (1 μg Hg/liter) for exposure periods of 24 hr at 10 and 18°C (Table 2).

When the temperature of the environment is reduced from 18°C (which is approximately the thermal preferendum of the species) to 10°C, there is a decrease in behavioral and metabolic activity in *Daphnia magna* and a considerable reduction in exchanges with the surrounding medium. The results obtained reflect the capacities of the two compounds to fix on the tegumen-

Table 1. Accumulation of Mercury Compounds by *Chlorella vulgaris* According to pH of the Environment (18°C)[a]

Contaminant	pH	Mercury content %	
		2 hr	24 hr
HgCl$_2$	5.0	44 ± 6	98 ± 4
	10.0	29 ± 5	36 ± 5
CH$_3$HgCl	5.0	82 ± 4	98 ± 5
	10.0	78 ± 5	98 ± 4

[a] From Ribeyre and Boudou, 1981b.

tary surfaces and with their ability to cross the barriers which separate the organisms from their environment (Boudou and Ribeyre, 1981).

Trophic transfers between *Chlorella vulgaris* and *Daphnia magna* were measured in relation to the nature of the mercury compound and the temperature (Fig. 3).

A comparative analysis of the results shows a very considerable difference between amounts bioaccumulated by the daphnia, the level in the case of methylmercury being much higher. These results seem to indicate that the intestinal barrier has the capacity to be very selective in the transfer of mercury between the contaminated prey and the organism's internal medium. At 18°C the transfer rate for CH$_3$HgCl is 58%, and for HgCl$_2$, 6%. In similar experiments where trophic relationships were optimized, rates of transfer for the organic compound were of the order of 100% (Delarche and Ribeyre, 1978).

Table 2. Direct Contamination of *Daphnia magna* (Levels Expressed as ng Hg/100 Daphniae)[a]

	Content in Medium ($t=0$) (ng Hg)	Contaminant	
		HgCl$_2$	CH$_3$HgCl
10°C	330	38.3 ± 7.1	61.1 ± 15.2
	(100%)	(11.6%)	(20.5%)
18°C	330	39.4 ± 6.3	159.0 ± 31.0
	(100%)	(11.9%)	(48.2%)
Ratio of contents (Hg) 18°C/10°C	1.00	1.03	2.30
		10°C	18°C
Ratio of contents CH$_3$HgCl/HgCl$_2$	1.00	1.80	4.04

[a] From Ribeyre and Boudou, 1981c.

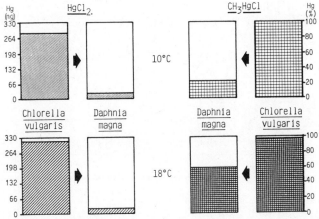

Figure 3. Comparative study of the trophic transfer of mercury between *Chlorella vulgaris* and *Daphnia magna* according to compound (CH₃HgCl and HgCl₂) and temperature (10 and 18°C) (Boudou and Ribeyre, 1981).

When these results are extrapolated to natural conditions, there is a very great imbalance in mercury transfers at the bottom of the alimentary chains, in favor of methylmercury. It would seem that the phytoplanktonic algae have a similar fixation capacity, which is approximately the same for the two compounds, and that it is only when these autotrophs are consumed by the zooplanktonic organisms that there is selectivity between transfer of the inorganic and organic compounds. Such a mechanism emphasizes the important fact that the amounts of methylmercury available in the aquatic environment, and especially the natural production of the metal by biological methylation, can have a bearing on the ecotoxicological consequences, and it would probably also help to explain the predominance of the CH_3Hg form in the terminal consumers in aquatic environment.

3.3.   Secondary Consumers: *Gambusia affinis* and *Salmo gairdneri*

In any medium-term or long-term study of direct contamination, we encounter the problem of keeping the toxic concentration of the environment constant throughout. With the two mercury compounds studied, there are several parameters which tend to exaggerate the diminution in the amount of metal in the experimental medium, and which usually affect $HgCl_2$ and CH_3HgCl in different ways. These parameters are adsorption on the walls of the tanks; volatilization; aeration of the environments; temperature; and accumulation in the organisms (Ribeyre and Boudou, 1981a).

For the experiments on the fish links in the chain, we set up automated modules for direct contamination. The function of these was to renew the environment periodically. They thus enabled us to establish and maintain

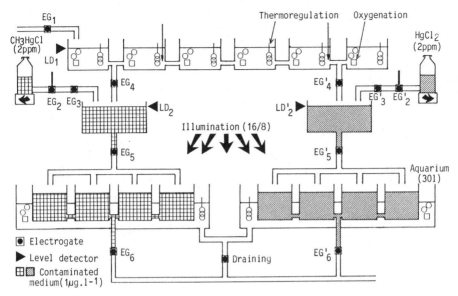

Figure 4. Simplified diagram of automated modules for direct contamination study (Ribeyre and Boudou, 1981a).

throughout the whole experimentation period a mercury concentration which was similar for both compounds, that is, 1.0 ± 0.1 ppb. At the same time they controlled and regulated the other parameters being studied (oxygen level, temperature, photoperiod). A diagram of these automated modules is shown in Fig. 4.

To illustrate direct contamination in a secondary consumer, we have selected experiments carried out on rainbow trout alevins (*Salmo gairdneri*) over a 60-day exposure period ($HgCl_2$ and CH_3HgCl, 1 ppb, 18°C). The difference between the two compounds becomes very clear when one examines the development of the bioaccumulation, expressed as a concentration (Fig. 5). After 60 days of exposure the ratio of $CH_3HgCl/HgCl_2$ concentrations is almost 7. The shape of the curve, and in particular the break observed between 15 and 30 days for the organic compound are due mainly to the relationship between the weight of the organisms and the mercury concentrations measured (Boudou and Ribeyre, 1982a). This relationship is expressed as a graph in Fig. 6 and it can be seen that there is a negative correlation between these two factors which diminishes as the exposure period increases. Most *in situ* studies have produced a positive relationship between the mercury concentrations in the fish and the age and the weight of the organism (Scott, 1974; Walter et al., 1974; Olsson, 1976; Stoeppler et al., 1979; Moore and Sutherland, 1980). However, this is not entirely inconsistent with our experimental results. For several reasons, in a natural aquatic environment all consumers are contaminated via two exposure routes— direct and trophic—which is not the case in our study. Also, the mercury

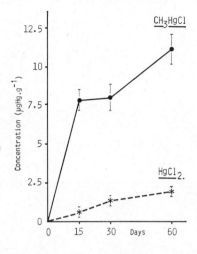

Figure 5. Bioaccumulation of the mercury compounds by *Salmo gairdneri* according to time, after direct contamination (Confidence intervals: $P = 0.05$) (Boudou and Ribeyre, 1982a).

remains in the organisms and thus the importance of contamination via the food chain increases with the age of the fish. Moreover, the negative correlation which we have observed between weight and concentration decreases progressively during the period of direct contamination (Boudou and Ribeyre, 1982a).

By using an experimental trophic chain, we were able to make a comparative analysis of the roles played by each exposure route in relation to the overall process of mercury bioaccumulation. As a preliminary step, a study was carried out on *Gambusia affinis* to compare contamination by the direct route (CH_3HgCl, 1 ppb in water) and contamination by the trophic route (consumption of contaminated daphnia; chain: water →chlorella→daphnia); the study was over a 30-day period, at 10, 18, and 26°C.

The evolution in the mercury concentrations is illustrated in Fig. 7. Contamination route and temperature are two parameters which have a very significant influence on the bioaccumulation processes. After 30 days of exposure at 26°C the amounts of mercury accumulated from the alimentary route are 8 times greater than those from the direct route, and the ratio of the overall concentrations measured at 26°C to those at 10°C is 9.0.

These experimental results underline the importance of the trophic route in the contamination of organisms by methylmercury. They also show the suitability of the ecotoxicological model which we set up in order to show the bioaccumulation of the metal: after 30 days at 26°C the concentration of mercury in the gambusia was 27,000 times greater than that in the environment; 90% of the contaminant had been introduced via preceding levels of the trophic chain (Boudou et al., 1979).

For the two compounds studied it is possible to estimate transfer rates between the primary producer, *Chlorella vulgaris,* and the terminal consumer, *Salmo gairdneri.*

Complementary experiments have been carried out involving trophic contamination only between the consumer levels (Boudou, 1982). The interlevel transfer rates were as follows: at 18°C, algae→daphnia, 6% for $HgCl_2$ and 58% for CH_3HgCl; daphnia→gambusia, 41% and 91%; gambusia→trout, 54% and 95%. From these results we can estimate the overall transfer rate, for the model as a whole: 1.5% for $HgCl_2$ and 50.5% for CH_3HgCl. This value can be as high as 70–80% for the organic compound, after taking into consideration an underestimation in the algae→daphnia transfer, because of an overabundant food supply.

4. ECOTOXICOLOGICAL ANALYSIS OF CONTAMINATION AND DECONTAMINATION PROCESSES IN *Salmo gairdneri*: ORGANISM AND ORGAN LEVELS

In the *Salmo gairdneri* level of the chain we analyzed the accumulation dynamics of $HgCl_2$ and CH_3HgCl during contamination by direct and trophic routes. Quantification of the contaminant was carried out in the whole organism and in the main organs (liver, brain, branchial arches, dorsal skeletal muscle, posterior intestine, kidney, spleen, and blood). The aim of our studies is to specify the ecotoxicological behavior of each organ in the processes of penetration, transport, storage, or elimination of the contaminants. As a typology of the organs is established during the different stages of contamination, the overall mechanisms involved can be better understood.

In parallel with these studies, we also carried out an analysis of decontamination dynamics in fish which had previously been contaminated by either the direct or the trophic route. When the remanence of a contaminant within an organism and the main organs is known, it is possible to estimate more accurately the risks involved in cumulative transfers between trophic levels. It also helps us understand the contamination processes. These processes are basically the results of, first, the contaminant entering the fish and being transported and stored in the fixation sites in the cells, and second, the liberation of a fraction of the accumulated pollutant molecules into the external medium (by excretion) or occasionally into other organs. Contamination and decontamination probably occur simultaneously and several ecotoxicological parameters can affect the respective importance of each. From this can be determined the capacity of the contaminant in question to bioaccumulate in the organism and the main organs.

4.1. Analysis of Contamination Processes

4.1.1. Direct Contamination

Direct contamination of *Salmo gairdneri* was done in automated modules (Fig. 4) at 10°C for a period of 30 days, and from a dynamic point of view for

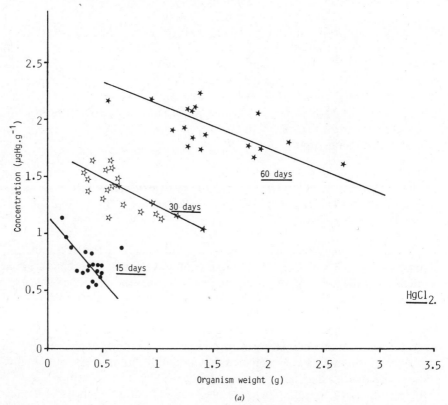

(a)

Figure 6. Relationship between weight of organism and mercury concentration after direct contamination. (a) with $HgCl_2$ (b) with CH_3HgCl (Boudou and Ribeyre, 1982a).

5, 10, 20, and 30 days. The media underwent a 6-hr renewal cycle producing a concentration of 1 ± 0.1 ppb of mercury for the two compounds and for the entire exposure period. After two weeks of acclimatization in the experimental conditions the average weight of the fish was 26 ± 4 g. This parameter increased very little during the contamination period, and there were no significant differences between the batches of fish (six trout for each of the eight experimental conditions).

The trend of the global mercury concentrations is similar to those for the mercury content of the fish as a whole (Fig. 8).

The mercury concentration expresses the extent to which the potential fixation sites are occupied and is thus related to the notion of toxicological risk. The values measured at the end of the contamination period (0.57 ± 0.12 ppm for $HgCl_2$ and 3.50 ± 0.56 ppm for CH_3HgCl) were sublethal in both cases.

The global mercury content gives the amount of mercury accumulated in the fish, which is potentially transferable into other compartments of the

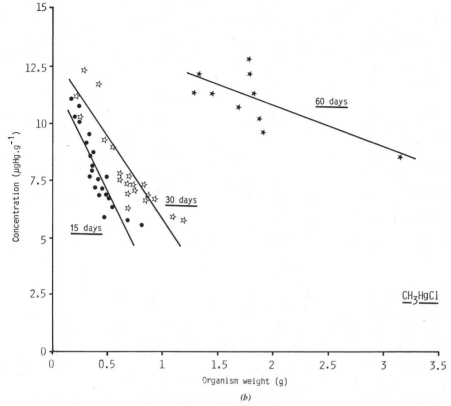

(b)

Figure 6. (*Continued*)

system: predators, decomposers, sediment, and so on. The curves shown in Fig. 8 when analyzed reveal a sigmoid trend for both compounds, and in the case of methylmercury the first phase is very markedly exponential. Although the existence of a "plateau" during the contamination period is a fairly traditional occurrence, the fact that the curves are nonlinear between 0 and 20 days is a much more difficult phenomenon to explain. By studying the evolution of the mercury content of the main organs of the fish, it should be possible to understand these results better. For all organs, higher values were obtained after contamination by methylmercury. The maximal concentrations observed after 30 days were between 5 and 7 ppm for $HgCl_2$ (gills > kidneys and spleen) and between 10 and 24 ppm for CH_3HgCl (spleen > gills > kidney > liver > blood). Such values, especially those obtained with the organic compound, are possibly the beginning of some fairly pronounced structural or biochemical changes (Ribeyre and Boudou, 1982b).

The respective weights of the organs were estimated and the mercury content of each was calculated, based on the concentrations already measured. In certain cases (brain, liver, and spleen) there was no linear

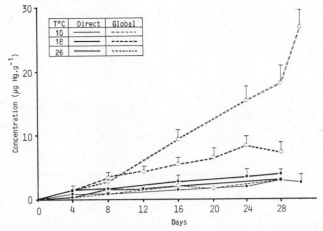

Figure 7. Accumulation of methylmercury in *Gambusia affinis*, according to time (Confidence intervals: $P = 0.05$) (Boudou et al., 1979).

relationship between the weight of the organ and the weight of the fish (Boudou, 1982).

An analysis of the evolution of the mercury content of the organs (Fig. 9) shows that four main trends can be defined. Type 1 is a curve with a very pronounced plateau and type 4 is an exponential curve (Fig. 10).

Our hypotheses on the different trends of these curves in relation to the contamination processes and the ecotoxicological role of each organ is presented with the synthetic approach to bioaccumulation (Section 4.3).

At this stage in the analysis it is possible to attempt an explanation of the global processes of mercury accumulation by the direct route (Fig. 8) from

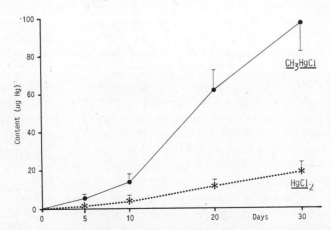

Figure 8. Mercury content of *Salmo gairdneri* (whole organism) after direct contamination (confidence intervals: $P = 0.05$) (Ribeyre and Boudou, 1982b).

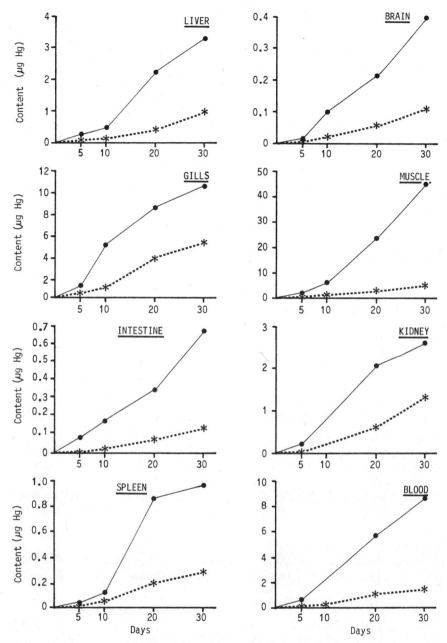

Figure 9. Evolution of mercury content of the organs of *Salmo gairdneri* during direct contamination (HgCl₂, ---; CH₃HgCl, ——) (Ribeyre and Boudou, 1982b).

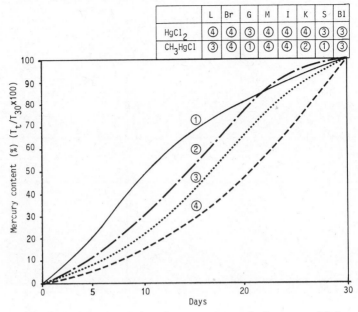

	L	Br	G	M	I	K	S	Bl
HgCl$_2$	④	④	③	④	④	④	③	③
CH$_3$HgCl	③	④	①	④	④	②	①	③

Figure 10. Trend synthesis of evolution of mercury content in the organs of *Salmo gairdneri* (direct contamination). L: liver; Br: brain; G: gills; M: muscle; I: intestine; K: kidney; S: spleen; BL: blood (Boudou and Ribeyre, 1982b).

the development of the mercury content of the organs. Some organs play only a very secondary role in the quantities of accumulated metal, in relation to the global mercury content (Table 3), in particular, the intestine, brain, and spleen. The skeletal muscles and the branchial arches, however, play a much more significant role; and the liver, kidneys, and blood play an intermediate role.

Thus the sigmoid trends of the curves showing the increase in global mercury content (Fig. 8) are the results of the sigmoid trends (type 1) and the exponential trends (type 4) of the two most important organs, the gills and the muscle.

In parallel with this study of direct contamination, we have analyzed the processes involved when the two compounds penetrate by the trophic route.

4.1.2. Trophic Contamination

Salmo gairdneri was contaminated by means of prey (alevins) exposed to HgCl$_2$ and CH$_3$HgCl, and the daily quantity of mercury administered was similar for both compounds (Boudou and Ribeyre, 1982b). The amounts of metal bioaccumulated were monitored after periods of 10 and 30 days, at 10°C, for both the whole organism and the main organs.

As was the case during direct exposure, the weight of the organism did not alter significantly during the 30-day exposure period (45 ± 9 g). Thus the

Table 3. Mercury Content (%) of the Organs of *Salmo gairdneri* During Direct Contamination[a]

Contaminant	Time (days)	L	Br	G	M	I	K	S	Bl
HgCl$_2$	5	2.0	0.3	40.4	16.4	0.7	2.3	0.6	3.5
	10	2.1	0.5	24.7	22.1	0.5	3.4	0.8	5.0
	20	3.5	0.5	31.6	18.5	0.6	5.3	1.6	8.9
	30	5.3	0.6	28.4	22.5	0.8	6.7	1.5	7.6
CH$_3$HgCl	5	4.5	0.3	21.9	35.2	1.6	4.0	0.6	11.7
	10	2.9	0.7	33.3	39.7	1.1	3.8	0.7	10.2
	20	3.6	0.4	13.7	37.3	0.6	3.3	1.4	9.1
	30	3.6	0.4	10.8	46.6	0.7	2.7	1.0	8.8

Note: L: liver; Br: brain; G: gills; M: muscle; I: intestine; K: kidney; S: spleen; Bl: blood
[a] From Ribeyre and Boudou, 1982b.

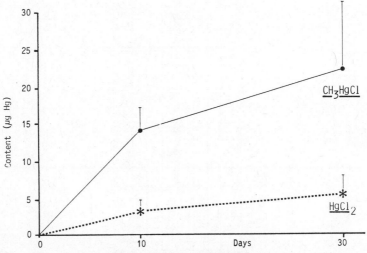

Figure 11.   Mercury content of *Salmo gairdneri* (whole organism) after trophic contamination (confidence intervals: $P = 0.05$) (Boudou and Ribeyre, 1982b).

concentration and the global mercury content follow a similar pattern, with a very pronounced plateau between 10 and 30 days (Fig. 11). The maximal concentration measured (0.48 ± 0.15 ppm CH_3HgCl, 30 days) is considerably below a level which could lead to any lethal effect on the fish.

The mercury concentrations in the eight organs selected displayed some considerable divergencies (Fig. 12). For the inorganic compound, there was a concentration of the order of 6 ppm in the intestine after 30 days. In the other organs, however, the levels are very low, with concentrations of less than 0.25 ppm.

For methylmercury there were five organs which had concentrations of 1–1.5 ppm (liver, posterior intestine, kidney, spleen, and blood) and the other three (brain, gills, and muscle) had concentrations of approximately 0.5 ppm.

After a comparative analysis of the evolution of the mercury content of the organs, a synthetic representation was produced of the main trends observed, as was the case for direct exposure (Fig. 9 and 10). Four types of curve were recorded (Fig. 13), the two extremes being a curve with a very pronounced plateau (type 1) and an exponential curve (type 4).

In examining the mercury content of each of the organs, it was observed that a very high proportion of mercury was to be found in the posterior intestine and the muscle after exposure to $HgCl_2$. For methylmercury the distribution is quite different; the muscle contains about 60% of the metal accumulated in the organism (Table 4).

The pattern of the curve of mercury content for the whole organism (Fig. 11) is mainly the result of the trends of the corresponding curves for the

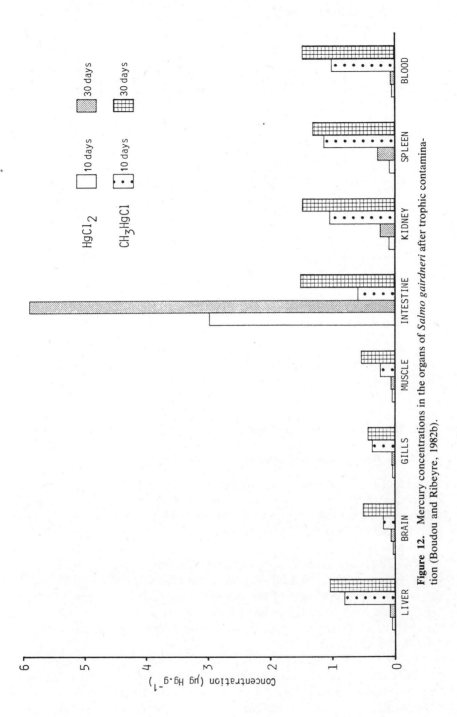

Figure 12. Mercury concentrations in the organs of *Salmo gairdneri* after trophic contamination (Boudou and Ribeyre, 1982b).

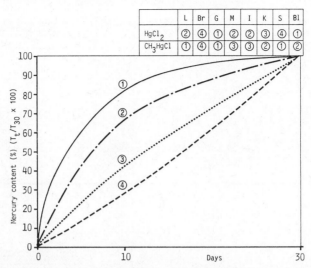

Figure 13.   Trend synthesis of evolution of mercury content in the organs of *Salmo gairdneri* (trophic contamination). L: liver; Br: brain; G: gills; M: muscle; I: intestine; K: kidney; S: spleen; Bl: blood (Boudou and Ribeyre, 1982b).

intestine and the muscle with $HgCl_2$, and the muscle and the blood for CH_3HgCl.

4.2.   Analysis of Decontamination Processes

4.2.1.   Decontamination after Direct Contamination

Two batches of 60 trout, with an average weight of 75 ± 9 g underwent direct contamination. This was done over a short term and using high concentrations of contaminant in order to begin decontamination at time zero with similar mercury concentrations and contents for $HgCl_2$ and CH_3HgCl. The fish were then placed in 1000-liter tanks, with continuous water renewal, at 10°C. The analysis of the decontamination process covered a period of 250 days, with samples of 10 fish being taken out after 0, 17, 31, 56, 120, and 250 days. The average weight of the organisms in both contaminated batches (Fig. 14) increased by a factor of 4 in relation to the weight at time zero, and this partly accounts for the decrease in the global concentrations, simply through "dilution" (Fig. 15).

The differences observed between the two curves which show experimental concentrations (Ce_t) and theoretical dilution concentrations (Cd_t) represent mercury elimination for the two contamination conditions.

Similarly, by calculating the global mercury content (Fig. 16) we are able to estimate decontamination rates. After 250 days, the decontamination rates measured were 28% for $HgCl_2$ and 37% for CH_3HgCl. The trends of

Table 4. Mercury Content (%) of the Organs of *Salmo gairdneri* During Trophic Contamination

Contaminant	Time (days)	L	Br	G	M	I	K	S	Bl
HgCl$_2$	10	0.5	0.07	0.5	25.2	40.0	0.7	0.1	1.4
	30	0.5	0.1	0.4	20.5	35.6	0.9	0.2	1.0
CH$_3$HgCl	10	2.9	0.2	2.4	39.0	1.7	2.1	0.4	9.5
	30	2.3	0.4	1.8	58.5	2.7	1.9	0.3	8.9

Note: L: liver; Br: brain; G: gills; M: muscle; I: intestine; K: kidney; S: spleen; Bl: blood

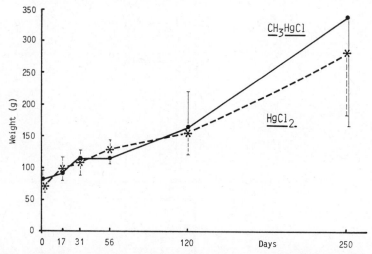

Figure 14. Evolution of average weight of *Salmo gairdneri* during decontamination, after direct contamination (confidence intervals: $P = 0.05$) (Ribeyre and Boudou, 1982c).

evolution of the two curves are different. The mercuric chloride curve drops very rapidly at first, then is almost linear after 56 days; the methylmercury curve decreases steadily.

These results enable us to consider the problem of measuring the biological half-life of mercury in *Salmo gairdneri,* which after 250 days was not reached for either of the two compounds. The asymptotic trend of the $HgCl_2$ decontamination curve in relation to the values of the confidence intervals

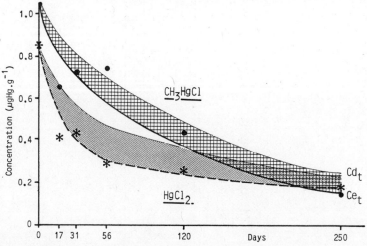

Figure 15. Comparison of experimental (Ce_t) and theoretical dilution (Cd_t) concentrations during 250 days decontamination (Ribeyre and Boudou, 1982c).

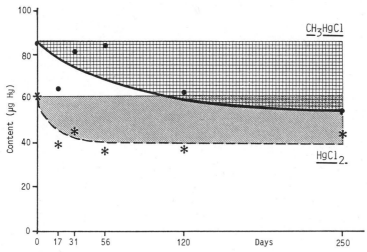

Figure 16. Mercury content of *Salmo gairdneri* (whole organism) during decontamination (Ribeyre and Boudou, 1982c).

assigned to each average can lead to considerable errors in estimating this factor. Where this ambiguity is combined with interspecific differences and the parameters of the environment, it probably accounts for the great diversity of values attributed to this factor in current literature, which range from a few days to several years (Huckabee et al., 1979).

Because these global phenomena result from the ecotoxicological responses of different compartments in the fish, we have analyzed the decontamination processes in the selected organs. For those organs which have a high accumulation potential and which represent a toxicological risk, the evolution of the concentration curves during the 250-day experimentation period (Fig. 17) showed one of two main trends: either a rapid decrease in concentration (e.g., gills and spleen) or a slow decrease (e.g., kidney, $HgCl_2$).

As was the case for the whole organism, the increase in the weight of the organs affects the mercury concentrations measured ("dilution" effect). By calculating the mercury content it is possible to discover the amounts of mercury accumulated in each organ (Fig. 18). Two main trends emerge: in some organs the mercury content decreases during the 250-day decontamination period and in others it increases. Since the fish are no longer subjected to mercury contamination, these results suggest that there are transfers between "donor" and "receiver" organs during the decontamination phase. These exchanges can be quantified by calculating the transfer rates for each organ, $\mathcal{T}_t = (T_t - T_0)/T_0 \times 100$. When these results are analyzed, five main trends emerge, as shown in Fig. 19.

For both compounds there are three organs which play a very important role in mercury distribution during the decontamination period: gills, mus-

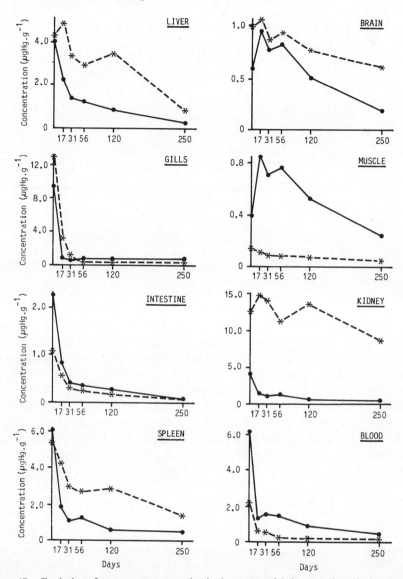

Figure 17. Evolution of mercury concentration in the organs of *Salmo gairdneri* during decontamination, after direct contamination (HgCl₂, ---; CH₃HgCl, ——) (Ribeyre and Boudou, 1982c).

cle, and kidneys for HgCl₂ and gills, muscle, and blood for CH₃HgCl (Table 5). It is the evolution of their mercury content levels which accounts for the evolution of the mercury content of the fish as a whole (Fig. 16). The asymptotic trend of the HgCl₂ curve is related to the very rapid decrease in the mercury content of the gills and the progressive increase in the mercury content of the muscle and kidneys.

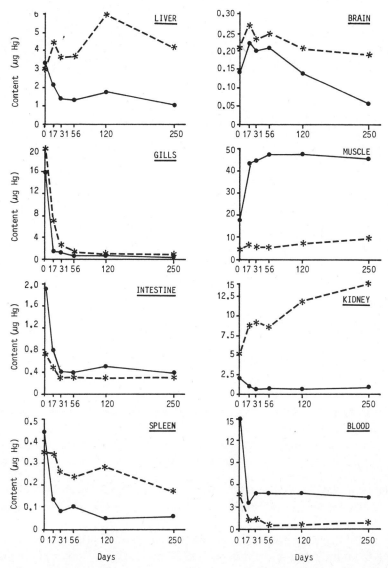

Figure 18. Evolution of mercury content in the organs of *Salmo gairdneri* during decontamination, after direct contamination (HgCl$_2$, ---; CH$_3$HgCl, ——) (Ribeyre and Boudou, 1982c).

4.2.2. *Decontamination after Trophic Contamination*

After consuming prey contaminated by the two mercury compounds (in a method similar to that described for contamination by the trophic route) the trout were placed in tanks in which the medium was at 10°C and was continually renewed. Decontamination was studied over a period of 60 days and

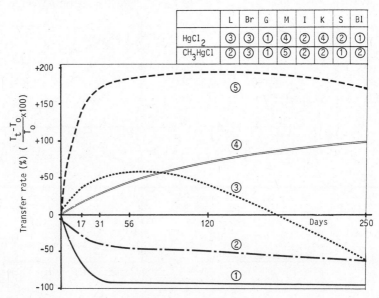

Figure 19. Trend synthesis of transfer rates ($\mathcal{T}_t$) evolution during decontamination, after direct contamination. L: liver; Br: brain; G: gills; M: muscle; I: intestine; K: kidney; S: spleen; Bl: blood (Ribeyre and Boudou, 1982c).

sample batches of eight fish were taken for each experimental condition: $HgCl_2$ and CH_3HgCl; time 0, 15, 30, and 60 days.

The evolution of the average weight of the organisms was identical for the two compounds and can be expressed as increasing by a factor of 2 between time zero and 60 days. This affects the value of concentrations measured ("dilution" effect) but by calculating the mercury contents we are able to estimate directly the decontamination phenomenon in the organism as a whole (Fig. 20).

The reason for the difference observed between the mercury content of the two populations at time zero is the considerable discrepancy between the amounts of mercury transferred by the trophic route, with more being transferred from the organic compound (see Section 3.3). A similar phenomenon is observed at the time of decontamination after direct contamination: for $HgCl_2$ the decrease is much more rapid and the biological half-life is reached before the tenth day.

When time was zero, the mercury concentration in the organs selected was less than 3 ppm, with the exception of the intestine with $HgCl_2$, where the concentration was 20 ppm. A synthetic analysis of the evolution of these concentrations revealed a decrease in each organ, which was particularly rapid in the case of the intestine (Boudou and Ribeyre, 1982c).

A dynamic study of the mercury content of the organs during the 60 days of experimentation does not reveal the transfer of important amounts of

Table 5. Mercury Content (%) of the Organs of *Salmo gairdneri* During Decontamination, After Direct Contamination[a]

Contaminant	Time (days)	L	Br	G	M	I	K	S	Bl
HgCl$_2$	0	5.0	0.3	33.9	8.1	1.1	8.8	0.6	7.3
	17	11.2	0.7	17.6	16.3	1.3	22.4	0.9	2.5
	31	7.8	0.5	6.0	12.3	0.7	20.5	0.6	2.9
	56	10.2	0.7	2.2	14.9	0.8	23.5	0.7	1.1
	120	16.0	0.6	1.6	18.5	0.8	32.3	0.8	0.8
	250	6.8	0.4	0.9	21.0	0.7	32.1	0.4	1.6
CH$_3$HgCl	0	3.9	0.2	19.6	20.8	2.3	2.4	0.5	17.8
	17	3.5	0.4	2.6	71.8	1.3	1.5	0.2	5.9
	31	1.7	0.2	1.5	55.6	0.5	0.7	0.1	6.1
	56	1.5	0.3	1.2	56.8	0.5	0.8	0.1	5.8
	120	2.5	0.2	1.3	76.6	0.8	1.0	0.1	14.6
	250	1.9	0.1	1.5	86.0	0.8	1.5	0.1	8.1

Note: L: liver; Br: brain; G: gills; M: muscle; I: intestine; K: kidney; S: spleen; Bl: blood.
[a]From Ribeyre and Boudou, 1982c.

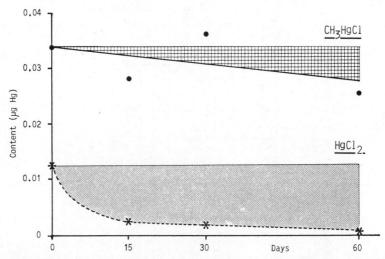

Figure 20. Mercury content of *Salmo gairdneri* (whole organism) during decontamination, after trophic contamination (Boudou and Ribeyre, 1982c).

mercury between organs. An analysis of the decontamination rates $(\mathcal{T}_t)$ reveals four main evolutionary trends for this parameter (Fig. 21).

These trends reflect the response of each organ during the decontamination phase. Besides their intrinsic value, these results will provide valuable information in a global approach to the bioaccumulation processes of the two mercury compounds in *Salmo gairdneri* (Section 4.3).

The distribution of the contaminant throughout the organism (Table 6) provides an explanation for the trends of the curves representing the global mercury content (Fig. 20). In the case of the organic mercury compound, the muscle represents approximately 60% of the total amount of mercury stored in the fish, and its mercury content remains practically constant throughout the period studied. As the other extreme, the considerable decrease in the level of mercury in the intestine for $HgCl_2$, from the high figure of 64% at time zero, is the reason for the rapid global decrease observed.

4.3.   Synthetic Approach to the Bioaccumulation Processes

From our studies of mercury contamination and decontamination in *Salmo gairdneri* via the two routes of exposure, we have been able to specify for each organ the trends in the changes in mercury content.

A comparative analysis of these trends over an identical period, 30 days for example, gives us a synthetic approach to these processes. The organs were grouped together according to their behavior during the eight experimental conditions selected (contamination and decontamination, via direct and trophic routes, and with $HgCl_2$ and CH_3HgCl). The basis for comparison

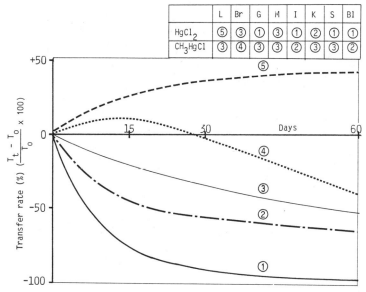

Figure 21. Trend synthesis of transfer rates ($\mathcal{T}_t$) evolution during decontamination, after trophic contamination. L: liver Br: brain; G: gills; M: muscle; I: intestine; K: kidney; S: spleen; Bl: blood (Boudou and Ribeyre, 1982c).

is the simultaneous emergence of the trends, during the exposure phase (accumulation speed $T_t/T_{30} \times 100$) and the decontamination phase (decontamination rate $(T_t - T_0)/T_0 \times 100$).

In the first set of curves (Figs. 10, 13, 19, and 21) there are six main types of response (Fig. 22). Type A represents organs in which the speed of mercury accumulation increased during the contamination period (cumulative process) and in which the overall transfer was positive ("receiver" organ). Graphs B, C, D, and E move progressively toward the other extreme, type F, a curve which forms a very pronounced plateau during the contamination period (limiting process) and where there is a rapid and total decontamination.

Between the two extreme trends, A and F, all the intermediate types of curve are present, suggesting that the exponential evolution observed in some organs during the contamination period is a trend which does not necessarily conflict with the trends observed in other organs. It may simply represent a deferred phenomenon, and a slowing down of accumulation rates may emerge in the longer term.

While these processes seem to depend on a number of parameters (e.g., nature of contaminants, exposure conditions, anatomical and physiological characteristics of the organ studied), the mercury accumulation capacity and its evolution should logically depend on the extent to which the sites in the cell structures for the fixing of the contaminant are occupied. The thioloprive capacity of mercury plays a dominant role in the fixing of the metal on

Table 6. Mercury Content (%) of the Organs of *Salmo gairdneri* During Decontamination, After Trophic Contamination

Contaminant	Time (days)	L	Br	G	M	I	K	S	Bl
HgCl$_2$	0	0.1	0.03	0.2	8.7	63.8	1.2	0.07	0.7
	15	1.0	0.09	0.2	39.0	49.5	2.8	0.1	0.2
	30	1.2	0.14	—	38.0	7.4	4.6	0.1	0.8
CH$_3$HgCl	0	2.5	0.4	2.0	63.4	1.5	1.4	0.3	9.5
	15	2.5	0.5	1.7	62.8	0.9	1.3	0.3	3.4
	30	1.3	0.3	1.0	47.9	0.6	0.8	0.1	3.8
	60	1.5	0.4	1.0	62.3	0.5	0.6	0.1	2.9

Note: L: liver; Br: brain; G: gills; M: muscle; I: intestine; K: kidney; S: spleen; Bl: blood

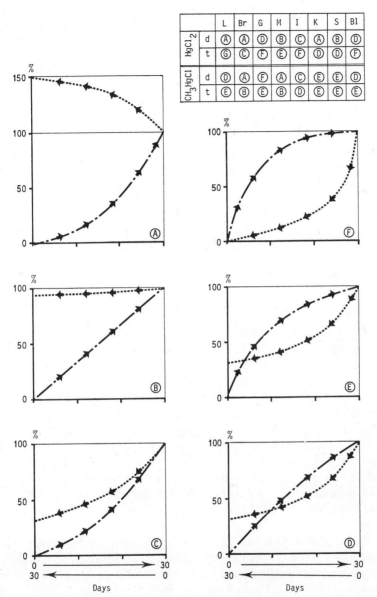

Figure 22. Synthetic trends of the evolution of mercury contents in the organs of *Salmo gairdneri* during contamination and decontamination (d, direct route; t, trophic route). L: liver; Br: brain; G: gills; M: muscle; I: intestine; K: kidney; S: spleen; Bl: blood (From Ribeyre and Boudou, 1982b).

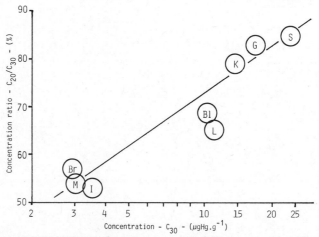

Figure 23. Relationship between speed of accumulation of methylmercury and mercury at the end of direct contamination period (30 days) for the organs of *Salmo gairdneri*. L: liver; Br: brain; G: gills; M: muscle; I: intestine; K: kidney; S: spleen; Bl: blood (Ribeyre and Boudou, 1982b).

the proteins; the membrane lipids, however, are also responsible in part for the storage of the metal (Suzuki and Matsushita, 1969; Reichert and Malins, 1974; Boudou et al., 1982). Various factors influence these processes, such as the accessibility of the different sites, the nature of the liaisons and their degree of reversibility, and the amount of exchange between the extra- and intracellular media.

The mercury concentration can be used as an indicator of the capacity of an organ to fix a contaminant, and as it increases it reflects the extent of this fixing capacity.

We have researched the relationships between the speed of mercury accumulation in an organ (C_t/C_{30}, t = 10 or 20 days) and the mercury concentration measured at the end of the exposure period (C_{30}). In the case of direct exposure to methylmercury (Fig. 23) there is a very clear relationship between these parameters: the greater the mercury concentration (spleen, gills, and kidney) the slower the accumulation. This relationship is the same for the other contamination conditions, but to a lesser degree. There is one exception to this trend: food chain contamination by mercuric chloride. In this case the influence of the intestine predominates and this explains the absence of any relationship between accumulation rate and mercury concentration in the organs (Boudou and Ribeyre, 1982b).

From an analysis of results obtained during the decontamination study, we observe that after direct or trophic contamination by methylmercury a similar relationship exists: the greater the initial mercury concentration, the greater the decontamination speed. For the inorganic compound this relationship is not evident (Boudou and Ribeyre, 1982c).

It would seem therefore that the mercury concentration does have an important role to play in the processes of bioaccumulation. It is not possible to generalize about this relationship, as variations have been observed in relation to this factor. These are due mainly to the characteristics of the different organs and the contamination mechanisms (nature of compound, penetration routes, method of transport by the blood, and so on).

Mercury accumulated in tissue is supplied by the blood, which ensures the distribution of the contaminant throughout the organism. The ratios between concentrations in the different organs and the blood were calculated for the four contamination conditions ($HgCl_2$ and CH_3HgCl, direct and trophic routes) and the results highlight three distinct groups of organs:

Ratio < 0.5: brain and muscle, for the four conditions; intestine after direct contamination; and gills after trophic contamination.

Ratio ≈ 1: liver.

Ratio > 1.5: kidney and spleen; gills after direct contamination; and intestine after trophic contamination by $HgCl_2$ (ratio > 100).

This classification seems to be independent of the experimental conditions (nature of compound, contamination routes) except for the two penetration barriers: gills and intestine. In the case of the muscle, kidney, liver, spleen, and gills after direct exposure, a relationship seems to exist between these ratios and the irrigation rates of the organs of *Salmo gairdneri* (Randall, 1970). However, this is not the case for all the tissues. The mercury concentration in the gills, for example, despite its extensive vascularization, is lower than that in the blood after trophic contamination. The blood provides only a "passive supply" of the contaminant it transports. The behavior of the cell barriers, the abundance and accessibility of the fixing sites, the penetration of the mercury into the tissue structures, all these are also processes which have a bearing on the amounts of metal accumulated in each organ of the fish.

From the preceding, the question to ask now is how should we view the bioaccumulation of mercury compounds in fish, ecotoxicologically. Different stages in the process can be distinguished, ranging from the penetration of the contaminant into the organism, to its storage or excretion.

Sources of Contamination.   In the case of direct exposure, the concentration of mercury present in the environment is usually fairly low; inorganic compounds are much more abundant than the organic form. Abiotic factors have a fundamental effect on the physico-chemical properties of the contaminants (chemical speciation). Mercury brought in via consumed prey, on the other hand, is usually in the organic form, and the percentage of methylmercury increases with the trophic position of the species in the food chains.

Crossing the Penetration Barriers.   The gills, being a respiratory organ, provide a vast surface area for exchanges between the external medium and the blood. The fixing and penetration of the mercury are thus favored by this epithelial structure and its plentiful irrigation. The secreted mucus has the capacity to retain the metal, a capacity which is greater for the inorganic compounds (Varanasi et al., 1975; Wobeser, 1975; Lock and Van Overbeeke, 1981). The branchial barrier in identical contamination conditions, via the direct exposure route, is permeable to the two mercury compounds, although CH_3HgCl has a greater penetration capacity than $HgCl_2$. The cutaneous surface of the fish has a limited ability to accumulate mercury, although there is some fixing on the mucus and exchange with some of scales' constituents (Van Coillie et al., 1974). However, for short exposure periods, and taking into consideration its extensive surface area, the skin probably plays a not insignificant part in the overall accumulation of metal in the organism as a whole.

During trophic contamination, the intestinal barrier is much more selective with regard to the two compounds. The consumption of prey contaminated by methylmercury results in almost 100% of the metal passing between the digestive tract and the internal medium (Boudou and Ribeyre, 1982b). These results are consistent with those obtained during perfusion of the mammalian digestive tract (Friberg and Vostal, 1972; Neathery et al., 1974; Sell and Davison, 1975). With $HgCl_2$, however, the amount of mercury transferred is very low, despite a fairly high degree of accumulation in the intestine. These results are identical to those observed in mammals and suggest that the digestive barrier is only very slightly permeable to inorganic compounds even when they are fixed on organic matter (contaminated prey). From studying the structure of this epithelium and from *in vivo* experiments carried out by perfusion in the intestine of *Salmo gairdneri* (Boudou, 1982) it appears that the mercuric chloride hardly penetrates at all into the intestinal wall. The presence of mucus, the abundant cell-coat on the external face of the absorbant cells, and also the physico-chemical conditions encountered, especially the pH, appear to be the reason for this retention with no transfer. This leads subsequently to the capacity of this organ in the trout to decontaminate very rapidly and extensively.

Transport by the Blood.   The blood plays a fundamental role in bioaccumulation processes since it ensures the liaison between the penetration routes of the contaminants and the storage and excretion organs. Its ability to transfer mercury depends not only on the relation to its capacity to fix it but also to the labile nature of liaisons established between the different sites and the toxic molecules. Several S-H groups are present on the proteins of the serum and the blood elements. The distribution of the two mercury compounds in the blood is quite different, depending on the contamination route involved: $HgCl_2$ is fixed on the plasmic proteins (mainly albumin and lipoproteins; Berg and Miles, 1978) whereas 80–90% of the methylmercury is to be found in the red blood cells (Olson et al., 1973; Naganuma and Imura, 1979). This distribution varies according to the species, the concentration of metal in the blood, and so on. It depends largely, however, on the physico-chemical properties of the two compounds and more especially on their ability to cross the erythrocyte membranes, and this is much easier for CH_3HgCl in the conditions found in the blood.

Thus the blood has a considerable capacity for storing mercury, and the S–Hg liaison is the basis of the fixing process. The reversibility of these covalent liaisons is the basis of mercury transfers into the organs. The work of Giblin and Massaro (1975) on the fixing and liberating of methylmercury by the erythrocytes of *Salmo gairdneri* illustrates perfectly the role played by the blood in mercury transportation and exchange.

Accumulation in the Organs. The irrigation characteristics of each organ are very important in transfer processes depending on volume of blood per unit weight, density of capillary network, flow, and so on. It is also probable that the position of the organs in relation to the circulatory system can influence the accumulation processes according to the contamination route. In the same way, the structural and metabolic specificities of the cells and the tissues dictate the accumulation capacity of an organ depending on properties of the membrane barriers (mercury fixing and penetration), number of sites and their accessibility, rate of cell renewal, and so on. Bioaccumulation, then, is the resultant process of many interactions within the compartments of the organism. The chemical affinity of mercury for the fixing sites, and the reversibility of established liaisons forms the basis for exchanges, while the blood ensures a link between the different organs.

Because conditions have been simplified and the main parameters of the medium are controlled, an experimental approach to ecotoxicological processes enables us to analyze in considerable depth the mechanisms involved. In the context of our own work on the bioaccumulation and transfer of mercury compounds within aquatic biocenoses, the results we have obtained have made clear the importance of each abiotic or biotic factor. As each factor is progressively taken into account, and in spite of the approach becoming more complex, we are able gradually to reach a better understanding of the respective roles of these factors. Besides our fairly well-advanced studies of the most important factors, such as pH, we are currently moving toward a systemic approach in which the parameter "interspecies competition" is a fundamental one to study in relation to contamination and transfer processes. In the context of this research program we have diversified the species representing the different trophic levels, and at the same time we intend to integrate the "sediment" compartment into our experimental models, because this would be an important mercury storage area and also a potential source for transfer of the contaminant into intra- or extrasedimentary organisms.

ACKNOWLEDGMENTS

Support of this research was derived partially from funds provided by the French Ministry of the Environment (trophic chain contamination research programs) and the Commission of the European Communities (environment and raw materials research programs). We should like to acknowledge the contribution of Mme. V. Serre who produced the illustrations for this chapter.

REFERENCES

Amiard-Triquet, C. and Foulquier, L. (1978). Modalités de la contamination de deux chaînes trophiques par le Cobalt 60. *Water Air Soil Pollut.* **9**, 475–489.

Andren, A. W. and Nriagu, J. O. (1979). The global cycle of mercury. In: J. O. Nriagu, Ed., *The biogeochemistry of mercury in the environment,* Elsevier/North Holland Biomedical Press, New York, pp. 1–23.

Astruc, M., Lecomte, J., and Mericam, P. (1981). Evaluation of methods for speciation of heavy metals in water. *Environ. Technol. Lett.* **2**(1), 1–8.

Aubert, M. (1972). Pollutions chimiques et chaînes trophodynamiques marines. *Rev. Intern. Océanog. Méd.* **28**, 9–25.

Bakir, F., Damluji, S. F., Amin-Zaki, A., Murtadha, M., Khalidi, A., Al-Rawi, N. Y., Tikriti, S., and Dhahir, H. I. (1973). Methylmercury poisoning in Iraq. *Science* **181**, 230–241.

Beijer, K. and Jernelov, A. (1979). Methylation of mercury in aquatic environments. In: J. O. Nriagu, Ed., *The biogeochemistry of mercury in the environment,* Elsevier/North Holland Biomedical Press, New York, pp. 203–210.

Benes, P. and Havlik, B. (1979). Speciation of mercury in natural waters. In: J. O. Nriagu, Ed., *The Biogeochemistry of mercury in the environment,* Elsevier/North Holland Biomedical Press, New York, pp. 175–202.

Berg, G. G. and Miles, E. F. (1978). Binding of mercurials to membrane suspensions and undenaturated proteins. *Memb. Biochem.* **2**(1), 117–134.

Bishop, J. N. and Neary, B. P. (1974). The form of mercury in freshwater fish. In: Proceedings International Conference on Transport of Persistent Chemical Aquatic Ecosystems. Ottawa, Canada, pp. 25–29.

Boudou, A., Delarche, A., Ribeyre, F., and Marty, R. (1977). Modèles expérimentaux en écotoxicologie: chaînes trophiques en milieu limnique. *Bull. Ecol.* **8**(4), 401–414.

Boudou, A., Delarche, A., Ribeyre, F., and Marty, R. (1979). Bioaccumulation and bioamplification of mercury compounds in a second level consumer, *Gambusia affinis.* Temperature effects. *Bull. Environ. Cont. Toxicol.* **22**, 813–818.

Boudou, A. and Ribeyre, F. (1981). Comparative study of the trophic transfer of two mercury compounds—$HgCl_2$ and CH_3HgCl—between *Chlorella vulgaris* and *Daphnia magna.* Influence of temperature. *Bull. Environ. Cont. Toxicol.* **27**(5), 624–629.

Boudou, A. (1982) Recherches en écotoxicologie expérimentale sur les processus de bioaccumulation et de transfert des dérivés du mercure, Thesis Dr. es-Sciences, University of Bordeaux I, Talence (France).

Boudou, A. and Ribeyre, F. (1983a). Influence of parameters "organism weight" and "exposure length" on the direct bioaccumulation of two mercury compounds by *Salmo gairdneri. Water Res.,* in press.

Boudou, A. and Ribeyre, F. (1983b). Processes of contamination by trophic route of *Salmo gairdneri* with mercury compounds; analysis at the global and organ levels. *Water Air and Soil Pollut.,* in press.

Boudou, A. and Ribeyre, F. (1983c). Processes of decontamination after trophic contamination ($HgCl_2$ and CH_3HgCl) in *Salmo gairdneri*: analysis at the global and organ levels. *Water Air Soil Pollut.,* in press.

Boudou, A., Desmazes, J. P., and Georgescauld, D. (1982). Fluorescence quenching study of mercury compounds and liposome interactions: effect of charged lipids and pH. *Ecotox. Environ. Safety,* **6,** 379–387.

Bryan, G. W. (1980). Recent trends in research on heavy metal contamination in the sea. *Holgol. Meeres.* **33**(1–4), 6–25.

Burton, J. D. (1979). Physico-chemical limitations in experimental investigations. *Phil. Trans. Roy. Soc. London* **286** (1015), 443–457.

Caballa, S. H., Patterson, M., and Kapoor, I. P. (1978). A terrestrial–aquatic model ecosystem for evaluating the environmental fate of drugs and related residus in animal excreta. In: M. A. Q. Khan, J. J. Lech, and J. J. Menn, Eds., *Pesticide and xenobiotic metabolism in aquatic organisms,* A.C.S. Symposium, No. 99, pp. 183–194.

Cabridenc, R. and Chouroulinkov, P. (1977). Tests biologiques d'évaluation d'effets toxiques de substances chimiques dans l'environnement. Coll. Recherche et Environnement No. 5, Documentation Française, Paris.

Cain, J. R. and Allen, R. K. (1980). Use of a cell wall-less mutant strain to assess the role of the cell-wall in cadmium and mercury tolerance by *Chlamydomonas reinhardtii.* Bull. Environ. Contam. Toxicol. **25,** 797–801.

Canton, J. H. (1975). Toxicity, accumulation and elimination studies of hexachlorocyclohexane (HCH) with freshwater organisms of different trophic levels. *Water Res.* **9**(12), 1163–1169.

Charlebois, C. T. (1978). High mercury levels in Indians and Inuits (Eskimos) in Canada. *Ambio* **7**(5–6), 204–210.

Craig, P. (1981). Biomethylation: pollution amplified. *New Scientist* **90,** 694–697.

Davies, A. G. (1978). Pollution studies with marine plankton. Part II: heavy metals. *Adv. Mar. Biol.* **15,** 381–508.

Davies, J. M. and Gamble, J. C. (1979). Experiments with large enclosed ecosystems. *Phil. Trans. Roy. Soc. London* **286,** 523–544.

Delarche, A. and Ribeyre, F. (1978). Chaîne trophique expérimentale en milieu limnique, Thèse No. 1436, University of Bordeaux I, Talence (France).

Engrand, P. (1982). Approche en écotoxicologie expérimentale des processus de bioaccumulation des dérivés du mercure par les végétaux aquatiques, D.E.A. Ecotoxicology, University of Bordeaux I, Talence (France).

Fillipis de, L. F. and Pallaghy, C. K. (1976). The effect of sublethal concentrations of mercury and zinc on Chlorella. *Z. Pflanz.* **78**(5), 197–207.

Frenet, M. (1979). Phénomènes de fixation-desorption du mercure sur les argiles dans les eaux à salinité variable. Application à l'estuaire de la Loire. Thesis Dr. es-Sciences, University of Nantes, France.

Friberg, L. and Vostal, J. (1972). *Mercury in the environment: an epidemiological and toxicological appraisal.* Chemical Rubber Company, Cleveland.

Gächter, R. (1979). Melimex, an experimental heavy metal pollution study. *Swis. J. Hydrol.* **41**(2), 165–314.

Gardner, W. S. (1978). The distribution of methylmercury in a contaminated salt marsh ecosystem. *Environ. Pollut.* **15,** 243–251.

Giblin, F. J. and Massaro, E. J. (1975). The erythrocyte transport and transfer of methylmercury to the tissues of the rainbow trout. *Toxicology* **5,** 243–254.

Glooschenko, W. A. (1969). Accumulation of Hg^{203} by the marine diatom *Chaetoceros costratum. J. Phycol.* **5,** 224–226.

Hahne, H. C. H. and Kroontje, W. (1973). The simultaneous effect of pH and chloride concentrations upon mercury(II) as a pollutant. *Soil Sci. Soc. Am. Proc.* **37,** 838–843.

Havlik, B., Stary, J., Prasilova, J., Kratzer, K., and Hanusova, J. (1979). Mercury circulation in aquatic biocenoses: metabolism in phytoplankton. *Acta. Hydroch. Hydrobiol.* 7(2), 215–223.

Huckabee, J. W., Elwood, J. W., and Hildebrand, S. G. (1979). Accumulation of mercury in freshwater biota. In: J. O. Nriagu, Ed., *The biogeochemistry of mercury in the environment,* Elsevier/North-Holland Biomedical Press, New York, pp. 277–303.

International Journal of Environmental Studies (1979). J. Rose, Ed., Special issue on microcosms, **13**, 83–182.

Isensee, A. R., Kearney, P. C., and Jones, G. E. (1978). Modeling aquatic ecosystems for metabolic studies. In: M. A. Q. Khan, J. J. Lech, and J. J. Menn, Eds., *Pesticide and xenobiotic metabolism in aquatic organisms,* A.C.S. symposium, No. 99.

Kudo, A., Akagi, H., Mortimer, D. C., and Miller, D. R. (1977). Equilibrium concentrations of methylmercury in Ottawa River sediments. *Nature* **270**, 419–420.

Kudo, A., Miller, D. R., Akagi, H., Mortimer, D. C., De Freitas, A. S., Nagase, H., Townsend, D. R., and Warnock, R. G. (1978). The role of sediments on mercury transport (total and methyl-) in a river system. *Prog. Water Tech.* **10**(5–6), 329–339.

Kudo, A., Miyahara, S., and Miller, D. R. (1981). Movement of mercury from Minamata bay into Yatsushiro sea. *Water Sci. Tech.* **13**(1), 509–524.

Lillelund, K. (1974). Considerations on testing the accumulation of pesticides by means of artificial food chains. *Ber. Wiss. Kom. Meer.* **23**, 317–325.

Lock, R. A. C. and Van Overbeeke, A. P. (1981). Effects of mercuric chloride and methylmercuric chloride on mucus secretion in rainbow trout, *Salmo gairdneri. Comp. Biochem. Phys.* **69**C, 67–73.

Luckinbill, L. S. (1979). Regulation, stability and diversity in a model experimental microcosm. *Ecology* **60**(6), 1098–1102.

Metcalf, R. L., Sangha, G. K., and Kapoor, I. P. (1971). Model ecosystem for the evaluation of pesticide biodegradability and ecological magnification. *Environ. Sci. Tech.* **5**(8), 709–713.

Moore, J. W. and Sutherland, D. J. (1980). Mercury concentrations in fish inhabiting two polluted lakes in northern Canada. *Water Res.* **14**(7), 903–908.

Naganuma, A. and Imura, N. (1979). Methylmercury binds to a low molecular weight substance in rabbit and human erythrocytes. *Toxicol. Appl. Pharmacol.* **47**, 613–616.

Neathery, M. W., Miller, W. J., Gentry, R. P., Stake, P. E., and Blackmon, D. M. (1974). Cadmium (109) and methylmercury (203) metabolism, tissue distribution and secretion into milk of cows. *J. Dairy Sci.* **57**, 1177–1183.

Northcote, D. H. and Goulding, K. J. (1958). The chemical composition and structure of the cell wall of *Chlorella pyrenoidosa. Biochem. J.* **70**, 391–397.

Nriagu, J. O. (1979). *The biogeochemistry of mercury in the environment.* Elsevier/North Holland Biomedical Press, New York.

Nunney, L. (1980). The stability of complex model ecosystems. *Amer. Natur.* **115**(5), 639–650.

Olson, K. R., Bergman, H. L., and Fromm, P. O. (1973). Uptake of CH_3HgCl and $HgCl_2$ by trout: a study of uptake pathways into the whole animal and uptake by erythrocytes in vitro. *J. Fish. Res. Board Can.* **30**, 1293–1299.

Olsson, M. (1976). Mercury level as a function of size and age in northern pike. *Ambio* **5**(2), 73–76.

Parrish, K. M. and Carr, R. A. (1976). Transport of mercury through a laboratory two-level food chain. *Mar. Pollut. Bull.* **7**(5), 90–91.

Petrocelli, S. R. (1975). Controlled food-chain transfer of dieldrin residus from phytoplankton to clams. *Mar. Biol.* **31**(3), 215–218.

Phillips, G. R., Lenhart, T. E., and Gregory, R. W. (1980). Relation between trophic position and mercury accumulation among fishes from the Tongue River Reservoir, Montana. *Environ. Res.* **22**, 73–80.

Potter, H. I., Kidd, E., and Standiford, D. (1974). Mercury levels in Lake Powell: Bioamplification of mercury in man-made desert reservoir. *Environ. Sci. Tech.* **8**(13), 41–46.

Rabenstein, D. L. (1978). The aqueous solution chemistry of methylmercury and its complexes. *Accounts Chem. Res.* **11**, 100–104.

Randall, D. J. (1970). Circulation. In: W. S. Hoar and D. J. Randall, Eds., *Fish physiology,* tome IV, Acad. Press, New York pp. 133–172.

Reichert, W. L. and Malins, D. C. (1974). Interaction of mercurials with salmon serum lipoproteins. *Nature* **247**, 569–570.

Reinert, R. E. (1972). Accumulation of dieldrin in an alga (*Scenedesmus obliquus*), *Daphnia magna* and the guppy (*Poecilia reticulata*). *J. Fish. Res. Board Canada* **29**(10), 1413–1418.

Ribeyre, F., Boudou, A., and Delarche, A. (1979). Interest of the experimental trophic chains as ecotoxicological models for the study of the ecosystem contamination. *Ecotox. Environ. Safety* **3**, 411–427.

Ribeyre, F. and Boudou, A. (1981a). Modules automatisés de contamination directe pour une étude de la bioaccumulation de deux dérivés du mercure—HgCl₂ et CH₃HgCl—par les maillons poissons. *Environ. Tech. Lett.* **2**, 425–432.

Ribeyre, F. and Boudou, A. (1981b). Contamination d'une chaîne trophique expérimentale par le méthylmercure: importance du système "Producteur–Consommateur primaire". *Environ. Pollut.* **24**, 193–206.

Ribeyre, F. and Boudou, A. (1981c). Bioaccumulation des dérivés du mercure par un consommateur primaire: *Daphnia magna.* Importance des voies de contamination et du facteur température. Colloque International d'Ecotoxicologie, Lille, France.

Ribeyre, F. and Boudou, A. (1982a). Study of the dynamics of the accumulation of two mercury compounds—HgCl₂ and CH₃HgCl—by *Chlorella vulgaris:* effect of temperature and pH factor. *Intern. J. Environ. Stud.,* 20, 35–40.

Ribeyre, F. and Boudou, A. (1982b). A study of the processes of decontamination in *Salmo gairdneri,* after direct or trophic contamination by mercury compounds. 3rd European Conference on Environmental Pollution, Nice, France.

Ribeyre, F. and Boudou, A. (1982c). Etude expérimentale des processus de décontamination chez *Salmo gairdneri* après contamination directe par les dérivés du mercure (HgCl₂ et CH₃HgCl). Analyse dynamique aux niveaux organisme et organes. 17ème Congrès Nat. Assoc. Franç. Limnology, Bordeaux, France.

Scott, D. P. (1974). Mercury concentration of white muscle in relation to age, growth and condition in four species of fishes from Clay Lake, Ontario. *J. Fish. Res. Board Can.* **31**(II), 1723–1729.

Sell, J. L. and Davison, K. L. (1975). Metabolism of mercury administered as methylmercuric chloride or mercuric chloride by lactating ruminants. *J. Agric. Food. Chem.* **23**, 803–808.

Shieh, Y. J. and Barber, J. (1973). Uptake of mercury by chlorella and its effect on K⁺ regulation. *Planta* **109**, 49–60.

Shin, E. B. and Krenkel, P. A. (1976). Mercury uptake by fish and biomethylation mechanisms. *J. Water Pollut. Cont. Fed.* **48**(3), 473–501.

Spehar, R. L., Holcombe, G. W., and Carlson, R. W. (1979). Effects of pollution on freshwater fish. *J. Water Pollut. Cont. Fed.* **51**(6), 1616–1694.

Steele, J. H. (1979). The uses of experimental ecosystems. *Phil. Trans. Roy. Soc. London* **286**, 583–595.

Stern, A. M. and Walker, C. R. (1978). Hazard assessment of toxic substances: environmental fate testing of organic chemicals and ecological effects testing. In: J. Cairns, K. L. Dickson, and A. W. Maki, Eds., *Estimating the hazard of chemical substances to aquatic life,* ASTM, Philadelphia, pp. 81–131.

Stoeppler, M., Bernhard, M., Bachhaus, F., and Schulte, E. (1979). Comparative studies on trace metal levels in marine biota. I: mercury in marine organisms from western Italian coast, the strait of Gibraltar and the north sea. *Sci. Total Environ.* **13,** 209–223.

Suzuki, Y. and Matsushita, H. (1969). Interactions of metal ions with phospholipid monolayer and their acute toxicity. *Ind. Health* **7,** 143–154.

Takisawa, Y. (1979). Epidemiology of mercury poisoning. In: J. O. Nriagu, Ed., *The biogeochemistry of mercury in the environment,* Elsevier/North Holland Biomedical Press, New York, pp. 325–366.

Tarifeno-Silva, E., Kawasaki, L. Y., Yu, D. P., Gordon, M. S., and Chapman, D. J. (1982). Aquacultural approaches to recycling of dissolved nutrients in secondarily treated domestic wastewaters. II: biological productivity of artificial food chain. *Water Res.* **16**(1), 51–58.

Terhaar, C. J. (1977). A laboratory model for evaluating the behavior of heavy metals in an aquatic environment. *Water Res.* **11,** 101–110.

Van Coillie, R., Lapointe, R., Rousseau, A., and Sasseville, J. L. (1974). Microanalyse de l'incorporation d'un métal lourd dans les écailles d'un poisson. Proc. Intern. Conf. Transport Persistent Chemicals in Aquatic Ecosystems. *Publ. Cons. Nat. Rech. Can.* **2,** 41–46.

Van Coillie, R. and Thellen, C. (1982). Capacité de méthylation du mercure chez *Salmo gairdneri,* in press.

Varanasi, U., Robish, P. A., and Malins, D. C. (1975). Structural alterations in fish epidermal mucus produced by water-borne lead and mercury. *Nature* **258,** 431–432.

Walter, C. M., Brown, H. G., and Hensley, C. P. (1974). Distribution of total mercury in the fishes of lake Oahe. *Water Res.* **8,** 413–418.

WHO (1976). *Environmental Health Criteria.* 1, Mercury. World Health Organization, Geneva.

Windom, H. L. and Kendall, D. R. (1979). Accumulation and biotransformation of mercury in coastal and marine biota. In: J. O. Nriagu, Ed., *The biogeochemistry of mercury in the environment,* Elsevier/North Holland Biomedical Press, New York, pp. 303–323.

Wobeser, G. (1975). Acute toxicity of methylmercury chloride and mercuric chloride for rainbow trout fry and fingerlings. *J. Fish. Res. Board Can.* **32,** 2005–2013.

4

ECOTOXICOLOGICAL ROLE OF THE MEMBRANE BARRIERS IN TRANSPORT AND BIOACCUMULATION OF MERCURY COMPOUNDS

A. Boudou

Animal Ecology and Ecophysiology Laboratory
Bordeaux I University
Talence, France

D. Georgescauld and J. P. Desmazès

Research Center Paul Pascal—CNRS
Bordeaux I University
Talence, France

1. INTRODUCTION

During any contamination process, the penetration of exogenous molecules across the biological barriers that separate the internal medium of organisms from the surrounding environment takes place. In the case of autotrophic organisms, only direct absorption of the contaminant assures its penetration into the tissues. In general, phytoplanktonic algae show high accumulation potential due to their vast surface exchange area exposed to the environment (Davies, 1978). The presence of the pecto-cellulose cell wall in many plants increases the complexity of the biological barrier. In *Chlorella vulgaris* (unicellular algae) this wall is 200 Å thick and the cell diameter is 3–4 μm (Northcote and Goulding 1958). However, in aquatic bryophytes it may be as much as 70 μm. The actual role of this membrane as a fixation site and barrier to the penetration of contaminants is not well known.

Filtering organisms (microphages) such as molluscs also show high accumulation potential due to the direct absorption of contaminants. Both the constancy and intensity of the exchange between the organism and the environment amplify the effect of contact between the contaminants and the barriers to penetration and so facilitate accumulation within the organism ("concentrating" organisms, according to Ramade, 1978).

In fish, contamination by direct absorption depends on the crossing of cutaneous and branchial epithelium by the pollutant. The importance of these with reference to the total entry is variable. In fact, these structures (derm and epiderm) are relatively impermeable to molecules present in the water, due to their covering with scales and mucus secretion. Usually, only a temporary accumulation of small quantities occurs via the replacement of certain natural constituents (Van Coillie et al., 1974). On the other hand, the branchial lamellae as a respiratory organ present a huge surface exchange area between the blood and the environment equal to 95% of the body surface of *Salmo gairdneri* (Lock et al., 1981). Branchial epithelium is extremely thin and the transfer of contaminants is increased by the magnitude of the exchange which depends on water debts in the respiratory cavity and irrigation of the gills by the capillaries.

All contaminants accumulated by direct absorption are also influenced by the abiotic factors present in the environment and by the physicochemical nature of the molecule concerned. The structural and functional characteris-

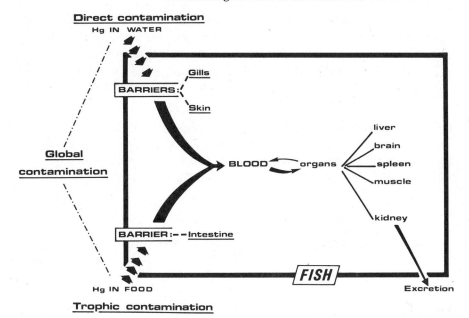

Figure 1. Principal process leading to bioaccumulation in a consumer (fish) in an aquatic environment.

tics of the biological membranes also exert a great influence on the level of contamination. This varies according to species, developmental stage of the organism, and so forth (Klein and Sheunert, 1978).

Contamination through indirect (trophic) route takes place in the intestine where the microvilli provide a large surface for contact between themselves and the food digested. The toxic molecules are brought in by food or water ingestion (especially in the case of marine organisms) and their entry into the blood depends on active or passive transport processes. As in the cutaneous and respiratory barriers, the characteristics of the contaminant and those of the food vector and the species involved are the cause of the great variability in penetration of toxic molecules by indirect absorption.

The concept of a biological barrier to the entry of contaminants into the organism may be applied to the different phases of the contamination process (Fig. 1).

1. *Transport via the circulatory system.* In many cases the blood constituents ensure accumulation of the contaminant within the system. This necessitates the crossing of the plasma membrane of the blood cells to reach intracellular fixation sites such as the hemoglobin (Giblin and Massaro, 1975).

2. *Accumulation in target organs.* This depends on the physicochemical properties of the contaminant, the level of irrigation, and the number of

fixation sites provided by the tissue. During this process, many biological barriers (capillary walls, plasma membranes) must be crossed in order that the contaminant can enter the cells of the organ.

3. *Excretion.* Among the elements concerned in the different processes the kidney is the most important. The passage of a contaminant into the urine depends on the crossing of the renal barrier.

The study of the interaction between contaminants and biological barriers is of major interest in the comprehension of ecotoxicological processes. Although dependent on a more or less complicated arrangement of cells, each barrier in fact rests on the same fundamental structure: the plasma membrane.

2. PLASMA MEMBRANES: STRUCTURE AND DYNAMICS

Plasma membranes are about 80 Å thick. Their extracellular surface is sometimes covered with a fibrous layer (cell coat) which may be 2000–3000 Å thick (intestinal epithelium). Plasma membranes are formed of proteins (2/3 of membrane mass) and lipids (Fig. 2). They also contain sugars which are covalently linked to glycoproteins and glycolipids (Nicolson et al., 1977).

The principal characteristic of these membranes is their phospholipid bilayer which is a planar molecular structure showing fluidity under physiological conditions (Singer and Nicolson, 1972; Nicolson, 1976; Kimelberg, 1977). In some cases the various types of phospholipids are distributed differently in the external and internal monolayers, thus giving the bilayer an asymmetrical structure (Kimelberg, 1977). The lipid bilayer is not a continuous structure; it is broken by proteins which are sunk into the lipid mass. These proteins may be roughly divided into two categories: integral proteins, which interact with the hydrophilic and hydrophobic lipid areas; and peripheral proteins, or those existing at the surface of the membrane and ionically bound to the proteins already mentioned or to the glycolipids (Singer and Nicolson, 1972). Thus, the plasma membrane may be regarded as two-dimensional solution of a mosaic of integral membrane proteins embedded in a fluid lipid bilayer with peripheral proteins bound loosely to either surface (Singer and Nicolson, 1972). This molecular structure allows the membrane components to be asymmetrically distributed. Perhaps the best example of this is the position of glycoproteins and glycolipids on the external surface of the membrane (Nicolson, 1976).

A wide variety of physical techniques have been used for the study of the structure and dynamics of biological membranes. Two classes may be distinguished: those which explore the membrane directly with minimum disturbance, such as $X_T$ray diffraction, nuclear magnetic resonance (NMR) spectroscopy, and Raman spectroscopy; and those which need the introduction of an extrinsic probe for the study of specific areas of the membrane, such as

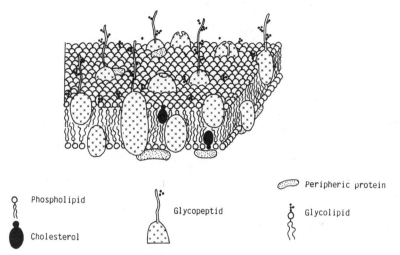

Figure 2.   Diagram of the molecular structure of the plasma membrane (Berkaloff et al., 1977).

electron-spin resonance (ESR) spectroscopy, and fluorescence (For a review see Nicolson et al., 1977).

Among the techniques listed, the use of fluorescent probes has a double advantage. First, the technique is very sensitive and needs only small quantities of membrane preparations. Second, short time constants may be used which are compatible with rapid molecular dynamics (Azzi, 1975). These probles may be used to explore either the lipid or protein regions of the membrane. At present, they are used to determine the microviscosity of the lipid core of biological membranes under steady-state or active conditions (Shinizki and Barenholz, 1974; Azzi, 1975; Georgescauld and Duclohier, 1978).

The study of the structure and dynamics of plasma membrane has progressed considerably due to the use of membrane models composed of phospholipids. When placed in water, these spontaneously form a bilayer.

Membrane models can be of two types: (1) vesicles, composed of one or more lipid bilayers (liposomes) (Huang et al., 1974); and (2) bimolecular lipid membranes (BLM) formed around a small orifice of about 1 mm^2 (Finkelstein, 1978).

Important information concerning the dynamics of membrane components have recently come to light. The flexibility of the aliphatic chains of lipid molecules increases toward the middle of the bilayer (flexibility gradient). It has now been shown that these exhibit rotational and lateral diffusion in relation to the plane of the membrane. Haphazard mobility of the aliphatic chains (membranar microviscosity) has been demonstrated, as has the jumping from one monolayer to another (flip flop) and the aggregation of certain lipids within membranes composed of lipids of a different type (separation of phase) (Nicolson et al., 1977; Wallach, 1979). All these movements are heavily dependent on the composition of the lipids and the cholesterol concentration. More and more results suggest that the fluidity of the lipid matrix plays an important part in the regulation of membrane function, especially in regard to transport.

Membrane proteins are also characterized by different movements, notably rotations around an axis perpendicular to that of the membrane and translation in the membrane plane (Edidin et al., 1976).

All plasma membranes are influenced by a strong electric field. This is due both to the negatively charged membrane components (charged phospholipids and proteins) and to the electrochemical gradient caused by the differing ionic concentrations on either side of it. Thus, at steady state, a difference of potential equal to about 70 mV is established between the environments. This corresponds to an electric field of 10^5 V/cm.

The interactions demonstrated between mercury derivatives and plasma membranes, can now be considered in terms of (a) the physicochemical properties of the contaminants in an aquatic environment in relation to abiotic factors, (b) the processes causing the fixation of mercury at membrane sites and its ensuing effects on cellular and tissue functions, and (c) the crossing of the plasma membrane by mercury compounds. This information comes chiefly from works on model membrane experiments.

3. PHYSICOCHEMICAL PROPERTIES OF MERCURY IN AQUATIC ENVIRONMENT

Mercury exists in three oxidized forms: Hg^0, Hg_2^{2+}, Hg^{2+}. Apart from its metallic form it is found in the environment in inorganic (mercurous or mercuric salts) and organic forms. Metallic mercury is practically insoluble in water but its transfer from the earth to the atmosphere stems principally from the high volatility of this form. The commonest inorganic forms of mercury are the mercuric halides. Their solubility in water is variable: low in the case of iodides and possibly as high as 73.3 g/liter for $HgCl_2$ at 25°C. The ecotoxicological properties of mercury depend principally on its capacity to complex with free radicals or with macromolecules (Engel et al., 1980). For example, it may exist in aqueous solution as hydroxide [$Hg(OH)_2$, $Hg(OH)^+$] or chloride ($HgCl^+$, $HgCl_2$, $HgCl_3^-$, $HgCl_4^{2-}$) complexes. The abiotic environmental factors affect the chemical speciation of mercury. The most common of these factors are pH, salinity, and redox potential (Hahne and Kroontje, 1973; Benes and Havlik, 1979; Burton, 1979; Engel et al., 1980; Hart, 1981). This fact has given rise to much research into the distribution of the various chemical species under different conditions. Studies of chemical speciation are extremely delicate, mainly due to the complex nature of the environment and the low concentration of the contaminants (Astruc et al., 1981). Under laboratory controlled conditions, experiments have given good results, which only serves to underline the importance of the control of the environmental physicochemical parameters during any ecotoxicological study.

Mercury forms mercurous organic compounds; symmetric (R-Hg-R) and asymmetric (R-Hg-R') compounds are the most unstable species and are very often photodegradable. The organic salts may complex with anions present in aqueous solution or with macromolecules (Zepp et al., 1974; Benes and Havlik, 1979).

The most common organomercuric compounds are methyl and phenyl mercury. Methylmercury accounts for 80% of the metal accumulated in terminal consumers (Bishop and Neary, 1974; Huckabee et al., 1979). This is caused by the methylation of inorganic mercury compounds by biological or chemical processes (Beijer and Jernelov, 1979). The contamination of the biocenotic system depends on the magnitude of the methylation and de-methylation processes (Bisogni, 1979).

The chemistry of mercury in an aquatic environment is therefore very complex and strongly influenced by biotic and abiotic factors. The concentrations of the free metal in water are therefore very low under normal conditions due to its predisposition to complex with other inorganic and organic material in suspension (Kudo et al., 1978; Bourg, 1979).

Because each mercury compound has specific physicochemical properties, its chemical form controls its distribution in aquatic systems. The eventual contamination of organisms and especially the interchanges occurring at the level of the membrane (adsorption and penetration) are therefore influenced by these mechanisms.

4. FIXATION OF MERCURY ON BIOLOGICAL BARRIERS AND ITS EFFECT ON MEMBRANE FUNCTIONS

The cells composing branchial or intestinal epithelium are not in contact directly with the external environment. In fact, the presence of scales, shells, and so forth, as well as the secretion of mucus, protect such structures. However, mercury may accumulate in the mucus chiefly due to the glycoprotein it contains. When the mercury concentrations become large enough, the properties of the mucus may be modified. For example, Varanasi et al. (1975) have observed an increase in the fluidity of mucus secreted by the epiderm of fish after contamination with $HgCl_2$. This affects the swimming speed of the fish and the efficiency of its defense against microorganisms. It has also been demonstrated that mercuric chloride has a higher capacity for accumulation in the branchial mucus than methylmercury. It also causes a more abundant secretion of mucus when contamination is direct (Kone et al., 1971; Wobeser, 1975; Lock and Van Overbeeke, 1981).

Some epithelia may have a cell-coat 500–2000 Å thick (e.g., amoeba or the apical surface of intestinal cells). These structures are rich in polysaccharides which have negatively charged acid groups. These may have a synergistic or antagonistic role in the accessibility of contaminants to the membrane itself.

In plants, the plasma membrane is reinforced by pecto-cellulosic membrane. The role of this is hard to determine. In general it is permeable to small molecules and plays a vital part in the mechanical support of the cell.

Studies of different phytoplanktonic species with and without cellulose membrane (such as *Chlamydomonas reinhardtii,* mutant species, Cain and Allen, 1980; *Isochrysis galbana* and *Dunaliella tertiolecta,* Davies, 1978) are unable precisely to attribute a fixation role to this structure in regard to mercury compounds.

The unicellular algae have a large capacity for accumulating pollutants because of their large surface exchange area. The analysis of membrane components in *Chlorella pyrenoidosa* shows that cellulose accounts for 40%, lipids 9.2%, and proteins 27% (Northcote et al., 1958). In spite of these potential fixation sites, it seems that mercury, whether in organic CH_3HgCl or inorganic $HgCl_2$ form, penetrates quickly into the cytoplasm as shown by electron microprobe (Boudou, 1982). In other aquatic plants, especially bryophytes, the thickness of the cell wall permits a high accumulation of heavy metals (Mouvet, 1982).

The plasmic membrane is the first site of action for toxic substances in the case of any cellular structure. The thioloprive property of mercury is responsible for its fixation capacity on proteins, which are potential targets for this contaminant. In this way, mercury affects the membrane functions which are protein dependent.

4.1. The Inhibition of Membrane Functions by the Fixation of Mercury on Proteins

The fixation of mercury on SH groups is closely related to its accessibility. This is dependent on the position of the protein within the membrane (i.e., whether it is located in the internal and external surfaces or whether it is integrated into the membrane structure); the position of its atoms in tertiary or quaternary structures of the molecule (hydrophobic or not, presence or absence of electrical charges); and the physicochemical properties of the structure concerned (molecular crowding, hydro and liposolubilities, electric charges) (Thrasher, 1973). The distribution of sulfhydryl groups within the plasma membrane is not homogeneous. In the case of red blood cells, only 3% are associated with the outer surface, 57% with the inner surface, and 40% with the interior of the membrane. The capacity of mercury compounds to occupy the SH sites is therefore influenced by this. This is shown by the work of Rothstein (1981) which illustrates the property of inorganic mercury to reach and titrate virtually all sulfhydryl groups of red cell ghosts. However, organic mercury (*p*-chloromercuribenzene sulfonic acid or chlormerodrin) can only interact with about 20% of the total.

4.1.1. Enzyme Activity

Any enzyme containing an SH group essential to its catalyzing activity (e.g., cholinesterase, and adenyl-cyclase) is a potential target for mercury (Salvaterra et al., 1973; Storm and Gunsalus, 1974; Mavier and Hanoune, 1975; Shamoo et al., 1976; Carty and Malone, 1979; Rothstein, 1981). Mercury chloride and methylmercury often have different inhibitory effects. This is due to liposolubility and the presence of charges which condition the accessibility of certain thiol groups. Although the fixation of mercury usually disturbs enzymatic functions, in some cases it may cause favorable conformational changes (Hatefi et al., 1969).

4.1.2. Transport Systems and Permeability

Many proteins are directly or indirectly associated with the passage of molecules across the membrane. In some cases, this process, which may be active or passive, is inhibited by mercury compounds. The transport of sugar, lactate, glycerol, cations are among those affected (Passow and Rothstein, 1960; Shamoo et al., 1976; Bogucka and Wojtczak, 1979; Arhem, 1980; Klip et al., 1980; Rothstein, 1981). However, not all transport processes (e.g., transport of anions and nonelectrolytes) are affected by these contaminants (Rothstein, 1981).

The action of mercury derivatives on transport processes is the origin of the effects, mainly irreversible, observed on excitable membranes. Mercury reduces sodium conductance and has a drastic effect on the resting membrane potential. This has been demonstrated on the giant axon of the squid, *Loligo pealei* (Pennock and Goldman, 1972; Shrivastav et al., 1976), and on the muscular fibers of the blue crab, *Callinectes sapidus* (Marco et al., 1979).

The effects of mercury on transport and permeability on the role of the branchial epithelium of fish in the process of osmoregulation have already been shown. *In vitro,* $HgCl_2$ and CH_3HgCl modify the active absorption of Na^+ and Cl^- by the gills of trout. Mercuric chloride has the greater effect of the two. On the other hand, *in vivo,* methylmercury is the more effective. This clearly shows the difference in the accessibility of membrane sites to the two derivatives (Lock et al., 1981).

4.1.3. Membrane Structure

Although microtubules play an important part in the maintenance of cell form, other structural proteins are also responsible for the stability of the membrane. Mercury compounds may cause changes in membrane deformability which is illustrated by a change in size in the case of erythrocytes. They also increase the osmotic fragility of these cells which may result in hemolysis (Tanaka and Nakai, 1977). Such modifications of the membranes may be caused by exposure to $HgCl_2$ concentrations as low as 10^{-9} M (Mel and Reed, 1981). Two peripheral proteins, spectrin and actin, play a part in the conservation of shape in red blood cells. These may be detached from the membrane by two organomercuric compounds (PMB or *p*-

mercuribenzoate and PMBS or *p*-mercuribenzene sulfonate); this process does not involve proteolysis. The distribution of mercury on membrane proteins shows a low level of fixation on actin and spectrin, but it is high on other species which probably play an important part in the stabilization of the cytoskeleton (Ralston and Crisp, 1981). The interaction of mercury with the S–S bridges may modify tertiary and quaternary protein structures to such an extent that a generalized breakdown of the membrane with release of cellular constituents may result (Rothstein, 1959). Thiol groups provide the chief sites for mercury fixation. Others, such as amino acid residues may be used, especially when system SH is absent. Arginine, lysine, aspartine, and histidine are thought to fill this role in the case of $HgCl_2$ (Carty and Malone, 1979).

This explains the difference observed between the quantity of mercury accumulated and the number of SH sites estimated (Kasuya, 1972; Wallach, 1979; Gruenwedel et al., 1981). In the case of certain derivatives, fixation may occur in the hydrophobic zones of the membrane via Van der Waal's forces.

4.2.   The interactions between mercury and membrane lipids

The interactions between mercury compounds and membrane lipids have been little studied even though these form the greater part of this structure. Segall and Wood (1974) have shown that methylmercury has a catalytic effect on the hydrolysis of plasmalogen which is an important constituent of neuronal membranes. Mercuric chloride is able to form reversible complexes with phospholipids (PC or phosphatidylcholine; PS or phosphatidylserine; PE or phosphatidylethanolamine) in chloroform solution. However, this does not occur with either cholesterol or oleic acid (Reichert and Malins, 1974). It has also been demonstrated that $HgCl_2$ concentration of $10^{-7} M$ causes an increase in surface tension of phospholipid monolayers ("animal cephalin"; or PE + PS). This parameter, which reflects the intramolecular distances within the monolayer is modified by many monovalent and divalent cations such as Na^+, Li^+, Ca^{2+}, Mn^{2+}, and Cd^{2+}. However, only mercury brings out a rigidification which indicates that the phospholipid–Hg^{2+} complex has a large polymeric arrangement. The interaction between metallic ions and the ionized lipid groups (phosphate and carboxyl groups being negatively charged while amino groups are protonated) is probably the cause of monolayer expansion (Suzuki and Matsushita, 1969). It has been demonstrated by Nakada et al. (1978) that the permeability of the lipid bilayer increased as a result of the exposure of liposomes to the mercury compounds $HgCl_2$ and CH_3HgCl. It was found that the release of glucose decreased with the increasing ratio of cholesterol in total lipids. The susceptibility of liposomes increased with the content of unsaturated fatty acid moieties in the lipids used. Consequently, membrane fluidity may play a significant role in the permeability change of liposomes caused by exposure to them. The presence of negatively charged lipids (dicetyl phosphate) increases the effect of both CH_3HgCl and $HgCl_2$ whereas positively charged ones (stearylamine) decrease it. This demonstrates the role played by positively charged mercury species. The results obtained are the same for both mercury compounds. Other divalent cations, notably Ba^{2+}, Cd^{2+}, Co^{2+}, Ca^{2+}, Mn^{2+}, Pb^{2+}, and Zn^{2+}, do not significantly influence the permeability of liposomes to glucose. These results clearly show the interactions between mercury derivatives and membrane phospholipids, whose charged polar heads attract them.

The use of fluorescent molecules (pyrene, benzo(a)pyrene, carbazoles, etc.) as hydrophobic probes allows the study of the accessibility of the regions of the membrane to the mercury compounds. The meeting of the labelled species with mercury (distance: 5–10 Å between the two molecules) causes a quenching of fluorescence proportional to the number of intramolecular collisions. Experiments carried out using liposomes labelled with pyrene have shown that these differ according to the derivative and the lipids used (PC, PS, PC-PS) and the pH of the environment (5.0 and 9.5). Under acid conditions, an increase in the quenching of pyrene occurs for both derivatives (Boudou et al., 1982).

Many of the physiological properties of the membrane are dependent on the negative charges carried by the polar heads of its phospholipids (especially phosphatidylserine). An example is given by the exchange of Ca^{2+} (Nash and Tobias, 1964; Seimiya and Ohki, 1973; Trauble et al., 1976). These negative charges seem to affect the chemical speciation of mercury by modulating the ionic forms it adopts. It is possible that the proteins, in particular glycoproteins, of the membrane surface may also have a similar effect.

By means of the processes just outlined, the mercury becomes fixed on the membrane before it is actually absorbed. This process can be reversible depending on the physicochemical conditions of the environment (especially pH) and the presence of different molecular species with which the mercury may complex. The study of the effect of pH on the bioaccumulation of mercury in phytoplankton carried out by Ribeyre and Boudou (1982a) illustrate this. One may conclude then, that from a toxicological point of view, the membrane is the first target for attack by mercury. However it also controls the penetration of this contaminant into the cell and into the organism.

5. TRANSPORT OF MERCURY COMPOUNDS ACROSS CELLULAR MEMBRANES

The crossing of the membrane by an exogenous molecule may take place in a variety of different ways: by diffusion due to a concentration gradient, displacement in an electric field, a difference in pressure, or the presence of a solvent. These are all passive transport mechanisms. Active mechanisms do however exist as does pinocytosis and phagocytosis (Berkaloff et al., 1977).

In the case of mineral and organic compounds, little is known of the actual process which allows their transport. According to Rothstein (1981), the penetration of erythrocytes by mercury occurs in three ways: nonionic forms pass through the membrane by partitioning into the lipid phase; anions pass via the anion transport system; a small fraction probably use another protein channel, possibly the cation permeation channel.

The phospholipids are a major obstacle to the crossing of these barriers by contaminants. In the case of methylmercury its high liposolubility is generally taken as the explanation for its high level of accumulation within organisms. However its partition coefficient in a water–lipid mixture is less than 2 (Lacowicz and Anderson, 1980). From the solubility and NMR data it appears that in fact this compound partitions weakly into lipid bilayers. Measures of lipid bilayer permeability (dimyristoyl and phosphatidylcholine vesicles) using the quenching of N-alkyl carbazole fluorescence, indicate that these model membranes are highly permeable to CH_3HgCl. The permeabilities are equal to 30% of that shown by an equivalent thickness of water or ethanol. It is probable that rapid diffusion across membranes rather than lipoid affinity is responsible for the transport of this compound (Lakowicz and Anderson, 1980).

The use of bimolecular lipid membrane (BLM) as membrane models permitted the study of the transport of inorganic mercury ($HgCl_2$) in relation to pH and chloride concentration (Gutnecht, 1981). These results show that $HgCl_2$ is a highly permeable species with a membrane permeability coefficient of about 10^{-2} cm/s. This is roughly 20-fold higher than the membrane permeability to water and a million times higher than the permeabilities to Na^+, K^+, and Cl^-. The other major mercuric complexes [Hg^{2+}, $HgCl_3^-$, $HgCl_4^{2-}$, $HgOHCl$, $Hg(OH)_2$] do not cross the membrane at a significant rate under physiological conditions.

The study of the transport of $HgCl_2$ and CH_3HgCl across BLMs in relation to pH confirms the importance of neutral forms in the crossing of lipid bilayers (Bienvenue et al., 1982). The influence of pH is more marked in the case of $HgCl_2$. At pH 9.5 the flux measured for mercuric chloride is 9 times less than at pH 5.0 (Table 1). It is interesting to note that the flux measured for CH_3HgCl and $HgCl_2$ crossing BLM is identical when CH_3HgCl is at pH 9.5 and $HgCl_2$ at pH 5.0. These pH-mediated flux differences may be related to the chemical speciation of these compounds. At pH 5.0 the predominant one is $HgCl_2$ whereas it is $CH_3Hg(OH)$ at pH 9.5.

The higher degree of transfer for the two chloride forms, especially in the case of the inorganic form, has been confirmed by experiments taking into account the chloride concentration as well as pH (Table 2). At pH 5.0 with Cl concentrations $<$ 100 mM, $HgCl_2$ is dominant. The flux measured is constant: 0.20–0.22. 10^{-9} M/cm$^2 \cdot$s^1. However at greater chloride concentra-

Table 1. Mercury Flux Measurements ($J_{Hg} \times 10^{-9}$ $M/cm^2 \cdot s$) for the System: Buffer + Hg ($5.10^{-4}M$)/BLM(PC–cholesterol)/Buffer[a]

	Contaminant			
	HgCl$_2$		CH$_3$HgCl	
pH	5.0	9.5	5.0	9.5
Mercury flux	0.075	0.008	0.112	0.072

[a] From Bienvenue et al., 1982.

tions, HgCl$_3^-$ and HgCl$_4^{-2}$ become dominant and the flux decreases abruptly (0.14 and $0.08.10^{-9}$ $M/cm^2 \cdot s^1$).

When the influence of the lipids (making up the BLM) on the flux of the two compounds crossing it was examined, it was found that neither the presence of PC, PS, nor cholesterol had a significant effect. The electric charges present in the membrane (PS), though having an effect on the organization of lipids in the bilayer by increasing the distance between polar heads (Trauble et al., 1976), do not seem to facilitate its crossing by the two mercury compounds.

Electrochemical measurements under the experimental conditions already outlined have shown that the specific resistance of BLMs remains high whether in the presence or absence of mercury compounds. Both HgCl$_2$ and CH$_3$HgCl must therefore be transported in an electrically neutral form. This agrees with results obtained by Gutnecht (1981) for HgCl$_2$. These neutral forms may be HgCl$_2$, Hg(OH)$_2$, CH$_3$HgCl, and CH$_3$HgOH according to the pH. However, it is possible that the transport of ionized forms of mercury does take place via ion pairing in the hydrophobic part of the membrane (dielectric constant $\simeq 2$). This process is electrically silent and so would agree with the electrochemical measurements obtained on BLMs (Gunn, 1978). The rate of this transmembrane transport seems to be determined by the rate of matter transport in the unstirred aqueous layers. This latter fact enables one to explain why a change in the nature of the lipids forming the BLM does not significantly change the values of the steady state value,

Table 2. Variation of the Unidirectional Flux of Mercury ($J_{Hg} \times 10^{-9}$ $M/cm^2 \cdot s$) as a Function of NaCl Concentration (pH 5.0), for the System: Buffer + NaCl (c) + HgCl$_2$ (c') / BLM (PC-cholesterol) / Buffer + NaCl (c) + HgCl$_2$ (c')

HgCl$_2$ (M)	NaCl (mM) (c)				
(c')	0	1	10	100	500
10^{-3}	0.20	0.22	0.22	0.14	0.08

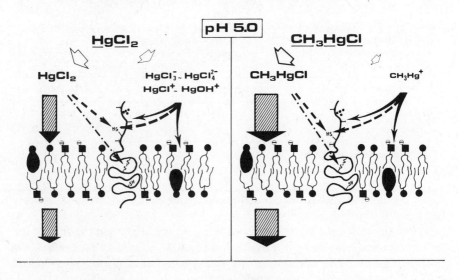

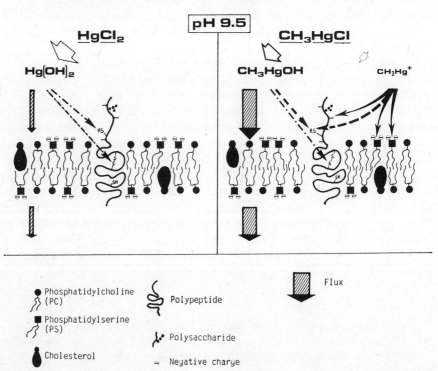

Figure 3. Fixation and transport of two mercury compounds, $HgCl_2$ and CH_3HgCl, across biological membranes, in relation to pH of medium (5.0 and 9.5).

while the quenching of pyrene fluorescence is modified. A transmembrane transfer of mercury only achieved by neutral species does not exclude the presence of free ionized species adsorbed at the membrane–solution interface.

If one considers all the information already discussed about the fixation of mercury and its transport across the membrane, the following theoretical explanation can be made:

1. The ionized species would probably interact with the charges present on the external surface of the membrane (glycoproteins, proteins, polar heads of lipids). This process of adsorption by electrostatic attraction could be one of the mechanisms by which fixation occurs in conjunction with the occupation of the SH sites on the proteins. This might affect the transport process because neutralization would then take place at the interface. As has already been demonstrated, the pH, chloride concentration, redox potential, as well as the characteristics of the membrane components, play an important role in these processes.

2. The neutral species such as CH_3HgCl and $HgCl_2$ would probably be responsible for the transport of most of the mercury across the lipid bilayer by diffusion rather than lipoid affinity. These processes are shown in Fig. 3 for the two mercury derivatives in relation to pH (5.0 and 9.5) and the presence or absence of charges on the membrane phospholipids.

The mercury, having crossed the membrane, then comes into contact with many intracellular sites. In the case of red blood cells, 95% of the thiol groups are present in the cytoplasm (Rothstein, 1981). The membrane of the organites (mitochondria, reticulum, nucleus, etc.) however, present other obstacles to access by the contaminant to certain storage areas (Thrasher, 1973; Dustin, 1978; Imura et al., 1980; Nakada, 1980; Ramanujam and Prasad, 1980).

6. CONCLUSION

The cell membrane is both a fixation site and a barrier to the penetration of mercury compounds into the cells and thus to the organism. Research in this field has revealed the complexity of these processes. At present, the role of proteins in the fixation of mercury has been well studied but the part played by lipids as ligands and as hydrophobic obstacles remains comparatively unknown.

It now seems definite that electrically neutral species are responsible for most of the transport of mercury by diffusion. Environmental factors, such as pH, have a great influence on these mechanisms and also on the speciation of mercury. In the case of methylmercury, it appears that its liposolubility, contrary to what has been generally accepted, is not the entire reason for its toxicity and does not play a major role in its transport.

To date, most research has been carried out on membrane models and it would therefore be of interest to carry out some experiments on live membranes.

REFERENCES

Arhem, P. (1980). Effects of some heavy metals ions on the ionic currents of myelinated fibers from *Xenopus laevis. J. Physiol.* **306,** 219–231.

Astruc, M., Leconte, J., and Mericam, P. (1981). Evaluation of methods for speciation of heavy metals in water. *Environ. Tech. Lett.* **2**(1), 1–8.

Azzi, A. (1975). The application of fluorescent probes in membrane studies. *Q. Rev. Biophys.* **8**(2), 237–316.

Beijer, K. and Jernelov, A. (1979). Methylation of mercury in aquatic environments. In: J. O. Nriagu, Ed., *The biogeochemistry of mercury in the environment,* Elsevier/North Holland Biomedical Press, New York, pp. 203–208.

Benes, P. and Havlik, B. (1979). Speciation of mercury in natural waters. In: J. O. Nriagu, Ed., *The biogeochemistry of mercury in the environment,* Elsevier/North Holland Biomedical Press, New York, pp. 175–202.

Berkaloff, A., Bourguet, J., Favard, P., and Lacroix, J. C. (1977). *Biologie et physiologie cellulaires, I: membrane plasmique,* Herman edit., Paris.

Bienvenue, E., Boudou, A., Desmazes, J. P., Gavach, C., Georgescauld, D., Sandeaux, J., Sandeaux, R., and Seta, P. (1983). Transport of mercury compounds across bimolecular lipid membranes: effect of lipid composition, pH and chloride concentration. *Chem. Biol. Interactions* (in press).

Bishop, J. N. and Neary, B. P. (1974). The form of mercury in freshwater fish. *Publ. Cons. Nat. Rech. Can.* 3, 25–29.

Bisogni, J. J. (1979). Kinetics of methylmercury formation and decomposition in aquatic environments. In: J. O. Nriagu, Ed., *The biogeochemistry of mercury in the environment,* Elsevier/North Holland Biomedical Press, New York, pp. 211–227.

Bogucka, K. and Wojtczak, L. (1979). On the mechanism of mercurial induced permeability of the mitochondrial membrane to K^+. *Febs Lett.* **100**(2), 301–304.

Boudou, A. (1982). Recherches en écotoxicologie expérimentale sur les processus de bioaccumulation et de transfert des dérivés du mercure, Thèse Doctorat d'Etat, Université de Bordeaux I (France).

Boudou, A., Desmazès, J. P., and Georgescauld, D. (1982). Fluorescence quenching study of mercury compounds and liposome interactions: effect of charged lipid and pH. *Ecotox. Environ. Safety* **6,** 379–387.

Bourg, A. (1979). Spéciation chimique des métaux traces dans les systèmes aquatiques. *J. Franc. Hydrologie* **10**(3), 159–164.

Burton, J. D. (1979). Physico-chemical limitations in experimental investigations. *Phil. Trans. Roy. Soc. London* **286**(1015), 443–457.

Cain, J. R. and Allen, R. K. (1980). Use of a cell wall-less mutant strain to assess role of the cell wall in cadmium and mercury tolerance by *Chlamydomonas reinhardtii. Bull. Environ. Contam. Toxicol.* **25,** 797–801.

Carty, A. J. and Malone, S. F. (1979). The chemistry of mercury in biological systems. In: J. O.

Nriagu, Ed., *The biogeochemistry of mercury in the environment,* Elsevier/North Holland Biomedical Press, New York, pp. 433–481.

Davies, A. G. (1978). Pollution studies with marine plankton. Part II, Heavy metals. *Adv. Mar. Biol.* **15**, 381–508.

Dustin, P. (1978). *Microtubules.* Springer-Verlag, Berlin, pp. 207–210.

Edidin, M., Zagyansky, Y., and Lardner, T. J. (1976). Measurement of membrane protein diffusion in single cells. *Science* **191**, 466–468.

Engel, D. W., Sunda, W. G., and Fowler, B. A. (1980). Factors affecting trace metal uptake and toxicity to estuarine organisms. In: *Biological monitoring of marine pollutants,* S. E. Fisheries CTR, Beaufort, pp. 127–144.

Finkelstein, A. (1978). Lipid bilayer membranes: their permeability properties as related to those of cell membranes. In: T. E. Andreoli, J. F. Hoffman, and D. D. Fanestil, Eds., *Physiology of membrane disorders,* Plenum Medical Book Company, New York, pp. 205–216.

Georgescauld, D. and Duclohier, H. (1978). Transient fluorescence signals from pyrene labeled pike nerves during action potential. Possible implications for membrane fluidity changes. *Biochem. Biophys. Res. Commun.* **85**, 1186–1191.

Giblin, F. J. and Massaro, E. J. (1975). The erythrocyte transport and transfer of methylmercury to the tissues of the rainbow trout, *Salmo gairdneri. Toxicology,* **5**, 243–254.

Gruenwedel, D. W., Glaser, J. F., and Cruikshank, M. K. (1981). Binding of methylmercury by Hela S3 suspension-culture cells: intracellular mercury levels and their effect on DNA replication and protein synthesis. *Chem. Biol. Interactions* **36**(3), 259–274.

Gunn, R. B. (1978). Electrically neutral ion transport in biomembranes. In: T. E. Andreoli, J. F. Hoffman, and D. D. Fanestil, Eds., *Physiology of membrane disorders,* Plenum Medical Book Company, New York, pp. 205–216.

Gutknecht, J. (1981). Inorganic mercury (Hg^{2+}) transport through lipid bilayer membranes. *J. Membrane Biol.* **61**, 61–66.

Hahne, H. C. H. and Kroontje, W. (1973). Effect of pH and chloride concentrations upon mercury (II). *Soil Sci. Soc. Am. Proc.* **37**, 838–843.

Hart, B. T. (1981). Heavy metals review paper: trace metal complexing capacity of natural waters. *Environ. Tech. Lett.* **2**(3), 95–110.

Hatefi, Y., Stemple, K. E., and Hanstein, W. G. (1969). Inhibitors and activators of the mitochondrial reduced diphosphopyridine nucleotide dehydrogenase. *J. Biol. Chem.* **244**, 2358–2365.

Huang, C. H., Sipe, J. P., Chow, S. T., and Martin, R. B. (1974). Differential interaction of cholesterol with phosphatidylcholine on the inner and outer surfaces of lipid bilayer vesicles. *Proc. Natl. Acad. Sci. USA* **71**, 359–362.

Huckabee, J. W., Elwood, J. W., and Hildebrand, S. G. (1979). Accumulation of mercury in freshwater biota. In: J. O. Nriagu, Ed., *The biogeochemistry of mercury in the environment,* Elsevier/North-Holland Biomedical Press, pp. 277–296.

Imura, N., Miura, K., Inokawa, M., and Nakada, S. (1980). Mechanism of methylmercury cytotoxicity by biochemical and morphological experiments using cultured cells. *Toxicology* **17**(2), 241–254.

Kasuya, M. (1972). Effects of mercury compounds on the outgrowth of cells and fibers from dorsal root ganglia in tissue culture. *Toxicol. Appl. Pharmacol.* **23**, 136–143.

Kimelberg, H. K. (1977). The influence of membrane fluidity on the activity of membrane-bound enzymes. In: G. Poste and G. L. Nicolson, Eds., *Dynamic aspects of cell surface organization,* Elsevier/North-Holland, Amsterdam, pp. 205–293.

Klein, W. and Scheunert, I. (1978). Environmental behaviour of pollutants: biotic processes.

In: G. C. Butler, Ed., *Principles of ecotoxicology* (scope 12), Wiley & Sons, Chichester, pp. 37–71.

Klip, A., Grinstein, S., Biber, J., and Semenza, G. (1980). Interaction of the sugar carrier of intestinal brush–border membranes with $HgCl_2$. *Biochim. Biophys. Acta* **548**, 100–114.

Kone Mc, C. E., Young, R. G., Bache, C. A., and Lisk, D. J. (1971). Rapid uptake of mercuric ion by goldfish. *Envir. Sci. Technol.* **5**, 1138–1139.

Kudo, A., Miller, D. R., Akagi, H., Mortimer, D. C., De Freitas, A. S., and Nagase, H. (1978). The role of sediments on mercury transport in a river system. *Prog. Water Technol.* **10**(5/6), 329–339.

Lakowicz, J. R. and Anderson, C. J. (1980). Permeability of lipid bilayers to methylmercuric chloride: quantification by fluorescence quenching of a carbazole-labeled phospholipid. *Chem. Biol. Interactions* **30**, 309–323.

Lock, R. A. C. and Van Overbeeke, A. P. (1981). Effects of mercuric chloride and methylmercuric chloride on mucus secretion in rainbow trout, *Salmo gairdneri Richardson. Comp. Biochem. Physiol.* **69C**, 67–73.

Lock, R. A. C., Cruijsen, P. M. J. M., and Van Overbeeke, A. P. (1981). Effects of mercuric chloride and methylmercuric chloride on the osmoregulation function of the gills in rainbow trout, *Salmo gairdneri Richardson. Comp. Biochem. Physiol.* **68C**, 151–159.

Marco, L. A., Isaacson, L., and Torri, J. C. (1979). Effects of $HgCl_2$ on the resting membrane potentials of blue crab muscle fibers. *Toxicology* **12**, 41–46.

Mavier, P. and Hanoune, J. (1975). Adenyl-cyclase from rat-liver plasma membrane: inhibition by mersalyl and other mercurial derivatives. *Europ. J. Biochem.* **59**(2), 593–599.

Mel, H. C. and Reed, T. A. (1981). Biophysical responses of red cell-membrane systems to very low concentrations of inorganic mercury. *Cell Biophys.* **3**(3), 233–251.

Mouvet, C. (1982). Utilisation d'un système de transplantation de bryophytes aquatiques pour le contrôle de la pollution des eaux courantes par les métaux lourds. XXVII congrès Assoc. Franç. Limnologie, Bordeaux, France.

Nakada, S., Inoue, K., Nojima, S., and Imura, N. (1978). Change in permeability of liposomes caused by methylmercury and inorganic mercury. *Chem. Biol. Interactions* **22**, 15–23.

Nakada, S. (1980). Methylmercury and inorganic mercury on protein synthesis in mammalian cells. *Ecotox. Environ. Safety* **4**(2), 184–190.

Nash, H. A. and Tobias, J. M. (1964). Phospholipid membrane model: importance of phosphatidylserine and its cation exchanger nature. *Proc. Nat. Acad. Sci. USA* **51**, 476–479.

Nicolson, G. L. (1976). Transmembrane control of the receptors on normal and tumor cells, I. Cytoplasmic influence over cell surface components. *Biochim. Biophys. Acta.* **457**, 57–108.

Nicolson, G. L., Poste, G., and Ji, T. H. (1977). The dynamic of cell membrane organization. In: G. Poste and G. L. Nicolson, Eds., *Dynamic aspects of cell surface organization,* Elsevier/North-Holland, Amsterdam, pp. 1–73.

Northcote, D. H. and Goulding, K. F. (1958). Chemical composition and structure of the cell wall of chlorella. *Biochemistry* **70**, 391–397.

Passow, H. and Rothstein, A. (1960). The binding of mercury by the yeast cell in relation to changes in permeability. *J. Gen. Physiol.* **43**, 621–633.

Pennock, B. E. and Goldman, D. E. (1972). The action of lead and mercury on lobster axon. *Fed. Proc.* **31**, 319–326.

Rabenstein, D. L. (1978). The aqueous solution chemistry of methylmercury and its complexes. *Accounts Chem. Res.* **11**, 100–104.

Ralston, G. B. and Crisp, E. A. (1981). The action of organic mercurials on the erythrocyte membrane. *Biochim. Biophys. Acta* **649**, 98–104.

Ramade, F. (1978). *Eléments d'écologie appliquée: action de l'homme sur la biosphère*, McGraw-Hill, Paris.

Ramanujam, M. and Prasad, K. N. (1980). Effect of methylmercuric chloride on gene expression in neuroblastoma and glioma cells after acute and chronic treatments. *Biochem. Pharmacol.* **29**(4), 539–552.

Reichert, W. L. and Malins, D. C. (1974). Interaction of mercurials with salmon serum lipoproteins. *Nature* **247**, 569–570.

Ribeyre, F. and Boudou, A. (1982a). Study of the dynamics of the accumulation of two mercury compounds—$HgCl_2$ and CH_3HgCl—by *Chlorella vulgaris:* effect of temperature and pH factor. *Intern. J. Environ. Stud.,* **20**, 35–40.

Ribeyre, F. and Boudou A. (1982b). A study of the processes of decontamination in *Salmo gairdneri*, after direct or trophic contamination by mercury compounds. 3rd European Conference on Environmental Pollution, Nice (France).

Robertson, J. D. (1959). The ultrastructure of cell membranes and their derivatives. Biochemical symposium, No. 16, 3–43.

Rothstein, A. (1959). Cell membrane as site of action of heavy metals. *Fed. Proc.* **18**, 1026–1035.

Rothstein, A. (1981). Mercurials and red cell membranes. In: A. R. Liss, Ed., *The function of red blood cells: erythrocyte pathobiology,* Inc., New York, pp. 105–131.

Salvaterra, P., Lown, B., Morganti, J., and Massaro, E. J. (1973). Alterations in neurochemical and behavioural parameters in the mouse induced by low doses of CH_3Hg. *Acta Pharmacol. Toxicol.* **33**, 177–190.

Segall, H. J. and Wood, J. M. (1974). Reaction of CH_3Hg^+ with plasmalogen suggests a mechanism for neurotoxicity of metal-alkyls. *Nature* **248**, 456–457.

Seimiya, T. and Ohki, S. (1973). Ionic structure of phospholipid membranes and binding of calcium ions. *Biochim. Biophys. Acta* **298**, 546–561.

Shamoo, A. E., MacLennan, D. H., and Eldefrawi, M. E. (1976). Differential effects of mercurial compounds on excitable tissues. *Chem. Biol. Interactions* **12**, 41–52.

Shin, E. B. and Krenkel, P. A. (1976). Mercury uptake by fish and biomethylation mechanisms. *J. Water Pollut. Cont. Fed.* **48**(3), 473–501.

Shinizki, M. and Barenholz, Y. (1974). Dynamics of the hydrocarbon layer in liposomes of lecithin and sphingomyelin in containing dicethylphosphate. *J. Biol. Chem.* **249**, 2652–2656.

Shrivastav, B. B., Brodwick, M. S., and Narahashi, T. (1976). Methylmercury: effects on electrical properties of squid axon membranes. *Life Sci.* **18**, 1077–1082.

Singer, S. J. and Nicolson, G. L. (1972). The fluid mosaic model of the structure of cell membranes. *Science* **175**, 720–731.

Storm, D. R. and Gunsalus, R. P. (1974). Methylmercury is a potent inhibitor of membrane adenyl-cyclase. *Nature* **250**, 778–779.

Suzuki, Y. and Matsushita H. (1969). Interaction of metal ions with phospholipid monolayer and their acute toxicity. *Ind. Health* **7**, 143–154.

Tanaka, R. and Nakai, K. (1977). Hemolysis and morphological changes in rat erythrocytes with mercurials. *Jap. J., Pharmacol.* **27**(3), 413–419.

Thrasher, J. D. (1973). The effect of mercuric compounds on dividing cells. In: A. M. Zimmerman, Ed., *Drugs and the cell cycle,* Academic Press, New York, pp. 25–48.

Trauble, H., Teubner, M., Woolley, P., and Eibel, H. (1976). Electrostatic interaction at charged lipid-membranes: effects of pH and univalent cations on membrane structure. *Biophys. Chem.* **4**, 319–342.

Van Coillie, R., Lapointe, R., Rousseau, A., and Sasseville, J. L. (1974). Microanalyse de l'incorporation d'un métal lourd dans les écailles d'un poisson. *Proc. Inter. Conf. Transport Persistent Chemicals in Aquatic Ecosystems. Publ. Cons. Nat. Rech. Can.* **2**, 41–46.

Varanasi, U., Robisch, P. A., and Malins, D. C. (1975). Structural alterations in fish epidermal mucus produced by water-borne lead and mercury. *Nature* **258**, 431–432.

Wallach, D. F. H. (1979). *Plasma membranes and disease,* Academic Press, London.

Wobeser, G. (1975). Acute toxicity of methylmercury chloride and mercuric chloride for rainbow trout fry and fingerlings. *J. Fish. Res. Board. Can.* **32**, 2005–2013.

Zepp, R. G., Baughman, G. L., Wolfe, N. L., and Cline, D. Q. (1974). Methylmercuric complexes in aquatic systems. *Environ. Lett.* **6**(2), 117–127.

5

TOXIC RESPONSES OF PLANARIANS TO VARIOUS WATERBORNE HEAVY METALS

Jay Boyd Best and Michio Morita

Department of Physiology and Biophysics
Colorado State University
Fort Collins, Colorado

1. INTRODUCTION

1.1. Ecological Distribution of Planarians

Freshwater planarians, such as *Dugesia dorotocephala* (Fig. 1), are a ubiquitous component of most unpolluted lakes and streams of the North American Continent, as well as Europe and Japan. Various planarian species can
be found inhabiting the head waters of streams at the edge of melting snow
fields up above the timberline where vegetation resembles arctic tundra.
Other free-living flatworm species can be found in brackish bays and estuaries. More detailed accounts of their ecological distribution have been
given previously (den Hartog, 1974; Hyman, 1951; Kawakatsu, 1974;
Teshirogi et al., 1981). In simplified miniature, they appear to possess useful
similarities to higher animals in their sensitivities and types of responses to a
variety of chemical toxicants (Best, 1983; Best and Morita, 1982; Best et al.,
1981a,b). Despite these characteristics, they are seldom included in limnological censuses used in environmental impact studies. Since no rational
explanation has been found for this omission, one can only conjecture the
reason; however, the most likely explanation may be the following. Free-
living flatworms such as planarians do not inhabit the free volume of aquatic
habitats, preferring instead to remain and move on the interfacial boundaries. They are thus unlikely to be collected by conventional sampling
procedures.

1.2. Previous Studies on Planarian Responses to Various Toxicants

Although planarians and other closely related free-living flatworms (e.g.,
marine polycads) have been utilized in numerous studies as model systems
and tested with various types of pharmacological and toxic agents, for example, actinomycin D, Puromycin, X-irradiation, cyanide, tetrodotoxin,
catecholamine and serotonin analogs, colchicine, DDT, chlordane, and
polyaromatic carcinogens (Best et al., 1968; Child, 1941; Coward, 1968;
Dubois, 1948; Flickinger, 1963; Foster, 1969; Keenan and Koopowitz, 1981;
Keenan et al., 1979; Lange, 1969a,b; LeMoigne and Gabriel, 1971; McWhinnie, 1955; Phillips et al., 1974; Wolff, 1962), there appear to be few data
regarding their toxic responses to heavy metal compounds.

This chapter will report some of our laboratory studies that were designed
for preliminary investigation of the toxic responses of asexual *Dugesia
dorotocephala* to graduated habitat water concentrations of some of the
various heavy metals apt to occur as environmental contaminants in the
vicinity of smelter operations. We have, with varying degrees of thor-
oughness, tested compounds of mercury, cadmium, copper, zinc, lead, and
arsenic, although, in the case of most of these, further and more thorough
testing is needed. Others, such as compounds of chromium, nickel, cobalt,

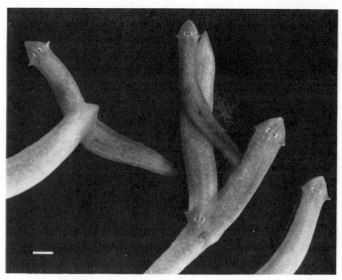

Figure 1. Dark field illumination photographs of normal asexual planarians of the species *D. dorotocephala*. The horizontal bar in the photograph denotes 1.0 mm. The two eyelike structures in the head really are eyes.

tin, molybdenum, beryllium, titanium, and uranium, have not yet been tested but need to be.

2. METHODS AND MATERIALS

Because dead planarians autolyze into a clump of debris within an hour, there is, in scoring lethality, seldom ambiguity in determining whether a planarian is dead or alive. Lethality is, of course, the least sensitive of the various types of available responses.

Asexual planarians of the type used for the present study do not differentiate gonads and do not reproduce sexually. Instead, they reproduce by fissioning, in which the caudal portion of the planarian tears asunder from the anterior portion. The head regenerates a new tail, and the tail fragment regenerates a new head, to yield two complete, but smaller, planarians. With other factors the same, longer planarians have a higher probability of fissioning than short ones (Best et al., 1969). Thus this factor was controlled by selecting only specimens of 15–18-mm lengths. Increasing the population density on the interfacial area of the test habitat suppresses fissioning; isolation or reduced population density releases it (Best et al., 1969, 1974). This negative feedback effect is mediated by the brain, but the segmental nervous system has all of the reflexes involved in executing the act of fissioning (Best et al., 1969, 1975; Pigon et al., 1974). Because this fissioning control and execution system involves both brain and segmental nervous system, changes in fissioning incidence vs. time curves, with other factors controlled, can indicate neurotoxicity of a toxicant at levels well below lethal levels. Thus, this indicator might be especially pertinent in regard to metals such as mercury and lead which are well known to target the nervous systems of higher animals for damage.

When such an asexual planarian fissions, the anterior portion, which usually contains about two-thirds or three-fourths of the original animal, as well as the head and brain, is refractory to fissioning again for the several weeks required to regenerate a new tail and grow longer to an approximation of its original length. For several days or a week following such fissioning, the caudal portion of such an anterior fragment appears truncated. To insure that the planarians initially selected for the test have not recently fissioned, and are competent to fission during the period of the experiment, only specimens that have tails tapering to a point in the normal morphological conformation are selected. Such selected specimens are habituated to specimen bowls, similar to those used for testing, for three days prior to zero time. During this habituation period, the planarians are maintained in groups of 50–70 specimens in 100 ml culture water in each specimen bowl, a population density adequate to almost completely suppress fissioning. Thus when, at time zero, the planarians are allocated into their respective test bowls, with 10 planarians and 50 ml of water or solution per bowl, the planarians are all competent to fission and fissioning is partially released from the suppressive effect of population density. Since anterior fission fragments normally do not undergo secondary or tertiary fissionings within the two-week time span of the tests, and since the tail fragments, which are capable of such secondary fissionings, are removed daily, each test subject can fission only once during the experimental period. Thus, fissioning will not exceed 100% in our experimental test situation.*

All of the glass specimen bowls used in the studies reported here had cylindrical interiors 105 mm in diameter. All of the planarians were last fed two days before selection; they were then not fed throughout the 3 days of habituation and 14 days of the experimental testing. This imposes no undue stress and simplifies the interpretation of the results.

3. TOXIC RESPONSES TO VARIOUS HEAVY METALS

3.1. Mercury

Toxic responses of planarians to various water concentrations of methylmercuric chloride (MMC) have been described previously (Best et al.,

---

*One exception to this was observed in tests on the pesticide chlordane, an excitatory neurotoxicant. Low concentrations caused an increased fissioning to more than 100% (Best et al., 1981a), but this result was unique and has not been observed in any of the other numerous similar studies we have performed on other compounds.

EFFECT OF METHYL MERCURY ON FISSIONING

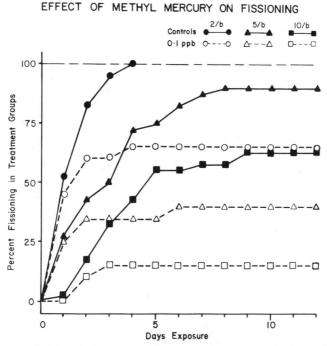

Figure 2. Shows the joint effects of group size and aquatic habitat methylmercury chloride (MMC) on the cumulative number of fissionings of asexual planarians of the species *D. dorotocephala* as a function of time. Increased group size and MMC both depress the rate of fissioning. (From Best et al., 1981b.)

1981b). Lethality was the predominant response observed with concentrations in the 0.5–2 ppm range, with a 5-day LC50 greater than 0.2 ppm but less than 0.5 ppm.

Grossly visible abnormalities in head regeneration of decapitated planarians were produced by concentrations of 0.1 and 0.2 ppm. Although concentrations of 20–80 ppb MMC did not cause morphologically visible abnormalities in the regenerate heads of such planarians, they did produce behavioral abnormalities in the regenerates. Such abnormalities were not observed in control planarians regenerating in ordinary culture water.

Such neurotoxicity is also clearly indicated by the effect of MMC on fissioning. Figure 2 shows the joint effects of population density and MMC on fissioning. Fissioning is progressively suppressed as the number of planarians per bowl is increased from 2 to 5 to 10. Fissioning is almost completely suppressed in all three population density groups after 2 days in 0.1 ppb of MMC in the culture water. Significant fissioning suppression was even observed at 0.03 ppb, which approximates the lower mercury levels found in "unpolluted" U.S. streams and ocean water. Such toxic sensitivities compare favorably with those reported for other assay systems; for example, no adverse effects were observed in brook trout, with two generations over a 2-

year period, maintained chronically in concentrations less than 0.3 ppb (Woebeser, 1973; Mount, 1976).

In a practical sense, the values just given for planarians and fish do not differ significantly, but two other factors, worth mentioning, do indicate significant advantages of planarians as water quality indicators, at least in regard to mercury. First, the testing paradigms yielding sensitivities of the order of 0.1 ppb required a year or two in the case of the fish tests, compared to only two weeks for the planarian test using fissioning suppression as the indicator. Second, the values for planarians were determined in a test protocol that involved changing the MMC solutions every third day instead of every day; subsequent studies have shown that daily changes of the MMC solutions in the planarian tests result in substantial increases in sensitivity, that is, the toxic effects of a solution of given concentration are enhanced.

3.2. Cadmium

Experimental tests were conducted to determine the toxic responses of planarians to various water concentrations of cadmium sulfate. These tests were conducted in the same way just described for mercury except that solutions were changed daily and a standardized population density of 10 planarians per specimen bowl were used throughout. A total of 40 planarians were used for each cadmium concentration and 80 as water controls. Results are shown in Figs. 3 and 4.

Figure 3 shows lethality as a function of time in various concentrations of cadmium. As the concentration decreases, the response latency increases and rate of rise decreases. No deaths were observed in the water controls. The data indicate the 5-day LC50 to be in the range of 2–3 ppm.

Figure 4 shows the effect of various cadmium concentrations on fissioning. Below 0.02 ppm, no effect is apparent; however, concentrations of 0.09 ppm or greater almost completely suppress fissioning. The steepness of the dose–response curve in this 0.02–0.09 ppm range is suggestive of a critical threshold of concentration for this neurotoxic effect. This is different from that observed in the case of copper (cf. Section 3.3). Since these values are somewhat less than those cadmium toxicity indices reported on various higher animal test species (Christensen, 1976), it would appear that planarians may be a useful indicator species for hazardous aquatic levels of cadmium.

3.3 Copper

Experimental tests, similar to those just described, were conducted to determine the toxic responses of planarians to various water concentrations of cupric sulfate. Solutions were changed daily and a standardized population

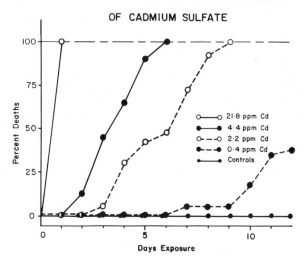

LETHALITY AS A FUNCTION OF DURATION

OF EXPOSURE TO AQUATIC CONCENTRATIONS

OF CADMIUM SULFATE

Figure 3. Cumulative lethality of asexual planarians of the species *D. dorotocephala* as a function of the duration of exposure to various habitat water concentrations of cadmium. No deaths occurred in the controls. All planarians exposed to 21.8 ppm of cadmic ion died within the first day. The 5-day LC50 estimate is greater than 2.2 and less than 4.4 ppm cadmium. Lag time decreases and rate of death increases with increasing cadmium concentration.

density of 10 planarians per bowl was used throughout. A total of 40 planarians were used for each copper concentration and 80 as water controls. Results are shown in Figs. 5 and 6.

Figure 5 shows percent lethality as a function of time in various concentrations of cupric sulfate. Both 4- and 5-day LC50s lie in the range of 0.5–1.3 ppm copper. No deaths were observed in the water controls or in test solutions containing less than 0.25 ppm copper. No real latent period is evident in the curves of lethality as a function of time. Rates of increase in percent lethality decrease as the concentration is decreased.

Figure 6 shows the effect of various copper concentrations on fissioning. The inhibition of fissioning appears to be a linear function of the habitat water concentration of copper from 0 to 0.5 ppm. Fissioning was completely suppressed by 0.5 ppm copper. No critical concentration threshold, of the type observed with cadmium (Fig. 4), was evident in these data on copper inhibition of fissioning.

3.4. Lead

Experimental tests, similar to those just described, were conducted to investigate the toxic responses of planarians to various water concentrations of

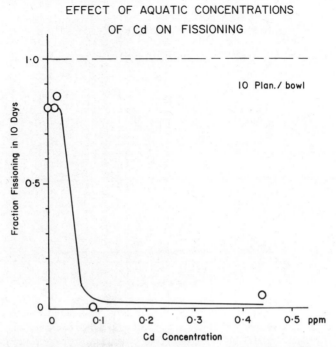

Figure 4. Effect of aquatic concentrations of cadmium on fissioning (asexual reproduction) of asexual planarians of the species *D. dorotocephala*. No effect on fissioning is observed at concentrations of 0.02 ppm or less. Cadmium concentrations of 0.1 ppm or greater suppress fissioning almost completely.

lead acetate. A standardized population density of 10 planarians per bowl was used throughout. Each concentration of lead acetate was tested with two different protocols: in one, solutions were changed daily; in the other, solutions were changed every third day except when deaths occurred in a bowl during the preceding 24 hr. Whenever debris of dead planarians was found in a test bowl in the daily observation, this debris was removed, the bowl cleaned, and the solution changed.

Twenty planarians were tested at each lead concentration and frequency of solution change. Forty planarians were used as water controls for each frequency of solution change schedule.

Results are shown in Figs. 7 and 8. Figure 7 shows the percent lethality as a function of time for each concentration of lead acetate and each frequency of solution change. Considering only those test groups in which the solution was changed daily (1/day), it is evident that the latency of the percent lethality vs. time curves increases, and the rate of rise decreases, with decreasing lead acetate concentration. No deaths occurred in the water controls or in those solutions with 5 ppm of lead acetate or less. The 5-day LC50 appears to lie in the range 20–50 ppm lead acetate for the daily solution change

LETHALITY AS A FUNCTION OF DURATION

OF EXPOSURE TO AQUATIC CONCENTRATIONS

OF CuSO$_4$

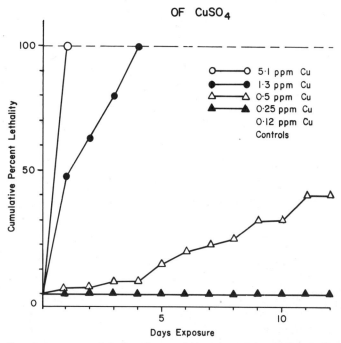

Figure 5. Cumulative percent lethality of asexual planarians of the species *D. dorotocephala* as a function of the duration of exposure to various habitat water concentrations of cupric ion. No deaths were observed in the controls, or at concentrations of copper of 0.25 ppm or less. All exposed to 5.1 ppm of copper died within the first day. The estimated 5-day LC50 is less than 1.3 and greater than 0.5 ppm of copper.

treatment groups. Comparison of the lethality vs. time curves, for those in which solutions were changed daily (1/day) with those in which solutions were changed every third day (1/3 days), shows a marked decrease in the apparent toxicity of a given lead concentration with less frequent solution changes.

Figure 8 shows the effect of lead acetate on fissioning in planarians. But since only 20 subjects were tested at each concentration and only 40 for water controls, the difference in fissioning between those in 1 ppm lead acetate and the controls is suggestive but not significant. However, the total suppression of fissioning by 5 and 10 ppm lead acetate is significant and probably mirrors the neurotoxic component of lead poisoning that is a dominant aspect of its toxic syndrome in higher animals. Daily solution changes were used for all treatment groups represented in Fig. 8.

Comparison of these toxic sensitivities of planarians in aquatic lead concentrations with various toxic indices of standard higher animal test species

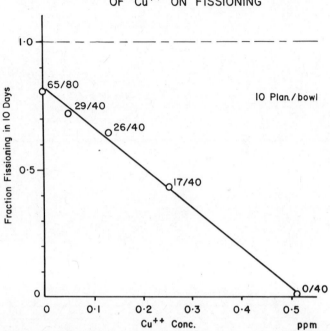

EFFECT OF AQUATIC CONCENTRATIONS

OF Cu^{++} ON FISSIONING

Figure 6.   Effect of aquatic habitat concentrations of cupric ion on fissioning (asexual reproduction) of asexual planarians of the species *D. dorotocephala*. The proportion of planarians
fissioning in 10 days is shown as a function of the copper concentration. The numerator of the
ratio by each data point indicates the number of fissionings, the denominator indicates the
number of subjects. Fissioning suppression appears to be a linear function of the copper concentration, with complete suppression at 0.5 ppm.

for lead (Christensen, 1976) indicates that planarians may be a useful indicator or assay species for hazardous levels of this heavy metal in water.

3.5.   Arsenic

Since arsenic is a common toxic contaminant associated with smelter operation, we have performed limited tests to obtain estimates of the toxicity of
some forms of arsenic, that is, arsenate, arsenite, and cacodylate, for planarians. No deaths were observed over a 10-day period in concentrations of
sodium arsenite less than 25 ppm. With 50 ppm water concentrations of
sodium arsenite, no deaths occurred in the first 4 days, but all test specimens
died by day 7. With 200 ppm water concentration, all died within the first
day. Fissioning was affected by lower concentrations: 10 ppm of sodium
arsenite suppressed fissioning to about 20% of control incidence over a 10-
day period; 5 ppm or less did not produce significant fissioning suppression.

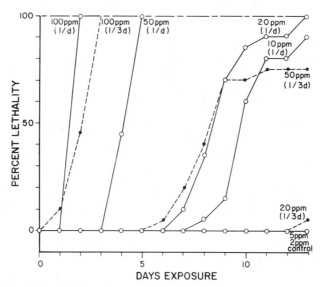

Figure 7. Cumulative lethality of asexual planarians of the species *D. dorotocephala* as a function of the duration of exposure to various habitat water concentrations of lead acetate. No deaths occurred in the controls. Apparent toxicity of a given lead solution is greater in those changed daily than in those changed every third day. Reducing the lead concentration increases the latency and decreases the slope of the dose–response curve.

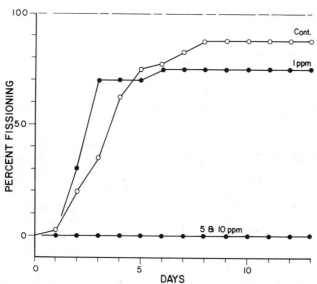

Figure 8. Effect of aquatic concentrations of lead on fissioning (asexual reproduction) of asexual planarians of the species *D. dorotocephala*. Fissioning was completely suppressed with lead acetate concentrations of 5 ppm or greater.

147

These values compare fairly well with an LD50 of 41 ppm (41 mg/kg) for oral administration to rat and an LD50 of 19 mg/kg (19 ppm) for intraperitoneal administration to mice (Christensen, 1976).

A 6-day LC50 of approximately 80 ppm was found for planarians exposed to water concentrations of cacodylate. Since cacodylate acts as a buffer, the relative proportions of cacodylic acid and cacodylate in such solutions will depend on the pH. This toxicity estimate for planarians can be compared with an LD50 of 1350 ppm (mg/kg) for oral administration to rat, 500 ppm (mg/kg) for intraperitoneal administration to mice, and an aquatic toxicity index of 10–100 ppm (Christensen, 1976).

On the other hand, preliminary studies to test the toxicity of water concentrations of sodium arsenate for planarians indicate a 6-day LC50 greater than 90 ppm. This value is greater than the LD50 of 12.5 mg/kg for oral administration to rabbit, the LD50 of 21 mg/kg (21 ppm) for intraperitoneal administration to mouse, and the TL_m96 generalized aquatic toxicity of 10–100 ppm (Christensen, 1976). Further tests of arsenate toxicity for planarians need to be conducted, but these data suggest that planarians may not be very sensitive to waterborne arsenic in the form of arsenate. This apparent relative insensitivity to arsenate may result from an impermeability of the planarian epidermis to this molecular species of arsenic.

In comparing the sensitivities of planarians with higher animals, it is well to consider whether the experimental determinations involved a route of administration comparable to those avenues that might be practically involved in exposures to waterborne arsenic. Oral administration is, for example, more pertinent for considerations of water quality than intraperitoneal or intravenous injection.

3.6. Zinc

Toxicological tests, similar to those just described, were conducted to investigate the responses of planarians to various water concentrations of zinc sulphate (Best and Morita, unpublished results). A standardized population density of 10 planarians in 50 ml of water or solution per bowl was used throughout. Water and solutions were changed daily at the same time each day. No deaths were observed in the 2-week test period at concentrations of zinc less than 0.68 ppm. The 5-day LC50 lies in the range of 1.1–2.3 ppm zinc. At 1.1 ppm zinc, there was a latency of 8 days before any deaths were observed.

Fissioning was progressively suppressed in a graduated manner as zinc concentrations were increased from 0.23 to 1.13 ppm. Thus, in 0.68 ppm Zn, fissioning was only 80% of that observed in controls, and only 10% of control values at 1.13 ppm Zn.

4. GENERAL DISCUSSION AND CONCLUSIONS

4.1. Gaps in the Data

Incomplete though they are, the foregoing results show that freshwater planarians are sensitive to relatively low water concentrations of common compounds of some heavy metals, such as mercury, cadmium, copper, lead, arsenic, and zinc, which are apt to be troublesome waterborne environmental contaminants associated with mining and smelter operations. Several important gaps in the data, requiring further study, should be indicated.

Other heavy metals, such as chromium, nickel, cobalt, tin, silver, vanadium, beryllium, titanium, molybdenum, and uranium, also can occur in various forms in conjunction with smelter operations. Various compounds of these also need to be tested with planarians.

There is some evidence that commonly measured water quality parameters such as hardness, total alkalinity, pH, dissolved O_2, and salinity (or conductance) have significant effects on the toxicities of these various heavy metal compounds. These effects need to be investigated more thoroughly in the case of planarians.

Environmental standards are usually stated in terms of permissible levels of individual elements or molecular species, and the foregoing tests using various concentrations of the individual compounds are consistent with such practices. However, there is evidence that mixtures of such compounds can be toxic even though each individual compound may be only present in amounts less than the maximum permissible concentration. Conversely, some such toxicants, for example, mercuric compounds and selenides, can antagonize each other. Since most toxic smelter effluents can, in practice, be expected to be mixtures of heavy metal compounds, the interactive effects of compounds in such mixtures should be investigated.

4.2. Other Types of Toxic Responses

Another type of omission in the data presented here should also be mentioned. This involves other kinds of toxic responses that we have observed in planarians. In addition to lethality and changes in fissioning incidence, planarians exhibit various other types of toxic responses not reported here for lack of space. For example, head resorptions, as well as other types of visible lesions and ulcerations, frequently occur at sublethal concentrations; the incidence and severity of these can be quantified (Best et al., 1981a,b). One also, in the case of compounds of heavy metals such as mercury, observes disturbances and abnormalities in the head regeneration that normally occurs in surgically decapitated planarians (Best et al., 1981b). Such effects may reflect the teratogenic hazard potential of such compounds (Best and Morita, 1982).

4.3. Comparisons with Other Indicator Species

It is worth comparing the toxicologic sensitivities of planarians with those of two commonly used water quality indicator species, Daphnia (Biesinger and Christensen, 1972) and the fathead minnow, *Pimophales promelas*, (Mount, 1969; Pickering and Gant, 1972), for some of these waterborne metallic compounds.

Acute static tests with fathead minnows and cadmium, in the Cd^{2+} form, showed that about 50% survive for 4 days at 30–32 ppm. Whereas, in continuous flow-through tests, there was 18% survival in 110 ppb and 63% survival in 57 ppb after 30 days. Long-term tests revealed no adverse effects on adults or embryos with concentrations in the 4.5–37 ppb range. The chronic Maximum Acceptable Toxicant Concentration (MATC) is in the range of 37–57 ppb, at which levels deleterious effects begin to become apparent in regard to embryo survival; these determinations involved more than 60 days exposure. The 4-day LC50 for *Daphnia magna* was reported to be 65 ppb cadmium (Biesinger and Christensen, 1972). Our results from toxicologic tests of cadmium with planarians indicate that the 15-day LC50 is approximately 0.4 ppm. Suppression of fissioning from control values provides a more sensitive response. The fraction of planarians fissioning in 10 days is unaffected by concentrations of cadmium up to 30 ppb, but is almost completely inhibited by 90 ppb or more. The cadmium MATC for minnows, 4-day LC50 for Daphnia, and the concentration required for fissioning suppression in planarians all appear to fall in the range of 30–90 ppb. Percent lethality observed in 2 or 4 days is, it should be noted, the toxic response of Daphnia most commonly used for routine assessment of water quality.

Acute static tests with fathead minnows and copper, in the cupric form, showed a 4-day TL_m of 84 ppb in soft water and 430 ppb in hard water (Mount, 1969). Similar minnow tests in a continuous flow-through system estimated a 4-day TL_m of 75 ppb Cu in soft water and 470 ppb Cu in hard water (Mount, 1969). *Daphnia magna* was found to be somewhat more sensitive to copper in the same form, with a 48-hr LC50 of only 10 ppb. Our results from toxicologic tests of copper with planarians indicate a 15-day LC50 of approximately 0.5 ppm and significant fissioning suppression over a 10-day period with 0.12 ppm. These tests were semistatic in that solutions were changed daily. The results indicate that planarians and fathead minnows have approximately the same sensitivity to copper, but neither appear to be as sensitive to it as Daphnia.

Methylmercuric chloride (MMC) was tested with fathead minnows in a full life cycle chronic toxicity study (Mount, 1976). Three months exposure to concentrations of 1.0 and 0.5 ppb of MMC caused 100% mortality. Exposure over the same period to 0.28 ppb of MMC caused 92% mortality. Spawning, as well as sexual development of males, was completely inhibited by 0.15 ppb of MMC. No toxic effects were observed with exposures to 0.09 ppb or less MMC. The toxicity of mercuric chloride for *Daphnia magna* has been investigated in both acute and chronic tests (Biesinger and Christensen, 1972). The 48-hr LC50 was found to be about 5 ppb mercury. A 16% reproductive impairment was caused by a 3-week exposure to 3.4 ppb mercury, and a 50% impairment resulted from similar exposure to 6.7 ppb. The diluent was Lake Superior water. Our results from toxicologic studies of planarians with MMC in static tests (solutions changed every third day) restricted to 2 weeks showed morphologic teratogenic effects on head regeneration of surgically decapitated planarians at 0.1 and 0.2 ppm of MMC, but not at 0.08 ppm or less. Fissioning was significantly suppressed at 0.1 and 0.03 ppb of MMC.

Subsequent studies have shown a marked enhancement of toxicity of a given water concentration with daily solution changes. For example, 60 ppb causes morphologic teratogenic effects on head regeneration of decapitated planarians and behavioral abnormalities are produced in the regenerates by 40 and 20 ppb of MMC.

In making these sensitivity comparisons, it is well to remember that all of the planarian toxicity studies described are acute studies. In view of the tendency of heavy metals to accumulate from relatively low water concentrations to much higher levels in tissues over protracted periods of time, one might anticipate sensitivities to lower water concentrations as the exposure time is increased from the 2-week periods used. Also, our tests were semistatic and, at least in the case of lead and methylmercury, increasing the frequency of solution change enhanced the toxicity of a given water concentration.

In addition to considerable expense and laboratory space required for the large flow-through systems appropriate for toxicity studies on fish such as trout, very large sample volumes are needed of the water to be assayed. Chronic studies, in which the greatest sensitivities to waterborne metals are manifested, also require exposure and observation periods that may extend to months and need even larger sample volumes. Such factors have led to increased interest in and use of less expensive species such as daphnia which have been shown to exhibit toxic sensitivities that correlate with those of fish for a wide variety of waterborne toxicants (Maki, 1979). Fathead minnows are intermediate between trout and daphnia in regard to such factors of expense, space, time, and sample volumes. Freshwater planarians such as *D. dorotocephala* are comparable to Daphnia in terms of cost and space requirements. Sample volumes and exposure times needed are relatively modest but greater than for daphnia.

4.4. Complementary Use of Planaria and Daphnia

Planarians present several features that suggest they may usefully complement daphnia as an inexpensive indicator species for assessment of water quality and environmental impact on aquatic ecosystems. In contrast to daphnia, planarians exhibit a considerable repertoire of quantifiable toxic responses that appear to reflect many of those that the various toxicants evoke in vertebrates. Position in the food chain is generally recognized as an important factor in the bioaccumulation of cumulative toxicants such as heavy metals. Daphnia are relatively low in the food chain and probably provide an important food source for trout fry and for fathead minnows which in turn provide an important food source for more mature trout, in nature. In laboratory tests, adult planarians readily captured and ingested daphnia, as well as mosquito larvae, tubifex worms, injured snails, and a variety of other small aquatic fauna. It would thus appear that planarians are somewhat higher in the food chain than daphnia. Since planarians are somewhat larger than daphnia, most toxic responses of interest are easily visible to the unaided eye.

It seems likely that joint use of bioassay results on inexpensive species such as daphnia and planaria in appropriate "discriminant functions" (Rao, 1952) could give better predictions of the toxicities of various waters for fish and higher animals than would be obtainable by use of either daphnia or planaria alone.

ACKNOWLEDGMENTS

This work was partially supported by Science and Education grants from the U.S. Department of Agriculture, BRSG funds to the Dean of the College of Veterinary Medicine and Biomedical Sciences of CSU from the National Institutes of Health, and a grant from Larimer County CETA.

REFERENCES

Best, J. B., Hand, S., and Rosenvold, R. (1968). Mitosis in normal and regenerating planarians. *J. Exp. Zool.* **168,** 157–168.

Best, J. B., Goodman, A. B., and Pigon, A. (1969). Fissioning in planaria: control by the brain. *Science* **164,** 565–566.

Best, J. B., Howell, W., Riegel, V., and Abelein, M. (1974). Cephalic mechanism for social control of fissioning in planarians. I. Feedback cue and switching characteristics. *J. Neurobiol.* **5,** 421–442.

Best, J. B., Abelein, M., Kreutzer, E., and Pigon, A. (1975). Cephalic mechanism for the social control of fissioning in planarians. III. CNS centers of facilitation and inhibition. *J. Comp. Physiol. Psychol.* **89,** 923–932.

Best, J. B., Morita, M., and Abbotts, B. (1981a). Acute toxic responses of the freshwater planarian, *Dugesia dorotocephala,* to chlordane. *Bull. Environ. Contam. Toxicol.* **26,** 502–507.

Best, J. B., Morita, M., Ragin, J., and Best, J. B., Jr. (1981b). Acute toxic responses of the freshwater planarian, *Dugesia dorotocephala,* to methylmercury. *Bull. Environ. Contam. Toxicol.* **27,** 49–54.

Best, J. B. (1983). Transphyletic animal similarities and predictive toxicology. In: A. Van der Merwe, Ed., *Old and new problems in physics, cosmology, philosophy and theoretical biology. Essays in honor of Wolfgang Yourgrau,* Plenum Press, New York, pp. 549–591.

Best, J. B. and Morita, M. (1982). Freshwater planarians for in vitro teratogenesis studies. *Teratogenesis, Carcinogenesis, Mutagenesis,* **2,** 277–291.

Biesinger, K. E. and Christensen, H. E. (1972). Effects of various metals on survival, growth, reproduction and metabolism of *Daphnia magna. J. Fish. Res. Board Can.* **29,** 1691–1700.

Child, C. M. (1941). *Patterns and problems of development,* University of Chicago Press, Chicago.

Christensen, H. E. (1976). *Registry of toxic effects of chemical substances.* U.S. Dept. Health, Education and Welfare, N.I.O.S.H., Rockville, Maryland.

Coward, S. J. (1968). Effects of actinomycin D on regeneration give evidence of sequential gene activation. *Nature* **219,** 1257–1258.

Dubois, F. (1948). Demonstration de la migration des cellules de regeneration des planaires par la methode des graffes et des irradiations combinees, *Compt. Rend. Acad. Sci.* **226,** 1316.

Flickinger, R. A. (1963). Cell differentiation, some aspects of the problem. *Science* **141,** 608–614.

Foster, J. (1969). Malformations and lethal growths in planarians treated with carcinogens. *Natl. Cancer Inst. Monograph 31,* 683–691.

den Hartog, C. (1974). Salt-marsh Turbellaria. In: N. W. Riser and M. P. Morse, Eds., *Biology of the Turbellaria,* McGraw Hill, New York, pp. 229–247.

Hyman, L. (1951). *The invertebrates: Platyhelminthes and Rhynchocoela,* Vol. 2, McGraw-Hill, New York.

Kawakatsu, M. (1974). Further studies on the vertical distribution of freshwater planarians in the Japanese Islands. In: N. W. Riser and M. P. Morse, Eds., *Biology of the Turbellaria,* McGraw-Hill, New York, pp. 291–338.

Keenan, L., Koopowitz, H., and Bernardo, K. (1979). Primitive nervous systems: action of aminergic drugs and blocking agents on activity in the ventral nerve cord of the flatworm, *Notoplana actiola. J. Neurobiol.* **10,** 397–407.

Keenan, L., and Koopowitz, H. (1981). Tetrodotoxin sensitive potentials in the first brains. *J. Exp. Zool.* **215,** 209–213.

Kenk, R. (1974). History of the study of Turbellaria in North America. In: N. W. Riser and M. P. Morse, Eds., *Biology of the Turbellaria,* McGraw-Hill, New York, pp. 17–22.

Lange, C. S. (1969a). Studies on the cellular basis of planarian radiation lethality. IV. Confirmation of the validity of the model and the effects of dose fractionation. *Intl. J. Radiat. Biol.* **14,** 539–551.

Lange, C. S. (1969b). Studies on the cellular basis of radiation lethality. V. A survival curve for the reproductive integrity of the planarian neoblast and the effect of polyploidy on the radiation response. *Intl. J. Radiat. Biol.* **15,** 51–64.

LeMoigne, A. and Gabriel, A. (1971). Action de l'actinomycine D sur la differenciatin cellulaire au cours de la regeneration de planaires qui viennent d'eclore. II. Etudes autoradio-

graphiques histologiques et ultra structurales de l'action de l'antibiotique sur les synth-
eses d'ARN, *Z. Zellforsche* **115**, 442–460.

Maki, A. W. (1979). Correlations between *Daphnia magna* and fathead minnow (*Pimephales
promelas*) chronic toxicity values for several classes of test substances. *J. Fish. Res.
Board Can.* **36**, 411–421.

McWhinnie, M. (1955). The effects of colchicine on reconstitutional development in *Dugesia
dorotocephala. Biol. Bull.* **108**, 54–65.

Mount, D. I. (1969). Chronic toxicity of copper to the fathead minnow, *P. promelas,* in soft
water. *J. Fish. Res. Board Can.* **26**, 2449–2457.

Mount, D. I. (1976). Testimony in the matter of the proposed effluent standards for Aldrin,
Dieldrin, et al. FWPCA (307). Docket No. 1, Exhibit No. 4, U.S. Congressional Regis-
ter.

Phillips, J., Wells, M., and Chandler, C. (1974). Metabolism of DDT by the freshwater planarian, *Phagocata velata. Bull. Environ. Contam. Toxicol.* **12**, 355–358.

Pickering, Q. H., and Gant, M. H. (1972). Acute and chronic toxicity of cadmium to the fathead
minnow, *P. promelas. J. Fish. Res. Board Can.* **29**, 1099–1106.

Pigon, A., Morita, M., and Best, J. B. (1974). Cephalic mechanism for the social control of
fissioning in planarians. II. Localization and identification of the receptors by electromi-
crographic and ablation studies. *J. Neurobiol.* **5**, 443–462.

Rao, C. R. (1952). *Advanced statistical methods in biometric research,* John Wiley & Sons, Inc.
New York.

Teshirogi, W., Sasaki, M., and Kawakatsu, M. (1981). Freshwater planarians from Lake
Usoriyama-ko and its lake-side area, the Shimokita Peninsula, in North Japan. *Sci. Rep.
Hirosaki Univ.* **28**(2), 84–96.

Woebeser, G. A. (1973). Aquatic mercury pollution. Studies of its occurrence and pathologic
effects on fish and mink. Thesis: Dept. Vet. Path., University of Saskatchewan, Saska-
toon, Canada.

Wolff, E. (1962). Recent researches on regeneration of planaria. In: D. Rudnick, Ed., *Regeneration,* The Ronald Press, New York, pp. 53–84.

6

VANADIUM IN THE AQUATIC ECOSYSTEM

Kenneth Lee*

Department of Botany
University of Toronto
Toronto, Ontario

*Present address: Ocean Chemistry Division, Institute of Ocean Sciences, P.O. Box 6000, Sidney, B.C., Canada V8L 4B2.

155

1. INTRODUCTION

Vanadium is one of the few metals whose anthropogenic input has led to a significant enrichment of the element in the environment (Goldberg et al., 1979; Briat, 1978; Duce and Hoffman, 1976; Zoller et al., 1974). This fact, coupled with recent data concerning the biological effects of vanadium at low concentrations, has resulted in a resurgence of interest in understanding the effects and biological fate of the element in the environment (van Zinderen Bakker and Jaworski, 1980; EPA, 1977; Bengtsson and Tyler, 1976; NRC, 1974).

In 1978 a water quality agreement for the Great Lakes was signed by Canada and the United States (IJC, 1978). After study of vanadium toxicity largely from data concerning humans, mammals, and higher plants, vanadium was classified as a hazardous polluting substance. Unfortunately, objectives were not set due to inadequate information on the possible degree of bioaccumulation or chronic effects of vanadium to aquatic organisms.

There is no history of vanadium-induced problems in the aquatic ecosystem, but at the same time, there have not been any thorough reviews concerning its potential environmental impact in this ecosystem. To date, the elements under intense ecotoxicological study have been those which have caused evident perturbations in the ecosystem. It would be much more satisfactory if the effects of potentially toxic substances such as vanadium could be assessed, and environmental standards established, to circumvent future problems.

2. SOURCES, CONCENTRATIONS, AND TRANSPORT

Vanadium enters aquatic ecosystems via leaching of parent rocks and soil, transport of water and sediments from contaminated areas, deposition of airborne particles, and direct dumping.

Vanadium occurs in the earth's crust at a concentration between 100 and 150 ppm, not as a free metal, but as relatively insoluble salts with copper, lead, zinc, ferric iron, uranium, manganese, calcium, and potassium (Vouk, 1979; Beliles, 1978; EPA, 1977; NRC, 1974; Schroeder, 1970; Cannon, 1963; Bertrand, 1954). Schroeder (1970) found average vanadium concentrations of 135 ppm in igneous rocks, 130 ppm in shale, and 20 ppm in sandstone and limestone. Vanadium concentrations in different soils of the world normally vary between 20 and 500 ppm (Hopkins et al., 1977; Schroeder, 1970; Bowen, 1966; Mitchell, 1964; Cannon, 1963).

A large fraction of vanadium released into the aquatic environment from natural sources originates from erosion of land surfaces by water. The concentration of dissolved vanadium salts in freshwater is largely dependent on the amount leached from the soil and rocks in the catchment area. This transition is thought to be aided by microorganisms, and vanadium is oxidized from the trivalent to the more soluble pentavalent state (Waters, 1977; EPA, 1977; Zajic, 1969).

Linstedt and Kruger (1970) have shown that mean vanadium concentrations in natural freshwaters range from 0.3 to over 20 ppb. High natural vanadium concentrations (7–300 ppb) have been reported in the Colorado River Basin by Kopp and Kroner (1968), who detected vanadium in only 3.4% of 1500 samples analyzed from rivers and lakes throughout the United States. Chau et al. (1970), in seasonal studies of Lake Ontario, reported vanadium concentrations from 0 to 0.1 ppb. Montiel (1975) has suggested that a natural vanadium removal system in aerobic river water exists which involves coprecipitation of vanadium with ferric hydroxide. Bengtsson and Tyler (1976) defined vanadium concentrations of 0.1–1.0 ppb as a normal range in freshwater. It was proposed that concentrations above 2 ppb indicated either a polluted state, or an exceptionally high vanadium content in the bedrock of the catchment area.

Schroeder (1974) and Bertine and Goldberg (1971) calculated that 2.8×10^5 tonnes of particulate and 3.2×10^4 tonnes of dissolved vanadium are annually transported by rivers to the oceans. However, much of the soluble vanadium in rivers is removed by precipitation when it reaches the sea. Bowen (1966) estimated that only 0.001% of the vanadium entering the ocean is retained in soluble form. In an attempt to explain the mechanisms responsible for the low vanadium concentrations in seawater, Krauskopf (1956) found that vanadium was insufficiently removed by precipitation as a sulfide or other insoluble forms or by adsorption on substances such as manganese or ferric hydroxides. Thus he suggested that biological processes were a major pathway for vanadium to sediments.

The total amount of vanadium in the oceans is estimated to be 7.5×10^{12} kg (Mason, 1966). The concentration in seawater generally averages between 1 and 3 ppb with no systematic variation with depth, although concentrations as high as 30 ppb have been reported (Sato and Okabe, 1978; Duce and Hoffman, 1976; Morris, 1975; Riley and Taylor, 1972; Piotrowicz et al., 1972; Burton, 1966; Chan and Riley, 1966).

Vanadium mobilization as a consequence of man's industrial activities occurs mainly in the form of particles emitted into the atmosphere. Environment Canada (1976) estimated that in Canada, during 1972, 2065 tonnes of vanadium were emitted into the atmosphere. In the United States, emissions were estimated to be about 17,000 tonnes in 1968 (EPA, 1977). Environmentally, the occurrence of vanadium in petroleum and coal is important because the combustion of these fuels constitutes the major source of vanadium emissions to the atmosphere. All crude oils of petroleum origin contain vanadium as an impurity, in concentrations from less than 1 to as high as 1600 ppm depending on the source of the crude oil (Bengtsson and Tyler, 1976; Hitchon et al., 1975; NRC, 1974). Vanadium concentrations in coal from numerous areas of the world are generally in the range of 10–200 ppm (Nadkarni, 1980; Ondov et al., 1979; Bengtsson and Tyler, 1976; NRC,

1974). However, concentrations as high as 2400 ppm have been reported by Schroeder (1970) in lignite deposits in Argentina.

The significance of anthropogenic inputs of vanadium into the atmosphere has been well documented. Data on vanadium concentrations in air indicate an annual mean of >100 ng/m^3 for most cities, and 0.5–2 ng/m^3 for continental air far from urban areas (EPA, 1977; McMullen and Faoro, 1977; Environment Canada, 1976; Duce et al., 1975; Chester and Stoner, 1974; NRC, 1974; Sugimae and Hasegawa, 1973; Lee and von Lehmden, 1973; Zoller et al., 1971). At the South Pole (i.e., far away from continents and anthropogenic sources) Zoller et al. (1974) found vanadium concentrations of only 0.001–0.002 ng/m^3. Zoller et al. (1971) and Duce et al. (1975) found that vanadium is present in atmospheric particles in concentrations too high to be explained by normal crustal weathering processes. Their data suggest that comparable amounts of atmospheric vanadium arise from petroleum combustion and natural sources. Bertine and Goldberg (1971) calculated the rate of vanadium mobilization from fossil fuels into the atmosphere to be about 12×10^9 g/yr.

Gravitational sedimentation removes a large fraction of atmospheric vanadium. Studies by Lee et al. (1972) and Montiel (1975) support the theory that the bulk of V_2O_5 emissions are removed by deposition of large aerosols close to industrial sources. Tuller and Suffet (1975) estimated the residence time of vanadium in the atmosphere of an urban air shed to be approximately one day. Precipitation removal processes may also represent an important factor. Hansen and Fisher (1980) and Sugawara et al. (1956) have found high vanadium values in snow and rain of Norway and Japan. Briat's (1978) studies of snow cores from Mt. Blanc in the high Alps, indicate that levels of atmospheric deposition of vanadium increased by a factor of two since 1950, paralleling the increase in the use of fossil fuels.

In aquatic systems, Montiel (1975) reported that vanadium in the Seine River was derived from atmospheric deposition of the metal. Gatz (1975) found that atmospheric inputs of pollutant aerosols into Lake Michigan were a significant fraction of the total metal inputs into the lake. Klein (1975) estimated the total annual aerosol deposition of vanadium into Lake Michigan to be 1.1×10^2 tonnes/yr. Kemp et al. (1978) calculated the sediment inputs of anthropogenic vanadium into Lake Superior, Lake Huron, Lake Erie, and Lake Ontario to be 0.05, 0.09, 2.4, and 0.80 $\mu g/cm^2 \cdot yr^1$, respectively. Recent analysis of vanadium concentrations in the Great Lakes (Lee, 1982) indicates the incidence of elevated dissolved vanadium concentrations in Lake Erie and Lake Ontario, at inshore areas close to highly populated or industrial sites (Fig. 1). In the Savannah River estuary, Goldberg et al. (1979) found that the concentrations of lead, chromium, and vanadium decreased with increasing depth in the sediment, suggesting an increased delivery of these elements to the system in recent years.

Chester and Stoner (1974) studied particulates from the lower troposphere over the Atlantic Ocean, Indian Ocean, China Sea, and various coastal

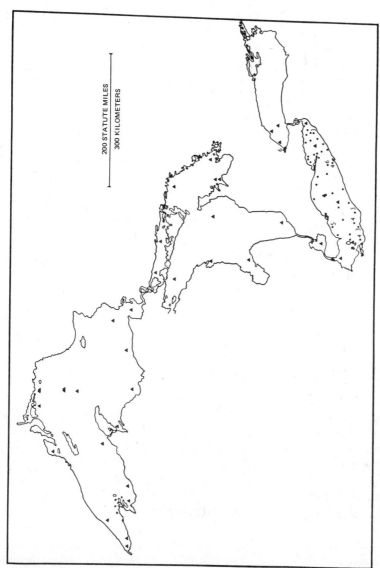

Figure 1. Vanadium concentrations in surface waters, at selected field sites in the Great Lakes. Absence of value (in ppb), next to data point, indicates that the concentration was below the detection limit (2.8 ppb). ▲, analysis by ICAP; ●, analysis by neutron activation.

areas. Vanadium concentration in the sand-sized particulates varied from 37–760 ppm with a mean of 163 ppm. The average crustal abundance in the study was found to be 135 ppm. The calculated vanadium enrichment factor in the particulates (1.2) indicated that in most marine areas there was no significant enrichment of vanadium over crustal material. In subsequent studies, Duce and Hoffman (1976) calculated the annual vanadium deposition from the air to the oceans between 30° and 60° north latitude to be 1.5–2.5 × 10^3 tonnes. This quantity was only 5% of the vanadium contributed to the region by all natural weathering processes; thus man's present contribution of vanadium to the global oceans is apparently small.

However, vanadium polluted sites in the marine environment exist. For example, Jaffe and Walters (1977) reported high vanadium concentrations in anaerobic sediments of an area of the Humber Estuary were the results of effluent discharge from a titanium dioxide processing plant. Piotrowicz et al. (1972) found that high vanadium enrichment in nearshore samples of the sea-surface microlayer was a result of extensive use of vanadium-rich heavy fuel oils. Bertine and Goldberg (1977) reported that the anthropogenic fluxes of vanadium, lead, and zinc to the sediments off the coast of southern California, 100 km from shore, were substantially lower than those in deposits 30 km from shore, and appeared to decrease with the square of the distance from shore. These results support the hypothesis that the transport of the metals was largely atmospheric. About 70% of anthropogenically derived vanadium-rich atmospheric particles are solubilized rapidly in seawater (Walsh and Duce, 1976; Duce and Hoffman, 1976). The majority of the vanadium in oceanic waters is in the dissolved form. The residence time for this fraction has been estimated to be 10^4–10^5 yr. (Goldberg et al., 1971; Walsh and Duce, 1976; Duce and Hoffman, 1976). The long residence time of the soluble vanadium species relative to particulates indicates that vanadium in the open ocean may be a long-term pollutant.

3. PHYSICAL AND CHEMICAL PROPERTIES

The physical and chemical states of vanadium in aquatic ecosystems are important factors, affecting uptake by organisms and processes controlling its residence time.

According to its position in the Vb-group of the first transition series, with niobium and tantalum, vanadium belongs to the transition elements with five valence electrons, giving rise to a maximum oxidation state of +5. Vanadium compounds with the metal in the oxidation states of 0, +2, +3, +4, and +5 have been found; however, it appears that the +4 and +5 valence states are the most stable (Meisch and Bielig, 1980; Waters, 1977; Schroeder, 1970). Discrete V^{4+} and V^{5+} ions are not known to exist, and vanadium is usually found bound to oxygen as a negatively charged polymeric oxy-anion. The element forms VO, V_2O_3, V_2O_4 and V_2O_5 when heated in the presence of oxygen (Shamberger, 1978; Waters, 1977; Eichhorn, 1973; Clark, 1968).

Under the extreme conditions of oil or coal combustion or gasification, the vanadium associated with the fuels would be liberated as an oxide in the flue gas (Kuntz et al., 1975). According to Tuller and Suffet (1975), the lower oxides of vanadium rapidly oxidize to V_2O_5 when heated in excess oxygen. Since V_2O_5 is soluble in water (Meyer and Aulich, 1930), airborne vanadium would likely dissolve and ionize in raindrops which enter directly into natural waters.

The characterization of various vanadium species in solution has been the subject of extensive research since the initial work of Berzelius in 1831 (Clark, 1968). Although vanadium has numerous oxidation states, it appears that only pentavalent (V^{5+}) vanadium is stable to any extent in natural freshwaters. Charlot and Bezier (1957) observed that the oxidation of vanadyl salt solutions to the pentavalent state was rapid even in the atmosphere. Remy (1961) stated that only vanadium oxides and salts in the tetravalent (V^{4+}) and pentavalent forms were likely to be soluble in aqueous media. Chau and Lum (1970) and Kalk (1963) noted that under normal aerobic conditions vanadate (V^{5+}) is the most probable species in natural waters, although the vanadyl (V^{4+}) cation was detected at concentrations of approximately 1% of total vanadium. Except in waters of unusually low pH, trivalent ions are found in extremely low concentrations (Chau and Lum, 1970). Kuntz et al. (1976) reported that the divalent (V^{2+}) vanadium cation was very unstable.

Vanadium is amphoteric in aqueous solution, and as the pH of the solution is varied, soluble vanadium will occur in many ionic species. A property of aqueous vanadate solution (V_2O_5 dissolved in alkali) is that, as acid is added, the vanadate ion undergoes various hydrolysis-polymerization reactions in specific pH regions. The principal solute species generated by such reactions is the isopoly anion, in which the metal atom occupies interstices of closely packed arrays of oxide ions (Pope and Dale, 1968; Clark, 1968). Despite extensive research on the nature of the V^{5+} species in aqueous solution, results and interpretation of data from different laboratories are not in agreement (Pope and Dale, 1968; Clark, 1968; Evans and Garrels, 1958; Schwarzenbach and Geier, 1963; Murmann and Giese, 1978). The impact of such complex chemistry, with the formation of numerous polynuclear species, on biological systems is largely unknown.

The known species of vanadium in aqueous equilibrium within the redox potential limits of natural limnological systems, as a function of pH and total vanadium concentration are illustrated in Fig. 2. Boundaries beween dissolved species are drawn where the molar concentration ratio of the two major ions is at unity. To construct Fig. 2, results from experiments using artificial media by several research groups have been used (Murmann and Giese, 1978; Rieger, 173; Pope and Dale, 1968; Schiller and Thilo, 1961; Ingri and Brito, 1959; Evans and Garrels, 1958). Therefore, such experimental

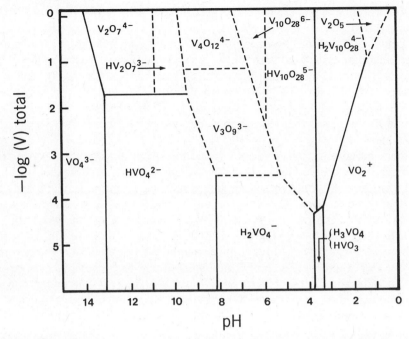

Figure 2. Major solute components of vanadates in solution at 25°C at various concentrations and pH values. Broken lines indicate doubtful demarcations (modified from Stendahl and Sprague, 1982).

data is not strictly comparable. For these reasons, dotted lines between species in the equilibrium diagram indicate uncertain boundaries.

It is apparent from Fig. 2 that in water between pH 4 to 13 and vanadium concentrations below 10^{-4} gram atoms/liter, only the simple orthovanadates (HVO_4^{-2}, $H_2VO_4^-$) exist. However, Burton (1966) has suggested that vanadium in the ocean may not be in thermodynamically stable states because the equilibration time of the metal could be longer than its residence time in the system. In addition, biochemical reactions mediated by living organisms may affect vanadium chemistry in aquatic ecosystems. For example, phytoplankton may excrete chelators which bind vanadium. In addition, biochemical processes may also alter chemical factors such as pH and Eh, which affect the forms of vanadium in solution. Goodman and Cheshire (1975) and Szalay and Szilagyi (1967) found that vanadium in the vanadyl form complexes with humic acids. In addition, it was postulated that humic acids in natural waters could reduce the vanadate ion VO_3^- to the vanadyl ion VO^{2+}.

Orvini et al. (1979) recently proposed a method of determining the chemical forms of dissolved vanadium in freshwater, utilizing ion exchange chromatography and neutron activation analysis. In contrast to past studies, they reported significant concentrations of cationic vanadium species (thought to be the vanadyl ion VO^{2+}) in natural waters. Utilizing Orvini's

Table 1.   Vanadium Speciation in Culture Media and Lakewater 2 hr after Spiking with 500 ppb of Vanadium from a Preequilibrated (pH 7.0) Stock Solution of Sodium Orthovanadate ($Na_3VO_4 \cdot nH_2O$)

Sample	% Residue	% neutral Complexed	% Cation	% Anion	% Recovery
Chu-10	N.D.	0.3	0.9	98.8	97.8
Arnon	N.D.	0.4	25.9	73.6	100.3
Lake Ontario (7/10/81)	N.D.	0.3	4.3	95.4	101.7
Lake Erie (6/10/81)	N.D.	0.2	3.4	96.5	98.4
Jack Lake (21/09/81)	N.D.	0.3	1.3	98.4	100.8

technique, Lee (1982) identified the vanadium species in algal culture media and natural lakewaters resulting from the addition of sodium orthovanadate (Table 1). In natural lakewaters and Chu-10 medium, more than 95% of the element added was retained as anionic vanadate forms two hours after 800 ppb vanadium addition. In contrast, in Arnon's medium, 25.9% of the vanadium added was found as cationic forms [such as VO^{2+}; $MgVO_3^+$; $Fe(VO_3)_2^+$]. These results suggest that further chemical studies are needed to elucidate the chemical nature of vanadium at low concentrations and its effects on aquatic organisms.

4.   OCCURRENCE AND EFFECTS IN PLANTS

Bowen (1966) estimated the vanadium content per unit dry weight of plant tissues to be of the order of 5 ppm in plankton, 2 ppm in brown algae, 2.3 ppm in bryophytes, 0.13 ppm in ferns, 0.69 ppm in gymnosperms, 1.6 ppm in angiosperms, and 0.67 ppm in fungi.

Since the studies of Witz and Osmond in 1886, extensive studies have been made on the effect of vanadium salts on the growth and metabolism of microorganisms and higher plants. The majority of such investigations (reviewed by van Zinderen Bakker and Jaworski, 1980; EPA, 1977; Cannon, 1963; Bertrand, 1954) indicate that vanadium concentrations of 10–20 ppm or greater were generally toxic, whereas in many cases lower concentrations were stimulatory.

4.1.   Bacteria and Fungi

Numerous reports have implicated vanadium in nitrogen fixation following Bortels' (1933) discovery that vanadium could substitute for molybdenum in the nitrogen fixation processes of *Azotobacter*. Further studies suggested that vanadium was a catalyst in chemical fixation of nitrogen in *A. vinelan-*

dii, A. agile, and *A. chroococcum.* Additions as small as 0.05 ppb vanadium could stimulate nitrogen fixation. However, vanadium was found to be capable of only partly replacing molybdenum, and was not required (Bové et al., 1957; Horner et al., 1942; Burk and Horner, 1935; Shibuya and Saeki, 1934). Furthermore, Becking (1962) observed inter- and intraspecific responses to vanadium. In a study of 10 *A. chroococcum* strains, three were unable to substitute vanadium for molybdenum in nitrogen fixation. In one of 20 *A. vinelandii* strains vanadium was able to replace molybdenum, and in one of 20 *A. agile* strains it was unable to replace molybdenum in nitrogen fixation.

From recent studies, in which the nitrogenase enzyme complex has been isolated, it is evident that the V-Nase isolated from vanadium-enriched, molybdenum-starved cultures is less active and stable than the Mo-Nase. It appears that vanadium does not substitute for molybdenum, but structurally stabilizes the nitrogenase–enzyme complex, allowing more effective utilization of molybdenum in molybdenum-starved cells and stimulates molybdenum uptake (Nagatani and Brill, 1974; Benemann et al., 1972; Burns et al., 1971; McKenna et al., 1970).

Lee et al. (1974) found that vanadium inhibited the formation of assimilatory NADPH–nitrate reductase and the growth of wild type *Neurospora crassa* in a nutrient medium containing nitrate, as the sole nitrogen source. Inhibition was prevented by addition of high levels of molybdate to the nutrient medium. These results implicate vanadium as a competitive inhibitor of molybdenum in nitrate reductase structure and function. For this system, vanadium appears to form an inactive analogue of nitrate reductase through replacement of molybdenum in the enzyme, in contrast to the nitrogenase system, in which it promotes effective utilization of available molybdenum.

The effects of vanadium on yeasts were first reported by Bokorny (1904), who found that a vanadium concentration of 260 ppm inhibited their growth, but not numerous bacteria which continued to multiply at vanadium concentrations as high as 2600 ppm. Sampath (1944) noted that sporulation of yeast cells was inhibited by 280 ppm vanadium, but favored by 140 ppm. Since yeast cells normally sporulate in unfavorable media, it was assumed that 140 ppm vanadium was above the optimum for growth. Crandall and Caulton (1973) found vanadium was functioning in the induction of the glycoprotein (5-factor), a cell wall factor necessary for the sexual agglutination reaction between opposite mating types of the yeast *Hansenula wingei.* No metal alone except vanadium could induce 5-f synthesis.

In ascomycetes, Frouin and Mercier (1914) found that sodium vanadate at concentrations from 2.5 to 645 ppm vanadium favored the growth of *Aspergillus niger,* increasing biomass by one third at the optimum concentration of 25 ppm. Anekwe (1976) found that V_2O_5 suppressed lipid biosynthesis. The mycelia of *Glomerella cingulata* grown in the presence of V_2O_5 $(2.8 \times 10^{-4}$ $M)$ were found to incorporate less $(2\text{-}^{14}C)$ acetate into lipids than mycelia grown in the absence of $V_2O_5.$ Nicholas and Commissiong (1957) suggested that metavanadate suppressed acid phosphatase *in vitro* in *Neurospora crassa,* by complex formation between vanadate and the substrate (*p*-nitrophenyl phosphate) used in their analysis. Further studies by Lopez et al. (1976) indicated that in *Escherichia coli* the oxovanadium (IV) ion (VO^{2+}) and vanadium (V) ion (VO_3^-) were potent competitive inhibitors of *p*-nitrophenyl phosphate hydrolysis by alkaline phosphatase. Their observations indicated that VO_3^- could bind specifically at the phosphate-binding site of the enzyme. Complementing these studies, Tyler (1976) suggested that anthropogenic inputs of vanadium from atmospheric deposition could suppress soil phosphatases. Subsequent studies by Tabatabai (1977) indicated that vanadium also inhibited soil urease activity.

Kanematsu and Kada (1978) assayed the mutagenicity of 77 metal compounds in *Bacillus subtilis* and found that vanadium as $VOCl_2$, V_2O_5, and NH_4VO_3 gave positive results.

4.2. Algae

Black and Mitchell (1952) found that several species of Scottish Laminariaceae and Fucaceae concentrated vanadium. A concentration factor (ratio of the vanadium concentration in the algae to the seawater content), of 100 was reported for *Pelvetia caniculata* and *Ascophyllum nodosum,* and 300 for *Fucus spiralis.* Aquatic plants are effective concentrators of chemical elements, especially those of physiological importance. In general, trace amounts of vanadium (>10 ppm), are found in phytoplankton and attached algae (Cockerill et al., 1978; Saenko et al., 1976; Udel'nova et al., 1974; Segar and Gilio, 1973; Martin and Knauer, 1973; Yamamoto et al., 1970; Sugawara et al., 1956).

The identification of vanadium as an essential micronutrient resulted from experiments on iron metabolism conducted by Arnon and Wessel (1953) with the green algae *Scenedesmus obliquus.* A marked increase in growth was found in cultures supplemented with the known higher plant micronutrients (manganese, boron, copper, zinc, and molybdenum) with increasing iron additions. Since the iron salts were not purified, it appeared that the increase in growth at high concentrations of iron was due to some essential micronutrient present as an impurity in the iron salt. Subsequent study indicated that vanadium could increase growth of algae. Of 16 other elements assayed including molybdenum, none were found capable of substituting for vanadium. Arnon and Wessel regarded this specificity of vanadium as evidence of essentiality. Maximum growth rates in *S. obliquus* were found with 0.1 ppm vanadium in the nutrient medium (Arnon, 1954).

Warburg et al. (1955) and Warburg and Knippahl (1954) confirmed the stimulatory effects of vanadium on photosynthetic gas exchange in *Chlorella* species. They postulated a participation of the metal in photosynthetic reduction of carbon dioxide. In subsequent studies by Arnon (1958), it was found that vanadium deficiency in *S. obliquus* resulted in lower chlorophyll content. In addition, the rate of photosynthesis per unit chlorophyll was twice as high in vanadium-enriched cultures under high light (20,000 lux) but not under low light (2000 lux) intensities. Payer and Trüeltzsch (1972) calculated the vanadium demand of *S. obliquus* to be 5 μg V/kg dry weight.

Stimulatory effects of vanadium on dry weight production and chlorophyll content have also been reported in *Bumilleriopsis filiformis, Chlorella vulgaris, Chlorella pyrenoidosa, Chlorella luteoviridis,* and *Chlamydomonas reinhardii* (Meisch and Bielig, 1975; Salageanu, 1973; Hesse, 1974; Boger, 1969). However, vanadium has not been found to be an essential trace element for *Nostic muscorum, Calothrix parietina,* and *Anabaena cylindrica* (Allen, 1956; Holm-Hansen, 1954).

Meisch, in a number of publications reported that trace amounts of vanadium (0.01–1000 ppb as NH_4VO_3) influenced biochemical processes in *Chlorella pyrenoidosa* and *Scenedesmus obliquus,* resulting in increased dry weight and chlorophyll content. It was suggested that vanadium metabolism may be closely related to iron, since chlorosis in algae due to iron deficiency could be relieved by the addition of 20 ppb vanadium as NH_4VO_3. Two different pH optima were observed for vanadium action on dry weight (pH 7) and chlorophyll biosynthesis (ph 7.5–8.0), thus suggesting two sites of action. Biochemical analysis indicated that 90% of the [48]V offered to *S. obliquus* was taken up by the culture in 5 days, 21% of the vanadium was in the chloroplast fraction. It was suggested that the algae possess an intracellular cytoplasmic pool with a specific binding site for vanadium and that only a specific quantity of vanadium was transported to the plastids, where photosynthesis and biosynthesis of chlorophyll required traces of the metal. Preliminary studies indicated that vanadium-stimulated chlorophyll formation was light dependent, but occurred to a small extent in the dark. Because vanadium stimulated both the formation of chlorophylls in the dark and the synthesis of the porphyrin protoporphyrin-IX in a mutant *Chlorella* (which had lost its ability to form any chlorophyll), it was assumed that vanadium influences the formation of a precursor of the chlorophylls, in the reaction sequence leading to the green pigments in a step prior to protoporphyrin-IX (Meisch et al., 1977; Meisch and Bielig, 1975; Meisch, 1970).

Subsequent studies by Meisch and Bellmann (1980) and Meisch and Bauer (1978) have shown that vanadium stimulated the δ-amino levulinic acid–transaminase pathway, an initial reaction of chlorophyll biosynthesis. This effect was positively correlated with illumination, with a 130% stimulation at 20,000 lux, but no effect in the dark. It was suggested that vanadium catalyzes the step in the transamination pathway from 4,5-dioxovaleric acid (DOVA) to δ-amino levulinic acid (δ ALA). The latter is an intermediate in the biosynthesis of porphyrins, known to play a key role in the regulation of chlorophyll and heme formation.

In support of previous evidence, Wilhelm and Wild (1980) found vanadium altered the CO_2 fixation rate, dry weight, chlorophyll content, and symptoms of chlorosis in *Chlorella*. Cells grown in high light conditions in a medium containing 20 ppb vanadium had thicker cell walls, higher starch content, and other biochemical components which contributed to a higher dry weight. With increasing concentrations of vanadium, chlorophyll content, and concentrations of the components of the electron transport chain, P-700 and cytochrome-f were also increased. At 20 ppb vanadium, P-700 was 4 times higher on a dry weight basis, and cytochrome-f was 3.4 times higher than in controls. Thus, vanadium appears to play a role in the central processes regulating growth of green algae.

Meisch et al. (1980) observed that vanadium deficiency caused intracellular starch accumulation in *Chlorella fusca*. Algae in the absence of vanadium appeared to have increased starch synthesis and were unable to utilize their carbohydrate pools as indicated by the occurrence of large deposits of intracellular starch. These symptoms were reversed by addition of trace amounts of the metal.

As expected, high concentrations of vanadium have toxic effects in algae. Upitis et al. (1974) found that growth of *Chlorella* decreased at vanadium concentrations as low as 100 ppb, and at 50–100 ppm production was lowered by 25–34% compared to the control. Different results were obtained by Meisch et al. (1977) for *Chlorella*. The maximum stimulatory effects on biomass production and chlorophyll synthesis were found at 500 ppb vanadium in the medium. Inhibitory effects on dry weight and chlorophyll content were found at concentrations about 25 ppm vanadium, and growth was found to cease at 100 ppm vanadium. The toxic threshold for vanadium content in the alga was determined to be 150–200 ng V/g dry weight. Bruno and McLaughlin (1977) found the growth of the dinoflagellate *Ceratium hirundinella* to be inhibited by 100 ppb vanadium. In marine studies, Miramand and Unsal (1978) performed acute toxicity tests on *Dunaliella marina, Prorocentrum micans,* and *Asterionella japonica* with sodium metavanadate. The 9-day LC50 values were 0.5 ppm, 3 ppm, and 2 ppm respectively. In general, these values were lower than those for the benthic invertebrates studied by the same researchers. In contrast, Ballaster and Castellvi (1979) reported that their cultures of *Dunaliella* no appreciable suppression in growth was observed up to 50 ppm vanadium.

Detailed growth and primary production experiments with algal cultures from various taxonomic groups by Lee (1982), confirmed the specificity of the species responses to vanadium. In addition, the chemistry of the culture media was found to affect the algal response to vanadium. In ^{14}C uptake studies, algae isolated from local lakes were found to be much more sensitive to vanadium than culture collection species. It is likely that these planktonic algae have more exacting nutritional requirements than culture collection species which comprise mainly of benthic or "weed" species. Phytoplankton maximize their chances of survival in their respective environments by responding to specific selection pressures. This suggests that algae grown under laboratory conditions for many generations in concentrated nutrient media with correspondingly high contaminant trace metal content, probably evolve higher tolerance to trace metals, including vanadium.

Vanadium appears to influence cell division processes in algae. Hesse (1974) reported that 3 ppb vanadium as sodium vanadate prevented complete synchronization of *Bumilleriopsis filiformis*. Meisch and Benzschawel (1978) found that in the range of vanadium concentration known to stimulate *Chlorella pyrenoidosa*; toxic effects on cell division were apparent. In continuous light, in the presence of 20 ppb vanadium as NH_4VO_3, mean cell size increased significantly. Maximal increase occurred at 500 ppb vanadium. These large cells had giant nuclei with multiple chromosomes. In addition, synchronous growth of the algae with vanadium ceased after three division periods, after which a division occurred, which generally produced larger than normal autospores. It was postulated that during growth, normal duplication of genetic material occurred, producing nuclei with multiple sets of chromosomes. However, subsequent nuclear division was inhibited by vanadium and the subsequent division of autospores did not occur, producing giant cells with large nuclei. Lee (1982) observed that ultrastructural changes in enlarged cells of *Scenedesmus obliquus* induced by growth at elevated concentrations of vanadium (0.8–9 ppm), included thickened cell walls, and larger numbers of vacuoles, starch granules, and lipid droplets.

Direct evidence of vanadium-inhibited cell division has been collected by Cande and Wolniak (1978). The mitotic spindle is responsible for equal partitioning of chromosomes during cell division. At anaphase, the sister chromatids separate, the chromosomes move to their spindle poles and the spindle elongates. Vanadate at 10–100 μM was found to reversibly inhibit anaphase movement of chromosomes, and spindle elongation in mitotic mammalian cells in tissue culture (PtK_1 cells).

Ramadoss (1979) found that 100 ppb vanadium ($NaVO_3$) inhibited nitrate reductase in *Chlorella vulgaris,* both *in vivo* and *in vitro,* by forming an inactive complex with the reduced enzyme. However, the inactiviated enzyme complex could be reactivated by the addition of ferrocyanide or EDTA, suggesting that the vanadate was relatively loosely bound.

Ever since Bortels in 1933 reported that vanadium could substitute for molybdenum in nitrogen fixation by *Azotobacter* species, contradictory observations have been made in algae. Arnon (1958), Allen (1956), and Holm-Hansen (1954) were unable to find conclusive evidence for the requirement of vanadium in nitrogen fixation by blue-green algae. Fay and De Vasconcelos (1974) noted that vanadium exerted an inhibitory effect on the nitrogen fixing ability of *Anabaena cylindrica,* and contrary to the effects in *Azotobacter,* the presence of vanadium in molybdenum-deficient cultures resulted in the amplification of molybdenum deficiency symptoms. It was postulated that vanadium substituted for molybdenum in the nitrogenase complex, forming a less active enzyme. Curiously, in all cultures containing vanadium, the rate of heterocyst production was higher, and nitrogenase activity and pigment concentration were lower, than when it was excluded from the medium. Increased frequency of heterocysts in *A. cylindrica* in filaments incubated with vanadium and without molybdenum indicated severe nitrogen starvation in the alga.

Phosphate uptake kinetics in natural waters may be investigated by the steady-state approach introduced by Rigler (1956), in which carrier free ^{32}P–PO_4 is added to lakewater samples, and the time-course of uptake is monitored. Field studies in lakes utilizing this technique have indicated that vanadium at concentrations >10 ppb decreases the $^{32}PO_4$–P influx of aquatic microorganisms, thus increasing the turnover time of the phosphate pool (Lee, 1982). The observed decrease of $^{32}PO_4$–P influx in these studies may be due to vanadium competing with phosphate for the same uptake sites in the phytoplankton. The predominant form of vanadium in lakewater is the orthovanadate ion $H_2VO_4^-$. The molecular orbital structures of phosphate and vanadate are similar; the oxygen is attached to the central atom in an sp^3 arrangement, thus forming tetrahedral structures. The V–O and P–O bond lengths, at 1.66 Å and 1.55 Å respectively, are similar (Biggs and Swinehart, 1976; Bailar et al., 1973; Hill and Matrone, 1970). Hansen (1979), Cantley et al. (1977), Lopez et al. (1976), and Van Etten et al. (1974) have proposed that vanadate substituted for phosphate in a number of phosphate-binding enzymes.

Lee (1982) investigated vanadium uptake by algae by use of the radioisotope ^{48}V (as $VOCl_2$). Culture experiments with *Chlorella pyrenoidosa, Scenedesmus basiliensis, Selenastrum capricornutum,* and *Scenedesmus obliquus* indicated that vanadium uptake was species specific, and also influenced by the chemical environment, that is, the type of media. For example, on a per-cell basis, after 10 days of growth in media containing 5 mg V/liter, *S. obliquus* accumulated 189 fg V/cell in Arnon's medium and 9 fg V/cell in Chu-10 medium, whereas *C. pyrenoidosa* accumulated less than 7 fg V/cell in both media. Further uptake experiments with heat-killed cultures of *S. obliquus* indicated that a large fraction of vanadium flux occurs by passive adsorption. Cellular component analyses of ^{48}V-labelled samples showed that 80% of the vanadium was associated with the polysaccharide fraction. The abundance of carboxylated polysaccharides in the external slime envelope of *Scenedesmus* (Pickett-Heaps, 1975) appears to account for its greater capacity for vanadium uptake in comparison to other algal species.

The relative importance of phytoplankton, bacteria, and detritus in vanadium uptake and transport in the aquatic ecosystem was estimated by size fractionation of ^{48}V- and ^{14}C-labelled lakewater samples (Lee, 1982). Most of the photosynthetic carbon uptake occurred in the 8–30 μm and 1–3 μm size ranges while much of the vanadium was incorporated into particles in the 0.2–8 μm size range. These results suggest that a large fraction of the vanadium was incorporated into nonphotosynthetic bacterial and/or detrital components. As previously suggested by Krauskopf (1956), biogenic detritus may be the principal agent in the vertical sedimentation of vanadium.

To be toxic, vanadium must reach its site of action within the cell, and attain a critical level to elicit a response. From considerations of the atomic structure of vanadium and its solution chemistry, Nieboer and Richardson (1980) concluded that it could bind to all categories of ligands. The upper limit of vanadium accumulation in algal cells is determined by the number of nondiffusable, ionizable ligands present in the cells to which vanadium ions can bind. The observed inter- and intraspecific differences in vanadium uptake by phytoplankton, and their response to the metal depends on species specific, as well as environmentally controlled, differences in the types and/ or concentrations of ligand present in the cells.

In applied ecological studies, Steenivasan et al. (1975) suggested the use of trace amounts of vanadium as a fertilizer in aquaculture, because the addition of 500 ppb vanadium increased primary production by stimulating growth of the blue-green alga *Microcystis aeruginosa*. Further studies by Lee (1982) and Montiel (1975) showed that the addition of trace amounts of vanadium (20–25 ppb) stimulated primary production and growth of natural phytoplankton populations. Hence, in natural waters, various algal species may be vanadium deficient.

Studies by Patrick (1978) and Patrick et al. (1975) clearly indicated that trace elements could determine the kinds of algal species dominant in natural algal communities. Seasonal field studies in streams indicated that additions of up to 20 ppb vanadium stimulated growth of benthic algae, particularly the diatom *Melosira varians* which dominated the natural population. At higher concentrations vanadium did not favor diatom growth, and other kinds of algae such as filamentous green algae and blue-green algae increased. At vanadium concentrations higher than 4 ppm, primary production was depressed and blue-green algae were found to out-compete the diatoms. Decreases in diatom growth appeared to be correlated with the concentration of vanadium associated with the cells. Similar observations were made by Lee (1982) in lakewater phytoplankton studies. Seasonal ^{14}C–primary productivity experiments in a variety of lakes indicated that vanadium at concentrations greater than 100 ppb significantly decreased photosynthesis whereas lower concentrations (25 ppb) were stimulatory. Statistical analysis of the seasonal field data on the effects of vanadium in relation to phytoplankton composition, revealed differences in responses to vanadium by various taxonomic groups. The diatoms (Bacillariophyceae) were extremely sensitive to vanadium, and were depressed at concentrations as low as 10 ppb. In contrast, the Chlorophyceae and Cyanophyceae appeared to be stimulated at various vanadium concentrations. Hence, vanadium at levels encountered as a result of industrial operations may have important effects on the population structure of ecosystems in the receiving waters.

Preliminary primary production experiments conducted at sites in the

Atlantic and Pacific oceans (Lee, 1982) indicated that marine algae were not as sensitive to vanadium as were their freshwater counterparts. This tolerance may be attributable to chemical reactions in seawater, which decrease concentrations of biologically available vanadium.

4.3. Higher Plants

The aquatic plants *Pontedaria cordata, Phyllospadix iwatensis,* and *Thalassia testudinum* have been found to have high vanadium content (Saenko et al., 1976; Cowgill, 1973; Segar and Gilio, 1973). These vanadium "accumulator" plants are characterized by their capacity to absorb and store large amounts of vanadium to levels not encountered in the rest of the population growing in the same environment.

Study of vanadium toxicity in aquatic higher plants has not been conducted to date.

5. OCCURRENCE AND EFFECTS IN ANIMALS

A large amount of information is available on vanadium in animals (Berman, 1980; Vouk, 1979; EPA, 1977; Hopkins et al., 1977; Bengtsson and Tyler, 1976; NRC, 1974; Schroeder, 1970; Faulkner Hudson, 1964).

In the majority of invertebrates, vanadium concentrations of 0.5–2.5 ppm dry weight appear to be the rule, whereas body concentrations in vertebrates appear to be lower, 0.4 ppm dry weight or less (Schroeder, 1970; Bowen, 1966; Bertrand, 1954).

5.1. Invertebrates

The first report of the presence of vanadium in the animal kingdom was made by Henze (1911), who found concentrations as high as 42,000 ppm in the blood of four species of ascidians, marine animals belonging to subphylum Tunicata. In subsequent studies Webb (1939) found vanadium to be located principally in the green blood cells called vanadocytes. In these blood cells the metal appears to be present in the trivalent state, complexed to pyrrole rings, and associated with high concentrations of sulfuric acid (Kustin et al., 1976; Biggs and Swinehart, 1976; Carlson, 1975; Levine, 1961).

Theories postulated for the function of vanadium in ascidians include a possible role in oxygen binding and transport (Carlisle, 1968; Faulkner Hudson, 1964), tunicin synthesis (Endean, 1960), and defense mechanisms (Stoecker, 1977; Brown and Davies, 1971). However, there is no conclusive evidence supporting any of these theories (Biggs and Swinehart, 1976; Goodbody, 1974).

Tunicates are not the only animals to accumulate vanadium in large quantities. Vinogradov (1934) and Noddack and Noddack (1940) reported the presence of large concentrations of the metal in the holothurians *Stichopus japonicus* and *S. tremulus*. However, vanadium accumulation does not appear to hold for all holothurians, since little vanadium accumulation has been observed in other genera (Bertrand, 1943; Webb, 1939). The bryozoan *Plumatella fungosa* was found to contain 16.8 ppm vanadium per unit dry weight, a value much higher than the 1–3 ppm range reported for most invertebrates (Bertrand, 1943, 1954).

Vanadium is commonly found in trace amounts in shell fish and crustaceans (La Touche et al., 1981; Blotcky et al., 1979; Ikebe and Tanaka, 1979). The uptake of vanadium in molluscs, crustaceans, and echinoderms indicated that besides the food pathway, direct surface sorption processes are of major importance in the bioaccumulation of the metal (Miramand et al., 1981; Miramand et al., 1982; Ballester and Castellvi, 1979, 1980; Unsal, 1978).

Very few vanadium toxicity tests have been conducted with invertebrates. Miramand and Unsal (1978) found that the 9-day LC50 values for *Nereis diversicolor* (worm), *Mytilus galloprovincialis* (mussel), and *Carcinus maenas* (crab) were 10, 35, and 65 ppm vanadium (as $NaVO_3$ in the seawater) respectively. These high values are supported by evidence from Ballester and Castellvi (1979) who found that the critical concentration for vanadium in *Mytilus edulis* was between 50 and 100 ppm.

Bovee (1978) assessed the toxicity of the heavy metals selenium, zirconium, and vanadium on the freshwater ciliated protozoan *Tetrahymena pyriformis*. The addition of 20 ppm vanadium as vanadyl sulfate significantly lowered the growth and locomotor rate (measured as swimming speed) of the organism. Experiments conducted by MacDonald (1979) indicated a MST (median survival time) of 8 hr for *Daphnia magna* in media containing 30 ppm vanadium added as vanadate.

Kuntz et al. (1976) outlined invertebrate species shifts in activated sludge communities as vanadium was added to the system. At approximately 15 ppm soluble vanadium, the rotifers died; and with decreased competition, other free-swimming ciliates appeared. At high concentrations of vanadium (>120 ppm) the flagellated protozoa were favored.

5.2. Vertebrates: Fish

Trace quantities of vanadium have been found in both freshwater and marine fish (Bertrand, 1943; Noddack and Noddack, 1940). The average value has been estimated by Bowen (1966) to be 0.14 ppm dry weight.

Tarzwell and Henderson (1956, 1960) reported for fathead minnow and bluegill in hard and soft waters 96-hour LC50 values ranging from 4.8 to 55 ppm vanadium, added as $VOSO_4$ or V_2O_5. With the increased concern over anthropogenic inputs of vanadium into the aquatic ecosystem, there has been a considerable increase in research on the toxic effects of vanadium on fish in recent years.

Studies with American flagfish (*Jordanella floridae*) by Holdway and Sprague (1979) indicated a 96-hour LC50 of 11.2 ppm vanadium. Growth and survival in 96-day tests was depressed, particularly in the larvae, at 0.17 ppm vanadium. At concentration of 0.041 ppm there was stimulation of growth and reproductive performance in female fish. The sublethal threshold for toxicity of vanadium was estimated to be 0.08 ppm.

Studies by Giles and Klaverkamp (1982) and Giles et al. (1979) reported that vanadium was moderately toxic to juvenile rainbow trout (*Salmo gairdneri*) and white fish (*Coregonus clupeaformis*), (96-hr LC50 of 6.4 and 17.4 ppm respectively), with toxicity increasing slightly with decreasing pH. Pronounced histopathological lesions were observed in gills and kidneys of trout exposed to sublethal concentrations of vanadium, with damage increasing with increased exposure to the metal. Vanadium induced premature hatching of eyed eggs at concentrations from 44 to 595 ppm. Curiously, eyed eggs of trout were 200–300 times more resistant to vanadium than fingerlings, and the metal did not appear to induce histopathological lesions in the developing embryos. It appeared that juvenile whitefish avoided vanadium concentrations of 500 ppb or higher in the test water.

Anderson et al. (1979) also reported dose-related histopathological effects on the lamellae of gills in juvenile rainbow trout, and suggested that the gills are a critical site for the lethal action of vanadium. Of the three toxicants tested (vanadium, nickel, and phenol), vanadium was the most potent lethal agent (96-hr LC50 of 10 ppm vanadium).

Stendahl and Sprague (1982) noted that the 7-day LC50 values for trout in waters ranging from 30 to 355 mg/liter total hardness and pH from 5.5 to 8.8 were within a narrow range, from 1.9 to 6.0 ppm vanadium, added as V_2O_5. Toxicity decreased with increasing water hardness, and was greatest at pH 7.7, where $H_2VO_4^-$ was predicted to be the predominant vanadium ion.

6. BIOCHEMICAL STUDIES

Extensive studies have been conducted on the biochemical action of vanadium in nonaquatic organisms. Of great biochemical interest concerning plants, are reports by Rosen et al. (1975) which indicate that ions of vanadium (IV) and (V) are specific ionic redox agents in photosynthetic reactions. Utilizing spinach chloroplasts, it was found the vanadyl sulfate in moderately high concentrations (0.03 M) resembles ferrocyanide and donates electrons to photosystem II. Decavanadate in the presence of 2,5-dibromothymoquinone accepts electrons in photosystem II, and in the absence of a block between the two photosystems, accepts electrons in photosystem I in the vicinity of plastocyanin or beyond. Vanadite and ferrocyanide in high concentrations (0.32 *M*) donate electrons to Photosystem I.

Mountain et al. (1953) showed that rats fed vanadium pentoxide had lower cystine content in their hair. It was postulated that vanadium partially blocked the utilization of methionine and its subsequent conversion to cystine in liver cells. Bergel et al. (1958) demonstrated that catabolism of cystine and cysteine increased in the presence of vanadium.

Mascitelli-Coriandoli and Citterio (1959) demonstrated a reduction of coenzyme A in the liver of rats treated with sodium vanadate. This effect was probably related to the effects of vanadium on cystine metabolism. Thioethanolamine, one of the compounds involved in the synthesis of coenzyme A, is derived from the decarboxylation of cysteine. Coenzyme A is known to be involved in biochemical processes in which acetate is the precursor. Curran (1954) demonstrated that the synthesis of cholesterol from ^{14}C-acetate in rat liver was depressed by vanadium.

Vanadium has also been reported to affect the synthesis of triglycerides and phospholipids, as expected from its effect on acetyl coenzyme A, which is a precursor of fatty acids (Bernheim and Bernheim, 1939; Curran et al., 1959; Snyder and Cornatzer, 1958; White and Dieter, 1978).

Aiyar and Sreenivasan (1961) reported that vanadium reduced synthesis of coenzyme Q (ubiquinone) in the mitochondrial electron transport chain. In addition, vanadium salts also inhibited succinic dehydrogenase in the tricarboxylic acid cycle. These reactions indicated that vanadium could reduce ATP synthesis.

Wright et al. (1960) demonstrated that vanadium uncouples mitochondrial oxidative phosphorylation in liver homogenates *in vitro,* thus depleting ATP energy stores. *In vivo* studies conducted subsequently by Hathcock et al. (1966) indicated uncoupling of oxidative phosphorylation in liver mitochondria of chicks fed NH_4VO_3 at 25 mg V/kg.

The enzyme (Na, K)-ATPase is vital in controlling and utilizing the energy stored in ATP to maintain cellular cation transport, salt homostasis, nerve conduction, and other bioelectrical phenomena (Nechay and Saunders, 1978). Cantley et al., in 1977, identified vanadate as a potent inhibitor of ATPase. Subsequent studies from a variety of organisms have concerned vanadium effects on (Na, K)-ATPase; Mg-ATPase and Ca-ATPase (Nelson and Blaustein, 1981; Buczek, 1980; Simons, 1979; Hansen, 1979; Beaugé and Glynn, 1978).

Schwabe et al. (1979) reported that vanadium produced significant activation of adenyl cyclase which in turn resulted in increased production of cyclic adenosine monophosphate. Cyclic AMP is known to mediate control of numerous energy-related homeostatic mechanisms in animals.

Recent work has shown that vanadium may exert both positive inotropic (increases in contraction forces) and negative inotropic effects in various tissues (Garcia et al., 1981; Bell et al., 1979; Grupp et al., 1979; Borchard et al., 1979). Intravenous injection of small doses in animals produced generalized vasoconstriction and elevated blood pressure (Inciarte et al., 1979; Schroeder and Perry, 1955).

Tolman et al. (1979) demonstrated that vanadium affected glucose metabolism directly in a number of *in vitro* rat assay systems, including the stimulation of glucose oxidation and transport in adipocytes, stimulation of glycogen synthesis in the liver and diaphrgm, and inhibition of hepatic gluconeogenesis and intestinal glucose transport. DeMaster and Mitchell (1973) reported that vanadate could replace phosphate as a substrate for glyceraldehyde-3-phosphate-dehydrogenase, forming an unstable analogue of 1,3-diphosphoglycerate, similar to that produced by arsenate.

Vanadium has also been shown to affect the following enzymes: ribonuclease (Cantley et al., 1977); acid phosphatase (Van Etten et al., 1974), alkaline phosphatase (Lopez et al., 1976), phosphofructokinase (Choata and Mansour, 1978), adenylate kinase (DeMaster and Mitchell, 1973), monoamine oxidase (Perry et al., 1955, 1969), and nitrate reductase (Buczek et al., 1980).

Vanadium has been found to occur naturally in mammalian muscle tissue and blood serum at concentrations great enough to partially inhibit (Na, K)-ATPase if present as vanadate (Post, 1979; Hamlyn and Duffy, 1978). Cell regulation could thus be provided by controlling the vanadyl/vanadate redox reaction. However, all that can be said at present is that there is no evidence for or against this hypothesis.

7. BIOACCUMULATION

Schroeder (1970) and Schroeder et al. (1963) indicated that vanadium accumulated in animal fats and serum lipids. In algae, Meisch and Bielig (1975) demonstrated that *Scenedesmus obliquus* in Arnon's medium containing 20 ppb vanadium (as NH_4VO_3) labelled with $^{48}VOCl_3$, incorporated 90% of the vanadium in solution after 5 days of growth. Recent laboratory studies conducted by Unsal (1982), indicate that vanadium accumulated by phytoplankton may be transferred through the food chain to final consumers such as terrestrial mammals. However, studies on the extent of vanadium bioaccumulation in aquatic ecosystems show little evidence of amplification of vanadium in different trophic levels. The concentrations in carnivorous groups were lower than in filter feeders, which obtain the element from particulate matter such as phytoplankton (Miramand et al., 1980; Ballester and Castellvi, 1979; Lutz and Henzel, 1977; Guthrie and Cherry, 1979; NRC, 1974; Copeland and Ayeres, 1972).

8. SYNERGISTIC AND ANTAGONISTIC EFFECTS

Most ecotoxicological data on metals have been obtained from bioassays of lethal and sublethal toxicity induced by individual metals. However, in natural ecosystems single metal occurrences are non-events. When metals are mixed together, they may have supplemented synergistic (effects of combined exposure is greater than the additive) or antagonistic (one factor reduces the effect of another) effects on the biota. Such factors with vanadium should be considered in greater detail, since industrial operations introduce an array of chemical substances simultaneously into the aquatic environment.

In aquatic organisms, Anderson et al. (1979) observed synergism in 96 hour LC50 lethal tests with juvenile rainbow trout in tertiary mixtures which contained vanadium, nickel, and phenol. Antagonistic effects in algae have been reported by Upitis et al. (1974), who noted that the toxicity of vanadium to *Chlorella* could be reduced by the addition of aluminum, chromium, nickel, and iron.

9.   EFFECT ON COMMUNITY STRUCTURE

The need for experimental studies of pollutant effects on whole communities and ecosystems have been emphasized by numerous ecologists (e.g., Marshall and Mellinger, 1980) and is now gaining wider recognition. There is no compelling evidence that single species tests can be used to accurately predict multispecies community or ecosystem responses.

In natural waters vanadium may be complexed with organic matter, chelated, absorbed into inorganic and organic particulates, or exist in an ionic form. As previously discussed, the bioavailability of such forms differs, hence, the absolute metal concentration in the system does not necessarily reflect the degree to which it affects the biological organisms. Therefore, the bioassay response of natural populations, which is an integration of the chemical, biological, and physical factors which influence vanadium toxicity, gives a more realistic result for assessment of the effects of vanadium on the biota.

Phytoplankton, being the main primary producers in aquatic ecosystems, are of great ecological significance. Although there have been numerous bioassay studies on the effects of vanadium on algae in cultures (Ramadoss, 1979; Ballester and Castellvi, 1979; Meisch and Benzschawel, 1978; Meisch et al., 1977), there have been very few field studies with natural phytoplankton communities. Most studies on the effects of metals on phytoplankton in the aquatic environment have been concerned with the overall decrease in biomass or productivity caused by the metal. However, when one considers an ecosystem and the importance of primary producers in its food web, it is apparent that one must consider not only the effects of vanadium on the quantity of phytoplankton, but also its effects on the quality or species composition.

Organisms in natural aquatic systems are subjected to a continuously changing environment which causes both spatial and temporal changes in species composition, standing crop and primary productivity, as a result of the inability of certain species to adapt to environmental changes. One would expect that in ecosystems under vanadium-contaminated conditions, the ecological balance would be shifted to the more tolerant organisms. This was apparent in studies conducted with natural algal populations, which indicated that at low concentrations of vanadium (<1 ppm), primary production and growth of diatoms (Bacillariophyceae) was suppressed whereas some of the green and blue-green algae appeared to be stimulated (Lee, 1982; Patrick et al., 1975).

Although low concentrations of vanadium may not be lethal to all phytoplankton, they can have quite drastic effects on the functioning of an ecosystem as a result of alterations in phytoplankton community structure. For example, Patrick (1978) suggested that the diatoms were the preferred food source of many aquatic invertebrates and vertebrates, while various filamentous green algae and blue-green algae were found to have little nutrient value or were toxic to the grazers. Hence, a decrease of diatoms as a consequence of vanadium toxicity, was hypothesized to reduce animal populations while large standing crops of greens and blue-green algae developed due to the reduced grazing pressure. In addition, the grazers may also be directly affected by vanadium as previously outlined.

ACKNOWLEDGMENTS

I would like to thank Drs. C. Nalewajko, T. R. Jack, and B. Imber for critically reading the manuscript.

REFERENCES

Aiyar, A. S. and Sreenivasan, A. (1961). Effect of vanadium administration on coenzyme Q metabolism in rats. *Proc. Soc. Exp. Biol. N.Y.* **107**, 914.

Allen, M. B. (1956). Photosynthetic nitrogen fixation by blue-green algae. *Sci. Monthly* **83**, 100–106.

Anderson, P. D., Spear, P., D'Apollinia, S., Perry, S., de Luca, J., and Dick, J. (1979). *The multiple toxicity of vanadium, nickel and phenol to fish.* Alberta Oil Sands Environmental Program, Report 79, pp. 1–109.

Anekwe, G. E. (1976). Effect of vanadium pentoxide on the incorporation of (2-^{14}C)-acetate into fungal lipids. *Physiol. Plant* **38**, 305–306.

Arnon, D. I. (1954). Some recent advances in the study of essential microelements for green plants. *Proc. 8th Intern. Congr. Bot. (Paris)* **11**, 73–80.

Arnon, D. I. (1958). The role of micronutrients in plant nutrition with special reference to photosynthesis and nitrogen assimilation. In: C. A. Lamb, O. G. Bentley, and J. M. Beattie, Eds., *Trace Elements,* Academic Press, New York, pp. 1–32.

Arnon, D. I. and Wessel, G. (1953). Vanadium as an essential element for green plants. *Nature* **172**, 1039–1040.

Bailar, J. C., Emelcus, J. H., Nyholm, R., and Trotman-Dichenson, A. F. (1973). *Comprehensive inorganic chemistry*, Vol. 3. Pergamon Press, New York, pp. 518–522.

Ballester, A. and Castellvi, J. (1979). Contribution to the biocynetic study of V and Ni uptake by marine organisms. *Inv. Pesq.* **43**, 449–478.

Ballester, A. and Castellvi, J. (1980). Bioaccumulation of V and Ni by marine organisms and sediments. *Inv. Pesq.* **44**, 1–12.

Beaugé, L. A. and Glynn, I. M. (1978). Commercial ATP containing traces of vanadate alters the response of ($Na^+ + K^+$) ATPase to external potassium. *Nature* **272**, 551–552.

Becking, J. H. (1962). Species differences in molybdenum and vanadium requirements and combined nitrogen utilization by *Azotobacteriaceae*. *Plant Soil* **16**, 171–201.

Beliles, R. P. (1978). The lesser metals. In: F. W. Oehme, Ed., *Toxicity of heavy metals in the environment*. Part 2. Marcel Dekker Inc., New York, pp. 547–615.

Bell, M. V., Kelly, K. F., and Sargent, J. R. (1979). Sodium orthovanadate, a powerful vasoconstrictor in the gills of the common eel, *Anguilla anguilla*. *J. Mar. Biol. Assoc. U.K.* **59**, 429–435.

Benemann, J. R., McKenna, C. E., Lie, R. F., Traylor, T. G., and Kamen, M. D. (1972). The vanadium effect in nitrogen fixation by *Azotobacter*. *Biochim. Biophys. Acta.* **264**, 25–38.

Bengtsson, S. and Tyler, G. (1976). *Vanadium in the environment*. The Monitoring and Assessment Research Centre, Chelsea College, Univ. of London. MARC Technical Report #2.

Bergel, F., Bray, R. C., and Harrap, K. R. (1958). A model system for cystine desulphydrase action: Pyridoxal phosphate-vanadium. *Nature* **181**, 1654–1655.

Berman, E. (1980). *Toxic metals and their analysis*. Cambridge University Press, Cambridge, pp. 221–232.

Bernheim, F. and Bernheim, M. L. (1939). The action of vanadium on the oxidation of phospholipids by certain tissues. *J. Biol. Chem.* **127**, 353–360.

Bertine, K. K. and Goldberg, E. D. (1971). Fossil fuel combustion and the major sedimentary cycle. *Science* **173**, 233–235.

Bertine, K. K. and Goldberg, E. D. (1977). History of heavy metal pollution in southern California coastal zone-reprise. *Environ. Sci. Technol.* **11**, 297–299.

Bertrand, D. (1943). Le vanadium chez les champignons et plus specialement chez les amanites. *Bull. Soc. Chim. Biol.* **25**, 194–197.

Bertrand, D. (1954). The biogeochemistry of vanadium. *Am. Mus. Nat. Hist. Bull.* **94**, 409–455.

Biggs, W. R. and Swinehart, J. H. (1976). Vanadium in selected biological systems. In: H. Sigel, Ed., *Metal ions in biological systems*. Vol. 6, *Biological action of metal ions*. Marcel Dekker, New York, pp. 141–196.

Black, W. A. P. and Mitchell, R. L. (1952). Trace elements in the common brown algae and in sea water. *J. Mar. Biol. Assoc. U.K.* **30**, 575–583.

Blotcky, A. J., Falcone, C., Medina, V. A., Rack, E. P., and Hobson, D.W. (1979). Determination of trace-level vanadium in marine biological samples by chemical neutron activation analysis. *Anal. Chem.* **51**, 178–182.

Boger, P. (1969). Photophosphorylierung mit chloroplasten aus *Bumilleriopsis filiformis* Vischer. *Z. Pflanzenphysiol. Bd.* **61.S.**, 85–97.

Bokorny, T. (1904). Einiges über die Wirkung der Vanadinsäure auf Mikroorganismen. Geringe antiseptische Kraft derselben. *Chem. Zeitig.* **28**, 596–597.

Borchard, U., Fox, A. A. L., Greeff, K., and Schlieper, P. (1979). Negative and positive inotropic action of vanadate on atrial and ventricular myocardium. *Nature* **279**, 339–341.

Bortels, H. (1933). Kurze Notiz über die Katalyse der biologischen Stickstoffbindung. *Zbl. Bakt. II. Abt.* **87**, 476–477.

Bové, J., Bové, C., and Arnon, D. I. (1957). Molybdenum and vanadium requirements of *Azotobacter* for growth and nitrogen fixation. *Plant Physiol.* **32**, supplement xxiii.

Bovee, E. C. (1978). *Effects of heavy metals, especially selenium, vanadium and zirconium on the movement, growth and survival of certain animal aquatic life.* Kansas Water Resources Research Institute, University of Kansas. Contribution No. 199. Consultant's Report to Office of Water Research and Technology, Dept. of the Interior, Oct. 1978, pp. 1–26.

Bowen, H. J. M. (1966). *Trace elements in biochemistry.* Academic Press, New York, 241 pp.

Briat, M. (1978). Evaluation of levels of Pb, V, Cd, Zn and Cu in the snow of Mt. Blanc during the last 25 years. In: Atmospheric Pollution 1978, Proc. 13th Internat. Colloquium, Paris, France, April 25–28, 1978, M. M. Benarie, Ed. *Stud. Environ. Sci.* **1**, 225–228.

Brown, A. C. and Davies, A. B. (1971). The fate of ThO₂ introduced into the body cavity of *Ciona intestinalis* (Tunicata). *J. Invertebr. Pathol.* **18**, 276–279.

Bruno, S. F. and McLaughlin, J. J. A. (1977). The nutrition of the freshwater dinoflagellate *Ceratium hirundinella*. *J. Protozool.* **24**, 548–553.

Buczek, J. (1980). Reduction of nitrates in *Cucumis sativus* L. seedlings. II. Influence of tungsten and vanadium on nitrate and adenosine triphosphatase activities. *Acta Soc. Bot. Pol.* **49**, 269–280.

Buczek, J., Kowalinska, E., and Kuczera, K. (1980). Reduction of nitrates in *Cucumis sativus* L. seedlings. I. Influence of tungsten and vanadium on adsorption and reduction of nitrates. *Acta Soc. Bot. Pol.* **49**, 259–267.

Burk, D. and Horner, C. K. (1935). The specific catalytic role of molybdenum and vanadium in nitrogen fixation and amide utilization by *Azotobacter*. *Trans. 3rd. Congr. Internat. Soc. Soil Sci.* **I**, 152–155.

Burns, E. C., Fuchsman, W. H., and Hardy, R. W. F. (1971). Nitrogenase from vanadium-grown *Azotobacter*: Isolation, characteristics, and mechanistic implications. *Biochem. Biophys. Res. Commun.* **42**, 353–358.

Burton, J. D. (1966). Some problems concerning the marine geochemistry of vanadium. *Nature* **212**, 976–978.

Cande, W. Z. and Wolniak, S. M. (1978). Chromosome movement in lysed mitotic cells is inhibited by vanadate. *J. Cell Biol.* **79**, 573–580.

Cannon, H. L. (1963). The biogeochemistry of vanadium. *Soil Sci.* **96**, 196–204.

Cantley, L. C., Josephson, L., Warner, R., Yanagisawa, M., Lechene, C., and Guidotti, G. (1977). Vanadate is a potent (Na, K)-ATPase inhibitor found in ATP derived from muscle. *J. Biol. Chem.* **252**, 7421–7423.

Carlisle, D. B. (1968). Vanadium and other metals in ascidians. *Proc. Roy. Soc. London Ser. B* **171**, 31–42.

Carlson, R. M. K. (1975). Nuclear magnetic resonance spectrum of living tunicate blood cells and the structure of the native vanadium chromogen. *Proc. Nat. Acad. Sci. USA* **72**, 2217–2221.

Chan, K. M. and Riley, J. P. (1966). The determination of vanadium in sea and natural waters, biological materials and silicate sediments and rocks. *Anal. Chim. Acta* **34**, 337–345.

Charlot, G. and Bezier, D. (1957). *Quantitative inorganic analysis.* John Wiley & Sons, New York, 624 pp.

Chau, Y. K. and Lum-Shue-Chan, K. (1970). Complex extraction of vanadium for atomic absorption spectroscopy: Determination of microgram quantities of vanadium in lake waters. *Anal. Chim. Acta* **50**, 201–207.

Chau, Y. K., Chawla, V. K., Nicholson, H. F., and Vollenweider, R. A. (1970). Distribution of trace elements and chlorophyll *a* in Lake Ontario. *Proc. 13th Conf. Great Lakes Res.*, 659–672.

Chester, R. and Stoner, J. H. (1974). The distribution of Mn, Fe, Cu, Ni, Co, Ga, Cr, V, Ba, Sr, Sn, Zn, and Pb in some soil-sized particulates from the lower trophosphere over the world ocean. *Mar. Chem.* **2**, 157–188.

Choata, G. L. and Mansour, T. E. (1978). Inhibition of sheep heart phosphofructokinase by ortho-vanadate. *Fed. Proc.* **37**, 1433.

Clark, R. J. H. (1968). The chemistry of titanium and vanadium. In: P. L. Robinson, Ed., *Topics in inorganic and general chemistry,* monograph II. Elsevier, Amsterdam, pp. 214–219.

Cockerill, B. M., Finch, P., and Percival, E. (1978). Vanadium in the brown seaweed, *Desmarestia firma. Phytochemistry* **17**, 2129.

Copeland, R. A. and Ayeres, J. C. (1972). *Trace element distributions in water, sediment, phytoplankton, zooplankton and benthos of Lake Michigan: A baseline study with calculations of concentration factors and buildup of radioisotopes in the food web.* Environmental Research Group Inc., ERG. Special Report #1, 1972, 271 pp.

Cowgill, V. M. (1973). The determination of all detectable elements in the aquatic plants of Linsley Pond and Cedar Lake (N. Bradford, Conn.) by x-ray emission and optical emission spectroscopy. *Appl. Spectrosc.* **27**, 5–9.

Crandall, M. and Caulton, J. H. (1973). Induction of glycoprotein mating factors in diploid yeast of *Hansenula wingei* by vanadium salts or chelating agents. *Exp. Cell Res.* **82**, 159–167.

Curran, G. L. (1954). Effect of certain transition group elements on hepatic synthesis of cholesterol in the rat. *J. Biol. Chem.* **210**, 765–770.

Curran, G. L., Azarnoff, D. L., and Boliner, R. E. (1959). Effect of cholesterol synthesis inhibition in normal cholestermic young men. *J. Clin. Invest.* **38**, 1251–1261.

DeMaster, E. G. and Mitchell, R. A. (1973). A comparison of arsenate and vanadate as inhibitors or uncouplers of mitochondrial and glycolytic energy metabolism. *Biochem.* **12**, 3616–3621.

Duce, R. A. and Hoffman, G. L. (1976). Atmospheric vanadium transport to the ocean. *Atmos. Environ.* **10**, 989–996.

Duce, R. A., Hoffman, G. L., and Zoller, W. H. (1975). Atmospheric trace metals at remote northern and southern hemisphere sites: pollution or natural. *Science* **187**, 59–61.

Eichhorn, G. L. (1973). *Inorganic biochemistry.* Elsevier, Amsterdam, p. 18.

Endean, R. (1960). The blood cells of the ascidian, *Phallusia mammillata. Q. J. Microsc. Sci.* **101**, 177–197.

Environment Canada, Environmental Protection Service (1976). *National inventory of sources and emissions of manganese, fluoride, and vanadium.* Summary of Emissions for 1972. Air Pollution Control Directorate, Economic and Technical Review Report. EPS 3-AP-76-1.

Environmental Protection Agency. (1977). *Scientific and technical assessment report of vanadium.* (Program Element #1AA601) U.S. EPA. EPA-600/6-77/002 STAR series.

Evans, H. T., Jr., and Garrels, R. M. (1958). Thermodynamic equilibria of vanadium in aqueous systems as applied to the interpretation of the Colorado Plateau ore deposits. *Geochim. Cosmochim. Acta* **15**, 131–149.

Faulkner Hudson, T. G. (1964). Vanadium: Toxicology and biological significance. Elsevier, New York, 140 pp.

Fay, P. and De Vasconcelos, L. (1974). Nitrogen metabolism and ultrastructure in *Anabaena cylindrica.* II. The effect of molybdenum and vanadium. *Arch. Microbiol.* **99**, 221–230.

Frouin, A. and Mercier, V. (1914). Action du vanadate de soude sur le developpement de l'*Aspergillus niger. Bull. Soc. Chim. Biol.* **1**, 8–13.

Garcia, A. G., Jurkiewicz, A., and Jurkiewicz, N. H. (1981). Contractile effect of vanadium and other vanadium compounds on the rat vas deferens. *Eur. J. Pharmacol.* **70**, 17–23.

Gatz, D. F. (1975). Pollutant aerosol deposition into southern Lake Michigan. *Water Air Soil Pollut.* **5**, 239–251.

Giles, M. A. and Klaverkamp, J. F. (1982). The acute toxicity of vanadium and copper to eyed eggs of Rainbow trout (*Salmo gairdneri*). *Water Res.* **16**, 885–889.

Giles, M. A., Klaverkamp, J. F., and Lawrence, S. G. (1979). *The acute toxicity of saline groundwater and of vanadium to fish and aquatic invertebrates.* Alberta Oil Sands Environmental Research Program Project AF 3.2.1., Report 56, pp. 1–216.

Goldberg, E. D., Broecker, W. S., Gross, M. G., and Turekian, K. K. (1971). Marine chemistry. In: *Radioactivity in the marine environment.* National Academy of Sciences, Washington, D.C., pp. 137–146.

Goldberg, E. D., Griffin, J. J., Hodge, V., Koide, M., and Windom, H. (1979). Pollution history of the Savannah River Estuary. *Environ. Sci. Technol.* **13**, 588–594.

Goodbody, I. (1974). The physiology of ascidians. *Adv. Mar. Biol.* **12**, 1–149.

Goodman, B. A. and Cheshire, M. V. (1975). The bonding of vanadium in complexes with humic acid: an electron paramagnetic resonance study. *Geochim. Cosmochim. Acta* **39**, 1711–1713.

Grupp, G., Grupp, I., Johnson, C. L., Wallick, E. T., and Schwartz, A. (1979). Effects of vanadate on cardiac contraction and adenylate-cyclase. *Biochem. Biophys. Res. Commun.* **88**, 440–447.

Guthrie, R. K. and Cherry, D. S. (1979). Trophic level accumulation of heavy metals in a coal ash drainage system. *Water Res. Bull.* **15**, 244–248.

Hamlyn, J. M. and Duffy, T. (1978). Direct stimulation of human erythrocyte membrane sodium-potassium, magnesium ATPase EC-3.6.1.3. activity *in vitro* by physiological concentrations of dextroaldosterone. *Biochem. Biophys. Res. Commun.* **84**, 458–464.

Hansen, L. D. and Fisher, G. L. (1980). Elemental distribution in coal fly ash particles. *Environ. Sci. Technol.* **14**, 1111–1117.

Hansen, O. (1979). Facilitation of ovabain binding to $(Na^+ + K^+)$-ATPase by vanadate at *in vivo* concentrations. *Biochim. Biophys. Acta* **568**, 265–269.

Hathcock, J. N., Hill, C. H., and Tove, S. B. (1966). Uncoupling of oxidative phosphorylation by vanadate. *Can. J. Biochem.* **44**, 983–988.

Henze, M. (1911). Die Vanadiumverbindung der Blutkorperchen. Hoppe-Seyler Zeitschr. f. *Physiol Chem.* **72**, 494–501.

Hesse, M. (1974). Wachstum und Synchronisierung der Alge *Bumilleriopsis filiformis* Vischer (Xanthophyceae). *Planta (Berl.)* **120**, 135–146.

Hill, C. H. and Matrone, G. (1970). Chemical parameters in the study of *in vivo* and *in vitro* interactions of transition elements. *Fed. Proc.* **29**, 1474–1481.

Hitchon, B., Filby, R. H., and Shah, K. R. (1975). Geochemistry of trace elements in crude oils, Alberta, Canada. In: T. F. Yen, Ed., *The role of trace metals in petroleum.* Ann Arbor Sci. Pub. Inc., pp. 111–121.

Hoffman, G. L., Duce, R. A., Walsh, P. R., Hoffman, E. J., Ray, B. J., and Fasching, J. L. (1974). Residence time of some particulate trace metals in the oceanic surface microlayer: significance of atmospheric deposition. *J. Rech. Atmos.* **8**: 745–759.

Holdway, D. A. and Sprague, J. B. (1979). Chronic toxicity of vanadium to flag fish. *Water Res.* **13**, 905–910.

Holm-Hansen, O. (1954). A study of major and minor element requirements in the nutrition of blue-green algae. Ph.D. thesis, University of Wisconsin, 200 pp.

Hopkins, L. L., Cannon, H. L., Musch, A. T., Welch, R. M., and Nielsen, F. H. (1977). Vanadium. *Geochem. Environ.* **2**, 93–107.

Horner, C. K., Burk, D., Allison, F. E., and Sherman, M. S. (1942). Nitrogen fixation by *Azotobacter* as influenced by molybdenum and vanadium. *J. Agr. Res.* **65**, 173–193.

182   Kenneth Lee

I.J.C. (1978). Great Lakes Water Quality Agreement of 1978, International Joint Commission of Canada and the United States, Windsor, Ontario, 51 pp.

Ikebe, K. and Tanaka, R. (1979). Determination of vanadium and nickel in marine samples by flameless and flame atomic absorption spectrophotometry. *Bull. Environ. Contam. Toxicol.* **21**, 526–532.

Inciarte, D. J., Steffen, R. P., Swindall, B. T., Johnson, J. R., Dobbins, D. E., and Haddy, F. J. (1979). Effects of intravenously infused vanadate on the circulation of the anesthetized dog. *Fed. Proc.* **38**, 1036.

Ingri, N. and Brito, F. (1959). Equilibrium studies of polyanions. VI. Polyvanadates in alkaline Na (Cl) medium. *Acta. Chem. Scand.* **13**, 1971–1996.

Jaffe, D. and Walters, J. K. (1977). Intertidal trace metal concentrations in some sediments from the Humber Estuary. *Sci. Total Environ.* **7**, 1–15.

Kalk, M. (1963). Absorption of vanadium by tunicates. *Nature* **198**, 1010–1011.

Kanematsu, N. and Kada, T. (1978). Mutagenicity of metal compounds. *Mutat. Res.* **54**, 215–216.

Kemp, A. L. W., Williams, J. D. H., Thomas, R. L., and Gregory, M. I. (1978). Impact of man's activities on the chemical composition of the sediments of Lakes Superior and Huron. *Water Air Soil Pollut.* **10**, 381–402.

Klein, D. H. (1975). Fluxes, residence times, and sources of some elements to Lake Michigan. *Water Air Soil Pollut.* **4**, 3–8.

Knudtson, B. K. (1979). Acute toxicity of vanadium to two species of freshwater fish. *Bull. Environ. Contam. Toxicol.* **23**, 95–99.

Kopp, J. F. and Kroner, R. C. (1968). A comparison of trace elements in natural waters, dissolved versus suspended. *Develop. Appl. Spectrosc.* **6**, 339–352.

Krauskopf, K. B. (1956). Factors controlling the concentrations of thirteen rare metals in seawater. *Geochim. Cosmochim. Acta* **9**, 1–32.

Kuntz, R. G., Giannelli, J. F., and Stensel, H. D. (1975). Vanadium removal from industrial wastewaters. *Proc. 30th Industrial Waste Conference,* Purdue Univ., W. Lafayette, Indiana, May 6–8, 1975, pp. 48–64.

Kuntz, R. G., Giannelli, J. F., and Stensel, H. D. (1976). Vanadium removal from industrial wastewaters. *J. Water Pollut. Control Fed.* **48**, 762–770.

Kustin, K., Levine, D. S., McLeod, G. C., and Curby, W. A. (1976). The blood of *Ascidia nigra:* Blood cell frequency distribution, morphology, and the distribution of valence of vanadium in living blood cells. *Biol. Bull.* **150**, 426–441.

La Touche, Y. D., Bennett, C. W., and Mix, M. C. (1981). Determination of vanadium in a marine mollusc using a chelating ion exchange resin and neutron activation. *Bull. Environ. Contam. Toxicol.* **26**, 224–227.

Lee, G. R., Friedrick, F. D., and Mitchell, F. D. (1961). Control of SO_3 in low pressure heating boilers by an additive. *J. Inst. Fuel.* **43**, 67.

Lee, K. (1982). The effects of vanadium on phytoplankton: field and laboratory studies. Ph.D. thesis, University of Toronto.

Lee, K.-Y., Erickson, R., Pan, S.-S., Jones, G., May, F., and Nason, A. (1974). Effects of tungsten and vanadium on the *in vitro* assembly of assimilatory nitrate reductase utilizing *Neurospora* mutant nit.-1. *J. Biol. Chem.* **249**, 3953–3959.

Lee, R. E., Goranson, S. S., Enrione, R. E., and Morgan, G. B. (1972). National air surveillance cascade impactor network. II. Size distribution measurements of trace metal components. *Environs. Sci. Technol.* **6**, 1025–1030.

Lee, R. E., Jr., and von Lehmden, D. J. (1973). Trace metal pollution in the environment. *J. Air Pollut. Control Fed.* **23**, 853–857.

Levine, E. P. (1961). Occurrence of titanium, vanadium, chromium, and sulfuric acid in the ascidian *Eudistoma ritteri. Science* **133**, 1352–1353.

Linstedt, K. D. and Kruger, P. (1970). Determination of vanadium in natural waters by neutron activation analysis. *Anal. Chem.* **42**, 113–115.

Lopez, V., Stevens, T., and Lindquist, R. N. (1976). Vanadium ion inhibition of alkaline phosphatase-catalyzed phosphate ester hydrolysis. *Arch. Biochem. Biophys.* **175**, 31–38.

Lutz, A. and Henzel, M. (1977). *A survey of baseline levels of contaminants in aquatic biota of the AOSERP study area*. Alberta Oil Sands Environmental Research Program. AOSERP Report #17, 51 pp.

MacDonald, C. (1979). Effects of complexation on metal toxicity to *Daphnia magna*. M.Sc. thesis, University of Western Ontario.

Marshall, J. S. and Mellinger, D. L. (1980). An *in situ* experimental method for toxicological studies on natural plankton communities. In: J. G. Eaton, P. R. Parrish, and A. C. Hendricks, Eds., *Aquatic toxicology*. American Society for Testing and Materials, pp. 27–39.

Martin, J. H. and Knauer, G. A. (1973). The elemental composition of plankton. *Geochim. Cosmochim. Acta* **37**, 1639–1653.

Mascitelli-Coriandoli, E. and Citterio, C. (1959). Effects of vanadium upon liver coenzyme A in rats. *Nature* **183**, 1527–1528.

Mason, B. H. (1966). *Principles of geochemistry*. John Wiley & Sons, New York, 329 pp.

McKenna, C. E., Benemann, J. R., and Traylor, T. G. (1970). A vanadium containing nitrogenase preparation: implications for the role of molybdenum in nitrogen fixation. *Biochem. Biophys. Res. Commun.* **41**, 1501–1508.

McMullen, T. B. and Faoro, R. B. (1977). Occurrence of eleven metals in airborne particulates and in superficial materials. *J. Air Pollut. Control Assoc.* **27**, 1198–1202.

Meisch, H.-U. (1970). Über die Funktion von Vanadin bei einzelligen Grunalgen. Dissertation, University of Saarbrücken.

Meisch, H.-U. and Bauer, J. (1978). The role of vanadium in green plants. IV. Influence on the formation of γ-aminolevulinic acid in *Chlorella*. *Arch. Microbiol.* **117**, 49–52.

Meisch, H.-U. and Bellman, I. (1980). Light dependence of the vanadium induced formation of chlorophyll and γ-aminolevulinic acid in *Chlorella*. *Z. Pflanzenphysiol. Bd.* **96**, 143–151.

Meisch, H.-U. and Benzschawel, H. (1978). The role of vanadium in green plants. III. Influence on cell division of *Chlorella*. *Arch. Microbiol.* **116**, 91–95.

Meisch, H.-U. and Bielig, H.-J. (1975). Effect of vanadium on growth, chlorophyll formation and iron metabolism in unicellular green algae. *Arch. Microbiol.* **105**, 77–82.

Meisch, H.-U. and Bielig, H.-J. (1980). Chemistry and biochemistry of vanadium. *Basic Res. Cardiol.* **75**, 413–417.

Meisch, H.-U., Becker, L. J. M., and Schwab, D. (1980). Ultrastructural changes in *Chlorella fusca* during iron deficiency and vanadium treatment. *Protoplasma* **103**, 273–280.

Meisch, H.-U., Benzschawel, H., and Bielig, H.-J. (1977). The role of vanadium in green plants. II. Vanadium in green algae—two sites of action. *Arch. Microbiol.* **114**, 67–70.

Meyer, J. and Aulich, M. (1930). Solubility of inorganic vanadium salts. *Z. Anorg. Alle. Chem.* **194**, 278–292.

Miramand, P. and Unsal, M. (1978). Acute toxicity of vanadium to some marine benthic and phytoplankton species. *Chemosphere* **7**, 827–832.

Miramand, P., Fowler, S. W., and Guary, J. C. (1982). Comparative study of vanadium biokinetics in three species of echinoderms. *Mar. Biol.* **67**, 127–134.

Miramand, P., Guary, J. C., and Fowler, S. W. (1980). Vanadium transfer in the mussel *Mytilus galloprovincialis*. *Mar. Biol.* **56**, 281–293.

Miramand, P., Guary, J. C., and Fowler, S. W. (1981). Uptake, assimilation and excretion of vanadium in the shrimp, *Lysmata seticaudata* (Risso), and the crab, *Carcinus maenas* (L.) *J. Exp. Mar. Biol. Ecol.* **49**, 267–287.

Mitchell, R. L. (1964). Trace elements in soil. In: F. E. Bear, Ed., *Chemistry of the soil*. Reinhold, New York, pp. 320–368.

Montiel, A. (1975). Vanadium in rainwater and effects on surface water. *Prog. Water Technol.* **7**, 743–751.

Morris, A. W. (1975). Dissolved molybdenum and vanadium in the northeast Atlantic Ocean. *Deep Sea Res.* **22**, 49–54.

Mountain, J. T., Delker, L. L., and Stokinger, H. E. (1953). Studies in vanadium toxicology: Reduction in the cystine content of rat hair. *A.M.A. Arch. Ind. Hyg. Occup. Med.* **8**, 406–411.

Murmann, R. K. and Giese, K. C. (1978). Mechanism of oxygen-18 exchange between water and the vanadium(V) oxyanion: $V_{10}O_{26}^{6-}$. *Inorg. Chem.* **17**, 1160–1166.

Nadkarni, R. A. (1980). Multitechnique multielemental analysis of coal and fly ash. *Anal. Chem.* **52**, 929–935.

Nagatani, H. H. and Brill, W. J. (1974). Nitrogenase V. The effect of Mo, W and V on the synthesis of nitrogenase components in *Azotobacter vinelandii*. *Biochim. Biophys. Acta* **362**, 160–166.

Nechay, B. R. and Saunders, J. P. (1978). Inhibition by vanadium of sodium and potassium dependent adenosine-triphosphatase derived from animal and human tissues. *J. Environ. Pathol. Toxicol.* **2**, 247–262.

Nelson, M. T. and Blaustein, M. P. (1981). Effects of ATP and vanadate on calcium efflux from barnacle muscle fibres. *Nature* **289**, 314–316.

Nicholas, D. J. D. and Commissiong, K. (1957). Effects of molybdenum, copper and iron on some enzymes in *Neurospora crassa*. *J. Gen. Microbiol.* **17**, 699–707.

Nieboer, E. and Richardson, D. H. S. (1980). The replacement of the nondescript term "heavy metals" by a biologically and chemically significant classification of metal ions. *Environ. Pollut. (Ser. B)* **1**, 3–26.

Noddack, I. and Noddack, W. (1940). Die Häufigkeiten der Schwermettale in Meerestieren. *Ark. Zool.* **32**, 1.

NRC, National Research Council. (1974). Committee on Biologic Effects of Atmospheric Pollutants. Vanadium (Medical and biological effects of environmental pollutants). National Academy of Sciences, Washington, D.C., ISBN 0-309-02218-5, 110 pp.

Ondov, J. M., Ragaini, R. C., and Biermann, A. H. (1979). Emissions and particle-size distributions of minor and trace elements at two western coal-fired power plants equipped with coal-side electrostatic precipitators. *Environ. Sci. Technol.* **13**, 946–953.

Orvini, E., Lodola, L., Sabbioni, E., Pietra, R., and Goetz, L. (1979). Determination of the chemical forms of dissolved vanadium in freshwater as determined by [48]V radiotracer experiments and neutron activation analysis. *Sci. Total Environ.* **13**, 195–207.

Patrick, R. (1978). Effects of trace metals in the aquatic ecosystem. *Am. Sci.* **66**, 185–191.

Patrick, R., Bott, T., and Larson, R. (1975). *The role of trace elements in management of nuisance growths*. U.S. EPA Tech. Ser. EPA-660/2-75-008.

Payer, H.-D. and Trueltzsch, U. (1972). Meeting the trace elements requirement of dense cultures of microalgae under special consideration of manganese and vanadium. *Arch. Mikrobiol.* **84**, 43–53.

Perry, H. M., Jr., Schwartz, P. L., and Sahagian, B. M. (1969). Effect of transition metals and of metal binding antihypertensive agents on tryptamine oxidase and dopa decarboxylase. *Proc. Soc. Exp. Biol. Med.* **130**, 273–277.

Perry, H. M., Jr., Teitlebaum, S., and Schwartz, P. L. (1955). Effect of antihypertensive agents on amino acid decarboxylation and amine oxidation. *Fed. Proc.* **14**, 113–114.

Pickett-Heaps, J. D. (1975). *Green algae structure reproduction and evolution in selected genera*. Sinauer Assoc., Sunderland, Massachusetts, 640 pp.

Piotrowicz, S. R., Ray, B. J., Hoffman, G. L., and Duce, R. A. (1972). Trace metal enrichment in the sea-surface microlayer. *J. Geophys. Res.* **77**, 5243–5254.

Pope, M. T. and Dale, B. W. (1968). Isopoly-vanadates, -niobates, and -tantalates. *Q. Rev. Chem. Soc.* **22**, 527–548.

Post, R. L. (1979). A model for regulation of vanadate inhibition of sodium potassium ATPase by reduction. *Fed. Proc.* **38** (3, part 1), 242.

Ramadoss, C. S. (1979). The effect of vanadium on nitrate reductase of *Chlorella vulgaris*. *Planta* **146**, 539–544.

Remy, H. (1961). *Treatise on inorganic chemistry.* Vol. 2. Elsevier, New York, pp. 92–104.

Rieger, P. H. (1973). Spectrophotometric studies of the metavanadate system. I. Solution equilibria. *Aust. J. Chem.* **26**, 1173–1181.

Rigler, F. H. (1956). A tracer study of the phosphorus cycle in lakewater. *Ecology* **27**, 550–562.

Riley, J. P. and Taylor, D. (1972). The concentrations of cadmium, copper, iron, manganese, molybdenum, nickel, vanadium and zinc in part of the tropical north-east Atlantic Ocean. *Deep Sea Res.* **19**, 307–317.

Rosen, D., Barr, R., and Crane, F. L. (1975). Vanadium compounds and ferrocyanide as ionic redox agents in photosynthesis. *Biochim. Biophys. Acta* **408**, 35–46.

Saenko, G. N., Koryakova, M. D., Makienko, V. F., and Dobrosmyslova, I. G. (1976). Concentration of polyvalent metals by seaweeds in Vostok Bay, Sea of Japan. *Mar. Biol.* **34**, 169–176.

Salageanu, V. (1973). Upon the optimal concentration of microelements salts occurring in experiments performed with *Chlamydomonas reinhardti, Chlorella vulgaris* and *Chlorella luteovirdis*. *Rev. Roum. Biol. Ser. Botan.* **18**, 171–177.

Sampath, S. (1944). Effect of vanadium on yeast cells. *Current Sci.* **13**, 47.

Sato, Y. and Okabe, S. (1978). Vanadium in sea waters and deposits from Tokyo Bay, Suruga Bay and Harima Nada. *J. Mar. Sci. Technol. Tokai Univ.* **11**, 1–19.

Schiller, K. and Thilo, E. (1961). Spektrophotometrische untersuchung von vanadatgleich-gewichten in verdünnten wä Brigen lösungen. *Z. Anorg. Chem.* **310**, 261–285.

Schroeder, H. A. (1974). *The poisons around us: Toxic metals in food, air and water.* Indiana University Press, Bloomington, pp. 1–144.

Schroeder, H. A. and Perry, H. M., Jr. (1955). The antihypertensive effects of metal binding agents. *J. Lab. Clin. Med.* **46**, 416.

Schroeder, H. A., Balassa, J. J., and Tipton, I. H. (1963). Abnormal trace metals in man: Vanadium. *J. Chron. Dis.* **16**, 1047–1071.

Schroeder, M. D. (1970). *Vanadium.* American Petroleum Institute, Air Quality Monograph #70-13, pp. 1–32.

Schwabe, U., Puchstein, C., Hannemann, H., and Sochtig, E. (1979). Activation of adenyl cyclase by vanadate. *Nature* **277**, 143–145.

Schwarzenbach, G. and Geier, G. (1963). Die raschacidifierung und-alkalisierung von vanada-ten. *Helvet. Chim. Acta* **46**, 906–926.

Segar, D. A. and Gilio, J. L. (1973). The determination of trace transition elements in biological tissues using flameless atom reservoir atomic absorption. *Intern. J. Environ. Anal. Chem.* **2**, 291–301.

Shamberger, R. J. (1978). Beneficial effects of trace elements. In: F. W. Oehme, Ed., *Toxicity of heavy metals in the environment,* Vol. 2. Marcel Dekker, New York, pp. 689–796.

Shibuya, K. and Saeki, H. (1934). Effect of vanadium on growth of plants. *J. Soc. Trop. Agr. Japan* **6**, 721.

Simons, T. J. B. (1979). Vanadate a new tool for biologists. *Nature* **281**, 337–338.

Snyder, F. and Cornatzer, W. E. (1958). Vanadium inhibition of phospholipid synthesis and sulphydryl activity in rat liver. *Nature* **182**, 462.

Sprague, J. B., Holdway, D. A., and Stendahl, D. H. (1978). *Acute and chronic toxicity of vanadium to fish*. Alberta Oil Sands Environmental Research Program Report #41, pp. 1–92.

Sreenivasan, A., Pillai, K. V., and Franklin, T. (1975). Role of trace elements in aquaculture. *J. Inland Fish. Soc. India* **7**, 204–208.

Stendahl, D. H. (1979). Acute toxicity of vanadium to rainbow trout (*Salmo gairdneri* Richardson) in waters of different hardness and pH. M.Sc. thesis, University of Guelph. pp. 1–105.

Stendahl, D. H. and Sprague, J. B. (1982). Effects of water hardness and pH on vanadium lethality to rainbow trout. *Water Res.* 16:1479–1488.

Stoecker, D. (1977). Chemical defenses against fouling organisms in the tunicate *Ascidia nigra* (Savigny). *Am. Zool.* **17**, 859.

Sugawara, K., Naito, H., and Yamada, S. (1956). Geochemistry of vanadium in natural waters. *J. Earth Sci. Nagoya Univ.* **4**, 44–61.

Sugimae, A. and Hasegawa, T. (1973). Vanadium concentrations in the atmosphere. *Environ. Sci. Technol.* **7**, 444–448.

Szalay, A. and Szilagyi, M. (1967). The association of vanadium with humic acids. *Geochim. Cosmochim. Acta* **31**, 1–6.

Tabatabai, M. A. (1977). Effects of trace elements on urease activity in soils. *Soil Biol. Biochem.* **9**, 9–13.

Tarzwell, C. M. and Henderson, C. (1956). The toxicity of some of the less common metals to fishes. *Trans. Seminar on Sanitary Engineering Aspects of the Atomic Energy Industry*. R. A. Taft Sanitation Engineering Center, TID-7517 (Pt. 1a), pp. 286–289.

Tarzwell, C. M. and Henderson, C. (1960). Toxicity of less common metals to fishes. *Indust. Wastes* **5**, 12.

Tolman, E. L., Barris, E., Burns, M., Pansini, A., and Partridge, R. (1979). Effects of vanadium on glucose metabolism *in vitro*. *Life Sci.* **25**, 1159–1164.

Tuller, I. V. and Suffet, I. H. (1975). The fate of vanadium in an urban air shed: The lower Delaware River valley. *J. Air Pollut. Control Assoc.* **25**, 282–286.

Tyler, G. (1972). Heavy metals pollute nature: May reduce productivity. *Ambio* **1**, 52–59.

Tyler, G. (1976). Influence of vanadium on soil phosphatase activity. *J. Environ. Qual.* **5**, 216–217.

Udel'nova, T. M., Pusheva, M. A., Laktionova, N. V., and Karyakin, A. V. (1974). Content of some polyvalent metals in blue-green algae. *Microbiology* **43**, 904–907.

Unsal, M. (1978). Study of the transfer pathways and the accumulation phenomena of vanadium in mollusca *Mytilus edulis*. *Rev. Int. Oceanogr. Med.* **51**, 71–81.

Unsal, M. (1982). The accumulation and transfer of vanadium within the food chain. *Mar. Pollut. Bull.* **13**, 139–141.

Upitis, V. V., Nollendorff, A. F., and Pakalne, D. S. (1974). Little studied trace elements in *Chlorella* culture: Vanadium. *Latvijas PSR Zinatnu Akademijas Vestis 11*, 15–22.

Van Etten, R. L., Waymack, P. P., and Rehkop, D. M. (1974). Transition metal ion inhibition of enzyme-catalyzed phosphate ester displacement reactions. *J. Am. Chem. Soc.* **96**, 6782–6785.

van Zinderen Bakker, E. M. and Jaworski, J. F. (1980). *Effects of vanadium in the Canadian environment*. Publication No. 18132 of the Environmental Secretariat, National Research Council of Canada, Associate Committee on Scientific Criteria for Environmental Quality.

Vinogradov, A. P. (1934). Distribution of vanadium in organisms. *C.R. Acad. Sci.* (URSS) **3,** 454.

Vouk, V. B. (1979) Vanadium. In: L. Friberg, G. Nordberg, and V. B. Vouk, Ed., *Handbook on the toxicology of metals.* Elsevier Press, New York, pp. 659–679.

Walsh, P. R. and Duce, R. A. (1976). The solubilization of anthropogenic atmospheric vanadium in sea water. *Geophys. Res. Letters* **3,** 375–378.

Warburg, O. and Krippahl, G. (1954). Über photosynthesefermente. *Angew. Chem.* **66,** 493–496.

Warburg, V. O., Krippahl, G. and Buchholz, W. (1955). Wirkung von Vanadium auf die Photosynthese. *Z. Naturforschg.* **106,** 422.

Waters, M. D. (1977). Toxicology of vanadium. In: R. A. Goyer and M. A. Mehlman, Eds., *Advances in modern Toxicology,* Vol. 2, Toxicology of Trace Elements. Holstad Press, John Wiley & Sons, New York, pp. 147–489.

Webb, D. A. (1939). Observations on the blood of certain Ascidians, with special reference to the biochemistry of vanadium. *J. Exp. Biol.* **16,** 499.

White, D. H. and Dieter, M. P. (1978). Effects of dietary vanadium in mallard ducks. *J. Toxicol. Environ. Health* **4,** 43–50.

Wilhelm, C. and Wild, A. (1980). The effect of vanadium on the content of chlorophyll, p-700 and cytochrome-f at different light intensities in *Chlorella fusca. Biochem. Physiol. Pflanzen* **175,** 163–171.

Wright, L. D., Li, L. F., and Trager, R. (1960). The site of vanadyl inhibition of cholesterol biosynthesis in liver homogenates. *Biochem. Biophys. Res. Commun.* **3,** 264–267.

Yamamoto, T., Fujita, T., and Ishibashi, M. (1970). Chemical studies on the seaweeds (25); vanadium and titanium contents in seaweeds. *Rec. Oceanogr. Works Japan* **10,** 125–135.

Zajic, J. E. (1969). *Microbiology and biogeochemistry.* Academic Press, New York, pp. 196–202.

Zoller, W. H., Gladney, E. S., and Duce, R. A. (1974). Atmospheric concentration and sources of trace metals at the South Pole. *Science* **183,** 198–200.

Zoller, W. H., Gordon, G. E., Gladney, E. S., and Jones, A. G. (1971). The sources of distribution of vanadium in the atmosphere. In: E. L. Kothny, Ed., *Advances in chemistry Series* #123, Trace Elements in the Environment. Symp. Washington, D.C., Sept. 1971.

7

INTRASPECIFIC DIFFERENCES IN SUSCEPTIBILITY TO TOXICANTS DUE TO SHORT-TERM OR CHRONIC PREEXPOSURE

Judith S. Weis

Department of Zoology and Physiology
Rutgers University
Newark, New Jersey

Peddrick Weis

Department of Anatomy
UMDNJ-New Jersey Medical School
Newark, New Jersey

1. INTRODUCTION

The toxicity of a substance to an organism can be altered by many factors including interactions with environmental variables, such as temperature, pH, salinity, and other pollutants (see Babich and Stotzky, this volume). Other factors which can affect the outcome of a bioassay are intraspecific variation in susceptibility. This variation has been tacitly acknowledged in toxicology and underlies the LC50 test, because, after a period of time, half the animals are dead and half are still alive. Nevertheless, it is often regarded as an inconvenience since it interferes with consistency of one's data and replication of results. This variation can be caused by naturally occurring sex and age differences in the organisms, and by previous exposure to toxicants and/or by genetic differences among populations. In this chapter we discuss effects of preexposure and genetic differences in tolerance.

2. SHORT-TERM PREEXPOSURE

2.1. Organics

Preexposure to organic pollutants can cause increased resistance through activation of a hepatic microsomal mixed-function oxidase system (MFO), which converts many organic agents into excretable metabolites. The MFO oxidizes petroleum compounds and chlorinated hydrocarbons to more polar derivatives that can be discharged by diffusion across membranes or conjugated with serum components and excreted. Lee et al. (1972) found that the rate of oxidation of benzopyrene in fish liver was fast enough to reach a steady state, balancing the uptake. The metabolites were rapidly transported and excreted in the urine.

This cytochrome P 450-linked enzyme system, which can detoxify a variety of compounds, was inducible in *Fundulus heteroclitus* in the laboratory and also by contamination of the aquatic environment with foreign hydrocarbons (Burns, 1976). Chambers and Yarbrough (1979) found higher levels of this enzyme system in insecticide-resistant mosquito fish (*Gambusia affinis*) compared to susceptible ones. Lee et al. (1979) have found that the MFO system in polychaete worms enables them to metabolize polycyclic aromatic hydrocarbons. The MFO system in *Nereis* was associated with the intestine and was induced by exposure to oil components. The third generation of exposed worms was found to have a much higher MFO activity, which may have been due to selection of a resistant strain. Lee et al. (1981) found that worms from oil-polluted areas had higher levels of MFO than those from a cleaner site. The MFO levels increased dramatically when worms were fed contaminated food. The MFO system also exists in bivalves (Bend et al., 1977; Khan et al., 1972a). It has its highest activity in the blood cells although the maximum capacity of the system appeared to be rather low compared with other organisms. Comparable detoxification systems have been found in crustaceans as well (Khan et al., 1972b).

Under some circumstances, however, preexposure can cause weakening and a lowering of tolerance. Embryonic exposure to the PCBs Aroclor 1254 and 1242 reduced the tolerance of *F. heteroclitus* larvae to subsequent PCB exposure (Weis and Weis, 1982b). Similarly, trout (*Salmo gairdneri*) preexposed to cyanide demonstrated decreased tolerance (Dixon and Sprague, 1981a). This was followed by a return to control levels.

2.2. Metals

In some species, tolerance to toxic effects of some metals can be increased by previous exposure to low sublethal concentrations. Lloyd (1960) showed that rainbow trout (*Salmo gairdneri*) were more resistant to zinc after preexposure. Beattie and Pascoe (1978) showed that pretreatment of rainbow trout eggs with cadmium made the larvae more resistant to subsequent Cd treatment. Similarly, Spehar et al. (1978) found that larvae of the flagfish, *Jordanella floridae,* initially exposed as embryos to zinc and to mixtures of Zn and Cd were much more tolerant than those not previously exposed, indicating acclimatization during embryonic exposure. Pascoe and Beattie (1979) pretreated *S. gairdneri* with low levels of Cd, exposed the pretreated and control fish to higher levels and found the LC50 for the pretreated fish was significantly higher. Brine shrimp (*Artemia salina*) preexposed to low levels of copper could tolerate higher levels than untreated controls (Saliba and Krzyz, 1976).

Dixon and Sprague (1981a) found that *S. gairdneri* preexposed to arsenic gradually increased their tolerance, as measured by incipient lethal level. These investigators (1981b) also found that *S. gairdneri* preexposed to Cu increased their tolerance, as measured by incipient lethal level (Fig. 1). This increase in tolerance was not retained after return to clean water. In addition, preexposure to Cu produced a decrease in tolerance to Zn. Furthermore, Dixon and Hilton (1981) found that Cu tolerance in this species could be affected by diet, with a high carbohydrate diet causing a decrease in Cu tolerance. They felt the decrease in tolerance was due to high liver glycogen which impaired the liver function.

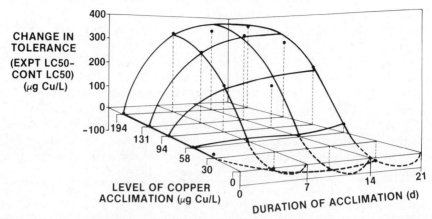

Figure 1. A response surface illustrating the change in incipient lethal levels of copper for rainbow trout acclimated to any combination of (a) copper from 0 to 194 µg/L with (b) time from 0 to 21 d. Observed values are points, predicted values intercepts. (From Dixon and Sprague, 1981b; reproduced by permission of the Government of Canada, Scientific Information and Publication Branch.)

The acclimatization to metals after preexposure was attributed by Pascoe and Beattie (1979) and Dixon and Sprague (1981c) to stimulation of the synthesis of metal-binding proteins, or metallothioneins, in the liver, which formed a nontoxic complex with the metal.

2.2.1.   Metal-Binding Proteins

Metallothioneins are small (6000–7000 daltons) proteins, rich in cysteine (19–20 of 61 amino acids), whose free thiol groups readily bind the heavy metal ions in trimercaptide linkages. The metals are thus sequestered within cytoplasm. It is thought that this system normally functions as a storage for essential trace metals (e.g., Zn and Cu) and only incidentally functions in heavy metal toxicity. There are numerous reviews of metallothionein biology and chemistry in recent years, most notably the report of a conference (Kägi and Nordberg, 1979). We are therefore not going to add to the list but, rather, point out salient features that are unique to or especially relevant for aquatic organisms.

Metallothioneins are found in a great diversity of species, including plants, animals, and protista. The mammalian metallothioneins have been studied in considerable depth by a number of investigators, so that it is known that the human, equine, and murine isometallothioneins have considerable homologies in their amino acid sequences (Huang et al., 1981), suggesting an early evolutionary development and a conservative genome, comparable to that of cytochrome *c. Neurospora* metallothionein has only 25 amino acid residues, but is basically similar to amino acid numbers 3–27 of the mammalian sequence (Lerch, 1979). Metallothioneins have recently been studied in an aquatic animal for amino acid sequences as well. Metallothioneins I and II from the hepatopancreas of the crab *Scylla serrata* were found to have 83% identity in sequence with mammalian metallothioneins, and all but one of the amino acid substitutions could have resulted from single base changes in the genome (Lerch et al., 1982).

Synthesis of metallothioneins is thought to occur in several tissues but is especially significant in the liver. Control of synthesis occurs at the transcriptional level (Durnam and Palmiter, 1981), and metallothionein synthesis is readily induced by several heavy metals, including Zn, Cu, Cd, Ag, and Hg. Induction by one metal may confer resistance to others because of the nonspecific nature of the ligand. That is, an organism normally exposed to Cu, for example, might be prepared for an influx of Hg into its environment.

Tissue levels of heavy metals tend to be significant in carnivores, because of biomagnification, and in marine organisms, because of the background levels in seawater. It was not unexpected, therefore, that Nöel-Lambot et al. (1978) should find metallothionein levels in untreated eels to be 350 μg/g liver, 2–3 times higher than values reported for many other species. When chronically exposed to 13 ppm Cd, the eels' metallothionein levels increased tenfold.

There are some other proteins which bind heavy metals, also. Molluscs, in particular, have developed unique metal-binding proteins. Roesijadi and Hall (1981) described a protein isolated from the gills of the mussel *Mytilus edulis* which is twice the size of metallothionein and contains relatively little cysteine. A specific Cd-binding protein is found in several marine bivalves and depends on acidic amino acids for its function (reviewed by Fowler et al., 1981). The methylmercuric ion differs from the inorganic Hg^{2+} and has an affinity for glutathione (Refsvik and Norseth, 1975). Some other heavy-metal-binding proteins are described in the final chapter of Kägi and Nordberg (1979).

Despite these apparently ubiquitous mechanisms for sequestering heavy metals, toxic situations still arise. There is, obviously, a finite limit to the ability of metallothioneins to bind metals beyond which the toxicants "spill over" and react with nonspecific proteins, thus changing their conformation and ability to function.

Another mechanism for dealing with heavy metals is by lysosomal storage. Lysosomes are membrane-bound cytoplasmic bodies, typically 0.25–0.50 μm in diameter, which contain hydrolytic enzymes and, at times, other soluble and insoluble items. They function in cell metabolism and digest substances taken into the cell by pinocytosis and phagocytosis. Insoluble materials may be stored in lysosomes indefinitely or may be removed from the cell by exocytosis of the lysosome. A number of reports have demonstrated that cations are compartmentalized in lysosomes (reviewed by Sternlieb and Goldfischer, 1976, and by Fowler et al., 1981). The metals may be transported to lysosomes via metallothioneins, but since Pb and Fe appear there in addition to Cu, Zn, and Hg, a separate or additional mechanism of cation transport must be involved.

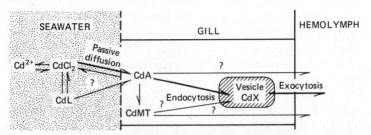

Figure 2. Proposed scheme for uptake of Cd by *M. edulis* gills. Cd enters the gill by passive diffusion with minimal membrane interaction, and is bound to ligand A. Cd exchanges between this ligand and metallothionein. CdA and/or CdMt are sequestered by a vesicle (or endocytosed if the vesicles are autophagic). Transport into the hemolymph can occur by exocytosis of CdA, CdMt or the vesicles. Key: A = soluble intracellular binding, L = external chelating ligand, Mt = metallothionein, X = intracellular vesicular binding ligand. (From Carpene and George, 1981; reproduced by permission of Elsevier Biomedical Press.)

When lysosomes accumulate metals in excessive concentrations, their normal structure and their enzymatic functions are interfered with (Sternlieb and Goldfischer, 1976).

Whether heavy metals are sequestered in tissues by metal-binding proteins or by lysosomes, the results are the same:

1. The organism is protected.
2. Because ions on the cytoplasmic side of cell membranes are immobilized, equilibria are changed so that the organism continues to take up the toxic ions from the environment against what would otherwise be a concentration gradient [see Fig. 2 (Carpene and George, 1981)]. The result is even higher concentrations to be passed up to higher trophic levels. Nonstorage protective methods (descriptions to follow) do not have these disadvantages.
3. Organisms utilizing these mechanisms exhibit tolerance to the toxicants.

2.2.2. Depuration

A unique mechanism for sequestering heavy metals from the intestinal lumen has recently been described in several marine teleosts by Nöel-Lambot (1981). Intestinal corpuscles consisting of a mucous envelope containing Mg- and Ca-rich granules (probably carbonates) were noted to bind large amounts of Cd, Zn, and Cu ions. Since these corpuscles are continuously eliminated from the fish, the author concluded that this is a method for limiting the uptake of these metals. Experimentally, *Anguilla* was shown to contain nearly 40% of its body burden of Cd in the corpuscles although they made up only 0.1% of the total weight of the fish.

Organisms have developed a variety of mechanisms for depurating heavy metal pollutants. Binding of toxic cations to metallothioneins in intestinal mucosa, first described by Cousins et al. (1977), can prevent low levels from entering the systemic circulation. An interpretation offered by Webb and Cain (1982) suggests that, since mucosal cells have a rapid turnover, metals bound to metallothioneins can then be eliminated by desquamation.

The biology of lysosomes includes the ability to leave the cell by the process of exocytosis. While the model proposed by Carpene and George (1981) suggests that lysosomes in *Mytilus* gill epithelium exocytose into the hemolymph, exocytosis from integumental, intestinal or renal epithelium would rid the organism of lysosomes with their stored cations. Large lysosomelike vesicles in *Mytilus* kidney, which contains 38% of the body burden of Cd^{2+} (George and Pirie, 1979), were shown to be shed into kidney lumen (George and Pirie, 1980). These authors have suggested, also, that metallothioneins are associated with these vesicles. Similar vesicles were described in gill epithelium (Fig. 2).

Glutathione-bound methylmercury has been reported to be significantly concentrated in the bile of methylmercury-treated animals (Refsvik and Norseth, 1975). Although many bile components are resorbed from the intestinal lumen, this can be considered a route of elimination of this toxic compound.

Calcium deposits, both intracellular and extracellular, sequester divalent cations in a number of marine invertebrates (Fowler et al., 1981). Since many of these animals deposit the calcareous compounds in shells which are metabolically inactive or in exoskeletons which are molted, the tissues are effectively rid of the heavy metals.

Mucus secretion is a common response of aquatic organisms to irritants. McKone et al. (1971) showed that Hg binds to fish mucus. Lock and Van Overbeeke (1981) demonstrated increased mucus secretion in trout exposed to specific mercury compounds. Presumably, the rate of secretion both prevents some of the uptake of and eliminates some of the body burden of the Hg to which the fish is exposed.

Therefore, by this variety of mechanisms of detoxification and of depuration, preexposed organisms can demonstrate increased resistance to heavy metal toxicity. However, despite the prevalence of these mechanisms, some studies have failed to show increased tolerance after preexposure. Green et al. (1976) found that preexposing white shrimp (*Penaeus setiferus*) to 0.5 and 1.0 ppb mercury for 57 days had no effect on the LC50 or on growth and molting in response to higher concentrations of Hg. Similarly, Corner and Sparrow (1956) found that short preexposure of *Artemia salina* nauplii to copper actually lowered their resistance to mercury exposure. The same was found when they were pretreated with mercury and then placed in copper. Weis (unpublished) found that treatment of fiddler crabs (*Uca pugilator*) with 0.06 or 0.1 ppm methylmercury for two weeks had no effect on their subsequent regenerative ability when exposed to 0.5 ppm.

3. LONG-TERM SELECTION AND POPULATION DIFFERENCES

3.1. Organics

Populations can develop tolerance to pollutants to which they have been chronically exposed. This tolerance can develop because of the existence of variation in response of members of a population. In polluted environments, selection for the more resistant genotypes should occur. Macek and Sanders (1970) reported considerable variation in susceptibility to DDT in different populations of invertebrates (amphipods, shrimp, daphnids, sowbugs, and damselflies) and fishes (bluegills, rainbow trout, fathead minnow, and channel catfish) from different locations, but did not state whether the more resistant populations were from more DDT-contaminated environments. Vinson et al. (1963) reported on increased resistance to DDT in the mosquitofish *Gambusia affinis* from areas with a history of treatment with DDT. Orciari (1979) described increased resistance to rotenone on the part of a chronically exposed population of golden shiners (*Notemigonus chrysoleucas*). Fish from acidic water have similarly been shown to be more acid tolerant (McWilliams, 1980).

3.2. Metals

Some populations living in water rich in metals have also become metal-resistant. Russell and Morris (1972) found genetically greater resistance to copper in the brown alga *Ectocarpus* from environments with elevated copper levels. Similarly, Stokes et al. (1973) isolated a nickel- and copper-resistant strain of the green alga *Scenedesmus* from a contaminated lake. Foster (1977) has reported that the mechanism of copper tolerance in the green alga *Chlorella vulgaris* from a Cu-polluted stream was to reduce greatly the accumulation of the metal.

Bryan and colleagues (reviewed by Bryan, 1976) have studied the polychaete *Nereis diversicolor* and have found populations from sediments rich in a particular metal to be resistant to that particular metal. Resistance to copper and zinc, possibly to silver and arsenic, but not to cadmium and lead, was demonstrated. Animals that were tolerant to zinc were also less permeable to the metal than were nontolerant worms. The differences in tolerance were believed to be genetic since the resistance was not changed by exposing tolerant and nontolerant worms to sediments of the opposite type (Bryan and Hummerstone, 1971).

Fraser et al. (1978) have demonstrated resistance to lead in the isopod *Asellus aquaticus* from sites with high lead concentrations. Brown (1976), in studying the related *Asellus meridianus,* found that strains tolerant to lead and copper could accumulate high levels which proved lethal to nontolerant animals. Tolerance to copper appeared to confer tolerance to lead, and the tolerance persisted into subsequent generations in the laboratory, indicating a genetic basis for the resistance. Moraitou-Apostolopoulou et al. (1979) determined that a population of the copepod *Acartia clausi* from a chronically Cd-polluted area was more resistant to Cd than a population from a nonpolluted area, but did not determine whether genetic adaptation was involved. Luoma et al. (in press) found increased resistance to Cu by the copepods *Acartia clausi* and *A. californiensis* and the bivalve *Macoma balthica* from regions where environmental Cu levels were high, even though they were not geographically isolated from nonexposed populations. They discussed the genetic plasticity of these species which allowed them to establish and maintain tolerant populations after only a few generations of larvae.

Callahan (1982) found greater resistance to the retarding effects of methyl-mercury on limb regeneration in fiddler crabs, *Uca pugnax,* from a polluted environment as compared to a nonpolluted area. Since earlier experiments (Weis, unpublished) had shown no enhancement of resistance in crabs after short-term preexposure to methylmercury, the increased resistance of the chronically exposed population was attributed to genetic selection.

The development of tolerance can help explain the survival of certain species in highly polluted environments. Another factor which can contrib-ute to their survival is the existence of some antagonistic interactions be-tween various pollutants, such that one can partially counteract the toxic effects of the other (Dixon and Compher, 1977; Kim et al., 1977; Roales and Perlmutter, 1974; Weis and Weis, 1980; Weis, 1978; Weis et al., 1981a).

Levinton (1980) described pollution as being a selective agent in estuaries, causing the more resistant genotypes to be prevalent in polluted areas. Nevo et al. (1981) studied allozymic variation of phosphoglucomutase (PGM) genotypes in the shrimp *Palaemon elegans*. They found differential toler-ance of certain genotypes to mercury, suggesting that they are adaptive (Fig. 3). Luoma (1977) discussed the potential use of toxicant resistance as a tool in assessing contaminant effects in natural ecosystems. He hypothesized that greater resistance to a toxicant in a population from one area as com-pared to another area is direct evidence that the toxicant was exerting selec-tive pressure at the first site, and stated that the level of resistance of the organisms should reflect the degree of contamination of the environment.

Although Luoma's (1977) ideas are conceptually appealing, one does not always find more resistant organisms on contaminated areas. Rahel (1981) selected for zinc tolerance in a laboratory population of flagfish, *J. floridae,* and found increased resistance after one generation. However, continued selection for three more generations failed to increase tolerance further, implying that the zinc exposure eliminated the weakest individuals but did not cause genetic changes specifically related to zinc tolerance. Further-more, shiners, *Notropus cornutus,* from a zinc-polluted stream were not more zinc tolerant (in terms of survival and swimming stamina) than those from unpolluted areas (Fig. 4). These results and a literature review sug-

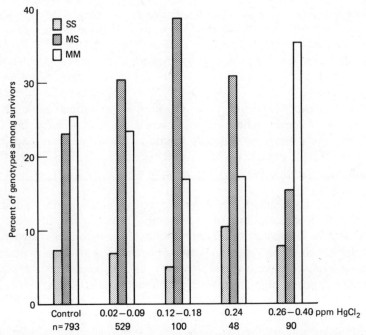

Figure 3. Differential survivorship of three PGM genotypes of *Palaemon elegans* as a function of increasing concentration of HgCl₂. (From Nevo et al., 1981; reproduced by permission of Birkhauser Verlag.)

gested to him that although fish have the genetic potential to evolve metal tolerance, they are unable to do so rapidly enough to survive in contaminated environments.

Research in our laboratory on *Fundulus heteroclitus* has shown the situation to be even more complicated. In studying the effects of methylmercury (meHg) on embryos from an unpolluted area (Montauk, N.Y.), we noted considerable variation in susceptibility. Some females produced eggs that were very tolerant, while others produced more susceptible eggs (Weis et al., 1982a). The abnormalities produced by mercury exposure were craniofacial, cardiovascular, and skeletal. We have devised indices to rate the relative severity of these defects. Craniofacial abnormalities, measured by a craniofacial index (CFI) on a scale of 0–6, involve progressive convergence of the eyes (0 = normal, 1 = slight convergence, 2 = greater convergence to touching, 3 = synophthalmic, 4 = fused with two lenses, 5 = cyclopic, and 6 = anencephalic). A cardiovascular index (CVI) similarly rates the severity of heart defects, and a skeletal index (SKI) rates the severity of skeletal malformations. Quantitation of teratogenic responses was thus possible within and between populations.

Tolerance of embryos was associated with the female's fin ray count, suggesting a genetic basis. No association of tolerance with traits of the male

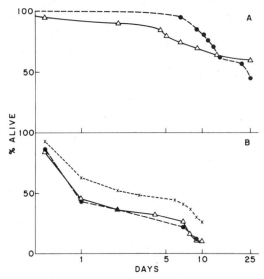

Figure 4. Survival of common shiners from zinc-contaminated Furnace Creek (△) and two uncontaminated streams, Mineral Point Branch (●) and Rock Branch (X) when exposed to toxic zinc concentrations. *A*, zinc = 1.7 mg/liter; *N* = 20 for Furnace Creek and *N* = 21 for Mineral Point Branch. *B*, zinc = 5.0 mg/liter, *N* = 31 for Furnace Creek, *N* = 14 for Mineral Point Branch, and *N* = 27 for Rock Branch. (From Rahel, 1981; reproduced by permission of the American Fisheries Society.)

was found. Susceptible clutches tended to incorporate higher levels of mercury than more resistant clutches.

In a population from Piles Creek in Linden, N.J., which is heavily impacted with metal and other pollution, very few females produced susceptible eggs, and most clutches were tolerant with respect to the production of malformations (Weis et al., 1981b) (Fig. 5). This species in clean environments has broad plasticity and therefore has a high probability of adapting. Mitton and Koehn (1975) felt that the polygynous mating system of this species allows for rapid evolutionary response to a variable environment. Different isozyme patterns were found in fish from the two locations (Heber, 1981) but these differences were correlated with geographic differences in genotypes of this species (Place and Powers, 1978) and were probably, therefore, not pollution related. The Piles Creek embryos developed somewhat more rapidly, which may have enabled them to pass through sensitive developmental stages faster and thus be less affected by the meHg. This fast developmental rate may be related to the earlier hatching time reported by DiMichele and Powers (1982) in *F. heteroclitus* with the LDH B^{a}B^a genotype, the one which was more prevalent at Piles Creek. In the Long Island population, tolerance of a clutch of embryos to meHg was correlated with its tolerance to HgCl$_2$, although the inorganic form was less teratogenic (Weis and Weis, 1982a). In Piles Creek embryos, however, the HgCl$_2$ was

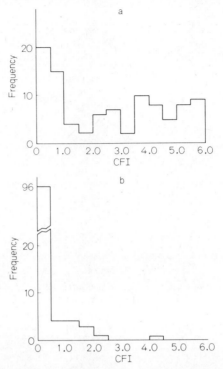

Figure 5. *Fundulus heteroclitus.* (*a*) Distribution of CFI among treated (0.05 ppm meHg) batches of eggs from Montauk (median value = 2.3). (*b*) Distribution of CFI among treated batches of eggs from Piles Creek (median value = 0.0). Chi-square for these distributions = 78.1, p < 0.001. The *y*-axis, "Frequency," represents the number of batches having that particular response. (From Weis et al., 1981b; reproduced by permission of Springer-Verlag).

consistently more toxic than meHg in terms of causing embryonic mortality (Weis et al. 1982b). It is interesting to note that in this population, tolerance existed to only one form of the metal. The tolerance to meHg but not $HgCl_2$ may indicate that the form of Hg available to the fish in their environment is primarily meHg, and that they have adapted to this specific toxicant. In the Long Island population, clutches of eggs that were more tolerant to meHg were generally less tolerant to Pb (Weis and Weis, 1982b), whereas in the Piles Creek population there was no correlation between meHg and Pb tolerance (Vaidya, in prep.).

In the Long Island population, clutches of eggs that were more meHg tolerant tended to become larvae that were likewise more tolerant (Weis and Weis, 1982a). Studies on adult tolerance, in terms of fin regeneration and survival, however, revealed that the Piles Creek adults were not more tolerant, but were, in fact, less tolerant than the unstressed population (Renna, 1982). Even control fish from Piles Creek regenerated fins more slowly and exhibited higher mortality than the Long Island fish.

Therefore, the increased tolerance to meHg which was evident in the embryos of the Piles Creek population was no longer present in adults. Adults appeared to be under stress and weaker than the fish from the cleaner environment. Therefore, Luoma's (1977) hypothesis is an oversimplification (at least regarding fish populations) and it is premature to state, after studying only one stage of its life history, that a population is or is not more resistant to a toxicant. The strong selection pressure for tolerance in the Piles Creek population would appear to be at the embryonic stages only.

The signs of stress and lowered resistance exhibited by the Piles Creek adult killifish are similar to the findings of McFarlane and Franzin (1978) on a population of white suckers (*Catostomus commersoni*) from a zinc-, copper-, and cadmium-polluted lake. This population showed reduced spawning success, increased larval mortality, and decreased longevity when compared to a population from a clean lake. They felt that these were signs of a population under stress. Likewise, Rahel (1981) found that the shiners from the zinc-polluted stream were less zinc-tolerant and appeared to be under chronic stress. It may be, therefore, that the ability of fish to develop tolerance to metals is restricted to certain early life history stages.

The ability to develop tolerance and adapt to pollution is certainly advantageous to the species which possess it. However, tolerant organisms in highly contaminated areas may accumulate high concentrations of toxicants, and these may be transmitted along the food chain to predatory species which may not be similarly adapted.

Intraspecific differences in tolerance, caused either by short-term preexposure, chronic weakening due to stress, or genetic variation and selection for tolerance, have major implications for bioassays, since the outcome of the assay is a result of the degree of tolerance of the organisms tested. Investigators who purchase organisms commercially may receive shipments collected from different locales and thereby organisms with differential tolerance. The use of inbred laboratory stocks can assure greater uniformity in response, but the question arises—of what relevance is their response to that of natural populations in the wild? (Cultured populations of laboratory stocks of fathead minnows were less resistant to hydrogen sulfide than field caught specimens, although none had any prior exposure to the toxicant; Smith et al., 1976).

Investigators concerned with bioassays must be aware of this variability when attempting to generalize from their data. One must remember that one effect of chronic exposure to pollution may be an alteration of the organism's tolerance to pollution.

ACKNOWLEDGMENT

The preparation of this manuscript was supported by a grant from NOAA Office of Sea Grant, NA 81AA-D-00065, Project No. R/F-4. This is New Jersey Sea Grant Publication NJSG 83-86.

REFERENCES

Beattie, J. N. and Pascoe, D. (1978). Cadmium uptake by rainbow trout, *Salmo gairdneri*, Richardson, eggs and alevins. *J. Fish Biol.* **13**, 631–637.

Bend, J. R., James, M. O., and Dansette, P. M. (1977). *In vitro* metabolism of xenobiotics in some marine animals. *Ann. N.Y. Acad. Sci.* **298**, 505–521.

Brown, B. E. (1976). Observations on the tolerance of the isopod *Asellus meridianus* Rac. to copper and lead. *Water Res.* **10**, 555–559.

Bryan, G. W. (1976). Some aspects of heavy metal tolerance in aquatic organisms. In: A. Lockwood, Ed., *Effects of pollutants on aquatic organisms*. Cambridge University Press, Cambridge, pp. 7–34.

Bryan, G. W. and Hummerstone, L. G. (1971). Adaptation of the polychaete *Nereis diversicolor* to sediments containing high concentrations of heavy metals. I. General observations and adaptation to copper. *J. Mar. Biol. Assoc. U.K.* **51**, 845–863.

Burns, K. (1976). Microsomal mixed function oxidases in an estuarine fish, *Fundulus heteroclitus*, and their induction as a result of environmental contamination. *Comp. Biochem. Physiol.* **53B**, 443–446.

Callahan, P. F. (1982). Differences in regeneration rate and response to methylmercury in fiddler crabs, *Uca pugnax*, from a polluted vs. non-polluted environment. M.S. Thesis, Rutgers University, Newark, New Jersey, 60 pp.

Carpene, E. and George, S. G. (1981). Absorption of cadmium by gills of *Mytilus edulis* (L.) *Molec. Physiol.* **1**, 23–34.

Chambers, J. E. and Yarbrough, J. D. (1979). A seasonal study of microsomal mixed function oxidase components in insecticide-resistant and -susceptible mosquitofish, *Gambusia affinis*. *Toxicol. Appl. Pharmacol.* **48**, 497–507.

Corner, E. D. and Sparrow, B. W. (1956). The modes of action of toxic agents. I. Observations of the poisoning of certain crustaceans by copper and mercury. *J. Mar. Biol. Assoc. U.K.* **35**, 531–548.

Cousins, R. J., Squibb, K. S., Feldman, S. L., DeBari, A., and Silbon, B. L. (1977). Biomedical responses of rats to chronic exposure to dietary cadmium fed ad libitum and equalized regimes. *J. Toxicol. Environ. Health* **2**, 929–943.

DiMichele, L. and Powers, D. A. (1982). LDH-B genotype-specific hatching times of *Fundulus heteroclitus* embryos. *Nature* **296**, 563–564.

Dixon, C. and Compher, K. (1977). Protective action of zinc against the deleterious effects of cadmium in the regenerating forelimb of the adult newt, *Notophthalmus viridescens*. *Growth* **41**, 95–103.

Dixon, D. G. and Hilton, J. W. (1981). Influence of dietary carbohydrate content on tolerance of waterborne copper by rainbow trout, *Salmo gairdneri*. *J. Fish Biol.* **19**, 509–518.

Dixon, D. G. and Sprague, J. B. (1981a). Acclimation-induced changes in toxicity of arsenic and cyanide to rainbow trout, *Salmo gairdneri* Richardson. *J. Fish Biol.* **18**, 579–589.

Dixon, D. G. and Sprague, J. B. (1981b). Acclimation to copper by rainbow trout (*Salmo gairdneri*)—a modifying factor in toxicity. *Can. J. Fish. Aquat. Sci.* **38**, 880–888.

Dixon, D. G. and Sprague, J. B. (1981c). Copper bioaccumulation and hepatoprotein synthesis during acclimation to copper by juvenile rainbow trout. *Aquat. Toxicol.* **1**, 69–81.

Durnam, D. M. and Palmiter, R. D. (1981). Transcriptional regulation of the mouse metallothionein—I gene by heavy metals. *J. Biol. Chem.* **256**, 5712–5716.

Foster, P. L. (1977). Copper exclusion as a mechanism of heavy metal tolerance in a green alga. *Nature* **269**, 322–323.

Fowler, B. A., Carmichael, N. G., Squibb, K. S., and Engel, D. W. (1981). Factors affecting trace metal uptake and toxicity to estuarine organisms. II. Cellular Mechanisms. In: F. J.

Vernberg, A. Calabrese, F. P. Thurberg, and W. B. Vernberg, Eds., *Biological monitoring of marine pollutants*, Academic Press, New York, pp. 145–163.

Fraser, J., Parker, T., and Vespoor, E. (1978). Tolerance to lead in the freshwater isopod *Asellus aquaticus*. *Water Res.* **12**, 637–641.

George, S. G. and Pirie, B. J. S. (1979). The occurrence of cadmium in subcellular particles in the kidney of the marine mussel, *Mytilus edulis*, exposed to cadmium. The use of electron microprobe analysis. *Biochim. Biophys. Acta* **580**, 234–244.

George, S. G. and Pirie, B. J. S. (1980). Metabolism of zinc in the mussel *Mytilus edulis* (L.): A combined ultrastructural and biochemical study. *J. Mar. Biol. Assoc. U.K.* **60**, 575–590.

Green, F. A., Jr., Anderson, J. W., Petrocelli, S. R., Presley, B. J., and Sims, R. (1976). Effects of mercury on survival, respiration and growth of postlarval white shrimp, *Penaeus setiferus*. *Mar. Biol.* **37**, 75–81.

Heber, M. A. (1981). Comparative embryonic methylmercury susceptibility and reproductive biology of two populations of the mummichog (*Fundulus heteroclitus*). M.S. Thesis. Rutgers University, Newark, New Jersey, 98 pp.

Huang, I.-Y., Kumura, M., Hata, A., Tsunoo, H., and Yoshida, A. (1981). Complete amino acid sequence of mouse liver metallothionein-II. *J. Biochem.* **89**, 1839–1845.

Kägi, J. H. R. and Nordberg, M., Eds. 1979. *Metallothionein*. Birkhauser Verlag, Basel, 378 pp.

Khan, M. A. Q., Coello, W., Khan, A., and Pinto, H. (1972a). Some characteristics of the microsomal mixed function oxidase in the freshwater crayfish, *Cambarus*. *Life Sci.* **11**, 405–415.

Khan, M. A. Q., Kamal, A., Wolin, R. J., and Runnels, J. (1972b). *In vivo* and *in vitro* epoxidation of aldrin by aquatic food chain organisms. *Bull. Environ. Contam. Toxicol.* **8**, 219–228.

Kim, J. H., Birks, E., and Heisinger, J. F. (1977). Protective action of selenium against mercury in northern creek chubs. *Bull. Environ. Contam. Toxicol.* **17**, 132–136.

Lee, R. F., Sauerheber, R., and Dobbs, G. H. (1972). Uptake, metabolism and discharge of polycyclic aromatic hydrocarbons by marine fish. *Mar. Biol.* **17**, 201–208.

Lee, R. F., Singer, S., Tenore, K., Gardner, W., and Philpot, R. (1979). Detoxification system in polychaete worms: Importance in the degradation of sediment hydrocarbons. In: W. B. Vernberg, F. Thurberg, A. Calabrese, and F. J. Vernberg, Eds., *Marine pollution: Functional responses*. Academic Press, New York, pp. 23–37.

Lee, R. F., Stolzenbach, J., Singer, S., and Tenore, K. (1981). Effects of crude oil on growth and mixed function oxygenase activity in polychaetes, *Nereis* sp. In: F. J. Vernberg, A. Calabrese, F. Thurberg, and W. B. Vernberg, Eds., *Biological monitoring of marine pollutants*. Academic Press, New York, pp. 323–334.

Lerch, K. (1979). Amino acid sequence of copper-metallothionein from *Neurospora crassa*. In: J. H. R. Kägi and M. Nordberg, Eds., *Metallothionein*. Birkhauser Verlag, Basel, pp. 173–179.

Lerch, K., Ammer, D., and Olafson, R. W. (1982). Crab metallothionein. Primary structures of metallothioneins 1 and 2. *J. Biol. Chem.* **257**, 2420–2426.

Levinton, J. S. (1980). Genetic divergence in estuaries. In: V. Kennedy, Ed., *Estuarine perspectives*. Academic Press, New York, pp. 509–520.

Lloyd, R. (1960). The toxicity of zinc sulfate to rainbow trout. *Ann. Appl. Biol.* **48**, 84–94.

Lock, R. A. C. and van Overbeeke, A. P. (1981). Effects of mercuric chloride and methylmercuric chloride on mucus secretion in rainbow trout, *Salmo gairdneri* Richardson. *Comp. Biochem. Physiol.* **69C**, 67–73.

Luoma, S. N. (1977). Detection of trace contaminant effects in aquatic ecosystems. *J. Fish. Res. Board Can.* **34**, 436–439.

Luoma, S. N., Cain, D., and Hutchinson, A. (1983). *Mar. Ecol. Prog. Ser.,* in press.

Macek, K. and Sanders, H. (1970). Biological variation in the susceptibility of fish and aquatic invertebrates to DDT. *Trans. Am. Fish. Soc.* **99,** 89–90.

McFarlane, G. A. and Franzin, W. G. (1978). Elevated heavy metals: A stress on a population of white suckers, *Catostomus commersoni,* in Hamell Lake, Saskatchewan. *J. Fish. Res. Board Can.* **35,** 963–970.

McKone, C. E., Young, R. G., Bache, C. A., and Lisk, D. J. (1971). Rapid uptake of mercuric ion by goldfish. *Environ. Sci. Technol.* **5,** 1138–1139.

McWilliams, P. (1980). Effect of pH on sodium uptake in Norwegian brown trout (*Salmo trutta*) from an acid river. *J. Exp. Biol.* **88,** 259–267.

Mitton, J. B. and Koehn, R. (1975). Genetic organization and adaptive response of allozymes to ecological variables in *Fundulus heteroclitus. Genetics* **79,** 97–111.

Moraitou-Apostolopoulou, M., Verriopoulos, G., and Lentzou, P. (1979). Effects of sublethal concentrations of cadmium as possible indicators of cadmium pollution for two populations of *Acartia clausi* (Copepoda) living at two differentially polluted areas. *Bull. Environ. Contam. Toxicol.* **23,** 642–649.

Nevo, E., Perl, T., Beiles, A., and Wool, D. (1981). Mercury selection of allozyme genotypes in shrimps. *Experientia* **37,** 1152–1154.

Noël-Lambot, F. (1981). Presence in the intestinal lumen of marine fish of corpuscles with a high cadmium-, zinc-, and copper-binding capacity: A possible mechanism of heavy metal tolerance. *Mar. Ecol. Prog. Ser.* **4,** 175–181.

Noël-Lambot, F., Gerday, Ch., and Disteche, A. (1978). Distribution of Cd, Zn, and Cu in liver and gills of the eel *Anguilla anguilla* with special reference to metallothioneins. *Comp. Biochem. Physiol.* **61C,** 177–187.

Orciari, R. D. (1979). Rotenone resistance of golden shiners from a periodically reclaimed pond. *Trans. Am. Fish. Soc.* **108,** 641–645.

Pascoe, D. and Beattie, J. H. (1979). Resistance to cadmium by pre-treated rainbow trout alevins. *J. Fish Biol.* **14,** 303–308.

Pederson, M. G., Hershberger, W., and Juchow, M. (1974). Metabolism of 3,4-benzpyrene in rainbow trout (*Salmo gairdneri*). *Bull. Environ. Contam. Toxicol.* **12,** 481–486.

Place, A. R. and Powers, D. A. (1978). Genetic bases for protein polymorphism in *Fundulus heteroclitus.* 1. Lactic dehydrogenase (Ldh-B), Malate Dehydrogenase (Mdh-A), Glucosephosphate Isomerase (Gpi-B) and Phosphoglucomutase (Pgm-A). *Biochem. Genet.* **16,** 577–607.

Rahel, F. J. (1981). Selection for zinc tolerance in fish: Results from laboratory and wild populations. *Trans. Am. Fish. Soc.* **110,** 19–28.

Refsvik, T. and Norseth, T. (1975). Methyl mercuric compounds in rat bile. *Acta Pharmacol. Toxicol.* **36,** 67–78.

Renna, M. (1982). Effects of polluted water and methylmercury on fin regeneration and swimming stamina in killifish (*Fundulus heteroclitus*): A comparison between two populations. M.S. Thesis, Rutgers University, Newark, New Jersey, 63 pp.

Roales, R. R. and Perlmutter, A. (1974). Toxicity of methylmercury and copper applied singly and jointly to the blue gourami, *Trichogaster trichopterus. Bull. Environ. Contam. Toxicol.* **12,** 633–639.

Roesijadi, G. and Hall, R. E. (1981). Characterization of mercury-binding protein from the gills of marine mussels exposed to mercury. *Comp. Biochem. Physiol.* **70C,** 59–64.

Russell, G. and Morris, O. P. (1972). Ship-fouling as an evolutionary process. In: *Proceedings of the Third International Congress on Marine Corrosion and Fouling,* Washington, D.C., pp. 719–730.

Saliba, L. J. and Krzyz, R. M. (1976). Acclimation and tolerance of *Artemia salina* to copper salts. *Mar. Biol.* **38**, 231–238.

Singer, S. C. and Lee, R. F. (1977). Mixed function oxygenase activity in the blue crab, *Callinectes sapidus:* Tissue distribution and correlation with changes during molting and development. *Biol. Bull.* **153**, 377–386.

Smith, L. L., Jr., Oseid, D. M., Adelman, I. R., and Broderius, S. J. (1976). Effect of hydrogen sulfide on fish and invertebrates. Part I. Acute and chronic toxicity studies. U.S. EPA Ecol. Res. Ser., EPA-600/3-76-062a.

Spehar, R., Leonard, E., and DeFoe, D. (1978). Chronic effects of cadmium and zinc mixtures on flagfish (*Jordanella floridae*). *Trans. Am. Fish. Soc.* **107**, 354–360.

Sternlieb, I. and Goldfischer, S. (1976). Heavy metals and lysosomes. In: J. T. Dingle and R. T. Dean, Eds., *Lysosomes in biology and pathology,* Vol. 5, pp. 185–200. North-Holland Publ., Amsterdam.

Stokes, P. M., Hutchinson, T. C., and Krauter, K. (1973). Heavy metal tolerance in algae isolated from contaminated lakes near Sudbury, Ontario. *Can. J. Bot.* **51**, 2155–2168.

Vinson, S. B., Boyd, C., and Ferguson, D. (1963). Resistance to DDT in the mosquitofish *Gambusia affinis. Science* **139**, 217–218.

Webb, M. and Cain, K. (1982). Functions of metallothionein. *Biochem. Pharmacol.* **31**, 137–142.

Weis, J. S. (1978). Interactions of methylmercury, cadmium and salinity on regeneration in the fiddler crabs *Uca pugilator, U. pugnax* and *U. minax. Mar. Biol.* **49**, 119–124.

Weis, J. S., Weis, P., and Ricci, J. (1981a). Effects of cadmium, zinc, salinity and temperature on the teratogenicity of methylmercury to the killifish (*Fundulus heteroclitus*). *Rapp. P.-V. Reun. Cons. Int. Explor. Mer.* **178**, 64–70.

Weis, J. S., Weis, P., Heber, M., and Vaidya, S. (1981b). Methylmercury tolerance of killifish (*Fundulus heteroclitus*) embryos from a polluted vs. nonpolluted environment. *Mar. Biol.* **65**, 283–287.

Weis, J. S., Weis, P., and Heber, M. (1982a). Variation in response to methylmercury by killifish (*Fundulus heteroclitus*) embryos. In: J. G. Pearson, R. Foster, and W. Bishop, Eds., *Aquatic toxicology and hazard assessment.* Fifth Conf. ASTM STP 766 American Society for Testing and Materials, pp. 109–119.

Weis, J. S., Weis, P., Heber, M. and Vaidya, S. (1982b). Investigations into mechanisms of methylmercury tolerance in killifish (*Fundulus heteroclitus*) embryos. In: WB Verberg, A. Calabrese, F. Thurberg, and F. J. Verberg, Eds. *Physiological Mechanisms of Marine Pollutant Toxicity.* Acad Press N.Y.

Weis, P. and Weis, J. S. (1980a). Effect of zinc on fin regeneration in the mummichog, *Fundulus heteroclitus,* and its interaction with methylmercury. *Fish. Bull.* **78**, 163–166.

Weis, P. and Weis, J. S. (1982a). Toxicity of the PCBs Aroclor 1254 and 1242 to embryos and larvae of the mummichog, *Fundulus heteroclitus. Bull. Environ. Contam. Toxicol.* **28**, 298–304.

Weis, P. and Weis, J. S. (1982b). Toxicity of methylmercury, mercuric chloride, and lead in killifish (*Fundulus heteroclitus*) from Southampton, New York. *Environ. Res.* **28**, 364–374.

8

PHYSIOLOGICAL EFFECTS OF CONTAMINANT DYNAMICS ON FISH

A. J. Niimi

Department of Fisheries and Oceans
Canada Centre for Inland Waters
Burlington, Ontario

1. INTRODUCTION

Historically, criteria for the study of the environmental toxicology of fishes included observations such as lethality and loss of equilibrium which were readily apparent to the observer (Ellis et al., 1937; Wuhrmann, 1952). These observations were used to quantify the response of fish to toxic substances. More recently, it has been generally recognized that toxicological measurements can be influenced by physiological and environmental factors. A protocol was suggested that would include the use of similar procedures to evaluate the hazard potential of a substance to ensure that the information derived from different sources would be comparable (Sprague, 1969; APHA, 1971). This approach has served well in establishing water quality guidelines for different substances (EPA, 1976).

A greater emphasis is now being made to examine the distribution and kinetics of toxic substances that occur at sublethal concentrations in the aquatic environment. To address this issue, the toxicological actions of a substance must now be viewed in the physiological context of the organism in its natural environment. Water temperature in the temperate zone varies by up to 25°C annually, and this has a significant influence on the physiological response of poikilotherms. Organisms, such as fish, exposed to a wide range of environmental conditions, will change their feeding chronology, increase in weight, and reproduce during their lifetime. These factors must be taken into consideration when extrapolating information derived from laboratory studies to the natural environment.

The variable toxicological behavior of a substance has led to the development of contaminant dynamics models which attempt to describe or predict the fate of a substance. Many of these models have been derived by integrating the physiological requirements of fish with the toxicological actions of the substance. Measurements on the physiological needs of fishes have received considerable attention, and the effects of toxic substances received perhaps slightly less attention; but there is relatively little substantive information on the sublethal behavior and effects of toxic substances in fish as viewed from the physiological perspective in response to environmental circumstances. A compilation of information on the more relevant issues on the whole fish response to toxic substances primarily at the sublethal level is presented in relation to the kinetics of a substance as they would apply in the natural environment.

2. PHYSIOLOGICAL RESPONSE

2.1. Metabolism

Oxygen consumption has commonly been used as a measure of the metabolic rate in organisms. The work of Fry and his co-workers has clearly demonstrated the effects variables such as temperature and body weight have on the O_2 requirements of fishes (Fry, 1947, 1957, 1971). Terms like "standard" and "active" metabolism describe the lower and upper respiratory limits of fish in response to environmental circumstances (Fry, 1957; Beamish, 1964a). In general, the rate of O_2 uptake for fish of a given size will increase with temperature and activity (swimming), and the relative rate of O_2 uptake, particularly at the standard level, will decrease with increasing body weight (Winberg, 1956; Beamish, 1964a; Brett, 1964). Respiratory measurements on fish under laboratory conditions have been reported with regularity and the results in most cases are comparable because similar methods have been used (Blazka et al., 1960; Muir et al., 1965).

There is now a sufficiently large information base available on O_2 uptake that a reliable estimate may be derived for many species under most environmental conditions (Fry, 1971; Brett and Groves, 1979; Holeton, 1980). In the natural environment, the rate of uptake is influenced by other factors that do not necessarily coincide with the activity level. Uptake rates at low activity levels may vary due to "spontaneous activity" and will be influenced by factors such as starvation and feeding (Beamish, 1964b; Beamish and Mookherjii, 1964; Muir and Niimi, 1972). Nevertheless, the metabolic range for many species can be defined under most environmental conditions.

2.1.1. Gill Surface Area

The gill surface is the principal site for oxygen exchange between the fish and its environment, and under certain conditions, the uptake of environmental contaminants from water. While much is known about the rate of O_2 uptake by fish under different conditions, there have been comparatively few studies that examine the functional aspects of the gills.

The relationship between gill surface area and body weight in fish can be expressed as $Y = aW^b$ where the rate constant b varies from 0.5 to 1.0 for different species (Muir, 1969; Hughes, 1972). The intercept a was observed to vary 22-fold among 41 species examined (Muir, 1969). There are interspecific differences in filament length, lamellae shape, and area (Hughes, 1966; Hughes and Morgan, 1973); intraspecific differences in distribution of surface area among the gill arches (Niimi and Morgan, 1980); and differences in ratios between portions of the gills used for filtering particulate materials and for gaseous exchange (Jirasek et al., 1982). The result is a large range in gill surface areas whose functional capacity varies among species under different conditions.

Oxygen uptake is influenced by factors such as surface area, gas pressure, respiratory demand, and lamellar configuration. Uptake rate may not be directly dependent on gill surface area. It has been estimated that the resting O_2 uptake among five species can range from 210 to 300 ml/hr $\cdot$ m^2 gill surface area (Hughes, 1978) and the percent of lamellar perfusion may vary from 58 to 70% in resting fish (Booth, 1978), but this would not adequately account for the O_2 uptake which varies at least several fold for fish at comparable activity levels. Factors that account for the increase in O_2 uptake include the differential pressure of CO_2 and O_2 at the gill surface–water interface, volume of water inspired, and the interlamellar spacing. Changes in these parameters in response to increased activity levels can result in a five-fold increase in oxygen transfer rate (Jones and Randall, 1978).

Changes in the volume of water inspired is one of the more noticeable responses to increased O_2 demand. Many species evolved mechanisms for active respiration while others like tunas and sharks lost the ability to respire in a stationary position and must swim continuously to respire passively (Hall, 1930; Brown and Muir, 1970). Some species respire actively when provided with a low velocity of water and respire passively as velocity is increased (Muir and Buckley, 1967), whereas most species increase the respiratory frequency to increase water intake. Other species increase respiratory volume more than respiratory frequency in order to meet the demand for increased water flow (Piiper et al., 1977).

Lamellae configuration can influence respiratory efficiency. Fish with high oxygen demands generally have a larger number of secondary lamellae that are spaced closer together than species with lower requirements (Gray, 1954; Hughes and Morgan, 1973). The number of secondary lamellae is known to range from 7/mm in sharks to 60/mm in tunas (Hughes and Morgan, 1973). A close interlamellae spacing is suggested to be a more efficient gaseous exchange system than a coarse arrangement (Hughes, 1966).

The net result of these interactive factors is the efficiency of O_2 uptake from water. There are several extrinsic and intrinsic factors that influence this estimate. Water samples in some studies have been collected from cannulated fish which yielded different estimates depending on the location of the cannula (Davis and Watters, 1970). Other studies used a membrane or saclike structure to contain the expired water (Piiper and Schumann, 1967; Kiceniuk and Jones, 1977). It has been suggested that uptake efficiency of fish in a hypoxic state is lower than a normoxic fish (Kerstens et al., 1979). Some studies have also shown that uptake efficiency decreases as the volume of water inspired increases (Saunders, 1962; Hanson and Johansen, 1970), while other studies reported that uptake efficiency in trout remained at 33% at different swimming speeds (Kiceniuk and Jones, 1977), and utilization remained at 40–45% as ventilation increased 3-fold in nonswimming fish (Davis and Cameron, 1971). Taking these factors into consideration, uptake efficiencies of 25–50% have been reported for sharks (Lenfant and Johansen, 1966; Piiper and Schumann, 1967), 11–55% for trout (Randall et al., 1967; Holeton and Randall, 1967; Kiceniuk and Jones, 1977), 56–78% for tuna (Stevens, 1972), 78% for yellowtail (Yamamoto et al., 1981), and up to 68–85% for suckers, bullhead, and carp (Saunders, 1962; Itazawa and Takeda, 1978).

2.2.   Feeding and Growth

Studies on feeding and growth in fishes have indicated a close relationship between temperature and body weight. In general, the amount of food consumed will increase with temperature over most of the range except near the upper lethal levels, and the relative rate of feeding will decrease with increasing body weight (Brett et al., 1969; Niimi and Beamish, 1974). Corresponding studies on digestion rates also indicate the clearance rate will increase with temperature, and will decrease as body weight increases (Molnar et al., 1967; Fange and Grove, 1979). The weight effect is most pronounced in daily food intake where young fish may consume in excess of 18% of their body weight in food while subadults and adults may consume only several percent (Brett, 1971, 1979).

An extensive review of the literature suggests that the gross growth efficiency (log K), which is a ratio between food consumption and weight increase, will decrease as food intake is increased (Paloheimo and Dickie, 1966). An analysis of fish growth in the natural environment also indicates that log K would decrease with increasing body weight (Niimi, 1981). Feeding and growth rates are influenced by the nutritional quality of the food, and the information available from the numerous studies can provide reliable estimates of growth for many species.

2.3.   Bioenergetics Models

The accumulated information derived from respiratory studies have been integrated with comparable studies on feeding and growth to provide an assessment of the total physiological requirements of fish. An oxycalorific coefficient of 3.42 mg O_2 consumed per calorie expended has been commonly applied to derive the energy equivalent of respiration (Brody, 1964). This bioenergetics approach has been used to identify the specific energy needs for the different fish activities (Beamish and Dickie, 1967; Kitchell et al., 1977; Brett, 1979; Brett and Groves, 1979).

Conceptual models which describe the growth and energetics of fishes are based on a balance between energy that is ingested and that which is deposited as growth, expended for activities such as swimming, and excreted through bodily processes (Beamish et al., 1975). One of the first models applied to fish attempted to achieve an energy balance between the food ingested and that deposited as growth (Ivlev, 1939), while others have examined the relationship between intake energy and that which is "physiologically useful" to fish (Winberg, 1956). Subsequent models have further examined energy losses attributable to nonfecal loss and specific dynamic action (Warren and Davis, 1967), and included variables to account for weight changes (Ursin, 1967).

Most bioenergetics models generally make use of equations of type:

$$Q_a = Q_b + Q_c + Q_d + Q_e + Q_f$$

where Q_a is the energy value of the food, Q_b the energy value of biomass retained as growth, Q_c the energy equivalent of fecal loss, Q_d the energy equivalent of nonfecal (urinary) loss, Q_e the energy dissipated through specific dynamic action or heat increment, and Q_f as the energy requirement for locomotory activities. Values of Q_a and Q_b can be measured relatively easily using a calorimeter, and estimates for Q_c, Q_d, and Q_e are available in the literature. Estimates of Q_c ranging from 15 to 25% and Q_d from 5 to 10% of intake energy have been reported for carnivorous species (Brett and Groves, 1979). Factors such as temperature and feeding level will affect digestion rates, but have no appreciable influence on the absorption efficiency of lipid, protein, and energy (Menzel, 1960; Davies, 1964; Beamish, 1972). The energy loss to specific dynamic action can account for 10–18% of the ingested energy (Muir and Niimi, 1972; Beamish, 1974; Jobling, 1981).

The energy expended for locomotory activity is the most difficult value to estimate. It has been partially derived by estimating the combined energy needs for Q_e and Q_f by calculating the difference in energy balance between Q_a and the sum of Q_b, Q_c, and Q_d (Warren, 1971; Niimi and Beamish, 1974). There have since been estimates that examined variables such as the quality and quantity of food consumed, and the influence of body weight that may provide an opportunity to specifically identify the energy requirements for Q_e (Smith et al., 1978; Tandler and Beamish, 1979). Values for Q_e and Q_f are derived from estimates of O_2 uptake that equate to their energy equivalent using the oxycalorific coefficient. It may prove difficult to derive an independent estimate of Q_f from field studies at the present time because natural fish movements are difficult to quantify. It may also be difficult to derive an estimate of O_2 uptake particularly at the low activity levels where uptake rates can easily vary several fold at nonswimming episodes and slow speeds (Beamish, 1964a; Smit, 1965; Muir and Niimi, 1972). Nevertheless, bioenergetics models can provide a reasonably accurate estimate of the physiological requirements of many fishes under most environmental conditions.

3. TOXICOLOGICAL RESPONSE

3.1. Temperature and Weight Effects

Many toxicological studies on fish indicate the toxicity response will increase with temperature. Studies at the sublethal and lethal levels have shown that the rate of uptake or time to death for waterborne substances such as lead, mercury, and zinc will increase with temperature (Somero et al., 1977; MacLeod and Pessah, 1973; Hodson, 1975). Reviews on the effect of metals on fish in general indicate a similar response, although there are some exceptions (Phillips and Russo, 1978; Eisler et al., 1979). This relationship has also been demonstrated in some studies on organic contaminants such as PCP and DDT (Crandall and Goodnight, 1959; Murphy and Murphy, 1971). These observations would be consistent with the bioconcentration factor, or amount accumulated, which has been shown to increase with temperature for mercury and DDT (Cember et al., 1978; Boudou ct al., 1980; Reinert et al., 1974). In contrast, studies on other organic contaminants have shown toxicity to decrease with increasing temperatures (Kumaraguru and Beamish, 1981; Brown et al., 1967). An assessment of the influence of temperature on contaminant toxicity to fish indicates that this response will increase over a wide temperature range; but there are some exceptions for different substances, particularly organic contaminants, which can vary among species (Johnson, 1968; Cairns et al., 1975).

Most studies that examined the influence of body weight observed that smaller fish are less tolerant to toxicants than larger fish (Howarth and Sprague, 1978; Kumaraguru and Beamish, 1981). Studies on mercury and DDT which examined this relationship over a weight range have reported regression coefficients of 0.75–0.77 of body weight (Murphy and Murphy, 1971; de Freitas and Hart, 1975). A more definitive study which examined six discrete substances reported regression coefficients which ranged from 0.30 for zinc to 0.81 for dieldrin (Anderson and Weber, 1975). Some studies also concluded that the size effect would be minimal under certain conditions (Adelman et al., 1976).

3.2. Water Chemistry

The chemical properties of water have a significant influence on the toxicological behavior of a substance (see Babich and Stotzky, this volume). For example, the rate of uptake of lead, cadmium, and PCB by fish is greater in freshwater than in seawater (Somero et al., 1977; Bengtsson, 1977; Tulp et al., 1979). In the freshwater environment, hardness and pH are the major factors that influence the toxicity of metals. Lethality studies have shown that the toxicity of many metals, including copper, cadmium, zinc, lead, chromium, and nickel, will increase with decreasing hardness (Pickering and

Henderson, 1966; Chakoumakos et al., 1979). The influence of pH is more complex because it will enhance the solubility, ionization, and speciation of metals and has been discussed by others in this series (see Borgmann, this volume).

3.3.   Contaminant Dynamics Models

Dynamic models of contaminants are generally based on an energetics and growth model with coefficients to describe the uptake and elimination of a substance. Some models examine the uptake and retention of a substance based on feeding rates, while others are based on metabolic rates or include a growth dependent term (Hartung, 1976; Carlsson, 1978; Norstrom et al., 1976).

A generalized model can include indices for the uptake of a substance from food and water, and its ultimate elimination, as noted in the following:

$$
\begin{aligned}
\begin{matrix}\text{Body burden} \\ \text{of substance}\end{matrix} = &\left[\begin{matrix}\text{Assimilation} \\ \text{efficiency}\end{matrix}\begin{pmatrix}\text{Residue level} \\ \text{and amount of} \\ \text{food consumed}\end{pmatrix} + \begin{matrix}\text{Extraction} \\ \text{efficiency}\end{matrix}\begin{pmatrix}\text{Residue level} \\ \text{and volume of} \\ \text{water respired}\end{pmatrix}\right. \\
&\left. + \begin{matrix}\text{Substance} \\ \text{accumulated}\end{matrix}\right] - \left[\begin{matrix}\text{Rate of} \\ \text{elimination}\end{matrix}\begin{pmatrix}\text{Substance} \\ \text{accumulated}\end{pmatrix}\right]
\end{aligned}
$$

The accuracy of the uptake component is largely dependent on estimates of the assimilation and extraction efficiencies for food and water respectively. The evidence on the physiological response of fish shows that factors such as temperature and body weight would influence uptake rate.

The elimination component of a contaminants model is not as well defined. Models that describe the elimination of cesium suggest the rate is metabolically dependent, whereas other models for PCB and mercury indicate clearance is influenced by body weight but not by metabolic rate (Carlsson, 1978; Norstrom et al., 1976). These observations indicate environmental variables like temperature, which influences metabolic rate, will have a direct effect on the elimination rate of some substances. The temperature effect would become an indirect factor in other cases such as in the weight-dependent model because of its influence through feeding and growth.

Estimates of elimination rates can also be influenced by methodology. Analytical procedures for these studies generally include chromatographic techniques and the use of ^{14}C-labelled substances. The former method can differentiate between the parent compound and its metabolites whereas the latter procedure cannot, but it does have the advantage of allowing smaller samples and rapid analysis (Niimi, 1979). It has been suggested that the elimination kinetics of a substance be defined by two constants, one describing that portion excreted as the "undamaged molecule," and the second describing that which is eliminated through biotransformation (Lech and Bend, 1980). This approach would be applicable to studies on organic contaminants that are analyzed by chromatography, but not suitable for studies using ^{14}C-labelled substances because the radioactive portion may not be representative of the entire substance (Metcalf et al., 1973; Lu and Metcalf, 1975). Perhaps these are some factors that contributed to the difficulties of describing the elimination components of a contaminant dynamics model.

3.4. Mode of Uptake

Food and water are the principal pathways for the uptake of a substance. There have been relatively few studies that examined both pathways to determine their importance, particularly under laboratory conditions that approximate the natural environment (Niimi and Cho, 1983). Some studies demonstrated that a substance like endrin can be accumulated from food and water, while other studies indicated that higher levels could be accumulated from water than from food (Argyle et al., 1973; Jarvinen and Tyo, 1978).

There have been differing views on the relative importance of each pathway particularly regarding the organic contaminants. These opinions have been based on laboratory studies to a large extent, which have unequivocally established that many substances can be accumulated from food and water; however, the application of these observations to the natural environment may not always be entirely accurate because exposure levels, particularly for waterborne substances, often greatly exceeds environmental concentrations. For example, the uptake of DDT and HCB from food and water has been demonstrated in the laboratory (Grzenda et al., 1970; Gakstatter and Weiss, 1967; Niimi and Cho, 1980; Oliver and Niimi, 1983). An examination of the kinetics of these and related substances such as PCBs in the Great Lakes environment in carnivorous species that occupy the higher trophic levels strongly suggests that uptake from food is substantially more important than uptake from water because environmental concentrations in food are in the µg/kg to mg/kg range, whereas levels in the water are measured in ng/liter or less (Thomann, 1981; Niimi and Cho, 1981). This observation does not diminish the importance of water as a pathway for these substances, but merely indicates that under these conditions one pathway becomes less important than the other. In contrast, PCP in certain localized areas of the Great Lakes can approach µg/liter and uptake from water becomes an important factor (Niimi and McFadden, 1982).

The relative importance of water and food for the uptake of elements further illustrates the difficulties in establishing the principal mode which is well defined for some but not for others. It should be noted that water quality criteria have been established for many metals by exposing fish to their dissolved salts to determine lethal concentrations. It can be inferred from this response that uptake from water is an important pathway for many metals. Corresponding studies that examined the importance of both pathways indicate water is the most important pathway for elements such as cadmium and lead (Williams and Giesy, 1978; Hodson et al., 1978). Elements such as calcium, manganese, and zinc can be accumulated by both pathways (Ophel and Judd, 1975; Miller et al., 1980; Hoss and Baptist, 1971; Merlini et al., 1975; Renfro et al., 1975). Mercury may be accumulated from food to a greater extent than from water (Jernelov and Lann, 1971; Lock, 1975; Phillips and Buhler, 1978). Studies on cesium indicate food is the most important pathway (King, 1964; Hewitt and Jefferies, 1976). Undoubtedly some of these observations will be modified because of the presence of other elements in the environment. The calcium content, or hardness of water, has been shown to have a strong influence on the uptake of lead, zinc, mercury, and strontium from food and water (Varanasi and Gmur, 1978; Rodgers and Beamish, 1981; Ophel and Judd, 1975). Thus, the mode of uptake should be viewed under conditions that approximate the natural environment. The primary pathway will not only influence the rate of uptake but may also affect the rate of elimination.

3.5.   Elimination (Half-life)

3.5.1.   Definition

The half-life ($T_{1/2}$) of a substance is described as the time required for the amount of a substance in a medium to be reduced to one-half of its former level. More specifically, half-life is defined as ''the time required for one-half of a given material to undergo chemical reactions,'' from a chemical perspective; or, ''the average time interval required for one-half of any quantity of identical radioactive atoms to undergo radioactive decay,'' from a radiological perspective; or, ''the time required by a body to eliminate half the amount of an administered substance through normal channels of elimination,'' from a biological perspective (Daniel, 1978). Biological half-life is also defined as ''the time required to reduce the concentration of a chemical by one-half in a designated medium or organism such as soil, water, and fish'' (ASTM, 1978).

The two definitions of biological half-life provide the opportunity for differing estimates of $T_{1/2}$ to be reported for the same substance. The former definition is concerned with the time required to eliminate one-half of the amount of the substance administered, whereas the latter is concerned with the time required for the concentration in an organism to be reduced by one-half. An apparent discrepancy between the definitions would not be a factor for inanimate media such as water and sediment, but could become an important factor in fish and other organisms whose weight changes during the observation period. The former definition of biological half-life monitors *quantity* which is "a positive or negative real number," or absolute amount, whereas the latter monitors *concentrations* which is "the mass, volume, or number of moles of solute present in proportion to the amount of solvent or total solution," or relative amount (Daniel, 1978). The quantity of a substance can be expressed as μg per fish, while its concentration may be expressed as μg/kg or parts per billion.

There have been several terms used in conjunction with half-life that distinguish absolute $T_{1/2}$ from relative values. Body burden, which is "the amount of radioactive material present in the body of a human or animal" (Daniel, 1978) or its equivalent for other substances, have been used to describe the quantity of substance in fish (Hakonson et al., 1975; Hansen et al., 1976). Whole body elimination or retention has also been used to imply the quantitative elimination of a substance (Sharpe et al., 1977; Guiney et al., 1979). These terms generally suggest a $T_{1/2}$ that is based on quantitative changes; however, there are no comparable terms commonly used that would specifically imply relative estimates.

3.5.2. *Estimation*

Biological half-life is determined by exposing fish to a substance, usually through water or food uptake, then systematically monitoring the levels to estimate the time required for the initial level to be reduced by one-half. The physical and chemical properties of the substance and the biochemical composition of the fish are important factors which can influence this duration. $T_{1/2}$ varies from less than 2 hr for carbon tetrachloride (CCl_4) to no apparent elimination of PCB in fishes (Statham et al., 1978; Lieb et al., 1974).

Half-life can be estimated using the relationship:

$$k = \frac{2.303}{t} \log \frac{C_0}{C}$$

and

$$T_{1/2} = \frac{-\ln(1/2)}{k} = \frac{-0.693}{k}$$

where C_0 is the initial amount or concentration, C the final amount or concentration at time t, and k is the specific rate constant.

The method of estimation and chemical analysis could also be a factor in determining if the $T_{1/2}$ reported is determined on an absolute or relative basis. Most analytical methods require a subsample of the fish. Estimates derived from this procedure could be based on relative levels if the fish changes in weight during the study. If there is no weight change, the $T_{1/2}$ based on relative and absolute levels would be the same. Absolute levels are derived by multiplying the concentrations by fish weight. Studies where measurements are made on whole fish provide estimates of absolute levels. This can be performed on small fish where the entire fish is sacrificed and analyzed, and the quantity of substance determined, or it may be derived from nondestructive studies such as the use of a gamma-emitting radionuclide substance that would allow a live fish to be counted then returned to its holding facility. Whole body counts are usually expressed as disintegrations or counts per minute, hence any change in body weight over the study period would not influence the quantity of labelled substance present, although adjustment would be required for the decay of the radionuclide.

3.5.3. Growth Effect on $T_{1/2}$

There are differences in $T_{1/2}$ estimates derived from relative and absolute levels unless the substance tested has a short half-life, a short observation period, or the study is conducted on fish held at a maintenance feeding level. If the study is conducted over a period where the fish increases in weight, the difference between the $T_{1/2}$ estimated using relative concentrations and that from absolute levels would be directly related to the rate of growth.

The influence of growth can be demonstrated by examining the levels of a substance similar to highly chlorinated PCB that is not readily excreted by fish. If juvenile trout of 1 g, which attain a body burden of 2 μg per fish, were maintained in a PCB-free environment, the average body weight could increase to 2 g after 14 days under laboratory conditions. It could be concluded that PCB concentrations decreased from 2 μg/g to 1 μg/g over the 14-day period; however, it is not entirely accurate to conclude that the half-life for PCB is 14 days. While trout did show a decrease in relative PCB levels, the quantity of PCB remains at 2 μg and the conclusion that there was no apparent elimination would also be correct. Similarly, if fish were monitored after 56 days and again after 154 days, the average body weight could increase to 10 g and 100 g, and PCB concentrations to 0.2 and 0.02 μg/g, respectively. The estimated $T_{1/2}$ on a relative basis would be 17 and 24 days for the respective intervals. In retrospect, the quantity of 2 μg PCB per fish would be retained over the 154-day period to suggest no apparent elimination and the differing conclusion of whether PCB is retained or eliminated, and the estimated $T_{1/2}$ of 14–24 days could be attributed entirely to growth. Thus, unless the experimental protocol and method of computation is explicitly described, it is apparent that the same study can derive two estimates of $T_{1/2}$ for the same substance.

This interactive effect between $T_{1/2}$ and growth becomes more difficult to interpret when a substance with a half-life of several weeks or more is monitored in fish whose body weight increases several fold over the study period. A fish could increase its body weight from 100 to 1000 g over a 500-day period under laboratory or natural conditions (Fig. 1A). If the levels of a group of substances whose half-lives range from 10 days to no apparent elimination were monitored over a 500-day period, the response of the substances expressed according to their concentrations (Fig. 1B) would differ from those expressed on the basis of their body burdens (Fig. 1C). The growth factor would accelerate the decrease in concentrations by imposing a "growth dilution" effect through increasing biomass that would otherwise be due only to the elimination of the substances; therefore, the estimates of

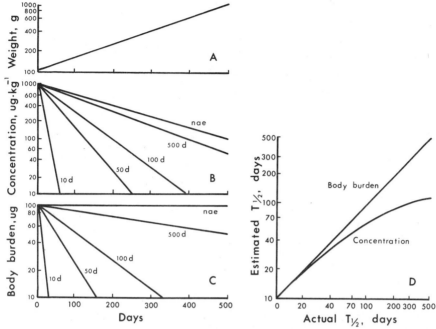

Figure 1. Effect of growth on the estimated half-life of a substance. *A*, the growth rate of a fish from 100 to 1000 g over a 500-day period. The 100-g fish has an initial concentration of 100 μg body burden, or 1000 μg/kg, and there is no additional uptake by the fish over the 500-day period. The interactive effect of growth and elimination on changes in tissue concentrations is demonstrated in *B*, where levels are expressed as μg/kg, but not in *C*, where levels are μg per fish, when $T_{1/2}$ is 10, 50, 100, 500 days, and no apparent elimination (nae) over the 500-day period. *D*, the difference between actual and estimated $T_{1/2}$ attributable to growth, where $T_{1/2}$ is estimated from body burden, and from tissue concentrations based on the growth rate of fish from *A*.

$T_{1/2}$ based on qualitative changes would be lower than estimates that were based on quantitative changes (Fig. 1*D*).

Estimates of $T_{1/2}$ that are based on concentrations may be recalculated to express $T_{1/2}$ on a body burden basis provided an estimate of the growth rate is available (Niimi and Cho, 1981). This relationship is described as

$$T_{1/2} = \frac{-\ln(1/2)}{k + \lambda}$$

where k is the rate constant for the decrease in concentration, and λ the rate constant of growth during the observation period.

3.5.4. First- and Second-Order Kinetics

Most dynamic models of contaminants generally assume a single compartment or first-order kinetic relationship (Hakonson et al., 1975; Norstrom et

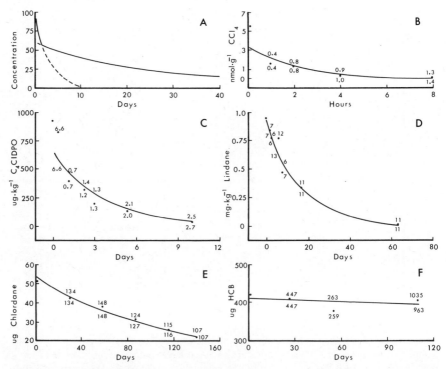

Figure 2. Relationship between sample frequency and number of sample intervals on the estimated half-life of a substance. (A) Hypothetical first- and second-order kinetics curves with $T_{1/2}$ of 3 and 15 days respectively. (B)–(F) Clearance curves of substances reported for fish whose estimated relative or absolute $T_{1/2}$ range from 1.4 hr to no apparent elimination. These include the elimination by rainbow trout of carbon tetrachloride (B) reported by Statham et al. (1978), *sec*-butyl-4-chlorodiphenyl oxide (C) by Blanchard et al. (1977), lindane (D) by Tooby and Durbin (1975), and hexachlorobenzene (F) by Niimi and Cho (1981). The elimination of chlordane by chiclids (E) was reported by Feroz and Khan (1979). Each curvilinear relationship was derived from the equation $Y = A_e BX$. Half-life was estimated as $T_{1/2} = [-\ln(1/2)]/k$, where k represents the specific rate constant B. All sample intervals were used to calculate the curvilinear relationship shown in each figure. The value at each data point below the regression line represents $T_{1/2}$ calculated from the cumulative sampling intervals up to that point. The value above the regression line represents the $T_{1/2}$ calculated only from the initial value and the level at the sample interval. F shows a relationship whose slope is not significantly different from zero ($P \geq 0.05$).

al., 1976; Carlsson, 1978). There is limited evidence to suggest a biphasic response which includes a short first-order elimination that is followed by a longer second-order release. A $T_{1/2}$ of 4.2 hr for PCP was observed in killifish which was followed by a $T_{1/2}$ of 4.7 days (Trujillo et al., 1982). This response was also observed for substances with longer half-lives. A $T_{1/2}$ of 39 days for mercury in sunfish was followed by a $T_{1/2}$ of 130 days (Burrows and Krenkel, 1973), similarly, a $T_{1/2}$ of 1.6 days preceded a second-order $T_{1/2}$ of 2.7 yr for PCB in trout (Guiney et al., 1977).

A reexamination of the elimination rates of substances reported whose $T_{1/2}$ varies from 1 hr to no apparent elimination in fish indicates only one elimination phase is evident which can be described by an exponential decline (Fig. 2). It is interesting to note that the $T_{1/2}$ calculated using the cumulative data over the observation period is in excellent agreement with the $T_{1/2}$ calculated using only the initial level and one other observation interval for most substances.

3.5.5.   Reported Values of $T_{1/2}$

Most values of $T_{1/2}$ are derived from observations based on whole fish or muscle (edible) portions. Studies on whole fish deal primarily with the kinetics of the substance in the organism or aquatic ecosystem, whereas studies on muscle samples are more concerned with the impact of the substance on human health. Most health warnings, guidelines, and regulations on specific substances are based on the concentration of the substance in the edible portion of the fish product. The present body of information in toxicology, particularly for organic contaminants, is not sufficiently advanced to extrapolate data derived from muscle samples to the kinetics and fate of a substance in the natural environment, or to provide the basis for extrapolating residue levels of potentially harmful substances from whole fish measurements to edible portions that would be used for human consumption. In view of the limited information that is presently available on the behavior of many substances, measurements on whole fish or muscle samples whose $T_{1/2}$ may be reported as relative or absolute values would serve as a useful indicator in future studies on the substance.

A compilation of the $T_{1/2}$ for the more relevant environmental organic and inorganic substances that have been reported for fishes is presented in Table 1. The criteria for data selection were: (1) fish were exposed to the substance through water or food to simulate natural conditions; (2) the observation period was long enough to span several half-lives for the short-lived substances, or were several months in duration for the more persistent substances; and (3) supporting information such as body weight and experimental temperature was reported where possible. The values listed include $T_{1/2}$ estimated from whole fish and muscle samples that were reported as relative or absolute values. Some relative estimates were recalculated where the necessary information was reported to provide comparative values on an absolute basis. Nearly all of the $T_{1/2}$ reported were presumed to have been estimated from a first-order elimination relationship unless noted otherwise.

3.5.6.   Related Effects

The mode of uptake, body weight, and temperature could also influence elimination rates although their roles are based on limited evidence. Laboratory studies suggest clearance rates of chlorinated and brominated hydrocarbons by salmon are longer when accumulated from food rather than from water (Zitko, 1977). Other studies suggest that the half-life of methylmercury

Table 1. Elimination Rates of Substances by Fish Taken Up from Food or Water under Different Conditions

Substance	Species	Mode of Uptake	Temperature (°C)	Initial Weight (g)	Study Period (days) Expose	Study Period (days) Observe	Muscle Conc.	Muscle Body Burden	Whole Fish Conc.	Whole Fish Body Burden	Comments	Source
Manganese	Sunfish	Water	10–30	2–5	7	56				4–18	Temp. dependent, biphasic	Miller et al., 1980
Selenium	Plaice	Water	10	30	267	91				166		Pentreath, 1973
	Plaice	Food	10	30	1	35				40		Pentreath, 1976a
	Trout	Water	15	3–6	28	28				29		Gissel-Nielsen and Gissel-Nielsen, 1978
	Carp	Water	24	3–26	49	35			28			Sato et al., 1980
	Eel	Food	INR[b]	INR	INR	21–42				27		Gissel-Nielsen and Gissel-Nielsen, 1973
Potassium	Pike	—	—	—	—	—				200	Natural fish, $T_{1/2}$ temperature and weight dependent	Carlsson, 1978
Zinc	Gambusia	Water	16–21	0.2	43	119				2,14,235	3 phases	Willis and Jones, 1977
	Pinfish	Water	12	INR	4	21				230[c]	Unrestrained	Hoss et al., 1978
	Plaice	Water	10	30	267	91				313		Pentreath, 1973
	Plaice	Food	10	30	1	35				52–196		Pentreath, 1976a
	Flounder	—	15	1	—	340				56–162	Natural fish	Renfro and Osterberg, 1969
Cesium	Trout	—	—	—	—	—	100–850					Nakatani, 1966
	Trout	—	—	—	—	—				134	Natural fish, $T_{1/2}$ varies seasonally	Hakonson et al., 1975
	Pike	—	8–10	500	—	—				475	Natural fish, $T_{1/2}$ and weight dependent	Carlsson, 1978
	Carp	—	12.5	—	—	120				174	Natural fish	Kevern, 1966
	Carp	—	20	—	—	72				98	Natural fish	Kevern, 1966

Compound	Species	Route								Notes	Reference
Lead	Trout	Water	15	20	10	7	1[c]		5–11	As Me_4Pb	Wong et al., 1981
	Goldfish	Water	19	INR	27	27					Merlini and Pozzi, 1977
Cadmium	*Fundulus*	Water	19	1	21	180					Eisler, 1974
	Cunner	Water	23	62	4	30	60[c]		2–4		Greig et al., 1974
	Plaice	Food	10	50	1	41			98–204		Pentreath, 1977
	Ray	Food	10	40	1	41			76–147		Pentreath, 1977
Mercury	Sunfish	Water	5–9	14–66	4	95			39–130	As $HgCl_2$, biphasic $T_{1/2}$	Burrows and Krenkel, 1973
	Plaice	Water	10	30	85	55–70	123[c]	693[c]		As CH_3HgCl	Pentreath, 1976b
	Trout	Food	16–18	177–595	360	180	217[c]	NAE[c,d]	275	Diff. conc.; As CH_3H_5Hg	Hartman, 1978
	Plaice	Food	10	50–70	1	38	730[c]	NAE[c]	163	As CH_3HgCl	Pentreath, 1976c
	Ray	Food	10	35–45	1	40			323	As CH_3HgCl	Pentreath, 1976d
	Plaice	Food	10	50–70	1	36			33	As $HgCl_2$	Pentreath, 1976c
	Ray	Food	10	35–45	1	38			62	As $HgCl_2$	Pentreath, 1976d
	Pike		—	4–22 kg	—	365		730[c]		Natural fish	Lockhart et al., 1972
	Perch		—	100–200	—	820	760[c]	NAE[c]		Natural fish	Laarman et al., 1976
	Bass		—	150–400	—	820	670[c]	NAE[c]		Natural fish	Laarman et al., 1976
	Eel		—	—	—	140	35			Natural fish	Kikuchi et al., 1978
PCP	Trout	Water	15	9	1	1	0.3				Glickman et al., 1977
	Eel	Water	12	65–130	8	8	8[c]			Seawater	Holmberg et al., 1972
	Eel	Water	12	65–130	4	55	17[c]			Freshwater	Holmberg et al., 1972
	Goldfish	Water	18	40	1	1	1[c]				Kobayashi and Akitake, 1975
Lindane	Sunfish	Water	17–21	16–42	16	16	5[c]				Pruitt et al., 1977
	Killifish	Water	INR	INR	7	18					Trujillo et al., 1982
	Trout	Water	13	140	4	73	11[c]			$T_{1/2}$ biphasic	Tooby and Durbin, 1975
	Goldfish	Water	18	5	1	4	1[c]				Gakstatter and Weiss, 1967
	Sunfish	Water	18	7	1	2	1[c]				Gakstatter and Weiss, 1967

Table 1. Continued

Substance	Species	Mode of Uptake	Temperature (°C)	Initial Weight (g)	Study Period (days) Expose	Study Period (days) Observe	Muscle Conc.	Muscle Body Burden	Whole Fish Conc.	Whole Fish Body Burden	Comments	Source
Endrin	Catfish	Food	28	2	198	28			6[c]			Argyle et al., 1973
	Catfish	Water	28	2	55	13			7[c]			Argyle et al., 1973
	Catfish	Food	30	INR	147	44			12			Jackson, 1976
Dieldrin	Trout	Food	16	95	140	90			40			Macek et al., 1970
	Goldfish	Food	15	INR	32	63	20					Grzenda et al., 1972
	Catfish	Food	27	600	210	56			10			Argyle et al., 1975
	Goldfish	Water	18	5	1	32			6[c]			Gakstatter and Weiss, 1967
	Sunfish	Water	18	7	1	32			10[c]			Gakstatter and Weiss, 1967
Chlordane	Goldfish	Water	21	15–29	1	35			35			Ducat and Khan, 1979
	Cichlid	Water	26	300	3	140				119		Feroz and Khan, 1979
	Sucker	Food	11	24–398	5	37						Roberts et al., 1977
DDT	Goldfish	Water	23	5	1	32			47[c]	60[c]		Gakstatter and Weiss, 1967
	Goldfish	Food	15	INR	128	100	30		160			Grzenda et al., 1970
	Trout	Food	16	95	140	90			34	428	Three	Macek et al., 1970
	Menhaden	Food	20	Juve.	48	109			24	64	initial	Warlen et al., 1977
									28	137	concs.	

Half-life of Substance (days)[a]

Compound	Species	Route									Notes	Reference
HCB	Sunfish	Food	23	INR	3	14	8		61	224		Sanborn et al., 1977
	Trout	Food	15	250	28	110			117	770	Two concs.	Niimi and Cho, 1981
Kepone	Spot	Water	23	1	30	24			21[c]			Bahner et al., 1977
Mirex	Mosquito-fish	INR	INR	INR	15	200			130			Ivie et al., 1974
Tetrachloro-biphenyl	Salmon	Food	10	8	42	55			71[c]	145[c]		Zitko, 1980
	Trout	Food	INR	149	104	385				NAE		Skea et al., 1981
	Trout	Water	10	Egg	1	54				231	Egg and sac fry	Guiney et al., 1980
	Trout	Water	10	Fry	1	51				15		Guiney et al., 1980
	Trout	Water	11	10	5	28						Branson et al., 1975
	Trout	Water	11	125	2	140	23[c]		90[c]	2–970	$T_{1/2}$ biphasic	Guiney et al., 1977
	Trout	Water	11	175	2	365	26[c]	44[c]	99–106[c]	522–642	Male and female fish	Guiney et al., 1979
TCB	Goldfish	Water	23	4	13	116			46–69			Brugeman et al., 1981
Aroclor 1242	Salmon	Water	11–15	Juve.	1	16			9			Zitko, 1977
	Salmon	Food	11–15	Juve.	1	42			35			
Aroclor 1248	Catfish	Food	25	47	140	56		NAE				Hansen et al., 1976
	Minnow	Water	24		66	28			93[c]			DeFoe et al., 1978
Aroclor 1254	Spot	Water	INR	Juve.	56	84	46[c]	135[c]	41[c]			Hansen et al., 1971
	Trout	Food	12	10	112	224				NAE		Lieb et al., 1974

[a]The half-lives reported are the estimated values for muscle and whole fish based on relative and absolute levels.

[b]INR = information not reported in the study.

[c]These values were estimated from the information reported.

[d]NAE = no apparent elimination.

accumulated from water is longer than that obtained from food (Pentreath, 1976b and c), and the half-life of mercury obtained from food in the methylated form is much longer than that obtained as inorganic mercury (Pentreath, 1976c). Some studies have used fish that had accumulated mercury in the natural environment and were then moved to another water body or the laboratory to estimate the rate of elimination (Lockhart et al., 1972; Laarman et al., 1976). There is insufficient evidence to determine if estimates of $T_{1/2}$ derived from laboratory studies are comparable with those from the field studies.

Body weight is also a contributing factor. The few studies that have examined this relationship indicate $T_{1/2}$ increases as fish weight increases. This relationship has been demonstrated for mercury (Sharpe et al., 1977; Norstrom et al., 1976), cesium and potassium (Hakonson et al., 1975; Carlsson, 1978), and for copper in fish gills (Anderson and Spear, 1980).

The influence of temperature is not as well defined. Studies on cesium (Kevern, 1966), naphthalene (Varanasi et al., 1981), and mercury (Jarvenpaa et al., 1970; Ruohtula and Miettinen, 1975) suggest $T_{1/2}$ increases as temperature decreases. Other studies on mercury (Sharpe et al., 1977) and PCB (Edgren et al., 1979) indicate that $T_{1/2}$ is not influenced by temperature. A study on manganese reported that $T_{1/2}$ in sunfish was slower at 10°C than at 20–30°C for the first two days, but was faster thereafter (Miller et al., 1980).

The concentration of a substance can also influence clearance rate. Studies on DDT and mercury indicate $T_{1/2}$ was longer at the lower concentrations (Warlen et al., 1977; Hartman, 1978). In contrast, fish with higher levels of HCB demonstrated a longer $T_{1/2}$ (Niimi and Cho, 1981). These observations were based on substances whose estimated $T_{1/2}$ ranged from many months to no apparent elimination, hence these may not have been the most appropriate examples to examine for this effect. Perhaps the influence of concentration on $T_{1/2}$ would best be examined for substances with a much shorter $T_{1/2}$.

3.5.7. Spawning

Persistent substances can also be eliminated during spawning. This mode of clearance is not considered in contaminant dynamics models, but represents a significant pathway by which highly persistent lipophilic substances such as PCB and DDT can be eliminated. It is estimated that eggs of species like trout may contain 6% of the total body burden of many organic contaminants, while the eggs of other species like perch may contain 26% of the parental residues (Niimi, 1983). The percent of residues transferred from females to eggs varies among species and is influenced by the ratio of egg weight to body weight and the relative concentration of lipid in eggs. Whole body elimination of PCB in trout has been estimated to be 1.4–1.8 yr in prespawning fish, and 0.5 yr following the spawning season (Guiney et al., 1979).

4. GENERAL OBSERVATIONS

4.1. Contaminants Uptake

It has been well established that factors like temperature and body weight have significant influence on the metabolic requirements of fishes. Concomitantly, these same factors must also influence the uptake component of a contaminant dynamics model where food and water are the principle modes of uptake. It is not difficult to establish the major uptake pathway at low level contaminants concentrations through laboratory studies, but determining the rate of uptake could be a difficult task.

Estimates of efficiency of assimilation from food would be less difficult to derive than the efficiency of extraction from water. Studies on the growth and energetics of fishes were sufficiently advanced that a good relationship was established between the amount and nutritional composition of food energy ingested and that which was retained (Brett and Groves, 1979). Substances like mercury have been found to be associated with protein and others such as PCB have been correlated with lipid component (Bishop and Neary, 1975; Lieb et al., 1974). If efficiency of assimilation from food is closely associated with the absorption of protein and lipid across the intestinal membrane in carnivorous species, efficiencies may approach 95% in fish (Beamish, 1972). If efficiencies are dependent on the energy available to the fish for growth and metabolism, then values of 80% for carnivores and 40% for herbivores would be applicable (Brett and Groves, 1979). These nutrient and energy absorption efficiencies are relatively consistent over a range of feeding levels, body weights, and temperatures for a given species fed the same diet.

There is limited information to assess the assimilation efficiencies of some environmental contaminants by fish fed a protein-rich diet. These usually range from 70 to 90% of that ingested for substances such as mercury, PCB, and HCB, which have long half-lives (Table 2). Estimates for less persistent substances such as dieldrin and DDT range from 10 to 30%. In retrospect, it is suggested that these estimates are conservative because the values were based on observations over extended periods during which some of the ingested substances were excreted. This effect would be most pronounced for those substances with relatively short half-lives whose assimilation efficiencies were estimated from a long-term study.

There is some evidence to suggest that the absorption efficiency of mercury from food will decrease as feeding duration is increased (Lock, 1975; Rodgers and Beamish, 1982). Nevertheless, a good approximation of the amount of a substance obtained from food can be derived for fish where growth and feeding rates, where possible, are measured, residue levels in food are known, and a reliable assimilation efficiency is available.

The efficiency of extraction of a substance from water is difficult to esti-

Table 2. Estimated Extraction Efficiency of Environmental Contaminants from Water and Assimilation Efficiency from Food Reported for Fish

Substance	Species	Days Exposed	Food	Mode of Uptake (%)		Source
				Water	Food	
Mercury	Trout	346		20 (mm)[a] / 0.2 (im)[b]		Hamelink et al., 1977
	Trout	1		8 (mm)		Rodgers and Beamish, 1981
	Shiner	1		17 (mm)		de Freitas and Hart, 1975
	Trout	24	Prepared	10 (mm)	70 (mm)	Phillips and Buhler, 1978
	Trout	269	Prepared		70 (mm)	Matida et al., 1971
	Trout	84	Prepared		70–80 (mm)	Rodgers and Beamish, 1982
		7	Daphnia		38–71 (mm)	Lock, 1975
	Goldfish	1	Prepared		70–90 (mm)	Sharpe et al., 1977
	Several	—	Fish		71–92 (mm)	de Freitas et al., 1977
	Yellowtail	—	Fish		67 (mm)	Suzuki and Hatanaka, 1975
	Pike	42	Fish		6–31 (mm)	Phillips and Gregory, 1979
Endrin	Trout	5		47–80		McKim, 1981
PCB	Goldfish	23	Prepared	>40	48–60	Bruggeman et al., 1981
	Trout	224	Prepared		68	Lieb et al., 1974
HCB	Trout	57	Prepared		80–90	Niimi and Cho, 1980
DDT	Trout	168	Prepared		20–24	Macek et al., 1970
	Menhaden	48	Prepared		17–27	Warlen et al., 1977
Dieldrin	Trout	168	Prepared		9–11	Macek et al., 1970

[a] Methylmercury (mm).
[b] Inorganic mercury (im).

mate because calculations are based on the volume of water respired and residue levels in fish. Although residue levels can be accurately measured, the volume of water respired is generally estimated from values of O_2 consumption and O_2 uptake efficiency. Relatively few studies have examined the efficiency of O_2 uptake from water. The results indicate that uptake efficiencies can range from 20 to 90%, and may vary according to respiratory requirements, volume of water respired, and swimming speed. Hence, the variability in O_2 consumption rates will be enhanced by the differences in O_2 uptake efficiencies to provide a gross estimate of the volume of water respired over a time interval.

There have been relatively few estimates on the efficiency of extraction of contaminants from water by fish. Estimates of 8–20% were reported for methylmercury, 40% for PCB, and 47–80% for endrin (Table 2). The adsorptive behavior of many organic contaminants may be a contributing factor influencing the estimated extraction efficiencies. It is probable that no differentiation could be made between the amount that is adsorbed on the gills from that absorbed from the water, particularly in studies where the observation period is relatively short.

4.2. Contaminants Elimination

The elimination of an environmental contaminant by fish may be viewed as a systematic clearance of a substance that cannot be entirely explained from the physiological and biochemical information that is available at the present time. Substances may be excreted or be retained by the fish as ingested, or be biotransformed by conjugation, hydrolysis, acetylation, oxidation, or dealkylation which would enhance elimination (Lech and Bend, 1980). The elimination rate of substances which have a short half-life of several hours could be correlated to the more obvious physiological processes such as metabolic rate. In contrast, the elimination rate of the more persistent substances with half-lives of many months or years may be correlated, but not necessarily attributable, to physiological processes that would be consistent within that time span.

Substances such as selenium, zinc, and potassium are considered "essential elements" and are always present in fish. Their concentrations are dependent on the homeostatic requirements of the fish, and can be eliminated through regulatory pathways as this need is exceeded. The kinetics of these substances should be examined to account for the internal needs as well as the response elicited once these bodily requirements have been exceeded. In contrast, substances such as cesium, lead, mercury, PCB, and HCB should be viewed as xenobiotics that ideally should not be present in fish. In the first case, a two-compartment model is required to describe their kinetics, whereas a single-compartment model may suffice for the latter.

The behavior of substances that are not readily eliminated, such as mercury and PCB, could be described from a mathematical perspective, but not necessarily supported by convincing biochemical and physiological evidence. Furthermore, the biochemical behavior of one substance can differ from another although their excretion rates may be similar. For example, it has been reported that mercury in muscle is eliminated at a slower rate than that from other tissues and organs (Burrows and Krenkel, 1973; Giblin and Massaro, 1973; Weisbart, 1973). This observation would be consistent with the hypothesis that most mercury in fish is likely to occur as a methylated product that is protein bound (Westoo, 1973; Matida et al., 1971; Suzuki et al., 1973). Analyses of mercury in fish tissues suggest levels in muscle are 60 times higher than those in stored lipid (Giblin and Massaro, 1973). Mercury-containing tissues that have been extracted by azeotropic distillation indicate 99% of the mercury is present in the proteinaceous material and 1% in the lipid and water fraction (Bishop and Neary, 1975).

These observations strongly suggest the elimination of mercury would more likely be associated with the dynamics of protein than of lipid. The biochemical behavior of mercury would be difficult to explain from a physiological view by relating elimination rates with biological rates such as respiratory metabolism because of the relatively long half-lives reported (Table 1). Perhaps one hypothesis that may be considered in the elimination of mercury is the correlation with protein synthesis. Limited estimates suggest protein synthesis (turnover) in tropical and subtropical species range from 4–20% per day in the liver to 0.3–1.3% in white epaxial muscle (Haschemeyer et al., 1979; Haschemeyer and Smith, 1979; Smith et al., 1980). Furthermore, the information on trout suggests most of the synthesis in epaxial muscle is deposited as growth rather than cellular turnover (Smith, 1981). Any reincorporation of the methylmercury present would further enhance mercury retention if protein synthesis does not preclude the complete elimination of mercury during cellular turnover. If the kinetics of mercury is associated with protein anabolism and catabolism to a large extent, the time factor of this biological process would be comparable to a half-life of many months, which would be in good agreement with the mathematical description of mercury elimination which indicates a uniform, long-term clearance process.

The behavior of a substance like PCB may not be physiologically comparable to that of mercury. Studies on its distribution in different tissues and organs in fish indicate concentrations in adipose is 18–50 times higher than that in muscle (Lieb et al., 1974; Gruger et al., 1975; Hansen et al., 1976; Guiney et al., 1977). This ratio would undoubtedly increase significantly if tissue samples were examined using a nonsolvent extraction method to first separate the lipid from muscle before residue analysis. Comparison of PCB levels in fish tissue and extractable fat indicate a $180 \times$ difference (Olsson and Jensen, 1975). This suggests that the behavior of PCB is more likely related to the dynamics of lipids than to protein. Some studies have examined the kinetics of organic contaminants such as PCB and related substances to lipid dynamics. A good correlation was demonstrated between the kinetics of chlordane and lipid levels in suckers (Roberts et al., 1977). It has been reported that triglycerides could influence the distribution of DDT in cod (Mitchell et al., 1977). Limited information also suggests that levels of PCB vary seasonally in fish (Olsson et al., 1978). These observations would be consistent with changes in quantity and quality of lipids in fish that are influenced by diet, temperature, feeding level, and season (Lovern, 1938; Brett et al., 1969; Love, 1970).

Estimates of half-life for substances such as PCB and DDT are even more difficult because they are composed of a mixture of related products. PCB analyses of trout captured from the natural environment indicated some fish contained a higher proportion of the more highly chlorinated isomers (Wszolek et al., 1979). Similarly, kinetic studies on chlorinated paraffins indicated the shorter-chain compounds were oxidized more readily than those with longer chains (Madeley and Birtley, 1980).

5. CONCLUSIONS

From a physiological perspective, it is apparent that there is a large body of information on the growth and energetics of fishes that could be applied to derive a better understanding of the kinetics of environmental contaminants in fish. Estimates of food consumption and respiration can be derived for many species, and extrapolated for others, under most environmental conditions. A reliable estimate of the assimilation efficiency of a substance from food can be made from the amount of food consumed and the percentage of residue retained with a reasonable degree of accuracy. Uptake from water would be more difficult to estimate. Gill performance studies have indicated that there is a range of O_2 uptake efficiencies from water. When the projected respiration rates are multiplied by these uptake efficiencies to estimate the volume of water respired, an even greater variation in efficiencies of contaminants extraction from water can be anticipated. The importance of water as a pathway for accumulation has been well established, but the rate of uptake under conditions that approximate the natural environment may not be as well defined as that derived from food.

The physiological and biochemical response of fish to environmental conditions strongly suggests that the dynamic models of contaminants should view the elimination component as a response distinct from the uptake phase. The evidence that is available suggests that the uptake component would be related to the energetic requirements of the fish. The contributions of food and water toward the uptake of a substance would depend on the environmental concentrations of the substance and the trophic position of the fish. Good correlations have been demonstrated between the uptake of waterborne DDT and mercury and respiration rates (Murphy and Murphy, 1971; Rodgers and Beamish, 1981). The high absorption efficiencies of contaminants from food would indicate this can be an important pathway in ecosystems where the food organisms contain high residue levels. It is also evident that there are a wide range of elimination rates for different substances and that which is ingested may not necessarily be retained for prolonged periods. Temperature and body weight has been shown to influence the half-life of some substances, but not others. Where temperature is an important factor, it is highly probable that the substance would be susceptible to biochemical degradation and have a relatively short half-life. The metabolic rate can be an important factor in the elimination of these substances. For example, fish exposed to naphthalene at 4°C retained higher levels of the parent compound than those held at 12°C (Varanasi et al., 1981). Concentrations of the total metabolites were comparable for the two groups, which would suggest that fish at the higher temperature hydrolyzed the substance at a faster rate. The half-life for naphthalene is estimated to be less than 24 hr (Melancon and Lech, 1978). Limited evidence indicates that the metabolic rate would not significantly influence the elimination rate of substances with long half-lives. The example of mercury has been discussed. Studies on zinc, DDT, and PCB, whose half-lives are in excess of 100 days, indicate no relationship between excretion rates and metabolic rates and temperatures (Hoss et al., 1978; Edgren et al., 1979).

A review of the literature indicates that the elimination rate of contaminants by fish has not been as well studied as have uptake rates. This can be attributed to factors associated with their measurements. Uptake studies expose fish with little or no residues initially, then monitor residue accumulation with time. The duration of exposure can range from several hours to several months, but in many cases the observation period is shorter than related studies on elimination rates. Estimates of elimination rates are derived by exposing fish to a substance until a desired concentration is attained. A single, multiple, or continuous exposure is necessary which requires one or more days. This can result in variations in residue concentrations among individuals at the start of the study which will increase as the observation period progresses. Lengthy sampling intervals may be required to ensure that the decline in levels is sufficient to derive a reliable estimate of $T_{1/2}$.

Information on the biochemical effects of a substance can be used to explain its effects on fish. This would include the impact on target organs and mode of action, which will be influenced by the duration and level of exposure. Information on the toxicity of metals indicates the target organ of fish exposed to lethal concentrations will differ from that exposed to chronic concentrations (Phillips and Russo, 1978). The gill assumes an important role in acute toxicity studies of metals, but organs such as the kidney and liver can become more susceptible at chronic exposure levels. This factor becomes an important issue in studies which examine the synergistic and antagonistic effects of metal mixtures.

The mode of action elicited by a substance may explain some of the responses observed in fish. Pentachlorophenol is an environmental contaminant that is readily metabolized by fish (Kobayashi and Akitake, 1975; Glickman et al., 1977). It acts primarily by uncoupling oxidative phosphorylation, which would require an animal to increase its metabolic expenditure to maintain its adenosine triphosphate (ATP) requirements (Weinbach, 1957). The observed deleterious effects of PCP on fish would be consistent with its mode of action. Fish treated with PCP showed increased O_2 consumption and fatty acid catabolism, and decreased growth rates (Holmberg and Saunders, 1979; Hanes et al., 1968; Webb and Brett, 1973; Hodson and Blunt, 1981).

The detoxification mechanisms of fish may explain some responses that do not appear consistent with those reported for other substances. It has been observed that the insecticide permethrin was more toxic to small fish at low temperatures than larger fish at higher temperatures (Kumaraguru and Beamish, 1981). This may be due to the higher rate of uptake by small fish relative to larger fish. Permethrin has been shown to be readily metabolized by hydrolysis and oxidation by microsomal enzymes (Glickman et al., 1979). The higher tolerance by larger fish can be explained by the lower relative rate of uptake and a greater production of liver microsomal enzymes to facilitate metabolism.

The extrapolation of laboratory observations to predict the biological effects and kinetics of contaminants in the natural environment should be viewed in accordance to the life history of the species. Most studies observed that adult fish are less susceptible to toxicants than young fish, although the egg stage tends to be more resistant than newly hatched fish (Olson and Marking, 1973; Schimmel et al., 1974; Niimi and LaHam, 1975). Young and juvenile fish have commonly been used for toxicological studies which provides information on the most sensitive life stage. But this practice may have been maintained because of the convenience of working with a large number of fish requiring fewer facilities. The results extrapolated from such studies using small fish may differ from those expected for large fish in the natural environment (Eberhardt, 1975).

Fish used in laboratory studies generally have not been exposed to the toxicant before the study period, while those in the natural environment may have been subjected to prolonged exposure and become acclimated. Recent studies demonstrated that the toxic response of fish exposed to a substance will be greater than in fish that were preexposed (Dixon and Sprague, 1981a and b). A similar response at the sublethal level indicated no difference in growth rates of fish exposed to copper after an initial decrease (Lett et al., 1976).

A further examination of the biology of a species will indicate that the contaminant kinetics for one species may not be applicable to other species even though they may occupy similar trophic levels (Fig. 3). The food chain relationship for related species such as salmon and trout can differ in the same water body (Niimi and Cho, 1981). Furthermore, trout will spawn for

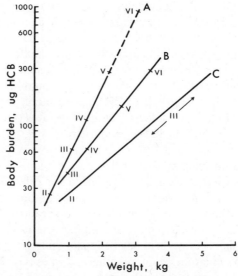

Figure 3. Relationship between body burden of hexachlorobenzene and body weight in lake trout (*A*), rainbow trout (*B*), and coho salmon (*C*) collected from Lake Ontario. The roman numerals represent fish age based on the mean weight at each age-class. (From Niimi and Cho, 1981.)

several years whereas most salmon cannot. The influence of spawning on contaminant dynamics has not received full attention, primarily because most laboratory studies are conducted on immature fish. The deposition of eggs can reduce the half-life of the more persistent substances (Guiney et al., 1979). The relationship between residue levels in fish and in eggs influences the kinetics of a substance. The relative concentration of a substance will increase in post-spawned fish if the residue levels in eggs is lower than that in the body. In contrast, levels in fish will decrease for species whose eggs contain higher residue levels than the body (Niimi, 1983).

Overall, a dynamic model of contaminants is only as accurate as the information available on the physiology, biochemistry, and life history of a species. There is a large body of information on these aspects which can be effectively applied to most species. It is suggested that substances with relatively long half-lives present the greatest challenge in developing a kinetics model that will be compatible with the existence of a species in its natural environment.

REFERENCES

Adelman, I. R., Smith, L. L., and Siesennop, G. D. (1976). Effect of size or age of goldfish and fathead minnows on use of pentachlorophenol as a reference toxicant. *Water Res* **10**, 685–687.

American Public Health Association (1971). *Standard methods for the examination of water and wastewater*. American Public Health Association, Washington, D.C.

American Society for Testing and Materials. (1978). Estimating the hazard of chemical substances to aquatic life. ASTM STP 657.

Anderson, P. D. and Spear, P. A. (1980). Copper pharmacokinetics in fish gills—I. Kinetics in pumpkinseed sunfish, *Lepomis gibbosus*, of different body sizes. *Water Res.* **14**, 1101–1105.

Anderson, P. D. and Weber, L. J. (1975). Toxic response as a quantitative function of body size. *Toxicol. Appl. Pharmacol* **33**, 471–483.

Argyle, R. L., Williams, G. C., and Daniel, C. B. (1975). Dieldrin in the diet of channel catfish. (*Ictalurus punctatus*): uptake and effect on growth. *J. Fish. Res. Board Can.* **32**, 2197–2204.

Argyle, R. L., Williams, G. C., and Dupree, H. K. (1973). Endrin uptake and release by fingering channel catfish (*Ictalurus punctatus*). *J. Fish. Res. Board Can.* **30**, 1743–1744.

Bahner, L. H., Wilson, A. J., Shepard, J. M., Patrick, J. M., Goodman, L. R., and Walsh, G. E. (1977). Kepone bioconcentration accumulation, loss, and transfer through estuarine food chains. *Chesapeake Sci.* **18**, 299–308.

Beamish, F. W. H. (1964a). Respiration of fishes with special emphasis on standard oxygen consumption. II. Influence of weight and temperature on respiration of several species. *Can. J. Zool.* **42**, 177–188.

Beamish, F. W. H. (1964b). Influence of starvation on standard and routine oxygen consumption. *Trans. Am. Fish. Soc.* **93**, 103–107.

Beamish, F. W. H. (1972). Ration size and digestion in largemouth bass, *Micropterus salmoides* Lacepede. *Can. J. Zool.* **50**, 153–164.

Beamish, F. W. H. (1974). Apparent specific dynamic action of largemouth bass, *Micropterus salmoides*. *J. Fish. Res. Board Can.* **31**, 1763–1769.

Beamish, F. W. H. and Dickie, L. M. (1967). Metabolism and biological production in fish. In: S. D. Gerking, Ed., *The biological basis of freshwater fish production*. Blackwell Scientific Publications, Oxford, pp. 215–242.

Beamish, F. W. H. and Mookherjii, P. S. (1964). Respiration of fishes with special emphasis on standard oxygen consumption. I. Influence of weight and temperature on respiration of goldfish, *Carassius auratas* L. *Can. J. Zool.* **42**, 161–175.

Beamish, F. W. H., Niimi, A. J., and Lett, P. F. K. P. (1975). Bioenergetics of teleost fishes: environmental influences. In: L. Bolis, H. P. Maddrell, and K. Schmidt-Nielson, Eds., *Comparative physiology—functional aspects of structural materials*. North-Holland Publishing Company, Amsterdam, pp. 187–209.

Bengtsson, B. E. (1977). Accumulation of cadmium in some aquatic animals from the Baltic Sea. *Ambio* **5**, 69–73.

Bishop, J. N. and Neary, B. P. (1975). The distribution of mercury in the tissues of freshwater fish. In: *Biological implications of metals in the environment*. Hanford Life Science Symposium, Richland, Wash. ERDA Symp. Series 42, CONF-750929, pp. 452–464.

Blanchard, F. A., Takahashi, I. T., Alexander, H. C., and Bartlett, E. A. (1977). Uptake, clearance, and bioconcentration of ^{14}C-*sec*-butyl-4-chlorodiphenyl oxide in rainbow trout. In: F. L. Mayer and J. L. Hamelink, Eds., *Aquatic toxicology and hazard evaluation*. ASTM STP 634. American Society for Testing and Materials, Philadelphia, Pennsylvania, pp. 162–177.

Blazka, P., Volf, M., and Cepela, M. (1960). A new type of respirometer for the determination of the metabolism of fish in an active state. *Physiol. Bohemoslov* **9**, 553–558.

Booth, J. H. (1978). The distribution of blood flow in the gills of fish: application of a new technique to rainbow trout (*Salmo gairdneri*). *J. Exp. Biol.* **73**, 119–129.

Boudou, A., Ribeyre, F., DeLarche, A., and Marty, R. (1980). Bioaccumulation et bioamplification des derives du mercure par un consommateur de troisieme ordre: *Salmo gairdneri*—incidences du faceur temperature. *Water Res.* **14**, 61–65.

Branson, D. R., Blau, G. E., Alexander, H. C., and Neely, W. B. (1975). Bioconcentration of 2,2',4,4'-tetrachlorobiphenyl in rainbow trout as measured by an accelerated test. *Trans. Am. Fish. Soc.* **104**, 785–792.

Brett, J. R. (1964). The respiratory metabolism and swimming performance of young sockeye salmon. *J. Fish. Res. Board Can.* **21**, 1183–1226.

Brett, J. R. (1971). Satiation time, appetite, and maximum food intake of sockeye salmon (*Oncorhynchus nerka*). *J. Fish. Res. Board Can.* **28**, 409–415.

Brett, J. R. (1979). Environmental factors and growth. In: W. S. Hoar, D. J. Randall, and J. R. Brett, Eds., *Fish physiology*, Vol. 8. Academic Press, New York, pp. 599–675.

Brett, J. R. and Groves, T. D. D. (1979). Physiological energetics. In W. S. Hoar, D. J. Randall, and J. R. Brett, Eds., *Fish physiology*, Vol. 8. Academic Press, New York, pp. 279–352.

Brett, J. R., Shelbourn, J. E., and Shoop, C. T. (1969). Growth rate and body composition of fingerling sockeye salmon, *Oncorhynchus nerka*, in relation to temperature and ration size. *J. Fish. Res. Board Can.* **26**, 2363–2394.

Brody, S. (1964). Bioenergetics and growth. Hafner Publishing Company, New York.

Brown, C. E. and Muir, B. S. (1970). Analysis of ram ventilation of fish gills with application to skipjack tuna (*Katsuwonus pelamis*). *J. Fish. Res. Board Can.* **27**, 1637–1652.

Brown, V. M., Jordan, D. H. M., and Tiller, B. A. (1967). The effect of temperature on the acute toxicity of phenol to rainbow trout in hard water. *Water Res.* **1**, 587–594.

Bruggeman, W. A., Martron, L. B. J. M., Kooiman, D., and Hutzinger, O. (1981). Accumulation and elimination kinetics of di-, tri- and tetra chlorobiphenyls by goldfish after dietary and aqueous exposure. *Chemosphere* **8**, 811–832.

Burrows, W. D. and Krenkel, P. A. (1973). Studies on uptake and loss of methylmercury-203 by bluegills (*Lepomis macrochirus* Raf.). *Environ. Sci. Technol.* **7**, 1127–1130.

Cairns, J., Heath, A. G., and Parker, B. C. (1975). The effects of temperature upon the toxicity of chemicals to aquatic organisms. *Hydrobiologia* **47**, 135–171.

Carlsson, S. (1978). A model for the turnover of ^{137}Cs and potassium in pike (*Esox lucius*). *Health Phys.* **35**, 549–554.

Cember, H., Curtis, E. H., and Blaylock, B. G. (1978). Mercury bioconcentration in fish: temperature and concentration effects. *Environ. Pollut.* **17**, 311–319.

Chakoumakos, C., Russo, R. C., and Thurston, R. V. (1979). Toxicity of copper to cutthroat trout (*Salmo clarki*) under different conditions of alkalinity, pH, and hardness. *Environ. Sci. Technol.* **13**, 213–219.

Crandall, C. A. and Goodnight, D. J. (1959). The effect of various factors on the toxicity of sodium pentachlorophenate to fish. *Limnol. Oceanogr.* **4**, 53–56.

Daniel, N., Ed. (1978). *McGraw-Hill dictionary of scientific and technical terms*. McGraw-Hill, New York.

Davies, P. M. C. (1964). The energy relations of *Carassius auratus* L. I. Food input and energy extraction efficiency at two experimental temperatures. *Comp. Biochem. Physiol.* **12**, 67–79.

Davis, J. C. and Cameron, J. N. (1971). Water flow and gas exchange at the gills of rainbow trout, *Salmo gairdneri*. *J. Exp. Biol.* **54**, 1–18.

Davis, J. C. and Watters, K. (1970). Evaluation of opercular catheterization as a method for sampling water expired by fish. *J. Fish. Res. Board Can.* **27**, 1627–1635.

DeFoe, D. L., Veith, G. D., and Carlson, R. W. (1978). Effects of Aroclor 1248 and 1260 on the fathead minnow (*Pimephales promelas*). *J. Fish. Res. Board Can.* **35**, 997–1002.

de Freitas, A. S. W. and Hart, J. S. (1975). Effect of body weight on uptake of methyl mercury by fish. In: *Water quality parameters*, ASTM STP 573, pp. 356–363.

de Freitas, A. S. W., Gidney, M. A. J., McKinnon, A. E., and Norstrom, R. J. (1977). Factors affecting whole-body retention of methyl mercury in fish. In: H. Drucker and R. E. Wildung, Eds., *Biological implications of metals in the environment*. ERDA Symp. Ser. 42. CONF-750929, pp. 441–451.

Dixon, D. G. and Sprague, J. B. (1981a). Acclimation-induced changes in toxicity of arsenic and cyanide to rainbow trout, *Salmo gairdneri* Richardson, *J. Fish Biol.* **18**, 579–589.

Dixon, D. G. and Sprague, J. B. (1981b). Acclimation to copper by rainbow trout (*Salmo gairdneri*)—a modifying factor in toxicity. *Can. J. Fish. Aquat. Sci.* **38**, 880–888.

Ducat, D. A. and Khan, M. A. Q. (1979). Absorption and elimination of ^{14}C-*cis*-chlordane and ^{14}C-photo-*cis*-chlordane by goldfish *Carassius auratus*. *Arch. Environ. Contam. Toxicol.* **8**, 409–417.

Eberhardt, L. L. (1975). Some methodology for appraising contaminants in aquatic systems. *J. Fish. Res. Board Can.* **32**, 1852–1859.

Edgren, M., Olsson, M., and Renberg, L. (1979). Preliminary results on uptake and elimination at different temperatures of *p,p'*-DDT and two chlorobiphenyls in perch from brackish water. *Ambio* **8**, 270–272.

Eisler, R. (1974). Radiocadmium exchange with seawater by *Fundulus heteroclitus* (L.) (Pices: Cyprinodontidae). *J. Fish Biol.* **6**, 601–612.

Eisler, R., Rossoll, R. M., and Gaboury, G. A. (1979). *Fourth annotated bibliography on biological effects of metals in aquatic environments* (No. 2247–3132). U.S. EPA, EPA-600/3-79-084.

Ellis, M. M., Motley, H. L., Ellis, M. D., and Jones, R. O. (1937). Selenium poisoning in fishes. *Proc. Soc. Exp. Biol. Med.* **36**, 519–522.

Environmental Protection Agency. (1976). *Quality criteria for water*. U.S. EPA, Washington, D.C. EPA-440/9-76-023.

Fange, R. and Grove, D. (1979). Digestion. In: W. S. Hoar, D. J. Randall, and J. R. Brett, Eds., *Fish physiology*, Vol. 8. Academic Press, New York, pp. 161–260.

Feroz, M. and Khan, M. A. Q. (1979). Metabolism, tissue distribution, and elimination of *cis*-[^{14}C] Chlordane in the tropical freshwater fish *Cichlasoma* sp. *J. Agric. Food Chem.* **27**, 1190–1197.

Fry, F. E. J. (1947). *Effects of the environment on animal activity*. University of Toronto Studies, Biol. Ser. No. 55.

Fry, F. E. J. (1957). The aquatic respiration of fish. In: M. E. Brown, Ed., *The physiology of fishes*, Vol. 1, Academic Press, New York, pp. 1–63.

Fry, F. E. J. (1971). The effect of environmental factors on the physiology of fishes. In: W. S. Hoar and D. J. Randall, Eds., *Fish physiology*, Vol. 6. Academic Press, New York, pp. 1–98.

Gakstatter, J. H. and Weiss, C. M. (1967). The elimination of DDT-C^{14}, dieldrin-C^{14}, and lindane-C^{14} from fish following a single sublethal exposure in aquaria. *Trans. Am. Fish. Soc.* **96**, 301–307.

Giblin, F. J. and Massaro, E. J. (1973). Pharmacodynamics of methyl mercury in the rainbow trout (*Salmo gairdneri*): tissue uptake, distribution and excretion. *Toxicol. Appl. Pharmacol.* **24**, 81–91.

Gissel-Nielsen, G. and Gissel-Nielsen, M. (1973). Ecological effects of selenium application to field crops. *Ambio* **2**, 114–117.

Gissel-Nielsen, M. and Gissel-Nielsen, G. (1978). Sensitivity of trout to chronic and acute exposure to selenium. *Agric. Environ.* **4**, 85–91.

Glickman, A. H., Shono, T., Casida, J. E., and Lech, J. J. (1979). In vitro metabolism of permethrin isomers by carp and rainbow trout liver microsomes. *J. Agric. Food Chem.* **27**, 1038–1041.

Glickman, A. H., Statham, C. N., Wu, A., and Lech, J. J. (1977). Studies on the uptake, metabolism, and disposition of pentachlorophenol and pentachloroanisole in rainbow trout. *Toxicol. Appl. Pharmacol.* **41**, 649–658.

Gray, I. E. (1954). Comparative study of the gill area of marine fishes. *Biol. Bull.* **107**, 219–226.

Greig, R. A., Adams, A. L., and Nelson, B. A. (1974). Physiological response of the cunner, *Tautogolabrus adspersus*, to cadmium. II. Uptake of cadmium by organs and tissues. NOAA Tech. Rep. NMFS SSRF 681, pp. 5–9.

Gruger, E. H., Karrick, N. L., Davidson, A. I., and Hruby, T. (1975). Accumulation of 3,4,3′,4′-tetrachlorobiphenyl and 2,4,5,2′,4′,5′,- and 2,4,6,2′,4′,6′-hexachlorobiphenyl in juvenile coho salmon. *Environ. Sci. Technol.* **9**, 121–127.

Grzenda, A. R., Paris, D. F., and Taylor, W. J. (1970). The uptake, metabolism, and elimination of chlorinated residues by goldfish (*Carassius auratus*) fed a ^{14}C-DDT contaminated diet. *Trans. Am. Fish. Soc.* **99**, 385–396.

Grzenda, A. R., Taylor, W. J., and Paris, D. F. (1972). The elimination and turnover of ^{14}C-dieldrin by different goldfish tissues. *Trans. Am. Fish. Soc.* **101**, 686–690.

Guiney, P. D., Lech, J. J., and Peterson, R. E. (1980). Distribution and elimination of polychlorinated biphenyl during early life stages of rainbow trout (*Salmo gairdneri*). *Toxicol. App. Pharmacol.* **53**, 521–529.

Guiney, P. D., Melancon, M. J., Lech, J. J., and Peterson, R. E. (1979). Effects of egg and sperm maturation and spawning on the distribution of a polychlorinated biphenyl in rainbow trout (*Salmo gairdneri*). *Toxicol. Appl. Pharmacol.* **47**, 261–272.

Guiney, P. D., Peterson, R. E., Melancon, M. J., and Lech, J. J. (1977).The distribution and elimination of 2,5,2′,5′-[^{14}C] tetrachlorobiphenyl in rainbow trout (*Salmo gairdneri*). *Toxicol. Appl. Pharmacol.* **39**, 329–338.

Hakonson, T. E., Gallegos, A. F., and Whicker, F. W. (1975). Cesium kinetics data for estimating food consumption rates of trout. *Health Phys.* **29**, 301–306.

Hall, F. H. (1930). The ability of the common mackerel and certain other marine fishes to remove dissolved oxygen from seawater. *Am. J. Physiol.* **93**, 417–421.

Hamelink, J. L., Waybrant, R. C., and Yant, P. R. (1977). Mechanisms of bioaccumulation of mercury and chlorinated hydrocarbon pesticides by fish in lentic ecosystems. In: I. H. Suffet, Ed., *Fate of pollutants in the air and water environments*, Vol. 8, Part 2. John Wiley & Sons, New York, pp. 261–281.

Hanes, D., Krueger, H., Tinsley, J., and Bond, C. (1968). Influence of pentachlorophenol on fatty acids in coho salmon (*Onchorynchus kisutch*). *West. Pharmacol. Soc. Proc.* **11**, 121–125.

Hansen, D. J., Parrish, P. R., Lowe, J. I., Wilson, A. J., and Wilson, P. D. (1971). Chronic toxicity, uptake, and retention of Aroclor 1254 in two estuarine fishes. *Bull. Environ. Contam. Toxicol.* **6**, 113–119.

Hansèn, L. G., Wiekhorst, W. B., and Simon, J. (1976). Effects of dietary Aroclor 1242 on channel catfish (*Ictalurus punctatus*) and the selective accumulation of PCB components. *J. Fish. Res. Board Can.* **33**, 1343–1352.

Hanson, D. and Johansen, K. (1970). Relationship of gill ventilation and perfusion in Pacific dogfish, *Squalus suckleyi*. *J. Fish. Res. Board Can.* **27**, 551–564.

Hartman, A. M. (1978). Mercury feeding schedules: effects on accumulation, retention, and behavior in trout. *Trans. Am. Fish. Soc.* **107**, 369–375.

Hartung, R. (1976). Pharmacokinetic approaches to the evaluation of methylmercury in fish. In: R. W. Andrew, P. V. Hodson, and D. E. Konasewich, Eds., *Toxicity to biota of metal forms in natural water*. Great Lakes Research Advisory Board, Stand. Comm. Res. Adv. Bd. Windsor, Ontario, pp. 233–248.

Haschemeyer, A. E. V. and Smith, M. A. K. (1979). Protein synthesis in liver, muscle and gill of mullet (*Mugil cephalus* L.) *in vivo. Biol. Bull.* **156**, 93–102.

Haschemeyer, A. E. V., Persell, R., and Smith, M. A. K. (1979). Effect of temperature on protein synthesis in fish of the Galapagos and Perlas Islands. *Comp. Biochem. Physiol.* **64B**, 91–95.

Hewett, C. J. and Jefferies, D. F. (1976). The accumulation of radioactive caesium from water by brown trout (*Salmo trutta*) and its comparison with plaice and rays. *J. Fish Biol.* **9**, 479–489.

Hodson, P. V. (1975). Zinc uptake by Atlantic salmon (*Salmo salar*) exposed to lethal concentrations of zinc at 3, 11, and 19 C. *J. Fish. Res. Board Can.* **32**, 2552–2556.

Hodson, P. V. and Blunt, B. R. (1981). Temperature-induced changes in pentachlorophenol chronic toxicity to early life stages of rainbow trout. *Aquat. Toxicol.* **1**, 113–127.

Hodson, P. V., Blunt, B. R., and Spry, D. J. (1978). Chronic toxicity of waterborne and dietary lead to rainbow trout (*Salmo gairdneri*) in Lake Ontario water. *Water Res.* **12**, 869–878.

Holeton, G. F. (1980). Oxygen as an environmental factor of fishes. In: M. A. Ali, Ed., *Environmental physiology of fishes*. Plenum Press, New York, pp. 7–32.

Holeton, G. F. and Randall, D. J. (1967). The effect of hypoxia upon the partial pressure of gases in the blood and water afferent and efferent to the gills of rainbow trout. *J. Exp. Biol.* **46**, 317–327.

Holmberg, B. and Saunders, R. L. (1979). The effects of pentachlorophenol on swimming performance and oxygen consumption in the American eel (*Anguilla rostrata*). *Rapp. P.V. Reun. Cons. Int. Explor. Mer* **174**,144–149.

Holmberg, B., Jensen, S., Larsson, A., Lewander, K., and Olsson, M. (1972). Metabolic effects of technical pentachlorophenol (PCP) on the eel *Anguilla anguilla* L. *Comp. Biochem. Physiol.* **43B**, 171–183.

Hoss, D. E. and Baptist, J. P. (1971). Accumulation of soluble and particulate radionuclides by estuarine fish. In: D. J. Nelson, Ed., *Radionuclides in ecosystems*. Third Nat. Symp. Radioecol. CONF-710501-P2, pp. 776–782.

Hoss, D. E., Peters, D. S., Hettler, W. F., and Clements, L. C. (1978). Excretion rate of ^{65}Zn: is it a useful tool for estimating metabolism of fish in the field? *J. Exp. Mar. Biol. Ecol.* **31**, 241–252.

Howarth, R. S. and Sprague, J. B. (1978). Copper lethality to rainbow trout in waters of various hardness and pH. *Water Res.* **12**, 455–462.

Hughes, G. M. (1966). The dimensions of fish gills in relation to their function. *J. Exp. Biol.* **45**, 177–195.

Hughes, G. M. (1972). Morphometrics of fish gills. *Resp. Physiol.* **14**, 1–25.

Hughes, G. M. (1978). On the respiration of *Torpedo marmorata. J. Exp. Biol.* **73**, 85–105.

Hughes, G. M. and Morgan, M. (1973). The structure of fish gills in relation to their respiratory function. *Biol. Rev.* **48**, 419–475.

Itazawa, Y. and Takeda, T. (1978). Gas exchange in the carp gills in normoxic and hypoxic conditions. *Resp. Physiol.* **35**, 263–269.

Ivie, G. W., Gibson, J. R., Bryant, H. E., Begin, J. J., Barnett, J. R., and Dorough, H. W. (1974). Accumulation, distribution, and excretion of Mirex^{14}C in animals exposed for long periods to the insecticide in the diet. *J. Agric. Food Chem.* **22**, 646–653.

Ivlev, V. S. (1939). [Balance of energy in carps.] (In Russian with English summary). *Zool. Zh.* **18**, 303–318.

Jackson, G. A. (1976). Biologic half-life of endrin in channel catfish tissues. *Bull. Environ. Contam. Toxicol.* **16**, 505–507.

Jarvenpaa, T., Tillander, M., and Miettinen, J. K. (1970). Methylmercury: half-time of elimination in flounder, pike and eel. *Suom. Kem. B* **43**, 439–442.

Jarvinen, A. W. and Tyo, R. M. (1978). Toxicity to fathead minnows of endrin in food and water. *Arch. Environ. Contam. Toxicol.* **7**, 409–421.

Jernelov, A. and Lann, H. (1971). Mercury accumulation in food chains. *Oikos* **22**, 403–406.

Jirasek, J., Hampl, A., and Sirotek, D. (1982). Growth morphology of the filtering apparatus of silver carp (*Hypohthalmichthys molitrix*). I. Gross anatomy state. *Aquaculture* **26**, 41–48.

Jobling, M. (1981). The influence of feeding on the metabolic rate of fishes: a short review. *J. Fish Biol.* **18**, 385–400.

Johnson, D. W. (1968). Pesticides and fishes—a review of selected literature. *Trans. Am. Fish. Soc.* **97**, 398–424.

Jones, D. R. and Randall, D. J. (1978). The respiratory and circulatory systems during exercise. In: W. S. Hoar and D. J. Randall, Eds., *Fish physiology*, Vol. 7. Academic Press, New York, pp. 425–501.

Kerstens, A., Lomholt, J. P., and Johansen, K. (1979). The ventilation, extraction and uptake oxygen in undisturbed flounders, *Platichthys flesus*: responses to hypoxic acclimation. *J. Exp. Biol.* **83**, 169–179.

Kevern, N. R. (1966). Feeding rate of carp estimated by a radioisotopic method. *Trans. Am. Fish. Soc.* **95**, 363–371.

Kiceniuk, J. W. and Jones, D. R. (1977). The oxygen transport system in trout (*Salmo gairdneri*) during sustained exercise. *J. Exp. Biol.* **69**, 247–260.

Kikuchi, T., Honda, H., Ishikawa, M., Yamanaka, H., and Amano, K. (1978). Excretion of mercury from fish. *Bull. Jap. Soc. Sci. Fish.* **44**, 217–222.

King, S. F. (1964). Uptake and transfer of Cesium-137 by *Chlamydomonas, Daphnia*, and bluegill fingerlings. *Ecology* **45**, 852–859.

Kitchell, J. F., Stewart, D. J., and Weininger, D. (1977). Applications of a bioenergetics model to yellow perch (*Perca flavescens*) and walleye (*Stizostedion vitreum vitreum*). *J. Fish. Res. Board Can.* **34**,1922–1935.

Kobayashi, K. and Akitake, H. (1975). Studies on the metabolism of chlorophenols in fish. II. Turnover of absorbed PCP in goldfish. *Bull. Jap. Soc. Sci. Fish.* **41**, 93–99.

Kumaraguru, A. K. and Beamish, F. W. H. (1981). Lethal toxicity of permethrin (NRDC-143) to rainbow trout, *Salmo gairdneri*, in relation to body weight and water temperature. *Water Res.* **15**, 503–505.

Laarman, P. W., Willford, W. A., and Olson, R. R. (1976). Retention of mercury in the muscle of yellow perch (*Perca flavescens*) and rock bass (*Ambloplites rupestris*). *Trans. Am. Fish. Soc.* **105**, 296–300.

Lech, J. J. and Bend, J. R. (1980). Relationship between biotransformation and the toxicity and fate of xenobiotic chemicals to fish. *Environ. Health Perspect.* **34**, 115–131.

Lenfant, C. and Johansen, K. (1966). Respiratory function in the elasmobranch *Squalus suckleyi* G. *Resp. Physiol.* **1**, 13–19.

Lett, P. F., Farmer, G. J., and Beamish, F. W. H. (1976). Effect of copper on some aspects of the bioenergetics of rainbow trout (*Salmo gairdneri*). *J. Fish. Res. Board Can.* **33**, 1335–1342.

Lieb, A. J., Bills, D. D., and Sinnhuber, R. O. (1974). Accumulation of dietary polychlorinated biphenyls (Aroclor 1254) by rainbow trout (*Salmo gairdneri*). *J. Agric. Food Chem.* **22**, 638–642.

Lock, R. A. C. (1975). Uptake of methylmercury by aquatic organisms from water and food. In: J. H. Koeman and J. J. T. W. A. Strik, Eds., *Sublethal effects of toxic chemicals on aquatic animals*. Elsevier, Netherlands, pp. 61–79.

Lockhart, W. L., Uthe, J. F., Kenney, A. R. and Mehrle, P. H. (1972). Methylmercury in northern pike (*Esox lucius*): distribution, elimination, and some biochemical characteristics of contaminated fish. *J. Fish. Res. Board Can.* **29**, 1519–1523.

Love, R. M. (1970). *The chemical biology of fishes.* Academic Press, London, 547 p.

Lovern, J. A. (1938). Fat metabolism in fishes. XIII. Factors influencing the composition of depot fat of fishes. *Biochem. J.* **32**, 1214–1224.

Lu, P. Y. and Metcalf, R. L. (1975). Environmental fate and biodegradability of benzene derivatives as studied in a model aquatic ecosystem. *Environ. Health Perspect.* **10**, 269–284.

Macek, K. J., Rodgers, C. R., Stalling, D. L., and Korn, S. (1970). The uptake, distribution and elimination of dietary ^{14}C-DDT and ^{14}C-dieldrin in rainbow trout. *Trans. Am. Fish. Soc.* **99**, 689–695.

MacLeod, J. C. and Pessah, E. (1973). Temperature effects on mercury accumulation, toxicity, and metabolic rate in rainbow trout (*Salmo gairdneri*). J. Fish. Res. Board Can. **30**, 485–492.

Madeley, J. R. and Birtley, R. D. N. (1980). Chlorinated paraffins and the environment. 2. Aquatic and avian toxicology. *Environ. Sci. Technol.* **14**, 1215–1221.

Matida, Y., Kawatsu, H., Kimura, S., Saiga, Y., Nose, T., Yokote, M., and Kawatsu, H. (1971). Toxicity of mercury compounds to aquatic organisms and accumulation of the compounds by the organisms. *Bull. Freshw. Fish. Res. Lab. Tokyo* **21**, 197–227.

McKim, J. M. (1981). A direct measure of the uptake efficiency of xenobiotic chemicals across the respiratory epithelium of brook trout (*Salvelinus fontinalis*). In: N. Bermingham, C. Blaise, P. Couture, B. Hummel, G. Joubert, and M. Speyer, Eds. *Proceedings of the seventh annual aquatic toxicity workshop:* Nov. 5–7, 1980, Montreal, Quebec. Can. Tech. Rep. Fish. Aquat. Sci. No. 990, pp. 111–112.

Melancon, M. J. and Lech, J. J. (1978). Distribution and elimination of naphthalene and 2-methylnaphthalene in rainbow trout during short- and long-term exposures. *Arch. Environ. Contam. Toxicol.* **7**, 207–220.

Menzel, D. W. (1960). Utilization of food by a Bermuda reef fish, *Epinephelus guttatus. J. Cons. Cons. Perma. Int. Explor. Mer* **25**, 216–222.

Merlini, M. and Pozzi, G. (1977). Lead and freshwater fishes: part 2—ionic lead accumulation. *Environ. Pollut.* **13**, 119–126.

Merlini, M., Pozzi, G., Brazelli, A., and Berg, A. (1975). The transfer of ^{65}Zn from natural and synthetic foods to a freshwater fish. In: C. E. Cushing, Eds., *Radioecology and energy resources.* The Ecological Society of America, Spec. Publ. No. 1. Dowden, Hutchinson & Ross, Inc., Stroudsburg, Pennsylvania, pp. 226–229.

Metcalf, R. L., Kapoor, I. P., Lu, P. Y., Schuth, C. K., and Sherman, P. (1973). Model ecosystem studies of the environmental fate of six organochlorine pesticides. *Environ. Health Perspect.* **4**, 35–44.

Miller, D. W., Vetter, R. J., and Atchison, G. J. (1980). Effect of temperature and dissolved oxygen on uptake and retention of ^{54}Mn in fish. *Health Phys.* **33**, 221–225.

Mitchell, A. I., Plank, P. A., and Thomson, I. M. (1977). Relative concentrations of ^{14}C-DDT and of two polychlorinated biphenyls in the lipids of cod tissues after a single oral dose. *Arch. Environ. Contam. Toxicol.* **6**, 525–532.

Molnar, G., Tamassy, E., and Tolg, I. (1967). The gastric digestion of living predatory fish. In: S. D. Gerking, Ed., *The biological basis of freshwater fish production.* Blackwell Scientific Publications, Oxford, pp. 135–149.

Muir, B. S. (1969). Gill dimensions as a function of fish size. *J. Fish. Res. Board Can.* **26**, 165–170.

Muir, B. S. and Buckley, R. M. (1967). Gill ventilation in *Remora remora. Copeia* **1967**, 581–586.

Muir, B. S. and Niimi, A. J. (1972). Oxygen consumption of the euryhaline fish, aholehole (*Kuhlia sandvicensis*), with reference to salinity, swimming, and food consumption. *J. Fish. Res. Board Can.* **22**, 67–77.

Muir, B. S., Nelson, G. J., and Bridges, K. W. (1965). A method for measuring swimming speed in oxygen consumption studies on the aholehole *Kuhlia sandvicensis*. *Trans. Am. Fish. Soc.* **94**, 378–382.

Murphy, P. G. and Murphy, J. V. (1971). Correlations between respiration and direct uptake of DDT in the mosquito fish *Gambusia affinis*. *Bull. Environ. Contam. Toxicol.* **6**, 581–588.

Nakatani, R. E. (1966). Biological response of rainbow trout (*Salmo gairdneri*) ingesting zinc-65. In: *Disposal of radioactive waste into seas, oceans and surface waters*. IAEA, Vienna, pp. 809–822.

Niimi, A. J. (1979). Quantitative analysis of carbon-[14] labelled polychlorinated biphenyls and hexachlorobenzene in biological samples using an oxidative combustion method. *Int. J. Environ. Anal. Chem.* **6**, 267–271.

Niimi, A. J. (1981). Examination of gross growth efficiency in fish (K_1) based on field observations of annual growth and kinetics of persistent environmental contaminants. *Can. J. Fish. Aquat. Sci.* **38**, 250–253.

Niimi, A. J. (1983). Biological and toxicological effects of environmental contaminants in fish and their eggs. *Can. J. Fish. Aquat. Sci.* **40**, 306–312.

Niimi, A. J. and Beamish, F. W. H. (1974). Bioenergetics and growth of largemouth bass (*Micropterus salmoides*) in relation to body weight and temperature. *Can. J. Zool.* **52**, 447–456.

Niimi, A. J. and Cho, C. Y. (1980). Uptake of hexachlorobenzene (HCB) from feed by rainbow trout (*Salmo gairdneri*). *Bull. Environ. Contam. Toxicol.* **24**, 834–839.

Niimi, A. J. and Cho, C. Y. (1981). Elimination of hexachlorobenzene (HCB) by rainbow trout (*Salmo gairdneri*), and an examination of its kinetics in Lake Ontario salmonids. *Can. J. Fish. Aquat. Sci.* **38**, 1350–1356.

Niimi, A. J. and Cho, C. Y. (1983). Laboratory and field analysis of pentachlorophenol (PCP) accumulation by salmonids. *Water Res.* (accepted for publication).

Niimi, A. J. and LaHam, Q. N. (1975). Selenium toxicity on the early life stages of zebrafish (*Brachydanio rerio*). *J. Fish. Res. Board Can.* **32**, 803–806.

Niimi, A. J. and McFadden, C. A. (1982). Uptake of sodium pentachlorophenate (NaPCP) by rainbow trout (*Salmo gairdneri*) exposed to concentrations in the ng/L range. *Bull. Environ. Contam. Toxicol.* **28**, 11–19.

Niimi, A. J. and Morgan, S. L. (1980). Morphometric examination of the gills of walleye (*Stizostedion vitreum vitreum*) and rainbow trout (*Salmo gairdneri*). *J. Fish Biol.* **16**, 685–692.

Norstrom, R. J., McKinnon, A. E., and de Freitas, A. S. W. (1976). A bioenergetics-based model for pollutant accumulation by fish. Simulation of PCB and methylmercury residue levels in Ottawa River yellow perch (*Perca flavescens*). *J. Fish. Res. Board Can.* **33**, 248–267.

Oliver, B. G. and Niimi, A. J. (1983). Bioconcentration of chlorobenzenes from water by rainbow trout: correlations with partition coefficients and environmental residues. *Environ. Sci. Technol.* **17**, 287–291.

Olson, L. E. and Marking, L. L. (1973). Toxicity of TFM (lampricide) to six early life stages of rainbow trout (*Salmo gairdneri*). *J. Fish. Res. Board Can.* **33**, 1047–1052.

Olsson, M. and Jensen, S. (1975). Pike as the test organism for mercury, DDT and PCB pollution. A study of the contamination in the Stockholm archipelago. *Inst. Freshw. Res., Drottningholm,* **54**, 83–106.

Olsson, M., Jensen, S., and Reutergard, L. (1978). Seasonal variation of PCB levels in fish—an important factor in planning aquatic monitoring programs. *Ambio* **7**, 66–69.

Ophel, I. L. and Judd, J. M. (1975). Strontium and calcium accumulation in fish as affected by food composition. In: C. E. Cushing, Ed., *Radioecology and energy resources*. The Ecological Society of America, Spec. Publ. No. 1, Dowden, Hutchinson & Ross Inc., Stroudsburg, Pennsylvania, pp. 221–225.

Paloheimo, J. E. and Dickie, L. M. (1966). Food and growth of fishes. III. Relations among food, body size, and growth efficiency. *J. Fish. Res. Board Can.* **23**, 1209–1248.

Pentreath, R. J. (1973). The accumulation and retention of ^{65}Zn and ^{54}Mn by the plaice, *Pleuronectes platessa* L. *J. Exp. Mar. Biol. Ecol.* **12**, 1–18.

Pentreath, R. J. (1976a). Some further studies of the accumulation and retention of ^{65}Zn and ^{54}Mn by the plaice, *Pleuronectes platessa* L. *J. Exp. Mar. Biol. Ecol.* **21**, 179–189.

Pentreath, R. J. (1976b). The accumulation of organic mercury from seawater by the plaice, *Pleuronectes platessa* L. *J. Exp. Mar. Biol. Ecol.* **24**, 121–132.

Pentreath, R. J. (1976c). The accumulation of mercury from food by the plaice, *Pleuronectes platessa* L. *J. Exp. Mar. Biol. Ecol.* **25**, 51–65.

Pentreath, R. J. (1976d). The accumulation of mercury by the thornback ray, *Raja clavata* L. *J. Exp. Mar. Biol. Ecol.* **25**, 131–140.

Pentreath, R. J. (1977). The accumulation of cadmium by the plaice, *Pleuronectes platessa* L., and the thornback ray, *Raja clavata* L. *J. Exp. Mar. Biol. Ecol.* **30**, 223–232.

Phillips, G. R. and Buhler, D. R. (1978). The relative contributions of methylmercury from food or water to rainbow trout (*Salmo gairdneri*) in a controlled laboratory environment. *Trans. Am. Fish. Soc.* **107**, 853–861.

Phillips, G. R. and Gregory, R. W. (1979). Assimilation efficiency of dietary methylmercury by northern pike (*Esox lucius*). *J. Fish. Res. Board Can.* **36**, 1516–1519.

Phillips, G. R. and Russo, R. C. (1978). *Metal bioaccumulation in fishes and aquatic invertebrates: a literature review*. U.S. EPA. EPA-600/3-78-103.

Pickering, Q. H. and Henderson, C. (1966). The acute toxicity of some heavy metals to different species of warmwater fishes. *Air Water Pollut. Int. J.* **10**, 453–463.

Piiper, J. and Schumann, D. (1967). Efficiency of O_2 exchange in the gills of the dogfish, *Scyliorhinus stellaris*. *Resp. Physiol.* **2**, 135–148.

Piiper, J., Meyer, M., Worth, H., and Willmer, H. (1977). Respiration and circulation during swimming activity in the dogfish *Scyliorhinus stellaris*. *Resp. Physiol.* **30**, 221–239.

Pruitt, G. W., Grantham, B. J., and Pierce, R. H. (1977). Accumulation and elimination of pentachlorophenol by the bluegill, *Lepomis macrochirus*. *Trans. Am. Fish. Soc.* **106**, 462–465.

Randall, D. J., Holeton, G. F., and Stevens, E. D. (1967). The exchange of oxygen and carbon dioxide across the gills of rainbow trout. *J. Exp. Biol.* **6**, 339–348.

Reinert, R. E., Stone, L. J., and Willford, W. A. (1974). Effects of temperature on accumulation of methylmercuric chloride and *p,p'* DDT by rainbow trout (*Salmo gairdneri*). *J. Fish. Res. Board Can.* **31**, 1649–1652.

Renfro, W. C. and Osterberg, C. (1969). Radiozinc decline in starry flounders after temporary shutdown of Hanford reactors. In: D. J. Nelson and F. C. Evans, Eds., *Symposium on radioecology*, Proc. Second Nat. Symp. CONF-67-503, pp. 372–379.

Renfro, W. C., Fowler, S. W., Heyraud, M., and La Rosa, J. (1975). Relative importance of food and water in long-term zinc-65 accumulation by marine biota. *J. Fish. Res. Board Can.* **32**, 1339–1345.

Roberts, J. R., de Freitas, A. S. W., and Gidney, M. A. J. (1977). Influence of lipid pool size on

244   A. J. Niimi

bioaccumulation of the insecticide chlordane by northern redhorse suckers (*Moxostoma macrolepidotum*). *J. Fish. Res. Board Can.* **34,** 89–97.

Rodgers, D. W. and Beamish, F. W. H. (1981). Uptake of waterborne methylmercury by rainbow trout (*Salmo gairdneri*) in relation to oxygen consumption and methylmercury concentration. *Can. J. Fish. Aquat. Sci.* **38,** 1300–1315.

Rodgers, D. W. and Beamish, F. W. H. (1982). Dynamics of dietary mercury in rainbow trout, *Salmo gairdneri*. *Aquat. Toxicol.,* **2,** 271–290.

Rodgers, D. W. and Beamish, F. W. H. (1983). Water quality modifies uptake of waterborne methylmercury by rainbow trout (*Salmo gairdneri*). *Can. J. Fish. Aquat. Sci.* **40,** 824–828.

Ruohtula, M. and Miettinen, J. K. (1975). Retention and excretion of ^{203}Hg-labelled methylmercury in rainbow trout. *Oikos* **26,** 385–390.

Sanborn, J. R., Childers, W. F., and Hansen, L. G. (1977). Uptake and elimination of [^{14}C] hexachlorobenzene (HCB) by the green sunfish *Lepomis cyanellus* Raf., after feeding contaminated food. *J. Agric. Food Chem.* **25,** 551–553.

Sato, T., Ose, Y., and Sakai, T. (1980). Toxicological effect of selenium on fish. *Environ. Pollut.,* Ser. A. **21,** 217–224.

Saunders, R. L. (1962). The irrigation of gills in fishes. II. Efficiency of oxygen uptake in relation to respiratory flow activity and concentrations of oxygen and carbon dioxide. *Can. J. Zool.* **40,** 817–862.

Schimmel, S. C., Hansen, D. J., and Forester, J. (1974). Effects of Aroclor 1254 on laboratory-reared embryos and fry of sheepshead minnow (*Cyprinodon variegatus*). *Trans. Am. Fish. Soc.* **103,** 582–586.

Sharpe, M. A., de Freitas, A. S. W., and McKinnon, A. E. (1977). The effect of body size on methylmercury clearance by goldfish (*Carassius auratus*). *Environ. Biol. Fish.* **2,** 177–83.

Skea, J. C., Simonin, H. J., Jackling, S., and Symula, J. (1981). Accumulation and retention of mirex by brook trout fed a contaminated diet. *Bull. Environ. Contam. Toxicol.* **27,** 79–83.

Smit, H. (1965). Some experiments on the oxygen consumption of goldfish (*Carassius auratus* L.) in relation to swimming speed. *Can. J. Zool.* **43,** 623–633.

Smith, M. A. K. (1981). Estimation of growth potential by measurement of tissue protein synthetic rates in feeding and fasting rainbow trout. *Salmo gairdneri* Richardson. *J. Fish Biol.* **19,** 213–220.

Smith, M. A. K., Mathews, R. W., Hudson, A. P., and Haschemeyer, A. E. V. (1980). Protein metabolism of tropical reef and pelagic fish. *Comp. Biochem. Physiol.* **65B,** 415–418.

Smith, R. R., Rumsey, G. L., and Scott, M. L. (1978). Heat increment associated with dietary protein, fat, carbohydrate and complete diets in salmonids: comparative energetic efficiency. *J. Nutr.* **108,** 1025–1032.

Somero, G. N., Chow, T. J., Yancey, P. H., and Snyder, C. B. (1977). Lead accumulation rates in tissues of the estuarine teleost fish, *Gillichthys mirabilis*: salinity and temperature effects. *Arch. Environ. Contam. Toxicol.* **6,** 337–348.

Sprague, J. B. (1969). Measurement of pollutant toxicity to fish. I. Bioassay methods for acute toxicity. *Water Res.* **3,** 793–821.

Statham, C. M., Croft, W. A., and Lech, J. J. (1978). Uptake, distribution, and effects of carbon tetrachloride in rainbow trout (*Salmo gairdneri*). *Toxicol. Appl. Pharmacol.* **45,** 131–140.

Stevens, E. D. (1972). Some aspects of gas exchange in tuna. *J. Exp. Biol.* **56,** 809–823.

Suzuki, T. and Hatanaka, M. (1975). Experimental investigation on the biological concentration of mercury. II. On the origin of mercury found in the body of young yellowtail. *Bull. Jap. Soc. Sci. Fish.* **41,** 225–231.

Suzuki, T., Miyama, T., and Toyama, C. (1973). The chemical form and bodily distribution of mercury in marine fish. *Bull. Environ. Contam. Toxicol.* **10**, 347–359.

Tandler, A. and Beamish, F. W. H. (1979). Mechanical and biochemical components of apparent specific dynamic action in largemouth bass, *Micropterus salmoides* Lacepede. *J. Fish Biol.* **14**, 343–350.

Thomann, R. V. (1981). Equilibrium model of fate of microcontaminants in diverse aquatic food chains. *Can. J. Fish. Aquat. Sci.* **38**, 280–296.

Tooby, T. E. and Durbin, F. J. (1975). Lindane residue accumulation and elimination in rainbow trout (*Salmo gairdneri* Richardson) and roach (*Rutilus rutilus* Linnaeus). *Environ. Pollut.* **8**, 79–89.

Trujillo, D. A., Ray, L. E., Murray, H. E., and Giam, C. S. (1982). Bioaccumulation of pentachlorophenol by killifish (*Fundulus similus*). *Chemosphere* **11**, 25–31.

Tulp, M. T. M., Haya, K., Carson, W. G., Zitko, V., and Hutzinger, O. (1979). Effect of salinity on uptake of ^{14}C-2,2',4,5,5'-pentachlorobiphenyl by juvenile Atlantic salmon. *Chemosphere* **4**, 243–249.

Ursin, E. (1967). A mathematical model of some aspects of fish growth, respiration, and mortality. *J. Fish. Res. Board Can.* **24**, 2355–2453.

Varanasi, U. and Gmur, D. J. (1978). Influence of water-borne and dietary calcium on uptake and retention of lead by coho salmon (*Oncorhynchus kisutch*). *Toxicol. Appl. Pharmacol.* **46**, 65–75.

Varanasi, U., Gmur, D. J., and Reichert, W. L. (1981). Effect of environmental temperature on naphthalene metabolism by juvenile starry flounder (*Platichthys stellatus*). *Arch. Environ. Contam. Toxicol.* **10**, 203–214.

Warlen, S. M., Wolfe, D. A., Lewis, C. W., and Colby, D. R. (1977). Accumulation and retention of dietary ^{14}C-DDT by Atlantic menhaden. *Trans. Am. Fish. Soc.* **106**, 95–104.

Warren, C. E. (1971). *Biology and water pollution control*. W. B. Saunders, Philadelphia, Pennsylvania.

Warren, C. E. and Davis, G. E. (1967). Laboratory studies on the feeding bioenergetics and growth of fish. In: S. D. Gerking, Ed., *The biological basis of freshwater fish production*. Blackwell Scientific Publications, Oxford, pp. 175–214.

Webb, P. W. and Brett, J. R. (1973). Effects of sublethal concentrations of sodium pentachlorophenate on growth rate, food conversion efficiency, and swimming performance in underyearling sockeye salmon (*Oncorhynchus nerka*). *J. Fish. Res. Board Can.* **30**, 499–507.

Weinbach, E. C. (1957). Biochemical basis for the toxicity of pentachlorophenol. *Proc. Nat. Acad. Sci. USA* **43**, 393–397.

Weisbart, M. (1973). The distribution and tissue retention of mercury-203 in the goldfish (*Carassius auratus*). *Can. J. Zool.* **51**, 143–150.

Westoo, G. (1973). Methylmercury as percentage of total mercury in flesh and viscera of salmon and sea trout of various ages. *Science* **181**, 567–568.

Williams, D. R. and Giesy, J. P., (1978). Relative importance of food and water sources to cadmium uptake by *Gambusia affinis* (Poecilidiidae). *Environ. Res.* **16**, 326–332.

Willis, J. M. and Jones, N. Y. (1977). The use of uniform labeling with zinc-65 to measure stable zinc turnover in the mosquito fish, *Gambusia affinis*. I. Retention. *Health Phys.* **32**, 381–387.

Winberg, G. G. (1956). [Rate of metabolism and food requirements of fishes.] Belorussian Univ. Minsk. (In Russian, *Fish. Res. Board Can. Transl. Ser.* 194).

Wong, P. T. S., Chau, Y. K., Kramar, O., and Bengert, G. A. (1981). Accumulation and depuration of tetramethyllead by rainbow trout. *Water Res.* **15**, 621–625.

Wszolek, P. C., Lisk, D. J., Wachs, T., and Youngs, W. D. (1979). Persistence of polychlorinated biphenyls and 1,1-dichloro-2,2-*bis*(*p*-chlorophenyl)ethylene (*p,p*-DDE) with age in lake trout after 8 years. *Environ. Sci. Technol.* **13**, 1269–1271.

Wuhrmann, K. (1952). Sur quelques principes de la toxicologie du poisson. *Bull. Cent. belge Docum. Eaux* **15**, 49. (*Fish. Res. Board Can. Transl. Ser.* 243.)

Yamamoto, K., Itazawa, Y., and Kobayashi, H. (1981). Gas exchange in the gills of yellowtail, *Seriola quinqueradiata*, under resting and normoxic condition. *Bull. Jap. Soc. Sci. Fish.* **47**, 447–451.

Zitko, V. (1977). Uptake and excretion of chlorinated and brominated hydrocarbons by fish. *Can. Fish. Mar. Ser. Tech. Rep.* 737.

Zitko, V. (1980). The uptake and excretion of mirex and dechloranes by juvenile Atlantic salmon. *Chemosphere* **9**, 73–78.

9

POLLUTANTS AND CHEMORECEPTION IN AQUATIC ORGANISMS

Toshiaki J. Hara, S. B. Brown, and R. E. Evans

Department of Fisheries and Oceans
Freshwater Institute
Winnipeg, Manitoba

---

1. INTRODUCTION

Trace levels of aquatic pollutants which do not directly impair health of animals have been observed to limit their feeding, distribution, orientation and migration, or reproductive behavior. Chemoreception plays a dominant role mediating behavior of aquatic animals, because vision and hearing have limited ranges. The ability to perceive and to use the information to select favorable conditions is of obvious importance to survival. An organism has acquired during its course of evolution the capability to behaviorally mitigate or entirely remove the effect of the environmental perturbation. However, the same capacity for behavioral change may or may not exist for man-made alterations in aquatic environments. These behavioral patterns are generally initiated by chemoreception, though less specific irritational responses mediated through general exteroceptors may also be involved. Chemoreceptive membranes are directly exposed to the environment and are not protected by external barriers or internal detoxifying systems. Therefore the physiological importance, chemical reactivity, structural complexity, and exposed location of chemosensory membranes combine to make them prime targets for interactions with pollutants.

This chapter reviews investigations of the effect of pollutants on chemoreceptive systems and on behavior mediated by chemoreception in aquatic organisms, with emphasis on studies from our laboratory with fish olfaction. This review will not cover aspects of pollution-altered physiology or behavior that do not likely involve the chemical senses directly. Reviews of the present subject have been provided by Sutterlin (1974), Olla et al. (1980), and Brown et al. (1982).

2. CHEMORECEPTION IN AQUATIC ORGANISMS

2.1. Chemical Control of Behavior

A comparative lack of sensitivity in human chemoreceptors has sometimes led us to underestimate the value and significance of the chemical senses to other organisms. Freshwater and marine animals use chemical senses to find foods, mates, and prey, or to escape from predators and other dangers (Lindstedt, 1971; Grant and Mackie, 1974; Bardach, 1975; Mackie, 1975; Hara 1981b, 1982a). The types of behavior elicited by the chemical signals in aquatic animals are summarized, though not exhaustively, in Table 1.

Numerous other behavioral changes that are no doubt elicited by chemicals, but the chemical stimuli have not been characterized and these are not considered here. Amino acids and related compounds clearly prevail as behavioral chemicals in many aquatic animal groups. However, other types of molecules also play important roles as chemical messengers.

2.2.   Chemosensory Systems and Mechanisms

Chemoreception by animals shows a wide range of sensitivity and specificity. On the basis of location and structure as well as the innervation, the chemical senses are generally divided into three categories: olfaction, gustation or taste, and the common or general chemical sense. In terrestrial animals, those receptors which have high sensitivity and specificity, and which are "distance" chemical receptors are distinguished as olfactory, and those receptors of moderate sensitivity and which are stimulated by dilute solutions are gustatory or contact chemical receptors. These distinctions, however, do not always hold in the aquatic environment, where chemical stimuli for both systems are mediated by water. For example, both the olfactory and the taste receptors on the barbel in the catfish (*Ictalurus punctatus*) are extremely sensitive (threshold ranging between 10^{-9} and $10^{-10}\,M$) to certain amino acids (Caprio, 1982); and some bile acids stimulate both the taste and olfactory systems of rainbow trout (*Salmo gairdneri*) at concentrations as low as $10^{-11}\,M$ (Hara and Marui, unpublished). Common chemical sense is mediated by free nerve endings located on an exposed body surface and relatively low sensitivity. Recent electrophysiological studies have also shown that the lateral-line organs of aquatic animals have a chemoreceptive function responding to changes in salt concentrations in the environment (Katsuki and Yanagisawa, 1982).

Although available information on the structural characteristics of metazoan chemoreceptors is limited to molluscs, arthropods and vertebrates, a homogeneity exists in morphology of the primary sensory neurons in the olfactory system (Fig. 1A). The receptor cell sends a slender dendrite toward the surface of the nasal cavity and in the other direction sends a fine axon conveying the coded sensory information directly to the brain (Fig. 1Ba,c). The dendrite terminates in a minute swelling or olfactory knob which bears a variable number of cilia or microvilli. The vertebrate taste system, on the other hand, is composed of elongated sensory cells that form clusters called taste buds typically protruded in the epithelial membranes in the mouth and in other body surfaces (Fig. 1Bb,d). The secondary nerve innervated at the taste receptor cells receives neural information and transmits them to the brain. A remarkable structural similarity has also been maintained throughout the vertebrate taste system. In crustaceans, chemosensory receptor cells are housed inside fine aesthetasc hairs (Fig. 1A). Each of these hairs, surrounded by a row of guard hair on the antennules, contains the fine branches of several hundred receptor cells.

Table 1. Behavior Mediated by Chemical Senses in Aquatic Organisms[a]

Taxonomic Category	Nature of Chemical	Function of Signal
Cnidaria		
Hydroids	Glutathione	Feeding response
Siphonophores	Proline, valine, tyrosine	Feeding response
Corals	Asparagine	Feeding response
Zoanthids	Glutathione and various amino acids	Feeding response
Sea anemones	Anthopleurine	Alarm response
Ctenophora		
Ctenophores	Various amino acids	Feeding?
Turbellaria		
Planarians	Lysine, glutamine, and unidentified large molecular weight compounds	Feeding response
Annelid		
Polychaetes	Various amino acids, glycoproteins, and polypeptides	Feeding response
	Di- and trivalent heavy metals (Zn, Hg, Fe, Cu)	Withdrawal response
Mollusca		
Gastropods	Organic and inorganic acids and bases, salts, sugars, quinine, skatol, glycerine, steroids, lactate, betaine, etc.	Attraction and feeding response

Crustacea		
Lobsters, crabs, shrimps	Glutathione, various amino acids, betaine, inosine, hypoxanthin	Feeding response
Barnacles	Crustecdysone	Mating
Crayfish	Dopachrome	Avoidance
	Carbohydrate	Reproductive behavior
Echinodermata		
Starfish	Niacine	Feeding response
Ophiuroids	Glycine, proline-OH, ornithine, and various other amino acids	Feeding response
	Saponin, steroid glycosides	Escape response
	Various amino acids	Repellent
Chordata		
Pisces (fishes)		
Cyclostomes (lampreys)	Isoleucine methyl ester	Prey location
	Various amino acids	Feeding?
Elasmobranchs (sharks)	Nucleotides, nucleosides, and various amino acids	Feeding response
Teleosts (salmonids, anguillids, cyprinids, ictalurids, tetraodontids, etc.)	Various amino acids, nucleotides, nucleosides, arcamine, and strombine	Feeding response
	Isoxanthopterin	Fright reaction?
	L-Serine	Predator avoidance
	Bile acids	Homing pheromone?

[a] Adapted from Hara (1981b).

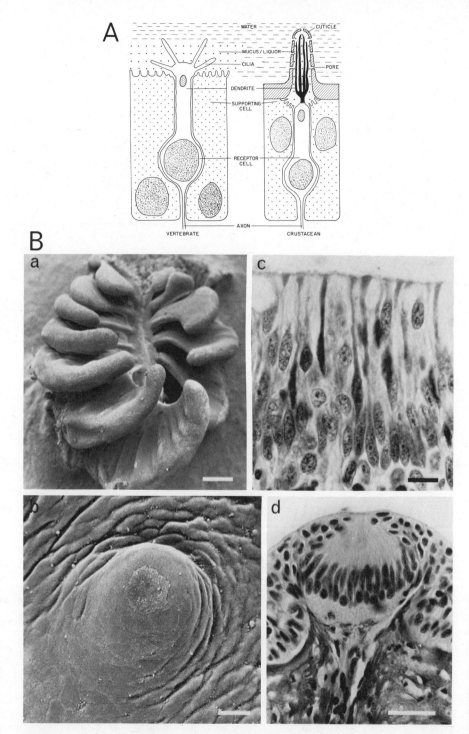

Figure 1. (*A*) Schematic comparison between vertebrate and crustacean olfactory receptors. (*B*) Olfactory and taste organs of rainbow trout (*Salmo gairdneri*). Scanning electron micro-

A common feature of the outer segments of chemoreceptor cells is the presence of cilia or microvilli which have been postulated for nearly 50 years to be the locus for the receptor sites. Recent biochemical studies have shown that olfactory receptor macromolecules are associated with the membrane of the cilia (Rhein and Cagan, 1980, 1981). It is generally assumed that the initial event of a chemoreceptive phenomenon is an interaction of the stimulus molecule(s) with the receptor; this interaction ultimately results in depolarization or hyperpolarization of the receptor cell membranes, which in turn modulates the generation of nerve impulses travelling to the central nervous system. The effectiveness of a stimulus molecule is probably dependent on its shape, size, and charge distribution. In fish, evidence has accumulated that structure–activity relationships exist among chemostimulatory amino acids (Hara, 1981b, 1982b).

3. INTERACTIONS BETWEEN POLLUTANTS, CHEMORECEPTORS, AND RESULTING BEHAVIOR

Because chemoreceptive membranes are relatively exposed to the environment and are protected in an only limited way by detoxifying systems, some compounds in the environment interfere with the functioning of the receptors and break down animal communications. Chemosensory disruption by pollutants can be caused by several ways: (1) overt avoidance or preference, (2) masking or counteracting biologically relevant chemical signals, and (3) directly damaging chemoreceptors (Sutterlin, 1974).

A change in behavior is the initial response of an animal to an environmental perturbation. The response may be movement toward (preference or attraction) or away from (avoidance) the area of perturbation. The consequences of avoiding toxic levels of pollutants would appear to be beneficial to an animal (adaptive), whereas attraction to pollutants renders them more hazardous. Obviously no behavioral reaction can be elicited if the perturbation is not detected or detected at a level which will not permit the animal to respond behaviorally (Fig. 2). These behavioral reactions are generally initiated by olfactory or gustatory reception, though avoidance may be induced by less specific irritative responses of mucous membranes (Hara, 1981a).

A second possible interaction of aquatic pollutants is the masking of biologically relevant chemical stimulants by competing for sites on the chemoreceptor membranes, or by coupling before the two ever come in contact with the receptor membrane. These types of interactions might result in altered sensitivity of the animal to important biological information by altering the threshold or the quality of the natural chemical stimuli.

---

graphs of an olfactory rosette (*a*) and taste bud (*b*). Cross sections of the olfactory epithelium (*c*) and taste bud (*d*). Scale bars = 500, 20, 10, and 30 μm in *a, b, c,* and *d,* respectively. (Scanning electron micrographs, courtesy of Barbara Zielinski.)

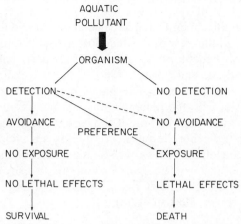

Figure 2. Possible behavioral responses of aquatic organisms to pollutants, and their consequences.

Pollutants may cause direct irreversible or reversible damage to the receptor cells. Persistent binding of a pollutant to receptor sites might also cause irreversible damage, resulting in death of functional chemoreceptor cells. Recent studies have shown the potential of the olfactory receptor cells for turnover and for regeneration after injury (Evans et al., 1982). The regenerative capacity of the olfactory neurons suggest that their continuous replacement may be an adapative process of the system to injury from the environment during the normal life of the animal (Graziadei and Monti Graziadei, 1978a, b).

In the following sections, each of these interactions will be discussed in detail, with special emphasis on studies from our own laboratory involving the fish olfactory system.

4. BEHAVIORAL STUDIES

4.1. Avoidance–Preference Reactions

A number of laboratory studies on the behavioral reactions of aquatic organisms to pollutants have employed an avoidance–preference trough. They may be divided into two categories: (1) those producing shallow gradients (relative general change in pollutant concentration), and (2) those with steep gradients (sharp separation of treated and untreated water) (Table 2). The shallow gradient system was first developed by Shelford and Allee (1913), who determined the reaction of fishes to dissolved gases. This gradient method was modified by Wells (1915) and further refined by Ishio (1960a,b, 1965), who eliminated vertical gradients and allowed more than one fish to be tested simultaneously. The steep gradient method was introduced by Takayasu and Sotooka (1924), who examined avoidance reactions of masou salmon (*Oncorhynchus masou*) to various industrial chemicals using a Y-maze trough. The counter current tube method initially proposed by Jones (1947) has been employed by Bishai (1962a,b) and later modified by Sprague (1964). Scherer and Nowak (1973) further advanced this method by adapting an automated recording system. Aquatic gradient avoidance response system developed by Cripe (1979) is a hybrid of the above two systems, allowing animals to choose between one uncontaminated zone and three increasingly toxic zones in a gradient trough that is monitored for extended time periods by infrared light sources, sensors, and a microprocessor.

Studies with lake whitefish (*Coregonus clupeaformis*) using a steep gradient avoidance–preference trough will be described later. The test procedures adapted are described by Kamchen and Hara (1980) and Hara (1981a). Briefly, water flows into each end of a trough and out of the center (Fig. 3). A test solution can be introduced at one end or the other. With an appropriate flow rate, a distinct separation between the two bodies of water at the center can be achieved. Following initial acclimatization, a fish generally swims back and forth across the boundary. Avoidance and preference reactions of fish are measured by comparing the amount of time that a fish spends in clean versus treated water.

4.1.1. Heavy Metals

Copper.   Test results with copper sulfate in whitefish are shown in Fig. 4. At the lowest concentration tested most fish show avoidance with logit % time response of -0.23. The lowest concentration of copper sulfate to induce appreciable avoidance is approximately 0.05 μM. The degree of avoidance increases with an increase in concentration, with the maximum avoidance at 25 μM. When the concentration is further increased the logit % time response increases indicating preference. This reversal in the response takes place between 25 and 100 μM. Ishio (1965) claims that attractive action of copper is attributable to their action of lowering the concentration of carbonic acid in water. However, with most natural waters, addition of $CuCl_2$ would be expected to result in liberation of carbonic acid from bicarbonates, and increase of total acidity, along with formation of basic copper carbonate and decline of pH.

The foregoing findings with whitefish correspond with some studies with other fish species where low levels of copper salts (25 μM) are avoided (Takayasu and Sotooka, 1924; Sprague, 1964; Westlake et al., 1974; Black and Birge, 1980) while higher levels (100 μM) are preferred (Jones, 1947; Ishio, 1965; Black and Birge, 1980). Generally higher avoidance threshold concentrations of copper are reported in some marine species (Syazuki, 1964). Extremely high concentrations (5000 μM) of copper sulfate are avoided by the ten-spined stickleback, *Pygosteus pungitilus* (Jones, 1947). Contrasting findings that lower levels of copper are attracted to goldfish

Table 2. Review of Experimental Designs of Avoidance–Preference Studies of Aquatic Organisms Exposed to Various Chemicals[a]

Chemical	Species	Reference
Shallow Gradients		
CO_2, O_2, N_2, acetic acid, NH_4	*Abramis crysoleucas, Ambloplites rupestris, Ameiurus melas, Catostomus commersoni, Etheostoma coeruleum, E. zonale, Hybopsis kentuckiensis, Lepomis cyanellus, Micropterus dolomieui, Notropis atherinoides, N. cornutus, Umbra limi*	Shelford and Allee, 1913, 1914
H_2S, salinity, alkalinity, acidity	*Clupea pallasii, Lepidapsetta bilineata, Oligocottus maculosus*	Shelford and Powers, 1915
H_2CO_3, H_2SO_4, NH_4OH, Na_2CO_3	*Ameiurus melas, Lepomis pallidus, Pomoxis annularis*	Wells, 1915
H^+, H_2CO_3, $CuCl_2$, NH_4OH, OH^-	*Acheilognathus limbata, Carassius auratus, Cyprinus carpio, Gnathopogon gracilis, Lebistes reticulatus, Lepomis macrochirus, Moroco steindachneri, Pimephales promelas, Pungtungia herzi, Sarcocheilichthys variegatus, Tribolodon hakonensis, Zacco platypus*	Ishio, 1960a,b, 1965
Chloroacetophenone, chlordane, etc.	*Lepomis cyanellus*	Summerfelt and Lewis, 1967
Steep Gradients		
Mercuric chloride, copper sulfate, zinc sulfate, HCl, CO_2, etc.	*Oncorhynchus masou*	Takayasu and Sotooka, 1924
Copper sulfate, zinc sulfate, lead nitrate, acids, alkalis, etc.	*Cyprinus carpio, Anguilla japonica, Meretrix meretrix*	Oya et al., 1939
Alcohol, chloroform, formalin, mercuric chloride	*Pygosteus pungitius*	Jones, 1947
Calcium nitrate, sodium sulfide, H^+, lead nitrate, zinc sulfate	*Gasterosteus aculeatus, Phoxinus phoxinus*	Jones, 1948

Toxicant/method	Species	References
Phenol, para-cresol, ortho-cresol, O_2 NaOH, H_2SO_4, sulfite pulp mill effluent, etc.	Phoxinus phoxinus, Gasterosteus aculeatus, Salmo trutta Carassius auratus, Fugu pardalis	Jones, 1951, 1952 Fujiya and Nitta, 1953
Sulfate waste, sulfite waste O_2, H^+	Oncorhynchus kisutch, O. tshawytscha, Salmo gairdneri Salmo salar, Salmo trutta	Jones et al., 1956 Bishai, 1962a,b
Copper sulfate, zinc sulfate, ABS, BKME, phenol, chlorine	Salmo gairdneri; Salmo salar	Sprague, 1964, 1968; Sprague et al., 1965; Sprague and Drury, 1969
DDT, endrin, dursban	Cyprinodon variegatus, Gambusia affinis	Hansen, 1969; Hansen et al., 1972
Mercuric chloride	Carassius auratus	Kleerekoper et al., 1970, 1973
Mercuric chloride, fenitrothion	Carassius auratus	Scherer and Nowak, 1973; Scherer, 1975
DDT, toxaphene, endrin	Gambusia affinis Rhinichthys atratulus	Kynard, 1974 Fava and Tsai, 1976
Total residual chlorine, free residual chlorine, etc.	Lagodon rhomboides, Fundulus grandis	Lewis and Livingston, 1977
BKME Copper sulfate	Gammarus lacustris	Maciorowski et al., 1977
Fluviarium Methods		
O_2, nickel nitrate, ferric nitrate	Leuciscus rutilus	Hoglund, 1951
2,4,6-Trinitrophenol	Leuciscus rutilus	Lindahl and Marcstrom, 1958
Sulfite waste liquor, HCl, O_2, NaOH, NaCl, pH, CO_2	Coregonus nasus, Esox lucius, Gasterosteus aculeatus, Leuciscus idvarus, Leuciscus rutilus, Perca fluviatilis, Salmo alpinus, Salmo salar, Salmo trutta, Salvelinus fontinalis, Tinca tinca	Hoglund, 1951, 1961; Hoglund and Hardig, 1969
Cadmium, copper, mercury, zinc, chloroform, dioctylphthalate, etc.	Lepomis macrochirus, Salmo gairdneri, Micropterus salmoides	Black and Birge, 1980

[a] Adapted from Larrick et al. (1978) and Cherry and Cairns (1982).

257

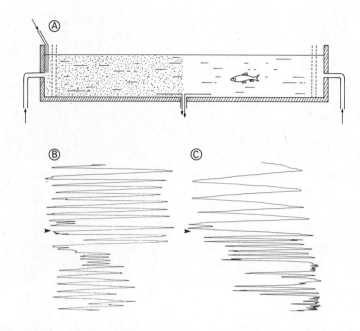

Figure 3. Schematic illustration of an avoidance–preference trough (*A*) and examples of tracings of preference (*B*) and avoidance (*C*) reactions of a fish to chemicals. In both recordings, chemical solutions are introduced at the left end (arrows). (From Hara, 1981a.)

(*Carassius auratus*) in both shallow (Kleerekoper et al., 1972) and steep gradient troughs (Timms et al, 1972; Westlake et al., 1974) may be related to the type of gradient developed in the testing apparatus and the availablility of other sensory cues. Avoidance reactions to copper are also influenced by the ambient temperature; when the presence of copper is associated with a 0.4°C (from 21.1 to 21.5°C) rise in temperature, avoidance reaction to copper by goldfish changes to attraction (Kleerekoper et al., 1973).

The avoidance of ethanol by juvenile Atlantic salmon (*Salmo salar*) is diminished in the presence of high concentration (25 μg/liter) of copper (Zitko and Carson, 1974). This is probably attributable to inhibitory effects of copper on the chemosensory systems (see Fig. 11). However, the elimination or suppression of copper avoidance by the same species in the presence of humic acid (Carson and Carson, 1973) would be explained by the complexation or chelation (Ramamoorthy and Kushner, 1975), or by their competition for the same receptor site.

In their natural habitat, Atlantic salmon ascending a stream for spawning showed avoidance reactions at about 0.4 toxic unit of copper and zinc; a level of 0.8 toxic unit blocked all upstream migration (Sprague et al., 1965; Saunders and Sprague, 1967). Large tank studies using the hatchery-reared Atlantic salmon returned to the hatchery demonstrated a clear-cut prefer-

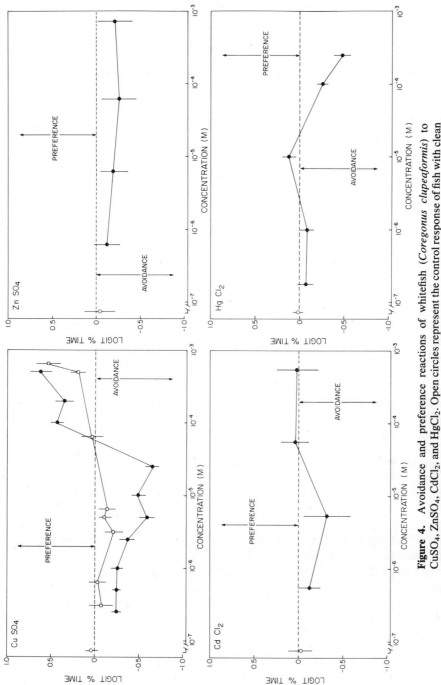

Figure 4. Avoidance and preference reactions of whitefish (*Coregonus clupeaformis*) to CuSO$_4$, ZnSO$_4$, CdCl$_2$, and HgCl$_2$. Open circles represent the control response of fish with clean water in both halves of the trough. Open squares represent fish whose nares were cauterized. (Adapted from Kamchen and Hara, 1980; Hara, 1981a; and Brown et al., 1982.)

ence for hatchery effluent. Addition of sublethal concentrations of $CuSO_4$ (44 µg/liter) to the effluent resulted in some degree of avoidance (Sutterlin and Gray, 1973).

Similar biphasic behavioral reactions to wide range of copper concentrations is also reported in an aquatic invertebrate *Gammarus lacuatris* (Maciorowski et al., 1977). *Gammarus pulex,* in contrast, showed avoidance at 10^{-4} $M,$ but the reaction was indifferent at 10^{-5} M (Costa, 1966).

The avoidance and preference reactions of whitefish to copper sulfate are essentially abolished after ablation or cauterization of the olfactory organ, except at the highest concentration (Fig. 4). The results indicate that olfaction is a principal mediator of the avoidance and preference responses to copper sulfate. Preference observed at 0.5 mM may be due to incomplete cauterization or to the function of other chemical senses, taste, and lateral-line organs. A potentiating effect of copper sulfate (1 mM) on the taste responses has been reported in Atlantic salmon (Sutterlin and Sutterlin, 1970).

Zinc. Whitefish significantly avoided zinc at all except the lowest (0.7 µM) concentration tested (Fig. 4). The threshold avoidance of whitefish to sublethal levels of zinc is similar to those reported for Atlantic salmon (Sprague, 1964) and rainbow trout (Black and Birge, 1980). However, rainbow trout examined by Sprague (1968) are 10 times more sensitive, avoiding zinc at 0.09 µM. Other species generally show higher avoidance thresholds for zinc than whitefish (Jones, 1947; Syazuki, 1964; Ishio, 1965; Summerfelt and Lewis, 1967; Black and Birge, 1980). *Gammarus pulex* avoided zinc sulfate with the threshold concentration of 1 mM. Further studies with antennulectomized and antennectomized gammarids indicate that these two appendages are the main chemoreceptors, but in addition, the mouth parts, gill, and other sensory areas of the body may also be involved in this recognition (Costa, 1966).

Cadmium. Whitefish slightly avoided cadmium chloride at low concentrations (10 µM); the averages were not significantly different from control at high concentrations (Fig. 4). These results indicate that whitefish do not avoid sublethal or lethal concentrations of cadmium. Comparable data are limited; however, Black and Birge (1980) showed that rainbow trout could avoid cadmium with a threshold of 0.5 µM, but that largemouth bass (*Micropterus salmoides*) and bluegill sunfish (*Lepomis macrochirus*) did not. Thus, there appears to be significant species differences in behavioral responses of fish to cadmium.

Mercury. The direct behavioral reactions of whitefish to mercuric chloride are shown in Fig. 4. Significant avoidance of mercury is not observed until the concentration reaches 0.1 mM. The ten-spined stickleback showed a similar avoidance threshold (20–150 µM) to mercury (Jones, 1947). Masou salmon showed clear avoidance at much lower concentrations ranging between 0.5 and 1.0 μM, which were approximately 20 times that of the lethal level for this species (Takayasu and Sotooka, 1924). Studies with green sunfish, *Lepomis cyanellus* (Summerfelt and Lewis, 1967) and goldfish (Scherer and Nowak, 1973), examining single concentrations of mercuric chloride, also reported avoidance at high concentrations. In contrast, Black and Birge (1980) demonstrated preference for low levels of mercury by rainbow trout; the threshold for attraction is estimated at 0.001 μM. The attraction of trout to sublethal or lethal levels of mercury and lack of avoidance by other species (e.g., largemouth bass and bluegill sunfish) appear to render this pollutant especially hazardous to fish. *Gammarus pulex* avoid mercury at lower concentrations down to 1 μM, but tend to exhibit a positive reaction at higher concentrations ranging between 1 and 10 mM (Costa, 1966).

4.1.2. Detergents

Behavioral reactions of whitefish to a detergent, sodium lauryl sulfate (SLS), are illustrated in Fig. 5 (Hara and Thompson, 1978). At the lowest and highest concentrations, 0.01 and 10 mg/liter, the overall response is neutral. At intermediate concentrations fish significantly prefer SLS. Reactions to commercial household detergents are biphasic; avoidance at the lowest (0.01 mg/liter) and highest (10 mg/liter) concentrations and preference at intermediate concentrations. These results can be contrasted with the general avoidance reactions elicited by exposure to sublethal levels of the detergents alkyl benzene sulfonate (ABS) and linear alkyl benzene sulfonate (LAS) in

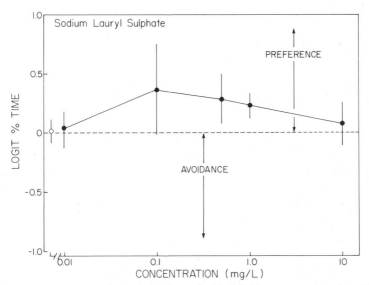

Figure 5. Avoidance and preference reactions of whitefish (*Coregonus clupeaformis*) to the anionic detergent sodium lauryl sulfate. Open circles represent the control response of fish with clean water in both halves of the trough. (From Hara and Thompson, 1978.)

rainbow trout (Sprague and Drury, 1969) and ayu, *Plecoglossus altivelis* (Tatsukawa and Hidaka, 1978), respectively. At 10 mg/liter ABS, nearly lethal, some rainbow trout showed avoidance, but others preferred it, resulting in neutral response. These data suggest that behavioral responses likely vary with detergent, species, and water quality factor. Marine invertebrates *Buccinum undatum, Chlamys opercularis, Pecten maximum, Ophiothrix fragilis,* and *Patella vulgata* are known to avoid predatory starfish (*Asterias rubens* and *Marthasterias glacialis*) and their extracts, an active component of which is a steroid glycoside with surface-active properties (Mackie et al, 1968; Mackie, 1970). Similar reactions can be mimicked with equal amounts (5 μg/mliter) of synthetic nonionic surfactants such as Triton X-100 and Tergitol NPX.

4.1.3. Chlorine

Avoidance has been well documented in a number of fish species at levels of chlorine which are not acutely toxic (Fava and Tsai, 1976; Cherry et al., 1977b; Larrick et al., 1978a; Cripe, 1979; Hose and Stoffel, 1980; Schumacher and Ney, 1980; Cherry and Cairns, 1982). Rainbow trout avoided chlorine at lowest (0.01 mg/liter) and highest (1.0 mg/liter) concentrations tested, but most preferred an intermediate lethal concentration of 0.1 mg/liter (Sprague and Drury, 1969). Other species have shown attraction or no avoidance at similar levels (Bogardus et al., 1978). Size of fishes (Meldrim et al., 1974; Hose and Stoffel, 1980) and environmental factors such as water temperature (Meldrim and Fava, 1977; Cherry et al., 1977b; Hose and Stoffel, 1980; Stober et al., 1980; Giattina et al., 1981), light (Meldrim and Fava, 1977), and salinity (Hose and Stoffel, 1980; Stober et al., 1980) have been found to influence behavioral reactions of fishes to chlorinated discharges. Cherry and Cairns (1982) describe variations in the avoidance response to chlorine due to species and the chlorine chemistry. The overall range in avoidance concentrations determined for 18 species varies from 0.05 to 0.43 mg/liter total residual chlorine (TRC). Salmonids are most sensitive, avoiding 0.05–0.10 mg/liter TRC, and cyprinids as a group are most variable, avoiding TRC concentrations as low as 0.05–0.20 mg/liter (rosyface shiner, *Notropis rubellus*) to as high as 0.21–0.43 mg/liter (*golden shiner, Notemigonus crysoleucas*).

The avoidance response of spotted bass (*Micropterus punctulatus*) and rosyface shiner were most closely associated with the calculated hypochlorus acid fraction of TRC (Cherry et al., 1977a). A greater concentration of TRC is necessary to initiate avoidance at higher acclimation temperature for the stenothermal species (rainbow trout and coho salmon, *Oncorhynchus kisutch*) and the eurythermal species (largemouth bass, bluegill, and mosquitofish, *Gambusia affinis*), although the amount of the hypochlorous acid within the TRC is approximately the same regardless of the acclimation temperature at each avoidance concentration (Cherry et al., 1982). Chlorine components were thought to be responsible for the behavioral reactions of fish towards sewage effluent (Fava and Tsai, 1976; Dinnel et al., 1979). However, the effects of other components of sewage (ammonia, turbidity, dissolved oxygen, and pH) have not been fully examined and may also influence behavior.

4.1.4. Oxygen, Carbon Dioxide, and pH

Dissolved-oxygen deficiency which can be lethal to fish frequently results from BOD and COD associated with pollution with domestic and industrial wastes. Detection and avoidance by fish of low oxygen concentrations before these result in fish mortality obviously can be beneficial. Many investigators have shown that fish avoid low concentrations of dissolved oxygen, but there is no clear consensus as to the nature of the response (Shelford and Allee, 1913; Jones, 1952; Whitmore et al., 1960; Hoglund, 1961; Hoglund and Hardig, 1969; Stott and Cross, 1973). Decrease in the dissolved oxygen concentration in a laboratory channel caused roach (*Rutilus rutilus*) and minnow (*Phoxinus phoxinus*) to move downstream to better oxygenated water by means of a predominantly appropriate response; the fall in oxygen level apparently being a directive stimulus. When an aerated water flow was restored the fish quickly reoccupied their original position (Stott and Cross, 1973; Stott and Buckley, 1979). These findings are in accord with those of Whitmore et al. (1960), who studied avoidance reactions of the chinook salmon (*Oncorhynchus tshawytscha*), coho salmon (*Oncorhynchus kisutch*), largemouth bass, and bluegill sunfish to low oxygen concentrations. However, these do not support Jones' (1952) and Hoglund's (1961) views that the driving force behind the attractions in oxygen gradients is random swimming caused by respiratory distress and incipient suffocation. Goldfish confined in deoxygenated water are capable of responding behaviorally to changes in oxygen levels and regulating their respiratory environment (van Sommers, 1962; Oglivie, 1982).

Fishes, if given the choice, avoid ambient water with unfavorably high levels of carbon dioxide and hydrogen ions (pH) (Shelford and Allee, 1913; Wells, 1915, 1918; Jones, 1948; Hoglund, 1961; Bishai, 1962a, b). Sticklebacks avoid water more acidic than pH 5.6 or more basic than pH 11.4, but they are indifferent or very vaguely positive over the pH range 5.8–11.2 (Jones, 1948). It has been suggested that a response to a carbon dioxide gradient is a dominant factor in the spawning migratory movement of fishes (Powers, 1941; Powers and Clark, 1943). Afferent receptors for carbon dioxide tension of the water are located in the lateral-line organs of brook trout and rainbow trout, since the response is lost when nerves leading to the organs are severed (Powers and Clark, 1943). Hoglund (1961) found that the main directive factor in combined pH/P_{CO_2} gradients is CO_2, particularly within the pH range of 7.4 to 5.5. In this range the fishes *Leuciscus rutilus* and *Salmo salar* are able to detect and avoid carbon dioxide separately from the accompanying pH, and they are largely indifferent to pH between the range approximately 5.5 to 10.5. Hoglund suggests that the avoidance reactions to CO_2 gradients may be attributable to chemoreceptors in the gill region, because ablation of the olfactory organs and the sectioning of the nerves innervating the later-line organs do not alter the reactions of fishes to CO_2. Taste receptors in the gill region and mouth of fishes are sensitive to CO_2 independent of pH (Konishi et al., 1969; Sutterlin and Sutterlin, 1970; Yoshii et al., 1980).

4.1.5. Other Pollutants

Behavioral investigations with other pollutants such as pulpmill effluents, pesticides, phenol, petroleum, and miscellaneous chemical toxicants consist largely of studies attempting to ascertain whether aquatic organisms will avoid lethal and sublethal exposures, and determination of environmental levels which would alter ecological distribution. Generally, the chemosensory systems involved have not been characterized and there is limited examination of the active ingredients of heterogeneous effluents.

Jones et al. (1956) observed that juvenile chinook salmon avoided 2.5% pulpmill effluents (PME) but coho salmon did not avoid them even at 10% dilution. Upstream addition of PME did not alter the progress of migrating coho and chinook salmon up a fish ladder (Brett and MacKinnon, 1954). Using ultrasonic transmitters, Kelso (1977) examined field avoidance and changes in population distribution due to PME. Avoidance reactions of minnows and roaches to sulfite waste liquor (SWL) was essentially abolished by the removal of the olfactory tissue (Hoglund, 1961). However, the avoidance reaction to SWL diminished with an increase in the gradient, indicating no direct relation between the presumed incipient lethal limits and the degree of avoidance. Atlantic salmon parr showed moderate avoidance to bleached Kraft mill effluent (BKME) throughout the sublethal range of 10 to 100,000 ppm (Sprague and Drury, 1969). Similar results for unbleached effluents suggest that avoidance is caused by material in the Kraft cooking wastes. Two marine species, pinfish (*Lagodon rhomboides*) and gulf killifish (*Fundulus grandis*), are reported to avoid BKME at 0.1% (Livingston et al., 1976; Lewis and Livingston, 1977). The data for herring (*Clupera harengus*) suggest that long-chain complex molecules such as lignosulfonates and lignin in PME are responsible for fish avoidance reactions (Wildish et al., 1977). However, the findings by Greer and Kosakoski (1978) with seawater-acclimated pink salmon (*Oncorhynchus gorbuscha*) fry indicate that avoidance of low salinity is the dominant response in avoidance of seawater dilutions of BKME.

Summerfelt and Lewis (1967) observed in laboratory studies that the green sunfish avoided chlordane but not lindane at concentrations close to the lethal level. Recent investigations have extended the number of fish species and pesticides examined (Hansen, 1969; Scherer, 1975; Granett et al., 1978). Grass shrimp (*Palaemonetes pugio*) avoided the herbicide 2,4-D at 1.0 and 10.0 ppm, but did not avoid insecticides DDT, endrin, dursban, malathion, and sevin (Hansen et al., 1973). Most of these insecticides are avoided by sheephead minnow (*Cyprinodon variegatus*) and mosquitofish (*Gambusia affinis*) (Hansen, 1969; Hansen et al., 1973). Avoidance studies with herbicides are widely varied; some herbicides are avoided at sublethal levels, but some are not avoided even at the lethal concentration (Folmar, 1976; Folmar et al., 1979).

There is limited but convincing evidence that petroleum and related hydrocarbons released into the marine environment may interfere with the normal behavior of certain organisms. This may be a consequence of a direct attraction or avoidance response to the presence of oil, or an indirect effect resulting from the masking or mimicking of natural chemical cues by specific components of the oil. The Arctic amphipods, *Onisimus affinis* and *Gammarus oceanicus,* were repelled by various crude oil masses, while the isopod *Mesidotea entomon* exhibited a essentially neutral response (Percy, 1976, 1977). The response was significantly diminished when the oil was weathered or if the animals were preexposed to light crude oil emulsions. Untainted food was preferentially selected over oil-tainted food. The blue crab (*Callinectes sapidus*) and Dungeness crab (*Cancer magister*) detected the petroleum hydrocarbon naphthalene, with the threshold concentration of 10^{-7} mg/liter (Pearson and Olla, 1979, 1980; Pearson et al., 1980; Pearson et al., 1981a).

Most of the studies investigating behavioral reactions of organisms to other miscellaneous chemicals (e.g., phenol, antitranspirant, etc.) are listed in Table 3.

Avoidance–preference tests *per se* monitor the ability of the test organism to detect the presence of a chemical, whether toxic or nontoxic, and to respond to the chemical by moving into or away from it. As examined previously, the degree of toxicity and the avoidance level of toxicants are not always correlated, and many toxicants are not avoided at concentrations exceeding the lethal level (Shelford, 1917; Sprague and Drury, 1969; Hara, 1981a; Brown et al., 1982). The relevance of these tests to toxicity testing is thus restricted to determine (1) whether the organism can detect a toxicant, and (2) if so, whether preference for the toxicant will render it more hazardous, or whether avoidance may provide a chance for escape.

4.2. Effects of Pollutants on Behavior Mediated by Chemoreception

Overt avoidance of pollutants may be advantageous to organisms by preventing their exposure to lethal or sublethal levels. However, more insidious hazards lie in the effects that unperceived or unavoidable toxicants may have on behavioral responses mediated by chemosensory systems (e.g., detection of predator or conspecifics, procurement of food, reproduction, and orientation and migration). Effects may be manifested directly or by modifying the organism's responses to its environment. Research into this area has received the least attention probably because of difficulties in quan-

Table 3. A Summary of Pollutant Effects on Chemoreception in Aquatic Organisms

Author	Species	Pollutant	Effective Level
	A. Preference–Avoidance		
	Invertebrates		
Costa, 1966	*Gammarus pulex*	Chloroform, alcohol, formalin	Variable
		Zinc sulfate	1 mM
		Lead nitrate	0.1 mM
		Mercuric chloride	1 M
		Copper sulfate	0.1 mM
Mackie et al., 1968	*Buccinum undatum*	Detergents (Triton X-100, Tween 80, etc.)	1–5 µg/liter
Mackie, 1970	*Buccinum undatum, Chlamys opercularis, Pecten maximus, Ophiothrix fragilis, Patella vulgata*	Detergents (Triton X-100, Tergitol NPX)	0.5–10 nM
Hansen et al., 1973	*Palaemonetes pugio*	DDT, Endrin, Dursban, Malathion, Sevin, 2,4-D	1–10 mg/liter
Maciorowski et al., 1977	*Gammarus lacustris*	Copper sulfate	0.15 mg/liter
Laughlin et al., 1978	*Callinectes sapidus*	Storm water runoff	pH 4.6
Pearson and Olla, 1979	*Callinectes sapidus*	Naphthalene	0.12 mg/liter
Pearson et al., 1980	*Cancer magister*	Naphthalene, water-soluble fraction of crude oil	10^{-2} mg/liter, 4×10^{-4} mg/liter
Pearson and Olla, 1980	*Callinectes sapidus*	Naphthalene	10^{-7} mg/liter
Pearson et al., 1981	*Callinectes sapidus*	Water-soluble fraction of crude oil	2×10^{-6} mg/liter

Fishes

Reference	Species	Substance	Concentration
Takayasu and Sotooka, 1924	Oncorhynchus masou	Copper sulfate	0.8 μM
		Zinc sulfate	50 μM
		Mercuric chloride	0.5 μM
Oya et al., 1939	Anguilla japonica	Copper sulfate	40 μM
	Cyprinus carpio	Zinc sulfate	180 μM
Jones, 1947	Pygosteus pungitius	Mercuric chloride	1 mM
		Zinc sulfate	0.3 mM
		Copper sulfate	0.1 M
Hasler and Wisby, 1950	Hyborhynchus notatus	Phenols	0.0005 mg/liter
Jones, 1951	Phoxinus phoxinus	Phenols	0.04%
Hiatt et al., 1953a,b	Kuhlia sandvicensis	Chlorine	1.0 mg/liter
		Cupric acetate	20 mg/liter
		Parathion	20 mg/liter
		Lindane	1.0 mg/liter
		Phenol	2.0 mg/liter
Jones et al., 1956	Oncorhynchus tshawytscha	Pulp mill effluents	1000 mg/liter
	Oncorhynchus kisutch		2000 mg/liter
Lindahl and Marcstrom, 1958	Leuciscus rutilus	Trinitrophenol	$3 \times 10^{-4}\ M$
Hoglund, 1961	Leuciscus rutilus	Sulfite waste liquor	?
	Salmo salar and others	CO_2	?
Syazuki, 1964	Chaenogobius heptacanthus	Copper sulfate	2.0 mg/liter
	Therapon jorbua	Zinc sulfate	24 mg/liter
	Mugil cephalus	Phenol	30 mg/liter
Sprague, 1964	Salmo salar	Crude petroleum	0.8 mg/liter
		Copper	2.3 μg/liter
		Zinc	53 μg/liter
		Copper and zinc	0.42 μg/liter + 6.1 μg/liter

Table 3. *(Continued)*

Author	Species	Pollutant	Effective Level
	Fishes Cont'd		
Summerfelt and Lewis, 1967	*Lepomis cyanellus*	Chlordane	20 mg/liter
		Pentachlorophenol	20 mg/liter
Sprague, 1968	*Salmo gairdneri*	Zinc	5.6 µg/liter
Hansen, 1969	*Cyprinodon variegatus*	DDT	0.005 mg/liter
		Endrin	0.0001 mg/liter
		Dursban	0.1 mg/liter
		2,4-D	0.1 mg/liter
Sprague and Drury, 1969	*Salmo gairdneri*	Detergent ABS	0.37 mg/liter
		Phenol	10 mg/liter, no effect
		Chlorine	0.01 mg/liter
		Bleached kraft pulp mill effluents	10 mg/liter
Hansen et al., 1972	*Gambusia affinis*	DDT	0.1 mg/liter
		Dursban	0.1 mg/liter
		Malathion	0.05 mg/liter
		Sevin	10.0 mg/liter
		2,4-D	1.0 mg/liter
Hansen et al., 1974	*Gambusia affinis*	Polychlorinated biphenyl (Arochlor 1254)	0.1 mg/liter
	Lagodon rhomboides		10.0 mg/liter
	Cyprinodon variegatus		10.0 mg/liter, no effect
Kynard, 1974	*Gambusia affinis*	Parathion	0.2 mg/liter
		Endorin, Toxaphene	0.25 mg/liter
		DDT	10.0 mg/liter
Lawrence and Scherer, 1974	*Coregonus clupeaformis*	Drilling fluids	1.0 mg/liter, preference
	Salmo gairdneri		10.0 mg/liter
Meldrim et al., 1974	*Morone americana*	Free chlorine	0.02 mg/liter

Reference	Species	Substance	Concentration
Westlake et al., 1974	*Carassius auratus*	Copper	0.005 mg/liter
Scherer, 1975	*Carassius auratus*	Fenitrothion	0.01 µg/liter
Fava and Tsai, 1976	*Rhinichthys atraculus*	Chlorinated sewage (total chlorine)	0.13 mg/liter
Folmar, 1976	*Salmo gairdneri*	Chloramines	0.18 mg/liter
		Free chlorine	0.61 mg/liter
		Copper sulfate	0.0001 mg/liter
		Acrolein, Emulsified xylene	0.1 mg/liter
		Dalapon, 2,4-dichlorophenoxy-acetic acid	1.0 mg/liter
Lewis, 1976	*Salmo gairdneri*	Glyphosate, Diquat	10.0 mg/liter, no effect
Livingston et al., 1976	*Lagodon rhomboides*	Aquathol K, Trichloroacetic acid	10.0 mg/liter, no effect
Updegraff and Sykora, 1976	*Oncorhynchus kisutch*	Manganous sulfate	10.0 mg/liter, no effect
Wildish et al., 1976	*Clupea harengus*	Pulp mill effluents	0.1%
		Neutralized iron hydroxide	4.2 mg/liter Fe
		Pulp mill effluent (sodium lignosulfonate)	2.5 mg/liter
Cherry et al., 1977a	*Notropis spilopterois* *Pimephalis notalis*	Total residual chlorine	0.1–0.2 mg/liter
Cherry et al., 1977b	*Micropterus punctatus* *Notropis rubellus*	Total residual chlorine	0.05 mg/liter
Johnson and Webster, 1977	*Salvelinus fontinalis*	pH	pH <4.5
Kelso, 1977	*Catostomus commersoni*	Pulp mill effluent	<15%
Lewis and Livingston, 1977	*Lagodon rhomboides* *Fundulus grandis*	Pulp mill effluent	0.06%
Meldrim and Fava, 1977	*Morone americana* *Menidia menidia* *Morone saxatilis*	Total residual chlorine	0.03 mg/liter
Middaugh et al., 1977a	*Leiostomus xanthurus*	Total residual chlorine	0.3 mg/liter
Middaugh et al., 1977b		Total residual chlorine	0.05 mg/liter
Wildish et al., 1977	*Clupea harengus*	Sodium lignosulfonate	0.1–0.3 mg/liter

Table 3. *(Continued)*

Author	Species	Pollutant	Effective Level
	Fishes (cont.)		
Bogardus et al., 1978	*Osmerus mordax*	Monochloramine (measured as total residual chlorine)	0.02 mg/liter
			<0.103 mg/liter, preference
			0.125 mg/liter
	Oncorhynchus kisutch		0.01 mg/liter
	Perca flavescens		0.002 mg/liter
	Alosa pseudoharengus		0.05 mg/liter
	Notropis hudsonius		
Grieve et al., 1978	*Morone chrysops*	Total residual chlorine	0.035 mg/liter
Granett et al., 1978	*Salmo salar*	Florex	0.01 mg/liter
		Dimilin-G1	No effect
Greer and Kosakoski, 1978	*Oncorhynchus gorbuscha*	Pulp mill effluents	0.8%
Hara and Thompson, 1978	*Coregonus clupeaformis*	Sodium lauryl sulfate	0.05 mg/liter, preference
Larrick et al., 1978a	*Pimephales promelas*	Total residual chlorine	0.115 mg/liter
Larrick et al., 1978b	*Noemigonus crysoleucas*	Total residual chlorine	0.199 mg/liter
Tatsukawa and Hidaka, 1978	*Plecoglossus altivelus*	Linear alkyl benzene sulfonate	0.0015 mg/liter
		Alkyl benzene sulfonate	0.011 mg/liter
Cripe, 1979	*Lagodon rhomboides*	Chlorine-produced oxidants	0.02–0.04 mg/liter
Dinnel et al., 1979	*Cymatogaster aggregata*	Chlorinated sewage	1–10%, preference
			15–20%, avoidance
Folmar et al., 1979	*Salmo gairdneri*	Glyphosate	10.0 mg/liter, no effect
McMahon and Kynard, 1979	*Gambusia affinis*	Folicote (antitranspirant)	0.75%
Stott and Buckley, 1979	*Phoxinus phoxinus*	Oxygen	low
		Phenol	10.0 mg/liter, no effect

Reference	Species	Substance	Value
Black and Birge, 1980	*Salmo gairdneri*	Copper	0.074 mg/liter
		Zinc	0.047 mg/liter
		Cadmium	0.052 mg/liter
		Mercury	0.0002 mg/liter, preference
	Lepomis macrochirus	Chloroform	11.9 mg/liter, preference
		Trisodium nitrilotriacetic acid	56.6 mg/liter
		Phenol	39.0 mg/liter
		Dioctyl phthalate	112.4 mg/liter, preference
Stevens et al., 1980	*Oncorhynchus kisutch, O. nerka, O. tshawytscha, Salmo gairdneri*	Air-supersaturated water	125–145%
Hose and Stoffel, 1980	*Chromis punctipinnis*	Total residual chlorine	0.08 mg/liter
Kamchen and Hara, 1980	*Coregonus clupeaformis*	Mercury	2×10^{-7} M, avoidance
			2.5×10^{-7} M, inhibition
Schumacher and Ney, 1980	*Salmo gairdneri*	Total residual chlorine	0.05 mg/liter
Stober et al., 1980	*Oncorhynchus kisutch*	Total residual chlorine	0.002 mg/liter
	Cymatogaster aggregata		0.175 mg/liter
Johnston and Wildish, 1981	*Clupea harengus*	Dredge spoil	9–12 mg/liter
Hara, 1981	*Coregonus clupeaformis*	Copper	1×10^{-7} M

B. Effects on Behavior Mediated by Chemoreception

Invertebrates

Reference	Species	Substance	Value
Takahashi and Kittredge, 1973	*Pachygrapsus crassipes*	Water-soluble extracts of crude oil	10^{-8} dilution
Jacobson and Boylan, 1973	*Nassarius obsoletus*	Seawater-soluble fraction of kerosene	1 µg/liter

Table 3. *(Continued)*

Author	Species	Pollutant	Effective Level
		B. Effects on Behavior Mediated by Chemoreception (cont.)	
	Invertebrates		
Atema et al., 1973	*Homarus americanus*	Seawater-soluble fraction of kerosene	60 µg/liter
	Nassarius obsoletus	Seawater-soluble fraction of kerosene	1 ng/liter
	Bdelloura candida	Mercuric chloride	1–100 mg/liter
		Ferric chloride	
		Detergents (and phosphate binders)	
McLeese, 1973	*Homarus americanus*	Bleached kraft mill effluent	2.0%, no effect
McLeese, 1974	*Homarus americanus*	Fenitrothion	25.4 µg/liter, no effect
Atema and Stein, 1974	*Homarus americanus*	Crude oil	10 µg/liter
McLeese, 1975	*Homarus americanus*	Copper	40–80 µg/liter
		Phosphamidon	32.5 µg/liter, no effect
Atema, 1976	*Nassarius obsoletus*	Water-solubles of kerosene	1.4 µg/liter
Percy, 1976, 1977	*Homarus americanus*	Crude oil	10 mg/liter
	Onisimus affinis	Crude oil	?
	Gammarus oceanicus		
	Mesidotea entomon		
Evans et al., 1977	*Crangon crangon*	Oil dispersants (Tween 80, BP1100×, Slickgone LT2)	1–100 mg/liter
Lyes, 1979	*Gammarus duebeni*	Surfactant Tween 80	10 mg/liter
Pearson et al., 1981	*Cancer magister*	Petroleum hydrocarbons	0.27 mg/liter

272

Fishes

Reference	Species	Substance	Concentration
Foster et al., 1966	*Jordanella floridae*	Detergent ABS	65 mg/liter
Kleerekoper et al., 1972	*Carassius auratus*	Copper	11–17 µg/liter
Symons, 1973	*Salmo salar*	Fenitrothion	1.0 mg/liter
Sutterlin and Gray, 1973	*Salmo salar*	Copper	44 µg/liter
Kleerekoper, 1974	*Mugil cephalus*	Parathion	0.33 mg/liter
Rand et al., 1975	*Carassius auratus*	Parathion	0.33 mg/liter
Bloom et al., 1978	*Brachydanio rerio*	Zinc	5.0 mg/liter
Kamchen and Hara, 1980	*Coregonus clupeaformis*	Mercury	$2 \times 10^{-5}\ M$, avoidance
			$2.5 \times 10^{-7}\ M$

C. Effects on Histology, Electrophysiology, and Biochemistry

Invertebrates

Reference	Species	Substance	Concentration
Bodammer, 1979	*Callinectes sapidus*	Copper sulfate	50–100 µg/liter
Derby and Atema, 1981	*Homarus americanus*	Drilling muds	10 mg/liter

Fishes

Reference	Species	Substance	Concentration
Bardach et al., 1965	*Ictalurus natalis*	Detergents ABS and LAS	0.5 mg/liter
Konishi et al., 1969	*Cyprinus carpio*	Carbon dioxide	0.5 vol %
	Protosus anguillaris		
Hidaka, 1970a	*Cyprinus carpio*	Carbon dioxide	1/100 saturation
		Mercuric chloride	$10^{-4}\ M$
		Cupric sulfate	$10^{-4}\ M$
		Zinc sulfate	$10^{-4}\ M$
Hidaka, 1970b	*Cyprinus carpio*	Silver nitrate	$10^{-5}\ M$
		Mercuric chloride	$10^{-4}\ M$
Sutterlin and Sutterlin, 1970	*Salmo salar*	Copper sulfate	$10^{-3}\ M$, augmentation
		Lead nitrate	$10^{-3}\ M$
Sutterlin and Sutterlin, 1971	*Salmo salar*	Mercuric chloride	$10^{-4}\ M$

Table 3. *(Continued)*

Author	Species	Pollutant	Effective Level
	C. *Effects on Histology, Electrophysiology, and Biochemistry* (cont.)		
	Fishes		
Sutterlin et al., 1971	*Salmo salar*	Alkyl benzene sulfonates	1–10 mg/liter
		Quaternary ammonium salts	
		Quaternary imidazolinium salts	
		Diamines	
Hara, 1972	*Oncorhynchus nerka*	Mercuric chloride	10^{-4} M (27 mg/liter) acute
	Oncorhynchus kisutch		0.1 mg/liter, chronic
	Salmo gairdneri		10^{-4} (16 mg/liter), acute
			0.1 mg/liter, chronic
Gardner and LaRoche, 1973	*Fundulus heteroclitus*	Copper sulfate	0.5 mg/liter
	Menidia menidia	Copper	0.5 mg/liter
Gardner, 1975	*Fundulus heteroclitus*	Mercury, copper, silver	0.5 mg/liter
	Menidia menidia	Crude oil	0.14 mg/liter
Haider, 1975	*Ameiurus nebulosus*	Lead acetate	10.6 mg/liter
	Tinca tinca		
Vijayamadhavan and Iwai, 1975	*Carassius auratus*	Mercury, copper, zinc, lead	10^{-4} M
Hara, 1976	*Salmo gairdneri*	pH	pH<4.0; pH>10.0
Hara et al., 1976	*Salmo gairdneri*	Copper sulfate	0.008 mg/liter
		Mercuric chloride	0.1 mg/liter
Daye and Garside, 1976	*Salvelinus fontinalis*	pH	pH<4.2; pH>10.0

Reference	Species	Substance	Electrophysiol.	Binding
Evans and Hara, 1977	*Salmo gairdneri*	Copper	0.05 mg/liter	
Thompson and Hara, 1977	*Salvelinus alpinus*	Natural water contaminated with heavy metals	0.1%	
Bloom et al., 1978	*Brachydanio rerio*	Zinc	5.0 mg/liter	
Cagan and Zeiger, 1978	*Salmo gairdneri*	Mercury	10^{-7} M	
		Copper	10^{-5} M	
		Cadmium	5×10^{-5} M	
		Silver, lead, zinc	10^{-3} M	
DiMichele and Taylor, 1978	*Fundulus heteroclitus*	Naphthalene	0.02 mg/liter	
Zelson and Cagan, 1979	*Ictalurus punctatus*	Mercury, *p*-mercurybenzoate, zinc, cadmium, copper	10^{-4} M	
Yoshii et al., 1980	*Anguilla japonica*	Carbon dioxide	2×10^{-5} M	
Borie et al., 1981	*Salmo gairdneri*	Atraxine, Lindane, Ethylparathion	1–10 mg/liter	
Cancalon, 1980	*Ictalurus punctatus*	Zinc	0.17–10 mM	
		Triton X-100	0.03–0.1%	
Suzuki and Suzuki, 1981	*Entosphenus japonicus*	Zinc sulfate	0.2 M	
Brown et al., 1982	*Salmo gairdneri*	Silver	0.03 μM	0.1 μM
		Mercury	0.4 μM	<0.1 μM
		Copper	0.2 μM	0.1 μM
		Cadmium	10 μM	10 μM
		Zinc	10 μM	10 μM
		Lead	100 μM	100 μM
		Cobalt	100 μM	100 μM
		Nickel	100 μM	100 μM

titative assessment, variability among individuals, and differences over time. In this section, selected examples that illustrate the effects of environmental perturbations on chemoreception-mediated behavior are presented.

One of the earliest studies that indicated the occurrence of chemosensory disruption was done by Takahashi and Kittredge (1973) with the shore crab, *Pachygrapsus crassipes*. The exposure of the crabs to the water-soluble extracts of crude oil completely inhibited both the feeding response to taurine and the mating stance response of the males when presented the sex pheromone. The threshold concentration of total water solubles that is effective in inhibiting chemoreception in this species is estimated below 10^{-8}. The polynuclear hydrocarbons, naphthalene, binaphthyl, and anthracene are suggested to be responsible for this inhibition.

A dilute seawater extract of kerosene consisting primarily of benzenes and naphthalenes (1 ppb) was found to inhibit attraction of mud snails (*Nassarius obsoletus*) to food extract (homogenates of oysters and scallop adductor muscles) (Jacobson and Boylan, 1973; Atema et al., 1973; Atema, 1976). On the contrary, whole kerosene and the branched-chain cyclic fractions induced searching and feeding behavior in the lobster (*Homarus americanus*) leading to ingestion of the test strips, but the water-soluble fraction of the same amount of crude oil caused no noticeable effects on chemosensory and feeding behavior (Atema et al., 1973; Atema and Stein, 1974). Feeding attraction is perhaps induced by the branched-cyclic fraction, while repulsion and feeding inhibition are caused by the polar-aromatic fraction of crude oil (Atema, 1976). Recently, Pearson et al. (1981b) observed that after 24-hr exposure to seawater contaminated with crude oil (0.27 ppm), the chemosensory antennular flicking response in the Dungeness crab was reduced, resulting in impaired feeding. In test runways the chemosensory response of *Homarus americanus* to food extracts (cod and herring muscles) is reduced by the simultaneous presentation of copper at concentrations estimated to be 4–80 times the lethal threshold (18 μg/liter) (McLeese, 1975). Bleached Kraft mill effluent and organophosphate insecticides fenitrothion and phosphamidon have no effect at concentrations higher than the lethal under the same experimental conditions (McLeese, 1973, 1974, 1975). Exposure of up to 48 hr to copper (12.5–32.5 μg/liter) causes a gradual decline in chemosensory response of lobsters, followed by gradual recovery in clean water (McLeese, 1975).

The heterocyclic amino acid proline and tripeptide glutathione elicit well-coordinated, stereotyped feeding responses in the zoanthid *Polythoa variabilis* and some Panamanian corals (*Pocillopora* cf. *damicornis, Pavona gigantea, Psammocora stellata,* and *Porites furcata*). These responses are essentially the same as the normal feeding reaction induced by food materials. Marine Diesel and Bunker-C oils can elicit a similar feeding reaction leading to ingestion in these species (Reimer, 1975a,b). However, the responses to oils are not normal in that ingestion takes a longer time to complete and, more significantly, it is followed by egestion. Brief exposure to oils (at concentration of 1/50 dilution for 30 min) retarded the feeding responses in *Polythoa variabilis*. Oil was retained in the coelenteron for several days following exposure and is periodically released in the form of tiny droplets. In corals the mouths were left opened for periods up to 17 days after exposure. Also, the feeding responses in Caribbean corals (*Porites porites, Agaricia agaricites, Favia fragum,* and *Madracis asperula*) were markedly reduced when exposed to crude oil and an oil-spill dispersant at concentrations as low as 50 ppm for 24 hr (Lewis, 1971).

In other studies with invertebrates, feeding behavior of brown shrimp (*Crangon crangon*) and reproductive behavior of *Gammarus duebeni* are decreased by exposure to sublethal concentrations of surfactants Tween 80, BP 1100X, and Slickgone LT2. The ability to locate food is largely recovered within a few hours of return of the animals to clean seawater (Evans et al., 1977; Lyes, 1979). Attraction of the flatworm *Bdelloura candida* to its host *Limulus polyphemus* is inhibited by the presence of $HgCl_2$, $FeCl_2$, detergents, and phosphate binders in detergents in concentrations ranging from 1 to 100 ppm (Atema et al., 1973). The surface-active agents appear to have a greater effect on chemosensory cells than on touch or pressure in the marine mollusc *Baccinum undatum* (Mackie, 1970).

In fish, impaired feeding behavior was observed after exposure of yellow bullheads, *Ictalurus natalis* (Bardach et al., 1965), and flagfish *Jordanella floridae* (Foster et al., 1966) to sublethal levels of detergents ABS and LAS. Food odor became unattractive and was significantly avoided after sublethal exposure of goldfish to parathion at 0.33 ppm (Kleerekoper, 1974; Rand et al., 1975). Zebrafish (*Brachydanio rerio*) possess a pheromonal sex attractant system that serves to maintain or limit sizes of schools or serves in attracting mature zebrafish to a spawning area (Bloom and Perlmutter, 1977). Exposing the fish to sublethal concentrations of zinc (76 μM) for 9 days abolished their preference for donor water containing pheromone (Bloom et al., 1978). As already mentioned, copper and zinc have detrimental effects on migration of Atlantic salmon to their spawning grounds (Saunders and Sprague, 1967; Sutterlin and Gray, 1973). Further, brook trout (*Salvelinus fontinalis*) show a strong preference for upwelling water in selection of spawning sites, and reducing the pH of the water to 4.5 causes avoidance of potential spawning areas (Johnson and Webster, 1977).

Kamchen and Hara (1980) examined the effects of mercuric chloride on behavioral reactions of whitefish to food extract. Whitefish show significant preference for food extract (dried food pellets) when tested using an avoidance–preference trough (see Fig. 3). Threshold preference estimated by regression analysis is 8×10^{-3} g/liter (Fig. 6). When the nares of whitefish are cauterized, the behavioral reactions to food extract are eliminated, indicating that the reactions to food extract are mediated through the olfactory system. Whitefish that are exposed to mercuric chloride (0.18 μM)

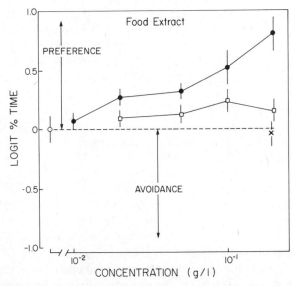

Figure 6. Behavioral reactions of whitefish (*Coregonus clupeaformis*) to food extract. Reactions of unexposed (solid circles) and fish preexposed (squares) to 0.25 μM HgCl$_2$ for 1–2 weeks are illustrated. Control response (open circle) with clean water in both halves of the trough and responses of nose-cauterized fish to food extract (cross) are also shown. (From Kamchen and Hara, 1980.)

for 1–2 weeks show greatly reduced behavioral responses to food extract; no significant preference is observed at any concentration (Fig. 6). In addition, no significant change in activity is recorded.

Recently, the effects of volcanic ash from the eruption of Mt. St. Helens, Washington, on the migration behavior of salmon were investigated using outdoor Y-maze raceways and displacement method (Whitman et al., 1982). Chinook salmon exhibited a strong preference for home water over nonnatal water source. The addition of ash to the home water significantly reduced preference for home water, apparently because of an avoidance response to ash, not an inability to recognize home water. Exposure to an ash suspension (approximately 650 mg/liter) for 7 days did not affect homing of salmon displaced downstream. The ash concentration used was substantially less than the lethal levels for this species, yet it was almost twice the level avoided in the Y-maze tests.

5.   HISTOPATHOLOGICAL STUDIES

Phospholipids stainable with Baker's acid hematein method are highly localized in the receptor neurons of the olfactory mucosa of several fish species, and alterations in phospholipid staining coincides well with changes

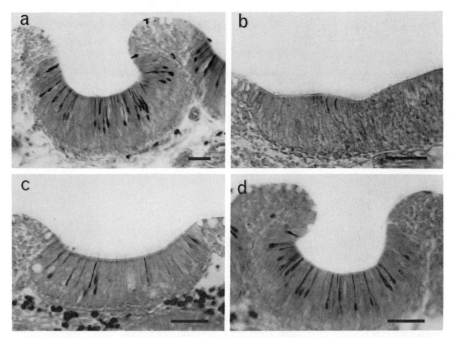

Figure 7. Cross sections (10 μM) of the olfactory neuroepithelium of whitefish (*Coregonus clupeaformis*), stained with Baker's acid hematein method. Control (*a*), with receptor neurons stained black after 2-week exposure to 2.4 μM copper sulfate (*b*), and after 4-week (*c*) and 12-week (*d*) recovery in clean water. Scale bars = 60 μm. (From Brown et al., 1982.)

in the electrophysiological activities of the olfactory epithelium following axotomy (Evans and Hara, 1977; Evans et al., 1982). Thus, the technique may be useful in monitoring histopathological and functional changes in the olfactory system caused by a deleterious environment.

The effects of exposure to copper sulfate (2.4 μM) on the olfactory epithelium of whitefish are illustrated in Fig. 7. The results show the formation of phospholipid stained granules in the necrotic receptors, followed by virtual elimination of stained elements after 2 weeks. The receptor cells containing stained granules gradually recover to near-normal levels by 12 weeks following removal of copper. Exposure to copper has no effect on the supporting cells. Results with rainbow trout are essentially the same as those with whitefish (Fig. 8). Degeneration of the olfactory sensory structures following exposure to copper has been previously reported in other species (Gardner and LaRoche, 1973; Gardner, 1975). After 24-hr exposure to 0.5 mg/liter (7.9 μM) copper sulfate, the receptor cells of *Fundulus heteroclitus* are necrotized and supporting cells are hyperplastic, effectively eliminating the sensory surface by overgrowth. Cystlike structures containing cellular debris and remnants of recognizable sensory tissue are formed. However, no noticeable injury is detected in the olfactory placode of *Fundulus* em-

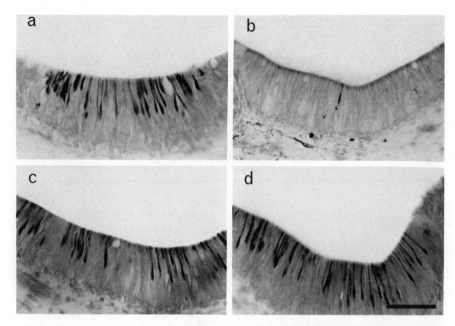

Figure 8. Cross sections (10 μM) of the olfactory neuroepithelium of rainbow trout (*Salmo gairdneri*), stained with Baker's acid hematein method. Control (*a*) with neuron stained black. The effects of exposure to 2.4 μM copper sulfate for 1 week (*b*), and 2-week exposure to 2.4 μM cadmium chloride (*c*) and mercuric chloride (*d*). Bar = 60 μm. (Modified from Brown et al., 1982.)

bryos under the light microscope. The olfactory epithelium of Atlantic silversides (*Menidia menidia*) is essentially destroyed after 6-hr treatment with 7.9 μM copper sulfate. In goldfish, copper sulfate at 200 μM, admittedly high, causes serious damage to taste buds within a few hours (Vijayamadhavan and Iwai, 1975). The chemoreceptors of the blue crab *Callinectes sapidus* appear susceptible to copper; exposure to 1000 μg/liter copper sulfate results in complete disruption of the integrity and disposition of the dendrites within the sensilla, but the majority of sensilla appear normal when exposed to 100 and 50 μg/liter copper sulfate (Bodammer, 1979).

Exposure of rainbow trout to sublethal levels of cadmium and mercury (0.8–2.4 μM) has proven to be less destructive than copper after 2 weeks (Fig. 8). In these fish there is only a slight reduction in the number of cells stained for phospholipids, though longer exposure time further diminishes staining. Mercury (2.5 μM) as well as silver (4.6 μM) are reported to cause severe degenerative changes in neurosensory cells from *Fundulus heteroclitus* olfactory organs within 96 hr, but cadmium chloride (5 μM) and zinc chloride elicit no morphological anomaly in these neurosensory structures (Gardner, 1975). Higher concentrations of mercuric chloride (100 μM) destroy taste buds and epithelial cells in the palatal organ of goldfish within 1 hr (Vijayamadhavan and Iwai, 1975). High concentrations of zinc (10–170 mM) produce degeneration specifically in the olfactory receptor cell of catfish, *Ictalurus punctatus* (Cancalon, 1980). The indifferent epithelium remains almost intact. A similar result is obtained using 0.1% Triton X-100. Recently Suzuki and Suzuki (1981) have demonstrated that irrigation of the nares of lampreys (*Entosphenus japonicus*) with 0.2 M ZnSO$_4$ causes a selective destruction of the olfactory receptor cells. Irrigation with 0.5 or 1.0 M ZnSO$_4$ causes severe and nonselective degeneration of the epithelium. Based on the high correspondence between morphological changes and amino acid binding activities (see Section 7) following zinc sulfate perfusion, Suzuki and Suzuki (1981) suggest that the essential structural component for amino acid binding is the distal segments of the olfactory receptor cilia. Sensory cell disintegration similar to the effects of heavy metals on olfactory tissues described previously is found in the taste receptors on the barbels and lips of catfish (*Ameiurus nebulosus*) and tench (*Tinca tinca*) exposed to lead acetate (50–100 μM) for up to 6 months (Haider, 1975).

Detergents ABS and LAS (4–5 ppm) produced a thickening of the border of sensory cells in the lamellae of the olfactory rosettes and a decrease in receptor cell numbers after 4 weeks in yellow bullheads (*Ictalurus natalis*). Erosions of taste buds were detected at lower concentrations (0.5–1.0 ppm) (Bardach et al., 1965). Crude oil and the saltwater-soluble and -insoluble fractions induced lesions in the olfactory organs of *Menidia menidia* similar to the lesions described earlier for copper (Gardner, 1975). Epithelial metaplasia induced in this manner either reduced or eliminated the surface area of sensory epithelium exposed to the aquatic environment. The necrocytosis encompassed both neurosensory and indifferent epithelia. Necrotic taste buds and neurosensory cells of the olfactory organ of *Fundulus heteroclitus* are observed after 15 day exposure to as low as 0.002 mg/liter (0.156 μM) naphthalene, a component of crude and refined oil–water mixtures (DiMichele and Taylor, 1978). Daye and Garside (1976) report increased mucous cell numbers and size in brook trout (*Salvelinus fontinalis*) at pH 4.2 and lower. Extreme alkaline conditions, above pH 9.5, create similar changes but to a lesser degree.

Due to the dynamic nature of the olfactory epithelium (Graziadei and Monti Graziadei, 1978a,b; Evans et al., 1982), cell renewal takes place once the toxicant is removed from the environment. Our studies on rainbow trout and whitefish exposed to copper sulfate indicate that 12 weeks is sufficient for return to near normal quantities of receptor cells (see Fig. 8). However, this does not imply functional recovery. Physiological measurements along with histochemical examination of regenerating cells in toxicant stressed fish are necessary to determine functional recovery. These studies should greatly enhance the usefulness of the histopathological methods as a predictive tool in the assessments of pollutant toxicity.

6. ELECTROPHYSIOLOGICAL STUDIES

Hara et al. (1976) have developed an electrophysiological method to monitor effects of sublethal concentrations of various toxicants on the olfactory responses of fishes. The method consists of recording of the olfactory epithelial or bulbar electrical responses to a standard stimulant (food extract, amino acid L-serine, etc.), while the olfactory organs are perfused with test toxicants of various levels (Fig. 9). In chronic exposure experiments responses to standard stimuli are normalized for both control and treated groups to constant instrument sensitivity. This facilitates comparison between two groups by analysis of variance.

6.1. Acute Effects of Heavy Metals

Figure 10 illustrates typical responses recorded from the olfactory bulb of rainbow trout when the nares are stimulated with L-serine (10 μM) before, during and after exposure to mercuric chloride (5.0 μM) for 30 min. The olfactory bulbar response normally starts declining within the first 2 min after infusion of mercuric chloride into the nares. The patterns of response and depression caused by mercuric chloride are qualitatively similar regardless of type of stimulant such as other amino acids or food extract. General patterns of the depression effects of silver, copper, and mercury on the bulbar response to L-serine are illustrated in Fig. 11 (Brown et al., 1982). Inhibition is usually followed by a stable period of 10–30 min when rinsing is initiated with fresh water. Partial recovery usually occurs with prolonged rinsing (Hara et al., 1976). Augmentation of the responses to L-serine sometimes occurs during treatment with high concentrations of metals; however, upon rinsing the response is left severely impaired. Zinc and lead are inhibitory only at the highest concentrations examined (0.5–1 mM). Elevated levels of cobalt and nickel cause some reduction of the bulbar response during treatment, but the responses tend to recover upon rinsing. Figure 12 summarizes the effects of all the various metals tested. Silver, mercury, and copper are the most effective inhibitors with IC50 (concentration which inhibits responses by 50%) values of 0.13–2.2 μM. The IC50 values for the other metals are greater than 100 μM. The threshold concentrations of silver, copper, and mercury needed to cause minimal inactivation are estimated at 0.03, 0.2, and 0.4 μM, respectively. These values are 2–5 times lower than lethal levels of the metals for rainbow trout (MacLeod and Pessah, 1973; Davies et al., 1978; Miller and MacKay, 1980). Inhibition of the bulbar response to chemical stimulant by cadmium, zinc, lead, cobalt, and nickel occurs at levels exceeding their lethal values. These data are in agreement with other studies in salmonids (Sutterlin and Sutterlin, 1970; Hara, 1972; Hara et al., 1976), indicating that olfactory responses to chemostimulants are depressed in fishes exposed to sublethal levels of mercury and

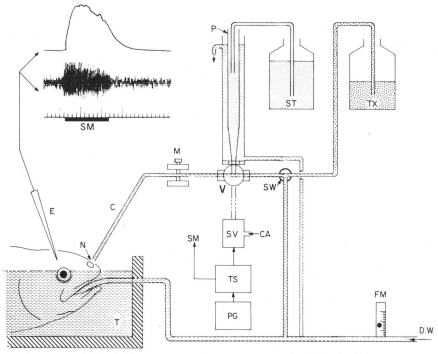

Figure 9. Experimental setup for electrophysiological recordings of olfactory responses and for toxicant infusion. The standard stimulant solution (ST) is led via plastic tubing into a glass pipette (P). By switching the three-way valve (V), stimulant is poured into the nares (N) through glass capillaries (C) adjusted by a micromanipulator (M). CA, compressed air; DW, dechlorinated water; E, recording electrodes; FM, flowmeter; SW, three-way valve; PG, programmer; SM, signal marker; SV, solenoid valve; T, trough; TS, time switch; TX, toxic chemical solution. (Modified from Hara et al., 1976.)

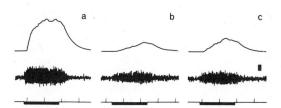

Figure 10. Electrical responses recorded from the olfactory bulb of rainbow trout (*Salmo gairdneri*) when nares were stimulated with L-serine (10 μM) before (*a*), during (*b*), and after (*c*) exposure to mercuric chloride (5 μM) for 30 min. The upper tracing of each pair is the integrated response of the lower. Duration of stimulation is indicated by heavy lines below each record. Time scale: each division = 5 sec. Calibration: 200 μV. (From Brown et al., 1982.)

283

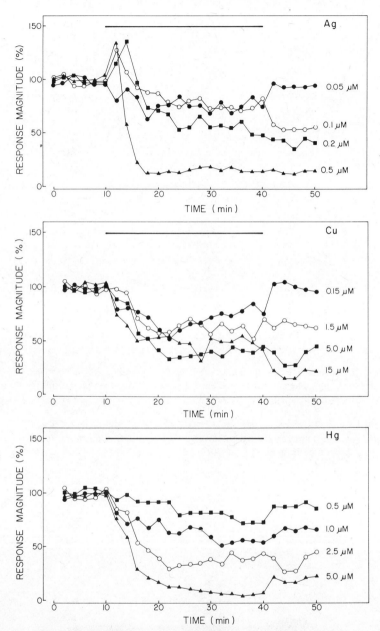

Figure 11. Effects of silver (Ag), copper (Cu), and mercury (Hg) on the olfactory bulbar response of rainbow trout (*Salmo gairdneri*) to L-serine (10 μ*M*). Horizontal bar indicates duration of treatment. The magnitude of the response is represented as a percentage of the control response before treatment. (From Brown et al., 1982.)

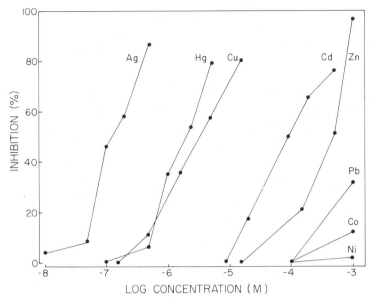

Figure 12. Inhibition of the olfactory bulbar response to L-serine (10 μ*M*) when the nares of rainbow trout (*Salmo gairdneri*) were exposed to various concentrations of heavy metals. Inhibition was determined from the average response (*n* = 5) to L-serine in the 10-min period following 30-min treatment with metals (see Fig. 11). (From Brown et al., 1982.)

copper. Although the concentrations used are not always realistic in terms of environmental contaminations, electrical recordings from the taste systems of carp, *Cyprinus carpio* (Hidaka and Yokota, 1967; Hidaka, 1970b), and Atlantic salmon (Sutterlin and Sutterlin, 1970) show that the heavy metals are also effective blocking agents of gustatory responses.

Incorporation of 100 μ*M*, 10 times the concentration used as the standard stimulant, along with the heavy metal protects the bulbar response from inhibition of copper (Fig. 13). This is probably due to competition between the stimulant and metal inhibitor for a receptor site. The relative inefficiency of copper, when presented simultaneously, to interfere with behavioral reactions of lobsters to food extracts in test runways is likely due to this type of competition between biological odors and pollutants (see Section 4.2; McLeese, 1975). Subsequent treatment of copper-exposed fish with dithiothreitol (1 m*M*), a thiol reagent, for 2 min reverses the effects of copper (Fig. 13). High concentrations of L-serine also protect the olfactory receptors from the effects of cadmium and zinc but not mercury or silver (Table 4). The inhibitory effects of all metals except mercury could be partially or totally reversed by subsequent treatment with dithiothreitol for various times after metal exposure. The effects of mercury cannot be reversed even with prolonged exposure to dithiothreitol. Previous work using the palatine nerve preparation from carp demonstrated that blocking effects of some

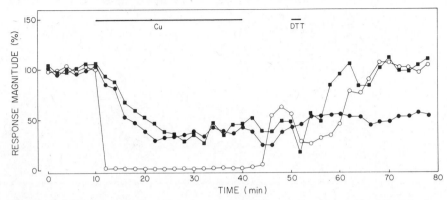

Figure 13. Olfactory responses of rainbow trout (*Salmo gairdneri*) to L-serine (10 μ*M*) when the nares were exposed to 1.5 μ*M* copper (solid circles) and 1.5 μ*M* copper plus 100 m*M* L-serine (open circles). The effects of treating the nares with dithiothreitol (DTT) after exposure to 1.5 μ*M* copper are also illustrated (squares). Duration of treatments is indicated by horizontal lines above records. (From Brown et al., 1982.)

metals on sugar receptors could be reversed by subsequent treatment with a thiol compound, cysteine (Hidaka, 1970b).

As previously shown, the behavioral reactions of whitefish to copper sulfate are of bimodal nature; they avoid it at lower concentrations but prefer it to the clean water at high concentrations (see Fig. 4). The effect of copper sulfate on the bulbar response induced by stimuli is also biphasic; the effect of lower concentrations is primarily inhibition, whereas the presence of excess copper sulfate augments the bulbar response (Hara, 1981a). Poten-

Table 4. Reversal of Metal Inhibition of the Olfactory Bulbar Response to L-Serine in Rainbow Trout (*Salmo gairdneri*) by High Ligand Concentration and Chelation[a]

	Response Magnitude[b]		
Metal (μ*M*)	Metal Alone	Metal + L-Serine (100 m*M*)	Dithiothreitol[c] (1 m*M*)
Mercury (2.5)	53 ± 11	47 ± 7	48 ± 17
Silver (0.5)	25 ± 5	29 ± 4	60 ± 8
Copper (1.5)	52 ± 11	101 ± 15	98 ± 15
Cadmium (200)	39 ± 8	69 ± 16	93 ± 29
Zinc (500)	50 ± 17	96 ± 9	92 ± 12

[a] From Brown et al. (1982).

[b] Values listed are the percentage ± S.D. (*n* = 3–5) of the olfactory bulbar response to L-serine (10 μ*M*) 35 min after cessation of metal exposure compared to control values prior to metal treatment.

[c] Treatment with dithiothreitol occurred subsequent to metal exposure. Time of dithiothreitol exposure was 2 min (copper), 4 min (zinc and silver), and 20 min (cadmium and mercury).

tiating effects of high concentrations of copper are also demonstrated in the responses from Atlantic salmon (Sutterlin and Sutterlin, 1970).

6.2. Chronic Effects of Heavy Metals

No behavioral act can be elicited if pollutants are not detected or are detected at levels which will not permit the animal to respond behaviorally before becoming debilitated. Chronic exposure to pollutants may result in receptor cell impairment due to membrane or organelle dysfunction or persistent binding of pollutants to receptor sites.

When rainbow trout are held for 2 weeks in water containing 0.15 mg/liter copper (2.4 μM), cadmium (1.3 μM), or mercury (0.75 μM) (sublethal except for cadmium), the olfactory rosettes accumulate the metals (Fig. 14; Brown et al., 1982). Total uptake after 2-week exposure is similar for all metals tested (120–160 nmol/g wet weight). The levels recorded are as high as those found in the gill. Only mercury is found in the brains of the exposed fish and maximal levels are 10% of those found in the olfactory rosettes. No difference in brain levels of copper between control (53.5 nmol/g) and treated (50.4 nmol/g) fish is evident. Brain cadmium is consistently below detection limit (0.36 nmol/liter; atomic absorption spectrometry) in all fish.

Figures 15 and 16 illustrate the effects on electro-olfactogram (EOG) of rainbow trout of exposure to 1.6 μM (0.1 mg/liter) copper sulfate. The EOG is a slow potential change evoked in the olfactory epithelium in response to chemical stimuli, and widely used as a measure of the receptor neuronal function. Little or no response either to food extract or L-serine at any concentration could be elicited after 1 week exposure. In other studies (Brown et al., 1982), exposure to 2.4 μM (0.15 mg/liter) copper progressively

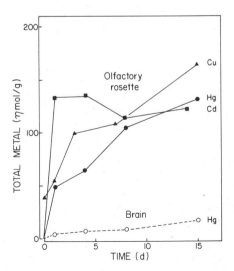

Figure 14. Total metal concentrations in olfactory rosette and brain tissues from rainbow trout (*Salmo gairdneri*) exposed to cadmium (Cd), copper (Cu), and mercury (Hg) at 0.15 mg/liter. No significant elevations above background levels were found for copper and cadmium levels in the brain. (From Brown et al., 1982.)

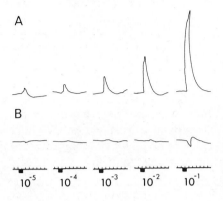

Figure 15. Electro-olfactogram (EOG) responses of rainbow trout (*Salmo gairdneri*) to food extract recorded from unexposed, control (*A*) and fish preexposed to 0.1 mg/liter (1.6 μ*M*) copper sulfate for 1 week (*B*). Duration of stimulation (heavy lines) and concentration (in g/liter) are indicated below each record. Time scale; each division = 5 sec.

inhibited the olfactory bulbar response of rainbow trout to L-serine (Fig. 17). The bulbar response was reduced by 42% after 1 week. Little response to L-serine at any concentration could be elicited after 2 weeks. Treatment of fish with 0.8 μ*M* (0.05 mg/liter) copper reduced the bulbar response to L-serine by 20% after 1 or 2 weeks (Fig. 17*C*). Cadmium at 1.3 μ*M* inhibited the L-serine response by 20% (Fig. 17*A*) and there was no difference in the extent of inhibition after 1 and 2 weeks. Mercury (0.75 μ*M*, or 0.15 mg/liter) inhibited the olfactory response by 30 and 40% after 1- and 2-week exposure, respectively (Fig. 17*B*). Exposure to 0.05 mg/liter mercury (0.25 μ*M*) or cadmium (0.44 μ*M*) did not significantly alter olfactory responses after 2 weeks.

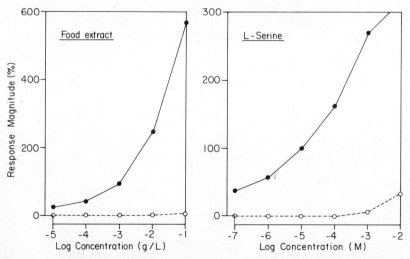

Figure 16. Inhibition of the EOG response of rainbow trout (*Salmo gairdneri*) to food extract (left) and L-serine (right) when fish were exposed to 0.1 mg/liter (1.6 μ*M*) copper sulfate for 1 week. The response magnitude is represented as a percentage of that of the control response to 10^{-5} *M* L-serine.

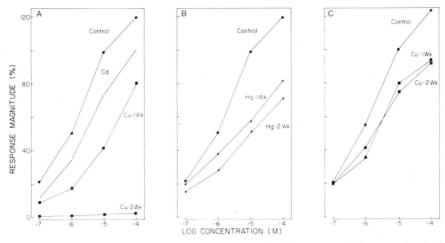

Figure 17. Effects on the olfactory bulbar response of rainbow trout (*Salmo gairdneri*) of exposure to 0.15 mg/liter cadmium, copper, or mercury. The effects of copper at 0.05 mg/liter are shown in (*C*). No difference in the effect of cadmium after 1 or 2 weeks was detected and the average of the two groups is shown (*A*). Abscissa, concentration of the standard stimulus L-serine. (From Brown et al., 1982.)

6.3.   Effects of Other Pollutants

Investigation examining the effects of other pollutants on chemosensory systems of aquatic organisms is limited. Electrical activities from the afferent nerve bundles of the barbel taste chemoreceptors in response to cystein (0.01 M) was impaired after a few hours of exposure to the detergent ABS at concentrations as low as 1 mg/liter in yellow bullhead (Bardach et al., 1965). Some ionic detergents (ABS, quaternary ammonium and imidazonium salts, and diamines) block the neural discharges evoked by amino acids in the olfactory epithelium of Atlantic salmon parr at 1 mg/liter or lower (Sutterlin et al., 1971). Most blocking effects are reversible following rinsing with clean water, and nonionic surfactants exhibit no blocking effects.

The effects of sodium lauryl sulfate (SLS) on the induced response of the olfactory bulb to food extract are illustrated in Fig. 18 (Hara and Thompson, 1978). These results clearly indicate that the olfactory response to chemical signals can be depressed by SLS at sublethal levels (lethal levels range between 1 and 10 mg/liter). Thus, the attractive effects of SLS shown previously (see Fig. 5) would render it hazardous to the normal function of the olfactory system of whitefish. The mechanisms by which detergents cause their observed toxic effects are not clear. The transient depression of olfactory responses by detergents at low concentrations is likely caused by simply washing off the mucus covering the epithelium. The mucus forms a reservoir of inorganic ions, needed for the electrical events associated with sensory transduction (Bannister, 1974). The mucus probably undergoes con-

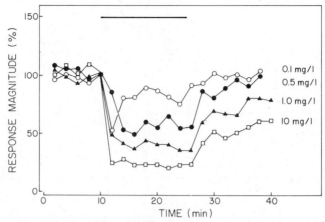

Figure 18. Effects of the anionic detergent sodium lauryl sulfate (0.1–10 mg/liter) on the olfactory bulbar response of rainbow trout (*Salmo gairdneri*) to food extract (5 mg/liter). Horizontal line indicates duration of treatment. The response magnitude is represented as a percentage of that of the control response before treatment. (From Hara and Thompson, 1978.)

tinual replacement. Prolonged exposure to high concentrations of detergents likely denatures receptor proteins and solubilizes chemosensory membranes. Irrigation of olfactory mucosa of catfish (*Ictalurus punctatus*) with 0.1% Triton X-100 removes membranous proteins and cellular process from the receptor and sustentacular cells (Cancalon, 1980). The EOG response is abolished within an hour of treatment but returns to 50–60% of the original activity level during the next hour.

The extent of injury to chemosensory systems in aquatic organisms subjected to abnormal levels of pH has not been examined in great detail. Increasing concentrations of hydrogen ion evoke electrical responses in taste preparations of several fish species (Konishi et al., 1969; Hidaka, 1970a, 1972; Sutterlin and Sutterlin, 1970; Yoshii et al., 1980; Marui and Hara, unpublished). However, electrophysiological studies dealing with the toxic effects of pH are lacking. Acute effects of pH on olfactory responses to amino acids and skin mucous substances in rainbow trout have been investigated (Hara, 1976; Hara and Macdonald, 1976). The olfactory bulbar responses are highly pH dependent, being inhibited below pH 4 and above pH 8 (Fig. 19). Changes in pH probably influence the ionization of both stimulant molecules and receptor sites, thus limiting their binding for sensory transduction. Most stimulatory amino acids showed peak activity near their isoelectric points at which dipolar ions bearing no net charge are at maximum concentration. Studies of chronic exposure will more adequately assess the effects of pH on the chemosensory systems.

The toxicity of natural lake waters contaminated with heavy metals from mining and smelting effluents has been investigated electrophysiologically in Arctic char, *Salvelinus alpinus* (Thompson and Hara, 1977). The depressive

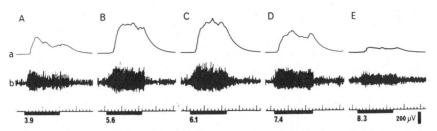

Figure 19. Electrical responses recorded from the olfactory bulb of rainbow trout (*Salmo gairdneri*) when the nares were stimulated with L-serine (10 μM) at different pH. The pH values are indicated below each heavy line (duration of stimulus). The upper tracing of each pair is the integrated response of the lower one. Time scale: each division = 1 sec. (From Hara, 1976.)

effect of lake waters on the olfactory bulb response is less than that of an artificial lake water composed of heavy metals based on the natural lake concentrations. Possible involvement of metal–organic complex formation is sought in the reduction of their toxicity. Borie et al. (1981) studied the olfactory bulb responses induced by nasal infusion of three pesticides (atrazine, lindane, and ethyl parathion) in rainbow trout. Amplitude and frequency changes were characteristic for each solution tested at concentrations between 10 ng/liter and 1 mg/liter. Recently, the effects of whole drilling muds on the activity of walking leg chemosensory neurons of the lobster have been examined electrophysiologically (Derby and Atema, 1981). Exposure of legs for 3–5 min to 10 mg/liter drilling mud suspended in seawater significantly reduced responses to food odors of some chemoreceptor neurons, while others were excited. However, no proof for a causal relationship between chemoreceptor interference and behavioral deficits was found.

7. BIOCHEMICAL STUDIES

Chemosensory receptors transduce a series of specific interactions between molecules into physiological and consequently behavioral responses. In the first step of information processing chemoreceptors detect extracellular chemical signals and send this information to the next element in the process. The presence of a component responsible for recognition of characteristic ligands is established for many neurotransmitter systems. The major unsolved problem in these systems is the complex process that translates the initial recognition of ligand into a final cellular response.

Recent biochemical studies in fish have begun to examine the initial interactions between amino acids and their putative receptors in the olfactory (Cagan and Zeiger, 1978; Cancalon, 1978; Novoselov et al., 1980; Rhein and Cagan, 1980, 1981; Suzuki, 1980; Suzuki and Suzuki, 1981; Brown and Hara, 1981, 1982) and taste (Krueger and Cagan, 1976; Cagan, 1979, 1981; Zelson and Cagan, 1979) systems using ligand-binding studies. In these studies the binding activity of a radioactively labelled amino acid with intact receptor cells or with isolated membrane preparations derived from such cells is measured. The binding is assumed to reflect specific receptor interaction if it demonstrates: (1) strict structural and steric specificity; (2) saturability, which indicates a finite and limited number of binding sites; (3) tissue specificity in accord with biological receptor cell sensitivity; (4) high affinity, in harmony with the physiological concentrations of the stimulus; and (5) reversibility which is kinetically consistent with the reversal of the physiological effects observed upon removal of the stimulus from the medium (Cuatrecasas, 1975; Burt, 1978; Hollenberg and Cuatrecasas, 1979). Binding studies are advantageous in that they give direct information on receptor occupation.

7.1. *In Vitro* Inhibition of Binding by Heavy Metals

Inhibition of L-[^{14}C] serine (10 μM) binding to the sedimentable fraction isolated from the olfactory rosettes of trout is shown in Fig. 20 (Brown and Hara, 1981, 1982; Brown et al., 1982). Mercury, silver, and copper are the most effective inhibitors; IC50 values are 1.0, 3.0, and 9.5 μM, respectively. Other metals inhibit L-serine binding with a decreasing order of potency as follows: cadmium > zinc > lead > nickel > cobalt. These data are in agreement with the results by Cagan and Zeiger (1978) on mercury inhibition of binding of L-alanine to a sedimentable fraction from the olfactory rosettes

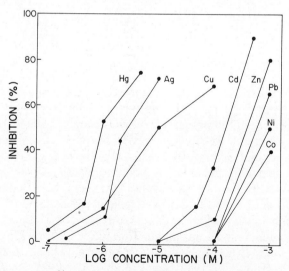

Figure 20.   Inhibition of L-[^{14}C]serine (10 μM) binding to a sedimentable fraction isolated from the olfactory rosettes of rainbow trout (*Salmo gairdneri*) by various concentrations of metals. (From Brown et al., 1982.)

of rainbow trout. However, Brown and Hara's (1982) data show that binding of L-serine is tenfold more sensitive to inhibition by copper and cadmium. Binding of L-alanine is not affected by sulfhydryl blocking reagents (iodoacetate and *N*-ethylmaleimide), being unfavorable for a widely accepted view that SH groups are involved in the binding interaction at olfactory receptor sites (Cagan and Zeiger, 1978).

7.2. *In Vivo* Effects of Metals on Binding

The binding of L-serine in fish exposed to 2.4 μM (0.15 mg/liter) copper shows significant reduction in maximal binding capacity (Fig. 21 and Table 5). There is no change in binding affinity. The binding data for cadmium and mercury are also summarized in Table 5.

The results indicate a parallelism between the inhibitory effects of metals on the electrophysiological responses (Section 6.2) and those on L-serine binding. The inhibition of electrophysiological responsiveness by copper and cadmium is accompanied by a simultaneous and equivalent reduction in the total number of L-serine binding sites. In mercury-exposed fish the reduction in L-serine binding is not significant after 1 week. By this time, however, mercury is accumulated in the brains of treated fish at the levels which are high enough to cause impairment of central nervous function (see

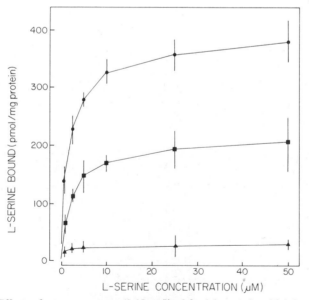

Figure 21. Effects of copper exposure (0.15 mg/liter) for 1 (squares) and 2 (triangles) weeks on the specific binding of L-[³H]serine to a sedimentable fraction from the olfactory rosettes of rainbow trout (*Salmo gairdneri*). Control binding (circles) is the mean of values determined from both weeks. (From Brown et al., 1982.)

Table 5. Apparent Dissociation Constant (K_d) and Maximal Binding Capacity (B_{max}) for Binding of L-Serine to the Sedimentable Fraction Isolated from Olfactory Rosettes of Rainbow Trout (*Salmo gairdneri*) Exposed to Copper, Cadmium and Mercury (0.15 mg/liter)[a]

Type of Exposure	K_d (μM)	B_{max} (pmol·mg/liter	% Change from Control
Copper			
Control	1.9	371	
1 week	2.0	210	-43^b
Control	1.6	402	
2 weeks	2.5	30	-93^b
Cadmium			
Control	2.4	460	
1 week	2.8	317	-31^b
Control	3.4	306	
2 weeks	3.4	198	-35^b
Mercury			
Control	2.7	332	
1 week	3.8	282	-15
Control	2.1	309	
2 weeks	2.0	250	-29^b

[a] From Brown et al. (1982).
[b] $P < 0.05$

Fig. 14; Fox et al., 1975; Verity et al., 1977; Aronstam and Eldefrawi, 1979; Bondy et al., 1979; von Burg et al., 1980). Thus, recorded bulbar activity in mercury-exposed fish may be attributable primarily to alteration in the central nervous system without comparable reduction in peripheral biochemical activity. Additional confirming evidence is supplied by histochemical investigations (see Section 5) which show that copper exposure reduces the number of neurons staining with Baker's acid hematein method. The reduction in staining has been related to lowered electrophysiological responsiveness and mercury does not reduce staining as effectively. In total, the data suggest that copper and cadmium reduce the number of functional receptor cells in the olfactory epithelium, whereas mercury may exert central inhibition as well as some peripheral effects.

7.3. Mode of Inhibitory Action of Heavy Metals

The ability of dithiothreitol, ethylenediamine tetraacetic acid (EDTA), washing, or the presence of high stimulus (amino acid) concentrations to reverse or protect from the inhibitory effects of metals on binding of L-serine to the sedimentable fraction from the olfactory rosettes is summarized in Table 6 (Brown et al., 1982). Dithiothreitol (1 mM) effectively reverses the inhibitory effects of silver, cadmium, zinc, and copper. Similar to the electrophysiological response, however, dithiothreitol is not effective in reversing the inhibition by mercury. EDTA is not as effective as dithiothreitol. Washing the sedimentable fraction with buffer increases control binding (30%) but does not reverse the effects of any metals examined. High concentrations of L-serine (10 mM) incorporated with the metal prior to washing the sedimentable fraction protects from the inhibitory effects of copper, cadmium, and zinc, but not those of silver or mercury.

In the fish olfactory epithelium at least one receptor site involving two charged subsites exists (Hara, 1975; 1982b). Metal binding to these charged subsites could explain some of the inhibitory effects observed. Because mercury is an irreversible inhibitor of both binding and electrophysiological response, this metal apparently denatures the olfactory receptor for L-serine or other amino acids. Results with group specific agents suggest that sulfhydryl groups are not involved in the amino acid binding in trout olfactory (Cagan and Zeiger, 1978) and catfish taste (Zelson and Cagan, 1979) systems. Perhaps mercury is reacting with disulfide bonds to change the conformation of the receptor–membrane complex (Cecil, 1963). Similar to mercury, inactivation by silver could not be prevented by high stimulus concentrations. However, silver does not appear to denature receptors, because its inactivation can be reversed by addition of dithiothreitol in both the electrophysiological and binding preparations. At present it is not totally clear whether high stimulus levels protect from the effects of metals by receptor occupation or by metal chelation.

8. CONCLUDING REMARKS

In this article, attempts have been made to show a variety of ways in which chemoreception may be used to assess and predict the effects of environmental perturbations. For organisms whose life is spent entirely in aquatic environment where vision can be limited, chemoreception plays a major and sometimes decisive role providing directive factors for behavior (Hara, 1975, 1981b, 1982a). Behavior is adaptive and natural selection has produced a capacity for behavioral response that permits an organism to perform its necessary life processes in the face of environmental perturbations (Olla et al., 1980). However, these behavioral responses are not always effective for man-made perturbations. When such responses fail, damage caused by the perturbation may become evident as behavioral changes that decrease survival potential. This will ultimately result in a altered distribution of a species, which may severely affect an ecosystem.

In spite of the great importance of chemoreception to behavioral reactions

Table 6. Reversal of Metal Inhibition of L-Serine Binding to the Sedimentable Fraction from the Olfactory Rosettes of Rainbow Trout (*Salmo gairdneri*) by Chelation, Washing or the Presence of High Ligand Concentrations[a]

Metal (μM)	Metal Alone	Specific L-Serine Binding[b]			
		Dithiothreitol[c] (1 mM)	Ethylenediamine tetraacetic acid[c] (1 mM)	Washing[d]	Metal[e] + L-Serine (10 mM)
Mercury (5)	46.9 ± 11.2	23.8 ± 11.7	10.0 ± 7.4	18.0 ± 9.0	27.6 ± 24.7
Silver (10)	11.2 ± 6.3	117.1 ± 13.2	47.1 ± 7.4	16.2 ± 9.2	8.1 ± 7.5
Copper (10)	56.9 ± 12.0	80.1 ± 12.2	53.9 ± 9.0	45.9 ± 13.1	98.8 ± 16.2
Cadmium (200)	44.8 ± 12.2	94.4 ± 15.5	86.8 ± 4.0	42.4 ± 10.6	95.9 ± 14.6
Zinc (500)	50.9 ± 11.3	96.4 ± 16.4	73.5 ± 10.7	52.7 ± 12.6	89.9 ± 8.0
No metal[f]	100.1 ± 11.8	117.5 ± 15.3	105.2 ± 12.0	130.5 ± 18.4	152.0 ± 13.5

[a]From Brown et al. (1982).

[b]Values listed are the percentage ± S.D. ($n = 4$) of specific L-[^{3}H] serine binding (0.02 μM) compared to the control values in the absence of any metal under the various treatment conditions.

[c]The sedimentable fraction was preincubated with metal for 15 min on ice and then treated with dithiothreitol or ethylenediamine tetraacetic acid for 15 min before L-serine binding was measured.

[d]The sedimentable fraction was preincubated with metal for 15 min then washed two times by suspension in 10 ml buffer and centrifuged at 20,000 × g for 10 min.

[e]The sedimentable fraction was preincubated with metal plus L-serine (10 mM) for 15 min then washed as in d.

[f]Values represent the level of L-serine binding in the presence of chelators or after washing procedure with no metals present, expressed as percentage of binding in untreated sedimentable fraction.

little research has been carried out to determine the mode and locus of toxicant reception. Behavioral responses, as evident from the preceding discussion, can be variable and not always related to lethal levels of pollutants. Therefore, physiological, biochemical, and histochemical studies of chemoreceptive mechanisms can provide other sensitive indicators of the effects of pollutants. They can indicate the modes and locus of toxicant influence and produce an understanding of mechanisms of toxicity. Each investigational approach requires the support of others and the fragmentary nature of information dealing with pollutants and chemoreceptive mechanisms is due, in part, to the lack of coordinated investigational approaches. Thus, combinations of methodologies (e.g., Bardach et al., 1965; Kamchen and Hara, 1980; Hara, 1981a; Derby and Atema, 1981; Brown et al., 1982) are most useful in attempting to understand interactions between pollutants and the chemical senses.

ACKNOWLEDGMENTS

We thank D. Klaprat, B. Thompson, and B. Zielinski, Freshwater Institute, for invaluable assistance in preparing this manuscript, and to Dr. B. Dronzek and Mr. B. Luit, Department of Plant Science, University of Manitoba, for the use of scanning electron microscope. We also thank Donna Laroque for typing the manuscript.

REFERENCES

Aronstam, R. S. and Eldefrawi, M. E. (1979). Transition and heavy metal inhibition of ligand binding to muscarinic acetylcholine receptors from rat brain. *Toxicol. Appl. Pharmacol.* **48**, 489–496.

Atema, J. (1976) Sublethal effects of petroleum fractions on the behavior of the lobster, *Homarus americanus,* and the mud snail, *Nassarius obsoletus.* In: M. Wiley, Ed., *Estuarine processes,* Vol. I. Uses, stresses, and adaptation to the estuary. Academic Press, New York, pp. 302–312.

Atema, J., and Stein L. S. (1974). Effects of crude oil on the feeding behavior of the lobster *Homarus americanus. Environ. Pollut.* **6**, 77–86.

Atema, J., Jacobson, S., Todd, J., and Boylan D. (1973). The importance of chemical signals in stimulating behavior of marine organisms: effects of altered environmental chemistry on animal communication. In: G. E. Glass, Ed., *Bioassay techniques and environmental chemistry.* Ann Arbor Science Publishers, Ann Arbor, Michigan, pp. 177–197.

Bannister, L. H. (1974). Possible functions of mucus at gustatory and olfactory surfaces. In: T. M. Poynder, Ed., *Transduction mechanisms in chemoreception.* Information Retrieval, London, pp. 39–48.

Bardach, J. E. (1975). Chemoreception of aquatic animals. In: D. A. Denton and J. P. Coghlan, Eds., *Olfaction and taste* V. Academic Press, New York, pp. 121–132.

Bardach, J. E., Fujiya, M., and Holl, A. (1965). Detergents: effects on the chemical senses of the fish *Ictalurus natalis* (le Sueur). *Science* **148**, 1605–1607.

Bishai, H. M. (1962a). The reactions of larval and young salmonids to water of low oxygen concentrations. *J. Cons. Cons. Int. Explor. Mer.* **27**, 167–180.

Bishai, H. M. (1962b). Reactions of larval and young salmonids to different hydrogen ion concentrations. *J. Cons. Cons. Int. Explor. Mer.* **27**, 181–191.

Black, J. A. and Birge, W. J. (1980). *An avoidance response bioassay for aquatic pollutants.* University of Kentucky, Water Resour. Res. Inst. Rep. No. 123, 34 p.

Bloom, H. D. and Perlmutter, A. (1977). A sexual aggregating pheromone system in the zebrafish, *Brachydanio rerio* (Hamilton-Buchanan). *Environ. Pollut.* **17**, 127–131.

Bloom, H. D., Perlmutter, A., and Seeley, R. J. (1978). Effect of a sublethal concentration of zinc on an aggregating pheromone system in the zebrafish, *Brachydanio rerio* (Hamilton-Buchanan). *Environ. Pollut.* **17**, 127–131.

Bodammer, J. E. (1979). Preliminary observations on the cytopathological effects of copper sulfate on the chemoreceptors of *Callinectes sapidus.* In: W. B. Vernberg, A. Calabrese, F. P. Thurberg, and F. H. Vernberg, Eds., *Marine pollution: functional responses.* Academic Press, New York, pp. 223–237.

Bogardus, R. B., Boies, D. B., Teppen, T. C., and Horvath, F. J. (1978). Avoidance of mono-chloramine: test tank results for rainbow trout, coho salmon, alewife, yellow perch and spottail shiner. In: R. J. Jolley, H. Gorcher, and D. H. Hamilton, Eds., *Water chlorination.* Environmental impact and health effects, Vol. II. Ann Arbor Science Publishers, Ann Arbor, Michigan, pp. 149–161.

Bondy, S. C., Anderson, C. L., Harrington, M. E., and Prasad, K. N. (1979). The effects of organic and inorganic lead and mercury on neurotransmitter high-affinity transport and release mechanisms. *Environ. Res.* **19**, 102–111.

Borie, F., Chantrier, N., Huve, J.-L., and Thomson, M.-A. (1981). Utilisation de l'activite bioelectrique du bulbe ofactif de la truite *Salmo gairdneri* dans la detection de pesticides. *C. R. Acad. Sci., Ser. III* **292**, 235–238.

Brett, J. R. and MacKinnon, D. (1954). Some aspects of olfactory perception in migrating adult coho and spring salmon. *J. Fish. Res. Board Can.* **11**, 310–318.

Brown, S. B. and Hara, T. J. (1981). Accumulation of chemostimulatory amino acids by a sedimentable fraction isolated from olfactory rosettes of rainbow trout (*Salmo gairdneri*). *Biochim. Biophys. Acta* **675**, 149–162.

Brown, S. B. and Hara, T. J. (1982). Biochemical aspects of amino acid receptors in olfaction and taste. In: T. J. Hara, Ed., *Chemoreception in fishes.* Elsevier Scientific Publishing, Amsterdam, pp. 159–180.

Brown, S. B., Evans, R. E., Thompson, B. E., and Hara, T. J. (1982). Chemoreception and aquatic pollutants. In: T. J. Hara, Ed., *Chemoreception in fishes.* Elsevier Scientific Publishing, Amsterdam, pp. 363–393.

Burt, D. R. (1978). Criteria for receptor identification. In: H. I. Yamamura, S. J. Enna, and M. J. Kuhar, Eds., *Neurotransmitter receptor binding.* Raven Press, New York, pp. 41–55.

Cagan, R. H. (1979). Biochemical studies of taste sensation. VII. Enhancement of taste stimulus binding to a catfish taste receptor preparation by prior exposure to the stimulus. *J. Neurobiol.* **10**, 207–220.

Cagan, R. H. (1981). Recognition of taste stimuli at the initial binding interaction. In: R. H. Cagan and M. R. Kare, Eds., *Biochemistry of taste and olfaction.* Academic Press, New York, pp. 175–203.

Cagan, R. H. and Zeiger, W. N. (1978). Biochemical studies of olfaction: binding specificity of radioactively labeled stimuli to an isolated olfactory preparation from rainbow trout (*Salmo gairdneri*). *Proc. Natl. Acad. Sci. USA* **75**, 4679–4683.

Cancalon, P. (1978). Isolation and characterization of the olfactory epithelial cells of the catfish. *Chem. Senses Flavour* **3**, 381–396.

Cancalon, P. (1980). Effects of salts, pH and detergents on the catfish olfactory mucosa. In: H. van der Starre, Ed., *Olfaction and taste* VII. IRL Press, London, pp. 73–76.

Caprio, J. (1982). High sensitivity and specificity of olfactory and gustatory receptors of catfish to amino acids. In: T. J. Hara, Ed., *Chemoreception in fishes*. Elsevier Scientific Publishing, Amsterdam, pp. 109–134.

Carson, W. G. and Carson, W. V. (1973). *Avoidance of copper in the presence of humic acid by juvenile Atlantic salmon.* J. Fish. Res. Board Can. MS Rep. 1237, 9 p.

Cecil, R. (1963). Intramolecular bonds in proteins. I. The role of sulfur in proteins. In: H. Neurath, Ed., *The proteins,* Vol. I. Acacemic Press, New York, pp. 379–476.

Cherry, D. S. and Cairns, J., Jr. (1982). Biological monitoring. Part V. Preference and avoidance studies. *Water Res.* **16,** 263–301.

Cherry, D. S., Larrick, S. R., Dickson, K. L., Hoehn, R. C., and Cairns, J., Jr. (1977a). Significance of hypochlorous acid in free residual chlorine to the avoidance response of spotted bass (*Micropterus punctulatus*) and rosyface shiner (*Notropis rubellus*). *J. Fish. Res. Board Can.* **34,** 1365–1372.

Cherry, D. S., Larrick, S. R., Giattina, J. D., Cairns, J., Jr., and van Hassel, J. (1982). Influence of temperature selection upon the chlorine avoidance of cold-water and warmwater fishes. *Can. J. Fish. Aquat. Sci.* **39,** 162–173.

Cherry, D. S., Hoehn, R. C., Waldo, S. S., Willis, D. H., Cairns, J., Jr., and Dickson, K. L. (1977b). Field-laboratory determined avoidances of the spotfin shiner and the bluntnose minnow to chlorinated discharges. *Water Res. Bull.* **13,** 1047–1055.

Costa, H. H. (1966). Responses of *Gammarus pulex* (L.) to modified environment. I. Reactions to toxic solutions. *Crustaceana* **11,** 245–256.

Cripe, C. R. (1979). An automated device (AGARS) for studying avoidance of pollutant gradients by aquatic organisms. *J. Fish. Res. Board Can.* **36,** 11–16.

Cuatrecasas, P. (1975). Criteria for and pitfalls in the identification of receptors. In: E. Usdin and W. E. Bunney, Eds., *Pre- and postsynaptic receptors*. Marcel Dekker, New York, pp. 245–264.

Davies, P. H., Goettl, J. P., and Sindey, J. R. (1978). Toxicity of silver to rainbow trout (*Salmo gairdneri*). *Water Res.* **12,** 113–117.

Daye, P. G. and Garside, E. T. (1976). Histopathologic changes in surficial tissues of brook trout, *Salvelinus fontinalis* (Mitchill), exposed to acute and chronic levels of pH. *Can. J. Zool.* **54,** 2140–2155.

DeGraeve, G. M. (1982). Avoidance response of rainbow trout to phenol. *Prog. Fish-Cult.* **44,** 82–87.

Derby, C. D. and Atema, J. (1981). Influence of drilling muds on the primary chemosensory neurons in walking legs of the lobster, *Homarus americanus. Can. J. Fish. Aquat. Sci.* **38,** 268–274.

DiMichele, L. and Taylor, M. H. (1978). Histopathological and physiological responses of *Fundulus heteroclitus* to naphthalene exposure. *J. Fish. Res. Board Can.* **35,** 1060–1066.

Dinnel, P. A., Stober, Q. J., and DiJulio, D. H. (1979). Behavioral responses of shiner perch to chlorinated primary sewage effluent. *Bull. Environ. Contam. Toxicol.* **22,** 708–714.

Evans, G. W., Lyes, M., and Lockwood, A. P. M. (1977). Some effects of oil dispersants on the feeding behaviour of the brown shrimp, *Crangon crangon. Mar. Behav. Physiol.* **4,** 171–181.

Evans, R. E. and Hara, T. J. (1977). Histochemical localization of phospholipids in the olfactory epithelium of fish. *Can. J. Zool.* **55,** 776–781.

Evans, R. E., Zielinski, B., and Hara, T. J. (1982). Development and regeneration of the olfactory organ in rainbow trout. In: T. J. Hara, Ed., *Chemoreception in fishes*. Elsevier Scientific Publishing, Amsterdam, pp. 15–37.

Fava, J. A. and Tsai, C. F. (1976). Immediate behavioral reactions of blacknose dace, *Rhinichthys atraturus*, to domestic sewage and its toxic constituents. *Trans. Am. Fish. Soc.* **105**, 430–441.

Folmar, L. C. (1976). Overt avoidance reaction of rainbow trout fry to nine herbicides. *Bull. Environ. Contam. Toxicol.* **15**, 509–514.

Folmar, L. C., Sanders, H. O., and Julin, A. M. (1979). Toxicity of the herbicide glyphosate and several of its formulations to fish and aquatic invertebrates. *Arch. Environ. Contam. Toxicol.* **8**, 269–278.

Foster, N. R., Scheier, A., and Cairns, J., Jr. (1966). Effects of ABS on feeding behavior of flagfish, *Jordanella floridae*. *Trans. Am. Fish Soc.* **95**, 109–110.

Fox, J. H., Patel, M. K., and Cohen, M. M. (1975). Comparative effects of organic and inorganic mercury on brain slice respiration and metabolism. *J. Neurochem.* **24**, 757–762.

Fujiya, M. and Nitta, T. (1953). Studies on avoidance reactions in fishes—I. *Bull. Naikai Reg. Fish. Res. Lab.* **3**, 12–14.

Gardner, G. R. (1975). Chemically induced lesions in estuarine or marine teleosts. In: W. E. Ribelin and G. Migaki, Eds., *The pathology of fishes*. University of Wisconsin Press, Madison, pp. 657–693.

Gardner, G. R. and LaRoche, G. (1973). Copper induced lesions in estuarine teleosts. *J. Fish. Res. Board Can.* **30**, 363–368.

Giattina, J. D., Cherry, D. S., Cairns, J., Jr., and Larrick, S. R. (1981). Comparison of laboratory and field avoidance behavior of fish in heated chlorinated water. *Trans. Am. Fish. Soc.* **110**, 526–535.

Granett, J., Morang, S., and Hatch, R. (1978). Reduced movement of precocious male Atlantic salmon parr into sublethal Dimlin-G1® and carrier concentrations. *Bull. Environ. Contam. Toxicol.* **19**, 462–464.

Grant, P. T. and Mackie, A. M., eds. (1974). *Chemoreception in marine organisms*. Academic Press, London, 295 pp.

Graziadei, P. P. C. and Monti Graziadei, G. A. (1978a). The olfactory system: a model for the study of neurogenesis and axon regeneration in mammals. In: W. Cotman, Ed., *Neural plasticity*. Raven Press, New York, pp. 131–153.

Graziadei, P. P. C. and Monti Graziadei, G. A. (1978b). Continuous nerve cell renewal in the olfactory system. In: M. Jacobson, Ed., *Handbook of sensory physiology*. IX. Development of sensory systems. Springer, Heidelberg, pp. 55–83.

Greer, G. L. and Kosakoski, G. J. (1978). *Avoidance of seawater dilutions of kraft pulp mill effluent by seawater acclimated pink salmon fry*. Can. Fish. Mar. Serv. Tech. Rep. 831, 11 pp.

Grieve, J. A., Johnston, L. E., Dunstall, T. G., and Minor, J. (1978). A program to introduce site-specific chlorination regimes at Ontario hydro generating stations. In: R. L. Jolley, H. Gorcher, and D. H. Hamilton, Eds., *Water chlorination*. Environmental impact and health effects. Vol. II. Ann Arbor Science Publishers, Ann Arbor, Michigan, pp. 77–94.

Haider, G. (1975). Die Wirkung subletaler Bleikonzentrationen auf die Chemorezeptoren zweier Susswasserfischarten. *Hydrobiologia* **47**, 291–300.

Hansen, D. J. (1969). Avoidance of pesticides by untrained sheephead minnows. *Trans. Am. Fish. Soc.* **98**, 426–429.

Hansen, D. J., Schimmel, S. C., and Keltner, J. M., Jr. (1973). Avoidance of pesticides by grass shrimp (*Palaemonetes pugio*). *Bull. Environ. Contam. Toxicol.* **9**, 129–133.

Hansen, D. J., Schimmel, S. C., and Matthews, E. (1974). Avoidance of Aroclor 1254 by shrimp and fishes. *Bull. Environ. Contam. Toxicol.* **12**, 253–256.

Hansen, D. J., Matthews, E., Nall, S. L., and Dumas, D. P. (1972). Avoidance of pesticides by untrained mosquitofish, *Gambusia affinis*. *Bull. Environ. Contam. Toxicol.* **8**, 46–51.

Hara, T. J. (1972). Electrical responses of the olfactory bulb of Pacific salmon *Oncorhynchus nerka* and *Oncorhynchus kisutch. J. Fish. Res. Board Can.* **29**, 1351–1355.

Hara, T. J. (1975). Olfaction in fish. In: G. A. Kerkut and J. W. Phyllis, Eds., *Progress in neurobiology,* Vol. 5. Pergamon Press, Oxford, pp. 271–335.

Hara, T. J. (1976). Effects of pH on the olfactory responses to amino acids in rainbow trout, *Salmo gairdneri. Comp. Biochem. Physiol.* **54A**, 37–39.

Hara, T. J. (1981a). Behavioural and electrophysiological studies of chemosensory reactions in fish. In: P. J. Laming, Ed., *Brain mechanisms of behaviour in lower vertebrates.* Cambridge University Press, Cambridge, pp. 123–136.

Hara, T. J. (1981b). Perception of behavior-altering chemicals in aquatic environments. In: D. M. Norris, Ed., *Perception of behavioral chemicals.* Elsevier/North-Holland, Amsterdam, pp. 29–57.

Hara, T. J., Ed. (1982a). *Chemoreception in fishes.* Elsevier Scientific Publishing, Amsterdam, 433 pp.

Hara, T. J. (1982b). Structure–activity relationships of amino acids as olfactory stimuli. In: T. J. Hara, Ed., *Chemoreception in fishes.* Elsevier Scientific Publishing, Amsterdam, pp. 135–157.

Hara, T. J. and Macdonald, S. (1976). Olfactory responses to skin mucous substances in rainbow trout *Salmo gairdneri. Comp. Biochem. Physiol.* **54A**, 41–44.

Hara, T. J. and Thompson, B. E. (1978). The reaction of whitefish, *Coregonus clupeaformis,* to the anionic detergent sodium lauryl sulphate and its effects on their olfactory responses. *Water Res.* **12**, 893–897.

Hara, T. J., Law, Y. M. C., and Macdonald, S. (1976). Effects of mercury and copper on the olfactory response in rainbow trout, *Salmo gairdneri. J. Fish. Res. Board Can.* **33**, 1568–1573.

Hasler, A. D. and Wisby, W. J. (1950). Use of fish for the olfactory assay of pollutants (phenols) in water. *Trans. Am. Fish. Soc.* **79**, 64–70.

Hiatt, R. W., Naughton, J. J., and Matthews, D. C. (1953a). Effects of chemicals on a schooling fish, *Kuhlia sandvicensis. Biol. Bull.* **104**, 28–44.

Hiatt, R. W., Naughton, J. J., and Matthews, D. C. (1953b). Relation of chemical structure to irritant responses in marine fish. *Nature (London)* **172**, 904–905.

Hidaka, I. (1970a). The effect of carbon dioxide on the carp palatal chemoreceptors. *Bull. Jap. Soc. Sci. Fish.* **36**, 1034–1039.

Hidaka, I. (1970b). The effects of transition metals on the palatal chemoreceptors of the carp. *Jap. J. Physiol.* **20**, 599–609.

Hidaka, I. (1972). Stimulation of the palatal chemoreceptors of the carp by mixed solutions of acid and salt. *Jap. J. Physiol.* **29**, 39–51.

Hidaka, I. and Yokota, S. (1967). Taste receptor stimulation by sweet tasting substances in the carp. *Jap. J. Physiol.* **17**, 652–666.

Hoglund, L. B. (1951). A new method of studying the reactions of fishes in stable gradients of chemical and other agents. *Oikos* **3**, 247–267.

Hoglund, L. B. (1961). *The reaction of fishes in concentration gradients.* Fish. Board Swed., Inst. Freshwater Res., Drottningholm, Rep. No. 43: 1–147.

Hoglund, L. B. and Hardig, J. (1969). *Reactions of young salmonids to sudden changes of pH, carbon dioxide tension and oxygen content.* Fish. Board Swed., Inst. Freshwater Res., Drottningholm, Rep. No. 49: 76–119.

Hollenberg, M. D. and Cuatrecasas, P. (1979). Distinction of receptor from non-receptor interactions in binding studies. In: R. D. O'Brian, Ed., *The receptors,* Vol. 1. Plenum Press, New York, pp. 193–214.

Hose, J. E. and Stoffel, R. J. (1980). Avoidance response of juvenile *Chromis punctipinnis* to chlorinated seawater. *Bull. Environ. Contam. Toxicol.* **25**, 929–935.

Ishio, S. (1960a). The reactions of fishes to toxic substances. I. New designed gradient tank for studying avoidance reactions of fishes. *Bull. Jap. Soc. Sci. Fish.* **26,** 349–353.

Ishio, S. (1960b). The reactions of fishes to toxic substances. II. The reactions of fishes to acids. *Bull. Jap. Soc. Sci. Fish.* **26,** 894–899.

Ishio, S. (1965). Behavior of fish exposed to toxic substances. *Adv. Water Pollut. Res.* **1,** 19–33.

Jacobson, S. M. and Boylan, D. B. (1973). Effect of seawater soluble fraction of kerosene on chemotaxis in a marine snail, *Nassarius obsoletus. Nature (London)* **241,** 213–215.

Johnson, D. W. and Webster, D. A. (1977). Avoidance of low pH in selection of spawning sites by brook trout (*Salvelinus fontinalis*). *J. Fish. Res. Board Can.* **34,** 2215–2218.

Johnston, D. W. and Wildish, D. J. (1981). Avoidance of dredge spoil by herring (*Clupea harengus harengus*). *Bull. Environ. Contam. Toxicol.* **26,** 307–314.

Jones, J. R. E. (1947). The reactions of *Pygosteus pungitius* L. to toxic solutions. *J. Exp. Biol.* **24,** 110–122.

Jones, J. R. E. (1948). A further study of the reactions of fish to toxic solutions. *J. Exp. Biol.* **25,** 22–34.

Jones, J. R. E. (1951). The reactions of the minnow, *Phoxinus phoxinus* (L.), to solutions of phenol, ortho-cresol and para-cresol. *J. Exp. Biol.* **28,** 261–270.

Jones, J. R. E. (1952). The reactions of fish to water of low oxygen concentration. *J. Exp. Biol.* **28,** 403–415.

Jones, B. F., Warren, C. E., Bond, C. E., and Doudoroff, P. (1956). Avoidance reactions of salmonid fishes to pulp mill effluents. *Sewage Indust. Wastes* **28,** 1403–1413.

Kamchen, R. and Hara, T.J. (1980). Behavioral reactions of whitefish (*Coregonus clupeaformis*) to food extract: an application to sublethal toxicity bioassay. *Can. Tech. Rep. Fish. Aquat. Sci.* **975,** 182–191.

Katsuki, Y. and Yanagisawa, K. (1982). Chemoreception in the lateral-line organ. In: T. J. Hara, Ed., *Chemoreception in fishes.* Elsevier Scientific Publishing, Amsterdam, pp. 227–242.

Kelso, J. R. M. (1977). Density, distribution, and movement of Nipigon Bay fishes in relation to a pulp and paper mill effluent. *J. Fish. Res. Board Can.* **34,** 879–885.

Kleerekoper, H. (1974). Effects of exposure to a subacute concentration of parathion on the interaction between chemoreception and water flow in fish. In: F. J. Vernberg and W. B. Vernberg, Eds., *Pollution and physiology of marine organisms.* Academic Press, New York.

Kleerekoper, H., Waxman, J. B., and Matis, J. (1973). Interaction of temperature and copper ions as orienting stimuli in the locomotor behavior of the goldfish (*Carassius auratus*). *J. Fish. Res. Board Can.* **30,** 725–728.

Kleerekoper, H., Westlake, G. F., Matis, J. H., and Gensler, P.J. (1972). Orientation of goldfish (*Carassius auratus*) in response to a shallow gradient of a sublethal concentration of copper in an open field. *J. Fish. Res. Board Can.* **29,** 45–54.

Konishi, J., Hidaka, I., Toyota, M., and Matsuda, H. (1969). High sensitivity of the palatal chemoreceptors of the carp to carbon dioxide. *Jap. J. Physiol.* **19,** 327–341.

Krueger, J. M. and Cagan, R. H. (1976). Biochemical studies of taste sensation. Binding of L-[^{3}H]alanine to a sedimentable fraction from catfish barbel epithelium. *J. Biol. Chem.* **251,** 88–97.

Kynard, B. (1974). Avoidance behavior of insecticide susceptible and resistant populations of mosquitofish to four insecticides. *Trans. Am. Fish. Soc.* **102,** 557–561.

Larrick, S. R., Cherry, D. S., Dickson, K. L., and Cairns, J. Jr., (1978a). The use of various avoidance indices to evaluate the behavioral response of the golden shiner to components of total residual chlorine. In: R. L. Jolley, H. Gorcher, and D. H. Hamilton, Eds., *Water chlorination.* Environmental impact and health effects, Vol. II. Ann Arbor Science Publishers, Ann Arbor, Michigan, p. 135–147.

Larrick, S. R., Dickson, K. L., Cherry, D. S., and Cairns, J., Jr. (1978b). Determining fish avoidance of polluted water. *Hydrobiologia* **61**, 257–265.

Laughlin, R. A., Cripe, C. R., and Livingston, R. J. (1978). Field and laboratory avoidance reactions by blue crabs (*Callinectes sapidus*) to storm water runoff. *Trans. Am. Fish. Soc.* **107**, 78–86.

Lawrence, M. and Scherer, E. (1974). *Behavioural responses of whitefish and rainbow trout to drilling fluids.* Can. Fish. Mar. Serv. Tech. Rep. 502, 47 pp.

Lewis, F. G. and Livingston, R. J. (1977). Avoidance of bleached kraft pulpmill effluent by pinfish (*Lagodon rhomboides*) and gulf killifish (*Fundulus grandis*). *J. Fish. Res. Board Can.* **34**, 568–570.

Lewis, J. B. (1971). Effect of crude oil and an oil-spill dispersant on reef corals. *Mar. Pollut. Bull.* **2**, 59–62.

Lewis, M. (1976). Effects of low concentrations of manganous sulfate on eggs and fry of rainbow trout. *Prog. Fish.-Cult.* **36**, 63–65.

Lindahl, P. E. and Marcstrom, A. (1958). On the preference of roaches (*Leuciscus rutilus*) for trinitrophenol, studied with the fluviarium technique. *J. Fish. Res. Board Can.* **15**, 685–694.

Lindstedt, K. J. (1971). Chemical control of feeding behavior. *Comp. Biochem. Physiol.* **39A**, 553–581.

Livingston, R. J., Cripe, C. R., Laughlin, R. A., and Lewis, F. G. (1976). Avoidance responses of estuarine organisms to storm water runoff and pulp mill effluents. In: M. Wiley, Ed., *Estuarine processes,* Vol. I. Uses, stresses, and adaptation to the estuary. Academic Press, New York, pp. 313–331.

Lyes, M. C. (1979). The reproductive behaviour of *Gammarus duebeni* (Lilljeborg), and the inhibitory effect of a surface active agent. *Mar. Behav. Physiol.* **6**, 47–55.

Maciorowski, H. D., Clarke, R. M., and Scherer, E. (1977). The use of avoidance–preference bioassays with aquatic invertebrates. Environ. Protect. Serv. Tech. Rep. No. EPS-5AR-77-1, Halifax, Canada, pp. 49–58.

Mackie, A. M. (1970). Avoidance reactions of marine invertebrates to either steroid glycosides of starfish or synthetic surface-active agents. *J. Exp. Mar. Biol. Ecol.* **5**, 63–69.

Mackie, A. M. (1975). Chemoreception. In: D. C. Malins and J. R. Sargeant, Eds., *Biochemical and biophysical perspectives in marine biology,* Vol. 2. Academic Press, London, pp. 69–105.

Mackie, A. M., Lasker, R., and Grant, P. T. (1968). Avoidance reactions of a mollusc *Buccinum undatum* to saponin-like surface-active substances in extracts of the starfish *Asterias rubens* and *Marthasterias glacialis*. *Comp. Biochem. Physiol.* **26**, 415–428.

McLeese, D. W. (1973). Response of lobsters *Homarus americanus* to odor solution in the presence of bleached kraft mill effluent. *J. Fish. Res. Board Can.* **30**, 279–282.

McLeese, D. W. (1974). Olfactory response and fenitrothion toxicity in American lobsters (*Homarus americanus*). *J. Fish. Res. Board Can.* **31**, 1127–1131.

McLeese, D. W. (1975). Chemosensory response of American lobsters (*Homarus americanus*) in the presence of copper and phosphamidon. *J. Fish. Res. Board Can.* **32**, 2055–2060.

McLeod, J. C. and Pessah, E. (1973). Temperature effects on mercury accumulation, toxicity, and metabolic rate in rainbow trout (*Salmo gairdneri*). *J. Fish. Res. Board Can.* **30**, 485–492.

McMahon, T. E. and Kynard, B. E. (1979). Avoidance of anti-transpirant by western mosquitofish, *Gambusia affinis affinis* (Pisces: Poeciliidae). *Southwest. Nat.* **24**, 87–92.

Meldrim, J. W. and Fava, J. A., Jr. (1977). Behavioral avoidance responses of estuarine fishes to chlorine. *Chesapeake Sci.* **18**, 154–157.

Meldrim, J. W., Grift, G. J., and Petrosky, B. R. (1974). *The effects of temperature and chemical pollutants on the behavior of several estuarine organisms.* Ichthyol. Assoc. Bull. 77, Ithaca, New York.

Middaugh, D. P., Couch, J. A., and Crane, A. M. (1977a). Responses of early life history stages of the striped bass, *Morone saxatilis* to chlorination. *Chesapeake Sci.* **18**, 141–153.

Middaugh, D. P., Crane, A. M., and Couch, J. A. (1977b). Toxicity of chlorine to juvenile spot, *Leostomus xanthurus. Water Res.* **2**, 1089–1096.

Miller, T. G. and MacKay, W. C. (1980). The effects of hardness, alkalinity and pH of test water on the toxicity of copper to rainbow trout (*Salmo gairdneri*). *Water Res.* **14**, 129–133.

Novoselov, V. I., Krapivinskaya, L. D., and Fesenko, E. E. (1980). Molecular mechanisms of odor sensing. V. Some biochemical characteristics of the alanineous receptor from the olfactory epithelium of the skate *Dasyatis pastinaca. Chem. Senses* **5**, 195–203.

Ogilvie, D. M. (1982). Behavioral response of goldfish (*Carassius auratus*) to deoxygenated water. *Copeia* **1982**(2), 434–439.

Olla, B. L., Pearson, W. H., and Studholme, A. L. (1980). Applicability of behavioral measures in environmental stress assessment. *Rapp. P.-V. Reun. Cons. Int. Explor. Mer.* **179**, 162–173.

Oya, T., Usui, Y., Kimata, M., and Ishikawa, K. (1939). Effects of chemical substances dissolved in water on Pisces and Mollusca. I. *Bull. Jap. Soc. Sci. Fish.* **7**, 281–287.

Pearson, W. H. and Olla, B. L. (1979). Detection of naphthalene by the blue crab, *Callinectes sapidus. Estuaries* **2**, 64–65.

Pearson, W. H. and Olla, B. L. (1980). Threshold for detection of naphthalene and other behavioral responses by the blue crab, *Callinectes sapidus. Estuaries* **3**, 224–229.

Pearson, W. H., Sugarman, P. C., Woodruff, D. L., and Blaylock, J. W. (1980). Detection of petroleum hydrocarbons by the dungeness crab, *Cancer magister. U.S. Nat. Mar. Fish. Serv. Fish. Bull.* **71**, 315–317.

Pearson, W. H., Miller, S. E., Blaylock, J. W., and Olla, B. L. (1981a). Detection of the water-soluble fraction of crude oil by the blue crab, *Callinectes sapidus. Mar. Environ. Res.* **5**, 3–11.

Pearson, W. H., Sugarman, P. C., Woodruff, D. L., and Olla, B. L. (1981b). Impairment of the chemosensory antennular flicking response in the dungeness crab, *Cancer magister,* by petroleum hydrocarbons. *U.S. Nat. Mar. Fish. Serv. Fish. Bull.* **79**, 641–647.

Percy, J. A. (1976). Responses of Arctic marine crustaceans to crude oil and oil-tainted food. *Environ. Pollut.* **10**, 155–162.

Percy, J. A. (1977). Responses of Arctic marine benthic crustaceans to sediments contaminated with crude oil. *Environ. Pollut.* **13**, 1–10.

Powers, E. B. (1941). Physico-chemical behaviors of waters as factors in the "homing" of the salmon. *Ecology* **22**, 1–16.

Powers, E. B. and Clark, R. T. (1943). Further evidence on chemical factors affecting the migratory movements of fishes, especially the salmon. *Ecology* **24**, 109–113.

Ramamoorthy, S. and Kushner, D. J. (1975). Heavy metal binding components of river water. *J. Fish. Res. Board Can.* **32**, 1755–1766.

Rand, G., Kleerekoper, H., and Matis, J. (1975). Interaction of odour and flow perception and the effects of parathion in the locomotor orientation of the goldfish *Carassius auratus* L. *J. Fish Biol.* **7**, 495–504.

Reimer, A. A. (1975a). Effects of crude oil on corals. *Mar. Pollut. Bull.* **6**, 39–43.

Reimer, A. A. (1975b). Effects of crude oil on the feeding behaviour of the zoanthid *Polythoa variabilis. Environ. Physiol. Biochem.* **5**, 258–266.

Rhein, L. D. and Cagan, R. H. (1980). Biochemical studies of olfaction: isolation, characterization, and odorant binding activity of cilia from rainbow trout olfactory rosettes. *Proc. Natl. Acad. Sci. USA* **77**, 4412–4416.

Rhein, L. D. and Cagan, R. H. (1981). Role of cilia in olfactory recognition. In: R. H. Cagan and M. R. Kare, Eds., *Biochemistry of taste and olfaction.* Academic Press, New York, pp. 47–68.

Saunders, R. L. and Sprague, J. B. (1967). Effects of copper-zinc mining pollution on a spawning migration of Atlantic salmon. *Water Res.* **1**, 419–432.

Scherer, E. (1975). Avoidance of fenitrothion by goldfish (*Carassius auratus*). *Bull. Environ. Contam. Toxicol.* **13**, 492–496.

Scherer, E. and Nowak, S. (1973). Apparatus for recording avoidance movements of fish. *J. Fish. Res. Board Can.* **30**, 1594–1596.

Schumacher, P. D. and Ney, J. J. (1980). Avoidance response of rainbow trout (*Salmo gairdneri*) to single-dose chlorination in a power plant discharge canal. *Water Res.* **14**, 651–655.

Shelford, V. E. (1917). An experimental study of the effects of gas waste upon fishes, with especial reference to stream pollution. *Bull. Ill. St. Lab. Nat. Hist.* **11**, 380–412.

Shelford, V. E. and Allee, W. C. (1913). The reactions of fishes to gradients of dissolved atmospheric gases. *J. Exp. Zool.* **14**, 207–266.

Shelford, V. E. and Allee, W. C. (1914). Rapid modification of the behavior of fishes by contact with modified water. *J. Anim. Behav.* **4**, 1–30.

Shelford, V. E. and Powers, E. B. (1915). An experimental study of the movements of herring and other marine fishes. *Biol. Bull.* **28**, 315–334.

Sprague, J. B. (1964). Avoidance of copper-zinc solutions by young salmon in the laboratory. *J. Water Pollut. Control Fed.* **36**, 990–1004.

Sprague, J. B. (1968). Avoidance reactions of rainbow trout to zinc sulphate solutions. *Water Res.* **2**, 367–372.

Sprague, J. B. and Drury, D. E. (1969). Avoidance reactions of salmonid fish to representative pollutants. *Adv. Water Pollut. Res.* **4**, 169–179.

Sprague, J. B., Elson, P. F., and Saunders, R. L. (1965). Sublethal copper-zinc pollution in a salmon river—a field and laboratory study. *Int. J. Air Water Pollut.* **9**, 531–543.

Stevens, D. G., Nebeker, A. V., and Baker, R. J. (1980). Avoidance responses of salmon and trout to air-supersaturated water. *Trans. Am. Fish. Soc.* **109**, 751–754.

Stober, Q. J., Dinnel, P. A., Hurlburt, E. F., and DiJulio, D. H. (1980). Acute toxicity and behavioral responses of coho salmon (*Oncorhynchus kisutch*) and shiner perch (*Cymatogaster aggregata*) to chlorine in heated seawater. *Water Res.* **14**, 347–354.

Stott, B. and Buckley, B. R. (1979). Avoidance experiments with homing shoals of minnows, *Phoxinus phoxinus* in a laboratory stream channel. *J. Fish Biol.* **14**, 135–146.

Stott, B. and Cross, D. G. (1973). The reactions of roach (*Rutilus rutilus* L.) to changes in the concentration of dissolved oxygen and free carbon dioxide in a laboratory channel. *Water Res.* **7**, 793–805.

Summerfelt, R. C. and Lewis, W. M. (1967). Repulsion of green sunfish by certain chemicals. *J. Water Pollut. Control Fed.* **39**, 2030–2038.

Sutterlin, A. M. (1974). Pollutants and the chemical senses of aquatic animals—perspective and review. *Chem. Senses Flavour* **1**, 167–178.

Sutterlin, A. M. and Gray, R. (1973). Chemical basis for homing of Atlantic salmon (*Salmo salar*) to a hatchery. *J. Fish. Res. Board Can.* **30**, 985–989.

Sutterlin, A. M. and Sutterlin, N. (1970). Taste responses in Atlantic salmon (*Salmo salar*). *J. Fish. Res. Board Can.* **28**, 565–572.

Sutterlin, A. M., Sutterlin, N., and Rand, S. (1971). *The influence of synthetic surfactants on the functional properties of the olfactory epithelium of Atlantic salmon.* J. Fish. Mar. Serv. Tech. Rep. 287, 8 p.

Suzuki, N. (1980). Binding activities of radioactively labeled amino acids to the lamprey olfactory tissue and its fractions. *Proc. Jap. Symp. Taste and Smell* **14**, 33–36.

Suzuki, N. and Suzuki, Y. (1981). Changes in epithelial structure and binding of amino acids followed by zinc sulfate irrigation of lamprey olfactory epithelium. *Proc. Jap. Symp. Taste and Smell* **15**, 48–51.

Syazuki, K. (1964). Studies on the toxic effects of industrial wastes on fishes and shell-fishes. *J. Shimonoseki Univ. Fish.* **13**, 157–211.

Symons, P. E. K. (1973). Behavior of young Atlantic salmon (*Salmo salar*) exposed to or force-fed fenitrothion, an organophosphate insecticide. *J. Fish. Res. Board Can.* **30**, 651–655.

Takahashi, F. T. and Kittredge, J. S. (1973). Sublethal effects of the water soluble component of oil: chemical communication in the marine environment. In: D. G. Ahearn and S. P. Meyers, Eds., *The microbial degradation of oil pollutants.* Louisiana State University, Baton Rouge, pp. 259–264.

Takayasu, S. and Sotooka, K. (1924). Experimental report on influence of industrial chemicals upon fishes. *Bull. Hokkaido Fish. Exp. Sta.,* pp. 1–70.

Tatsukawa, R. and Hidaka, H. (1978). Avoidance of chemical substances by fish—avoidance of detergents by ayu (*Plecoglossus altivelis*). *J. Agric. Chem. Soc. Jap.* **52**, 263–270.

Thompson, B. E. and Hara, T. J. (1977). Chemosensory bioassay of toxicity of lake waters contaminated with heavy metals from mining effluents. *Water Pollut. Res. Can.* **12**, 179–189.

Timms, A. M., Kleerekoper, H., and Matis, J. (1972). Locomotor responses of goldfish, channel catfish, and largemouth bass to a "copper-polluted" mass of water in an open field. *Water Resour. Res.* **8**, 1574–1580.

Updegraff, K. F. and Sykora, J. L. (1976). Avoidance of lime-neutralized iron hydroxide solutions by coho salmon in the laboratory. *Environ. Sci. Technol.* **10**, 51–54.

van Sommers, P. (1962). Oxygen-motivated behavior in the goldfish, *Carassius auratus. Science* **137**, 678–679.

Verity, M. A., Brown, W. J., Cheung, M., and Gzer, G. (1977). Methyl mercury inhibition of synaptosome and brain slice protein synthesis: in vivo and in vitro studies. *J. Neurochem.* **29**, 673–679.

Vijayamadhavan, K. T. and Iwai, T. (1975). Histochemical observations on the permeation of heavy metals into taste buds of goldfish. *Bull. Jap. Soc. Sci. Fish.* **41**, 631–639.

von Burg, R., Northington, F. C., and Shamoo, A. (1980). Methyl mercury inhibition of rat brain muscarinic receptors. *Toxicol. Appl. Pharmacol.* **53**, 285–292.

Wells, M. M. (1915). Reactions and resistance of fishes in their natural environment to acidity, alkalinity and neutrality. *Biol. Bull.* **29**, 221–257.

Wells, M. M. (1918). The reactions and resistance of fishes to carbon dioxide and carbon monoxide. *Bull. Ill. St. Lab. Nat. Hist.* **11**, 557–578.

Westlake, G. F., Kleerekoper, H., and Matis, J. (1974). The locomotor response of goldfish to a steep gradient of copper ions. *Water Resour. Res.* **10**, 103–105.

Whitman, R. P., Quinn, T. P., and Brannon, E. L. (1982). Influence of suspended volcanic ash on homing behavior of adult chinook salmon. *Trans. Am. Fish. Soc.* **111**, 63–69.

Whitmore, C. M., Warren, C. E., and Doudoroff, P. (1960). Avoidance reactions of salmonid and centrarchid fishes to low oxygen concentrations. *Trans. Am. Fish. Soc.* **89**, 17–26.

Wildish, D. J., Akagi, H., and Poole, N. J. (1977). Avoidance by herring of dissolved components in pulp mill effluents. *Bull. Environ. Contam. Toxicol.* **18**, 521–525.

Yoshii, K., Kashiwayanagi, M., Kurihara, K., and Kobatake, Y. (1980). High sensitivity of eel palatine receptors to carbon dioxide. *Comp. Biochem. Physiol.* **66A**, 327–330.

Zelson, P. R. and Cagan, R. H. (1979). Biochemical studies of taste sensation. VIII. Partial characterization of alanine-binding taste receptor sites of catfish *Ictalurus punctatus* using mercurials, sulfhydryl reagents, trypsin and phospholipase C. *Comp. Biochem. Physiol.* **64B**, 141–147.

Zitko, V. and Carson, W. G. (1974). *Avoidance of organic solvents and substituted phenols by juvenile Atlantic salmon.* J. Fish. Res. Board Can. MS Rep. 1327, 6 p.

10

ADENYLATE ENERGY CHARGE AND ATPASE ACTIVITY: POTENTIAL BIOCHEMICAL INDICATORS OF SUBLETHAL EFFECTS CAUSED BY POLLUTANTS IN AQUATIC ANIMALS

K. Haya and B. A. Waiwood

Fisheries and Environmental Sciences
Department of Fisheries and Oceans
Biological Station
St. Andrews, New Brunswick

1. INTRODUCTION

The potential hazard of xenobiotics in the aquatic environment is assessed mainly on the basis of data on acute toxicity, bioavailability, bioaccumulation, and persistence. Use of these data is indispensable in predicting lethal levels of pollutants; however, acute effects, such as massive fish kills, are seen rarely (Waldichuk, 1979). Sublethal effects of pollutants, such as decrease in reproduction efficiency, increase in susceptibility to disease and predators, or decrease in adaptability to changes in the environment, probably occur more frequently and often may go unnoticed. Thus, there is a need to develop indicators of sublethal effects in aquatic organisms to allow more accurate prediction of acceptable levels of xenobiotics in the aquatic biosphere.

Stresses inflicted by toxicants on an organism's mechanism for maintaining a healthy or normal physiological state may manifest themselves as biochemical sublethal effects. A knowledge of the biochemical events that occur as a result of pollution is helpful in understanding the molecular mode of action of the pollutant, but altered biochemical parameters may also indicate unfavorable living conditions. Biochemical parameters, as indices of sublethal effects, will find application in:

1. Assessing the overall health of fish communities and populations.
2. Monitoring, as an early warning signal for potential pollution problems.
3. Serving as a tool in the development and assessment of specific water quality criteria.
4. Assessing the hazard potential of xenobiotics.

Two biochemical parameters will be evaluated in this paper, the adenylate energy charge (AEC) and adenosine triphosphatase (ATPase) activity. AEC and ATPase are related biochemically. AEC is indicative of the metabolic energy available to the organism from the adenine nucleotide pool, mainly in the form of ATP (Atkinson, 1977). ATPase specifically hydrolyzes ATP to obtain the energy required for cation transport (Schuurmans Stekhoven and

Bonting, 1981). For clarity the two biochemical parameters will be discussed separately.

2. METHODS

2.1. Determination of AEC

As stated by Ivanovici (1981), "reliable estimates of adenylate energy charge approximating *in vivo* values depend on careful extraction and accurate determination of the concentrations of ATP, ADP, and AMP." The method which follows is used in our laboratory and appears to be applicable to a wide variety of species.

The animal may require anesthesia. The tissue or organ is excised quickly and immediately freeze-clamped at $-196°C$, using liquid N_2 (Hess and Brand, 1974). The tissues are ground to a fine powder with a porcelain mortar and pestle cooled with liquid N_2. The samples are stable at $-80°C$ for at least 6 months before or after pulverization.

Approximately 1 g (accurately weighed) of pulverized tissue is homogenized, at ice-bath temperature, in 2 ml of 6% $HClO_4$ with a Brinkman Polytron. The homogenate is allowed to stand at 25°C for 30 min to ensure destruction of ATPases (this step should be checked carefully for recovery of adenine nucleotides with each type of tissue or species). The homogenate is centrifuged at 30,000 × G and 4°C for 15 min. The supernatant is collected, and the pellet is suspended in 2 ml of 6% $HClO_4$. After centrifugation, the supernatants are pooled and 0.5 ml of 1 M MOPS buffer added. The extract is neutralized (pH 6.8–7.4) with 3 N KOH and the resulting precipitate is removed by centrifugation. The adenylates are stable in this neutralized extract for at least 1 week at $-80°C$.

The concentration of ATP, ADP, and AMP in the neutralized extract is determined by enzymatic methods (Lamprecht and Trautschold, 1974; Jaworek et al., 1974), using a spectrophotometer. These methods depend on the stoichiometric formation of NADPH or disappearance of NADH. Linear responses in absorbance are obtained for adenine nucleotide concentrations in the final assay medium of 10–100 nmole/ml. The assay is sensitive enough to measure adenine nucleotides in most aquatic animals.

More sensitive techniques may be required with organ or tissue samples that have low adenine nucleotide levels. The foregoing method can be adapted for fluorometric analysis with a sensitivity range of 0.1–10.0 nmole/ml. Quantitation of ATP by measurement of the bioluminescence formed in the reaction of ATP with luciferin-luciferase is specific and sensitive (0.1–80.0 pmole/assay; Lust et al., 1981; Strehler, 1974). ADP and AMP can be measured by this procedure after enzymatic conversion to ATP. However, luciferase is susceptible to general anion inhibition and sensitivity of the ATP assay varies with different buffers (Webster et al., 1980) or with the presence of inorganic or organic acids (Nichols et al., 1981). A sensitive (1–50 pmole/assay), but somewhat more complicated procedure, is fluorometric analysis combined with enzyme cycling (Lust et al., 1981). A radioenzymatic method which depends on the phosphorylation of a radioactively labelled sugar can be used to quantify levels of ATP at 3 pmole/assay (Gonzalez and Garcia-Sancho, 1981). The adenine nucleotides also can be analyzed by high-pressure liquid chromatography (Leray, 1979; Taylor et al., 1981). As a precautionary note, it should be mentioned that commonly used glass syringes adsorb adenine nucleotides and can cause pipetting errors (Goswami and Pande, 1981).

2.2. Determination of ATPase Activity

Procedures to determine gill ATPase activity will be described briefly (for details see Haya et al., 1980, 1983) with a brief discussion of variations in methodology used by other workers.

Gill filaments are homogenized in an ice-cold solution of 250 mM sucrose and 5 mM Na_2EDTA (40 mg/ml). A 0.2-ml aliquot of the crude homogenate is added to 0.6 ml of the assay medium and preincubated for 5 min at 37°C. Then the reaction is started by adding 0.2 ml $MgCl_2$-ATP solution. The final concentration in the assay mixture is 50 mM NaCl, 10 mM KCl, 4 mM $MgCl_2$, 6 mM Na_2ATP, and 90 mM pH 7.6 Tris buffer. To determine Na,K ATPase and residual ATPase activities the reaction is run with and without ouabain. The ATPase reaction is linear for at least 30 min and the inorganic phosphate formed is measured by a modified colorimetric procedure of Fiske and Subbarow (1925). The protein content is determined by a modification of the Lowry method (Hartree, 1972) and ATPase activity is expressed as μmole P_i/mg protein · hr.

Gill filaments can be freeze-clamped in liquid N_2, frozen in sucrose-EDTA solution prior to homogenization (Zaugg, 1982), or freeze-dried after homogenization (Neufeld et al., 1980) and stored at −80°C for at least 2 months without loss of activity. However, Mg ATPase and Ca ATPase in *Gillichthys mirabilis* gills showed significant losses in activity after freezing (Doneen, 1981). Many laboratories use a detergent such as Na-deoxycholate to disrupt membranes and to allow the substrate better access to the enzyme. This detergent enhanced Na,K ATPase activity greatly but inhibited Mg and Ca ATPases of *G. mirabilis* gills (Doneen, 1981). Deoxycholate also inhibited Na,K ATPase activity of gill homogenates from *Pseudopleuronectes americanus* (Janicki and Kinter, 1971). Detergents must be used with caution because solubilized proteins are no longer in a native state and as a result specific enzyme activity may be altered artificially (Askari, 1974). Gill ATPase activities can vary with incubation temperature of the assay and the response of ATPase to modifiers may be dissimilar (Watson and Beamish, 1980, 1981). If physiologically meaningful results are to be obtained, Watson and Beamish recommended that ATPase assays be performed at the preferred temperature of the fish.

Procedures for the preparation of gill subcellular fractions have been reported (Lock et al., 1981; Watson and Beamish, 1980; Doneen, 1981). A simplified procedure for the preparation of gill homogenates of comparable specific activity to that of microsomal fractions has been decribed (Zaugg, 1982). This method eliminates the long, complex procedure of subcellular fractionation and thus allows for more samples.

Various modifications of the Fiske and Subbarow method of inorganic phosphate determination are used because the method is simple and rapid. Disadvantages of the procedure are: instability of the color reagent which must be prepared fresh daily; color development is time and temperature dependent; color instability; acid-labile phosphates are hydrolyzed. Similar colorimetric procedures that have overcome some of the problems have been reported (Riedel and Christensen, 1979; Peterson, 1978; Heinonen and Lahti, 1981; Zaugg, 1982). Heinonen's method is simple, sensitive, and reliable. A method without preliminary harsh treatment to the tissue and carried out at neutral pH is the enzymatic procedure which depends on the phosphorolytic cleavage of glycogen by phosphorylase a. In this coupled enzyme system NADPH is formed stoichiometrically and is quantitated by fluorometry (Passonneau and Schulz, 1974) or spectrophotometry (Gawehn, 1974). ATPase activity also may be determined by a coupled enzymatic procedure using pyruvate kinase and lactic dehydrogenase (Saintsing and Towle, 1978; Schwartz et al., 1969). This procedure relies on the stoichiometric oxidation of NADH and is measured by spectrophotometric or fluorometric methods. A disadvantage of this method is that pyruvate kinase is affected by a wide range of metabolic modifiers. By far the most sensitive technique is the use of γ-^{32}P-ATP as the substrate for ATPase (Ghiasuddin and Matsumura, 1979); however, the isotope is expensive and has a short half-life (14.3 days).

3. ADENYLATE ENERGY CHARGE

All biochemical pathways are ultimately dependent on the adenine nucleotide pool to provide energy. AEC is an indicator of the metabolic energy state of cells and is defined as a ratio of the concentrations of the adenine nucleotides (Atkinson, 1977). By this definition, AEC = (ATP + 0.5 ADP) ÷ (ATP + ADP + AMP), and can vary between 0 and 1. Studies of enzyme kinetics and concentrations of adenine nucleotides of cells have revealed that metabolic activities are more dependent on AEC than on the concentration of individual adenine nucleotides (Atkinson, 1969; Swedes et al., 1975; Chapman et al., 1971).

AEC is homeostatically controlled at some optimum value and thus is a prime factor in the mechanisms which control the flux of energy through anabolic (energy-utilizing) and catabolic (energy-forming) cellular processes (Atkinson, 1977; Dickson and Franz, 1980). Any factor that upsets the homeostatic process will be reflected in an altered AEC (usually decreased) and thus would indicate suboptimal cellular energy metabolism.

AEC has been correlated with viability of microorganisms (Chapman et al., 1971; Wiebe and Bancroft, 1975). Values between 0.8 and 0.95 were found in cells that were actively growing and dividing. Values between 0.5 and 0.75 are indicative of cells in stationary growth phase. Those cells with values below 0.5 are usually moribund, no recovery occurring when the cells are placed in optimal environmental conditions. The use of AEC in ecological studies to determine the state of growth of microbial communities has been reviewed recently (Karl, 1980) and will not be discussed here.

Wiebe and Bancroft (1975) suggested that changes in AEC may be useful in detecting the effect of pollutants on microbial communities. For example, with the unicellular organism *Euglena gracilis,* cultures were incubated for 10 days in sublethal concentrations of Zn, 3 ppm; Hg, 20 ppb; or Cd, 1 ppb (De Filippis et al., 1981). In all treatments the ATP levels were decreased, ADP levels increased, and AMP levels were similar to those of control *Euglena.* Total adenylate concentrations (ATP + ADP + AMP) with Zn and Cd remained the same as in controls but not with Hg, where the total adenylate concentrations were 29% lower. AEC values of 0.8 were found for the steady state growth phase in control *Euglena,* but stabilized at 0.6 for cells exposed to the metals.

AEC appears to be a useful indicator of physiological status in multicellular organisms. Ivanovici (1979, 1980a,b) assessed AEC as a potential indicator of sublethal stress caused by pollutants in aquatic animals. However, the numerical criteria of AEC for physiological status of microorganisms may not be strictly valid for multicellular organisms because values below 0.8 have been reported for apparently healthy organisms (Table 1). Decreases in AEC occur in aquatic animals during physiological stress (salinity, temperature, pH, anoxia) or stress induced by xenobiotics.

3.1. Effect of Salinity

The adaptation of rainbow trout, *Salmo gairdneri,* to abrupt changes in salinity is reflected in AEC (Leray et al., 1981). Gill AEC was decreased from 0.91 to 0.88 72 hr after transfer from fresh- to seawater, but returned to initial values after 10 days. By this time, other physiological measurements indicated that the rainbow trout had become fully adapted to seawater.

In three estuarine molluscs, *Pyrazus ebeninus, Anadara trapezia,* and *Saccastrea commercialis,* the mean AEC decreased by 17% or more in columellar or adductor muscle when salinity was reduced from 35‰ to 10‰ (Rainer et al., 1979). The AEC values were below 0.75 after exposure to 10‰ salinity. With *P. ebeninus* the AEC fell below 0.7 at 17‰ salinity (Ivanovici, 1980c). Such low values are indicative of suboptimal physiological status. The data from these studies suggested that AEC below 0.55 will not sustain life in *P. ebeninus*.

3.2. Effect of Temperature

The effect of temperature on AEC has been noted in several studies. Brook trout, *Salvelinus fontinalis*, acclimated for 10 weeks to 4°C, had lower AEC (0.89) in white muscle compared to those at 24°C (AEC of 0.93; Walesby and Johnston, 1980). The AEC was approximately 20% less in molluscs, *P. ebeninus*, kept at 29°C than at 20°C (Ivanovici, 1980c). The AEC was well within the optimum range at both temperatures in both these studies. However, this was not the case for a bivalve, *Trichomya hirsuta*, collected from the inlet and outlet sides of a water-cooled power plant. The AEC of the bivalves was 0.78 on the inlet site and was 0.68 on the outlet side where the temperature was 8° higher (Ivanovici, 1979, 1980b).

3.3. Effect of pH

Exposure of gulf killifish, *Fundulus grandis*, to low pH resulted in decreased AEC in brain, liver, gills, and muscle (MacFarlane, 1981). The amount of change in the adenine nucleotides and AEC was related to the degree of acidity and duration of exposure. The greatest changes were found in killifish after 96 hr exposure to pH 4, the lowest pH tested. For example, total adenylates decreased from controls (20 μg/mg protein) by 18%, 30%, and 44% in brains of killifish exposed to pH 6.5, 5, and 4, respectively, for 96 hr. Brain AEC of controls was 0.835, and after 96 hr at pH 6.5, AEC was 0.75; at pH 5, 0.62; at pH 4, 0.574. Similar results were found for total adenylates and AEC of liver and gills from the acid-exposed fish. Acid treatment produced the greatest effects on adenylate metabolism and AEC (0.526) of gills compared with the other tissues of killifish after 96 hr at pH 4. Adenylates in muscle were affected differently than in the other tissues. The level of total adenylates in the muscle was altered only slightly; however, alterations in relative proportions of the adenine nucleotides occurred and caused AEC to fall from 0.828 initially to 0.546 after 96 hr at pH 4. The disruption of adenylate metabolism by low pH may result from hypoxia or loss of Na ions. These data indicate that there is a dose–response relationship between degree of acidity and extent of AEC depression.

3.4. Effect of Anaerobic Metabolism

A summary of AEC during anoxia in aquatic animals is given in Table 1. Abnormally low values of AEC in normoxic *Mytilus galloprovincialis* may be due to inadequate analytical techniques (Ivanovici, 1981). Depression of

Table 1. Adenylate Energy Charge in Aquatic Animals under Normoxic and Anoxic Conditions

Animal	Adenylate Energy Charge		Time (hr) Anoxic	Tissue Analyzed	Reference
	Normoxic	Anoxic			
Bivalvia					
Mytilus edulis	0.85	0.68	72	Whole body	Wijsman, 1976
	0.91	0.67	72	Posterior adductor muscle	Wijsman, 1976
	0.69	0.55	72	Hepatopancreas	Wijsman, 1976
	0.88	0.67	72	Mantle	Wijsman, 1976
Mytilus galloprovincialis	0.43	0.29	72	Whole body	Calculated from Zs-Nagy and Ermini, 1972
	0.43	0.30	1–3	Gills	Shapiro, 1981
Oligochaeta					
Tubifex sp.	0.84	0.69	9	Whole body	Schöttler, 1978
Polychaetae					
Arenicola marina	0.89	0.75	48	Whole body	Schöttler and Wienhausen, 1981
	0.85	0.68	24	Body wall musculature	Pörtner et al., 1979

Nereis diversicolor	0.88	0.70	72	Whole body	Schöttler, 1979
Nereis virens	0.90	0.70	72	Whole body	Schöttler, 1979
Nereis pelagica	0.88	0.66	36	Whole body	Schöttler, 1979
Anthozoa					
Bunodosoma cavenata	0.78	0.53	3	Whole body	Ellington, 1981
Crustacea					
Cirolana borealis	0.73	0.25	96	Whole body	Skjöldal and Bakke, 1978
Pisces					
Carassius auratus	0.99	0.82	8(mean)	Dorsal white muscle	Van den Thillart et al., 1976
	0.60	0.32	12	Liver	Van den Thillart et al., 1980
Platichthys flesus	0.73	0.36	29	Liver	Jorgensen and Mustafa, 1980
	0.86	0.74	29	Kidney	Jorgensen and Mustafa, 1980
	0.91	0.86	29	Muscle	Jorgensen and Mustafa, 1980

AEC during anoxia occurs in the whole body of invertebrates and in verte-brates the depression is greatest in the liver. Generally there is a fairly rapid decrease in AEC during the initial phase of anoxia, followed by a stable period at the decreased level. Prolonged anoxia will lead to death (Wijsman, 1976), since all animals ultimately depend on oxygen for sustaining life. Upon transfer of sea anemone, *Bunodosoma caverata,* from anoxic to nor-moxic conditions, the AEC returned to normal values within 12 hr (Elling-ton, 1981). The degree of depression of AEC among the polychaetes may be related to their relative resistance to anoxia (Schöttler, 1979). *Nereis pelagica* is sensitive to anoxia whereas *Nereis virens* and *Nereis diversicolor* are more resistant. The decrease in AEC upon exposure to anoxia was more rapid and more extensive in *N. pelagica* than in the other two polychaetes (Table 1).

Escape swimming in molluscs requires large bursts of energy and the ATP required is produced through anaerobic glycogen metabolism. Thus, exhaus-tive stimulation of "escape" muscles will decrease AEC. For example, squid, *Loligo pealeii,* which were induced to swim vigorously for 10 sec showed AEC of 0.52 in mantle muscle compared with 0.90 in that of resting individuals (calculated from Storey and Storey, 1978). Scallops, *Chlamys opercularis,* forced to swim until exhausted, had lower AEC (0.42) in adduc-tor muscle than that for resting scallops (0.93; Grieshaber, 1978). During rest AEC returned to optimum values within 30 min, but complete recovery of the adenylate metabolic system and AEC values required 120 min.

3.5.   Effect of Organic Xenobiotics

The use of AEC as an indicator of anaerobic metabolism in toxicological studies will provide a better understanding of toxicant mechanisms of action and anaerobic energy-producing metabolic pathways. Changing from aerobic to anaerobic metabolism results in a decrease of AEC from 0.78 to 0.53 in sea anemone (Ellington, 1981). Iodoacetate inhibits glycolysis and the AEC of sea anemone fell further to 0.3 in the presence of 10 ppm iodoacetate after 6 hr of anoxia. This dramatic reduction in AEC indicated that anaerobic glycolysis is the most important energy-yielding process in sea anemone during anoxia and may have been the cause of death of sea anemone during the exposure to iodoacetate (10 ppm) under anoxic condi-tions (Mangum, 1980).

3-mercaptopicolinic acid (3-MPA) was useful in the studies on anaerobic metabolism of *Arenicola marina* and *N. virens* (Schöttler and Wienhousen, 1981). 3-MPA is an inhibitor of gluconeogenesis of which phosphoenolpyru-vate carboxykinase is the key regulatory enzyme. In *N. virens* there was no difference in AEC between animals treated with 3-MPA and anoxic or nor-moxic controls. With *A. marina* AEC decreased much more under the in-fluence of 3-MPA than controls, especially during the first 24 hr of anaerobic

Table 2.   Adenylate Energy Charge of Polychaetes, *Nereis virens,* **Exposed to 11 ppm Endosulfan under Normoxic and Anoxic Conditions**

Time of Exposure (hr)	Mean ± Standard Error (n)			
	Control		Endosulfan-Treated	
	Normoxic	Anoxic	Normoxic	Anoxic
0	0.885 ± 0.004 (5)	0.885 ± 0.004 (5)	0.885 ± 0.004 (5)	0.885 ± 0.004 (5)
6	0.844 ± 0.035 (4)	0.891 ± 0.003 (5)	0.884 ± 0.007 (6)	0.797 ± 0.016 (5)
12	0.835 ± 0.016 (3)	0.817 ± 0.018 (4)	0.852 ± 0.010 (5)	0.795 ± 0.050 (5)
24	0.884 ± 0.006 (5)	0.849 ± 0.016 (5)	0.878 ± 0.003 (6)	0.813 ± 0.049 (6)
48	0.863 ± 0.021 (4)	0.908 ± 0.007 (4)	0.872 ± 0.013 (4)	0.877 ± 0.019 (4)
72	0.877 ± 0.034 (4)	0.905 ± 0.008 (4)	0.788 ± 0.035 (5)	0.730 ± 0.040 (5)
96	0.870 ± 0.004 (6)	0.875 ± 0.004 (6)	0.796 ± 0.011 (4)	0.737 ± 0.018 (6)

incubation. These data helped to identify differences in anaerobic metabolism between these two species of similar habitat.

In our laboratory, polychaetes, *N. virens,* were exposed to endosulfan (11 ppm) for 96 hr under anoxic and normoxic conditions. Periodically, AEC in whole polychaetes was determined (Table 2). Analysis of variance of the data within each exposure with time and between groups at each time period was performed for significance at $p < 0.05$. There were no differences in AEC with time of exposure in the normoxic or anoxic control groups. In endosulfan-treated polychaetes, both the anoxic and normoxic groups showed a significant decrease of AEC after 72 and 96 hr of exposure. After 72 hr of exposure the anoxic endosulfan-treated group had significantly lower AEC than the control anoxic or normoxic polychaetes. After 96 hr of exposure the normoxic endosulfan-exposed polychaetes had a significantly lower AEC than the control normoxic or anoxic group. The AEC of anoxic endosulfan-exposed polychaetes was significantly lower than in the other three groups. These results indicated that anoxia alone did not affect AEC in *N. virens* under the conditions of this experiment. However, sublethal levels of endosulfan decrease AEC in *N. virens* and the decrease is greater in anoxic conditions. Thus, endosulfan must interfere with some energy-producing metabolic pathway which appears to be more susceptible under anoxic conditions.

Several field studies with molluscs have been reported. *Pyrazus ebeninus* samples from an area of low hydrocarbon pollution were transferred to an area of high hydrocarbon pollution (Ivanovici, 1979, 1980b). After 24 hr AEC decreased from 0.81 to 0.64. When *P. ebeninus* were transferred after 2 weeks in the highly polluted area back to the area of low hydrocarbon pollution, the AEC returned to 0.80 within 2 weeks. Although details are not given, Phelps et al. (1981) reported that the AEC values for mussels from Narragansett Bay, Rhode Island, did not reflect suboptimal physiological status as indicated by other physiological data. The area in the Bay where the mussels were sampled is polluted heavily with petroleum hydrocarbons, heavy metals, and pesticides.

Exposure of the marine isopod *Cirolana borealis* to 12.5 ppm toluene led to a progressive decrease in ATP and AEC, and all individuals were dead by 8 days (Bakke and Skjöldal, 1979). By 48 hr ATP was reduced markedly while AEC was lowered only slightly. Upon exposure of isopods to 125 ppm toluene, ATP remained constant but AEC was decreased after 24 hr. Narcotization of the isopods exposed to 125 ppm toluene occurred after 1 hr; therefore, narcotization appears to be a more sensitive index than AEC for toluene intoxication with isopods.

3.6. Effect of Metals

During May 1980, Cd pollution associated with the effluent of a lead smelter at Belledune Harbour, N.B., resulted in the closure of lobster fishing in the harbor area (Uthe and Zitko, 1980). There was no apparent health problem to the resident lobsters, *Homarus americanus*; however, Cd in the hepatopancreas had accumulated to levels considered undesirable for human consumption. Cd levels in the gills, hepatopancreas, and tail muscle of the lobsters from Belledune Harbour were 16–20 times higher than in lobsters from nearby Stonehaven (Table 3).

The AEC of gills, hepatopancreas, and tail muscle of lobsters from the harbor were measured and compared with those of lobsters from Stonehaven (Table 4) in an attempt to identify possible sublethal effects (Haya et al., 1980). No differences were observed in the adenylate pool or AEC in the hepatopancreas or tail muscle of the lobsters from the two areas. AEC

Table 3. Levels of Cd and Zn in Gill, Hepatopancreas, and Tail Muscle of Lobster, *Homarus americanus*, from Belledune Harbour and Stonehaven, N.B., Canada, and Maine, United States

| Tissue | Metal | Mean ppm Dry Wt ± Standard Error (n) | | |
		Stonehaven[a]	Belledune Harbour[a]	Maine[b]
Gills	Cd	4 ± 1 (12)	70 ± 27 (17)	4 ± 1 (9)
	Zn	112 ± 6 (11)	203 ± 10 (16)	111 ± 7 (14)
Hepatopancreas	Cd	30 ± 10 (12)	483 ± 153 (17)	22 ± 7 (9)
	Zn	98 ± 14 (12)	133 ± 19 (17)	79 ± 3 (14)
Tail muscle	Cd	0.10 ± 0.06 (12)	2.18 ± 1.28 (17)	0.05 ± 0.01 (9)
	Zn	92 ± 7 (12)	155 ± 14 (17)	104 ± 21 (14)

[a]Cd data from Haya et al. (1980).
[b]Cd data from Ray et al. (1981).

Table 4. **Adenine Nucleotide Levels and Adenylate Energy Charge in Gills, Tail Muscle, and Hepatopancreas of Lobster, *Homarus americanus*, from Stonehaven and Belledune Harbour, N.B., Canada, and Maine, United States** [a]

Tissue	Parameter	Stonehaven ($n = 12$)	Belledune Harbour ($n = 17$)	Maine ($n = 10$)[b]
Gills	ATP[c]	0.74 ± 0.03	0.55 ± 0.02	0.26 ± 0.03
	ADP[c]	0.09 ± 0.01	0.09 ± 0.01	0.04 ± 0.01
	AMP[c]	0.08 ± 0.01	0.07 ± 0.01	0.02 ± 0.01
	Total adenylates[c]	0.91 ± 0.03	0.71 ± 0.03	0.32 ± 0.04
	AEC[d]	0.866 ± 0.006	0.844 ± 0.008	0.874 ± 0.018
Tail muscle	ATP	4.67 ± 0.24	4.68 ± 0.25	4.54 ± 0.26
	ADP	0.75 ± 0.04	0.78 ± 0.03	0.83 ± 0.09
	AMP	0.12 ± 0.01	0.12 ± 0.01	0.11 ± 0.02
	Total adenylates	5.61 ± 0.21	5.58 ± 0.28	5.48 ± 0.31
	AEC	0.911 ± 0.003	0.905 ± 0.009	0.904 ± 0.007
Hepatopancreas	ATP	1.10 ± 0.04	1.05 ± 0.03	0.63 ± 0.04
	ADP	0.29 ± 0.02	0.28 ± 0.02	0.14 ± 0.01
	AMP	0.11 ± 0.01	0.10 ± 0.01	0.03 ± 0.01
	Total adenylates	1.50 ± 0.06	1.43 ± 0.04	0.80 ± 0.05
	AEC	0.836 ± 0.014	0.831 ± 0.013	0.871 ± 0.007

[a] Data from Haya et al. (1980, 1983).
[b] $n = 9$ for gills.
[c] Mean μmole/g wet wt ± standard error.
[d] Mean ± standard error.

values of the gills of lobsters from Belledune Harbour were significantly ($p <$ .001) lower than those of lobsters from Stonehaven. The total adenylates were 20% less in the gills of lobsters from Belledune Harbour than in the lobsters from Stonehaven, and this was due mostly to a 24% decrease in ATP levels. Since these changes did not correlate with Cd concentrations in the tissues and the AEC was well within the optimum range for healthy individuals, it was concluded that the high level of Cd found in Belledune Harbour does not affect energy metabolism in lobsters.

Cd exposure has been reported to cause significant decreases in AEC of the foot muscle of clam, *Corbicula menilensis* (Bingham et al., 1978), and certain tissues of crayfish, *Procambarus pubescens* (Duke et al., 1978). The crayfish were exposed to 10 or 30 ppb Cd for short periods. Cd concentrations in water at Belledune Harbour ranged from 25 to 125 ppb (Loring et al., 1980). However, the reports of Bingham et al. (1978) and Duke et al. (1978) are abstracts and no other details were given; therefore, it is impossible to compare these studies.

High levels of Zn were also found in water at Belledune Harbour (260 ppb; Loring et al., 1980) and Zn concentrations of the gills, hepatopancreas, and tail muscle of lobsters from Belledune Harbour were higher than in those of lobsters from Stonehaven (Table 3). As part of a follow-up study, lobsters were exposed to sublethal levels of Zn under laboratory conditions. Lobsters from Maine were exposed to Zn for 96 hr followed by 168 hr depuration in a flow-through system (Haya et al., 1983). The measured concentration of Zn in seawater was 60 ppm initially and fell to 25 ppm by 12 hr and remained at this concentration. Lobsters were sampled periodically and the AEC determined. Zn concentration, adenine nucleotide levels, and AEC of the gills, hepatopancreas, and tail muscle are given in Tables 3 and 4 for control lobsters. A one-way analysis of variance showed no significant change in adenine nucleotide levels or AEC which correlated with time up to 96 hr of exposure. It was concluded that AEC is not an indicator of Zn intoxication in lobsters at or below the concentrations used in the study.

Comparison of adenine nucleotide levels in lobsters from the three areas indicates that differences may occur in these levels with habitat. The adenylate profile is identical in the tail muscle of lobsters from all three areas (Table 4) and similar to the values reported for the European lobster *Homarus vulgaris* (Beis and Newsholme, 1975). The adenine nucleotide levels of the gills and hepatopancreas of lobsters from Maine are approximately half the level of those from the other areas. The differences in the adenylate levels may be due to habitat variability (chemical, physical, biological) which can involve adjustment in behavior, physiology, and biochemistry. Two closely related crayfish species displayed differences in energy flow resulting from habitat adaptation (Dickson and Franz, 1980). However, AEC of lobsters from three locations in our studies, of clams, *Mya arenaria,* from three locations (unpublished results), of five species of crayfish from different habitats (Dickson and Giesy, 1981), and of two species of freshwater clams from two locations (Giesy and Dickson, 1981), did not vary with location and AEC values, indicating optimal physiological status were usually found. There seems to be, however, some variation in AEC with season (reproductive cycle) in clams (Giesy and Dickson, 1981). The insensitivity of AEC to habitat adaptations will allow for a more general application of AEC in pollution monitoring.

In summary, xenobiotics can alter adenylate energy metabolism during sublethal intoxication in one of four ways:

1. AEC decreases while the level of total adenylates remains constant (e.g., Ivanovici, 1980a; Rainer et al., 1979; MacFarlane, 1981; Storey and Storey, 1978).
2. AEC remains constant while the level of total adenylates decreases (e.g., Dickson and Giesy, 1981; Haya et al., 1980; Schöttler, 1978; Chapman and Atkinson, 1973).
3. AEC and total adenylates decrease (e.g., Van den Thillart et al., 1976; Jorgensen and Mustafa, 1980; Schöttler, 1979; Sharpe and Lee, 1981).
4. Total adenylates and AEC remain constant (or AEC remains in optimum range), but precursors (arginine phosphate in invertebrates or creatine

phosphate in vertebrates) or end products (e.g., lactate, pyruvate, succinate, inosine, alanine) of adenylate energy metabolism are altered (e.g., Dickson and Franz, 1980; Gäde, 1980; Grieshaber and Gäde, 1977).

Which of the four effects is observed depends on the toxicant, species, and organ or tissue analyzed for AEC. Therefore, to get a more complete picture of the effects of xenobiotics on adenylate energy state of multicellular organisms, other parameters as well as AEC must be determined.

4. SODIUM, POTASSIUM-ACTIVATED ADENOSINE TRIPHOSPHATASE

Most animal cells maintain a high intracellular K^+ concentration and a low Na^+ concentration. The surrounding interstitial fluid has high Na^+ and low K^+ concentrations. This is accomplished by movement of Na^+ and K^+ across the cellular membranes against an electrochemical gradient by an active transport (energy-requiring) process. The active transport mechanism involving Mg^{2+}-dependent, Na^+-, and K^+-activated adenosine triphosphatase (Na,K ATPase) provides the largest contribution to the maintenance of Na^+ and K^+ transmembrane gradients (Trachtenberg et al., 1981). Maintaining this Na^+ and K^+ gradient has a central role in, or is required for, the uptake by cells of metabolites such as glucose and amino acids, regeneration of transmembrane potential during nerve excitation, transmembrane movement of Ca^{2+} during muscle stimulation, maintenance of osmotic equilibrium in cells, and control of transcellular ion movement.

Several reviews on Na,K ATPase and its function have been published recently (Schuurmans Stekhoven and Bonting, 1981; Towle, 1981; Yates, 1980; Trachtenberg et al., 1981) and a brief overview will be presented here.

Na,K ATPase is an intrinsic membrane-bound protein which hydrolyzes ATP to ADP and inorganic phosphate and, in the process, makes the energy from ATP available for active cation transport. In reacting with a molecule of ATP, three Na^+ are transported across the membrane from the intracellular fluid to the interstitial fluid and two K^+ move in the opposite direction. The reaction is under control of the ligands, ATP, Na^+, K^+, and Mg^{2+}. Each ligand binds to a specific site on the ATPase molecule. Concentrations of interstitial K^+ and Na^+ regulate ATPase and Mg^{2+} catalyzes the hydrolysis of ATP during the phosphorylation (activation) of ATPase. This catalysis by Mg^{2+} is inhibited by some divalent ions (Fe^{2+}, Ca^{2+}, Zn^{2+}, Cu^{2+}, Ba^{2+}, Sr^{2+}, and Be^{2+}). Ouabain prevents the binding of ATP to the enzyme and is a highly specific and potent inhibitor of Na,K ATPase. Ion-regulating ATPases which are not inhibited by ouabain are mostly Mg^{2+}-activated ATPase but also include other ion-sensitive ATPases (e.g., Ca^{2+}, NH_4^+, HCO_3^-) and are collectively referred to as residual ATPase.

In an assessment of the data on the role of Na,K ATPase in osmoregulation and salinity adaptation of aquatic animals, Towle (1981) concluded that

Na,K ATPase plays a central role in whole body ion regulation. Thus, any toxicant that interferes with ionic homeostasis may be reflected as altered Na,K ATPase activity at sublethal concentrations. The xenobiotic can interact directly with the enzyme or alter Na,K ATPase activity due to disruption of energy producing metabolic pathways (Watson and Beamish, 1980; Verma et al., 1978). For example, ATP stores are reduced by increased energy demand in response to a physiologically stressful condition. Since Na,K ATPase turnover rate is extremely rapid (Hossler, 1980), Na,K ATPase would be sensitive to factors affecting protein biosynthetic pathways. Altered Na,K ATPase activity can arise in response to a wide variety of toxicants.

This chapter is restricted to Na,K ATPase of gills of aquatic animals because gills are the major osmoregulatory organ whether the animal is an hypo- or hyperosmoregulator or an osmoconformer. The major amount of Na,K ATPase of the teleost and probably invertebrate gill is found in the basolateral membrane of chloride cells and therefore in close contact with the blood, interstitial fluid, and external water (Towle, 1981). In addition, gill epithelium comprises approximately 95% of the body surface of fish (Parry, 1966), is relatively permeable to water, and is the main site of osmotic water movement (Evans, 1969; Motais et al., 1969). Since, for most pollutants, uptake from water is the most important route, gills are a primary target organ and may be one of the first organs to exhibit symptoms of sublethal toxicity.

4.1. Effect of Organic Xenobiotics

Inhibition of gill ATPases by 1,1,1-trichloro-2,2-*bis*(*p*-chlorophenyl) ethane (DDT) has been studied both *in vitro* and *in vivo*. Addition of 50 ppm DDT to incubations of gill homogenates from winter flounder, *P. americanus,* resulted in 54% inhibition of Na,K ATPase activity and 25% inhibition of residual ATPase activity (Janicki and Kinter, 1971). Total ATPase activity of rainbow trout, *Salmo gairdneri,* gill microsomal preparations was inhibited with DDT, and the concentration required for 50% inhibition was 1×10^{-4} M (Davis and Wedemeyer, 1971). In an *in vivo* study, DDT (2.75 or 8.3 mg/kg) in gelatin capsules was administered orally to freshwater- and seawater-adapted rainbow trout. The Na,K and residual ATPase activities of the gills were inhibited by 65% and 55%, respectively (averages estimated from Leadem et al., 1974).

Gill Na,K ATPase activities of several species of crabs were inhibited by DDT. In whole homogenates of gills from blue crab, *Callinectes sapidus,* ATPases were reduced by 1 ppm DDT (Neufeld and Pritchard, 1979a). Maximum inhibition (30%) was obtained with 9 ppm DDT in these *in vitro* studies. Blue crab were transferred from 100% seawater to 20% seawater after injection of 0.3 mg/kg body weight DDT (Neufeld and Pritchard, 1979a). By

28 hr after transfer the blue crabs had adapted to the hypoosmotic conditions and the gill Na,K ATPase activity of the DDT-treated crabs was the same as those without DDT. On the other hand, in shore crab, *Carcinus maenas,* gill Na,K and residual ATPase activities increased with decreasing salinity, but this response of gill ATPases was inhibited in the presence of 0.2 ppb DDT (Jowett et al., 1981). A single injection of 0.1 mg/kg body weight DDT into the pericardial sinus of rock crab, *Cancer irroratus,* inhibited gill ATPase up to 48 hr (Neufeld and Pritchard, 1979b).

Effects of other organochlorine pesticides on ATPases have been reported. Na,K ATPase activity in gill homogenates of channel catfish, *Labeo rohita,* was enhanced by low concentrations (0.06 μM) of aldrin and dieldrin (Verma et al., 1978). However, higher concentrations (1.66 μM) caused 50% inhibition of Na,K and residual ATPase activities. After exposure of a freshwater teleost, *Channa gachua,* to sublethal levels of endosulfan (2–5 ppb) for 30 days, gill Na,K and residual ATPases were reduced by 20–50% (Dalela et al., 1978). Crabs, *Cancer magister,* exposed to 0.01 ppm methoxychlor and low salinity were less resistant than control crabs exposed to low salinity (Caldwell, 1974). Total ATPase activity of the gills was 37% lower in crabs exposed to methoxychlor than in unexposed ones.

Pacific staghorn sculpin, *Leptocottus armatus,* were exposed to petroleum refinery waste water at various concentrations (1–100%) (Boese et al., 1982). The mean gill Na,K ATPase inhibition was 35% and inhibition of residual ATPase activity was 22%. While Na,K ATPase activity was reduced during exposure to refinery waste water, no deleterious effect on the ability of sculpin to osmoregulate under laboratory conditions was noticed. The constituents of refinery waste water responsible for the inhibition of ATPases were not identified.

4.2.   Effect of Metals

In *in vitro* experiments with gill whole homogenates from rock crab, inhibition of Na,K ATPase occurred to the extent of 37% in the presence of 10 ppm Cd but not Pb (Tucker and Matte, 1980). Residual ATPase was inhibited up to 13% by both Cd and Pb (1 and 10 ppm). This is in contrast to *in vivo* experiments with lobster, *Homarus americanus,* gill ATPases. Exposure of lobsters to 6 ppb Cd resulted in 25% increase in residual ATPase activity, but Na,K ATPase activity was the same as for controls (Tucker, 1979). The concentration of Cd in the gills was 1.3–3.4 ppm (Thurberg et al., 1977) and thus not too dissimilar from the *in vitro* rock crab experiments.

In our studies with lobsters from Belledune Harbour, the concentration of Cd in gills was 10 ppm (wet weight) [equivalent to 70 ppm (dry weight) since gills contained 86% moisture; Haya et al., 1980]. However, no differences in Na,K or residual ATPase activities were found between lobsters for the two areas (Table 5). The Na,K ATPase activity of these lobsters was similar to

Table 5.   Na,K and Residual ATPase Activities of Lobster, *Homarus americanus*, Gills from Stonehaven and Belledune Harbour, N.B., Canada, and Maine, United States [a]

		Mean μmole P_i/mg protein · hr ± Standard Error	
Location	*n*	Na,K ATPase	Residual ATPase
Belledune Harbour	16	5.1 ± 0.7	14.7 ± 2.7
Stonehaven	12	4.9 ± 1.2	14.9 ± 2.1
Maine	15	3.6 ± 0.3	2.3 ± 0.1

[a]Data from Haya et al. (1980, 1983).

those from Maine. However, the residual ATPase activity was much lower in gills of lobsters from Maine. This may be because of induction of residual ATPase activity in these lobsters from New Brunswick by some pollutant or other variable such as habitat, season, temperature, or salinity.

Exposure of lobsters to sublethal concentrations of Zn in a flow-through seawater system resulted in inhibition of Na,K ATPase activity in the gills (Fig. 1). Initial control lobsters had a mean activity of 4.51 μmole P_i/mg protein · hr. By 12 hr, a *t*-test of the Na,K ATPase activity of Zn-exposed lobster gills, compared to controls, indicated that the decrease to 1.85 μmole P_i/mg protein · hr was significant ($p < 0.01$); the concentration of Zn in the gills was 650 ppm (dry weight) at this time. Na,K ATPase activity continued to decline in the Zn-exposed lobster gills until 48 hr of depuration to 0.85

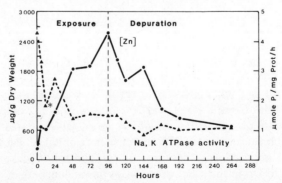

Figure 1.   Na,K ATPase activity and Zn concentration of gills during 96-hr exposure to sublethal levels of Zn and 168-hr depuration of lobster, *Homarus americanus*. Each point represents a mean of five lobsters; asterisk indicates point at which significant ($p < 0.01$) inhibition of NA,K ATPase activity first occurs when compared to controls. Mean activities of controls at 0, 96, 192 hr were 4.5 ± 0.2, 3.3 ± 0.4, and 3.4 ± 0.2 μmole P_i/mg protein · hr, respectively; mean Zn concentration in controls at 0, 96, 192 hr were 126 ± 34, 102 ± 11, and 106 ± 19 ppm, dry wt, respectively.)

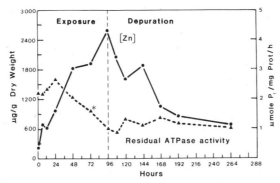

Figure 2. Residual ATPase activity and Zn concentration of gills during 96-hr exposure to sublethal levels of Zn and 168-hr depuration of lobster, *Homarus americanus*. Each point represents a mean of five lobsters; asterisk indicates point at which significant ($p < 0.1$) inhibition of residual ATPase activity first occurs compared to controls. Residual ATPase activities at 0, 96, 192 hr were 2.3 ± 0.2, 2.4 ± 0.1, and 2.6 ± 0.1 μmole P_i/mg protein · hr, respectively; mean Zn concentrations in controls at 0, 96, 192 hr were 126 ± 34, 102 ± 11, and 106 ± 19 ppm, dry wt, respectively.)

μmole P_i/mg protein · hr or 25% of the activity of the 96-hr control lobster gill Na,K ATPase. Na,K ATPase remained significantly depressed after 168 hr of depuration.

Similar results were obtained with residual ATPase activity (Fig. 2). The initial control level of gill residual ATPase activity was 2.25 μmole P_i/mg protein · hr, which was significantly decreased at 72 hr in the gills of the Zn-exposed lobsters to 1.59 μmole P_i/mg protein · hr. The concentration of Zn in the gills was 1900 ppm (dry weight) at this time. Maximum inhibition occurred at 12 hr depuration and the ATPase activity of Zn-exposed lobster gills of 0.86 μmole P_i/mg protein · hr was 35% of the activity of 96-hr control lobster gills. Residual ATPase activity did not recover after 168 hr of depuration.

Probably the reason for the inability of the ATPases to recover after 168 hr of depuration is that the gills still contained 675 ppm Zn compared with the initial control level of 126 ppm (dry weight). These data also indicate that the Zn levels in gills of lobsters from Belledune Harbour and Stonehaven (Table 3) were not high enough to cause inhibition of Na,K or residual ATPase.

The effects of Hg, Zn, and Cr on ATPases of rainbow trout, *S. gairdneri*, are variable. *In vitro* studies, in which gill microsomes of rainbow trout were incubated with Zn, resulted in significant inhibition of Na,K ATPase activity with Zn at 1 ppm and almost 100% inhibition at 50 ppm (Watson and Beamish, 1981). But, *in vivo* exposure of rainbow trout to 0.29–1.98 ppm Zn for 30 days resulted in stimulation of gill ATPase (Watson and Beamish, 1980). Exposure of rainbow trout to 2.5 ppm Cr had no effect on gill Na,K or residual ATPases up to 48 hr, by which time the Cr concentration in the gills was 2.14 ppm (wet weight) (Kuhnert and Kuhnert, 1976). However, Na,K ATPase activity of liver, kidney, and intestine was significantly inhibited. Gill perfusion or *in vivo* exposure of rainbow trout to methylmercuric or mercuric chloride inhibited Na,K ATPase (Lock et al., 1981). However, significant inhibition occurred only with Hg at lethal concentrations of Hg, while depressed levels of Na^+ and Cl^- in blood were found at sublethal concentrations of Hg. Thus, disruption of osmoregulation in these rainbow trout was attributed to permeability changes in gill epithelial cell membranes rather than to inhibition of Na,K ATPase. Treatment of winter flounder, *P. americanus,* with sublethal concentrations of methylmercury for 8 days did not affect gill Na,K ATPase activity (Schmit-Nielsen et al., 1977).

5. EVALUATION OF AEC AND ATPase ACTIVITY AS INDICATORS OF SUBLETHAL EFFECTS CAUSED BY XENOBIOTICS IN AQUATIC ANIMALS

On the basis of theoretical considerations, AEC and ATPase activity have potential as indicators of sublethal toxicity in aquatic animals. At present, the data base on the effects of toxicants on these two biochemical parameters in aquatic animals is small. For example, AEC is correlated with physiological status in microorganisms but, with multicellular aquatic organisms, the values of AEC that constitute a healthy physiological status are less well defined. There is considerable variability in the effects of xenobiotics or physiological stressors on AEC and Na,K ATPase. These effects also vary with species, organ or tissue sampled, geographical area, or habitat and concentration of the toxicant. However, AEC shows less variability than the individual adenine nucleotides. Very few dose–response relationships have been reported for xenobiotics versus AEC and ATPase activity. More information is needed (e.g., variability with season or reproductive status, relationship to effects on reproduction, changes during the life cycle, adaptation during chronic intoxication, greater number of xenobiotics to be tested) before these two biochemical parameters can be applied to routine monitoring programs.

Both AEC and ATPase may be affected by a wide variety of pollutants and natural stressors (e.g., salinity, temperature, tidal effects such as temporary anoxia). Thus, these nonspecific parameters are more applicable as a general indicator of the health of aquatic communities. Any effects on AEC or Na,K ATPase caused by natural stressors, such as sudden salinity change, should be relatively easy to identify as they generally vary within ranges of adaptability of the resident organisms. Therefore, any unexpected alteration in AEC or ATPase activity can be attributed to the effects of pollution. Identification of the pollutant would require more specific chemical and biological techniques. These biochemical parameters would be most useful as early warning indicators of unfavorable physiological conditions.

The analytical techniques involved in determination of AEC and ATPase activity require highly trained personnel. The assays can be time-consuming, but the high precision of this technique and small variability between individuals, at least for AEC (Ivanovici, 1980a,b), mean a small sample size may be adequate. Probably the most limiting factor, especially with field studies, is the need for liquid nitrogen or ice in sample preparation and for freezers capable of maintaining at least $-40°C$ for storage of the samples. These or similar problems are common in the analyses of most biochemical parameters. As technological advances occur in biochemistry, these factors may become less limiting.

At present, AEC and ATPase activity are useful toxicological tools for more basic studies, such as the determination of mechanisms of toxicant action, intricacies of energy metabolism, and osmoregulation. As more basic information is obtained, these parameters can be developed as useful sublethal indicators in screening programs for the assessment of hazard of Sxenobiotics and in the development of specific water quality criteria.

Similar to the conclusion reached by Ivanovici (1980b) for AEC, it seems unlikely that a single parameter will be able to indicate sublethal intoxication for all types of pollutants in aquatic animals. What may develop is a series of tests, similar to clinical procedures and tests with humans, but possibly more complex due to the diversity of species in the aquatic biosphere. For example, arginine or creatine phosphate measurements performed with AEC or osmolality of blood with ATPase activity may constitute part of such a series of tests for the indication of a pollution problem. However, positive identification of the pollutant can be accomplished only in conjunction with chemical analyses. Therefore, until more studies are completed on the effects of xenobiotics on biochemical parameters, AEC and ATPase activity remain categorized as potentially useful sublethal indicators of xenobiotic intoxication in aquatic animals.

6. SUMMARY

Indicators of sublethal effects caused by pollutants in aquatic animals will be helpful in predicting the acceptable level of xenobiotics for the aquatic biosphere. Two biochemical parameters which potentially can be developed as nonspecific indicators are the adenylate energy charge (AEC) and the sodium, potassium-activated adenosine triphosphatase (Na,K ATPase) activity. AEC is a measure of the metabolic energy state of cells and may be an indicator of the physiological status of multicellular organisms. Na,K ATPase is the prime mediator of ion transport across epithelial membranes in gills and is a key enzyme for whole body osmoregulation of aquatic animals. Recent studies showed that changes in AEC and Na,K ATPase occur in aquatic biota during physiological stress (e.g., salinity change, anoxia). Both parameters are altered during exposure of aquatic animals to organic and inorganic compounds. However, the data base on AEC and Na,K ATPase of aquatic fauna is small and more research, especially on the effects of xenobiotics on them, is required before they can be useful in hazard assessment of pollutants.

ACKNOWLEDGMENTS

We thank Drs. V. Zitko and D. W. McLeese for critical comments and for reviewing the manuscript, Ms. R. Garnett for editorial comments, Ms. B. Fawkes and J. Hurley for typing, and Mr. B. McMullon for preparing the figures.

REFERENCES

Askari, A., Ed. (1974). Properties and functions of $(Na^+ + K^+)$-activated adenosinetriphosphatase. *Ann. N.Y. Acad. Sci.* **242**, 1–741.

Atkinson, D. E. (1969). Regulation of enzyme function. *Annu. Rev. Microbiol.* **23**, 47–68.

Atkinson, D. E. (1977). *Cellular energy metabolism and its regulation.* Academic Press, New York, pp. 85–107.

Bakke, T. and Skjöldal, H. R. (1979). Effects of toluene on the survival, respiration, and adenylate system of a marine isopod. *Mar. Pollut. Bull.* **10**, 111–115.

Beis, I. and Newsholme, E. A. (1975). The contents of adenine nucleotides, phosphagens and some glycolytic intermediates in resting muscles from vertebrates and invertebrates. *Biochem. J.* **152**, 23–32.

Bingham, R. D., Duke, C. S., and Giesy, J. P. (1978). Changes in adenylate energy charge of *Corbicula manilensis* (Pelecypoda) foot muscle tissue due to cadmium exposure. *Assoc. Southeast Biol. Bull.* **25**, 39.

Boese, B. L., Johnson, V. G., Chapman, D. E., Ridlington, J. W., and Randall, R. (1982). Effects of petroleum refinery waste water exposure on gill ATPase and selected blood parameters in the Pacific staghorn sculpin (*Leptocottus armatus*). *Comp. Biochem. Physiol.* **71C**, 63–67.

Caldwell, R. S. (1974). Osmotic and ionic regulation in decapod crustacea exposed to methoxychlor. In: F. J. Vernberg and W. B. Vernberg, Eds., *Pollution and physiology of marine organisms.* Academic Press, New York, pp. 197–223.

Chapman, A. G. and Atkinson, D. E. (1973). Stabilization of adenylate energy charge by the adenylate deaminase reaction. *J. Biol. Chem.* **248**, 8309–8312.

Chapman, A. G., Fall, L., Atkinson, D. E. (1971). Adenylate energy charge in *Escherichia coli* during growth and starvation. *J. Bacteriol.* **108**, 1072–1086.

Dalela, R. C., Bhatnagar, M. C., Tyagi, A. K., and Verma, S. R. (1978). Adenosine triphosphatase activity in few tissues of a fresh water teleost, *Channa gachua* following *in vivo* exposure to endosulfan. *Toxicology* **11**, 361–368.

Davis, P. W. and Wedemeyer, G. A. (1971). Na^+, K^+-activated-ATPase inhibition in rainbow trout: A site for organochlorine pesticide toxicity? *Comp. Biochem. Physiol.* **40B**, 823–827.

De Filippis, L. F., Hampp, R., and Ziegler, H. (1981). The effect of sublethal concentrations of zinc, cadmium and mercury on *Euglena*. Adenylates and energy charge. *Z. Pflanzenphysiol.* **103**, 1–7.

Dickson, G. W. and Franz, R. (1980). Respiration rates, ATP turnover and adenylate energy charge in excised gills of surface and cave crayfish. *Comp. Biochem. Physiol.* **65A**, 375–379.

Dickson, G. W. and Giesy, J. P. (1981). Variation of phosphoadenylates and adenylate energy charge in crayfish (Decapoda: Astacidae) tail muscle due to habitat differences. *Comp. Biochem. Physiol.* **70A**, 421–425.

Doneen, B. A. (1981). Effects of adaption to sea water, 170% sea water and to fresh water on activities and subcellular distribution of branchial Na^+-K^+-ATPase, low- and high-affinity Ca^{++}-ATPase, and ouabain-insensitive ATPase in *Gillichthys mirabilis*. *J. Comp. Physiol.* **145**, 51–61.

Duke, C. S., Giesy, J. P., Dickson, G. W., Leversee, G. J., and Bingham, R. D. (1978). Effects of cadmium on adenylate energy charge in the crayfish, *Procambarus pubescens*. *Assoc. Southeast Biol. Bull.* **25**, 40.

Ellington, W. R. (1981). Effect of anoxia on the adenylates and the energy charge in the sea anemone, *Bunodosoma cavernata* (Bosc). *Physiol. Zool.* **54**, 415–422.

Evans, D. H. (1969). Studies on the permeability to water of selected marine, fresh water and euryhaline teleosts. *J. Exp. Biol.* **50**, 689–703.

Fiske, C. H. and Subbarow, Y. (1925). The colorimetric determination of phosphorus. *J. Biol. Chem.* **66**, 375–400.

Gäde, G. (1980). The energy metabolism of the foot muscle of the jumping cockle, *Cardium tuberculatum:* Sustained anoxia versus muscular activity. *J. Comp. Physiol.* **137**, 177–182.

Gawehn, K. (1974). Inorganic phosphate. UV-spectrophotometric method. In: H. U. Bergmeyer, Ed., *Methods of enzymatic analysis*. Academic Press, New York, pp. 2234–2238.

Ghiasuddin, S. M. and Matsumura, F. (1979). DDT inhibition of Ca-ATPase of the peripheral nerves of the American lobster. *Pestic. Biochem. Physiol.* **10**, 151–161.

Giesy, J. P. and Dickson, G. W. (1981). The effect of season and location in two species of fresh water clams. *Oecologia* **49**, 1–7.

Gonzalez, C. and Garcia-Sancho, J. (1981). A sensitive radioenzymatic assay for ATP. *Anal. Biochem.* **114**, 285–287.

Goswami, T. and Pande, S. V. (1981). Syringes are unsuitable for pipetting submicromolar solutions of nucleoside triphosphates because of adsorption. *Anal. Biochem.* **117**, 336–338.

Grieshaber, M. (1978). Breakdown and formation of high-energy phosphates and octopine in the adductor muscle of scallop, *Chlamys opercularis* (L.), during escape swimming and recovery. *J. Comp. Physiol.* **126**, 269–276.

Grieshaber, M. and Gäde, G. (1977). Energy supply and the formation of octopine in the adductor muscle of the scallop, *Pecten jacobaeus* (Lamarck). *Comp. Biochem. Physiol.* **58B**, 249–252.

Hartree, E. F. (1972). Determination of protein: A modification of the Lowry method that gives a linear photometric response. *Anal. Biochem.* **48**, 422–427.

Haya, K., Johnston, C. E., and Waiwood, B. A. (1980). Adenylate energy charge and ATPase activity in American lobster (*Homarus americanus*) from Belledune Harbour. In: J. F. Uthe and V. Zitko, Eds., *Cadmium pollution of Belledune Harbour, New Brunswick, Canada*. Can. Tech. Rep. Fish. Aquat. Sci. 963, pp. 85–91.

Haya, K., Waiwood, B. A., and Johnston, D. W. (1983). Adenylate energy charge and ATPase activity of lobster (*Homarus americanus*) during sublethal exposure to zinc. *Aquat. Toxicol.* **3**, 115–126.

Heinonen, J. K. and Lahti, R. J. (1981). A new and convenient colorimetric determination of inorganic orthophosphate and its application to the assay of inorganic pyrophosphatase. *Anal. Biochem.* **113**, 313–317.

Hess, B. and Brand, K. (1974). Methods for animal tissues and microorganisms. In: H. U. Bergmeyer, Ed., *Methods of enzymatic analysis*. Academic Press, New York, p. 400.

Hossler, F. E. (1980). Gill arch of the mullet, *Mugil cephalus*. III. Rate of response to salinity change. *Am. J. Physiol.* **7**, R160–R164.

Ivanovici, A. M. (1979). Adenylate energy charge: potential value as a tool for rapid determination of toxicity effects. In: P. T. S. Wong, P. V. Hodson, A. J. Niimi, V. W. Cairns, and U. Borgmann, Eds., *Proc. Fifth Annu. Aquatic Toxicity Workshop, Hamilton, Ontario.* Fish. Mar. Serv. Tech. Rep. 862, pp. 241–255.

Ivanovici, A. M. (1980a). Adenylate energy charge: an evaluation of applicability to assessment of pollution effects and directions for future research. *Rapp. P.-V. Réun. Cons. Int. Explor. Mer* **179**, 23–28.

Ivanovici, A. M. (1980b). Application of adenylate energy charge to problems of environmental impact assessment in aquatic organisms. *Helgol. Meeresunters.* **33**, 556–565.

Ivanovici, A. M. (1980c). The adenylate energy charge in the estuarine mollusc, *Pyrazus ebeninus*. Laboratory studies of responses to salinity and temperature. *Comp. Biochem. Physiol.* **66A**, 43–55.

Ivanovici, A. M. (1981). *A method for extraction and analysis of adenine nucleotides for determination of adenylate energy charge in molluscan tissue*. Rep. Div. Fish. Oceanogr. CSIRO, Cronulla, 118, 27 pp.

Janicki, R. H. and Kinter, W. B. (1971). DDT inhibits Na^+, K^+, Mg^{2+}-ATPase in the intestinal mucosae and gills of marine teleosts. *Nature* **233**, 148–149.

Jaworek, D., Gruber, W., and Bergmeyer, H. U. (1974). Adenosine-5'-diphosphate and adenosine-5'-monophosphate. In: H. U. Bergmeyer, Ed., *Methods of enzymatic analysis*. Academic Press, New York, pp. 2127–2131.

Jorgensen, J. B. and Mustafa, T. (1980). The effect of hypoxia on carbohydrate metabolism in flounder (*Platichthys flesus* L.). II. High energy phosphate compounds and the role of glycolytic and gluconeogenetic enzymes. *Comp. Biochem. Physiol.* **67B**, 249–256.

Jowett, P. E., Rhead, M. M., and Bayne, B. L. (1981). *In vivo* changes in the activity of gill ATPases and haemolymph ions of *Carcinus maenas* exposed to *p,p'*-DDT and reduced salinities. *Comp. Biochem. Physiol.* **69C**, 399–402.

Karl, D. M. (1980). Cellular nucleotide measurements and applications in microbial ecology. *Microbiol. Rev.* **44**, 739–796.

Kuhnert, P. M. and Kuhnert, B. R. (1976). The effect of *in vivo* chromium exposure on Na/K- and Mg-ATPase activity in several tissues of rainbow trout (*Salmo gairdneri*). *Bull. Environ. Contam. Toxicol.* **15**, 383–390.

Lamprecht, W. and Trautschold, I. (1974). Adenosine-5'-triphosphate, determination with hexokinase and glucose-6-phosphate dehydrogenase. In: H. U. Bergmeyer, Ed., *Methods of enzymatic analysis*. Academic Press, New York, pp. 2101–2110.

Leadem, T. P., Campbell, R. D., and Johnson, D. W. (1974). Osmoregulatory responses to DDT and varying salinities in *Salmo gairdneri*. I. Gill Na-K-ATPase. *Comp. Biochem. Physiol.* **49A**, 197–205.

Leray, C. (1979). Patterns of purine nucleotides in fish erythrocytes. *Comp. Biochem. Physiol.* **64B**, 77–82.

Leray, C., Colin, D. A., and Florentz, A. (1981). Time course of osmotic adaption and gill energetics of rainbow trout (*Salmo gairdneri* R.) following abrupt changes in external salinity. *J. Comp. Physiol.* **144**, 175–181.

Lock, R. A. C., Cruijsen, P. M. J. M., and van Overbeeke, A. P. (1981). Effects of mercuric chloride and methylmercuric chloride on the osmoregulatory function of the gills in the rainbow trout, *Salmo gairdneri* Richardson. *Comp. Biochem. Physiol.* **68C**, 151–159.

Loring, D. H., Bewers, J. M., Seibert, C., and Kranck, K. (1980). A preliminary survey of circulation and heavy metal contamination in Belledune Harbour and adjacent areas. In: J. F. Uthe and V. Zitko, Eds., *Cadmium pollution of Belledune Harbour, New Brunswick, Canada*. Can. Tech. Rep. Fish. Aquat. Sci. 963, pp. 35–47.

Lust, W. D., Feussner, G. K., Barbehenn, E. K., and Passonneau, J. V. (1981). The enzymatic measurement of adenine nucleotides and P-creatine in picomole amounts. *Anal. Biochem.* **110**, 258–266.

MacFarlane, R. B. (1981). Alterations in adenine nucleotide metabolism in the gulf killifish (*Fundulus grandis*) induced by low pH water. *Comp. Biochem. Physiol.* **68B**, 193–202.

Mangum, D. C. (1980). Sea aneome neuromuscular responses in anaerobic conditions. *Science* **208**, 1177–1178.

Motais, R., Isaia, J., Rankin, J. C., and Maetz, J. (1969). Adaptive changes of the water permeability of the teleostean gill epithelium in relation to external salinity. *J. Exp. Biol.* **51**, 529–546.

Neufeld, G. J. and Pritchard, J. B. (1979a). An assessment of DDT toxicity on osmoregulation and gill Na,K-ATPase activity in the blue crab. In: L. L. Marking and R. A. Kimerle, Eds., *Aquatic toxicology*, ASTM STP 667. American Society for Testing and Materials, Philadelphia, Pennsylvania, pp. 23–34.

Neufeld, G. J. and Pritchard, J. B. (1979b). Osmoregulation and gill Na,K-ATPase in the rock crab, *Cancer irroratus:* response to DDT. *Comp. Biochem. Physiol.* **62C**, 165–172.

Neufeld, G. J., Holliday, C. W., and Pritchard, J. B. (1980). Salinity adaption of gill Na,K-ATPase in the blue crab, *Callinectes sapidus*. *J. Exp. Zool.* **211**, 215–224.

Nichols, W. W., Curtis, G. D. W., and Johnston, H. H. (1981). Choice of buffer anion for the assay of adenosine-5'-triphosphate using firefly luciferase. *Anal. Biochem.* **114**, 396–397.

Parry, G. (1966). Osmotic adaption in fishes. *Biol. Rev.* **41**, 392–444.

Passonneau, J. V. and Schulz, D. W. (1974). Inorganic phosphate. Fluorometric method. In: H. U. Bergmeyer, Ed., *Methods of enzymatic analysis*. Academic Press, New York, pp. 2229–2234.

Peterson, G. L. A. (1978). Simplified method for analysis of inorganic phosphate in the presence of interfering substances. *Anal. Biochem.* **84**, 164–172.

Phelps, D. K., Galloway, W., Thurber, F. P., Gould, E., and Dawson, M. A. (1981). Comparison of several physiological monitoring techniques as applied to blue mussel, *Mytilus edulis*, along a gradient of pollutant stress in Narragansett Bay, Rhode Island. In: F. J. Vernberg, A. Calabrese, F. P. Thurberg, and W. B. Vernberg, Eds., *Biological monitoring of marine pollutants*. Academic Press, New York, pp. 335–355.

Pörtner, H., Surholt, B., and Grieshaber, M. (1979). Recovery from anaerobiosis of the lungworm, *Arenicola marina* L.: Changes of metabolite concentrations in the body-wall musculature. *J. Comp. Physiol.* **133**, 227–231.

Rainer, S. F., Ivanovici, A. M., and Wadley, V. A. (1979). Effect of reduced salinity on adenylate energy charge in three estuarine molluscs. *Mar. Biol.* **54**, 91–99.

Ray, S., McLeese, D. W., and Burridge, L. E. (1981). Cadmium in tissues of lobsters captured near a lead smelter. *Mar. Pollut. Bull.* **12**, 383–386.

Riedel, B. and Christensen, G. (1979). Effect of selected water toxicants and other chemicals upon adenosine triphosphatase activity in vitro. *Bull. Environ. Contam. Toxicol.* **23**, 365–368.

Saintsing, D. G. and Towle, D. W. (1978). Na$^+$ + K$^+$-ATPase in the osmoregulating clam, *Rangia cuneata*. *J. Exp. Zool.* **206**, 435–442.

Schmidt-Nielsen, B., Sheline, J., Miller, D. S., and Deldonno, M. (1977). Effect of methylmercury upon osmoregulation, cellular volume and ion regulation in winter flounder, *Pseudopleuronectes americanus*. In: F. J. Vernberg, A. Calabrese, F. P. Thurberg, W. V. Vernberg, Eds., *Physiological responses of marine biota to pollutants*. Academic Press, New York, pp. 105–117.

Schöttler, U. (1978). The influence of anaerobiosis on the levels of adenosine nucleotides and some glycolytic metabolites in *Tubifex* sp. (Annelida, Oligochaeta). *Comp. Biochem. Physiol.* **61B**, 29–32.

Schöttler, U. (1979). On the anaerobic metabolism of three species of *Nereis* (Annelida). *Mar. Ecol. Prog. Ser.* **1**, 249–254.

Schöttler, U. and Wienhausen, G. (1981). The importance of the phosphoenolpyruvate carboxykinase in the anaerobic metabolism of two marine polychaetes. *In vivo* investigations of *Nereis virens* and *Arenicola marina*. *Comp. Biochem. Physiol.* **68B**, 41–48.

Schuurmans Stekhoven, F. M. A. H. and Bonting, S. L. (1981). Sodium-potassium-activated adenosine triphosphatase. In: S. L. Bonting and J. J. H. H. M. DePont, Eds., *Membrane transport*. Elsevier/North-Holland Biomedical Press, Amsterdam, pp. 159–182.

Schwartz, A., Allen, J. C., and Harigaya, S. (1969). Possible involvement of cardiac Na^+,K^+-adenosine triphosphatase in the mechanism of action of cardiac glycosides. *J. Pharmacol. Exp. Ther.* **168**, 31–41.

Shapiro, A. Z. (1981). Content of high-energy compounds in mussel tissues under standard and hypoxic conditions. *Biol. Morya* (Vladivostok) **2**, 69–75. Through *Chem. Abstr.* (1981) **95**, 58580s.

Sharpe, M. J. and Lee, D. L. (1981). The effect of anaerobiosis on adenosine nucleotide levels in *Nematospiroides dubius* and *Trichostrongylus colubriformis* in vitro. *Parasitology* **83**, 425–433.

Skjöldal, H. R. and Bakke, T. (1978). Relationship between ATP and energy charge during lethal metabolic stress of the marine isopod *Cirolana borealis*. *J. Biol. Chem.* **253**, 3355–3356.

Storey, K. B. and Storey, M. M. (1978). Energy metabolism in the mantle muscle of the squid, *Loligo pealeii*. *J. Comp. Physiol.* **123**, 169–175.

Strehler, B. L. (1974). Adenosine-5'-triphosphate and creatine phosphate determination with luciferase. In: H. U. Bergmeyer, Ed., *Methods of enzymatic analysis*. Academic Press, New York, pp. 2112–2121.

Swedes, J. S., Sedo, R. J., and Atkinson, D. E. (1975). Relation of growth and protein synthesis to the adenylate energy charge in an adenine-requiring mutant of *Escherichia coli*. *J. Biol. Chem.* **250**, 6930–6938.

Taylor, M. W., Hershey, H. V., Levine, P. A., Coy, K., and Olivelle, S. (1981). Improved method of resolving nucleotides by reverse-phase high-performance liquid chromatography. *J. Chromatogr.* **219**, 133–139.

Thurberg, F. P., Calabrese, A., Gould, E., Greig, R. A., Dawson, M. A. and Tucker, R. K. (1977). Response of the lobster, *Homarus americanus*, to sublethal levels of cadmium and mercury. In: F. J. Vernberg, A. Calabrese, F. P. Thurberg, and W. B. Vernberg, Eds., *Physiological responses of marine biota to pollutants*. Academic Press, New York, pp. 185–197.

Towle, D. W. (1981). Role of $Na^+ + K^+$-ATPase in ionic regulation by marine and estuarine animals. *Mar. Biol. Lett.* **2**, 107–122.

Trachtenberg, M. C., Packey, D. J., and Sweeney, T. (1981). *In vivo* functioning of the Na^+,K^+-activated ATPase. In: B. L. Horecker and E. R. Stadtman, Eds., *Current topics in cellular regulation*, Vol. 19. Academic Press, New York, pp. 159–217.

Tucker, R. K. (1979). Effects of *in vivo* cadmium exposure on ATPases in gill of the lobster, *Homarus americanus*. *Bull. Environm. Contam. Toxicol.* **23**, 33–35.

Tucker, R. K. and Matte, A. (1980). *In vitro* effects of cadmium and lead on ATPases in gill of the rock crab, *Cancer irroratus*. *Bull. Environm. Contam. Toxicol.* **24**, 847–852.

Uthe, J. F. and Zitko, V., Eds. (1980). *Cadmium pollution of Belledune Harbour, New Brunswick, Canada*. Can. Tech. Rep. Fish. Aquat. Sci. 963, v + 107 p.

Van den Thillart, G., Kesbeke, F., and Van Waarde, A. (1976). Influence of anoxia on the energy metabolism of goldfish *Carassium auratus* (L.). *Comp. Biochem. Physiol.* **55A**, 329–336.

Van den Thillart, G., Kesbeke, F., and Van Waarde, A. (1980). Anaerobic energy-metabolism of goldfish, *Carassius auratus* (L.). Influence of hypoxia and anoxia on phosphorylated compounds and glycogen. *J. Comp. Biochem.* **136**, 45–52.

Verma, S. R., Gupta, A. K., Bansal, S. K., and Dalela, R. C. (1978). *In vitro* disruption of ATP dependent active transport following treatment with aldrin and its epoxy analog dieldrin in a fresh water teleost, *Labeo rohita*. *Toxicology* **11**, 193–201.

Waldichuk, M. (1979). Review of the problems. Discussion meeting on the assessment of sublethal effects of pollutants in the sea. *Phil Trans. Roy. Soc. London Ser. B.* **286**, 399–424.

Walesby, N. J. and Johnston, I. A. (1980). Temperature acclimation in brook trout muscle: adenine nucleotide concentrations, phosphorylation state and adenylate energy charge. *J. Comp. Physiol.* **139**, 127–133.

Watson, T. A. and Beamish, F. W. H. (1980). Effects of zinc on branchial ATPase activity *in vivo* in rainbow trout, *Salmo gairdneri*. *Comp. Biochem. Physiol.* **66C**, 77–82.

Watson, T. A. and Beamish, F. W. H. (1981). The effects of zinc on branchial adenosine triphosphatase enzymes *in vitro* from rainbow trout, *Salmo gairdneri*. *Comp. Biochem. Physiol.* **68C**, 167–173.

Webster, J. J., Chang, J. C., Manley, E. R., Spivey, H. O., and Leach, F. R. (1980). Buffer effects on ATP analysis by firefly luciferase. *Anal. Biochem.* **106**, 7–11.

Wiebe, W. J. and Bancroft, K. (1975). Use of adenylate energy charge ratio to measure growth state of natural microbial communities. *Proc. Nat. Acad. Sci. USA* **72**, 2112–2115.

Wijsman, T. C. M. (1976). Adenosine triphosphates and energy charge in different tissues of *Mytilus edulis* L. under aerobic and anaerobic conditions. *J. Comp. Physiol.* **107**, 129–140.

Yates, F. E., Ed. (1980). Biology of the chloride cell: Jean Maetz memorial symposium. *Am. J. Physiol.* **7**, R139–R276.

Zaugg, W. S. (1982). A simplified preparation for adenosine triphosphatase determination in gill tissue. *Can. J. Fish. Aquat. Sci.* **39**, 215–217.

Zs-Nagy, I. and Ermini, M. (1972). ATP production in the tissues of the bivalve *Mytilus galloprovincialis* (Plecypoda) under normal and anoxic conditions. *Comp. Biochem. Physiol.* **43B**, 593–600.

11

FISH CELL CYTOGENETICS: A MEASURE OF THE GENOTOXIC EFFECTS OF ENVIRONMENTAL POLLUTANTS

Marsha L. Landolt

School of Fisheries
University of Washington
Seattle, Washington

Richard M. Kocan

School of Fisheries and Department of Pathology
University of Washington
Seattle, Washington

1. INTRODUCTION

1.1. Use of Cytogenetics for Toxicological Studies

The field of genetic toxicology is the branch of toxicology which identifies and analyzes the action of agents whose toxicity is directed toward the hereditary components of living organisms. Although it is true that many substances with broad spectrum toxicity can damage genetic material in a nonspecific manner, this discipline focuses only on those agents which are highly specific in their attack on nucleic acids and which are capable of producing deleterious effects at sublethal levels (Brusick, 1980).

Chemical and physical agents which can produce genetic alterations at subtoxic concentrations and which can result in altered hereditary characteristics are referred to as being genotoxic. Genotoxic agents generally possess specialized chemical or physical properties which facilitate their interaction with nucleic acids. Because of the universality of the DNA molecule, agents which are genotoxic for one group of living organisms typically are genotoxic for others.

Although genetic toxicological studies date to the 1920s, the field has only come into its full development in the past 10 or 12 years. Beginning with the founding of the Environmental Mutagen Society in 1969, the field has experienced tremendous growth. One reason for that growth has been the development of short-term test systems which incorporate the use of host-mediated or *in vitro* microsome activation systems. These activating agents free investigators from the need to work with *in vivo* systems and allow them to circumvent many of the limitations that are inherent in other genetic assays.

The short-term tests that have been developed utilize a wide variety of species ranging from nonvascular (e.g., *Neurospora*) and vascular (e.g., *Tradescantia*) plants to bacteria (e.g., *Salmonella*), insects (e.g., *Drosophila*), fish (e.g., *Umbra*), and mammals (e.g., Chinese hamster cells). The tests measure a diverse array of genotoxic effects which, depending upon the method, may indicate gene mutation, chromosome damage, primary DNA damage, or oncogenesis (Brusick, 1980).

A rapid proliferation of short-term test systems has resulted in a surfeit of methods which must be sorted through if one is charged with responsibility for selecting a means by which to evaluate the potential hazard posed by a pure chemical or a complex mixture. Two major philosophies concerning method selection have arisen and both incorporate recognition of the fact that a single test system is seldom sufficient and that several assays must be used in order to ensure adequate sensitivity and accurate interpretation. The first philosophy consists of a hierarchical or tier approach in which one initially uses rapid, inexpensive tests to screen a large number of samples and then gradually progresses to longer-term, more costly tests as samples are eliminated from consideration based on the results of the early tests. The second philosophy consists of a battery approach in which tests representing several levels of evaluation are conducted simultaneously rather than in a multiphase system. The tier approach is cost effective; however, it is time consuming and prone to error if false negatives or false positives occur during the early phases. For these reasons the battery approach is more commonly used.

A battery of short-term tests should consist of several screening tests and several risk assessment tests. Screening tests, frequently conducted *in vitro,* measure the ability of a substance to produce genotoxic effects. Risk assessment assays generally must be conducted *in vivo* and must demonstrate the genotoxic potential of the test substance for a given biological species.

Each test that is selected for inclusion in a battery should satisfy several criteria. The test should specifically identify genotoxic agents rather than agents with nonspecific toxicity. The test should contain or incorporate a system for metabolically bioactivating test substances. Finally the test should be sufficiently validated to minimize the possibility of obtaining false results and it should be suitable for performance by investigators in a variety of laboratories.

1.2. Limitations of Short-Term Tests

Short-term cytogenetic assays have vastly expanded our knowledge of genotoxic agents; however, certain limitations are inherent in these tests and must be understood if one is to attempt extrapolation of the data obtained from them to a human or animal population at risk.

Most short-term tests, especially *in vivo* procedures, are conducted using a limited number of organisms and a high toxicant exposure level. To accurately extend the results of such studies to a large population that is exposed to low levels of a given compound is extremely difficult and relies heavily on selection of a proper statistical model. A second limitation of these tests arises from the fact that pharmacodynamic differences exist among species, even between very closely related ones. These differences can modify the effect which a substance has on the DNA molecule and can modify the animal's ability to repair DNA damage. Similarly, physiological differences among species complicate risk assessment. Finally, the actual basis of some of the tests is poorly understood. By way of example, the biological consequence of sister chromatid exchange is not known.

In spite of these limitations the tests are useful tools which have gained widespread acceptance both by researchers and by regulatory agencies.

1.3. Use of Cytogenetic Assays in Aquatic Toxicology

Short-term cytogenetic tests have been extensively used by mammalian toxicologists, but relatively few aquatic toxicologists have incorporated their use. A few investigators have employed these tests in their original form (e.g., Ames *Salmonella* assay using rat liver microsomes) to screen water or sediment contaminants, but it is only in very recent years that they have begun to incorporate aquatic species into existing test systems or into new test systems.

Even though DNA is chemically a relatively universal molecule, metabolic and physiological differences among species make it critical that tests based on tissues or cells derived from the species at risk be incorporated into any battery of tests. The development of aquatic animal-derived tests opens the door for more extensive use of short-term cytogenetic assays in the complex field of aquatic toxicology.

2. CYTOGENETIC TEST SYSTEMS

2.1. Introduction

The cytogenetic test systems which have been developed by toxicologists are classified into several broad categories depending upon the type of damage which is measured. Principal among these are tests which detect primary DNA damage, tests designed to detect chromosomal microlesions and tests which detect chromosomal macrolesions (Brusick, 1980). These three categories of cytogenetic assays are described in the succeeding sections and examples of specific tests which fall into each category and which are in use by aquatic toxicologists are given.

2.2. Primary DNA Damage

Cytogenetic assays of primary DNA damage represent a highly diverse group of tests which includes measures of DNA repair processes, mitotic recombination, mitotic gene conversion, unscheduled DNA synthesis, sister chromatid exchange, and spermhead abnormalities. Because of the critical role played by repair processes following low-dose exposure to contaminants, many toxicologists feel that some of these assays are particularly relevant for accurate interpretation of risk assessment.

2.2.1. Sister Chromatid Exchange

The sister chromatid exchange (SCE) assay combines the incorporation of a thymidine analog into cellular DNA with the use of a specialized staining procedure to permit visualization of exchanges of genetic material between the two sister chromatids of a given chromosome. To perform the test, one exposes dividing cells (*in vivo* or *in vitro*) to the thymidine analog 5-bromodeoxyuridine (BrdU) for at least one round of DNA replication, and then allows the cells to undergo a second round of DNA replication. During the second replication the presence of BrdU is optional. During replication in the first cell cycle, BrdU is incorporated into the newly synthesized strands of DNA in the place of normally incorporated thymidine so that each chromatid contains one BrdU-substituted DNA strand. Substituted chromosomes stain much more lightly than unsubstituted chromosomes because the alteration of the DNA molecular structure following substitution with BrdU reduces its staining affinity (Goto et al., 1975). If BrdU is removed during the second cell cycle, new thymidine-containing DNA strands are synthesized resulting in only one BrdU-substituted strand among the four strands. The substituted chromatid will stain lightly as before; however, the unsubstituted chromatid will stain darkly allowing differentiation between the two chromatids (sister chromatid differentiation, SCD). Exchanges between chromatids (sometimes called crossovers) can be detected by the presence of a piece of darkly stained chromatid attached to a lightly stained chromatid (Fig. 1).

Latt (1974) was the first to apply this new technique to study the effects of mutagens on chromosomes. Using mitomycin *C*, an agent which is known to cross-link complementary DNA strands, he demonstrated the sensitivity of this technique by showing that significant increases in the number of SCE could be detected when as little as 0.003 µg mitomycin *C*/ml culture medium was applied to cells, while concentrations of 0.01–0.1 µg/ml were required to produce large numbers of gross chromosomal breaks.

The chromosomal damage leading to the production of SCEs has been correlated with mutations. Carrano et al. (1978) found a linear relationship between induced SCEs and mutations occurring at a particular locus when Chinese hamster ovary cells were treated with alkylating agents (ethyl methanesulphonate and *N*-ethyl-*N*-nitroso-urea) and a cross-linking agent (mitomycin *C*). They also determined this relation to be dose-responsive; that is, a linear increase in both SCE rate and mutation rate was observed.

The technique of sister chromatid exchange can be a valuable tool for screening organisms for exposure to environmental pollutants. It can reveal

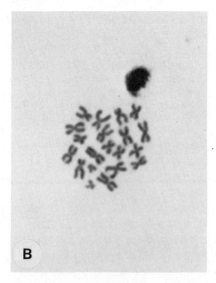

Figure 1. A comparison of the relative sizes of Chinese hamster (*A*) and Pacific sanddab (*Citharichthys sordidus*) (*B*) chromosomes. Resolution of SCEs is dependent upon the ability of the investigator to visualize differences between adjacent chromatids. (Photographs courtesy of H.R. Zakour, School of Fisheries, University of Washington.)

damage caused by relatively recent exposure to chemical mutagens; it is dose-responsive; and it is sensitive to very low concentrations of a substance, at which no gross chromosomal aberrations are detected. An important application of this technique has been to the study of the effects of carcinogens on human chromosomes. Rudiger et al. (1976) determined a doubling of the SCE rate in cultured human lymphocytes after 70 hr incubation in benzo(*a*)pyrene. Significant increases in SCEs were observed by Latt (1974) after exposure of cultured human lymphocytes to 3 μg/ml of mitomycin *C*, while few gross chromosomal aberrations were seen in cells that had as many as 100 SCEs. SCE has also been used to screen humans for exposure to carcinogenic chemicals (Murthy, 1979). For example, lymphocytes cultured from workers exposed to industrial chemicals show increased SCE rates as do those cultured from other members of their families (Funes-Cravioto et al., 1977). Patients undergoing treatment with cytostatic drugs such as adriamycin also exhibit increases in the SCE rates of their lymphocytes and marked decreases in the rate when taken off the drug (Perry and Evans, 1975; Musilova et al., 1979).

The majority of aquatic toxicologists utilizing the SCE assay perform the test *in vivo*. In a typical protocol fish are injected intraperitoneally with 5-bromodeoxyuridine and held for 5–6 days. Six hours prior to sacrifice the fish are injected with a spindle poison (colchicine or colcemid) to arrest actively dividing cells in metaphase. After sacrifice, tissues which normally have high mitotic activity (e.g., anterior kidney, gill, intestine) are excised, placed in a hypotonic solution (e.g., 0.07m KCl) to swell the cells and then fixed in a mixture of acetic acid and methanol 1:3. Dissociated cells are placed on glass slides, stained with Giemsa's solution and the cells are then examined microscopically for the presence of metaphases which display sister chromatid differentiation and sister chromatid exchange (Kligerman and Bloom, 1976, 1977; Stromberg et al., 1981). Most aquatic SCE studies have, to date, been conducted *in vivo*; however, Maddock and Kelly (1980) and Zakour et al. (1982) have developed *in vitro* procedures which utilize peripheral blood leucocytes and which allow for repeated sampling of a single individual over time. In addition, Barker and Rackham (1979) have used cultured fish cells for *in vitro* SCE studies.

Tests conducted utilizing central (*Umbra limi*) and eastern (*Umbra pygmaea*) mudminnows, English sole (*Parophrys vetulus*), *Ameca splendens,* oyster toadfish (*Opsanus tau*), and a freshwater aquarium fish (*Notobranchius rachowi*) have shown fish chromosomes to be very sensitive to induction of SCE following exposure to chemical agents. Kligerman and Bloom, (1976) were the first to demonstrate SCE in fish. Using the central mudminnow as a model species techniques were developed (Kligerman and Bloom 1976, 1978) and the sensitivity of the system was demonstrated by showing an increase in the frequency of SCE following exposure to methyl methanesulfonate (MMS), cyclophosphamide, or neutral red (Kligerman and Bloom, 1978; Kligerman, 1979, 1982). Stromberg et al. (1981) extended the use of the SCE test to cold-water marine fish and demonstrated a significant increase in the SCE rate in English sole which had been exposed to benzo(*a*)pyrene (BaP). In addition, they were able to demonstrate a statistical elevation in SCE rates in fish collected from the Duwamish River, a contaminated waterway leading into Puget Sound, Washington, over those found in fish collected in a pristine site. Prein et al. (1978), Alink et al. (1980), and Hooftman and Vink (1981), working with the eastern mudminnow, were able to increase by 2–3 times the frequency of SCE by exposing the fish to water from the Rhine River, Netherlands. Hooftman and Vink (1981) obtained similar results when they exposed eastern mudminnows to BaP and ethyl methanesulfonate (EMS), as did Hooftman (1981) when he exposed *Notobranchius rachowi* to the same two compounds. Both EMS and MMS have been used *in vitro* to induce SCEs in leucocytes (Maddock and Kelly, 1980) and cultured fibroblasts (Barker and Rackham, 1979) of fish, as have mitomycin *C* and *N*-methyl-*N'*-nitro-*N*-nitrosoguanidine (MNNG) in cultured fibroblasts (Barker and Rackham, 1979). Bromoform, however, did not induce *in vitro* SCE formation in oyster toadfish leucocytes (Maddock and Kelly, 1980).

2.2.2.   Unscheduled DNA Synthesis (Repair)

Carcinogenic agents have been shown to cause an elevation in the rate of induction of non-semiconservative DNA synthesis. This unscheduled DNA synthesis (UDS) occurs independently of normal replicative synthesis and can be monitored by the use of radioactive thymidine incorporation into nonreplicating cells. The procedure is usually carried out *in vitro* on cultured cells which have been exposed to a test agent, followed by inhibition of normal replicative DNA synthesis in the presence of ^{3}HTdR. Replicative synthesis can be blocked by deprivation of some essential amino acid such as arginine or by addition of a chemical inhibitor such as hydroxyurea. The unscheduled incorporation of ^{3}HTdR can then be measured by radioautography or in a scintillation counter.

The majority of research utilizing this technique has employed cultured human or rodent fibroblasts. However, since replicative and non-replicative DNA synthesis are essentially identical in all species, the technique can be adapted to any system the investigator chooses to employ.

At this time only a limited amount of UDS research has been done using fish cells *in vitro*. Mano et al. (1980) established a goldfish-fin cell line (CAF-MM1) which they used to study the effects of ultraviolet irradiation. This same cell line was later used by Mitani et al. (1982) and Mitani and Egami (1982) to study the resistance of the cells to gamma irradiation and their ability to repair DNA damaged by the radiation. Their findings showed that cultured goldfish cells were much less sensitive to the effects of gamma irradiation than were mouse L cells, a phenomenon that parallels the relatively high resistance to whole body radiation generally observed in fish. They were also able to show that the level of initial DNA strand breakage was the same in CAF-MM1 and mouse L cells immediately after irradiation, but that the amount of residual DNA strand breaks present after 7 hr incubation was higher in the fish cells than in the mouse cells. They concluded that certain basic similarities exist between the UDS process in fish and mammals and that the cellular and whole animal resistance of fish to radiation is not related to a more efficient DNA repair process.

The use of UDS in aquatic animal toxicology is in its infancy. Further development of this technique should make it an exciting system for study of pollution in marine and freshwater ecosystems.

2.3. Chromosomal Microlesions

Chromosomal microlesions result when DNA damage occurs at the level of the nucleotide. Microlesions consist primarily of qualitative changes in the nucleotide composition of a codon (base-pair substitution) or of additions/deletions of one or several nucleotide pairs from the nucleotide complement of a gene (frame shift). These two types of changes are induced by different classes of chemical mutagens and both can have profound consequences.

2.3.1. Ames Test

Although the Ames test is a bacterial mutagen system, it has been success-fully used with some components derived from fishes. The basic test system consists of various strains of *Salmonella typhimurium* which have been genetically engineered to be highly sensitive and responsive to a wide vari-ety of mutagens/carcinogens (Ames et al., 1973). Since some chemicals are inert and must be bioactivated before they exhibit any mutagenic capability, a rat liver microsome mixture has been added to biotransform these com-pounds from promutagens to mutagens.

In an attempt to capitalize on an already proven system, Kurelec et al. (1979) substituted carp liver microsomes into the Ames test system. By first treating carp with hexane extracts of seawater (HESW) to induce the mixed-function oxygenase enzyme system, then using the livers as a source of microsomes, they were able to show that the microsomes of some fish are suitable as a substitute for mammalian microsome systems in the Ames test. Benzo(*a*)pyrene, aflatoxin, and HESW were all positive in the Ames test following bioactivation by fish liver microsomes.

This early attempt at using fish-derived substitutes for mammalian com-ponents in mutagen test systems shows that aquatic ecosystems can be examined by using species, or components derived from species, which are relevant to the aquatic environment being tested. The great diversity in metabolic activities observed among the numerous fish species studied pre-cludes any generalized use of a "standard" fish enzyme system, but does offer a wide choice of systems for use in the complex field of aquatic toxicology.

2.3.2. Fish Cell Mutations

Eukaryotic cells have been used for *in vitro* mutagenicity studies for over 10 years. The vast majority of this work has been done with rodent (Arlett, 1977) and human cells (Jacobs and DeMars, 1977). The basic principal of *in vitro* mutagenesis experiments is to expose normal diploid cells to a muta-gen, allow the surviving cells to replicate through one or more cell cycles, and then expose the cultures to a selective agent which measures some predetermined mutational event. The list of selective agents that have been employed is extensive, but the two most popular agents have been ouabain and 8-azaguanine (Arlett et al., 1975). Ouabain is a Na,K ATPase inhibitor which is used to select cells which are insensitive to its effect through a mutation in that particular enzyme system. In normal cells 8-azaguanine is converted into a toxic ribonucleotide by hypoxanthine-guanine-phos-phoribosyltransferase (HGPRT). Since loss of the enzyme under normal culture conditions has no adverse effect on cells, mutants which have lost their HGPRT system grow out as colonies in the presence of 8-azaguanine.

Because cell culture has rarely been employed in aquatic toxicology it is not surprising that mutagenesis experiments have not become popular in studies of aquatic contaminants. Some of the early attempts to use cultured fish cells showed that they did respond similarly to mammalian cells, but that there was much greater diversity in the type of response due to the more pronounced differences in biochemical and physiological makeup of different species of fish. Bourne and Jones (1973) looked at the response of trout (RTG-2) and fathead minnow (FHM) cells following exposure to 7,12-dimethylbenz(a)anthracene (DMBA) in vitro. Their basic conclusion was that trout cells (RTG-2) were more sensitive to the mutagen/carcinogen than were the FHM cells. In light of the findings of Diamond and Clark (1970), this difference is not surprising. In their study, trout cells were found to metabolize BaP to its water soluble phenolic form much more efficiently than did cells derived from bluegill sunfish (BF-2). The effect of this high rate of hydroxylation of BaP was greater toxicity to the RTG-2 cells. A similar difference in metabolic capacity was found for three fish cell lines which had been exposed to eight organic mutagens/carcinogens (Kocan et al., 1979). In a later study by Kocan et al. (1981) bluegill sunfish cells (BF-2) were used for in vitro mutagenesis studies because of their ability to produce clones under dilute plating conditions. In this study the direct acting alkylating agent MNNG and the polycyclic aromatic hydrocarbon, BaP, were used as mutagens. Ouabain was chosen as the selective agent because the cells were resistant to the toxic effect of 8-azaguanine, presumably due to a lack of the HGPRT enzyme system. The spontaneous (background) mutation rate to ouabain resistance in BF-2 cells was found to be about 1×10^{-6}. Following mutagen treatment and selection, the cells were capable of resisting 100 times higher concentrations of ouabain than the wild type (nonmutant) cells.

Considering the large number of fish cell lines available, the diversity of biochemical and physiological responses exhibited by different fish species and the ease with which fish cells can be adapted to standard genotoxicity test procedures, it seems likely that a large number of unique systems are available to aquatic toxicologists who are willing to explore the area of fish cell culture.

2.4. Chromosomal Macrolesions

Chromosomal macrolesions are visible chromosome defects that can be detected through cytologic analysis. Macrolesions typically result either in changes in chromosome number (gain or loss of chromosomes) or in changes in chromosome structure (breaks, deletions). Changes in chromosome number may arise from incomplete dissociation of one or more sets of chromosomes at metaphase and can result in aneuploidy, monosomy, trisomy, or other defects. Changes in chromosome structure vary depending upon the nature of the chromosome-breaking agent (clastogen) and the time in the cell cycle at which damage occurs. Typically if injury occurs during the G_1

portion of the cell cycle, one sees whole chromosome effects, whereas if it occurs during the G_2 portion, chromatid effects are seen. Although both types of lesions can be found, chemical mutagens most commonly produce chromatid effects.

2.4.1. Micronucleus Formation

Micronucleus formation occurs during anaphase when, because of chromosome breakage or malfunction of the spindle apparatus, a bit of chromatin lags behind the other chromosomes as they migrate away from the metaphase plate. The lagging fragment is subsequently incorporated into one of the daughter cells where it may either fuse with the principal nucleus or remain as a separate, small secondary nucleus. When the latter situation occurs, the micronucleus can be easily visualized after one or more cell cycles. Micronuclei vary in their size and shape and may be present as acentric, dicentric, or multicentric fragments (when arising from chromosome breakage) or as whole chromosomes (when arising from spindle malfunction). In addition, more than one micronucleus may be present in a given cell.

The origin and nature of micronuclei have been known to biologists for many years. Perhaps their presence was best known by hematologists who, when micronuclei occurred in human red blood cells, referred to them as Howell-Jolly bodies. However, in spite of this awareness of their existence, the use of micronucleus formation as a toxicological assay is a relatively new development (Schmid, 1976). Jenssen and Ramel (1980) correlated data obtained from the micronucleus and Ames test for 143 chemicals and found that the micronucleus test showed the same specificity (80%) and predictive value (90%) as the Ames test, but that it showed diminished sensitivity. This meant that higher concentrations of chemicals had to be used for an observed effect in the micronucleus test, and the authors explained this to be the result of differences in the promutagen-metabolizing capabilities of the two systems.

Micronucleus formation can occur in any mitotically active cell type; however, most of the studies utilizing the technique to date have been performed *in vivo* using erythroblasts. This cell preference arose because the majority of the studies which have been conducted have used mammalian species and because mammalian erythroblasts give rise to anucleate cells in which micronuclei can be readily seen. In a typical mammalian procedure, bone marrow cells are aspirated into a tube containing fetal calf serum, pelleted by centrifugation, and spread onto a glass slide. After air drying, the cells are stained with May-Gruenwald and Giemsa solutions, cover slipped, and examined microscopically for the presence of micronuclei.

Although mammalian erythrocytes are particularly well suited for this test, they are not its sole province. Hooftman and de Raat (1982) successfully applied the micronucleus test to the nucleated red blood cells of eastern mudminnows (*Umbra pygmaea*) which had been exposed continuously to waterborne concentrations of EMS for 3–6 weeks. Examination of Feulgen-stained blood smears showed that EMS damaged the nucleus of the red blood cells. After 3 weeks exposure to 0, 8, and 40 mg/liter EMS, no micronuclei were seen; however, 3 weeks exposure to 200 mg/liter resulted in an incidence of 1.6 ± 1.2‰. The incidence of micronucleus formation after six weeks exposure to 0, 8, and 40 mg/liter EMS was 0.07 ± 0.04, 0.4 ± 0.2, and 3.7 ± 1.8‰, respectively. In addition to finding well-defined micronuclei, Hooftman and de Raat also noted other nuclear abnormalities including the presence of irregular Feulgen-positive structures in the cytoplasm and the loss of normal nuclear structure. The incidence of these irregular particles was low: 0.2 ± 0.4‰ after three weeks exposure to 200 mg/liter EMS, 1.3 ± 1.4‰ after 6 weeks exposure to 40 mg/liter EMS, 0 in all other concentrations and time periods.

2.4.2. Anaphase Aberrations

The anaphase aberration test (AAT) is a relatively simple procedure which allows one to visualize the segregation of chromosomes prior to telophase. Chromosome breakage, spindle malfunction, and chromosome stickiness are among the factors that can lead to production of the attached/lagging fragments, bridges, and multipolar figures that one sees at anaphase (Fig. 2). It appears that these aberrations are a measure of the events that ultimately lead up to the formation of micronuclei; however, because micronucleus formation accounts for only a portion of the outcome of the aberrations seen at anaphase, the AAT may be a much more sensitive indicator of damage.

The anaphase aberration test is a simple procedure that can be performed either *in vitro* or *in vivo*. The only requirement for the assay is large numbers of dividing cells; this requirement results from the fact that one cannot arrest cells in anaphase and thereby accumulate numbers sufficient for study. To perform the test *in vitro,* one cultures a desired cell type on glass microscope slides or coverslips and exposes the growing cells to a test compound. The cells are then fixed, stained with Giemsa solution and examined microscopically at 200–430× magnification. The technique does not require the use of spindle poisons or mechanical squashing, nor does it require specialized equipment. To perform the test *in vivo,* one exposes rapidly dividing tissues (e.g., embryos, regenerating tissue) to a test compound, fixes the tissue, and then makes a squash preparation. The preparation is stained, typically with aceto-orcein dye, and examined at 430–1000× magnification (Fig. 3).

The anaphase aberration test has been shown to be responsive to a wide variety of organic mutagens and it has been recommended for use by the Ad Hoc Committee of the Environmental Mutagen Society and the Institute for Medical Research (1972) as an integral part of any battery of mutagenicity tests.

The earliest uses of this test by aquatic toxicologists arose through *in vivo* exposure of fish to ionizing radiation (reviewed by Kligerman, 1982). Belyaeva and Pokrovskaia (1958, 1959) reported dose-dependent increases in

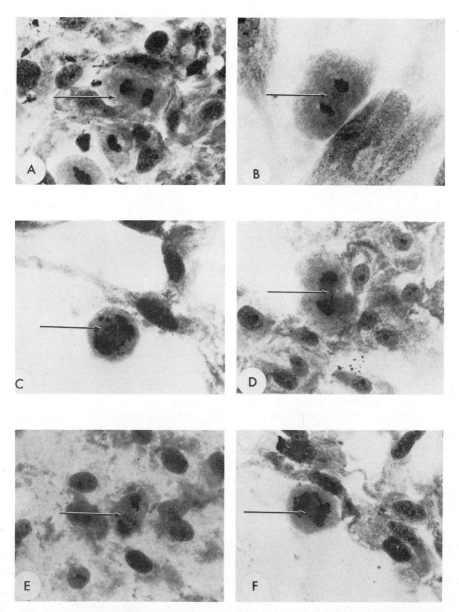

Figure 2. Normal and aberrant anaphase figures seen in rainbow trout (RTG-2) cells *in vitro* following exposure to a number of different classes of chemical mutagens/carcinogens. (*A*) Normal anaphase, (*B*) acentric chromosome fragment; (*C*) whole chromosomes, fragments and nondisjunctions; (*D*) attached fragments; (*E*) multiple acentric fragments; (*F*) bridges and fragments. (Photographs by R. M. Kocan.)

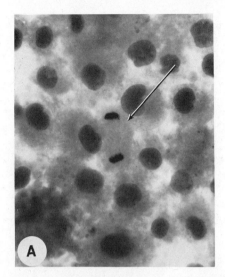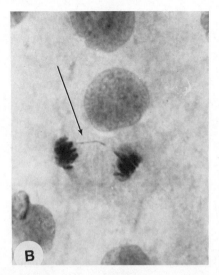

Figure 3. Normal (*A*) and abnormal (*B*) anaphase figures seen in developing trout embryos treated with *N*-methyl-*N'*-nitro-*N*-nitrosoguanidine (MNNG). (Photographs courtesy of V. M. Liguori, School of Fisheries, University of Washington.)

the number of chromosome bridges and fragments in anaphase cells of loach (*Misgurnus fossilis*) embryos which had been exposed to x-irradiation (during blastogenesis), and Pankova (1965), also working with loach, showed a similar phenomenon when ova were irradiated at the four-blastomere stage. A number of other Soviet workers confirmed the sensitivity of the anaphase and telophase stages to radiation-induced injury in fish embryos and were able to draw a correlation between the degrees of chromosome damage and ultimate embryonic damage (Vakhrameeva and Neifakh, 1959; Romashov et al., 1960; Prokof'yeva-Bel'govskaya, 1961; Bakulina et al., 1962; Romashov et al., 1963; Romashov and Belyaeva, 1964, 1966; Migalovskaya, 1973).

Only a limited number of reports have been published on the *in vivo* induction of anaphase aberrations following exposure to chemical agents. Tsoi and his co-workers (Tsoi, 1970, 1974; Tsoi et al., 1975) found that dimethyl sulfate and nitrosomethyl urea induced the formation of chromosomal bridges in *Salmo irideus* and *Coregonus peled* embryos that developed from normal eggs that had been fertilized with chemically treated sperm. Similar results were obtained in *Cyprinus carpio* when eggs were fertilized with sperm that had been exposed to dimethyl sulfate, nitrosomethyl urea or 1,4-*bis*-diazoacetyl butane. Hose et al. (1981) demonstrated maternal transfer of BaP to developing eggs of English sole (*Parophrys vetulus*) and showed (Hose et al., 1982) that embryos developing in the presence of BaP had an increase in the number of developmental anomalies and an increase (36.4% vs. 4.3%) in the number of telophase bridges, micronuclei, and lagging chromosomes over those of control fish. Longwell (1977) and Longwell and Hughes (1980) working with Atlantic mackerel (*Scomber scombrus*) eggs collected from the polluted New York Bight demonstrated a variety of cytogenetic defects including chromosome breakage, loss, and stickiness.

In addition to the *in vivo* studies just described, an *in vitro* assay has been developed which employs the use of cultured fish cells (Kocan et al., 1982). Using rainbow trout gonad (RTG-2) cells Kocan and his co-workers were able to demonstrate incidences of anaphase aberrations as high as 95% when cells were exposed for 24 or 48 hr to a variety of mutagenic agents including benzo(*a*)pyrene, 3-methylcholanthrene, 9-amino acridine, mitomycin *C* and *N*-methyl-*N*'-nitro-*N*-nitrosoguanidine. However, when the cells were exposed to two aromatic hydrocarbons (1-naphthol and anthracene) which were structurally similar to some of the test compounds, but which were nonmutagenic, anaphase aberration levels were equivalent to background ($\approx 12\%$).

3. CONCLUSION

Short-term cytogenetic tests have played a very useful role in the detection of sublethal toxic effects in mammalian systems. They have been routinely included in batteries of tests as a means of measuring genetic damage at the cellular and molecular level and have contributed a vast amount of information on the effects of environmental mutagens/carcinogens on eukaryotic organisms. Those tests which employ whole animals are useful for measuring the ultimate effect of a genotoxic agent on an intact animal. They are, however, expensive and time consuming when compared to the *in vitro* genotoxic tests. The *in vitro* tests are generally more sensitive than whole animal systems, less expensive to carry out, and of shorter duration. Their drawbacks are also obvious. They lack the numerous defense mechanisms found in intact animals and frequently they are chosen on the basis of convenience and availability rather than relevance to the ecosystem under investigation. Aside from these drawbacks, *in vitro* systems still offer the greatest flexibility for the testing and study of environmental contaminants. They can be chosen in such a fashion as to be relevant to the species of interest in a given area, and multiple types of measurements can be taken from a single test system (e.g., metabolic products, mitotic activity, cytotoxicity, and genetic damage).

What is needed most critically at this time are comparative studies between *in vitro* and *in vivo* systems using the same species to validate the findings of the *in vitro* system as well as to correlate and relate the changes which occur in each system.

ACKNOWLEDGMENTS

Portions of the research described in this chapter were supported byS grants from the National Institute of Environmental Health Sciences (5-P30-ES-02190-02), the Office of Marine Pollution Assessment, NOAA (NA80RAD00053), and the Marine Ecosystems Analysis Program, NOAA (04-78-BO1-13). We are grateful to Mr. Vincent M. Liguori and to Dr. Helen R. Zakour for their photographic assistance and to Ms. Valerie Munzlinger for secretarial assistance.

REFERENCES

Ad Hoc Committee of the Environmental Mutagen Society and the Institute for Medical Research. (1972). Chromosome methodologies in mutation testing. *Toxicol. Appl. Toxicol.* **22**, 269–275.

Alink, G. M., Frederix-Wolters, E. M. H., van der Gaag, M. A., van de Kerkhoff, J. F., and Poels, C. L. M. (1980). Induction of sister-chromatid exchanges in fish exposed to Rhine water. *Mut. Res.* **78**, 369–374.

Ames, B. N., Durston, W. E., Yamasaki, E., and Lee, F. D. (1973). Carcinogens are mutagens: a simple test system combining liver homogenates for activation and bacteria for detection. *Proc. Nat. Acad. Sci. USA* **70**, 2281–2285.

Arlett, C. F. (1977). Mutagenicity testing with V79 Chinese hamster cells. In: B. J. Kilbey, M. Legator, W. Nichols, and C. Ramel, Eds., *Handbook of mutagenicity test procedures,* Elsevier, New York, pp. 175–192.

Arlett, C. F., Turnbull, D., Harcourt, S. A., Lehmann, A. R., and Colella, C. M. (1975). A comparison of the 8-azaguanine and ouabain-resistance systems for the selection of induced mutant Chinese hamster cells. *Mut. Res.* **33**, 261–277.

Bakulina, E. D., Pokrovskaia, G. L., and Romashov, D. D. (1962). On radiosensitivity of loach (*Misgurnus fossilis* L.) spermatozoa. *Radiobiology* **2**, 135–147.

Barker, C. J. and Rackham, B. D. (1979). The induction of sister chromatid exchanges in cultured fish cells (*Ameca splendens*) by carcinogenic mutagens. *Mut. Res.* **68**, 381–387.

Belyaeva, V. N. and Pokrovskaia, G. L. (1958). Arrest of mitosis by X-rays at early developmental stages in loach spawn. *Dokl. Akad. Nauk SSSR* **119**, 149–155.

Belyaeva, V. N. and Pokrovskaia, G. L. (1959). Changes in the radiation sensitivity of loach spawn during the first embryonic mitoses. *Dokl. Akad. Nauk SSSR* **125**, 192–195.

Bourne, E. W. and Jones, R. W. (1973). Effects of 7,12-dimethylbenz(*a*)anthracene (DMBA) in fish cells in vitro. *Trans. Am. Micros. Soc.* **92**, 140–142.

Brusick, D. (1980). *Principles of genetic toxicology.* Plenum Press, New York, 279 pp.

Carrano, A. V., Thompson, L. H., Lindl, P. A., and Minkler, J. L. (1978). Sister chromatid exchange as an indicator of mutagenesis. *Nature* **271**, 551–553.

Diamond, L. and Clark, H. F. (1970). Comparative studies on the interaction of benzo(*a*)pyrene with cells derived from poikilothermic and homeothermic vertebrates. I. Metabolism of benzo(*a*)pyrene. *J. Nat. Cancer Inst.* **45**, 1005–1011.

Funes-Cravioto, F., Kolmodin-Hedman, B., Lindsten, J., Nordenskjold, M., Zapata-Gayon, C., Lambert, B., Norberg, E., Olin, R., and Swenson, A. (1977). Chromosome aberrations and sister-chromatid exchange in workers in chemical laboratories and a rotoprinting factory and in children of women laboratory workers. *Lancet* (August 13), 322–325.

Goto, K., Akematsu, T., Shimazu, H., and Sugiyama, T. (1975). Simple differential Giemsa staining of sister chromatids after treatment with photosensitive dyes and exposure to light and the mechanism of staining. *Chromosoma* **53**, 223–230.

Hooftman, R. N. (1981). The induction of chromosome aberrations in *Notobranchius rachowi* (Pisces: Cyprinodontidae) after treatment with ethyl methanesulfonate or benzo(*a*)pyrene. *Mut. Res.* **91**, 347–352.

Hooftman, R. N. and de Raat, W. K. (1982). Induction of nuclear anomalies (micronuclei) in the peripheral blood erythrocytes of the Eastern mudminnow *Umbra pygmaea* by ethyl methanesulfonate. *Mut. Res.* **104**, 147–152.

Hooftman, R. N. and Vink, G. J. (1981). Cytogenetic effects on the Eastern mudminnow, *Umbra pygmaea*, exposed to ethyl methanesulfonate, benzo(*a*)pyrene, and river water. *Ecotoxicol. Environ. Safety* **5**, 261–269.

Hose, J. E., Hannah, J. B., Landolt, M. L., Miller, B. S., Felton, S. P., and Iwaoka, W. T. (1981). Uptake of benzo(*a*)pyrene by gonadal tissue of flatfish (Family Pleuronectidae) and its effects on subsequent egg development. *J. Toxicol. Environ. Health* **7**, 991–1000.

Hose, J. E., Hannah, J. B., DiJulio, D., Landolt, M. L., Miller, B. S., Iwaoka, W. T., and Felton, S. P. (1982). Effects of benzo(a)pyrene on early development of flatfish. *Arch. Environ. Contam. Toxicol.* **11**, 167–171.

Jacobs, L. and DeMars, R. (1977). Chemical mutagenesis with human diploid fibroblasts. In: B. J. Kilbey, M. Legator, W. Nichols, and C. Ramel, Eds., *Handbook of mutagenicity test procedures,* Elsevier, New York, pp. 193–220.

Jenssen, D. and Ramel, C. (1980). The micronucleus test as part of a short-term mutagenicity test program for the prediction of carcinogenicity evaluated by 143 agents tested. *Mut. Res.* **75**, 191–202.

Kligerman, A. D. (1979). Induction of sister chromatid exchanges in the central mudminnow following *in vivo* exposure to mutagenic agents. *Mut. Res.* **64**, 205–217.

Kligerman, A. D. (1982). The use of cytogenetics to study genotoxic agents in fishes. In: T. C. Hsu, Ed., *Cytogenetic assays of environmental mutagens.* Allanheld, Osmun, Totowa, New Jersey, pp. 161–181.

Kligerman, A. D. and Bloom, S. E. (1976). Sister chromatid differentiation and exchanges in adult mudminnows (*Umbra limi*) after *in vivo* exposure to 5-bromodeoxyuridine. *Chromosoma* **56**, 101–109.

Kligerman, A. D. and Bloom, S. E. (1977). Rapid chromosome preparations from solid tissues of fishes. *J. Fish. Res. Board Can.* **34**, 266–269.

Kligerman, A. D. and Bloom, S. E. (1978). An *in vivo* aquatic system for detecting water-borne mutagens. *Can. J. Genet. Cytol.* **20**, 447.

Kocan, R. M., Landolt, M. L., and Sabo, K. M. (1979). In vitro toxicity of eight mutagens/carcinogens for three fish cell lines. *Bull. Environ. Contam. Toxicol.* **23**, 269–274.

Kocan, R. M., Landolt, M. L., Bond, J. A., and Benditt, E. P. (1981). *In vitro* effect of some mutagens/carcinogens on cultured fish cells. *Arch. Environ. Contam. Toxicol.* **10**, 663–671.

Kocan, R. M., Landolt, M. L., and Sabo, K. M. (1982). Anaphase aberrations: a measure of genotoxicity in mutagen-treated fish cells. *Environ. Mutagenesis* **4**, 181–189.

Kurelec, B., Matijasevic, Z., Rijavec, M., Alacevic, M., Britvic, S., Muller, W. E. G., and Zahn, R. K. (1979). Induction of benzo(*a*)pyrene monooxygenase in fish and the Salmonella test as a tool for detecting mutagenic/carcinogenic xenobiotics in the aquatic environment. *Bull. Environ. Contam. Toxicol.* **21**, 799–807.

Latt, S. A. (1974). Sister chromatid exchanges, indices of human chromosome damage and repair: detection by fluorescence and induction by mitomycin C. *Proc. Natl. Acad. Sci. USA* **71**, 3162–3166.

Longwell, A. C. (1977). A genetic look at fish eggs and oil. *Oceanus* **20**, 45–58.

Longwell, A. C. and Hughes, J. B. (1980). Cytologic, cytogenetic and developmental state of Atlantic mackerel eggs from sea surface waters of the New York Bight, and prospects for biological effects monitoring with ichthyoplankton. *Rapp. P.-V. Reun. Cons. Int. Explor. Mer* **179**, 275–291.

Maddock, M. B. and Kelly, J. J. (1980). A sister chromatid exchange assay for detecting genetic damage to marine fish exposed to mutagens and carcinogens. In: R. L. Jolley, W. A. Brunes, R. B. Cumming, and V. A. Jacobs, Eds., *Water chlorination: environmental impact and health.* Ann Arbor Science Publishers, Ann Arbor, Michigan, pp. 835–844.

Mano, Y., Mitani, H., Etoh, H., and Egami, N. (1980). Survival and photoreactivability of ultraviolet-irradiated cultured fish cells (CAF-MMl). *Radiat. Res.* **84**, 514–522.

Migalovskaya, V. N. (1973). Effect of X-irradiation on the gametes and embryonal cells of the Atlantic salmon. In: B. P. Sorokin, Ed., *Effect of ionizing radiation on the organism,* AEC-tr-7418, Washington, D.C., pp. 100–112.

Mitani, H. and Egami, N. (1982). Rejoining of DNA strand breaks after gamma-irradiation in cultured fish cells, CAF-MMl. *Int. J. Radiat. Biol.* **41**, 85–90.

Mitani, H., Etoh, H., and Egami, N. (1982). Resistance of a cultured fish cell line (CAF-MMl) to gamma irradiation. *Radiat. Res.* **89**, 334–347.

Murthy, P. B. K. (1979). Frequency of sister chromatid exchanges in cigarette smokers. *Hum. Genet.* **52**, 343–345.

Musilova, J., Michalova, K., and Urban, J. (1979). Sister-chromatid exchanges and chromosomal breakage in patients treated with cytostatics. *Mut. Res.* **67**, 289–294.

Pankova, N. (1965). Damage to the chromosomes in a series of cellular generations in irradiated loach embryos. *Radiobiology* **5**, 127–133.

Perry, P. and Evans, H. J. (1975). Cytological detection of mutagen-carcinogen exposure by sister chromatid exchange. *Nature* **258**, 121–125.

Prein, A. E., Thie, G. M., Alink, G. M., Koeman, J. H., and Poels, C. L. M. (1978). Cytogenetic changes in fish exposed to water of the river Rhine. *Sci. Total Environ.* **9**, 287–291.

Prokof'yeva-Bel'govskaya, A. A. (1961). Radiation injury to chromosomes at early stages of development of the salmon. *Tsitologiya* **3**, 437–445.

Romashov, D. D. and Belyaeva, V. N. (1964). Cytology of radiation gynogenesis and androgenesis in the loach (*Misgurnus fossilis* L.). *Dokl. Akad. Nauk SSSR* **157**, 503–506.

Romashov, D. D. and Belyaeva, V. N. (1966). On the conservation of radiation damage to the chromosomes in fish embryogenesis. *Sov. Genet.* **2**, 1–10.

Romashov, D. D., Golovinskaia, K. A., Belyaeva, V. N., Bakulina, E. D., Pokrovskaia, G. L., and Cherfas, N. B. (1960). Diploid radiation gynogenesis in fish. *Biophysics* **5**, 524–532.

Romashov, D. D., Nikolyukin, N. I., Belyaeva, V. N., and Timofeeva, N. A. (1963). Possibilities of producing diploid radiation-induced gynogenesis in sturgeon. *Radiobiology* **3**, 145–154.

Rudiger, H. W., Kohl, F., Mangels, W., von Wichert, P., Bartram, C. R., Wohler, W., and Passarge, E. (1976). Benzpyrene induces sister chromatid exchanges in cultured human lymphocytes. *Nature* **262**, 290–292.

Schmid, W. (1976). The micronucleus test for cytogenetic analysis. *Chem. Mutagens* **4**, 31–53.

Stromberg, P. T., Landolt, M. L., and Kocan, R. M. (1981). *Alterations in the frequency of sister chromatid exchanges in flatfish from Puget Sound, Washington following experimental and natural exposure to mutagenic chemicals.* NOAA Technical Memorandum, Office of Marine Pollution Assessment – 10, Boulder, Colorado, 43 pp.

Tsoi, R. M. (1970). Effect of nitrosomethyl urea and dimethyl sulfate on sperm of rainbow trout

(*Salmo irideus* Gibb.) and peled (*Coregonus peled* Gmel.). *Dokl. Akad. Nauk SSSR* **189,** 849–851.

Tsoi, R. M. (1974). Chemical gynogenesis in *Salmo irideus* and *Coregonus peled*. *Sov. Genet.* **8,** 275–277.

Tsoi, R. M., Men'shova, A. I., and Golodov, Y. F. (1975). Specificity of the influences of chemical mutagens on spermatozoids of *Cyprinus carpio* L. *Sov. Genet.* **10,** 190–193.

Vakhrameeva, N. A. and Neifakh, A. A. (1959). Comparison of changes in radiation and thermal sensitivity during cleavage of the loach egg (*Misgurnus fossilis*). *Dokl. Akad. Nauk SSSR* **128,** 779–782.

Zakour, H. R., Landolt, M. L., and Kocan, R. M. (1982). In vitro studies of marine toxicology: peripheral blood studies. 1981 Research in Fisheries, Annual Report of the School of Fisheries, University of Washington, Seattle, p. 48.

12

REACTIONS OF AQUATIC ECOSYSTEMS TO PESTICIDES

Charles W. Heckman

Institut für Hydrobiologie und Fischereiwissenschaft
der Universität Hamburg
Hamburg, Federal Republic of Germany

356   Charles W. Heckman

1. INTRODUCTION

It would now be extremely difficult to find a natural ecosystem anywhere in the world that has not been exposed to traces of modern pesticides. DDT, for example, has been used in great quantities on six continents. It persists even where its use has been forbidden for more than a decade and could still be found in aquatic invertebrates about 12 years after its last application to nearby fruit trees (Caspers and Heckman, 1982). In well-drained terrestrial locations, it decomposes very slowly, and considerable amounts were found in well-aerated soils 17 years after the last application (Nash and Woolson, 1967). Not only do the organochlorine pesticides enter the water with runoff, they are also transported through the atmosphere (Wheatley, 1973) and have spread over the entire surface of the earth. DDT has been found in whales from the Arctic Ocean (Addison and Brodie, 1973), fresh Antarctic snow (Peterle, 1969), Wedell seals (Brewerton, 1969), and in waters of the Sargasso Sea (Bidleman and Olney, 1974). Dieldrin is also ubiquitous (Brown, 1978). Obviously, if pesticide use were discontinued, many of the substances already used would be important environmental pollutants for a long time to come.

Since their debut shortly before the middle of this century, the new generation of pesticides have suffered a gradual decline in public esteem, from "wonder drugs of agriculture" to "major environmental problem." A general decrease in effectiveness due to an increasing resistance by the pests (Heckman, 1982a) has made each new pesticide little more than a means of short-term control rather than a permanent solution. At the same time, an ever-increasing number of chemicals are being released into the air and surface waters in large amounts. Even the pesticides already strictly forbidden in most industrial lands are still being used in vast quantities where laws to protect the environment are less stringent (Weir and Schapiro, 1981).

There is certainly an overwhelming body of evidence that pesticides, when properly used, can greatly increase agricultural productivity and aid in the control of serious insect-borne diseases. A blanket condemnation of these chemicals can in no way be justified. It is also obvious that competent professional supervision is necessary to prevent any serious environmental consequences of pesticide misuse and to protect human beings from accidental intoxication (Heckman, 1982a). This supervision has been lacking in the past, and it is unfortunate to note that the need to control pesticide use was only recognized after an alarming number of tragedies occurred, some of which were described by Muirhead-Thomson (1971). Producing food for a growing world population and promoting public health can scarcely be given lower priority than other activities. Offering the choice of less food and more disease or a liberal application of pesticidal chemicals is a faulty dilemma, however. It is becoming obvious that these substances are limited to a period of effectiveness, after which the target species will no longer respond to the treatment. A very long list of target pests have produced resistant populations after a few years' exposure to a particular pesticide, and many species are already immune to a variety of chemicals formerly effective for their control. Moreover, some species that failed to develop resistance were simply displaced by similar pests that did develop resistance (Brown, 1978). Just as bacteria have become insensitive to antibiotics (Mitsuhashi et al., 1976), insects have become resistant to individual insecticides; rodents, to rodenticides; fungi, to fungicides; mites, to acaricides; and plants, to herbicides (Brown, 1978). In light of the knowledge obtained over the last three decades, it is absolutely necessary to carefully evaluate a wide variety of factors before deciding on the application of a toxic chemical to eliminate an unwanted plant or animal. Some of these factors are economic and others agronomic. The ecological side effects also must be carefully considered, not only for aesthetic reasons, but also because they affect the overall economics of a crop protection or disease control program.

If a farmer includes only the cost of a pesticide and his expected increased harvest in his calculations, he may find that his monoculture system would bring him considerably more profit if the pesticide were employed. If his calculations were made on a regional basis, however, the results could very easily be different. Losses to commercial or sport fisheries, to beekeepers, to stocks of commercially valuable game birds, and to the health of farm workers applying the chemical could very well tip the balance into the red. Yunus and Lim (1971), for example, noted a great loss of important food fishes after a spraying program was initiated to increase rice production in Malaysia. The fish are more vital to the health of the farmers in many parts of Southeast Asia than the rice because of their high protein content (Heckman, 1979).

As production costs are increased by the need to continually develop new pesticides to replace those which are no longer effective, the great margin between the price of the chemical and the profit from the increased yield decreases. Moreover, the complaint is sometimes heard that many of the newer pesticides lack the effectiveness of the older ones. McEwen and Stephenson (1979), for example, wrote that no satisfactory substitute for

DDT in the program to control *Anopheles* mosquitoes had yet been found, although dieldrin and a few other insecticides had to be used in regions inhabited by DDT-resistant mosquitoes (Learmonth, 1977).

As the costs of pesticides increase and the returns decline, the losses from environmental side effects will become the factors that determine whether or not the use of pesticides remains profitable. Unfortunately, the environmental damage caused by toxic chemicals has proven to be one of the most difficult factors to evaluate. It is a hard enough job to calculate losses to hunters, fishermen, beekeepers, and water supply authorities, but estimating the losses to the general public from changes in environmental quality and long-term exposure to various chemical residues with any degree of accuracy is still impossible. First, there are no generally agreed upon values placed on such qualities as health and the presence of attractive wildlife species. Second, it is greatly disputed as to what degree pesticides endanger human health and environmental quality, and finally, relatively little is known about economic losses caused by the elimination of natural predators, saprophytic fungi, and members of the food webs supplying the nourishment for valuable fish and game.

Among the vast body of literature on pesticides, a very small proportion concerns the long-term changes in natural ecosystems brought about by chronic exposure to modern agricultural chemicals. The reasons for this are obvious. Most institutions do not plan experiments that require 10 to 20 years to complete in a relatively large tract of land or water body in which conditions can be carefully controlled. Field investigations can yield useful results only when the *status quo ante* is known, and there are not many places in the world that have been subjected to thorough ecological study. Furthermore, it is very difficult to account for all factors that may have brought about ecological changes, so a positive proof that pesticides produce an observed alteration cannot be obtained. Field studies must therefore involve a good deal of detective work to rule out as many factors as possible, and by comparative investigations identify the most probable cause for an observed change. Statistical studies of different regions also face the difficulty of ruling out all possibility that causes other than the suspected one are responsible for a particular phenomenon.

Gaining information by empirical methods is facilitated by large amounts of data. The imbalance between the number of ecological studies and the number of pesticides in use precludes authoritative assessments of the impact each of these chemicals will have on the various ecosystems to which they are applied. DDT is certainly the best investigated insecticide, yet transcripts of the hearings on whether or not to ban DDT in the United States clearly show that there was by no means a full consensus of opinion on the danger of this chemical (Dunlap, 1981). Perkow (1971–1979) has compiled a list of over 126 insecticides and 134 herbicides, in addition to a variety of other pesticides. Many of these chemicals decompose into other toxic substances. The detection of so many different organic chemicals in the environment alone would be a mammoth undertaking. The amount of ecological research already completed is miniscule compared to that still required to elucidate the numerous aspects of the pesticide impact on biotic systems and the reaction of these systems to reestablish an equilibrium.

This chapter confines itself to reviewing some of the ways aquatic ecosystems react after accidental or intentional introductions of pesticides bring about changes in the biotic communities. Terrestrial studies are also mentioned when necessary to support the theoretical concepts that apparently apply to all ecosystems. Several comprehensive works (Muirhead-Thomson, 1971; Brown, 1978; McEwen and Stephenson, 1979) provide enormous amounts of information on the effects of pesticides on aquatic life. A brief review of these effects and lists of the chemicals most frequently applied to water bodies is provided in the following two sections. The reactions of ecosystems to short- and long-term contamination by these pesticides is discussed in depth, both from the theoretical viewpoint and based on findings of studies in the field. These considerations are applied to practical problems of wildlife conservation, biological and integrated pest control programs, and agronomy in general. It is hoped that attention can be drawn to some of the largest gaps in the knowledge needed to assess the interaction between pesticides and natural ecosystems, such as the quantitative comparisons of the saprophytic fungi and the bacteria as agents of detrital decomposition processes, and the general ecological relationships in tropical water bodies.

2. PESTICIDES INTENTIONALLY APPLIED TO AQUATIC HABITATS

2.1. Herbicides

The chemicals listed in Table 1 are among those most frequently used to kill unwanted green plants in water bodies. Aquatic weeds are most frequently a problem in tropical and semitropical impoundments and waterways. They sometimes interfere with boat traffic, clog the inlet screens to the turbines at hydroelectric plants, block irrigation channels, and compete with commercially important crops, especially rice. In the temperate zones, herbicides are sometimes used against algae to improve the appearance of lakes.

More caution has been exercised in the selection and use of herbicides than in other activities involving pesticides, with only a few notable exceptions. The reason is obvious. A mistake can destroy a farmer's crop (Kates, 1965). Hence, selectivity is required, and chemicals are usually chosen that decompose rapidly, precluding their transportation through the air or water to fields of sensitive cultivated plants. The herbicides are also among the least harmful pesticides to human health, although cases of serious intoxication and even death from these chemicals have been reported (Staiff et al., 1973). Some herbicides are also particularly dangerous to vertebrates during

Table 1. Some Herbicides Commonly Used to Kill Aquatic and Semiaquatic Plants (Formulae and general information were provided by Wegler and Eue, 1970, and Perkow, 1971–1979).

Herbicide	Use
Inorganic Herbicides	
CuSO$_4$	Used to kill algae, keeps lake water clear; kills snails and increases the copper content of the water and sediment
NaAsO$_2$	Kills submerged plants; toxic to many organisms and increases the arsenic content of sediments
NaSCN	Applied mainly to kill reeds and other marsh plants
Organic Herbicides	
Acrylaldehyde (acrolein)	Recommended for killing submerged plants
2,3-dichloro-1,4-naphthoquinone (dichlone)	Used against submerged plants, including algae
Sodium 2,2-dichloropropionate (dalapon)	Kills littoral monocots
2,4-dichlorophenyl-4′-nitrophenyl ether (NIP or nitrofen)	Used to kill weeds in rice fields
2,4-dichloro-6-fluorophenyl-4′-nitrophenyl ether (MO 500)	Employed chiefly in Japan to selectively kill certain grasses and sedges in rice fields
2,4,6-trichlorophenyl-4′-nitrophenyl ether (MO 338)	Used in Japan to kill rice field weeds
3-methyl-4′-nitro-diphenyl ether	Selective herbicide, non-toxic to fish, used in rice fields
3,4-dichlorobenzyl-N-methylcarbamate (DMBC)	Weed killer in rice fields
Hexahydro-1-H-azepin-1-carbamyl thioester (molinate)	Selectively kills the grass, *Echinochloa crus-galli*, in rice fields

2,4-dichlorophenoxyacetic acid (2,4-D)	Kills weeds in rice fields and canals
2,3,6-trichlorophenylacetic acid (fenac)	Used to kill aquatic weeds in the United States
2-(2,4,5-trichlorophenoxy)-propionic acid (fenoprop)	Applied against woody plants in rice fields
Maleic hydrazide (MH)	Kills water plants in Great Britain
N-3-chlorophenyl-isopropylcarbamate (CIPC, chlor-propham)	Used in Great Britain to kill water plants
3,6-endo-oxo-hexahydrophthalic acid (ASA or endothal)	Contact herbicide used against aquatic plants
2,6-dichlorobenzonitrile (2,6-DBN or dichlobenil)	Selective herbicide in rice fields
3,4-dichloropropionanilide (propanil)	General aquatic herbicide and in rice fields
2-tertiary butyl-4-(2,4-dichloro-5-isopropyloxy-phenyl)-1,3,4-oxadiazoin-5-on (oxadiazon)	Employed in rice culture
2,6-dichlorobenzoic acid thioamide (chlorthiamid)	Kills water plants in Europe
2-methylthio-4-ethylamino-6-tertiary butylamino-1,3,5-triazine (terbutryn)	Kills water plants in Europe
2-(dichloroacetylamino)-3-chloronaphthoquinone (quinonamid)	Used to kill algae, especially in rice fields
6,7-dihydropyridol-1(2-a:2′, 1′c) pyrazine-diium di-bromide (diquat dibromide, deiquat)	Nonselective, kills water plants, phytoplankton, and some young fish
1,1′-dimethyl-4,4′-bipyridinium-di-(methyl sulfate) (paraquat)	Nonselective against water plants, including grasses
6-chloro-N,N′ diethyl-1,3,5-triazine-2,4-diamine (simazine)	Persistent weed killer occasionally used to kill aquatic plants

their early developmental stages. Paraquat, for example, was found to be particularly toxic to mallard duck embryos (Hoffman and Eastin, 1982) and to cause histological and biochemical changes in the lungs of neonatal rats (Hunter and Prahlad, 1981). Courtney et al. (1970) reported 2,4,5-T to have teratogenic effects on rodents, but the substance responsible was later suspected to be 2,3,7,8-tetrachlorodibenzo-*p*-dioxin (TCDD), a contaminant of the 2,4,5-T (McEwen and Stephenson, 1979). Still controversial is the increase in birth defects among Vietnamese civilians and the families of American military personnel who were exposed to large quantities of herbicides during the large-scale defoliation program in Vietnam. There is certainly strong circumstantial evidence to support the implication of the herbicides in the increased rates of miscarriages and birth defects in this population group.

For the past two decades, herbicides have increasingly replaced mechanical plant removal methods along water courses. In Great Britain, there has been a trend to employ more persistent and less selective weed killers (Newbold, 1977) because no aquatic plants of commercial importance are present in the habitats treated.

Due to the rapid growth of plants in the tropics, there are far more potential uses of herbicides than in the temperate zones. Robson (1976) reviewed the distribution of some aquatic plants that are frequent targets of eradication programs. It is evident that herbicides will probably be used in many parts of the world where aquatic plants provide valuable food items, such as taro, water chestnuts, edible lotus, and rice. Should the trend toward persistent and nonselective herbicides be carried over to the warm climatic zones, there is a high probability that some useful plants far from the points of weed killer applications will also be eliminated.

2.2. Fungicides

Deliberate fungicide applications to aquatic habitats are confined almost exclusively to rice fields. In Japan, organomercury compounds, particularly a mixture of phenyl mercury acetate (PMA) and slaked lime, were widely used to control rice blast, until it was found that the mercury was being transferred to the rice grains (Ishikura, 1972). Since the mid-1960s, antibiotics, such as blasticidin and kasugamycin, have come into general use, together with pentachlorobenzene compounds and the organophosphorus compounds: *S*-benzyl ethyl phenylphosphonothiolate (Inezin), *S*-benzyl diisopropyl phosphorothiolate (Kitazin), and *O*-ethyl diphenyl phosphorodithiolate (Hinosan). Arsenical compounds are also sometimes used against sheath blight (Ishikura, 1972). A group of fungicides called thiophenates have been developed and applied to rice fields since the late 1960s (Noguchi, 1972). In the United States, the organotin fungicide, triphenyl tin hydroxide (fentin hydroxide), is used in rice fields (McEwen and Stephenson, 1979).

2.3. Molluscicides

There are not a great many molluscicides in general use against aquatic snails and bivalves. $CuSO_4$ is toxic to snails as well as to algae, and it is the molluscicide longest in use (Muirhead-Thomson, 1971). Other chemicals introduced into water bodies to kill snails include sodium pentachlorophenate (sodium PCP); niclosamine, sold under the name Bayluscide; N-tritylmorpholine, sold as Frescon; copper compounds, such as Cu_2O and CuCl; herbicides that also kill snails, including diquat and paraquat; and organotin and organolead compounds. Chloramines are frequently used to kill bivalves that colonize water pipes (Beger, 1966). The greatest quantities of molluscicides are applied to tropical waters inhabited by various snails that serve as intermediate hosts for parasites of humans and commercially important animals. In North America, snails are sometimes poisoned to prevent "swimmers' itch," a cercarial dermatitis presenting little danger to humans (Harman, 1974).

2.4. Insecticides

Many different insecticides are applied to surface waters and marshlands throughout the world. The chlorinated hydrocarbons have been used in the greatest quantities, but these are being replaced, when possible, by less persistent compounds. Some sprays are used to protect rice and other aquatic plants, but most are intended to control mosquitoes, black flies, other insect vectors of pathogens, and even the harmless aquatic species that some people living near lakes happen to find annoying. Table 2 provides a list of some important insecticides that have been deliberately applied to surface waters.

Obviously, insecticides have been vital to the health and well-being of humans in many areas of the world where insect-borne parasites and pathogens are endemic. Malaria was temporarily brought under control (Learmonth, 1977), and moderate success was achieved in combatting yellow fever through mosquito control (Brown, 1977). The species of *Simulium* that carry infectious stages of onchocercid nematodes and transmit them to humans in tropical Africa and America have also long been suppressed by the treatment of rivers and streams with DDT (McMahon, 1967). Some uses of insecticides in agriculture have brought great increases in production and caused only minimal environmental side effects. The great disappointment with the insecticides came when it was realized that the gains were not

Table 2. Some of the Insecticides That Have Been Intentionally Applied to Surface Waters Most Frequently[a]

Insecticide	Use
Chlorinated Hydrocarbons	
DDT	Mosquito and black fly control
Aldrin	Rice culture
Endrin	Rice culture, but its use is very limited due to its toxicity
Dieldrin	Control of DDT-resistant mosquitoes
Telodrin	Rice culture
Hexachlorocyclohexane (lindane)	Limited use in rice culture
Carbamates	
Hopcide	Rice culture
Propoxur (Baygon®)	Control of DDT and dieldrin-resistant mosquitoes
Carbofuran	Control of insects and nematodes in rice
2(1′-methylpropyl)-phenylmethyl-carbamate	Rice culture
Organophosphorus Compounds	
Temephos (Abate®)	Mosquito larvicide
Fenthion (Baytex®)	Mosquito control
Fenitrothion	Mosquito control
Chlorpyrifos (Dursban®, Lorsban®)	Mosquito control
Chlorthion	Mosquito control
Inorganic Insecticides	
Paris Green	Mosquito control

[a]A large number of substances have been tested for their effectiveness in controlling mosquitoes, including various pyrethroids (Service, 1977b).

permanent. Meanwhile, the users had been seduced by the early successes to forsake the many good practices that had been developed before the insecticides had been discovered. Concentrating the bulk of the available resources on programs to eradicate the insect vectors with DDT seemed more practical than tedious education programs to encourage the drainage of standing water pools near houses, screening of windows, the use of mosquito nets when sleeping, and the available prophylactic methods. Perhaps the greatest mistake of all was the neglect of support for medical research programs designed to find patient-oriented methods of combatting the many widespread tropical diseases with effective medicines or vaccinations. While programs to eradicate the *Aedes* mosquitoes that carry yellow fever viruses brought only temporary local success, vaccination campaigns eliminated the disease from a large part of Africa (Brown, 1977). In fact, insecticides have never provided the means to fully eradicate any diseases of humans, while vaccinations, antibiotics, and public sanitation measures have made many of the plagues of yesteryear all but forgotten today.

Besides the applications of insecticides to promote public health and increase agricultural production, there are a good many questionable uses to which these chemicals have been put. For example, over 120,000 pounds of DDT were dumped into Clear Lake, California, in an attempt to kill a completely harmless chaoborid gnat because residents found it annoying that they congregated around electric lights at night. The program was terminated after losses of valuable wildlife were noticed (Rudd and Herman, 1972).

It is clear that the application of insecticides to surface waters has been undertaken for a wide variety of purposes, from very important to trivial. The substances used vary greatly in persistence, and some chlorinated hydrocarbons have already become significant contaminants of river sediments, such as the case of endrin and dieldrin in the lower Mississippi River (Matsumura, 1972). These have apparently made extracts from the sediments lethal to healthy fish (Cottam, 1965).

2.5. Piscicides

Apparently, the first piscicides were used as a means of catching fish. The extraction of rotenone and its use as a fish poison have been known to the natives of Asia and South America since ancient times (Holden, 1973). Only in the last few decades, mainly in the United States and the Soviet Union, have piscicides come into general use to fully eliminate species of fish deemed undesirable from freshwater bodies (Muirhead-Thomson, 1971). Ironically, the carp, *Cyprinus carpio*, is one of the chief targets for elimination in the United States (Mulla et al., 1967), although in Europe and Asia it is a prized food fish that is frequently raised commercially.

Rotenone has been largely replaced by other piscicides. Toxaphene is usually employed to rid lakes of all fish. It is relatively nontoxic to human beings, but it has the disadvantage of being persistent (Johnson et al., 1966), so restocking must be delayed. A chemical similar to toxaphene, polychlorpynene, is used for fish elimination in the Soviet Union (Burmakin, 1968).

A variety of selective fish poisons are now available. These are used to kill unwanted fish without harming the other species sharing the habitat. Generally, the dosages must be carefully controlled. Examples of selective piscicides are antimycin, azinphosmethyl, dichlorvos, and trifluoro methyl nitrophenol (TFM). Particularly large amounts of TFM have been used in streams feeding the Great Lakes of North America to kill young lampreys (Lennon et al., 1971). The selective toxicity to the lampreys is enhanced by the addition of small amounts of niclosamine, a molluscicide mentioned previously.

3. UNINTENTIONAL CONTAMINATION OF SURFACE WATERS WITH PESTICIDES

3.1. Accidents

Although damage caused by accidents involving pesticides are seldom included in cost calculations, they occur frequently enough to rate more consideration than they are generally given. Not only is the damage to wildlife a factor that is very difficult to place a monitary value on, it is something that is not easy to detect at all, except when the sudden death of a large number of animals occurs. Moreover, the death or ruined health of human beings accidentally exposed to toxic doses of pesticides are also very difficult to evaluate in terms of money. In spite of the difficulties, however, all of these factors must be added in the balance to determine whether the use of a pesticide for a particular purpose is warranted.

With the increase in pesticide use during the past three decades, there has been an alarming increase in the number of accidents. While the most public attention has been given to the large-scale contamination of towns and cities through industrial accidents, a few major disasters involving river systems are also worthy of mention. Muirhead-Thomson (1971) reported that 50,000 fish were killed in an English waterway when thionazin, a nematocide, was spilled into the water. This accident was repeated in the same waterway, and thousands of fish were again killed. Many fish were killed in the Rhine due to the release of endosulfan in 1969. The drinking water authorities in The Netherlands were obliged to use emergency water sources (Muirhead-Thomson, 1971). In the Mississippi River, an enormous fish kill was reported after endrin was discharged from a chemical plant (Mount and Putnicki, 1966). The same river received an industrial discharge of pentachlorophenol about a decade later, again with devastating results for the aquatic fauna (Pierce and Victor, 1978). Recently, the James River in Virginia was contaminated with kepone from a factory (Sanders et al., 1981). Through industrial accidents, even pesticides that are forbidden for use can contaminate the environment because there are still considerable export markets (Weir and Schapiro, 1981).

Although disasters related to the manufacture of pesticides are often the most spectacular, agricultural activities are no less prone to human failure. When a spray plane crashed into the Mississippi River, its load of endrin caused the death of a great many fish far downstream (Wade, 1969). Most agricultural accidents, however, are on a smaller scale, and the great majority of them apparently go unreported. The statistics provided by Davies et al. (1975) show that there are a great many cases of chlorinated hydrocarbon intoxication, some involving fatalities, among agricultural workers in developing countries. A great many other cases go unreported due to a lack of doctors able to diagnose them correctly and laboratories equipped to detect residues of the many different chemicals being used. An estimated 500,000 people are poisoned by pesticides each year around the world, and about 5000 of them die (WHO, 1973). Although the accuracy of such figures is open to doubt, there is certainly ample evidence that a danger to the health of farm workers exists.

Relatively small-scale accidents involving the loss of wildlife are more likely to go unreported than cases of injury to human beings. For example, washing of the spraying equipment and disposing of the sacks that contained pesticides in ponds and lakes are by no means minor sources of toxic substances in surface waters (McEwen and Stephenson, 1979). When hexachlorocyclohexane intended for the treatment of sheep was spilled into a British stream, a variety of insects and crustaceans were eliminated (Hynes, 1961), and for the few such incidents that come to the attention of scientists, there are certainly hundreds that do not.

3.2. Fallout, Leaching, and Aerial Transport

It is safe to say that significant quantities of every persistent pesticide applied to terrestrial crops will reach surface waters. Nonpersistent substances, on the other hand, contaminate only those water bodies near enough to cultivated lands to receive direct fallout. The ultimate sink for the most persistent pesticides is the ocean (Kerr and Vass, 1973), but their effects on marine organisms have received relatively little attention. Johannes (1975) reviewed the available reports on pelagic fish and coral communities, making it apparent that chlorinated hydrocarbons are already being accumulated by organisms in the sea.

Much more is known about the toxicity of pesticides to estuarine and mud-flat species (Butler, 1968, 1969; Eisler, 1969; Portmann and Wilson, 1971; Ishikura, 1972; Brown, 1978), and residues of chlorinated hydrocarbons are usually found in these organisms (Kerr and Vass, 1973). If the inhabitants of deeper waters react to pesticides in a way similar to their littoral relatives, the impact of pesticides on the biota of the oceans must be considerable.

Direct fallout introduces the highest dosages and greatest variety of pesticides to surface waters near cultivated land. Sieber and Woodrow (1981) recommended protective measures for persons within 400 m downwind from paraquat spraying operations, based on their studies of airborne distribution. Ponds, ditches, and canals directly beside sprayed fields are therefore treated with pesticides every time the fields are, the dosage depending on prevailing wind conditions. Of course, aerial sprayings of large areas also involve contamination not only of the surface waters directly beneath the aircraft, but also the streams and river systems downstream from the points of contamination (Kerswill and Elson, 1955).

The distribution of the pesticides can continue through the large inland drainage systems and eventually enter the sea. Although the water soluble substances may reach significant concentrations in lakes, pesticides are seldom detected in appreciable amounts by analysis of water alone (Hartung, 1975). On entering the water, most of these chemicals are quickly adsorbed on particles (Miles, 1980) or taken up by living organisms. The particles may remain suspended or join the sediment to be resuspended at a later date (Pionke and Chesters, 1973). Because of their feeding habits and affinities for the pesticidal chemicals, certain organisms tend to concentrate much greater amounts of particular residues than are found in the surrounding habitat, and this biomagnification of the concentration can be repeated at several levels along the food chain (Rudd, 1964). Thus, the residues spread downstream with the flowing water and also upstream with highly contaminated migratory organisms.

Pesticides are not only spread within the aqueous media of great watersheds, many are also transported through the atmosphere as vapors or adsorbed to dust particles (Junge, 1975; Slater and Spedding, 1981). Considerable amounts are often found in rain or snow (Strachan et al., 1980), and the winds seem to have carried significant amounts of various pesticides to oceanic regions far from the lands to which they were applied (Risebrough et al., 1968). Wheatley (1973) provided a review on various aspects of atmospheric pesticide distribution.

A final method of distribution is the importation of contaminated foodstuffs. Many persistent pesticides now forbidden in the industrial lands are still used in enormous quantities in the developing countries (Weir and Schapiro, 1981), and the crops exported to the industrial lands can be contaminated with considerable amounts of these chemicals. These eventually find their way into domestic sewage that is released into waterways or dumped offshore. Thus, it is clear that environmental contaminants do not confine themselves within political entities, and they must therefore be treated on a global basis.

4. SHORT-TERM EFFECTS OF PESTICIDES

4.1. Single Applications

Almost all the standard testing until fairly recently involved the effects of single applications of chemicals on previously unexposed individuals. The standard LD50 tests, regardless of the exposure times and other experimental parameters, are basically one-time exposures of test animals from captive populations. Even tests for sublethal effects are generally not continued for more than one or two generations. Before selective processes can manifest themselves, the tests are discontinued.

There are a great many field investigations of pesticide effects for the first few weeks after exposure. Even so, a glance at the long list of chemicals on the market (Perkow, 1971–79) and the number of new compounds being discovered each year shows that the research effort in this field is still not adequate. Studies of the flora and fauna in water bodies contaminated by specific chemicals permit evaluations of damage to useful nontarget populations, distortions of trophic relationships, and biomagnification of the residue concentrations, not to mention the usefulness of the chemicals in combatting pests under natural conditions. Field studies, however, are always open to question because so many uncontrolled variables are involved. Nevertheless, the results are often so unequivocal that the interpretations can scarcely be doubted. For example, the death of large percentages of mayfly, stonefly, and caddisfly larvae in a stream shortly after a DDT application to kill *Simulium* larvae can, without any reasonable doubt, be attributed to the presence of the DDT (Hatfield, 1969). The same degree of certainty can be assumed for the conclusions of Springer and Webster (1951), who observed considerable mortality among nontarget salt marsh species in New Jersey after DDT was applied to the habitat.

Other studies have not provided such unequivocal results. When Ames (1966) reported a correlation between the amount of DDT residues in osprey eggs and the rate of premature shell cracking, he could not show any direct causal relationships between the insecticide and the shell thickness. Laboratory experiments were necessary to dispel the doubts. DDE, one of the breakdown products of DDT (Klein and Korte, 1970), was found to have the greatest effect on mallard eggs, causing a significant thinning of the shells and increased rate of cracking (Heath et al., 1972). Dieldrin has the same effect on mallard eggs (Lehner and Egbert, 1969). These examples show that even where field studies fail to provide positive proof of a pesticide effect, situations are often indicated that bear further investigation.

It is not possible to adequately treat the enormous body of literature on short-term pesticide effects in these few introductory paragraphs. Reviews have been provided by Brown (1978), McEwen and Stephenson (1979), and Muirhead-Thomson (1971), among others. Corbett (1974) reviewed the information available on the biochemical mode of pesticide action, and it is clear that there is still a great deal to be learned about how the various pesticides kill their victims. The toxicology of pesticides relevant to individual taxa has been treated by the following authors: green plants, Fedtke (1982); fungi, Grewe (1970); crustaceans, Ruber and Baskar (1968) and Eisler (1969); insects, O'Brien (1967), Metcalf (1971), and Kuhr and Dorough (1976); fish, Walsh and Ribelin (1975); birds, Ohlendorf et al. (1974); just to mention a few.

4.2. Ecosystem Reactions to Single Pesticide Applications

After exposure to a toxic substance, a stable ecosystem tends to return itself to its state of equilibrium. The course of recovery is determined by the degree of injury. This, in turn, depends on the spectrum of organisms killed by the exposure, the dosage, the length of time required for the substance to decompose or be transported away, and the extent of the sublethal effects that manifest themselves later. Obviously, a highly selective pesticide that decomposes quickly to nontoxic chemicals would have relatively little impact on the ecosystem, even though it could be extremely deadly to the target pest. General ecosystem poisons, on the other hand, have the greatest effects and require the longest periods of recovery.

After the accidental release of chlorine from a drinking water pipeline being purged of fouling organisms, nearly all of the aquatic plants and animals in a small stream in northern Germany were killed. An investigation revealed that after an initial period during which massive populations of chironomids and simuliids developed, the community that had occupied the stream before the accident was able to reestablish itself. This complete recovery was facilitated by the presence of an intact community upstream from the contaminated section of stream and the rapid removal of the chlorine and organochlorine residues. Within 4 months (May to September) the aquatic plants had regenerated themselves and the invertebrate fauna had recovered its full diversity. Fish had migrated into the stream again to replace the large number killed by the chlorine, and only the pike (*Esox lucius*) would apparently require several years to recolonize the stream due to its territorial habits and relatively slow growth (Heckman, 1983).

Similar recoveries of various populations within a few weeks of pesticide applications have been reported by various authors (Hurlbert, 1975; Hurlbert et al., 1970; Peterle and Giles, 1964). In cases where the pesticide is somewhat persistent and the organisms rather sensitive, recovery takes longer (Patterson and von Windeguth, 1964).

Much more severe ecological disturbances result when an entire watershed is treated, because breeding stocks of some species are no longer present in any part of the habitat. For example, Hastings et al. (1961) reported the complete disappearance of caddisfly larvae belonging to the genus *Leptocerus* after the application of DDT, and their failure to return to the area. Larvae of *Chimarra* failed to return after DDT treatment of a Pennsylvania stream (Hoffmann and Drooz, 1953), and phosphamidon killed all caddisfly larvae in a British Columbian creek (Schouwenburg and Jackson, 1966).

It is well to remember that persistent pesticides, particularly the chlorinated hydrocarbons, have a more protracted period of influence on water bodies when applied to adjacent terrestrial habitats than when poured directly into the water. In streams, the current rapidly carries contaminants away, while the anerobic sediments in eutrophic ponds with their rich bacteria populations are media in which decomposition of many pesticides, including DDT, occurs most rapidly (Pionke and Chesters, 1973; Matsumura, 1974). In well-aerated lake sediments, on the other hand, considerable concentrations of pesticides can build up (Frank et al., 1977); but of the studies already conducted, very few have attributed high sedimentary concentrations of pesticides to direct treatment of the water body. One notable exception is found in Clear Lake, California (Rudd and Herman, 1972).

Runoff from terrestrial soils treated with pesticides brings these substances into lakes and streams repeatedly as long as the residues persist. Thus, a single application to a field can result in repeated contamination of a nearby stream with a persistent pesticide that adheres to soil particles. With this, however, the discussion enters the realm of chronic pesticide pollution.

5. LONG-TERM EFFECTS OF PESTICIDES

5.1. Chronic Exposure

At the present time, it would be extremely difficult to find an aquatic ecosystem that was exposed only once to a single pesticide. Not only are pesticides usually applied repeatedly, they are also frequently applied in combination as part of a program to protect specific crops during the growing season. For example, orchard ditches in northern Germany were exposed to fungicide sprays about 16 times each year, insecticides 5 times, and herbicides, acaricides, and a rodenticide once each. The farmers had about 30 different active ingredients in preparations on the local market to choose from (Heckman, 1981). DDT and lindane had not been used for about 10 years, yet significant amounts of these substances could still be found in aquatic animals from the region, even those from a protected watershed area in which the use of pesticides was forbidden (Caspers and Heckman, 1982). Obviously, field investigations of such highly contaminated water bodies cannot distinguish the long-term effect of one pesticide alone, but they indicate problems that must be solved by laboratory experiments. On the other hand, experiments have not yet been designed that can duplicate the multiplicity of factors encountered in natural ecosystems.

Not only do substances applied and residues from past applications directly affect aquatic biota, they also decompose into various chemicals with lethal or sublethal effects on living organisms (Matsumura, 1975). Experiments have demonstrated that some breakdown products are responsible for negative effects on wildlife associated with pesticides, such as the thinning of birds' eggshells caused by DDE (Stickel, 1973).

For the purposes of this discussion, many theoretical aspects of pesticide application are considered without regard to the substance applied or the target organisms. A hypothetical aquatic system is considered that has been exposed over a long term to a broad spectrum of toxic chemicals, and expected changes in the community structure are described. Examples are used to illustrate the model systems as they function in actual biotic communities.

5.2. The Wonder-Drug Model

The initial reaction to DDT, the first of the highly effective modern pesticides to come into general use, was one of euphoria. Very small amounts killed most insect pests on contact, and sprayed on a surface, it continued to kill any passing insect for weeks or months. The pre-DDT insecticides were not particularly effective, and Decker (1974) provided a vivid description of the difficulties farmers had had with insects before effective chemical agents to combat them became available. The initial gains in production achieved after the introduction of DDT were amazing. Although system modelling was not in vogue during the late 1940s, it is rather easy to formulate a model agricultural system according to the prevailing beliefs of that time.

DDT was thought to be highly toxic to almost all insects but safe for human beings and other vertebrates, even in relatively high concentrations. Therefore, a moderate amount applied to a cultivated field would free the crops from insect pests and persist for a long while to kill all insects that arrived later. Its slowness to decompose was viewed as desirable because its toxic effect would last longer. The destruction of nontarget arthropods, including predatory species, was not viewed with concern because a fully eliminated pest requires no biological control. The spraying of uncultivated fields and woodlands was also desirable, according to this model, since pests that might be hiding there would be killed. Environmental damage was not considered serious because DDT was believed not to harm vertebrates, and insects were considered to be so prolific that their complete extinction was impossible.

Using this model, the malaria control program, spruce budworm elimination plan, and a series of other public health, forestry, and agricultural projects involving massive amounts of DDT, were undertaken with great optimism. The reappearance of a pest indicated only that the pesticide had not been applied in sufficient quantity or often enough. Initial successes led to even more optimistic predictions of complete eradication of insect pests and the diseases they carry.

That this model failed to reflect reality became apparent during the 1950s and 1960s. The programs designed according to its premises failed to fulfill the early expectations. Not only was the "wonder-drug" model an extreme oversimplification, many of the ideas on which it was based proved false. DDT and its chemical relatives did prove harmful to certain vertebrates, including many valuable wildlife species, and it failed to maintain its effectiveness against the pests. *Silent Spring* (Carson, 1962) has to be viewed as a milestone in shaping public opinion on pesticides because it fully smashed the image of these chemicals as saviors of mankind from the prolific arthropod hordes that devour crops and spread disease.

Unfortunately, the wonder-drug model has not been replaced by a better one, and the place of pesticides in the world is still hotly debated. A few diehards still hold to this discredited model, perhaps because they remember and were strongly impressed by the effectiveness of DDT during the 1940s. The attempt to eradicate a stubborn pest by using more of a chemical control agent, however, invariably fails and often causes severe environmental damage, as in the case reported by Vaughan and Leon (1976). The reason is the selection process that leads to the development of resistant populations.

5.3. Resistance

One of the first deficiencies of the wonder-drug model to be noted was its failure to account for diminished toxicity of a pesticide against a pest. A poisonous substance was generally regarded as always being poisonous, and although a few reports of isolated pest populations developing resistances to inorganic poisons had been published early in the century (Brown, 1978), this was viewed more as a curiosity than a serious problem. The rapid development of resistant populations is now threatening the entire economic basis of chemical crop protection (Oppenoorth, 1976) and has dashed the hopes of an easy conquest of insect-borne diseases (Brown, 1977; Learmonth, 1977). At the same time, it has also allowed many nontarget species to survive so that the spring is still not completely silent.

A good many monographs on resistance are available, and it suffices to say here that it is achieved in different physiological, biochemical, or behavioral ways (Corbett, 1974), it is inherited and not acquired (Plapp, 1976), and it occurs in some species but apparently not in others (Brown, 1978). A number of species have developed resistance to every pesticide employed against them. Relatively little is known about resistance in nontarget species, except those with known economic value, such as fish (Yarbrough, 1974). In orchard drainage ditches that received large doses of different pesticides each year, a few insect species were just as abundant and widespread as in unsprayed ditches (Heckman, 1981; Caspers and Heckman, 1982). The majority of insects and all of the water mites that had been present in the 1950s could no longer be found in the habitats exposed to the pesticides, however.

5.4. Elimination of Pests' Natural Enemies

According to Boyce (1976), university, state, and federal entomologists in the United States regarded control by natural enemies to be the most effective means of minimizing damage caused by insect pests until about 1940, when the great success achieved with DDT seemed to be the proof that they were wrong. In recent years, as the effectiveness of insecticides diminished alarmingly, the use of predatory arthropods, fish, and birds to control harmful insects has again come into vogue (Ridgway and Vinson, 1977). It may be that those nineteenth-century entomologists were right all along.

Under the conditions assumed in the wonder-drug model, the complete destruction of the pest populations by the chemical pesticides made the promotion of predator populations superfluous. The destruction of a great many different nontarget organisms was viewed as a small price to pay for the benefits gained. Aesthetic factors generally rank behind economic ones. Early reports of insectivorous bird mortalities (Robbins and Stewart, 1949) therefore did little to dampen the enthusiasm of the DDT users. The results are evident today when waters in agricultural regions are found to lack large numbers of predatory beetle, dragonfly, and water mite species that had been abundant before the advent of modern pesticide use (Heckman, 1981).

Many cases have been reported of pesticides having effects opposite from those intended because of predator elimination. For example, Hurlbert (1975) referred to an application of fenthion to control a mosquito that resulted in the doubling of the mosquito population within a month due to the elimination of two predaceous beetles and one dragonfly species. The release of a pest from its natural biological control aggravates the resistance problem, since highly prolific insects resistant to the chemicals that formerly controlled them and freed from their natural enemies can quickly produce enormous populations.

Resistance develops most rapidly in habitats receiving the largest amounts of a pesticide (Brown, 1978), and these habitats are also the ones in which the greatest numbers of a pest's natural enemies are killed. The reasons that a pest usually develops resistance more rapidly than its natural enemies are related to the specific population dynamics. In a stable biotic community, feedback controls prevent populations of species from exhausting their food supplies (Odum, 1971). The standing stocks of plants must therefore remain greater than the stocks of herbivores that consume them, and the prey must outnumber the predators. Because the resistant populations must develop from individuals within the wild population that have abnormally high powers of resistance due to hereditary factors (Georghiou, 1972), and because such individuals are generally rare until the pesticides are applied and the selection process begins, the probability of encountering potential founders of resistant lines can be considered greater if the wild population is large than if it is small. Thus, the higher on the food chain a species occurs, the smaller are its numbers within a given area and the less are the chances of its regionally limited wild population having a sufficient number of abnormally resistant members to act as ancestors of selectively resistant populations. Of course, all species do not have equal numbers of resistant individuals among their wild populations, as evidenced by the success of some species and failure of others to develop resistance. Nevertheless, when considering a large number of species, those with more individuals to select from will tend to be more successful at surviving in habitats contaminated with pesticides.

A second factor to consider is the reproduction rate of the species. If a pest produces more offspring than its natural enemies, which is usually the case in stable biotic communities, a few resistant survivors of a pesticide application will be able to produce an enormous population of pests before the natural enemy has been able to appear again in sufficient numbers to act as a control.

The decisive factor, however, is probably the alteration of the natural trophic relationships. If a pest and a predator, both arthropods, are equally sensitive to an insecticide and have an equal percentage of resistant individuals among their populations, a liberal application of the insecticide will leave only those few of both species with the natural resistance. The pest will find its food supply intact, since insecticides harm neither the cultivated plants on which agricultural pests feed nor the detritus and saprophyte aggregation on which many aquatic Diptera larvae subsist. The predators, however, lose the great majority of their natural prey when the sensitive pests and nontarget insects are killed, and they must either migrate to untreated regions or starve. The few surviving pests can then begin to reproduce and generate fully resistant populations without interference from natural enemies or competitors. This process is interrupted by the immigration of more sensitive pests, which interbreed with the resistant individuals and produce partially sensitive populations. If the insecticide is used frequently, however, the sensitive individuals, as well as predators from unsprayed habitats, are killed off, and the process of selection and resistance development is accelerated. Only after a large population of fully resistant pests is present can the predators begin to develop resistant populations.

5.5. The Displacement of One Pest by Another

As a rule, any substance of nutritional value to living organisms will be utilized rapidly if it does not have some effective form of protection. Large deposits of a single food item are particularly attractive for species capable of consuming it. The extensive monoculture systems are therefore especially susceptible for attack by species that specialize in consuming the particular plant or animal being cultivated. To control the species competing with the farmer for the crop, pesticides are used. Although they kill the target pest, they do nothing to make the crop less available to other would-be consumers. Thus, the farmer is confronted with the need to constantly be on guard to protect his or her monoculture from insects, mites, nematodes, fungi, bacteria, weeds, and other possible pests trying to detract from his or her harvest.

Obviously, the introduction of a pesticide greatly increases the distortion of the ecosystem caused by the monoculture. Not only is the pest killed but a considerable number of nontarget species are also eliminated. A consequence of this noted not too long after DDT came into use was the displacement of one pest by another species that had never caused any notable trouble before. Collyer (1953) reported that the unobtrusive red spider mite, *Panonychus ulmi* (Koch), developed enormous populations in orchards that had been sprayed with DDT. She attributed this population explosion to the elimination of the many arthropods, particularly predatory mites, that normally prey on the red spider mite. Similar outbreaks of this species and its relatives occurred around the world (Brown, 1978) from time to time, necessitating the use of acaricides in many fruit orchards to eliminate harmful, DDT-resistant mites (Sasse and Unterstenhöfer, 1970).

In places where the human population is dense, humans have become a potential food supply for various parasites and pathogens. Pesticides applied for the protection of human health have sometimes also led to the inadvertent promotion of serious pests. For example, the insecticides sprayed to control mosquitoes bearing malaria and yellow fever have frequently eliminated the target species, but the "vacuum" left is quickly filled by a related species that is resistant but was formerly not abundant in the habitat because of the presence of natural enemies that the insecticide is also effective against. It would be difficult to prove that such a clear-cut case of one mosquito displacing another actually resulted from pesticide use because the *status quo ante* of the mosquito populations is rarely known, and resistance has been developed by almost all important vector species for malaria (Brown et al., 1976) and yellow fever (Brown, 1977) against both DDT and dieldrin. Nevertheless, the use of insecticides has certainly resulted in changes in the relative importance of the different *Anopheles* and *Aedes* species as disease vectors in many lands. Giglioli (1963) reported an unusual case of one species, *Anopheles aquasalis,* suddenly starting to bite human beings instead of cattle in Guyana and spreading malaria in a region that had been free from the disease for years after another vector, *A. darlingi,* had been eliminated. Another unusual report concerned the retreat of *Anopheles maculipennis* from the lowlands to the mountains of Corsica, where it had not been a problem before, after its breeding places in the lowlands were treated with larvicides (Roubaud and Toumanoff, 1954).

Displacements of one pest by another do not necessarily have to involve related species or even competitors for a single niche. They are basically the results of disturbances to the ecological equilibrium of a biotic community. For example, Hollis (1972) reported that the application of nematocides to rice fields promoted weeds. It can also be postulated that water bodies liberally sprayed with insecticides will also support luxuriant growth of water plants. Indeed, the remarkable success achieved at controlling a species of *Salvinia* on a lake using curculionid beetles (Room et al., 1981) would scarcely have been possible had the lake been regularly sprayed with broad-spectrum insecticides. Chapin and Wasserstrom (1981) blamed the excessive use of pesticides in agriculture for the resurgence of malaria in Central America and India. Various *Anopheles* mosquito species developed resistance to the insecticides rapidly because of their frequent exposure to the sprays, so attempts by health authorities to control them in buildings with the same sprays invariably failed.

A pattern of pesticide proliferation is frequently evident as the use of one pesticide promotes a different kind of pest, creating the need for still another toxic chemical. Before long, an arsenal of diverse substances must be available for use each year (Heckman, 1981).

5.6. Thienemann's Principle

Observations by limnologists early in this century revealed that there are fundamental characteristics of biotic communities living under conditions of stress. One of these characteristics, outlined by Thienemann (1918), is the reduction of species diversity accompanied by significant increases in the populations of a few species. "Stress" has been rather loosely defined as a negative influence of adverse environmental conditions, such as extreme temperatures, periodic desiccation, or pollution. It is distinct from the term "stress" used in a physiological sense.

The theoretical explanation of this principle is easy to understand. As conditions in the habitat deviate increasingly from the ideal, fewer species are able to adapt to them. Because food supplies are not necessarily affected by the stress factor, surviving species are frequently promoted by enormous amounts of nutrients that were formerly consumed by a variety of competing species. Thus, those few populations that can cope with the stress are able to increase enormously.

There are certain species that specialize particularly well in invading habitats that are hostile to most other organisms. Among the insects, many members of the Diptera are noted for their abundance in highly polluted or otherwise adversely influenced water bodies. Unfortunately, many Diptera are serious pests, and some of these are among the most successful insects at surviving under hostile conditions. In fact, the larvae of many mosquito, midge, and fly species are so attractive to predators and easy to catch that they are almost never found in diverse biotic communities. On the other hand, massive numbers of mosquito larvae characteristically develop in temporary puddles and polluted pools of foul-smelling waste water. The rat-tail larvae of many eristaline syrphids develop in highly polluted stagnant water or liquid manure. They are so resistant to external conditions that they have survived and continued their development during the passage through the human digestive tract after being accidentally swallowed (Coe, 1953). Other Diptera families also include many species that pass their larval stages under various extreme conditions. Among others, the Limoniidae, Psychodidae,

Ptychopteridae, Anisopodidae, and Muscidae are generally tolerant of highly polluted muds and water bodies, while many members of the Chironomidae are typical of habitats exposed to temporary dryness or to periodic chemical treatments that kill off most of the biota (Heckman, 1983). Simuliid larvae inhabit flowing water, frequently under extreme environmental conditions, from the tundra to the tropics.

With such a great adaptability to extreme environmental conditions, it is not surprising that many members of the Diptera have been able to cope with the whole spectrum of modern pesticides. Under the principle outlined by Thienemann, therefore, the insect group most likely to benefit from the stress placed on a biotic community is this one. Thus, the use of a pesticide, after a period of adjustment, can be expected to promote the development of enormous populations of many fly and mosquito species rather than act to control them. Many examples of this phenomenon have been reported. Service (1977a), for example, reported that the application of larvicides to kill a species of *Anopheles* in Kenya resulted in an increase of its population within a month. During a recent study of orchard drainage ditches that had been thoroughly investigated for about five years during the 1950s (Garms, 1961), it was found that the number of species in seven insect orders inhabiting the water had decreased, most significantly, after about 25 years of exposure to a variety of pesticides. An increase from three to four collembolan species was noted because the fauna occurring in winter was intensively investigated (Heckman, 1982b). The only order to show a significant increase in species diversity was the Diptera (Heckman, 1981). When a parallel investigation was made of nearby ditches in a protected watershed district in which pesticides had been forbidden, an even richer insect fauna was found than had inhabited the orchards during the 1950s. A surprising finding, however, was that even more Diptera species were found in the unsprayed habitats (Caspers and Heckman, 1982). Because of the great difficulty experienced in identifying many Diptera taxa, it was assumed that the fauna list for this order compiled by Garms (1961), which included many elements identified only to genus or family, would have been considerably longer if the individual congeneric and confamilial species could have been included in the list. Nevertheless, 41 Diptera species were identified from the heavily pesticide contaminated orchard ditches from 1978 to 1980, compared to 39 species from all other insect orders (Caspers and Heckman, 1981). In contrast, the unsprayed ditches in the protected watershed district contained 119 Diptera species in 1980–81 and 132 species belonging to all other insect orders. Thus, there was a slight increase in the proportion of Diptera among the insect fauna of the less diverse biotic community in the habitats strongly influenced by pesticides. More significant than the number of species, however, was the abundance of the individuals. Many of the species in the orchard ditches were rare, indicating that they may have immigrated from unsprayed habitats. The great majority of abundant insect species in the orchards were members of the Diptera, and several species of Syrphidae and

Chironomidae were extremely numerous. Among the other orders, the Heteroptera seemed to be the most resistant to pesticides, and a variety of species were more abundant in the orchards than in unsprayed habitats nearby (Caspers and Heckman, 1982).

The comparisons of the similar habitats with and without direct pesticide fallout conform with Thienemann's principle. While the species diversity in the orchard ditches has significantly decreased since the 1950s, enormous populations of certain species can still survive. In contrast, unsprayed habitats contain significantly more species, and a clear dominance of the biotic community by a few was observed in none of the ditches.

It might be added that monoculture itself employs Thienemann's principle. The farmer attempts to stress and distort a natural habitat in a way that conditions become conducive to one species alone, namely, the particular plant or animal that is being cultured. Pesticides are one of the means employed to make the survival of unwanted organisms difficult. The problem with this form of agriculture, however, is that useful species are destroyed as well. The merits of monoculture and polyculture will be discussed briefly later (Section 7).

5.7. Concentration and Accumulation of Toxic Substances in the Food Chain

For many years it was generally believed that toxic substances could be fully eliminated by dilution in large volumes of water. Toxic wastes were routinely dumped into large rivers and lakes in the belief that their concentrations would rapidly drop below harmful, and even detectable, levels. The dilution capacity of the oceans was thought to be limitless.

The belief that the surface waters of the earth are limitless waste receptacles had to be abandoned when the phenomenon called "bioconcentration" or "biomagnification" was discovered. There is a large body of literature on the concentration and accumulation of heavy metals by aquatic organisms, but the discussion here is confined to pesticides. One of the best documented cases, which came to the attention of scientists during the 1950s and was later extensively described by Rudd (1964), is the poisoning of the fish-eating grebes in Clear Lake, California. Relatively low concentrations of DDT in the lake plankton were concentrated in organisms that consumed it. The animals on the next level of the food chain concentrated it even more, and this "magnification" of the DDT content on each trophic level eventually resulted in the species at the top having 80,000 times more of the insecticide in their fatty tissues than was found in the lake water. As might be expected, this killed the grebes. It is not at all surprising that DDT behaved this way; it is known to be quite soluble in fats and oils.

The bioconcentration of chlorinated hydrocarbon pesticides was thoroughly reviewed by Kenaga (1972). This phenomenon also has some ecological aspects that deserve mention.

First of all, many nontarget organisms relatively high on the food chain continually consume considerable amounts of pesticides with their food. Moore (1967) mentioned some of the sublethal effects that these residues can have, and it is evident that pesticides can threaten the survival of a species by reducing its rate of reproduction or increasing the mortality of its young, even when adult individuals show no apparent ill effects. It is doubtful that any sublethal effects manifest themselves over a long term. A species must either develop resistance to the concentrated residues in its food or be exterminated from the habitats where the residues occur. A particular insecticide may be acutely toxic to mosquitoes initially but not harm birds at the concentrations applied, but after years of use, highly resistant mosquitoes would still be abundant and the birds would have been fully eliminated by biomagnified concentrations of the insecticides in their foods. This is exactly the situation frequently reported in regions of intensive DDT use. After almost 40 years of use against mosquitoes throughout the world, DDT has made very few mosquito species less abundant for more than a few years, and many resistant populations are apparently larger now than ever before. Several species of fish-eating raptors, on the other hand, are facing extinction due to the sublethal eggshell thinning effects of DDE received in high concentrations through the food chains (Hickey, 1969). The ban on DDT in many countries gave cause for optimism among conservationists, but the problem is by no means solved. DDT and its breakdown products, DDD and DDE, were still found in significant amounts in various invertebrates from the waters of northern Germany more than 10 years after they were banned (Caspers and Heckman, 1981, 1982), and a Cooper's hawk died of DDT poisoning in the United States in 1980, almost a decade after the insecticide was prohibited (Prouty et al., 1982). Although the authors conjectured that the bird might have been poisoned in Mexico, its death could just as easily have been due to the bioconcentrated persistent residues in its food chain.

An interesting phenomenon that bears further investigation is the acquired toxicity of species that accumulate high concentrations of a pesticide from the environment. Rosato and Ferguson (1968) reported that the mosquitofish, *Gambusia affinis,* had not only developed a very high resistance to endrin, it was also able to accumulate enough of the chemical to poison largemouth bass or water snakes that preyed on it. The selective advantage of poisonous species is well recognized, and it should be determined whether certain pesticide-resistant insect pests can store up enough of a pesticide to kill their nonresistant natural enemies.

A somewhat similar phenomenon is the accumulation of heavy metals by eels inhabiting the Elbe River in Germany. The fish populations in the Elbe have suffered general declines for several decades due to pollution and overfishing (Riedel-Lorjé and Gaumert, 1982). The eels seem to have adapted to heavy metal pollution and usually contain concentrations of mercury in their flesh above the legal limit. Their ban from the market has released them from the fishing pressure that formerly decimated their numbers. Thus, the bioconcentration of a toxic pollutant has freed them from heavy predation by their greatest natural enemy—humans.

There is a danger even to human beings from concentrated and biomagnified pesticides in fish or wild game. When animal species at the end of long food chains are included in our diet, we expose ourselves to the same risk of consuming considerable amounts of pesticides as raptors and other large vertebrate predators face. Whether these substances do any harm is still hotly debated. From all available evidence, DDT and a good many other commonly used pesticides present no serious danger whatever to human beings (Kilgore and Li, 1973; Mellanby, 1977); although endrin and dieldrin are considerably more toxic, there is little positive indication that their residues cause mortalities (Davies, 1973). The prolonged exposure of a great many people to these chemicals and some suggestion of possible carcinogenic properties have given cause for concern (Brown, 1978). The ban on these chemicals in many countries has by no means eliminated them from the environment, and residues will continue to be a cause for concern for years to come.

5.8.   The Selective Elimination of Species

It is obvious after several decades of use that modern pesticides do not eliminate all species from a habitat. It is now also apparent that the species eliminated are not usually the ones the treatment was meant to kill. The foregoing information provides some of the reasons for this situation.

Holling (1973) provided a theoretical discussion on resilience and stability in natural ecosystems. He concluded that populations of species displaying a high degree of stability are those most vulnerable to extinction as a result of an environmental disturbance. Highly unstable populations, on the other hand, are much more resilient and will again become abundant after periods of great scarcity. As an example of an unstable but resilient population, he chose the spruce budworm, which has been the target of massive spray campaigns since about 1944 involving first DDT, then fenitrothion, trichlorfon, dimethoate, and phosphamidon (McEwen and Stephenson, 1979). The results of the program have been disappointing, and considerable damage has been done to the biota of the forest streams (Hobart, 1977). Way and Bevan (1977) suggested that a new strategy in harvesting the trees might solve the problem where pesticides have failed, but it is no longer believed that this insect can be eliminated chemically.

The spruce budworm exhibits a "boom or bust" type of population dynamics typical of many animal pests, weeds, and pathogenic fungi. For a long period of time, a species remains rare and scarcely noticed. Then, taking advantage of particularly favorable conditions, it suddenly appears in great abundance and causes damage to some economically important population. After decimating its food supply or provoking a population explosion of a natural enemy, the undesirable species suddenly reverts to being an inconspicuous element of the flora or fauna. Pesticide applications that kill some of the large pest population simply delay the process, and the unwanted species remains abundant longer.

Many natural populations exhibit a great deal of stability. The species of undisturbed biotic communities are often maintained at nearly constant densities by a restricted availability of food and predation. The predator populations are maintained within limits by the same factors. Population fluctuations are limited within rather narrow ranges and generally follow a cyclical pattern. Such populations can adapt to outside disturbances through adjustments in their reproduction and juvenile mortality rates as long as the disturbance is not too great. If it is, according to Holling (1973), such species face extinction, or at least local extermination.

In predicting which species a pesticide is likely to eliminate, the following general guidelines can be used. Normally, the taxa against which a particular chemical is most toxic will include the greatest number of species eliminated after that chemical is applied over a long term. For example, orchard drainage ditches receiving large amounts of insecticide and acaricide sprays contained no water mites and a greatly reduced species diversity of insects. Other species had also been eliminated, but they generally represented only a small proportion of their phyla (Heckman, 1981).

Some taxa seem to be better able to develop resistance to pesticides than others. Many Diptera families, for example, seem to rapidly adjust to a wide spectrum of pesticides, whereas the Trichoptera and Neuroptera are eliminated relatively easily (Caspers and Heckman, 1982).

Finally, species high on the food chain with rather low rates of reproduction are eliminated much more readily than most pests, which usually reproduce rapidly and consume food items containing relatively low concentrations of pesticides, such as a food crop or detritus.

6. PRACTICAL ASPECTS OF PESTICIDE USE

From the foregoing discussion, it might seem that the dangers and disadvantages of pesticides are so great, that their use should be abandoned immediately, and there are people who recommend this. From a consideration of the present ecological situation and the population dynamics of a great many species affected, however, it is clear that the use of pesticides will be indispensable for years to come. The ecological impact of pesticides has obviously been enormous, and many of the delicate biological equilibria among pests, pathogens, and natural enemies that existed 40 years ago no longer function today because a great many species have been locally eliminated. Even the industrial lands that now have enormous food surpluses today could not afford to lose the major part of the harvests for several years while waiting for natural ecological balances to reestablish themselves. Some predator–prey equilibria reestablish themselves within a year after pesticide use is replaced by biological control (MacPhee and MacLellan, 1971), but in other cases, abnormally large pest populations remain to damage crops for several years (Hoyt and Caltagirone, 1971). Furthermore, there are many pests that have always been able to inflict considerable damage on crops, even in the presence of their natural enemies (Wilson and Huffaker, 1976), and the use of pesticides required to control these in the near future (Newsom et al., 1976) reduces the effectiveness of the biological control in many cases (Messenger et al., 1976).

It might well be that DDT and its successors would have served mankind better if reserved exclusively for the treatment of buildings and clothing, keeping the fields, forests, and surface waters free from contamination. It can scarcely be doubted that agronomists and public health officials would have found sounder, if less spectacular, methods of dealing with pests and pathogens. Dismounting from the pesticide tiger is proving much more difficult than climbing on.

First of all, there are many pests that have failed to develop resistance to certain pesticides (Oppenoorth, 1976). Their sudden release from pesticide control would result in rapid increases of their populations. Other harmful species that are partially suppressed by the pesticides would also multiply rapidly. Some time would be required for the natural enemies to return to the habitats and begin to bring the pests under control, and a number of large arthropod predators have been eliminated from much of their former ranges and would probably not return for many years (Caspers and Heckman, 1982). Dragonflies and large predatory beetles, for example, formerly took a great toll of mosquito larvae, and the gap left by their elimination has been closed by a series of larvicides, to which the mosquitoes have successively developed resistance. Metcalf (1976) blamed the increase in the annual malaria infection rate on Sri Lanka from 17 to over a million within a decade on the "premature termination of DDT spraying . . . in 1963." Although it is the consensus of opinion among a great many scientists familiar with the problem that the resurgence of malaria was inevitable as long as the efforts to control the disease centered around mosquito control with pesticides to which the insects had developed resistance (Perry, 1974; Springett, 1975; Service, 1977b; Learmonth, 1977; McEwen and Stephenson, 1979), the termination of the insecticide applications probably allowed the increase in the mosquito population to occur suddenly rather than gradually.

It seems likely that the abandonment of routine pesticide applications will be brought about by economic rather than environmental concerns. The newer pesticides cost more and do not bring the spectacular returns that DDT once did. The damage to the environment caused by the nonpersistent organophosphorus insecticides and various fungicides that do not contain heavy metals is relatively minor, but Moore (1977) stressed the problems to be faced as the target organisms develop resistance; cross-resistance is likely due to the chemical similarity of many of the organophosphorus compounds. Moreover, some of the organophosphorus insecticides, particularly parathion, are very toxic, and many human deaths have resulted from their use (Mellanby, 1977).

Biological control methods are being sought today, and there have been many successful cases of combatting pests using their natural enemies (De-Bach, 1974). There are also a few cases of large-scale success employing pathogens (Falcon, 1971), sterilized males (Waterhouse et al., 1976), and pheromone traps (Roelofs, 1976). A particularly promising method of pest control in agriculture is the cultivation of resistant crops (Beck and Maxwell, 1976). Although the progress being made is impressive, there are still many problems to be solved before pesticide-free agriculture is possible. In the meantime, many authors have recommended that "integrated pest control methods" be employed to gain the greatest benefit from both biological and chemical agents. Unfortunately, every author seems to have his or her own definition of "integrated." To some it simply means using a greater variety of pesticides, while to others, biological methods take priority, and chemicals are reserved only for emergencies.

For everyone's good, except perhaps a few special interest groups, pesticide use should be abandoned as quickly as practical. Admittedly, this goal cannot be reached in the next few years, but much more emphasis should be placed on research to develop pesticide-free agriculture. The greatest limitation on the implementation of biological control methods is the lack of enough knowledgeable experts to directly supervise the operations on a day-to-day basis. First, the essential feature of biological and integrated methods is a continual monitoring of the pest and pathogen populations to detect increases that might pose economic danger. A spraying schedule for pesticides, on the other hand, may be made years in advance. Second, biological control experts must be familiar with a variety of species that threaten a crop, and they usually have to know a good deal about the natural enemies of the various pests. Pesticide users require only a general knowledge of plant or animal species that they are trying to eradicate, and seldom pay any attention to other organisms that are killed. Third, the field of biological control is one of constant change, and a great many experimental methods must still be tested in the field. This requires experts to read and digest a tremendous amount of literature to remain abreast of the latest developments. Pesticide users can rely on salesmen and advertisements to provide them with information on the latest products available. Finally, highly trained and educated experts must have enough clients to pay the costs of their consultation services or to justify their employment by the local government. Some farmers might find the services of a spray machine operator more economical, at least until the biological expert can guarantee results.

It is not sufficient to deal in generalities when planning pest control programs. Each species of pest has its own peculiarities and must be dealt with individually. Resourcefulness and flexibility are required to develop sound tactics. One of the great deficiencies in the planning of the early pesticide application programs was the lack of adaptability to changing conditions and different situations. One recipe was used for all dishes. A liberal application of DDT was thought to solve all problems.

A lack of enough qualified personnel can also have serious economic consequences for biological control programs. This is best illustrated by the California "medfly" debacle. Because insufficient checks on the insects were made, a large number of supposedly sterile flies that were released turned out to be fertile, and a small outbreak turned into a major plague for the fruit growers (Dickson, 1981). After much debate between the federal and state governments over who was to blame, the government in Washington forced the state to allow massive aerial applications of poisonous baits designed to minimize the damage to the fruit crop. In spite of fears that great environmental damage would result, the state was blanketed with the insecticidal paste. At last reports, however, the medflies were still moving northward, destroying much of the fruit crop in the state.

In the search for natural enemies and pathogens, many species are being transported from one part of the world to another in the hopes that they will attack a particular weed or animal pest (Zwölfer et al., 1976). This is also a dangerous activity, as past experiences have proven. Most imported species fail to establish themselves, while others multiply rapidly, often with unexpected consequences. There are more than enough examples that come to mind: the rabbits in Australia, mongooses in the West Indies, the tent caterpillar of the gypsy moth in the United States, and the water hyacinth, *Eichhornia crassipes,* that has become a troublesome weed throughout much of the world. Unintentional introductions of species have also caused countless problems.

It is hoped that integrated pest control programs will minimize pesticide use in the immediate future. There are also other ways in which the unnecessary contamination of the environment can be minimized. As much as 20% of the pesticides used during the early 1970s were applied in private homes and gardens (McEwen and Stephenson, 1979). Those chemicals that do not rapidly decompose eventually find their way into the sewers and storm drains and finally contaminate the surface waters into which the wastewater or sewage sludge is emptied. Even chemicals that do rapidly decompose may be dangerous contaminants of the receiving waters. Fungicides containing mercury can contribute significantly to the heavy-metal contamination of a water body (Fukunaga et al., 1972), and the herbicides that are inactivated on contact with soil can remain adsorbed to particles for many months, and have harmful effects on various aquatic animals (Brown, 1978). In the long run, the liberal use of garden pesticides certainly favors the populations of prolific pests, such as aphids, which are released from their normal biological controls, and the amount of labor that these chemicals save each gardener is minimal. It would certainly be wise to consider restricting the use of such pesticides and permitting the sale only of such substances that rapidly decompose to simple, nontoxic chemicals.

A particular problem is the use of pesticides in the developing countries (Weir and Schapiro, 1981). The lack of legislation, as well as the complete absence of institutes capable of making independent evaluations of pesticide effects, has opened the way for the same indiscriminate use of DDT and other persistent substances in much of Asia, Africa, and South America that was typical for Europe and North America during the 1950s. Obviously, one country does not learn from the other's mistakes. Some of the consequences are already apparent. Adkisson (1971) reported the economic collapse of the cotton-growing industry in northeastern Mexico when the natural enemies of the tobacco budworm were eliminated by heavy insecticide applications, and this insect, which prefers to consume other crops, ravaged the cotton monoculture. The budworm is highly resistant to all insecticides and is therefore impossible to control.

Enormous amounts of pesticides are now being exported from the industrial lands to the developing countries, and aside from the economic consequences, there is an aspect of this situation that I find particularly regrettable. Having done research on the freshwater flora and fauna in Southeast Asia (Heckman, 1974, 1979), I know of the enormous gaps in the scientific knowledge of a great many taxa. In many tropical lands, including Laos and Thailand, extensive collection and study by specialists invariably lead to the discovery of a large number of previously undescribed species. It seems particularly sad that enormous amounts of pesticides are being dumped into the surface waters of such countries, probably wiping out scores of isolated populations of rare species that are the relics of otherwise extinct taxa. The argument that such a sacrifice is necessary to save human life is no longer convincing since it is now clear that attempts to control disease through the elimination of intermediate hosts are at best temporarily or locally successful, and that the resources would be better employed finding a more promising way of preventing or treating the disease. Moreover, the amount of pesticides employed in the tropics for public health projects is only a small proportion of the total. Most is used in attempts to introduce monoculture.

It would be a good general rule not to introduce pesticides into habitats that have not yet been exposed to them. No one could reasonably object to treating the walls of houses with DDT, but once the dumping of larvicides into natural water bodies begins, the project has simply begun to produce resistant mosquito populations. Shortly before the termination of DDT use in the United States, I visited a salt marsh in southern New Jersey. The region had always been known for its mosquitoes, and I was met by great swarms of them. The fact that the swamps had been heavily treated with DDT and other insecticides for about 20 years had made no inroads against the mosquito populations at all, but it had certainly cost the taxpayers a great deal of money. The severe effects of the treatments on the other salt marsh fauna had been reported by Springer and Webster as early as 1951.

7. ADVANTAGES OF NOT USING PESTICIDES

The advantages and disadvantages of using pesticides are well known and still hotly discussed, but as mentioned earlier, they cannot be dispensed with in the lands that have come to depend on them until a suitable substitute is found. There are some definite benefits in not using pesticides, and these deserve some mention. Some of these can be seen in regions where pesticides have not yet been introduced. They are distinct from the financial gains made by the so-called "organic" farmers, who, in Germany and other industrial countries, sell their crops for prices far above the market averages because they were grown without artificial fertilizers or pesticides. The fact that their harvests are nearly as good as their neighbors' who spray their crops can be explained by the suppression of the regional pest populations by their "inorganic" neighbors. The real advantages of pesticide-free agriculture on a regional basis, particularly as they concern aquatic habitats, can be grouped under two general topics: polyculture and conservation.

7.1. Polyculture

Day (1978) acknowledged the criticisms that are often made of monoculture, but he regards this system of agriculture as good because it provides high yields for low cost. This indicates a major problem of communication among agronomists and ecologists. Essentially, both the critics of monoculture and Day are correct, depending upon the context. For an industrial land with a highly mechanized agriculture, such as the United States, monoculture offers the best returns. Modern industrial farmers are concerned chiefly with finding buyers for their crops and holding labor costs down. They usually have large tracts of land at their disposal and are not forced to put fields to more than one use. In parts of the world where dense populations must be nourished and the available land for agriculture is limited, a maximum efficiency in land use is imperative, and polyculture is preferable to monoculture. Thus, where land is available in surplus and human labor is limited, monoculture is superior, while polyculture is the better system where land is limited and labor plentiful.

Some countries prefer to set large tracts of land aside for wildlife refuges, parks, and recreation areas. This voluntary limitation on the land available for agriculture can also make it desirable to develop polyculture systems. Another incentive for polyculture is the saving on feed or fertilizer costs when the waste product from one culture can be used as nutrients for another.

As a general rule, species diversity increases from the poles toward the equator. Consequently, the potential number of species available for culture is usually greater in the tropics than in temperate regions. Some tropical countries have already developed elaborate polyculture systems, but because many of the species cultured are used exclusively by the farmers or sold on the local markets, statistics on the production are unavailable. At least 19 different species, from green vegetables to ducks, were raised or caught in a rice field near Udorn Thani, Thailand, and used as food by the local farmers (Heckman, 1979). Furthermore, the rice stubble itself was a dry season food supply for cattle and water buffaloes.

Pesticides significantly reduce species diversity as well as the diversity of potential food items that can be cultivated in a particular habitat. A model comparison showed that the applications of various pesticides to the rice fields would significantly reduce the production of other edible species (Heckman, 1982c). Some of the fish and invertebrates eliminated are more important food sources for the farmers than the rice because they supply the protein that would otherwise be lacking in their diets. Insecticide sprays used in West Malaysia actually did eliminate many of the fish from the rice fields (Yunus and Lim, 1971), so the present form of pesticide-free rice polyculture practiced in much of Thailand can be considered as satisfactory for the local needs.

Not only do pesticides limit polyculture by directly or indirectly harming the animals cultured, they also contaminate aquatic species to the extent that they are no longer safe for human consumption. Fortunately, Thai surface waters seem to contain relatively low levels of chlorinated hydrocarbon residues (Huschenbeth and Harms, 1975), but in countries where pesticide use is more widespread, it is unlikely that symptoms of pesticide intoxication from contaminated fish or vegetables would be correctly diagnosed. The detection of high pesticide levels would automatically force the removal of the food items from the market in many countries, but in the developing nations, the means of detection are simply unavailable, and large doses of dieldrin, endrin, parathion, or other substances relatively toxic to man, may be inadvertently administered to the family of a fisherman who sets his nets in a ditch beside a newly sprayed field of crops. Even in Japan, it was only with difficulty that the cause of the Minamata disease could be identified as methylmercury residues in fish (Skerfving, 1972), and the source of much mercury contamination in Japan was the organomercury fungicides used on rice fields (Ukita, 1972). In simple terms, pesticides make polyculture products dangerous.

There are a wide variety of possible polyculture combinations possible when the use of pesticides can be avoided. A few of those that have been investigated are rice and various fish, rice and shrimp, ducks together with rice and fish, and fish with hydroponically grown vegetables. A great variety of polyculture combinations are practiced in East Asia, and the minor losses from one crop that could be avoided with pesticides are more than compensated for by the secondary crops.

In some parts of the world, notably South America, much uncultivated land is available. Labor is also relatively cheap. There is a trend in some of these underpopulated countries to develop large monoculture enterprises. In many cases, the deforestation, as well as the massive applications of pesticides, will make radical changes in the ecological equilibria that can only have disastrous results. At tropical temperatures, many insects have remarkably short periods of development, and resistant populations can appear much more rapidly than in temperate zones. Thus, the agricultural concerns that clear the land are able to make large profits for the first few years, benefitting from the effectiveness of the pesticides against previously unexposed pests. After a few years, however, they leave behind a fully useless tract of land and large pest populations. The effect of such monoculture enterprises on the soil of former rainforests, which is beyond the scope of this discussion, is an additional ground for classifying these activities as "slash and burn" farming. An example was provided by van den Bosch et al. (1976), who described how one valley in Peru after another was used for growing cotton, then abandoned, as the heavy applications of pesticides paved the way for the invasion of resistant pests.

The situation is different in other parts of the world and with different crops, but certain pests will always benefit when natural communities are replaced by populations of single species (Gibson and Jones, 1977). Some pests, however, are not well adapted to take advantage of monocultures, stressing the need for careful investigation of each species (Emden and Williams, 1974; Way, 1977). McVicar and MacKenzie (1977) reported that cultured fish suffered from a lower incidence of diseases than wild ones, indicating that the care given to the cultured species can offset some disadvantages of its concentration at one location. Once a disease or parasite appears, however, it can spread rapidly through the entire crowded population.

Since many projects in developing lands are financed by industrial nations, agricultural experts accustomed to monoculture systems are often sent to give advice on how agriculture should be developed in tropical countries. Failure to understand that great differences exist between the ecology and economy of the developed and the developing nation, and a complete faith in the superiority of monoculture in all situations, can result in the formulation of programs poorly suited to the local needs. Export crops are often given priority over items that the natives require for subsistence. A similar problem is encountered when programs to eliminate disease vectors eradicate instead the fish in rivers and lakes, that provide the most reliable protein supplies (Heckman, 1979, 1982a,c).

7.2. Conservation

Conserving resources is difficult in the face of an ever-expanding demand for the available materials on and in the earth's crust. One of the most vital substances is water in a pure enough state to support terrestrial and freshwater life. The elimination of pesticides would by no means guarantee the purity of surface waters. There are many other contaminants that make water unsafe for humans and animals. Nevertheless, in many places, pesticides are or have been the most serious sources of pollution. In addition to the many examples given above, various wells used to supply irrigation and drinking water were found to be highly contaminated by different pesticides (Brown, 1978). The irrigation water from some wells in Colorado contained enough 2,4-D to damage the crops (Nicholson, 1969).

Biological resources also require conservation, and a great deal of criticism from environmentalists is directed at the extremely negative effects pesticides are having on wildlife. The concern of conservationists and environmentalists about the impoverishment of the flora and fauna represents one view of the problem. Another facet, primarily the concern of ecologists, is how the elimination of many different species will affect the ecosystem that serves as the life support system for humans. While large vertebrates attract the most attention from conservation groups, the ecologist must also determine the role of each tiny alga and microscopic invertebrate and calculate the impact of its elimination on the entire community. Even unobtrusive aquatic fungi play a vital role in breaking down the organic polymers, such as lignin and chitin, that can only be attacked very slowly by most saprophytic bacteria. The elimination of these fungi by fungicide residues can greatly delay the recycling of the inorganic nutrients incorporated in detritus.

From the viewpoint of most conservationists, every species is an irreplaceable resource. While the mortality of individuals can be compensated for by normal reproduction, a species cannot be replaced at all once it is extinct. Some people therefore object to the loss of these biotic resources on aesthetic grounds, while others regret the loss of potential subjects of scientific study. Corbet (1958) suggested that perhaps a few undescribed species would have to be sacrificed to permit the black fly vectors of river blindness (onchocerciasis) to be eliminated from the Nile. This argument was tacitly accepted by conservationists for many years, but as it became apparent that no permanent victories over tropical diseases were being won by such methods, the acceptability of this sacrifice became a topic of debate.

For ecologists, the main item of concern is not the aesthetic or scientific value of individual species but rather the total effect on the ecosystem of a change in the structure of biotic communities. They must be able to recognize situations in which a few years of remarkable food production or disease control will be followed by the degeneration of a habitat to a state of complete uselessness. They should be able to recognize conditions under which the wrong kind of agricultural methods are likely to produce an Oklahoma dust bowl, a rapid expansion of the Sahara Desert, or a "dead sea" in Lower New York Bay.

There is a great lack of understanding among the general public of the basic relationships within biotic communities. Some farmers are glad to kill any insects for which they see no use, but they are careful not to contaminate their waters with any insecticides that are harmful to fish. It is banal to say that fish have to eat, but the importance of mayflies, caddisflies, midges, and even mosquitoes as fish food very often goes unrecognized. The size and number of fish that can inhabit a water body is not determined by how many fish fry are purchased in the fish hatchery, but rather by the physical and chemical characteristics of the habitat and by the number of insects and other small invertebrates that are available as food. For an ecologist, the toxicity of a pesticide to fish is no more important than its toxicity to the animals or plants that the fish consumes.

The use of piscicides is questionable in most cases ecologically. Killing off cyprinids that are adapted to mesotrophic or eutrophic waters with relatively high summer temperatures and low oxygen concentrations does not make the ponds more suitable for the salmonid game fish, most of which prefer oligotrophic waters with their characteristically high oxygen concentrations (Schindler, 1975). In many cases, however, the stocked fish are removed so rapidly by anglers that the establishment of populations in the ponds or lakes is scarcely possible anyway. Like some other pesticide uses, fish poisoning seems to be a standard procedure done in imitation of others rather than to satisfy a real economic need.

The greatest problem confronted by ecologists investigating the effects of pesticides on various microorganisms and nontarget invertebrates is finding data for comparison. The ranges and relative abundances of many taxa are very poorly known, even in western Europe and North America, where studies have been conducted for over 200 years. The list of endangered species in the Federal Republic of Germany, for example, includes information on very few insect orders and other invertebrate phyla (Blab et al., 1978), and although it is obvious to many naturalists who have been regularly collecting and observing these animals for years that some formerly abundant species are becoming very rare, it is difficult to quantify this with figures on former and present populations.

It would certainly be beneficial from a conservationist's viewpoint if the use of pesticides could be discontinued. As long as they are necessary, however, it would be well to consider establishing pesticide-free zones, the value of which as wildlife preserves for endangered invertebrates was discussed by Caspers and Heckman (1982). They should be large enough to allow the normal migratory activities of the flying species, and should be upstream from any areas subject to pesticide treatment. Of course, they should be free from cultivated plant species to prevent their acting as reservoirs of the pests, as well.

8. CONCLUSIONS

The widespread use of a great many toxic chemicals to eliminate unwanted plant or animal species has resulted in the contamination of most aquatic habitats with these substances on a regular basis. The biotic communities inhabiting such waters are initially disrupted, but an equilibrium is gradually reestablished. Generally, the pesticide-adapted community has a reduced species diversity and increased numbers of certain species that benefit from the lack of competitors or natural enemies. Taxa most likely to be eliminated are those to which the pesticides are most toxic, but many initially suscepti- ble species may become highly resistant and remain. Other species to which the pesticides were not acutely toxic at the concentrations applied may be eliminated due to sublethal effects, particularly on their reproductive capac- ity, and by especially large doses in their prey after a bioconcentration of the residues along the food chain. Some of the predators may become scarce due to the elimination of their main food species. Usually, species high on the food chain with relatively low rates of reproduction are the most likely to be eliminated.

After a restabilization of the ecological equilibrium, the pesticide applica- tions have relatively little effect. Therefore, when agricultural pests, weeds, pathogens, or vectors of diseases have established themselves in the resis- tant community, further attempts to eradicate them will have little effect. Introductions of new pesticides seem to have only temporary effect, and many undesirable species have been among those to show a long-term popu- lation increase as a result of pesticide use.

The protection of aquatic resources requires the quantities of pesticides used to be held to the minimum possible. The replacement of chemical with biological methods of pest control is recommended as soon as practical and effective biological controls are developed.

REFERENCES

Addison, R. F. and Brodie, P. F. (1973). Occurrence of DDT residues in beluga whales from the Mackenzie Delta. *J. Fish. Res. Board Can.* **30**, 1733–1736.

Adkisson, P. L. (1971). Objective uses of insecticides in agriculture. In: J. E. Swift, Ed., *Agricultural chemicals—harmony or discord for food, people and environment*. Univer- sity of California Division of Agricultural Science, Berkeley, pp. 43–51.

Ames, P. L. (1966). DDT residues in the eggs of the osprey in the northeastern United States and their relation to nesting success. *J. Appl. Ecol.* **3** (Suppl.), 87–97.

Beck, S. D. and Maxwell, F. G. (1976). Use of plant resistance. In: C. B. Huffaker and P. S. Messenger, Eds., *Theory and practice of biological control*. Academic Press, New York, pp. 615–636.

Beger, H. (1966). *Leitfaden der Trink- und Brauchwasserbiologie*. 2nd ed. Gustav Fischer Verlag, Stuttgart.

Bidleman, T. F. and Olney, C. E. (1974). Chlorinated hydrocarbons in the Sargasso atmosphere and surface water. *Science* **183**, 516–518.

Blab, J., Nowak, E., Trautmann, W., and Sukopp, H. (1978). *Rote Liste der gefährdeten Tiere und Pflanzen in der Bundesrepublik Deutschland*. IUCN, Morges, Switzerland.

Boyce, A. M. (1976). Historical aspects of insecticide development. In: R. L. Metcalf and J. J. McKelvey, Jr., Eds., *The future for insecticides: needs and prospects*, R. L. Metcalf and

J. J. McKelvey, Jr., Eds. Vol. 6, *Advances in Environmental Science and Technology,* John Wiley & Sons, New York, pp. 469–488.

Brewerton, H. V. (1969). DDT in fats of Antarctic animals. *New Zealand J. Sci.* **12,** 194–199.

Brown, A. W. A. (1977). Yellow fever, dengue and dengue haemorrhagic fever. In: G. M. Howe, Ed., *A world geography of human diseases.* Academic Press, London, pp. 271–318.

Brown, A. W. A. (1978). *Ecology of pesticides.* John Wiley & Sons, New York.

Brown, A. W. A., Haworth, J., and Zahar, A. R. (1976). Malaria eradication and control from a global standpoint. *J. Med. Ent.* **13,** 1–25.

Burmakin, E. V. (1968). Chemical methods of lake rehabilitation and preparation of new fish fauna in lakes. 1st and 2nd group fellowship study tours on inland fisheries research, management and fish culture in the Union of Soviet Socialist Republics, 1965–66. *FAO Rome* No. TA 2547, 109–123.

Butler, P. A. (1968). Pesticides in the estuary. In: *Proceedings of the Marsh and Estuary Management Symposium, Baton Rouge,* July 19–20, 1967. Louisiana State University, Baton Rouge, pp. 120–124.

Carson, R. (1962). *Silent spring.* Houghton-Mifflin, Boston.

Caspers, H. and Heckman, C. W. (1981). Ecology of orchard drainage ditches along the freshwater section of the Elbe Estuary. *Arch. Hydrobiol.* Suppl. 43 (Untersuch. Elbe-Aestuar 4), 347–486.

Caspers, H. and Heckman, C. W. (1982). The biota of a small standing water ecosystem in the Elbe flood plain. *Arch. Hydrobiol.* Suppl. 61 (Untersuch. Elbe-Aestuar 5), 227–316.

Chapin, G. and Wasserstrom, R. (1981). Agricultural production and malaria resurgence in Central America and India. *Nature (London)* **293,** 181–185.

Coe, R. L. (1953). Diptera. Syrphidae. *Handbooks for the identification of British insects,* 10, Part 1. Royal Entomological Society, London.

Collyer, E. (1953). Biology of some predatory insects and mites associated with the fruit tree red spider mite (*Metatetranychus ulmi* (Koch)) in South-Eastern England. IV. The predator-mite relationship. *J. Hortic. Sci.* **28,** 246–259.

Corbet, P. S. (1958). Some effects of DDT on the fauna of the Victoria Nile. *Rev. Zool. Bot. Afr.* **57,** 73–95.

Corbett, J. R. (1974). *The biochemical mode of action of pesticides.* Academic Press, London.

Cottam, L. (1965). The ecologists' role in problems of pesticide pollution. *Bioscience* **15,** 457–463.

Courtney, K. D., Gaylor, D. W., Hogan, M. D., Falk, H. L., Bates, R. R., and Mitchell, I. (1970). Teratogenic evaluation of 2,4,5-T. *Science* **168,** 864–866.

Davies, J. E. (1973). Pesticide residues in man. C. A. Edwards, Ed., *Environmental pollution by pesticides.* Plenum Press, London, pp. 313–333.

Davies, J. E., Poznanski, S. A., Smith, R. F., and Freed, V. H. (1975). International dynamics of pesticide poisoning. In: R. Haque and V. H. Freed, Eds., *Environmental dynamics of pesticides.* Plenum Press, New York, pp. 275–287.

Day, B. E. (1978). The status and future of chemical weed control. In: E. H. Smith and D. Pimentel, Eds., *Pest control strategies.* Academic Press, New York, pp. 203–213.

DeBach, P. (1974). *Biological control by natural enemies.* Cambridge University Press, London.

Decker, G. C. (1974). Costs and benefits of pesticides: an overview. In: M. A. Q. Khan and J. P. Bederka, Jr., Eds., *Survival in toxic environments.* Academic Press, New York, pp. 447–471.

Dickson, D. (1981). California's medflies: who to blame? *Nature (London)* **293,** 178–179.

394   Charles W. Heckman

Dunlap, T. R. (1981). *DDT: Scientists, citizens and public policy*. Princeton University Press, Princeton, New Jersey.

Eisler, R. (1969). Acute toxicities of insecticides to marine decapod crustaceans. *Crustaceana* **16**, 302–310.

Emden, H. F. van and Williams, G. F. (1974). Insect stability and diversity in agro-ecosystems. *Annu. Rev. Ent.* **19**, 455–475.

Falcon, L. A. (1971). Microbial control as a tool in integrated control programs. In: C. B. Huffaker, Ed., *Biological control*. Plenum Press, New York.

Fedtke, C. (1982). *Biochemistry and physiology of herbicide action*. Springer-Verlag, Berlin.

Frank, R., Thomas, R. L., Holdrinet, M., Kemp, A. L. W., Braun, H. E., and Jaquat, J. M. (1977). Organochlorine insecticides and PCBs in sediments of Lake St. Clair (1970 and 1974) and Lake Erie (1971). *Sci. Total Environ.* **8**, 205–227.

Fukunaga, K., Tsukano, Y., and Kanazawa, J. (1972). Residue analysis of organomercury fungicides sprayed on rice plants. In: F. Matsumura, G. M. Boush, and T. Misato, Eds., *Environmental toxicology of pesticides*. Academic Press, New York, pp. 177–191.

Garms, R. (1961). Biozönotische Untersuchungen an Entwässerungsgräben in Flußmarschen des Elbe-Aestuars. *Arch. Hydrobiol.* Suppl. **26**, 344–462.

Georghiou, G. P. (1972). The evolution of resistance to pesticides. *Annu. Rev. Ecol. Syst.* **3**, 133–168.

Gibson, I. A. S. and Jones, T. (1977). Monoculture as the origin of major forest pests and diseases. In: J. M. Cherrett and G. R. Sagar, Eds., *Origins of pest, parasite, disease and weed problems*. Blackwell Scientific Publishers, London, pp. 139–161.

Giglioli, G. (1963). Ecological change as a factor in renewed malaria transmission in an eradicated area: a localized outbreak of *An. aquasalis* transmitted malaria on the Demerara River estuary, British Guiana, in the fifteenth year of *An. darlingi* and malaria eradication. *Bull. WHO* **29**, 131–145.

Grewe, F. (1970). Fungi und Fungizide. In: R. Wegler, Ed., *Chemie der Pflanzenschutz- und Schädlingsbekämpfungsmittel*, Vol. 2. Springer-Verlag, Berlin, pp. 3–43.

Harman, W. N. (1974). Snails (Mollusca: Gastropoda). In: C. W. Hart and L. N. Fuller, Eds., *Pollution ecology of freshwater invertebrates*. Academic Press, New York, pp. 275–312.

Hartung, R. (1975). Accumulation of chemicals in the hydrosphere. In: R. Haque and V. H. Freed, Eds., *Environmental dynamics of pesticides*. Plenum Press, New York, pp. 185–198.

Hastings, E., Kittams, W. H., and Pepper, J. H. (1961). Repopulation by aquatic insects in streams sprayed with DDT. *Ann. Entomol. Soc. Am.* **54**, 436–437.

Hatfield, C. T. (1969). Effects of DDT larviciding on aquatic fauna of Bobby's Brook, Labrador. *Can. Fish Cult.* **40**, 61–72.

Heath, R. G., Spann, J. W., Hill, E. F., and Kreitzer, J. F. (1972). *Comparative dietary toxicities of pesticides to birds*. U. S. Fish and Wildlife Service, Bureau of Sport Fish and Wildlife Special Sci. Report—Wildlife, No. 152.

Heckman, C. W. (1974). The seasonal succession of species in a rice paddy in Vientiane, Laos. *Int. Rev. gesamten Hydrobiol.* **59**, 489–507.

Heckman, C. W. (1979). *Rice field ecology in northeastern Thailand*. Monographiae Biologicae, Vol. 34. Dr. W. Junk, The Hague.

Heckman, C. W. (1981). Long-term effects of intensive pesticide applications on the aquatic community in orchard drainage ditches near Hamburg, Germany. *Arch. Environ. Contam. Toxicol.* **10**, 393–426.

Heckman, C. W. (1982a). Pesticide effects on aquatic habitats. *Environ. Sci. Technol.* **16**, 48A–57A.

Heckman, C. W. (1982b). Ecophysiological and phylogenetic characterization of a wintertime biotic community in shallow freshwater habitats near Hamburg. *Int. Rev. gesamten Hydrobiol.* **67,** 361–386.

Heckman, C. W. (1982c). Problems of pesticide application on cultivated aquatic ecosystems. In: B. Gopal, R. E. Turner, R. G. Wetzel, and D. F. Whigham, Eds., *Wetlands: ecology and management. Proc. 1st Intl. Wetlands Conf., New Delhi,* pp. 435–445.

Heckman, C. W. (1983). The recovery of the biotic community in a lotic freshwater habitat after extensive destruction by chlorine. *Int. Rev. gesamten Hydrobiol.* **68,** 207–226.

Hickey, J. J., Ed. (1969). *Peregrine falcon populations: their biology and decline.* University of Wisconsin Press, Madison.

Hobart, J. (1977). Pesticides in forestry: an introduction. In: F. H. Perring and K. Mellanby, Eds., *Ecological effects of pesticides.* Academic Press, London, pp. 61–88.

Hoffman, D. J. and Eastin, W. C., Jr. (1982). Effects of lindane, paraquat, toxaphene, and 2,4,5-trichlorophenoxyacetic acid on mallard embryo development. *Arch. Environ. Contam. Toxicol.* **11,** 79–86.

Hoffmann, C. H. and Drooz, A. T. (1953). Effects of a C-47 airplane application of DDT on fish food organisms in two Pennsylvania watersheds. *Am. Midl. Nat.* **50,** 172–188.

Holden, A. V. (1973). Effects of pesticides on fish. In: C. A. Edwards, Ed., *Environmental pollution by pesticides.* Plenum Press, London, pp. 213–253.

Holling, C. S. (1973). Resilience and stability of ecological systems. *Annu. Rev. Ecol. Syst.* **4,** 1–23.

Hollis, J. P. (1972). Nematicide-weeds interaction in rice fields. *Plant Dis. Reporter* **56,** 420–424.

Hoyt, S. C. and Caltagirone, L. E. (1971). The developing programs of integrated control of pests of apples in Washington and peaches in California. In: C. B. Huffaker, Ed., *Biological control.* Plenum Press, New York, pp. 395–421.

Hunter, G. S. and Prahlad, K. V. (1981). The effects of paraquat on neonatal rat lung: a histological and biochemical study. *Arch. Environ. Contam. Toxicol.* **10,** 151–158.

Hurlbert, S. H. (1975). Secondary effects of pesticides on aquatic ecosystems. *Residue Rev.* **57,** 82–148.

Hurlbert, S. H., Mulla, M. S., Keith, J. O., Westlake, W. E., and Duesch, M. E. (1970). Biological effects and persistence of Dursban in freshwater ponds. *J. Econ. Entomol.* **63,** 43–52.

Huschenbeth, E. and Harms, U. (1975). On the accumulation of organochlorine pesticides, PCB and certain heavy metals in fish and shellfish from Thai coastal and inland waters. *Arch. FischWiss.* **25,** 109–122.

Hynes, H. B. N. (1961). The effect of sheep-dip containing the insecticide BHC on the fauna of a small stream. *Ann. Trop. Med. Parasit.* **55,** 192–196.

Ishikura, H. (1972). Impact of pesticide use on the Japanese environment. In: F. Matsumura, G. M. Boush, and T. Misato, Eds., *Environmental toxicology of pesticides.* Academic Press, New York, pp. 1–32.

Johannes, R. E. (1975). Pollution and degradation of coral reef communities. In: E. J. F. Wood and R. E. Johannes, Eds., *Tropical marine pollution.* Elsevier, Amsterdam, pp. 13–51.

Johnson, W. D., Lee, G. F., and Spyradikis, D. (1966). Persistence of toxaphene in treated lakes. *Int. J. Air Water Pollut.* **10,** 555–560.

Junge, C. E. (1975). Transport mechanisms for pesticides in the atmosphere. *Pure Appl. Chem.* **42,** 95–104.

Kates, A. H. (1965). A note on damage to tobacco by lateral movement of picloram. *Proc. N.E. Weed Control Conf.* **19,** 393–396.

Kenaga, E. E. (1972). Factors related to bioconcentration of pesticides. In: F. Matsumura, G. M. Boush, and T. Misato, Eds., *Environmental toxicology of pesticides*. Academic Press, New York, pp. 193–228.

Kerr, S. R. and Vass, W. P. (1973). Pesticide residues in aquatic invertebrates. In: C. A. Edwards, Ed., *Environmental pollution by pesticides*. Plenum Press, London, pp. 134–180.

Kerswill, C. J. and Elson, P. F. (1955). Preliminary observations on effects of 1954 DDT spraying on Miramichi salmon stocks. *Fish. Res. Board Can. Prog. Rep.* **62**, 17–23.

Kilgore, W. W. and Li, M. Y. (1973). The carcinogenicity of pesticides. *Residue Rev.* **48**, 141–161.

Klein, W. and Korte, F. (1970). Metabolismus von Chlorkohlenwasserstoffen. In: R. Wegler, Ed., *Chemie der Pflanzenschutz- und Schädlingsbekämpfungsmittel*. Vol. 1. Springer-Verlag, Berlin, pp. 199–218.

Kuhr, R. J. and Dorough, H. W. (1976). *Carbamate insecticides: chemistry, biochemistry and toxicology*. CRC Press, Cleveland.

Learmonth, A. T. A. (1977). Malaria. In: G. M. Howe, Ed., *A world geography of human diseases*. Academic Press, London, pp. 61–108.

Lehner, P. N. and Egbert, A. (1969). Dieldrin and eggshell thickness in ducks. *Nature (London)* **224**, 1218–1219.

Lennon, R. E., Hunn, J. B., Schnick, R. A., and Burress, R. M. (1971). *Reclamation of ponds, lakes, and streams with fish toxicants: a review*. FAO Technical Paper No. 100. FIRI/T100.

MacPhee, A. W. and MacLellan, C. R. (1971). Cases of naturally occurring biological control in Canada. In: C. B. Huffaker, Ed., *Biological control*. Plenum Press, New York, pp. 312–328.

Matsumura, F. (1972). Current pesticide situation in the United States. In: F. Matsumura, G. M. Boush, and T. Misato, Eds., *Environmental toxicology of pesticides*. Academic Press, New York, pp. 33–60.

Matsumura, F. (1974). Microbial degradation of pesticides. In: M. A. Q. Khan and J. P. Bederka, Jr., Eds., *Survival in toxic environments*. Academic Press, New York, pp. 129–154.

Matsumura, F. (1975). *Toxicology of insecticides*. Plenum Press, New York.

McEwen, F. L. and Stephenson, G. R. (1979). *The use and significance of pesticides in the environment*. John Wiley & Sons, New York.

McMahon, J. P. (1967). A review of the control of *Simulium* vectors of onchocerciasis. *Bull. WHO* **37**, 415–430.

McVicar, A. H. and MacKenzie, K. (1977). Effects of different systems of monoculture on marine fish parasites. In: *Origins of pest, parasite, disease and weed problems*. Blackwell Scientific Publishers, London, pp. 163–182.

Mellanby, K. (1977). The future prospect for man. In: F. H. Perring and K. Mellanby, Eds., *Ecological effects of pesticides*. Academic Press, London, pp. 181–184.

Messenger, P. S., Biliotti, E., and van den Bosch, R. (1976). The importance of natural enemies in integrated control. In: C. B. Huffaker and P. S. Messenger, Eds., *Theory and practice of biological control*. Academic Press, New York, pp. 543–563.

Metcalf, R. L. (1971). Chemistry and biology of pesticides. In: R. White-Stevens, Ed., *Pesticides in the environment,* Vol. 1, Part 1. Marcel Dekker, New York, pp. 1–144.

Metcalf, R. L. (1976). Organochlorine insecticides, survey, and prospects. In: R. L. Metcalf and J. J. McKelvey, Jr., Eds., The future for insecticides: needs and prospects, Vol. 6, *Advances in Environmental Science and Technology,* John Wiley & Sons, New York, pp. 223–285.

Miles, J. R. W. (1980). Adsorption of insecticide residues—importance in environmental sampling and analysis. In: B. K. Afghan and D. Mackay, Eds., *Hydrocarbons and halogenated hydrocarbons in the aquatic environment*. Plenum Press, New York, pp. 81–90.

Mitsuhashi, S., Inoue, M., Oshima, H., Okubo, T., and Saito, T. (1976). Epidemiologic and genetic studies of drug resistance in staphylococci. In: J. Jeljaszewicz, Ed., *Staphylococci and staphylococcal diseases*. Gustav Fischer, Stuttgart, pp. 255–274.

Moore, N. W. (1967). A synopsis of the pesticide problem. *Adv. Ecol. Res.* **4**, 75–129.

Moore, N. W. (1977). The future prospects for wildlife. In: F. H. Perring and K. Mellanby, Eds., *Ecological effects of pesticides*. Academic Press, London, pp. 175–180.

Mount, D. I. and Putnicki, G. J. (1966). Summary report of the 1963 Mississippi fish kill. *Trans. North Am. Wildl. Nat. Resour. Conf.* **31**, 177–184.

Muirhead-Thomson, R. C. (1971). *Pesticides and freshwater fauna*. Academic Press, London.

Mulla, M. S., Amant, J. St., and Anderson, L. D. (1967). Evaluation of organic pesticides for possible use as fish toxicants. *Progve. Fish Cult.* **29**, 36–42.

Nash, R. G. and Woolson, E. A. (1967). Persistence of chlorinated hydrocarbon insecticides in soils. *Science* **157**, 924–927.

Newbold, C. (1977). Aquatic herbicides: possible future developments. In: F. H. Perring and K. Mellanby, Eds., *Ecological effects of pesticides*. Academic Press, London, pp. 119–131.

Newsome, L. D., Smith, R. F., and Whitcomb, W. H. (1976). Selective pesticides and selective use of pesticides. In: C. B. Huffaker and P. S. Messenger, Eds., *Theory and practice of biological control*. Academic Press, New York, pp. 565–591.

Nicholson, H. P. (1969). Occurrence and significance of pesticide residues in water. *J. Washington Acad. Sci.* **59**, 77–85.

Noguchi, T. (1972). Environmental evaluation of systemic fungicides. In: F. Matsumura, G. M. Boush, and T. Misato, Eds., *Environmental toxicology of pesticides*. Academic Press, New York, pp. 607–632.

O'Brien, R. D. (1967). *Insecticides: action and metabolism*. Academic Press, New York.

Odum, E. P. (1971). *Fundamentals of ecology*. 3rd ed. W. B. Saunders, Philadelphia.

Ohlendorf, H. M., Klaas, E. E., and Kaiser, T. E. (1974). Environmental pollution in relation to estuarine birds. In: M. A. Q. Khan and J. P. Bederka, Jr., Eds., *Survival in toxic environments*. Academic Press, New York, pp. 53–81.

Oppenoorth, F. J. (1976). Development of resistance to insecticides. In: R. L. Metcalf and J. J. McKelvey, Eds., *The future for insecticides: needs and prospects*, Vol. 6, Advances in Environmental Science and Technology. John Wiley & Sons, New York, pp. 41–59.

Patterson, R. S. and Windeguth, D. L. von. (1964). The effect of Baytex on some aquatic organisms. *Mosquito News* **24**, 46–49.

Perkow, W. (1971–79). *Wirksubstanzen der Pflanzenschutz- und Schädlingsbekämpfungsmittel*. Paul Parey, Hamburg.

Perry, A. S. (1974). Insecticide resistance and its ecological and economic thrust. In: M. A. Q. Khan and J. P. Bederka, Jr., Eds., *Survival in toxic environments*. Academic Press, New York, pp. 399–445.

Peterle, T. J. (1969). DDT in Antarctic snow. *Nature (London)* **224**, 620.

Peterle, T. J. and Giles, R. H. (1964). *New tracer techniques for evaluating the effects of an insecticide on the ecology of forest fauna*. Ohio State University Research Foundation Rep. 1207 (to U.S. Atomic Energy Commission).

Pierce, R. H. and Victor, D. M. (1978). The fate of pentachlorophenol in an aquatic ecosystem. In: K. R. Rao, Ed., *Pentachlorophenol. Chemistry, pharmacology, and environmental toxicology*. Plenum Press, New York, pp. 41–52.

Pionke, H. B. and Chesters, G. (1973). Pesticide–sediment–water interactions. *J. Environ. Quality* **2**, 29–45.

Plapp, F. W. (1976). Biochemical genetics of insecticide resistance. *Annu. Rev. Ent.* **21**, 179–197.

Portmann, J. E. and Wilson, K. W. (1971). *The toxicity of 140 substances to the brown shrimp and other marine animals.* Min. Agri. Fish. Food, U.K., Shellfish Info. Leafllet No. 22.

Prouty, R. M., Pattee, O. H., and Schmeling, S. K. (1982). DDT poisoning in a Cooper's hawk. *Bull. Environ. Contam. Toxicol.* **28**, 319–321.

Ridgway, R. L. and Vinson, S. B., Eds. (1977). *Biological control by augmentation of natural enemies.* Plenum Press, New York.

Riedel-Lorjé, J. C. and Gaumert, T. (1982). 100 Jahre Elbeforschung. *Arch. Hydrobiol.* Suppl. 61(Untersuch. Elbe-Aestuar 5), 317–376.

Risebrough, R. W., Huggett, R. J., Griffin, J. J., and Goldberg, E. D. (1968). Pesticides: transatlantic movements in the Northeast Trades. *Science* **159**, 1233–1235.

Robbins, C. S. and Stewart, R. E. (1949). Effects of DDT on bird population of scrub forest. *J. Wildl. Management* **13**, 11–16.

Robson, T. O. (1976). A review of the distribution of aquatic weeds in the tropics and subtropics. In: C. K. Varshney and J. Rzóska, Eds., Aquatic weeds of South East Asia, Dr. W. Junk, The Hague, pp. 25–41.

Roelofs, W. L. (1976). Pheromones. In: R. L. Metcalf and J. J. McKelvey, Eds., *The future for insecticides: needs and prospects.* Vol. 6, Advances in Environmental Science and Technology. John Wiley & Sons, New York, pp. 445–461.

Room, P. M., Harley, K. L. S., Forno, I. W., and Sands, D. P. A. (1981). Successful biological control of the floating weed salvinia. *Nature (London)* **294**, 78–80.

Rosato, P. and Ferguson, D. E. (1968). The toxicity of endrin-resistant mosquitofish to eleven species of vertebrates. *Bioscience* **18**, 783–784.

Roubaud, E. and Toumanoff, C. (1954). Dé placements des Anophèles consécutifs aux traitements larvicides. *Bull. Soc. Path. Exotiq.* **47**, 91–97.

Ruber, E. and Baskar, J. (1968). Sensitivity of selected microcrustacea to eight mosquito toxicants. *Proc. N.J. Mosq. Exterm. Assoc.* **55**, 99–103.

Rudd, R. L. (1964). *Pesticides and the living landscape.* Faber and Faber, London.

Rudd, R. L. and Herman, S. G. (1972). Ecosystemic transferal of pesticides residues in an aquatic environment. In: F. Matsumura, G. M. Boush, and T. Misato, Eds. *Environmental toxicology of pesticides.* Academic Press, New York, pp. 471–485.

Sasse, K. and Unterstenhöfer, G. (1970). Akarizide. In: R. Wegler, Ed., *Chemie der Pflanzenschutz- und Schädlingsbekämpfungsmittel.* Vol. 1. Springer-Verlag, Berlin, pp. 525–570.

Sanders, H. O., Huckins, J., Johnson, B. T., and Skaar, D. (1981). Biological effects of Kepone and Mirex in freshwater invertebrates. *Arch. Environ. Contam. Toxicol.* **10**, 531–539.

Schindler, O. (1975). *Unsere Süßwasserfische.* 5th ed. Kosmos, Franckh'sche Verlagshandlung, Stuttgart.

Schouwenburg, W. J. and Jackson, K. J. (1966). A field assessment of the effects of spraying a small coastal coho salmon stream with phosphamidon. *Can. Fish Cult.* **37**, 35–43.

Service, M. W. (1977a). Mortalities of the immature stages of species B of the *Anopheles gambiae* complex in Kenya: comparison between rice fields and temporary pools, identification of predators, and effects of insecticidal spraying. *J. Med. Ent.* **13**, 535–545.

Service, M. W. (1977b). Some problems in the control of malaria. In: F. H. Perring and K. Mellanby, Eds., *Ecological effects of pesticides.* Academic Press, London, pp. 151–164.

Sieber, J. N. and Woodrow, J. E. (1981). Sampling and analysis of airborne residues of paraquat in treated cotton field environments. *Arch. Environ. Contam. Toxicol.* **10,** 133–149.

Skerfving, S. (1972). Organic mercury compounds—relation between exposure and effects. In: L. Friberg and J. Vostal, Eds., *Mercury in the environment.* CRC Press, Cleveland, pp. 141–168.

Slater, R. M. and Spedding, D. J. (1981). Transport of dieldrin between air and water. *Arch. Environ. Contam. Toxicol.* **10,** 25–33.

Springer, P. F. and Webster, J. R. (1951). Biological effects of DDT applications on tidal salt marshes. *Mosquito News* **11,** 67–74.

Springett, J. A. (1975). Problems of insect vector control. In: N. F. Stanley and M. P. Alpers, Eds., *Man-made lakes and human health.* Academic Press, London, pp. 323–335.

Staiff, D. C., Irle, G. K., and Felsenstein, W. C. (1973). Screening of various absorbents for protection against paraquat poisoning. *Bull. Environ. Contam. Toxicol.* **10,** 193–199.

Stickel, L. F. (1973). Pesticide residues in birds and mammals. In: C. A. Edwards, Ed., *Environmental pollution by pesticides.* Plenum Press, London, pp. 254–312.

Strachan, W. M. J., Huneault, H., Schertzer, W. M., and Elder, F. C. (1980). Organochlorines in precipitation in the Great Lakes region. In: B. K. Afghan and D. Mackay, Eds., *Hydrocarbons and halogenated hydrocarbons in the aquatic environment.* Plenum Press, New York, pp. 387–396.

Thienemann, A. (1918). Lebensgemeinschaft und Lebensraum. *Naturwiss. Wochenschrift* N.F., 282–290, 297–303.

Ukita, T. (1972). Research on the distribution and accumulation of organomercurials in animal bodies. In: F. Matsumura, G. M. Boush, and T. Misato, Eds., *Environmental toxicology of pesticides.* Academic Press, New York, pp. 135–164.

Van den Bosch, R., Beingolea, G. O., Hafez, M., and Falcon, L. A. (1976). Biological control of insect pests of row crops. In: C. B. Huffaker and P. S. Messenger, Eds., *Theory and practice of biological control.* Academic Press, New York, pp. 443–456.

Vaughan, M. A. and Leon, G. (1976). Pesticide management on a major crop with severe resistance problems. *Trans. 15th Int. Congr. Entomol.* pp. 812–815.

Wade, R. A. (1969). *Ecology of juvenile tarpon and effect of dieldrin on two associated species.* U.S. Dept. Interior, Bureau Sport Fish. Wildl. Tech. Paper No. 41.

Walsh, A. H. and Ribelin, W. E. (1975). The pathology of pesticide poisoning. In: W. E. Ribelin and G. Migaki, Eds., *The pathology of fishes.* University of Wisconsin Press, pp. 515–557.

Waterhouse, D. F., LaChance, L. E., and Whitten, M. J. (1976). Use of autocidal methods. In: C. B. Huffaker and P. S. Messenger, Eds., *Theory and practice of biological control.* Academic Press, New York, pp. 637–659.

Way, M. J. (1977). Pest and disease status in mixed stands vs. monocultures; the relevance of ecosystem stability. In: J. M. Cherrett and G. R. Sagar, Eds., *Origins of pest, parasite, disease and weed problems.* Blackwell Scientific Publishing, London, pp. 127–138.

Way, M. J. and Bevan, D. (1977). Dilemmas in forest pest and disease management. In: F. H. Perring and K. Mellanby, Eds., *Ecological effects of pesticides.* Academic Press, London, pp. 95–110.

Wegler, R. and Eue, L. (1970). Herbizide. In: R. Wegler, Ed., *Chemie der Pflanzenschutz- und Schädlingsbekämpfungsmittel.* Vol. 2. Springer-Verlag, Berlin, pp. 165–395.

Weir, D. and Schapiro, M. (1981). *Circle of poison: pesticides and people in a hungry world.* Inst. for Food and Development Policy/Third World Publications, San Francisco.

Wheatley, G. A. (1973). Pesticides in the atmosphere. In: C. A. Edwards, Ed., *Environmental pollution by pesticides.* Plenum Press, London, pp. 365–408.

Wilson, F. and Huffaker, C. B. (1976). The philosophy, scope, and importance of biological control. In: C. B. Huffaker and P. S. Messenger, Eds., *Theory and practice of biological control*. Academic Press, New York, pp. 3–15.

World Health Organization. (1973). *Safe use of pesticides*. WHO Tech. Rep. Ser. No. 513.

Yarbrough, J. D. (1974). Insecticide resistance in invertebrates. In: M. A. Q. Khan and J. P. Bederka, Eds., *Survival in toxic environments*. Academic Press, New York, pp. 373–397.

Yunus, A. and Lim, G. S. (1971). A problem in the use of insecticides in paddy fields in West Malaysia. A case study. *Malay Agric. J.* **48**, 168–178.

Zwölfer, H., Ghani, M. A., and Rao, V. P. (1976). Foreign exploration and importation of natural enemies. In: C. B. Huffaker and P. S. Messenger, Eds., *Theory and practice of biological control*. Academic Press, New York, pp. 189–207.

13

AQUATIC TOXICOLOGY OF NITROGEN HETEROCYCLIC MOLECULES: QUANTITATIVE STRUCTURE-ACTIVITY RELATIONSHIPS

T. Wayne Schultz

Department of Animal Science
College of Veterinary Medicine
University of Tennessee
Knoxville, Tennessee

1. INTRODUCTION

1.1. Structure–Activity Relations

Over a century ago it was proposed that the biological activity manifested by exposure to a molecule is a function of that molecule's chemical structure. This structure activity concept has been broadened to include biological activity as a function of physiochemical properties. Thus a structure–activity relationship (SAR) is a correlation between a single or set of molecular descriptors (structural, physical, or chemical properties), of a group of molecules and some uniform measurement of their biological activity which in aquatic toxicology is typically the LC50 values.

Quantifying, studying, and interpreting such molecular structure-related changes in biological activity is the practice of QSAR, quantitative stucture–activity relationships. The first QSAR work was done by Richardson (1869) who demonstrated a direct linear relationship between the narcotic effects of fatty alcohols and the number of carbon atoms in each molecular structure. Since this initial finding, numerous similar linear correlations have been described between a variety of molecular descriptors and a number of biological end-points. Such chemical structure–biological activity relationships have the potential to predict or rank the activity of untested molecules and thus aid the decision making process concerning safeguarding man's health and environment.

Two major bits of information are required for each molecule used to generate a QSAR: one, some measurement of biological activity, which is derived quantitatively from a dose–response relationship and possesses some measure of confidence; second, one or more molecular descriptors which are quantitations of chemical structure or physiochemical properties. Molecular descriptors used in QSAR investigations are of two general classes. One group consists of free-energy related physiochemical properties including electronic, steric, and hydrophobic parameters (for review see Hansch and Leo, 1979). The leading physiochemical descriptor has been the hydrophobic parameter, the logarithm of 1-octanol/water partition coefficient (log K_{ow}) (Hansch, 1969). The success in using this hydrophobic parameter has been due, in a large part, to the facts that the rate of movement of organic molecules through biological materials is approximately proportional to their partition coefficient (Collander, 1954) and the 1-octanol/water partitioning is a good index of partitioning in biological systems (Leo et al., 1971). In addition to experimental determination, 1-octanol/water partition coefficients can be calculated by the substituent or π method (Fujita et al., 1964; Leo et al., 1971; Hansch and Leo, 1979) where the parameter π is defined in the expression:

$$\pi_x = \log K_{ow}^X - \log K_{ow}^H \tag{1}$$

where K_{ow}^X is the partition coefficient of the derivative, and K_{ow}^H is the partition coefficient of the parent molecule. Because of the additive nature of log K_{ow} values, partition coefficients can be calculated by summing appropriate structural elements or fragments. This fragment method (Leo, 1975; Hansch and Leo, 1979) is based on a set of molecular fragment values using the following formula:

$$\log K_{ow} = \sum_1^n x_n f_n \tag{2}$$

where x is the number of times fragment f of structural type n appears in the molecule in question.

Other important free-energy-related molecular descriptors which demonstrate substituent addability include the Hammett electronic constant σ (Hammett, 1937), the polar electronic constant F (Swain and Lupton, 1968), the resonance electronic constant R (Swain and Lupton, 1968), the Taft steric constant E_s (Taft, 1952), and the molar refractivity constant MR (Hansch et al., 1973), a corrected term for molar volume.

The second molecular descriptor group, quantitation of molecular structure, includes a simple count of the atoms in the molecule, molecular weight, molecular connectivity, molecular orbital theory, and quantum mechanics. Although more sophisticated than simple counts of atoms or molecular weight, molecular connectivity is less rigorous then either molecular orbital theory or quantum mechanics. Molecular connectivity (Kier and Hall, 1976; Kier, 1980) describes the molecule in question by its topological characteristics. The molecular connectivity method results in descriptors consisting of numerical indices which are generated on the assumption that it is possible to differentiate molecular structure by abstract numerical means.

Since molecular structure is simply a topological graph, that is, a set of vertices (points; atoms) connected by edges (lines; bonds), numerical indices, which are counts of sigma electrons other than those bonding to hydrogen atoms can be easily generated. These indices, based on 0, 1, 2, 3, or 4 bond subgraphs, are numerical encodings of structural information concerning number and types of atoms, branching, cyclization, and saturation level, as well as other properties. In order to minimize isomeric redundancies in molecular connectivity indices, a reciprocal square root transformation of the product of the vertex valences is done.

The most commonly used molecular connectivity index in aquatic toxicology is the $^1\chi^v$ (one-chi-v) index. The $^1\chi^v$ term is a sum over all the bonds in the molecule, weighted by the reciprocal square root valencies. The only type of molecular fragment (subgraph) is the bond(s) between two atoms. This index is described by the equation:

$$^1\chi^v = \sum_{s=1}^{N_b} (\delta_i^v \delta_j^v)_s^{-\frac{1}{2}} \qquad (3)$$

where bond b_s is between atoms a_i and a_j. The number of bonds in the molecule is N_b. δ_i^v and δ_j^v (valence delta) is the hydrogen suppressed valence of each atom and an index of multiple bonds. Common δ^v values include: C, 4; N, 5; 0, 6; S, 3.56.

1.2.   The *Tetrahymena* Bioassay System

The use of the free-living ciliate *Tetrahymena pyriformis* (Fig. 1) as a model in toxicity testing has been demonstrated for a variety of materials. Hunter and his co-workers have discussed much of the earlier screening work especially with carcinogens and antitumor agents (Hunter et al., 1973). *Tetrahymena* also has been used as a bioassay system to examine effects of other chemicals including trace elements and heavy metals (Thrasher and Adams, 1972; Apostol, 1973; Carter and Cameron, 1973; Tingle et al., 1973; Buergquest and Bovee, 1976; Bovee, 1978), organic contaminants (Cooley et al., 1972, 1973; Geike and Parasher, 1976; Schultz and Dumont, 1977; Geike, 1978; Schultz et al., 1978c, 1980, 1981, 1982; Schultz and Allison, 1980; Schultz and Cajina-Quezada, 1982), food-related compounds (Surak et al., 1976; Surak and Schifanella, 1979), and complex environmental mixtures (Kennedy and Elliot, 1970; Gray and Kennedy, 1974; Schultz et al., 1978a, b, d; Schultz and Dumont, 1978; Schultz, 1982).

As a toxicity test system, *Tetrahymena* cultures present several advantages. Bioassay with *Tetrahymena* allows for the examination in a short time period a large number of independent cells which concomitantly possesses features of single eucaryotic cells and whole organisms. *Tetrahymena*, a representitive microfauna of aquatic ecosystems, plays an important role in the turnover of organic detritus (Persone and Dive, 1978). As a zooplankter it occupies an important trophic level where bioaccumulation and/or bioconcentration are potential problems (Cooley et al., 1972). *Tetrahymena* is widely distributed in nature and is an index of a healthy aquatic environment (Carter and Cameron, 1973). As noted by Burbank and Spoon (1967) for ciliates in general, *Tetrahymena* lacks a sophisticated homeostatic mechan-

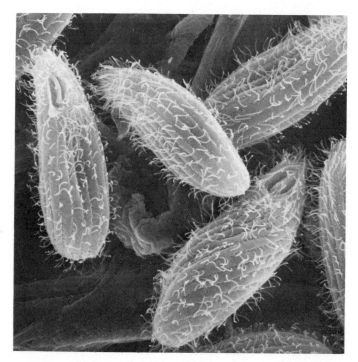

Figure 1.   Scanning electron micrograph of *Tetrahymena pyriformis*.

ism for adjusting to environmental alterations, thus it responds rapidly and in a relatively easily discernable fashion to environmental stress. *Tetrahymena* is one of the most extensively studied eucaryotes and a vast literature has been amassed on virtually every aspect of its biology (see the reviews of Hill, 1972; Elliott, 1973). In the laboratory it can be cultured axenically both easily and economically. In addition, a number of quantifiable bioassay end points including lethality, population growth and density, respiration, and several biochemical parameters can be rapidly obtained. *Tetrahymena* thus provides a bioassay system that is: (1) appropriate not only as a eucaryotic cytotoxicity model but also as a protozoan zooplankter aquatic toxicity test system, (2) inexpensive, (3) rapid, (4) well characterized, and (5) lends itself to quantitative dose–response relationships for a number of biological responses.

While it is possible to monitor a number of biological end points (Schultz et al., 1981), the most sensitive and often used is population growth impairment, quantitated as the IGC50 (inhibitor growth concentration for 50% of control populations). Sprague (1971) pointed out that reproduction impairment should be regarded as among the most important in determining relative hazard. As he further stated, even with invertebrates and algae, tests of sublethal effects such as abnormal growth and development are more mean-

406   T. Wayne Schultz

ingful than tests of acute toxicity, and decreased reproductive ability appears to be one of the most sensitive of the sublethal responses (Sprague 1970, 1971).

As stressed by Levy (1973), in using *Tetrahymena* as a research tool, the exact growing conditions should be noted. These include: (1) formulation of the medium; (2) growth temperature and pH; (3) the age and size of the inoculating cell suspension; (4) volume and shape of the culture container; and (5) amount of medium.

An examination of the literature reveals that there are almost as many recipes for culture media as there are investigators. Hunter et al. (1973) suggest this may be due to the variability of iron content between batches of proteose-peptone and yeast extract which affects population growth (Conner and Cline, 1964). Review of the nutritional requirements of *T. pyriformis* reveals it requires a purine and a pyrimidine nitrogenous base, water-soluble vitamins, a carbohydrate source such as glucose, and trace elements (Holz, 1973). All of these requirements are met by a solution of proteose-peptone, yeast extract, glucose, and Fe-EDTA (Sequestrine) (Cameron, 1973).

For most strains of *Tetrahymena* the optimal growth temperature occurs between 27 and 35°C (Holz et al., 1959; Rosenbaum et al., 1966). Elliott (1933) and Prescott (1958) report that the pH growth range for *Tetrahymena* is between pH 5.0 and 8.6 with the optimum being 7.25–7.30.

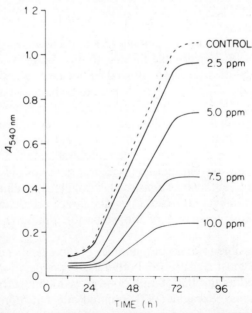

Figure 2.   Effects of acridine on population growth and densities of *Tetrahymena pyriformis* at 28°C. Slopes of the mean log-phase-growth lines for control populations and those exposed to 2.5, 5.0, 7.5, and 10.0 ppm acidine are 0.020, 0.018, 0.014, 0.011, and 0.003, respectively.

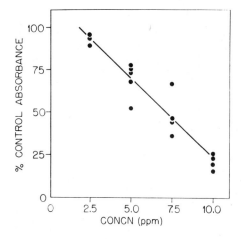

Figure 3. Least-squares linear regression analysis of mid-region of the concentration–response curve for population growth of *Tetrahymena pyriformis* exposed to acridine for 60 hr. The regression equation is Y 116.82 − 9.39X, $r = -0.958$, $n = 17$.

The effects of the age and size of the inoculum have been investigated by Phelps (1935) and Prescott (1958). Prescott (1958) observed that the age of the inoculum had a direct and linear effect on the length of the log-growth-phase. On the other hand, Phelps (1935) and Cameron (1973) observed no effect on the length of the log-growth-phase with inoculum ranging from 10 to 42,000 cells per milliliter. Inoculation with lower cell numbers, however, permits a longer log-growth-phase (Phelps, 1935).

Since the concentration of *Tetrahymena* in culture is directly proportional to the optical density (Cameron, 1973), a plot of absorbance versus time is a rapid means of estimating population growth rates and cell densities (Fig. 2). The word "estimate," however, should be noted for the size of the cells (Levy, 1973) as well as the glycogen content (Levy and Schabaum, 1965; Ryley, 1952) increase as the population enters stationary-growth-phase. Similarly, a plot of absorbance versus toxicant concentration yields a dose–response curve whose linear portion can be quantitated by regression analysis (Fig. 3). Thus, the relative toxicity for a number of compounds can be quantitated with confidence intervals in both a time- and cost-effective manner.

1.3. Nitrogen Heterocyclic Molecules

Classically, organic molecules are subdivided into three main divisions: (1) acyclic molecules, straight or branch-chain compounds; (2) homocyclic molecules, compounds having an alicyclic or aromatic ring, in practice, formed only of carbon atoms; and (3) heterocyclic molecules, compounds having a ring formed of more than one kind of atom. In addition to carbon, this is typically nitrogen, oxygen and/or sulfur. Because of the diversity of atoms and ring size, the latter division contains the greatest number of different kinds of compounds. The studies described here include nitrogen-substituted analogs and aromatic ring addition homologs of the alkaline nitrogen-heterocyclic pyridine and the neutral nitrogen-heterocyclic pyrrole.

Previously, Schultz et al. (1978c) have revealed structure–activity correlations for a number of organic contaminants, including pyridines and quinolines using the hydrophobic parameter, the logarithm of the 1-octanol/water partition coefficient. This work was expanded by Schultz et al. (1980) who have shown linear structure–activity relationships for alkyl-substituted neutral and basic nitrogen-heterocyclic molecules using a number of co-linear molecular descriptors. Recently these studies were diversified to include dinitrogen-containing molecules (Schultz and Cajina-Quezada, 1982). More recently Schultz et al. (1982) have correlated biological response with molecular connectivity using the $^1\chi^v$ index. Reported in this study are correlations between five general molecular descriptors of 26 selected single- and multi-nitrogen-containing heterocyclic molecules and acute cellular response monitored as population growth of the ciliate *Tetrahymena pyriformis*. In addition, six oxygen- and sulfur-containing heterocyclic molecules are examined.

2. MATERIALS AND METHODS

2.1. Test System and Chemicals

In these investigations the amicronucleated strain GL-C of the fresh water holotrich ciliate *Tetrahymena pyriformis* was used as an aquatic toxicity test system. Cultures were grown axenically in 50 ml of a 2% proteose-peptone medium (Table 1) in 250 ml Erlenmeyer flasks at 28°C (Schultz et al. (1980). The molecules tested, purchased from Aldrich Chemical Co., Milwaukee, Wisconsin, USA, were not repurified prior to testing. The test molecules included a series of 26 aromatic nitrogen-containing heterocyclic molecules which are mono-, di-, and tri-ringed homologs, analogs, and isomers.

Table 1. *Tetrahymena* Growth Medium

Component[a]	Amount
Distilled water	1 liter
Proteose-peptone	20 g
Glucose	5 g
Yeast extract	1 g
Sequestrine (ethylenediamine tetraacetic acid ferric salt)	0.03 g[b]

[a] Initial pH ≃ 6.9; pH to 7.3 with 10 N NaOH, filter, and autoclave: 20 min at 15 psi.
[b] One ml/liter of 3% aqueous stock stored at 4°C.

2.2.   Biological Response Analyses

Based on studies with acridine (Schultz et al., 1981), the biological response of population growth was selected for examination in these studies. Population growth analyses were conducted using a modified method of Cooley et al. (1972) with cell density being measured spectrophotometrically as optical density at 540 nm. A minimum of three replicates of two runs each of a four-step concentration series were assayed. Each flask was inoculated with 0.2 ml of log-growth-phase culture and incubated for 60 hr. Cultures without toxicant served as controls. Absorbance values were converted to percent control values prior to being transformed to probit (Finney, 1971). The linear portion of the concentration–response curve was generated for each test molecule by the least-squares method linear regression and the concentration in mmol/liter, which elicits 50% impairment of population growth in 48–72 hr (60-hr IGC50) calculated. In addition, 95% confidence intervals were also determined for each test molecule (Litchfield and Wilcoxin, 1949).

2.3.   Quantitative Structure–Activity Analyses

For quantitative structure–activity correlations the log of the inverse of the 60-hr IGC50 values were used as the log BR (biological response). Regression analysis was used to examine the correlations between the molecular descriptors: log 1-octanol/water partition coefficient, molecular weight, boiling point, number of carbon atoms per molecule, and the $^1\chi^v$ molecular connectivity index, and biological activity, log BR. The log K_{ow} values were, when possible, obtained from Appendix II of Hansch and Leo (1979). When not available in the literature they were calculated by the substituent method (Leo et al., 1971). The molecular weight, boiling point, and number of carbon atoms for each molecule were obtained from the *Handbook of Chemistry and Physics* (Weast, 1980). The $^1\chi^v$ values were calculated using the heteroatom δ^v values listed by Kier (1980) and following the methodology of Kier and Hall (1976).

3.   RESULTS

3.1.   Biological Response

In Table 2 are listed, in increasing order of activity, the 26 aromatic nitrogen heterocyclic molecules tested, their Chemical Abstract Services (CAS) registry number, population growth regression equation, correlation coefficient, number of regression data points, calculated 60-hr IGC50 value (mmol/liter) and 95% confidence limits. Excellent linearity for each concen-

Table 2. Population Growth Impairment to *Tetrahymena* of Selected *N*-heterocyclic Molecules

Molecule	CAS Number	Population Growth Regression Equation	Correlation Coefficient	n	60-hr IGC50[a] (mmol/liter)
1. Pyrazine[b]	290-37-9	$Y = 7.4767 - 0.0373X$	−0.977	23	66.36 (47.72–92.20)
2. Pyrimidine[b]	289-95-2	$Y = 8.4984 - 0.0619X$	−0.939	10	56.50 (40.56–79.71)
3. Pyrazole[b]	288-13-1	$Y = 7.1021 - 0.0006X$	−0.969	25	51.86 (38.84–69.20)
4. Pyridazine[b]	289-80-5	$Y = 6.6460 - 0.0645X$	−0.957	26	25.51 (14.91–43.60)
5. Pyridine[c]	110-86-1	$Y = 7.8980 - 0.1983X$	−0.969	15	15.32 (11.18–20.99)
6. Pyrrole[c]	109-97-7	$Y = 8.0019 - 0.2351X$	−0.979	17	12.75 (9.41–17.28)
7. Imidazole[b]	288-32-4	$Y = 6.5768 - 0.0023X$	−0.943	23	9.99 (5.74–17.38)
8. Purine	120-73-0	$Y = 6.9758 - 0.3198X$	−0.924	28	6.17 (4.38–8.67)
9. 4-Azabenzimidazole	273-21-2	$Y = 7.9293 - 0.5742X$	−0.977	34	5.10 (4.12–6.32)
10. 1,2,3-Benzotriazole	97-14-7	$Y = 6.7775 - 0.6790X$	−0.962	30	2.60 (1.74–3.89)
11. Phthalazine[b]	253-52-1	$Y = 6.4275 - 0.6576X$	−0.945	22	2.17 (1.21–3.88)
12. Benzimidazole	51-17-2	$Y = 6.5289 - 0.7443X$	−0.944	27	2.07 (1.32–3.24) 2.05

	CAS No.	Equation	r	n	95% confidence limits
13. Indoline	496-15-1	$Y = 6.6641 - 0.8127X$	−0.906	27	(1.38–3.03) 2.01
14. Quinoxaline[b]	91-19-0	$Y = 6.7129 - 0.8502X$	−0.961	23	(1.23–3.29) 1.95
15. Quinazoline[b]	253-82-7	$Y = 6.5999 - 0.8195X$	−0.946	22	(1.06–3.58) 0.97
16. Quinoline[c]	91-22-5	$Y = 7.2265 - 2.2887X$	−0.955	20	(0.67–1.41) 0.97
17. Isoquinoline	119-65-3	$Y = 7.8472 - 2.9423X$	−0.966	42	(0.80–1.17) 0.79
18. 1,10-Phenanthroline	66-71-7	$Y = 7.3374 - 2.9735X$	−0.961	30	(0.60–1.01) 0.71
19. 7-Azaindole	271-63-6	$Y = 7.0172 - 2.8350X$	−0.987	24	(0.51–1.00) 0.70
20. Indazole	271-44-3	$Y = 7.5224 - 3.6033X$	−0.988	32	(0.54–0.90) 0.62
21. Indole[c]	120-72-9	$Y = 7.3672 - 3.8190X$	−0.977	14	(0.44–0.87) 0.55
22. 1,2,3,4-Tetrahydro-quinoline	635-46-1	$Y = 6.5147 - 2.7570X$	−0.925	25	(0.28–1.08) 0.12
23. Carbazole[c]	86-74-8	$Y = 6.9653 - 15.9262X$	−0.942	40	(0.09–0.16) 0.04
24. Phenazine[b]	2-82-0	$Y = 6.2657 - 34.0250X$	−0.904	26	(0.01–0.07) 0.04
25. Phenanthridine	229-87-8	$Y = 7.2536 - 58.7842X$	−0.987	28	(0.03–0.05) 0.04
26. Acridine[c]	260-94-6	$Y = 7.0986 - 51.7633X$	−0.965	17	(0.03–0.06)

[a]95% confidence limits in parenthesis.
[b]From Schultz and Cajina-Quezada (1982).
[c]From Schultz et al. (1980).

411

tration–response curve is indicated by the fact that every correlation coefficient is better than − .900.

A cursory examination of Table 2 shows some general trends of chemical structure biological activity. Comparisons of homologs (molecules 1, 14, and 24; 3 and 20; 5, 16, and 26; 6, 21, and 23; 7 and 12) show that activity increases with an increase in number of aromatic ring systems within any given homologous series.

Comparisons of molecules 1 and 5, 2 and 5, 3 and 6, 4 and 5, 8 and 9, 8 and 10, 9 and 12, 9 and 19, 9 and 20, 10 and 12, 10 and 19, 10 and 20, 11 and 16, 11 and 17, 12 and 21, 14 and 16, 14 and 17, 15 and 16, 15 and 17 reveal that when additional nitrogen atoms are substituted into molecules of the same general structure, biological response decreases. Two exceptions to this trend are noted: (1) comparison of molecules 6 and 7, two of the smallest molecules tested; and (2) comparisons of molecules 24 and 25 with molecule 26, three of the largest molecules tested.

The comparison of multi-nitrogen-substituted indole analogs (molecules 8, 9, 10, 12, 19, 20, and 21) discloses not only that activity is reduced with in-ring nitrogen addition, but also points to the importance of substituent positioning (e.g., conformational isomerism) in determining biological response. Comparison of molecules 9 and 10 as well as 12, 19, and 20 suggests that the clustering of nitrogen atoms within a molecule increases the activity. Although the results are less definitive, comparisons of molecules 1, 2, and 4 support this premise. However, no such relationship can be drawn from a comparison of molecules 11, 14, and 15.

3.2. Quantitative Structure–Activity Relationships

Since previous studies had shown excellent correlations between the log K_{ow} and molecular weight (MW), boiling point (BP) and number of carbon atoms per molecule (#C-atoms) and biological activity (Schultz et al., 1980; Schultz and Cajina-Quezada, 1982) and the $^1\chi^v$ molecular connectivity index and biological activity (Schultz et al., 1982), these five parameters were selected as molecular descriptors for quantitative structure activity analyses. The biological response monitored as log BR as well as the five molecular descriptors are presented in Table 3.

A plot of log BR vs. log K_{ow} demonstrates a direct linear relationship. Least-squares linear regression of these data yields the equation:

$$\log BR = 0.7450 \, (\log K_{ow}) - 1.2984 \quad r = 0.949 \qquad (4)$$

Equation 4 explains 90.1% of the variation in the observed biological activity.

As demonstrated in Table 4 there is substantial co-linearity between the five molecular descriptors, especially MW, #C-atoms, and $^1\chi^v$. The quantita-

Table 3. Biological Activity and Molecular Descriptors of Selected N-heterocyclic Molecules

Molecule	log BR	log K_{ow}	MW	BP	#C-atoms	$^1\chi^v$
1. Pyrazine	−1.822	−0.22	80.09	115.5	4	1.699
2. Pyrimidine	−1.752	−0.40	80.09	123.5	4	1.699
3. Pyrazole	−1.715	0.02	68.08	187.0	3	1.437
4. Pyridazine	−1.407	−0.72	80.09	208.0	4	1.716
5. Pyridine	−1.185	0.64	79.10	115.0	5	1.850
6. Pyrrole	−1.106	0.75	67.09	131.0	4	1.577
7. Imidazole	−1.000	−0.08	68.08	256.0	3	1.427
8. Purine	−0.790	0.70	120.12	—	5	2.558
9. 4-Azabenzimidazole	−0.708	0.82	119.13	—	6	2.702
10. 1,2,3-Benzotriazole	−0.415	1.39	119.13	—	6	2.725
11. Phthalazine	−0.336	0.60	130.15	175.0	8	3.121
12. Benzimidazole	−0.316	1.38	118.14	>360.0	7	2.848
13. Indoline	−0.312	1.18	119.17	229.5	8	3.285
14. Quinoxaline	−0.303	1.10	130.15	241.5	8	3.124
15. Quinazoline	−0.290	0.92	130.15	229.0	8	3.114
16. Quinoline	−0.003	2.04	129.16	237.0	9	3.264
17. Isoquinoline	−0.003	2.09	129.16	243.3	9	3.254
18. 1,10-Phenanthroline	0.102	1.78	180.21	>300.0	12	4.311
19. 7-Azaindole	0.149	1.82	118.14	—	7	2.848
20. Indazole	0.155	1.82	118.14	—	7	2.848
21. Indole	0.208	2.13	117.15	253.5	8	2.988
22. 1,2,3,4-Tetrahydro-quinoline	0.260	2.29	133.19	249.0	9	3.785
23. Carbazole	0.921	3.59	167.21	355.0	12	4.405
24. Phenazine	1.398	2.84	180.21	>360.0	12	4.549
25. Phenanthridine	1.398	3.40	179.22	360.0	13	4.679
26. Acridine	1.398	3.40	179.22	360.0	13	4.679

Table 4. Molecular Descriptors r^2 Matrix

	log K_{ow}	MW	BP	#C-atoms	$^1\chi^v$
log K_{ow}	1.00	0.72	0.61	0.80	0.80
MW		1.00	0.63	0.93	0.97
BP			1.00	0.60	0.63
#C-atoms				1.00	0.97
$^1\chi^v$					1.00

tive structure–activity relationships between MW, BP, #C-atoms, and $^1\chi^v$ and log BR are presented in Eqs. (5), (6), (7), and (8), respectively.

$$\log BR = 0.0235 \,(\text{MW}) - 3.1223 \quad r = 0.904 \tag{5}$$

$$\log BR = 0.0104 \,(\text{BP}) - 2.7913 \quad r = 0.846 \tag{6}$$

$$\log BR = 0.2791 \,(\text{#C-atoms}) - 2.3701 \quad r = 0.926 \tag{7}$$

$$\log BR = 0.8450 \,(^1\chi^v) - 2.7734 \quad r = 0.935 \tag{8}$$

Equations (5), (6), (7), and (8) explain 81.7, 71.6, 85.9, and 87.4% of the observed variation in log BR, respectively. Attempts to develop higher-order (2–4) polynomial predictive equations did not increase the variance after adjusting for degrees of freedom.

Of the five molecular descriptors examined in these investigations log K_{ow} and BP are free-energy related parameters and thus represent the first general class of molecular descriptors. Because of the problems of sublimation and thermal decomposition, boiling point values, especially at atmospheric pressure, are difficult to ascertain, especially for larger and/or multiple substituted heterocyclic molecules. Thus, log K_{ow} appears to be the best free-energy related descriptor.

The remaining three descriptors, MW, #C-atoms, and $^1\chi^v$, are representative of the second general class of molecular descriptors. While strongly co-linear (see Table 4), when presented in the order #C-atoms, MW, and $^1\chi^v$, they reflect a progressive refinement and quantitation of the same basic data. Since $^1\chi^v$ encodes more structure information, thus having the best discriminating power, it is the best of the latter three descriptors.

Log K_{ow} and $^1\chi^v$ provided the best two descriptor model. A three-dimensional plot of log K_{ow} vs. log BR vs. $^1\chi^v$ is presented in Fig. 4. The regression equation of these data is:

$$\log BR = 0.4446 \,(\log K_{ow}) + 0.3866 \,(^1\chi^v) - 2.0282 \quad r = 0.968 \tag{9}$$

In Eq. (9) both log K_{ow} and $^1\chi^v$ are significant with P values of 0.0001 and 0.0013, respectively. Addition of a third descriptor from the other three does

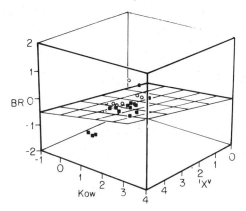

Figure 4. Least-squares linear regression analysis of log K_{ow} vs. log BR vs. $^1\chi^v$. The regression equation is presented in Eq. (9). Open squares above the plane, closed squares below the plane.

not increase the variance for the predictive equation. Statistical analysis of residual values based on Eqs. (4), (8), and (9) reveals that none of the observed log BR values are significantly different from their predicted values at the 0.05 level.

3.3. Oxygen and Sulfur Heterocyclic Molecules

Since in-ring nitrogen substitution causes a predictable linear nonspecific response modification (see Section 3.2 and Schultz and Cajina-Quezada, 1982), two questions that arose were: (1) does in-ring oxygen and sulfur substitution elicit the same type of response, and (2) can Eq. (9) predict these responses. In an effort to examine these questions, six additional molecules were bioassayed. The molecules tested were the oxygen-containing heterocyclic 1,2-benzofuran, the sulfur-containing heterocyclic 1-benzothiophene, the oxygen- and nitrogen-containing heterocyclics benzoxazole and benzoisoxazole, and the sulfur- and nitrogen-containing heterocyclics benzothiazole and 2,1,3-benzothiadiazole.

In Table 5 are listed the CAS number, population growth regression equation, correlation coefficient, number of regression data points, calculated 60-hr IGC50 value (mmol/liter), and 95% confidence interval for these six oxygen- or sulfur-containing molecules. The log K_{ow} and $^1\chi^v$ molecular descriptors, as well as log BR observed, log BR predicted, and residual value for each test molecule, are compared in Table 6. The residual values show good predictability for these molecules using Eq. (9). Thus, a similar mode of action can be assumed. The only possible exception is benzofuran which is less toxic than predicted.

Table 5. Growth Inhibition to *Tetrahymena* of Selected Oxygen- and Sulfur-containing Heterocyclic Molecules

Molecule	CAS Number	Population Growth Regression Equation	Correlation Coefficient	n	60-hr IGC50[a] (mmol/liter)
2,3-Benzofuran	271-89-6	$Y = 9.8106 - 3.9459X$	-.916	37	1.22 (1.07–1.39)
1-Benzothiophene	95-15-8	$Y = 8.9598 - 8.7767X$	-.907	28	0.45 (0.38–0.54)
Benzoxazole	273-53-0	$Y = 6.1753 - 0.5670X$	-.869	31	2.07 (1.02–4.22)
Benzoisoxazole	271-59-9	$Y = 6.0820 - 0.7505X$	-.980	25	1.44 (0.48–4.28)
Benzothiazole	95-16-9	$Y = 6.9386 - 2.2523X$	-.971	21	0.86 (0.58–1.29)
2,1,3-Benzo-thiadiazole	273-13-2	$Y = 7.5280 - 2.0427X$	-.959	24	1.23 (0.94–1.62)

[a]95% confidence interval in parenthesis.

416

Table 6. Comparison of Molecular Descriptors and Log Biological Response of Selected Oxygen- and Sulfur-Containing Heterocyclic Molecules

Molecule	$\log K_{ow}$	$^1\chi^v$	$\log BR$ (obs)	$\log BR^a$ (pred)	Residual Values
2,3-Benzofuran	2.67	2.889	-0.086	0.276	-0.362
1-Benzothiophene	3.11	3.020	0.347	0.522	-0.175
Benzoxazole	1.64	2.749	-0.316	-0.236	-0.080
Benzoisoxazole	1.52	2.759	-0.158	-0.286	0.128
Benzothiazole	2.02	2.937	0.066	0.005	0.061
2,1,3-Benzothiadiazole	1.74	2.749	-0.090	-0.192	0.102

[a] Based on Eq. (9).

4. DISCUSSION

4.1. Biological Response and Structure–Activity

Since the biological response testing conducted in these experiments is static in design, the abiotic loss of test molecules, especially the more volatile single-ring species, is a potential variable. However, Davis et al. (1981) studied the aquatic persistence of several nitrogen-containing compounds including pyridine and quinoline and found them to be highly resistant to abiotic loss. Pyridine, which had the highest rate of loss, had a half-life of 11.4 ± 1.2 days. Additionally, Schultz and Cajina-Quezada (1982), in examining the aqueous persistence of 12 dinitrogen heterocyclic molecules, found no significant change in concentration over 48 hr. Therefore, it is assumed that the concentration of each of the molecules assayed in this study was not altered by abiotic means.

The strong correlation of biological activity with log K_{ow} [see Eq. (4)] indicates that passive cellular uptake of the test molecules is the rate-limiting step governing biological response. Linear relationships between nonspecific biological response (e.g., cell membrane perturbation, aquatic systems narcosis) have been recognized in a number of studies including the investigations of Kopperman et al. (1974), Zitko et al. (1976), McLeese et al. (1979), and Könemann (1980).

Recently Schultz and Cajina-Quezada (1982) addressed, without much success, the question of which molecular descriptor best describes the biological response for conformational isomers. The present work allows for an expanded evaluation of this question. As evident from an examination of the data in Table 3, some disparity exists between the five molecular descriptors and log BR, especially within isomeric groups and nitrogen-heterocyclic analogs. As noted in section 3, an increase in nitrogen atom content generally causes a decrease in activity, whereas crowding of in-ring nitrogen causes an increase in activity.

Molecular weight, because of the problem of isomeric redundancy (see Table 2) and the fact that replacing a (=CH—) group with a (=N—) group causes only a − 1.01 unit change in molecular weight [i.e., C(12.01) + H(1.01) − N(14.01) = − 1.01], shows little if any change for the different ring shaped analogs (compare molecules 1, 2, 4, and 5; 3, 6, and 7; 8, 9, 10, 12, 13, 19, 20, and 21; 11, 14, 15, 16, 17, and 22; 18, 24, 25, and 26). This is in contrast to log BR which often varies markedly within such subsets as most dramatically seen with the indole analogs (molecules 8, 9, 10, 12, 19, 20, and 21).

The strong correlation between the number of carbon atoms per molecule and biological activity is somewhat surprising in light of the fact that the #C-atoms show such redundancy (see Table 3) and is the crudest of the five descriptors examined in these studies. While the greatest disparity in using this descriptor lies with 1,10-phenanthroline and imidazole, molecules 18, and 7, respectively, it does do a good job in explaining the response to the indole analog series molecules.

The $^1\chi^v$ molecular connectivity index is highly co-linear to both #C-atoms and MW (see Table 4). Despite the use of reciprocal square root, $^1\chi^v$, like #C-atoms and MW, has the problem of isomeric redundancy (see molecules 1 and 2; 12, 19, and 21; 25 and 26). This problem is most acute for di-substituted multi-ringed systems where spatial difference can be amplified (see molecules 12, 19, and 21).

Log K_{ow} is the best single molecular descriptor of log BR [see Eq. (4)]. However, dissection of the data into subsets reveals some variability. For the di-ringed isomers (molecules 9 and 10; 11, 14, and 15; and 12, 19, and 20), log K_{ow} does directly correlate with the observed biological activity. Similarly, log K_{ow} does show a direct linear relationship with the activity elicited by the indole analog series (molecules 8, 9, 10, 12, 19, 20, and 21). In addition, within the tri-ringed series (molecules 18, 24, 25, and 26), log K_{ow} separates molecule 18 from the other three, which tend to be aggregated at the upper end of the value spectrum for both log K_{ow} and log BR. However, examination of the data for mono-ring isomers (molecules 1, 2, and 4; 3 and 7) shows log K_{ow} to be inversely related to activity.

Previous investigations of log K_{ow}-dependent quantitative structure–activity correlations have dealt with alkyl-substituted mononitrogen heterocyclic molecules (Schultz et al., 1980) and alkyl-substituted dinitrogen heterocyclic molecules (Schultz and Cajina-Quezada, 1982). These data exhibit similar quantitative relationships to that described in Eq. (4). That is to say, a slope of 0.7 with an intercept of 1.2 [see Eq. (11); Schultz and Cajina-Quezada, 1982]. Similarly, Schultz et al. (1982) show a $^1\chi^v$-dependent quantitative correlation for the alkyl-substituted mono- and dinitrogen heterocyclic molecule data, which is in agreement with Eq. (8) of this study.

Due to the three dimensions of Fig. 4, it is difficult to accurately visualize the scatter of the data. No molecule is considered an outlier. The molecules whose observed biological response is farthest from the plane, predicted by Eq. (9), are molecule 7, imidazole, which is 0.512 log unit more active than predicted, and molecule 24, phenazine, which is 0.405 log unit less active than predicted.

Response modifications caused by alkyl and/or in-ring nitrogen substitution as well as hydrocarbon aromatic ring addition is linearly related to either the log K_{ow} or $^1\chi^v$ molecular descriptor. Equations such as (4), (8), and (9) are able to describe the vast majority of the variability in the observed biological response monitored in these investigations because all three types of chemical structure modifications (e.g., alkyl substitution, in-ring nitrogen substitution, and aromatic hydrocarbon ring addition) cause general membrane perturbation rather than altering a specific biochemical pathway such as replication, transcription, translation, or energetics. In addition, since none of the molecules tested interact very much with water (i.e., all have weak hydrogen bonding), the only chemical form to which the cell is exposed is the basic molecule itself and not a hydrated or ionic species. Similarly, the limited work with oxygen and sulfur heterocyclics (Section 3.3) suggests the same linear relationships and thus the same mode of action. The major problem that arises from the use of such relationships for predictive purposes is that with complex conformational isomers where steric and electronic effects can become important in determining biological activity and thus log K_{ow} values could be incorrectly calculated.

4.2. The *Tetrahymena* Bioassay System

As noted earlier when using the *Tetrahymena* population growth end point as a bioassay, it is important to note the exact rearing conditions. The medium formulation (see Table 1) used in these studies meets all the nutritional requirements of the cell. However, with this formulation a potential problem arises, for glucose suppresses the utilization of serine (Dewey and Kidder, 1966), an important amino acid derived from proteose-peptone (Cox et al., 1968). In addition, high glucose levels lead to large amounts of acid being formed (Rockland and Dunn, 1949). This acidic condition is not the case with the present growing conditions because the pH changes little (i.e., 60-hr control cultures with an optical density of 0.70 have pH values greater than 6.0) and stays well within the *Tetrahymena* pH growth range (Elliott, 1933; Prescott, 1958).

While *Tetrahymena* grows well at low oxygen tensions, depletion of oxygen can lead to the production of acids from glucose and peptone (Rockland and Dunn, 1949; Levy, 1973). These potential difficulties appear to be sharply decreased by culturing the ciliates in Erlenmeyer flasks containing relatively little medium. This allows for a large surface-to-volume ratio which provides ample gaseous exchange as is indicated by more or less uniform population distribution rather than the apical crowding observed with tube-grown cultures. Although Levy and Scherbaum (1965) pointed out that populations grown as shaken cultures attain a greater density than static cultures, shaking was not employed in these studies so as not to magnify possible toxicant volatilization or purging.

With the culturing conditions described here, stationary-growth phase with an absorbance of 0.75–0.80 is attained in approximately 72 hr. Thus, recording absorbance at 60 hr reduces errors in population estimations due to size and glycogen content alterations. In addition, this time format allows for late afternoon inoculations and early morning readings and thus, two set-ups per week, optimizing time usage. Although only experiments with 60-hr control absorbances of between 0.65 and 0.75 were used in these investigations, conversion of absorbance values to percent control values was done to standardize the experiments. Initially triplicate, and as of late duplicate, flasks for each concentration of each replicate are assayed. The variation between replicates is always equal to or greater than that within replicates.

Organic molecules of interest in aquatic toxicology are often not soluble in water at the concentration required of a stock solution. These can often be solubilized in acetone, ethanol, propylene glycol, or dimethyl sulfoxide. These carriers, when added in small concentrations to cultures of *Tetrahymena,* have no effect on population growth (Hunter et al., 1973; Geike and Parasher, 1976; Geike, 1978; Schultz and Cajina-Quezada, 1982). Of the four, dimethyl sulfoxide appears to be the one of choice.

4.3. Summary

In summary, it has been demonstrated that the *Tetrahymena* bioassay system is a time-, cost-, and man-power-effective model for aquatic toxicity testing. In addition, the standardized protocol described in this chapter provides a meaningful biological end point, growth impairment. This biological activity is generated from quantitative dose–response data which allows for the relative ranking of toxic potential of a variety of molecules as well as complex environmental mixtures.

Quantitative structure–activity relationships between biological response and several co-linear molecular descriptors for 26 nitrogen heterocyclic molecules show that activity is linearly related to hydrophobicity, with log 1-octanol/water partition coefficient and the $^1\chi^v$ molecular connectivity index being the best descriptors. Biological activity increases with ring addition and decreases with in-ring nitrogen addition. The crowding of nitrogen within a molecule increases activity.

ACKNOWLEDGMENTS

The author is grateful to Drs. T. C. Allison, J. N. Dumont, and L. B. Kier for their constructive criticism and assistance in the analyses of these studies. Special thanks go to Ms. M. Cajina-Quezada for her assistance and patience during the development and standardization of the bioassay.

REFERENCES

Apostol, S. (1973). A bioassay of toxicity using protozoa in the study of aquatic environment pollution and its prevention. *Environ. Res.* **6,** 365–372.

Bergquist, B. L. and Bovee, E. C. (1976). Cadmium: Quantitative methodology and study of its effect upon the locomotor rate of *Tetrahymena pyriformis. Acta Protozool.* **15,** 471–483.

Bovee, E. C. (1978). *Effects of heavy metals, especially selenium, vanadium and zirconium, on the movement, growth and survival of certain animal aquatic life.* Consultant's Report to Office of Water Research and Technology, Department of the Interior, October 1978, Washington, D.C., 26 pp.

422   T. Wayne Schultz

Burbank, W. D. and Spoon, D. M. (1967). The use of sessile ciliates collected in plastic petri
dishes for rapid assessment of water pollution. *J. Protozool.* **4**, 739–744.

Cameron, I. L. (1973). Growth characteristics of *Tetrahymena*. In: A. M. Elliott, Ed., *Biology
of Tetrahymena*. Dowden, Hutchinson & Ross, Stroudsburg, Pennsylvania, pp. 199–
226.

Carter, J. W. and Cameron, I. L. (1973). Toxicity bioassay of heavy metals in water using
Tetrahymena pyriformis. *Water Res.* **7**, 951–961.

Collander, R. (1954). The permeability of *Nitella* cells to non-electrolytes. *Physiol. Plant* **7**,
420–445.

Conner, R. L. and Cline, S. G. (1964). Iron deficiency and the metabolism of *Tetrahymena
pyriformis*. *J. Protozool.* **11**, 486–491.

Cooley, N. R., Keltner, J. M., Jr., and Forester, J. (1972). Mirex and Aroclor 1254: Effects on
and accumulation by *Tetrahymena pyriformis* strain W. *J. Protozool.* **18**, 636–638.

Cooley, N. R., Keltner, J. M., Jr., and Forester, J. (1973). Polychlorinated biphenyls, Aroclors
1248 and 1260: effects on and accumulation by *Tetrahymena pyriformis*. *J. Protozool.* **26**,
443–445.

Cox, D., Frank, O., Hunter, S. H., and Baker, H. (1968). Growth of *Tetrahymena* in carbohy-
drate-free high-glutamate media. *J. Protozool.* **15**, 713–716.

Davis, K. R., Schultz, T. W., and Dumont, J. N. (1981). Toxic and teratogenic effects of
selected aromatic amines on embryos of the amphibian *Xenopus laevis*. *Arch. Environ.
Contam. Toxicol.* **10**, 371–391.

Dewey, V. C. and Kidder, G. W. (1960). Serine synthesis in *Tetrahymena* from non-amino acids
sources: compounds derived from serine. *J. Gen. Microbiol.* **22**, 79–92.

Elliott, A. M. (1933). Isolation of *Colpidium striatum* Stokes in bacteria-free culture and the
relation of growth of pH of the medium. *Biol. Bull.* **65**, 45–56.

Elliott, A. M., Ed. (1973). *Biology of Tetrahymena*. Dowden, Hutchinson & Ross, Stroudsburg,
Pennsylvania. p. 508.

Finney, D. J. (1971). *Probit analysis*. 3rd Ed. Cambridge University Press, Cambridge, p. 333.

Fujita, T., Iwasa, J., and Hansch, C. (1964). A new substituent constant, π, derived from
partition coefficients. *J. Am. Chem. Soc.* **86**, 5175–5180.

Geike, F. (1978). Effect of hexachlorobenzene (HCB) on the activity of some enzymes from
Tetrahymena pyriformis. *Bull. Environ. Contam. Toxicol.* **20**, 640–646.

Geike, F. and Parasher, C. D. (1976). Effect of hexachlorobenzene (HCB) on growth of *Tetrahymena pyriformis*. *Bull. Environ. Contam. Toxicol.* **16**, 347–354.

Gray, J. P. and Kennedy, J. R., Jr. (1974). Ultrastructure and physiological effects of non-
tobacco cigarettes on *Tetrahymena*. *Arch. Environ. Health* **28**, 283–291.

Hammett, L. P. (1937). Effect of structure upon the reactions of organic compounds: benzene
derivatives. *J. Am. Chem. Soc.* **59**, 96–103.

Hansch, C. (1969). A quantitative approach to biochemical structure–activity relationships.
Acc. Chem. Res. **2**, 232–239.

Hansch, C. and Leo, A. (1979). *Substituent constants for correlation analysis in chemistry and
biology*. Wiley-Interscience, New York, p. 339.

Hansch, C., Leo, A., Unger, S. H., Kim, K. H., Nikaitoni, D., and Lien, E. J. (1973). "Aromatic" substituent constants for structure–activity correlations. *J. Med. Chem.* **16**,
1207–1216.

Hill, D. L. (1972). *The biochemistry and physiology of Tetrahymena*. Academic Press, New
York, p. 230.

Holz, G. G., Jr. (1973). The nutrition of *Tetrahymena:* Essential nutrients, feeding, and digestion. In: A. M. Elliott, Ed., *Biology of Tetrahymena*. Dowden, Hutchinson & Ross,
Stroudsburg, Pennsylvania, pp. 89–98.

Holz, G. G., Jr., Erwin, J. A., and Davis, R. J. (1959). Some physiological characteristics of the mating types and varieties of *Tetrahymena pyriformis*. *J. Protozool.* **6**, 149–156.

Hunter, S. H., Baker, H., Frank, O., and Cox, D. (1973). *Tetrahymena* as a nutritional pharmacological tool. In: A. M. Elliott, Ed., *Biology of Tetrahymena*. Dowden, Hutchison & Ross, Stroudsburg, Pennsylvania, pp. 411–434.

Kennedy, J. R., Jr. and Elliott, A. M. (1970). Cigarette smoke: The effect of residue on mitochondrial structure. *Science* **168**, 1097–1098.

Kier, L. B. (1980). Molecular connectivity as a description of structure for SAR analysis. In: S. Yalkowsky, Ed., *Physical chemical properties of drugs*. Marcel Dekker, New York, pp. 277–319.

Kier, L. B. and Hall, L. H. (1976). *Molecular connectivity in chemistry and drug research*. Academic Press, New York, p. 257.

Könemann, H. (1980). Structure–activity relationships and additivity in fish toxicity of environmental pollutants. *Ecotox. Environ. Safety* **4**, 415–421.

Kopperman, H. L., Carlson, R. M., and Caple, R. (1974). Aqueous chlorination and ozonation studies. I. Structure–toxicity correlations of phenolic compounds to *Daphnia magna*. *Chem. Biol. Interact.* **9**, 245–251.

Leo, A. J. (1975). Calculation of partition coefficients useful in the evaluation of the relative hazards of various chemicals in the environment. In: G. D. Veith and D. E. Konasewich, Eds., *Symposium on structure–activity correlations in studies of toxicity and bioconcentration with aquatic organisms*, pp. 151–176.

Leo, A. J., Hansch, C., and Elkins, D. (1971). Partition coefficients and their uses. *Chem. Rev.* **71**, 525–616.

Levy, M. R. (1973). Effects of some environmental factors on the biochemistry, physiology and metabolism of *Tetrahymena*. In: A. M. Elliott, Ed., *Biology of Tetrahymena*. Dowden, Hutchinson & Ross, Stroudsburg, Pennsylvania, pp. 227–258.

Levy, M. R. and Scherbaum, O. H. (1965). Glyconeogenesis in growing and nongrowing cultures of *Tetrahymena pyriformis*. *J. Gen. Microbiol.* **38**, 211–230.

Litchfield, J. R. and Wilcoxin, F. (1949). A simplified method of evaluating dose-effect experiments. *J. Pharmacol. Exp. Ther.* **96**, 99–113.

McLeese, D. W., Zitko, V., and Peterson, M. R. (1979). Structure–lethality relationships for phenols, anilines and other aromatic compounds in shrimp and clams. *Chemosphere* **2**, 53–57.

Persoone, G. and Dive, D. (1978). Toxicity tests on ciliates—A short review. *Ecotoxicol. Environ. Safety* **2**, 105–114.

Phelps, A. (1935). Growth of protozoa in pure culture. I. Effect upon the growth curve of the age of the inoculum and of the amount of the inoculum. *J. Exp. Zool.* **70**, 109–130.

Prescott, D. M. (1958). The growth rate of *Tetrahymena geleii* HS under optimal conditions. *Physiol. Zool.* **31**, 111–117.

Richardson, B. W. (1869). Physiological research on alcohols. *Med. Times Gaz.* **2**, 703.

Rockland, L. B. and Dunn, M. S. (1949). Growth studies on *Tetrahymena geleii*. *J. Biol. Chem.* **179**, 511–521.

Rosenbaum, N., Erwin, J., Beach, D., and Holz, G. G., Jr. (1966). The induction of a phospholipid requirement and morphological abnormalities in *Tetrahymena pyriformis* by growth at supraoptimal temperature. *J. Protozool.* **13**, 115–123.

Ryley, J. F. (1952). Studies on the metabolism of the protozoa. 3. Metabolism of the ciliate *Tetrahymena pyriformis (Glaucoma pyriformis)*. *Biochem. J.* **52**, 483–492.

Schultz, T. W. (1982). Acute cytotoxicity of fossil-energy-related comparative research materials. *J. Environ. Sci. Health* **A17**, 153–167.

Schultz, T. W. and Allison, T. C. (1980). Toxicity and toxic interaction of aniline and pyridine. *Bull. Environ. Contam. Toxicol.* **23**, 814–819.

Schultz, T. W. and Cajina-Quezada, M. (1982). Structure–toxicity relationships of selected nitrogenous heterocyclic compounds II. Dinitrogen molecules. *Arch. Environ. Contam. Toxicol.* 11, 353–361.

Schultz, T. W., Cajina-Quezada, M., and Dumont, J. N. (1980). Structure–toxicity relationships of selected nitrogenous heterocyclic compounds. *Arch. Environ. Contam. Toxicol.* 9, 591–598.

Schultz, T. W. and Dumont, J. N. (1977). Cytotoxicity of synthetic fuel products on *Tetrahymena pyriformis*. 1. Phenol. *J. Protozool.* 24, 164–172.

Schultz, T. W. and Dumont, J. N. (1978). Cytotoxicity of untreated coal liquefaction process water (and a comparison with gasification process water). *J. Environ. Sci. Health* A13, 641–651.

Schultz, T. W., Dumont, J. N., and Kyte, L. M. (1978a). Cytotoxicity of untreated coal-conversion gasifier condensate. In: J. H. Thorp and J. W. Gibbons, Eds., *Energy and environmental stress in aquatic systems*. DOE Symposium Series. (Conf.-771114) National Technical Information Service. Springfield, Virginia, pp. 502–518.

Schultz, T. W., Dumont, J. N., and Kyte, L. M. (1978b). Cytotoxicity of synthetic fuel products on *Tetrahymena pyriformis*. II. Shale oil retort water. *J. Protozool.* 25, 502–509.

Schultz, T. W., Kier, L. B., and Hall, L. H. (1982). Structure–toxicity relationships of selected nitrogenous heterocyclic compounds. III. Relationships using molecular connectivity. *Bull. Environ. Contam. Toxicol.* 28, 373–378.

Schultz, T. W., Kyte, L. M., and Dumont, J. N. (1978c). Structure–toxicity correlations of organic contaminants in aqueous coal-conversion effluents. *Arch. Environ. Contam. Toxicol.* 7, 457–463.

Schultz, T. W., Perry, S. T., and Dumont, J. N. (1978d). Reduced toxicity of an aqueous coal-conversion effluent following waste disposal treatment. *Bull. Environ. Contam. Toxicol.* 20, 633–639.

Schultz, T. W., Richter, C. S., and Dumont, J. N. (1981). Cytotoxicity of acridine, a synfuel component, to *Tetrahymena*. *Environ. Pollut. Ser. A.* 26, 215–226.

Sprague, J. B. (1970). Measurement of pollutant toxicity to fish. II. Utilizing and applying bioassay results. *Water Res.* 4, 3–32.

Sprague, J. B. (1971). Measurement of pollutant toxicity to fish. III. Sublethal effects and safe concentrations. *Water Res.* 5, 245–266.

Surak, J. G., Bradley, R. L., Jr., Branen, A. L., and Shrago, E. (1976). Effects of butylated hydroxyanisole on *Tetrahymena pyriformis*. *Food Cosmet. Toxicol.* 14, 277–281.

Surak, J. G. and Schifanella, A. V. (1979). The toxicity of α-tomatine to *Tetrahymena pyriformis*. *Food Cosmet. Toxicol.* 17, 61–67.

Swain, C. G. and Lupton, E. C., Jr. (1968). Field and resonance components of substituent effects. *J. Am. Chem. Soc.* 90, 4328–4337.

Taft, R. W. (1952). Polar and steric substituent constants for aliphatic and *o*-benzoate groups from rates of esterification and hydrolysis of esters. *J. Am. Chem. Soc.* 74, 3120–3128.

Thrasher, J. D. and Adams, J. F. (1972). The effects of four mercury compounds on the generation time and cell division in *Tetrahymena pyriformis,* WH 14. *Environ. Res.* 5, 443–450.

Tingle, L. E., Paulet, W. A., and Cameron, I. L. (1973). Sublethal cytotoxic effects of mercuric chloride on the ciliate *Tetrahymena pyriformis*. *J. Protozool.* 20, 301–304.

Weast, R. C., Ed. (1980). *CRC handbook of chemistry and physics,* 61st ed. CRC Press, Boca Raton, Florida.

Zitko, V., McLeese, D. W., Carson, W. G., and Welch, H. E. (1976). Toxicity of alkyldinitrophenols to some aquatic organisms. *Bull. Environ. Contam. Toxicol.* 5, 508–515.

14

TOXICOLOGY OF CHRONIC CRUDE OIL EXPOSURE: SUBLETHAL EFFECTS ON AQUATIC ORGANISMS

J. W. Kiceniuk

Research and Resource Services
Department of Fisheries and Oceans
St. John's, Newfoundland

R. A. Khan

Department of Biology and Marine Sciences Research Laboratory
Memorial University of Newfoundland
St. John's, Newfoundland

1. INTRODUCTION

Crude oil is a mixture with complexity little realized by most biologists. This mixture contains compounds ranging from low-molecular-weight hydrocarbons to very complex polynuclear aromatic hydrocarbons containing numerous isomers. Some of these compounds are essentially insoluble in water (e.g., paraffin waxes), while others (phenols, quinolines) are very soluble (Lysyj et al., 1980). When crude oil is mixed with water, a much more physically and chemically complicated mixture is formed. The bulk of the oil is mostly nonpolar and forms into spheres of various sizes. Compounds then partition between the oil droplets and the water (Shaw, 1977). It has been shown that crude oil droplets in water are coated by a layer of water molecules (Malcolm and Commaert, 1981) which prevents the droplets from coalescing on contact with each other. Apart from tending to keep oil in an emulsion, these water jackets on the oil droplets could be important in increasing contact between oil and biological components such as mucus.

Crude oil in water not only provides difficulties for analytical chemists (Lysyj et al., 1980) but it also creates formidable problems for environmental toxicologists who not only have to report concentrations of toxicants but also have to design dosing systems that provide concentrations in the range of those found or expected in the real world. One approach in evaluating the effects of a complex toxicant on organisms is to examine the toxicity of each of the constituents and combine the results. This is an attractive approach because of its simplicity, but because there are probably a million compounds or isomers in crude oil, a very large number of tests would be required. Even if such tests were conducted, how well could results be related to animals exposed to crude oil in water? Interactions of constituents of the complex mixture would probably make interpretation of single-compound tests uninterpretable in the real world context. For example, Hoffman (1979), in testing the embryotoxicity and teratogenicity of a mixture of aromatic hydrocarbons and its constituent parts, found that the mixture was more toxic than the combination of any two constituent compounds. In a study of dimethylnaphthalene metabolite secretion into bile, Gruger et al. (1981) reported a different metabolite pattern in fish pretreated with a combination of p-cresol and naphthalene than with either compound alone. It is therefore clear that predictions of effects of a crude oil on aquatic organisms cannot be based on toxicity of individual compounds alone. The study of metabolism of individual compounds must be integrated with the more "clinical" observation of the effects on aquatic organisms of mixtures of hydrocarbons that reflect more accurately their condition in the aquatic environment.

In this chapter we do not review all the work that has been done in this relatively new field, but rather attempt to integrate results from various studies and extract some of the basic themes which we feel are emerging in the field of sublethal toxicology of chronic oil exposure of aquatic animals.

It is often quoted that fish are generally considered to be motile and have the capacity of avoiding an unsuitable environment (Anderson et al., 1979). This view is not supported by experimental findings in flatfish behavior. For example, Weber et al. (1979) found that juvenile English sole do not avoid oil-contaminated sediment. In the case of animals such as flatfish, which live in contact with sediments, it may be immaterial in the long term whether the fish are able to avoid oiled areas. If they stay, they will be affected by the oil (Fletcher et al., 1981) and if they avoid the area they will lose that amount of habitat. Either way, there is an impact on the population until hydrocarbons return to a no-effect level. The no-effect level is, at this time, undetermined.

2. EFFECTS OF CHRONIC OIL EXPOSURE ON PHYSIOLOGY, HISTOPATHOLOGY, AND MORPHOLOGY OF FISH

Hawkes (1977) reported that five days of exposure of starry flounder *Platichthys stellatus* to 100 ppb of water-soluble fraction of crude oil caused sloughing of gill epithelium. This study was, however, complicated by the presence of *Gyrodactylus* sp. on the gills. Our own studies, which involved exposing cod, *Gadus morhua,* to Venezuelan crude oil at concentrations of 150–300 ppb in water for 13 weeks, produced fusion of gill filaments and edema in many of the secondary lamellae (Khan et al., 1981). Similarly, Woodard et al. (1981) reported hyperplasia, edema, and fusion of gill lamellae of groups of *Salmo clarki* exposed to 450 and 520 ppb of oil for 90 days. It is therefore likely that the sloughing observed by Hawkes (1977) after only five days exposure was an initial stage in gill filament degeneration resulting from oil exposure. Alteration of gill structure was not apparent in cunner, *Tautoglabrus adspersus* (Payne et al., 1978), or in sculpins, *Myoxocephalus octodecemspinosus* (Kiceniuk et al., 1982), under similar exposure conditions (in the case of sculpins, identical to exposure conditions for cod) using the same type and batch of crude oil. This indicates a real species difference in response. It is likely that the species difference is due to a difference in threshold for the species, as was found by Solangi (1980) in examining gill damage in *Menidis seryllina* and *Trinectes manulatus* upon exposure to different concentrations of oil for various lengths of time.

Chronic exposure of cod to 150–300 ppb of Venezuelan crude and as little as 50 ppb of Hibernia crude causes enlargement of the heart (up to 50%, $p <$ 0.002) (Khan et al., 1981). We believe that this heart enlargement is due to the damage of gill lamellae, which results in increased gill resistance, thus increasing the load on the heart. It is interesting that we found no gill damage or heart enlargement in sculpins and cunners exposed to water-accommodated oil, or flounder, *Pseudopleuronectes americanus,* exposed to oiled sediment. We have not yet examined the histological sections of gills of flounder from these experiments, but as already mentioned, no alterations were found in gills of sculpins or cunner. In the cod, Khan et al. (1981)

observed large hematomas in the secondary lamellae of the oil-exposed group. It is possible that these hematomas form by the coincidence of tissue weakening and blood pressure elevation, which normally occurs during activity or excitement, being further increased by increased gill vascular resistance.

3. GONAD MATURATION

Possibly one of the most interesting effects of oil on organs is that on fish testes. Payne et al. (1978) reported a decrease in testes size of cunner after 6 months of exposure to oil.

Winter flounder exposed to oiled sediment during the gonad maturation had decreased testes size (Fletcher et al., 1982). Flounder exposed to the same oiled sediment after it had been allowed to age for one year had less reduction in testes size but a significant reduction nevertheless. Recently, we have found that testes somatic indices in cod exposed to 50–100 ppb of Hibernia crude oil in seawater during the early stages of gonad maturation (August–November), were reduced sevenfold relative to control fish. In a similar exposure during the late stages of gonad maturation (December–May), testis maturation was somewhat retarded relative to both the control male fish and to egg maturation of the females in the oil-treated group, but maturation did occur and resulted in functional sperm. Fertilization and hatching was accomplished in oil-treated and control fish, but percentage of fertilization and hatching was not quantitated. The retardation of testes development could be serious if the males get too far out of synchrony with the females.

4. LIVER STRUCTURE AND FUNCTION

Ingestion of 122 mg/kg · day of crude oil in food for up to 75 days was reported to cause depletion of liver glycogen as well as liver lipid (Hawkes, 1977). Eurell and Haensly (1981) found a biphasic response in liver lipid content. After 14–21 days exposure to 5% water-soluble fraction, liver lipids were depressed relative to controls, whereas with 10% water-soluble fraction lipids content was increased. It is interesting that although the response of lipid content was biphasic, the vacuolation which they found in the hematocytes was not. This suggests that the observed vacuole formation is not directly related to lipid accumulation.

Stegeman and Sabo (1976) reported a decrease in liver lipid in oil-exposed *Stenotomus*. They also found that the exposed fish had depressed lipogenesis. Cod exposed to 150–300 ppb crude oil for 13 weeks had smaller hepatocytes but liver size and total lipid content were not significantly different (Khan et al., 1981).

We have found that in cunner exposed to repeated doses of crude oil at concentrations of 50–200 ppb in water, the total liver lipid contents are not significantly different but densitometry of some fractions of the mixture separated by thin layer chromatography are significantly different. Similarly, we found that cod exposed to 50–100 ppb of crude oil in water had a significant change in lipid fractions but not in total lipid content (Dey et al., 1983). These fish were exposed at low winter temperature which reduced feeding to below maintenance levels (fish lost weight) and abolished the effect of oil treatment on feeding. It is therefore apparent that the effect of oil treatment on lipid fractions is not secondary by way of level of feeding. Since lipids seem to be the favored energy reserve in fish (Cowey and Sargent, 1977) it is to be expected that any interference with lipid metabolism would be detrimental to the fish. Other than the investigation of lipogenesis by Stegeman and Sabo (1976), in which they examined the rates of incorporation of ^{14}C-acetate into lipids, we are not aware of any work on effects of hydrocarbons on lipid metabolism. Chambers et al. (1979) found decreased malate dehydrogenase (MDH) activity in the supernatant fraction of muscle and gill of mullet after exposure to crude oil for eight months. This is an interesting finding since extramitochondrial MDH is involved in fatty acid synthesis and in mammals is thought to be one of the control sites of this pathway (Lane and Moss, 1971). It is known that in a variety of fish, epinephrine, norepinephrine, ACTH, and glucagon do not stimulate lypolysis from adipose tissue as they do in mammals (Farkas 1967a,b, 1969). The control of lipid metabolism in fish has been aptly termed "obscure" (Driedzic and Hochachka, 1978).

Gall bladder size is affected by oil exposure in cunner (Kiceniuk et al., 1980), winter flounder (Fletcher et al., 1982), and sculpins (Kiceniuk et al., 1982), and is not related to feeding in the case of cunner (Kiceniuk et al., 1980). In the studies mentioned previously, gall bladders in cod and cunner increased in size whereas in flounder and sculpins they decreased in size. Whether this species difference is indicative of differences in hydrocarbon metabolism or in other liver functions is not known but the large change in gall bladder size ($p < 0.006$ in all species examined on $n < 10$) together with the changes in liver histology and liver lipids suggests liver damage at oil concentrations as low as 50–100 ppb (Kiceniuk et al., unpublished).

5. HEMATOLOGICAL CHANGES

Hematocrit was reported to increase in cunner after two weeks exposure to oil in water (Kiceniuk et al., 1980) but not after six months exposure under similar conditions in the same species (Payne et al., 1978). In recent exposures of cod to 150–300 ppb of Venezuelan crude oil in water, hematological variables including hematocrit were examined at monthly intervals but no changes were found (Khan et al., 1981). In some of our other long-term low

hydrocarbon exposures of fish (sculpins and cod) there was a trend for
increased hematocrit in the first 2–4 weeks of exposure but the increase was
generally not statistically significant.

Thurberg et al. (1978), working on fish from the Argo Merchant fuel oil
spill area and a clean area, reported reduced plasma sodium in yellowtail
flounder and haddock from the oil-exposed area. They also found reduced
potassium in yellowtail, winter flounder, and haddock and reduced plasma
osmolality in yellowtail and haddock from the exposed area. Plasma copper
and chloride levels were also depressed in cunner exposed to crude oil for 6
months (Fletcher et al., 1979) but not after only 14 days exposure to similar
concentrations of oil (Kiceniuk et al., 1980). The reasons for the observed
depression of blood electrolytes by oil exposure have not been investigated
in fish, but in birds it has been found that crude oil can interfere with
intestinal Na^+ and with water transport (Crocker et al., 1975).

6. IMPLICATIONS OF CHRONIC OIL EXPOSURE ON FEEDING AND GROWTH OF FISH

Productivity of a fish stock depends on the number of individuals and growth
rate. Growth rate in fish is determined largely by food supply. Both growth

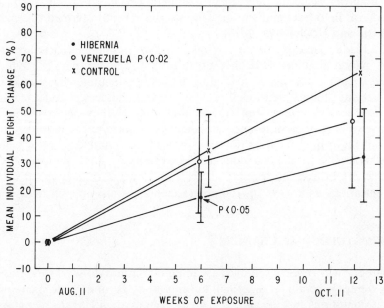

Figure 1.   Growth rate of individual cod during summer and fall feeding experiment. The "P"
value in the key is from a t-test of mean fish weight at week 0 and at week 6 in the "Venezuela"
group. The "P" value in the body of the graph is for t-test comparison of "Hibernia" group with
the parallel control group. "Venezuela" and "Hibernia" groups were exposed to 50-100 ppb of
the respective crude oils as water-accommodated fraction.

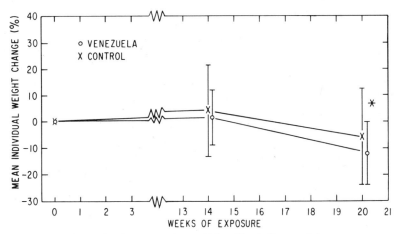

Figure 2. Weight change in winter experiment (3°C and less). Venezuela group was exposed to 50–100 ppb of water-accommodated crude oil. The asterisk indicates significance at 5% level in a *t*-test.

rate and feeding rate are therefore important variables in determining long-term effects of any toxicant on fish stock productivity.

McCain et al. (1978) suggested that flatfish exposed to oiled sediment reduced food intake. Fletcher et al. (1981) reported that food intake and condition factor of winter flounder were reduced by exposing the animals to oiled sediment. However, ageing the oil in the sediment for one year diminished its effectiveness to inhibit feeding. Similarly, Atlantic cod exposed to 150–300 ppb of water-accommodated oil for 13 weeks ate only 53% per unit body weight as much food as control fish and increased in weight by only 11% during the experimental period compared to 79% weight increase in the controls (Khan et al., 1981). In another long-term feeding experiment on cod, we have found that as little as 50 ppb of Hibernia or Venezuelan crude oil can inhibit feeding and growth (Fig. 1) with Hibernia crude oil being more potent (unpublished data). We also found that when cod are kept in cold water (3°C and less) they tended to lose weight and the percentage of weight loss over a given period of time was greater in chronically oil-treated fish than in controls (Fig. 2). Therefore, not only is growth inhibited but during periods of very low feeding, body resources are used up more quickly. Effects on something as fundamental as growth of such low levels of water-accommodated oil are worrying since it is not known at present which components of the oil are responsible, nor is the no-effect level known.

7. INVERTEBRATES

Gilfillan et al. (1976) reported a reduction in growth rate and increased respiration in *Mya arenaria* after a fuel oil spill in Casco Bay, Maine, and Gilfillan and Vandermeullen (1978) noted reduced growth in *M. arenaria*

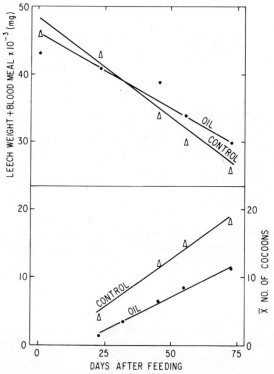

Figure 3. The effect of Venezuelan crude oil (~50 ppb) at 0°C on blood meal digestion and cocoon deposition in the hematophagous fish leech *Johanssonia arctica*.

following chronic Bunker *C* exposure in Chedebucto Bay, Nova Scotia. In studies on scallops exposed to weekly pulses of oil accommodated in water at concentrations of 60 ppb at the start of the week, falling to 14 ppb at the end of the week, we found that food intake, measured as rate of removal of algae from water, was reduced, probably due to physical damage to gills. The scallops were also observed to be irritable and expended a considerable amount of energy in attempts to escape.

One of us (R.A.K.) recently studied the effect of Venezuelan crude oil (~50 ppb) as a water-accommodated fraction (WAF) on the hematophagous fish leech *Johanssonia arctica* at 0°C over a period of 69 days. Adult leeches (~25 mm) were first permitted to feed to repletion on Atlantic cod, then were weighed and exposed in groups of 20 to 25 to WAF in a flow-through system. Control leeches were treated similarly except they were held in oil-free seawater. Digestion was more rapid in control leeches (Fig. 3) and was completed in 70% of the leeches after 69 days of exposure, whereas only 30% of oil-treated leeches digested the blood meal in this time. Moreover, control leeches produced about three times the cocoons (egg cases) that oil-treated leeches did after 69 days. These results suggest some effect on the digestive and reproductive systems following chronic oil exposure.

We have also observed that winter flounder infected with the gastrointestinal nematode *Fellodistomum furcigerum* and exposed to newly oiled sediment (2.7 mg/g) for 160 days had a lower incidence of the parasites ($\bar{X}$ = 1.47 worms) than flounder exposed to oiled sediment which had been weathered for one year (2.6 mg/g, $\bar{X}$ = 3.95 worms) or control flounder kept on clean sand ($\bar{X}$ = 6.84). Similarly, cod, harboring natural infections of an acanthocephalan parasite, *Echinorhynchus gadi*, were exposed to Venezuelan and Hibernia crude oils (water-accommodated fraction) for 81 days (~50 ppb) in a flow-through seawater system; they tended to lose the parasites. Control cod were infected more often and contained more parasites ($\bar{X}$ = 4.89) than fish exposed to Venezuelan ($\bar{X}$ = 3.20) or hibernia ($\bar{X}$ = 2.04) crude oils. A number of heterocyclic and aromatic compounds are used as antinematodal drugs due to their anesthetic action on worms (Robertson, 1977). Since marine fish must drink to osmoregulate, some of the ingested hydrocarbons may likely cause the worms to be released and be lost from the fish in the same way as antinematodal drugs act. This is, as a matter of fact, an old "farmers' remedy" for worms in livestock which calls for administration of a jigger of oil to the animal to rid it of worms.

8. CONCLUSIONS

Most of the sublethal effects of chronic oil exposure are on growth, feeding, and liver function. These may have a common general mode of action or they may be affected by several modes of action. The more relationships we can develop between affected variables under given treatment conditions the better we are able to predict the effects of complex pollutants on animals under different conditions.

In pharmacology it is recognized that a material seldom has just one site of action. More commonly a substance acts mostly at one site, but also has side effects (Goodman and Gilman, 1975). In our investigations of the effects of oil on organisms as a whole or even on the relationships of organisms (ecological effects) we must be careful not to pursue too blindly "the effect" and miss all the side effects in the process. Medical diagnosis is now a very well established art, but there is no single magic test for any disease, except maybe some biochemical disorders. Diagnoses are done by careful matching of symptoms and various test results. In the same way, research into effects of introduced materials on aquatic organisms should be broadly based, investigating as many variables as is practical so that various responses can be related to each other. Similarly, investigations should be conducted at realistic concentrations (preferably a range of concentrations); no effects on reproduction will be found if the animals die before gonads can be affected. Exposures must be long enough for symptoms to develop. It is also important that investigators think in terms of integrating the changes they find in a number of variables, not just enzyme "A." Multivariate experiments and their analyses are complicated and painstaking, but in a complex field there are no simple answers.

ACKNOWLEDGMENT

We gratefully acknowledge word processing by Karen Harding.

REFERENCES

Anderson, J. W., Birchard, E., Bourne, W. R. P., Gusey, W. F., Hughson, W. B., Kelly, G. F., McNulty, K., St. Amant, L., Sails, S. B., and Seymour, D. (1979). Fish, birds, marine mammals and sea turtles. *J. Environ. Pathol. Toxicol.* **3**, 119–148.

Chambers, J. E., Heitz, J. R., McCorckle, F. M., and Yarbrough, J. D. (1979). Enzyme activities following chronic exposure to crude oil in a simulated ecosystem. II. Striped mullet. *Environ. Res.* **20**, 140–147.

Cowey, C. B., and Sargent, J. R. (1977). Lipid nutrition in fish. *Comp. Biochem. Physiol* **57B**, 269–273.

Crocker, A. D., Cronshaw, J., and Holmes, W. N. (1975). The effect of several crude oils and some petroleum distillation fractions on intestinal absorption in ducklings (*Anas platyrhynchos*). *Environ. Physiol. Biochem.* **5**, 92–106.

Dey, A. C., Kiceniuk, J. W., Williams, U. P., Khan, R. A., and Payne, J. F. (1983). Long term exposure of marine fish to crude petroleum: I. Studies on lipids and fatty acids in cod (*Gadus morhua*) and winter flounder (*Pseudopleuronectes americanus*). *Comp. Biochem. Physiol.* (in press).

Driedzic, W. R. and Hochachka, P. W. (1978). Metabolism in fish during exercise. In: W. S. Hoar and D. J. Randall, Eds., *Fish physiology,* Vol. VII. Academic Press, New York, pp. 503–543.

Eurell, J. A. and Haensly, W. E. (1981). The effects of exposure to water-soluble fractions of crude oil on selected histochemical parameters of the liver of Atlantic croaker, *Micropogon undulatus* L. *J. Fish. Dis.* **4**, 187–194.

Farkas, T. (1967a). The effect of catecholamines and adrenocorticotrophic hormone on blood and adipose tissue FFA levels in the fish *Cyprinus carpio* L. *Prog. Biochem. Pharmacol.* **3**, 314–319.

Farkas, T. (1967b). Examinations of the fat metabolism in freshwater fishes—the sympathetic nervous system and the mobilization of fatty acids. *Ann. Biol. (Tihany)* **34**, 129–138.

Farkas, T. (1969). Studies on the mobilization of fats in lower vertebrates. *Acta Biochim. Biophys. Acad. Sci. Hung.* **4**, 237–249.

Fletcher, G. L., Kiceniuk, J. W., King, M., and Payne, J. F. (1979). Reduction of blood plasma copper concentrations in a marine fish following a six month exposure to crude oil. *Bull. Environ. Contam. Toxicol.* **22**, 548–551.

Fletcher, G. L., Kiceniuk, J. W., and Williams, U. P. (1981). Effects of oiled sediments on mortality, feeding and growth of winter flounder, *Pseudopleuronectes americanus. Mar. Ecol. Prog. Ser.* **4**, 91–96.

Fletcher, G. L., King, M. J., Kiceniuk, J. W., and Addison, R. F. (1982). Liver hypertrophy in winter flounder following exposure to experimentally oiled sediments. *Comp. Biochem. Physiol.* 73C, 457–462.

Gilfillan, E. S., Mayo, D., Hanson, S., Donovan, D., and Jiang, L. C. (1976). Reduction in carbon flux in *Mya arenaria* caused by a spill of No. 6 fuel oil. *Mar. Biol.* **37**, 115–123.

Gilfillan, E. S. and Vandermeulen, J. H. (1978). Alterations in growth and physiology of soft-shell clams, *Mya arenaria*, chronically oiled with Bunker C from Chedabucto Bay, Nova Scotia, 1970–1976. *J. Fish. Res. Board Can.* **35**, 630.

Goodman, L. S. and Gilman, A. (1975). *The pharmacological basis of therapeutics.* MacMillan Publishing, New York.

Gruger, E. H., Jr., Schnell, J. V., Fraser, P. S., Brown, D. W., and Malins, D. C. (1981). Metabolism of 2,6-dimethylnaphthalene in starry flounder (*Platichthys stellatus*) exposed to naphthalene and p-cresol. *Aquat. Toxicol.* **1**, 37–38.

Hawkes, J. W. (1977). The effects of petroleum hydrocarbon exposure on the structure of fish tissue. In: D. A. Wolfe, Ed., *Fate and effects of petroleum hydrocarbons in marine organisms and ecosystems.* Pergamon Press, New York, pp. 115–128.

Hoffman, D. J. (1979). Embryotoxic and teratogenic effects of petroleum hydrocarbons in mallards (*Anas platyrhynchos*). *J. Toxicol. Environ. Health* **5**, 835–844.

Khan, R. A., Kiceniuk, J., Dawe, M., and Williams, U. (1981). *Long term effects of crude oil on Atlantic cod.* ICES C.M. 1981/E:40, 10 pp.

Kiceniuk, J. W., Fletcher, G. L., and Misra, R. (1980). Physiological and morphological changes in cold torpid marine fish upon acute exposure to petroleum. *Bull. Environ. Contam. Toxicol.* **24**, 313–319.

Kiceniuk, J. W., Khan, R. A., Dawe, M., and Williams, U. (1982). Examination of interaction of trypanosome infection and crude oil exposure on hematology of the longhorn sculpin (*Myoxocephalus octodecemspinosus*). *Bull. Environ. Contam. Toxicol.* **28**, 435–438.

Lane, M. D. and Moss, J. (1971). Regulation of fatty acid synthesis in animal tissues. In: H. J. Vogel, Ed., *Metabolic pathways,* Vol. 5. Academic Press, New York, pp. 23–54.

Lysyj, I., Rushworth, R., Melvold, R., and Russell, E. C. (1980). A scheme for analysis of oily waters. In: L. Petrakis and F. T. Weiss, Eds., *Petroleum in the marine environment.* American Chemical Society, Washington, D.C., pp. 246–266.

Malcolm, J. D. and Cammaert, A. B. (1981). Transport and deposition of oil and gas spills under sea ice. In: *Proceedings of the fourth Arctic marine oilspill program technical seminars, Edmonton, Alberta.* June 16–18, 1980, pp. 45–74.

McCain, B. B., Hodgkins, H. O., Gronlund, W. D., Hawkes, J. W., Brown, D. W., Meyers, M. S., and Vandermeulen, J. H. (1978). Bioavailability of crude oil from experimentally oiled sediments to English oil from experimentally pathological consequences. *J. Fish. Res. Board Can.* **35**, 657–664.

Payne, J. F., Kiceniuk, J. W., Squires, W. R., and Fletcher, G. L. (1978). Pathological changes in a marine fish after a 6-month exposure to petroleum. *J. Fish. Res. Board Can.* **35**, 665–667.

Roberson, E. L. (1977). Antinematodal drugs. In: L. J. Jones, N. H. Booth, and L. E. McDonald, Eds., *Veterinary pharmacology and therapeutics.* Iowa State University Press, pp. 994–1051.

Shaw, D. G. (1977). Hydrocarbons in the water column. In: D. A. Wolfe, Ed., *Fate and effects of petroleum in marine organisms and ecosystems.* Pergamon Press, New York, pp. 8–18.

Solangi, M. A. (1980). Histopathological changes in two estuarine fishes exposed to crude oil and its water soluble fractions. Ph.D. dissertation, University of Southern Mississippi.

Stegeman, J. J. and Sabo, D. J. (1976). Aspects of the effects of petroleum hydrocarbons on intermediary metabolism and xenobiotic metabolism in marine fish. In: *Sources, effects and sinks of hydrocarbons in the aquatic environment.* American Institute of Biological Science, Washington, D.C., pp. 423–436.

Thurberg, F. P., Gould, E., and Dawson, M. A. (1978). Some physiological effects of the Argo Merchant oil spill on several marine teleosts and bivalve molluscs. In: *The wake of the Argo Merchant*. University of Rhode Island Press.

Weber, D., Gronlund, W., Scherman, T., and Brown, D. (1979). Non-avoidance of oil-contaminated sediment by juvenile English sole (*Paraphrys vetulus*). In: A. Calabrese and F. P. Thurberg, Eds., *Proceedings of the symposium on pollution and physiology of marine organisms*. Milford, Connecticut.

Woodward, P. F., Mehrle, P. M., Jr., and Mauck, W. L. (1981). Accumulation and sublethal effects of a Wyoming crude oil in Cutthroat trout. *Trans. Am. Fish. Soc.* **110**, 437–445.

15

REVIEW OF ECOTOXICITY OF MATACIL IN FRESHWATER ENVIRONMENT: CHEMICAL AND PHYTOBIOLOGICAL IMPACT STUDIES

Pearl Weinberger

Biology Department
University of Ottawa
Ottawa, Ontario

Roy Greenhalgh

Chemistry and Biology Research Institute
Canada Agriculture
Ottawa, Ontario

1. INTRODUCTION

For the past three decades, North American forests have suffered considerable damage due to lepidopterous defoliators. One of the most serious and widespread of these pests is the spruce budworm, *Choristoneura fumiferana* (Clemens), which has ravaged large areas of spruce and fir forests in Canada.

In an effort to combat the potential economic loss, controlled applications of various insecticides have been tested. The major criteria used to evaluate insecticides were high toxicity to the target insect, and minimal toxicity to nontarget organisms, with few harmful residual effects (Sundaram and Hopewell, 1977). Prior to 1969, organochlorine insecticides such as aldrin, dieldrin, toxaphene, heptachlor, BHC, and DDT were widely used. Their persistence and potential for biomagnification in the environment became recognized after a period of time and these chlorinated insecticides were replaced by organophosphorus and carbamate compounds. The latter insecticides are readily degraded and hence less persistent, resulting in fewer undesirable ecological consequences. One of these chemicals is the carbamate, aminocarb (4-dimethylamino-*m*-tolyl-*N*-methylcarbamate), which was introduced into Canada in 1973. It is registered as a formulation containing aminocarb dissolved in nonyl phenol and carries the trade mark Matacil 1.8D OSC (for operational use it is mixed with diluent oil No. 585), Matacil 1.8 OSC, and an older formulation, 1.68 OSC. Under current Canadian registration for forest use, Matacil is applied at rates of 52–87 g active ingredient (aminocarb) in 1.1–1.4 liters of mix per hectare (0.74–1.23 oz in 16–20 fl. oz per acre). Repeat applications at 5-day intervals are permissible. Prior to 1978, the carrier diluent used was No. 2 fuel oil, since then however, the more refined diluent, 585 oil has been employed.

Matacil reaches forest aquatic water systems by three principal routes: leaching to ground waters, by direct spray, and drift. The tank-mixed Matacil is applied to the forest aerially. The droplets from tank-mixed Matacil spray range in size from less than 10 μm (0.0004 in.) diameter to larger than 200 μm (0.008 in.) diameter. Depending on the conditions of atomization and formulation of insecticide, different ranges of size droplets will be obtained. Generally, 10% of the droplets will be less than 10 μm in size, representing about 1% of the tank mix. Larger droplets contain more formulation by cubic proportions. The percentage of the spray lost by vaporization as the spray descends is not known. Similarly, there is very little information on evaporation of pesticide from surfaces such as leaves as a result of aerosol deposits. Under ideal conditions, it has been found that 30–50% of the spray reaches the forest canopy. A detailed survey indicated that large forest spray operations normally contribute only small amounts of insecticide to atmospheric contamination and little to nontarget sites outside the area of spray (Varty, 1980).

In addition to its use in the Canadian forests, Matacil is used agriculturally for the control of insects on fruit, tobacco, and cotton in many countries including Germany, Australia, New Zealand, Israel, Mexico, and Peru. In these cases the application rates are greater than those used for forestry in Canada. To control apple pests, for example, repeat applications of up to 8.4 kg aminocarb per hectare were used. Food residue tolerances have been established in New Zealand, Germany, and Australia with the maximum permissible residue on apples as 4 mg/ml, with a 3-day preharvest interval.

2. PROPERTIES OF MATACIL

2.1. Chemical Properties

Aminocarb is a waxy white solid, mp 93–94°C, with vapor pressure $< 7.5 \times 10^{-5}$ mm Hg (20°C). It is slightly soluble in water < 2000 μg/ml, with a log K_{ow} in the range 1–2 at 25°C, depending on pH (Greenhalgh and Weinberger, 1982). It is moderately soluble in aromatic solvents and soluble in most polar organic solvents.

2.2. Volatilization

The volatility of aminocarb is a function of both temperature and surface texture, and with Matacil, the adjuvants must also be taken into account. Adbul-Wahab et al. (1966) indicated the disappearance of aminocarb at 25°C to be pseudo first-order. The estimated $t_{1/2}$ (half-life) from a glass surface was 1.6 hr, and from bean leaves, 4 hr. The rate of volatilization from water will depend upon Henry's law constant, which is the ratio of vapor pressure and water solubility (Mackay and Leinone, 1975). Generally, compounds with $H < 10$ torr · liter/mole may be considered to have little tendency to volatilize from water to air (Smith et al., 1980). For aminocarb, the value for H is of the order of 2×10^3 torr · liter/mole (v.p. 2×10^{-5} mm, Addison, 1981; water solubility 2000 μg/ml). Although this is 200-fold greater than the value suggested by Smith et al. (1980), other observation suggests that aminocarb appears to have a low volatility from clear water surfaces. In lake and distilled water, for aminocarb added as a tank mix with nonyl phenol and No. 585 oil, volatilization at 25°C is of the order of $t_{1/2}$ = 3–6 hr (Weinberger et al., 1982).

2.3. Partition Coefficient

Partition between octanol and water, which is used as an indication of its solubility into membrane lipids, is dependent on pH (Table 1). At pH 8, when aminocarb is in the free base form, the K_{ow} value is 70 ± 10 determined by use of GC analysis (Greenhalgh and Weinberger, 1982). However, McLeese et al. (1979), have calculated $\log K_{ow}$ = 2.91 (K_{ow} = 813), based on Hansch lipophylic substitution values.

2.4. Hydrolysis

Hydrolytic cleavage of aminocarb gives 4-(dimethylamino)-3-methyl phenol and methyl carbamic acid, the latter being further degraded into carbon dioxide and methylamine (Patel, 1978). The rate of hydrolysis decreases as both the temperature and pH decrease (Murphy et al., 1975). The estimated $t_{1/2}$ for aminocarb in 0.2 M phosphate buffers, pH of 5–9 and in the dark, ranged from $t_{1/2}$ = 90 hr (pH 5 at 20°C) to $t_{1/2}$ = 0.6 hr (pH 9.0 at 30°C). The persistence of Matacil in any environment compartment will be dependent on both the pH and temperature.

Environmental concern has been raised as to the possibility that some carbamates may hydrolyze slowly and be more persistent in natural waters than is commonly believed. The alkaline hydrolysis rates for carbamates has been shown to be structure dependent (Wolfe et al., 1978). At pH 9.0 and 27°C, the half-life for carbaryl (N-methyl carbamate) was 0.15 days, whereas for propam (N-phenyl carbamate) it was 5 orders of magnitude greater (1 × 10^4 days). The structural activity relationship of a number of carbamates can be used to predict their hydrolytic half-lives. Only N-substituted phenols with pK_a less than 12 might have rates of hydrolysis that could be considered to be ecologically relevant. This approach has been applied to Matacil (Fig. 1). The pK_a of 4-dimethylamino-3-methyl-phenol is 10.8, low enough to suggest that persistence may well be a factor in natural waters. In a recent study, Weinberger et al. (1980) followed the hydrolytic fate of tank-mixed (^{14}C-ring) aminocarb in lake water (pH 7.4, specific conductance 61 ± 2 μmho/cm) at different temperatures. Degradation was rapid at 50°C and the reaction followed first-order kinetics. After 13 hr only 70% of the substrate could be extracted with ethyl acetate. This fraction contained approximately 20% unchanged aminocarb with the remainder mostly aminocarb phenol and

Table 1.   Effect of pH on Aminocarb Partition Coefficient

pH	4.0	5.0	6.0	7.0	8.0	9.0
K_{ow}	1.8 ± 0.3	8.2 ± 1.8	30 ± 10	58 ± 6	70 ± 10	80 ± 10

some 4-amino-3-methylphenol. When aminocarb alone was used, as compared with formulated aminocarb, more aminocarb phenol and more organo soluble compounds were observed. Values for the half-life of tank-mixed aminocarb in lake water are shown in Table 2.

The active role played by natural assemblages of endemic microphyta in the lake water was evident when, in a parallel experiment, ^{14}C-ring aminocarb was introduced into distilled water. Post treatment (35 hr), in the absence of natural microbiota, only 3% of the total ^{14}C activity was not soluble in ethyl acetate whereas in natural waters, 88% was in this fraction.

2.5.   Photolysis

The photolytic stability of aminocarb has been investigated under a wide range of light conditions (Fig. 2, Table 3). Many studies have used wavelengths that are outside the range (290–450 nm) that normally reach the earth and thus provide little information of use environmentally. These studies, such as the photolysis of aminocarb in organic solvents, can provide data on the potential degradation products (Crosby et al., 1965; Mulkey et al.,

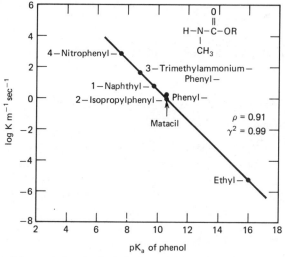

Figure 1.   Plots of the second-order hydrolysis rate constants of some N-methyl carbamates vs. pk_a of the resulting phenol of a range of carbamates, including aminocarb, in water at 25°C.

Table 2.   Estimated $t_{1/2}$ (days) for Aminocarb Formulated and Nonformulated in Distilled or Lake Water in Dark Systems as a Function of Temperature

Water	Temperature (°C)	Half-Life Formulated	Nonformulated
Lake	50	0.2	0.16
Lake	33	6.0	—
Lake	25	9.3[a]	10.5
Distilled	25	20.6	

[a]Does not fit first-order kinetics well.

1978). Abdul-Wahab and Casida (1967) tentatively identified four photo-products resulting from sunlight-irradiation of aminocarb on bean leaves; they were 4-(methylformamido)-3-methylphenyl-N-methylcarbamate, 4-formamido-3-methyl-phenyl-N-methylcarbamate, 4-amino-3 methylphenyl-N-methylcarbamate, and 4-methylamino-m-tolyl-N-methylcarbamate, the major photolysis product. In distilled water (Addison et al., 1974) and in natural lake water, in both the absence and presence of aquatic phytobiota, 4-(dimethylamino)-3-methylphenol was the major product (Greenhalgh and Weinberger, 1982). In lake water (pH 6.8), the $t_{1/2}$ for formulated Matacil was 24 hr in 5 klux fluorescent light as compared with 3–6 hr in bright natural sunlight. The rate of photolytic degradation was a function of pH (Fig. 2). At pH 7, the $t_{1/2} = 3$ hr, whereas at pH 3 the estimated $t_{1/2} = 15$ hr.

Although photolysis was the major process by which aminocarb degraded in lake water, the rate of degradation was reduced by the presence of aquatic macrophytes. By providing a "sink" for the pesticide, its concentration in the water compartment was reduced and the rate of photolysis was then related to the desorption coefficient (Weinberger et al., 1982).

2.6.   Absorption

2.6.1.   Polymers

The fate and transport of Matacil has been investigated in microcosms fabricated from one or more polymers (Weinberger et al., 1982). It was shown that after 24 hr, aminocarb is extensively absorbed from water by Tygon® (47%), and to a lesser extent by Teflon® (6%), Parafilm® (0.01%), and polyethylene (0.01%) (Weinberger et al., 1982).

2.6.2.   Soils

At 25°C and in the concentration range of 0.2–5.0 μg/ml, about 75% of applied aminocarb was bound to loam soil containing 42% organic matter

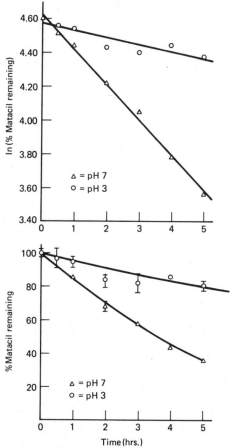

Figure 2.   Photolysis of Matacil (aminocarb in nonyl phenol) in natural sunlight at pH 7.0 and pH 3.0.

(Atwell, 1978). The Freudlich constants K and $1/n$ were 12.9 and 0.9, respectively, for 16 hr-agitated soil–water (10:50) mixtures.

2.6.3.   Sediments

In static two-compartment aquatic systems at 25°C and subject only to convection current mixing, 20% of applied Matacil was absorbed into sediment

Table 3. Photolysis of Aminocarb in Lake Water[a]. Estimated $t_{1/2}$ (hr) in Overcast Sunlight (July, Ottawa, Canada) at 23°C

pH	3	5	6	7	8
$t_{1/2}$	33	33	8.8	7.6	6.1

[a] Specific conductance 61 ± 2 μmho/cm; turbidity 10–25 FTU.

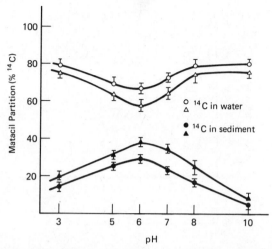

Figure 3. Partitioning characteristics of matacil into sediment as a function of pH. O = day 1 and Δ = day 2 post treatment.

(containing 5% organic matter) within 2 days. The amount sequestered in the sediment was a function of pH. Partitioning into the sediment was highest at pH 6.0 when aminocarb is in the free base form and lowest at pH 3.0 when protonated, and at 10.0, where some rapid hydrolysis in the water compartment could have occurred (Fig. 3). In three-compartment systems (water pH 6.8/sediment/phytobiota), only 10–15% of the added aminocarb (1 μg/ml) was in the sediment after 21 days. Partitioning into, and retention by, the phytobiota was found to be a function of taxa and genera (Weinberger et al., 1982).

3.   AQUATIC PHYTOBIOTA

3.1.   Microphytes, Macrophytes, Population Dynamics, Ultrastructure, and Physiology

Aminocarb (at concentrations of 1 and 10 μg/ml) stimulated the growth of the algal microphyte *Chlorella pyrenoidosa* Chick, when formulated or added as the tank mix; the same range of concentrations were algicidal. The latter activity was attributed to the nonyl phenol in the tank mix (Weinberger and Rea, 1982). Nonformulated aminocarb (<100 μg/ml) did not affect photosynthesis or population growth, whereas formulated (10 μg/ml) aminocarb or 0.75 μg/ml nonyl phenol, after 1 hr post treatment, caused extensive damage of chloroplast thylakoid membranes and the plasmalemma and resulted in flagellar distortion in *Chlamydomonas reinhardtii* Dang (Weinberger and Rea, 1982). The same concentrations of aminocarb did not affect the population growth, nor net photosynthesis of *Lemna minor*. Formulated aminocarb (3 µg/ml), in contrast, reduced the population growth of the duckweed. Growth reduction was preceded by the partial bleaching of the fronds, a reduction in total ATP content, and fragility of the rooting system. The toxicant present in the formulation appears to be nonyl phenol. Matacil was found to synergize the toxicity of nonyl phenol in *Lemna minor*. Population growth, as measured by frond production, was not affected by >10 µg/ml aminocarb but was reduced by 50% after 96-hr exposure to 5.6 µg/ml nonyl phenol or 1.3 µg/ml aminocarb formulated with 3.25 µg/ml nonyl phenol, (Weinberger and Iyengar, 1982).

3.2. Bioaccumulation

The aquatic macrophyte *Ceratophyllum demersum* retained 75% (as determined by GC analysis) of 1 µg/ml formulated and nonformulated aminocarb after 20 days when kept in sunlight, but only 39% if kept in the dark. Plants treated with formulated Matacil senesced in both the light and dark by 20 days post treatment, and also lost chlorophyll to the bathing lake water medium. When the plants were treated with nonformulated aminocarb, all sets remained healthy. *Ceratophyllum demersum* had a large capacity for the absorption of Matacil (> 1000 µg/g fresh weight), whereas the capacity of the vascular aquatics *Lloydella* and *Valisneria* and the microphytes *Chlorella* and *Chlamydomonas* was one third of this (>300 µg/g fresh weight) (Weinberger and Latourneau, 1982).

3.3. Biodegradation

The unicellular alga *Chlorella* and the aquatic macrophytes *Lloydella* and *Valisneria* retained approximately 3% of the aminocarb added to aquatic systems containing these organisms. They degraded more than 70% of the pesticide whether present as aminocarb or its formulation. The aminocarb appeared to be absorbed, degraded, and then desorbed back into the lake water, with only 3% being retained in the macrophytes. In *Ceratophyllum demersum* (the common aquatic weed, hornwort), little aminocarb was desorbed; most was retained (>70%), and released from the plant material only upon senescence. Loss from the algae was also evident on death (Weinberger et al., 1982). The major derivative found was Matacil phenol.

3.4. Fish–Algal Systems

Algal cells containing 0.3 µg/ml aminocarb augmented with [14]C-(2000 dpm/ml) was used as the sole food for guppies over a 7-day period. No aminocarb was detected (< 100 ppb) in the guppies by gas chromatographic analysis or by scintillation counting. Guppies immersed in water containing nonformulated aminocarb, (1–10 μg/ml) showed no behavioral aberrances nor any detectable retention of the aminocarb. However, when they were exposed to formulated, or tank-mixed aminocarb, swimming, feeding, and socially aberrant behavior was common. These abnormal behavioral changes can be attributed directly to the nonyl phenol in the formulation (Weinberger et al., 1982).

4. ECOTOXICITY ASSESSMENT

It is evident that exposure to nonformulated aminocarb within the permissible range of concentrations has few long-term effects on natural aquatic ecosystems in terms of acute toxicity. In acidic aquatic medium, the pesticide will persist longer in the system, which may slightly perturb the population dynamics of some aquatic unicellular algae by enhancing growth and net productivity. These effects, however, would be limited by the persistence of the chemical at the stimulative level of 0.5–1.0 μg/ml. Under natural pH conditions, degradation by hydrolysis and photolysis would reduce the time scale of potential perturbance to less than 2 days. In aquatic systems of pH 7, partitioning into sediment is greater than in acidic or alkaline systems. The effects of the pH range of 4–9 (found in nature) on partitioning, hydrolysis, and photolysis are of a time scale that has no significance to long-term community changes. The only sources of possible long-term perturbation derive from the degradative potential of many aquatic phyto micro- and macrophytes that can form an array of polar derivatives, most notably phenolic products, that may be desorbed back into the water medium. They have the potential to influence biotic vigor or to provide a new food resource for some food specialists in the aquatic system. The more potent sources of perturbance are the aquatic vascular macrophytes, such as *Ceratophyllum demersum,* which are able to provide a sink for the pesticide.

In practice, aminocarb is sprayed into the forest systems formulated in nonyl phenol. This surfactant is a mixture of para-substituted monoalkyl phenols, which also contain about 3% of the ortho isomer and 4% of 2,4-dinonyl phenol. The tank mix also contains a refined No. 585 fuel oil distillate. The formulation in current use for aminocarb, the 1.8D oil soluble concentrate, consists of 19.5% by weight active ingredient, 50.5% nonyl phenol, and 30.0% diluent 585 oil. The anticholinesterase activity of the tank mix against the pest larvae is due to aminocarb. However, the most biologically active ingredient in the tank mix, with respect to aquatic phytobiota, is the "inert" surfactant nonyl phenol. Whereas the long-term effects of exposure to aminocarb in forest ecosystems are assessed as minor, multiple exposures to formulated or tank-mixed Matacil may lead to significant perturbations of an aquatic environment.

REFERENCES

Abdul-Wahab, A. M. and Casida, J. E. (1967). Photooxidation of two 4-methylaminoaryl methylcarbamate insecticides (Zectran and Matacil) on bean foliage and of alkylaminophenyl methylcarbamates on silica gel chromoplates. *J. Agric. Food Chem.* **15**, 479–487.

Abdul-Wahab, A. M., Kuhr, R. J., and Casida, J. E. (1966). Fate of ^{14}C-carbonyl-labelled insecticide chemicals in and on bean plants. *J. Agric. Food Chem.* **14**, 290–298.

Addison, J. B. (1981). Measurement of vapour pressure of Fenitrothion and Matacil. *Chemosphere* **10**, 355–364.

Addison, J. B., Silk, P. J., and Unger, I. (1974). The photochemical reactions of carbamates II. Solution photochemistry of Matacil (4-methylamino-*m*-tolyl-*N*-methylcarbamate) and Landrin (3,4, 5-trimethylphenyl-*N*-methylcarbamate), *Bull. Environ. Contam. Toxicol.* **11**, 250–255.

Atwell, S. H. (1978). *Soil adsorption and desorption of ^{14}C-Matacil.* Mobay Chemical Corporation Rept. 66424, July.

Crosby, D. G., Leitis, E., and Winterlin, W. L. (1965). Photodecomposition of carbamate insecticides. *J. Agric. Food Chem.* **13**, 204–207.

Greenhalgh, R. and Weinberger, P. (1983). The fate of Matacil in an aquatic environment. *J. Environ. Sci. Health,* (in press).

Mackay, D. and Leinone, P. J. (1975). Rate of evaporation of L_{ow} solubility contaminants from water bodies to atmosphere. *Environ. Sci. Technol.* **9**, 1178–1180.

McLeese, D. W., Zitko, V., and Peterson, M. R. (1979). Structure–lethality for phenols, anilines and other aromatic compounds in shrimp and clams. *Chemosphere* **2**, 53–57.

Mulkey, N. S., McPaul, L., Augenstein, L. L., and Margo, J. P., Jr. (1978). *Photodegradation of* [^{14}C] *Matacil in aqueous solution.* Mobay Chemical Corporation, Chemagro Agricultural Chemicals Division, Rept. 50447, Oct.

Murphy, J. J., Minor, R. G., Jacobs, K., and Shaw, H. R., III. (1975). *Persistence of Matacil in soil.* Mobay Chemical Corporation, Chemagro Agricultural Chemicals Division, Rept. 43444, Jan.

Patel, N. (1978). *The composition of technical Matacil.* Mobay Chemical Corporation, Chemagro Agricultural Chemicals Division, Rept. 67418.

Smith, J. H., Bomberger, D. C., and Haynes, D. L. (1980). Prediction of the volatilization rates of high-volatility chemicals from natural water bodies. *Environ. Sci. Technol.* **14**, 1332–1337.

Sundaram, K. M. S. and Hopewell, W. W. (1977). *Fate and persistence of aminocarb in conifer foliage and forest soil after simulated aerial spray application.* Environment Canada Forest Pest Management Institute Rept. FPM-X-66.

Sundaram, K. M. S., Volpe, Y., Smith, G. G., and Duffy, J. R. (1976). *A preliminary study on the persistence and distribution of Matacil in a forest environment.* Canadian Forestry Service, Environment Canada Rept. CC-X-116, Jan.

Varty, I. W. (1980). *Environmental surveillance in New Brunswick, 1978–1979. Effects of Spray Operations for Forest Protection. Rept. by Committee for Environmental Monitoring of Forest Insect Control Operations, Dept. Forest Resources, University of New Brunswick, Fredericton, N. B.*

Weinberger, P., Engelhardt, R., Philogène, B., and Qadri, S. (1980). *The fate of Matacil in aquatic ecosystems.* Mid-grant report 95/307/92 Stat. 353 16 USC 1600. Ottawa University, Ottawa, Ontario.

Weinberger, P., Greenhalgh, R., Sher, D. and Ouellette, M. (1982). *The fate of Matacil in an aquatic environment.* Final grant report 97/308/92 Stat. 35516 USC 1700. Ottawa University, Ottawa, Ont.

Weinberger, P. and Rea, M. (1982). Population growth and ultrastructural effects of Matacil and its formulation adjuncts on *Chlorella pyrenoidosa* and *Chlamydomonas reinhardii. Environ. Exp. Botany* **22,** 491–496.

Weinberger, P. and Iyengar, S. (1983). Effects of Aminocarb. Matacil and Nonylphenol on *Lemna minor.* In *Developments in Arid Zone Ecology and Environmental Quality,* Vol. 11.

Weinberger, P. and Latourneau, C. (1982). The pesticide-absorptive capacity of some vascular aquatic macrophytes. Unpublished results.

Wolfe, N. L., Zepp, R. G., and Paris, D. F. (1978). Use of structure–reactivity relationships to estimate hydrolytic persistence of carbamate pesticides. *Water Res.* **12,** 561–563.

16

THE USE OF ALGAL BATCH AND CONTINUOUS CULTURE TECHNIQUES IN METAL TOXICITY STUDY

P. T. S. Wong

Great Lakes Biolimnology Laboratory
Canada Centre for Inland Waters
Burlington, Ontario

Y. K. Chau

National Water Research Institute
Canada Centre for Inland Waters
Burlington, Ontario

D. Patel

Great Lakes Biolimnology Laboratory
Canada Centre for Inland Waters
Burlington, Ontario

1. INTRODUCTION

Many studies have been conducted on the effects of toxic chemicals on algae (Wong et al., 1978b; Rai et al., 1981). The studies are usually carried out in a closed system (batch culture technique). The batch culture technique involves growing the algae in a closed container with no addition of fresh medium or removal of catabolic waste in the experiment. The algae go through the characteristic pattern of growth cycle, namely the lag, exponential, stationary, and death phases (Fogg, 1975). The technique is the most commonly used method because of its simplicity and relatively low cost. However, it has a number of inherent shortcomings which have been discussed in detail by Fogg (1975) and Rhee (1980). The continuous culture system involves a continuous supply of fresh medium to the cells allowing optimal growth and removal of catabolic waste. The technique was first used for bacterial cultures (Monod, 1950) and is relatively new for algal cultures. The theoretical analyses of continuous culture system were comprehensively treated by Malek and Fencl (1966). Two devices are available for this system: the turbidostat and the chemostat.

In a turbidostat, the cell concentration is maintained at a constant level by means of a photoelectric attachment. When the cell density exceeds the predetermined value, the photocell will cause the solenoid valve to open and let in fresh medium from a reservoir to dilute the cell density in the culture vessel and simultaneously allow overflow of an equal volume of the cells and the medium (Munson, 1970; Rhee, 1980). The first turbidostat was designed by Myers and Clark (1944) for the continuous culture of *Chlorella*. Now several types of turbidostat are available from commercial (Techtum Instrument, Umeà, Sweden) or individual investigators (Premazzi et al., 1978; Ferrara et al., 1975). The present status and future prospects of the turbidostat have been reviewed by Watson (1972).

The chemostat also involves the addition and removal of medium from a culture vessel. However, the cell density is controlled by the rate of nutrient addition. The faster the fresh medium is delivered to the culture vessel, the faster the cell growth rate. Apparatus suitable for the growth of algae has been described by Fay and Kulasooriya (1973) and Ukeles (1973). The concept and problems of the chemostat have been discussed by Solomons (1972).

Metals are known to be toxic to algae especially at high concentrations (Sorentino, 1979; Rai et al., 1981). Although there is a growing fund of information on the toxicity of individual metals to algae, not much is known about the interactive effects when the metals are present together. Since in natural waters, metals always occur together and not in isolation, it is important to study their interactions. Indeed, metals are known to have synergistic (Hutchinson and Stokes, 1975) and antagonistic (Stratton and Corke, 1979) toxicity on algae. A mixture of 10 metals was found to inhibit primary productivity, growth, and enzyme activities of several freshwater algae when the metals were present together (Wong et al., 1978a, 1983). The results were obtained from algae incubated under batch culture technique. In this study, the toxicity of the metal mixture was evaluated with a common freshwater green alga, *Ankistrodesmus falcatus*, grown under both batch and continuous culture techniques.

2. MATERIALS AND METHODS

2.1. Culture

Ankistrodesmus falcatus var. *acicularis* (Ontario Ministry of Natural Resources, P.O. Box 213, Rexdale, Ontario) was maintained in a modified CHU-10 medium at pH 8 (Wong et al., 1978a). The inoculum was prepared by growing the culture in 100 ml of CHU-10 medium at 20°C on a rotary shaker (100 rpm) under conditions of 18 hr of light (5000 lux) and 6 hr of darkness. When the cells reached the logarithmic phase of growth (about 1 week), they were used as inoculum.

2.2. Metal Mixture

The concentrations of the metal mixture were prepared according to the recommended Great Lakes Water Quality Objective levels (International Joint Commission, 1976). A full strength (1 ×) of the metal mixture contained the following metal and metalloid concentrations in µg of the metal per liter of medium: As, 50 (sodium arsenate); Cd, 0.2 (cadmium nitrate); Cr, 50 (potassium dichromate); Cu, 5 (copper sulfate); Fe, 300 (ferrous sulfate); Pb, 25 (lead nitrate); Hg, 0.2 (mercury chloride); Ni, 25 (nickel sulfate); Se, 10 (sodium selenite); and Zn, 30 (zinc chloride). The metal mixture of $0.5 \times$ and $0.1 \times$ represented half-strength and one-tenth of the strength of the metal mixture. The metal solutions were prepared by dissolving reagent-grade compounds in doubly distilled water.

2.3. ^{14}C-NaHCO$_3$ Uptake

The ^{14}C-NaHCO$_3$ uptake by the cells was used as an indicator of algal primary production. One ml of the inoculum (4×10^5 cells/ml) was added to 13.9 ml of modified CHU-10 medium or lake water from Hamilton Harbour with or without the addition of the metal mixture. After a 24-hr incubation at 20°C under conditions described previously, a 0.1-ml aliquot of 2 µCi/ml ^{14}C-NaHCO$_3$ (Amersham/Searle, 58.8 mCi/mmole) was added to each flask. The flasks were tightly capped with rubber stoppers which were wrapped in aluminum foil. A similar set of flasks was incubated in the dark. After a 4-hr incubation, the cells were fixed with 0.05 ml of neutralized formalin. The cells were separated from the medium by filtering through a 0.45-µm membrane filter, rinsed rapidly with 10 ml fresh CHU-10 medium to remove extracellular ^{14}C-NaHCO$_3$. Filters containing the radioisotope-labelled cells were dissolved in 10 ml PCS scintillation counting fluor (Amersham/Searle). Radioactivity was measured by a liquid scintillation counter (Beckman model LS8100) and the amount in the algae without exposure to metal mixture (Control) was calculated as 100%. Radioactivity taken up by algae in the dark represented less than 5% of the total and was subtracted from the total radioactive counts.

2.4. Reproduction

2.4.1. Optical Measurement

The effects of the metal mixture on algal reproduction were also measured spectrophotometrically with a Klett-Summerson photoelectric colorimeter with filter (#66). One ml of the inoculum was added to 49 ml of modified CHU-10 medium with and without the metal mixture in a 300-ml Nephelo culture flask with a side-arm (Bellco Co., Vineland, New Jersey). The rate of algal reproduction was measured at various time intervals by tilting the growth medium into the side-arm which was then inserted into the colorimeter for optical density readings. The readings in Klett units (K.U.) were converted to cell number, using a previously constructed standard curve relating K.U. to cell number (10 K.U. were equivalent to 1.2×10^5 cells/ml).

A growth curve of cells versus time was then plotted in a semi-log (base 10) paper. The growth rate (k) was calculated from values in the straight part of the curve (logarithmic phase). Two values were chosen (the higher and the lower cell numbers in the logarithmic phase) and the growth rate was calculated according to the formula (Guillard, 1973):

$$k = \frac{\log_2 (N_1/N_0)}{t_1 - t_0}$$

where k = growth rate
N_1 = the higher cell number in the logarithmic phase
N_0 = the lower cell number in the logarithmic phase
t_1 = time for the higher cell number
t_0 = time for the lower cell number

From K, the generation time (time for cell to multiply once) was computed as $Tg = 1/k$ days per division.

The effects of a metal mixture on the growth rate of algae can be calculated as follows:

$$\% \text{ inhibition} = \left(1 - \frac{k_1}{k_2}\right) \times 100$$

where k_1 = growth rate in the presence of metal mixture
k_2 = growth rate in the control.

2.4.2. Cell Count

The effects of the metal mixture on algal reproduction were followed by counting the number of cells at various time intervals. One ml of the inoculum was added to 9 ml of modified CHU-10 medium with or without the metal mixture in a 25-ml Erlenmeyer flask capped with a foam stopper. The flasks were incubated on a shaker under 18 hr of light and 6 hr of darkness as described previously. At different time intervals, a 0.5-ml subsample was taken and cell numbers were counted with a Petroff-Hausser counting chamber and a phase-contrast microscope. The growth rate and percent inhibition by the metal mixture were then calculated as described before.

2.5. Turbidostat

The turbidostat system (Techtum Instrument, Umeà, Sweden) consists of an algal cultivation controller unit and five cultivation tubes with optical heads (Fig. 1). Four hundred forty ml of CHU-10 medium with and without the metal mixture were added to the cultivation tube and 2 liters of the respective medium and metal solution were dispensed to the storage bottle. One tube was used as the control and two tubes for 0.5× metals and two for

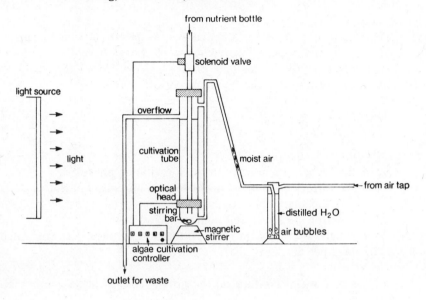

TURBIDOSTAT

Figure 1. A diagrammatic scheme of the turbidostat.

1.0× metals. The medium, chemicals, glasswares, and tubings were sterilized by autoclaving and the solenoid valves were sterilized with 70% ethanol and rinsed thoroughly with sterile distilled water. Ten ml of inoculum (2×10^6 cells/ml) were added into each of the five cultivation tubes. The medium and the cells were mixed rapidly with the magnetic stirrer and a stream of moist and cotton-filtered air. The algae were grown at 20°C under continuous illumination by a row of fluorescent lights (21,000 lux). When the cell number in the cultivation tube exceeded a preset value in the controller, the solenoid valve would open. The fresh medium in the storage bottle flowed into the tube by gravity and diluted the cells to the preset value. The excessive cell suspension flowed through an overflow to the waste bottle and the volume and the cell count were recorded daily. The growth rate and % inhibition by the metal mixture were calculated.

2.6. Chemostat

The design of the chemostat is shown in Fig. 2. Three experimental vessels (Bellco Co., Vineland, New Jersey), each containing 900 ml CHU-10 medium with and without the metal mixture, were inoculated with 10 ml of the algal culture. The medium and the cells were mixed rapidly with a magnetic stirrer and aerated with a stream of moist and filter-sterilized air. The medium with and without the metal mixture in the 2-liter reservoir was

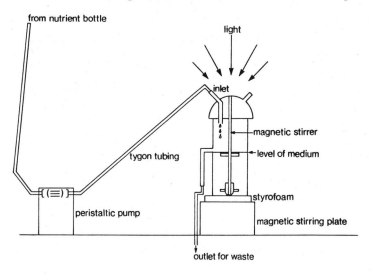

from nutrient bottle

light

inlet

magnetic stirrer

tygon tubing

level of medium

styrofoam

peristaltic pump

magnetic stirring plate

outlet for waste

CHEMOSTAT

Figure 2. A diagrammatic scheme of the chemostat.

introduced to the experimental vessel by a rate adjustable 4-channel peristaltic pump (Buchler, New Jersey). The rate of medium input varied from
experiment to experiment ranging from a low of 100 ml to a high of 700 ml
per day. Fast flow-rates would result in the "wash out" of the cells from the
experimental vessel. The excessive medium would flow through an overflow
to the waste bottle. The volume in the waste bottle was measured and the
cells in the experimental vessel were counted. Growth rate and percent
inhibition by the metal mixture were calculated.

3.   RESULTS AND DISCUSSION

The effects of a mixture of 10 metals at the recommended Great Lakes
Water Quality Objective levels (International Joint Commission, 1976) were
determined on the primary productivity and cell reproduction of *A. falcatus*
under static and continuous culture conditions.

3.1.   Primary Productivity

Ankistrodesmus falcatus exposed to the metal mixture for 24 hr in a CHU-10
laboratory medium lost its ability to take up ^{14}C-NaHCO$_3$ by 30% as compared to the control without metal treatment (Table 1). One-half of the metal
mixture also reduced the ^{14}C-uptake by 11%. However, one-tenth of the

Table 1. Effects of a Mixture of Metals on the Primary Productivity of
Ankistrodesmus falcatus **in CHU-10 Medium and Hamilton Harbour Water**

	Primary Productivity (% ± SE)[a]	
Metal Mixture	CHU-10	Hamilton Harbour Water
Control (no metal)	100	100
0.1× metals	105 ± 4	86 ± 5
0.5× metals	89 ± 3	81 ± 7
1.0× metals	70 ± 3	64 ± 5

[a] Mean and standard error of five samples.

concentration had no inhibitory effect, but instead was slightly stimulatory. The metal toxicity was more pronounced when lake water from Hamilton Harbour area was used as the incubation medium. The enhanced toxicity was probably due to the presence of other toxic elements in the lake water (Chau et al., 1970) which would have an additive toxic effect on the alga. The metal mixture was also found to reduce the primary productivity of four other freshwater algae as well as natural phytoplankton from Lake Ontario water (Wong et al., 1983).

The advantages and disadvantages of this technique are shown in Table 2. The major advantages are its sensitivity, short experimental time, and bacterial contamination is not a major problem. However, since the technique measures only a short physiological response, the longer reproduction time and the ability of the organism to tolerate the metal mixture cannot be tested. Experiments were, therefore, carried out to determine the reproduction of the alga incubated under static or continuous culture conditions.

Table 2. Primary Production (^{14}C-NaHCO$_3$)

Advantages	Disadvantages
1. Short time—4 hours	1. Physiological response
2. Sensitive	2. Adaptation or mutation not tested
3. Handles large number of samples	3. Cost of expensive counter and filtration apparatus
4. Not labor intensive	4. Slightly hazardous radioactivity
5. Contamination not a major problem	
6. Samples can be stored for a longer time before actually counting.	

3.2. Batch Culture

3.2.1. *Optical Density Measurement*

In this experiment, the cells were exposed to the metal mixture in an Erlenmeyer flask fitted with a side-arm. No fresh medium or metal mixture was added to or withdrawn from the flask during the course of the experiment. The effects of the metal mixture on the algal reproduction were followed by daily measurement of the optical density changes in the side-arm of the flask. The optical density units were converted to cell number to facilitate the calculation of cell growth rate.

The results in Fig. 3 demonstrate the toxic effects of the metal mixture on algal reproduction. The addition of the recommended level of the metal mixture ($1 \times$) decreased both the rate and the total amount in the steady state of the algal reproduction. Such a decrease in the total amount of algal biomass suggested that the alga did not adapt to the metal toxicity. Algae are known to have the capacity to become tolerant to individual metals (Stokes et al., 1973) by exclusion (DeFilippis and Pallaghy, 1976) or by internal detoxifying mechanism (Silverberg et al., 1977). It is unlikely that *A. fal-*

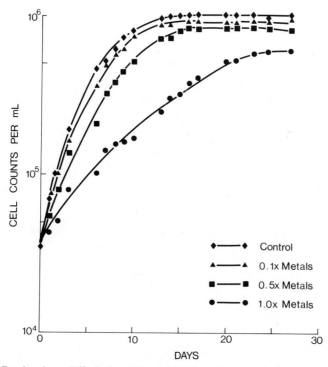

Figure 3. Batch culture. Effect of a mixture of metals on the reproduction of *A. falcatus*. The rate of reproduction was measured spectrophotometrically and converted to cell number.

Table 3. Summary of the Toxicity of a Mixture of Metals on the Reproduction of *A. falcatus* Using Batch and Continuous Culturing Techniques

Metal Mixture	Batch Culture						Continuous Culture					
	Optical			Cell Count			Turbidostat			Chemostat		
	A[a]	B[b]	C[c]	A	B	C	A	B	C	A	B	C
Control (no metal)	0.66	36	0	0.74	32	0	0.55	43	0	0.76	32	0
0.1× metal	0.60	40	9	—	—	—	—	—	—	—	—	—
0.5× metal	0.37	64	44	0.55	43	26	0.36	65	35	0.45	53	41
1.0× metal	0.17	136	74	0.22	109	71	0.16	150	71	0.23	106	70

[a]A = cell growth rate (*k*)/day.

[b]B = generation time (hr).

[c]C = % growth inhibition as compared with the controlled cells.

458

Table 4.   Reproduction (Optical Density Measurement)

Advantages	Disadvantages
1. Convenient	1. Nutrients depleted
2. Low cost	2. Metabolic wastes accumulated
3. Contamination not a major problem	3. No distinction in dead and live cells
4. Adaptation or mutation can be tested	4. Less sensitive measurement
5. Large sample sizes can be easily determined	

catus could tolerate a mixture of 10 metals simultaneously. In contrast with the primary productivity (Table 1), the reproduction was slightly inhibited by the presence of one-tenth of the concentration of the metal mixture (Fig. 3), suggesting that the reproduction process was more sensitive to the metals. The effects of the metal mixture on algal growth rate, generation time, and percent growth inhibition calculated according to equations in Section 2 are summarized in Table 3. Exposing the cells to $0.1\times$, $0.5\times$, $1.0\times$ metal mixture decreased the growth rate from 0.66 to 0.60, 0.37, and 0.17 division per day respectively. In terms of generation time (time for cell to multiply once), the metal mixture caused the cells to have a longer generation time (i.e., a slower reproduction rate). The use of optical density measurement to follow cell reproduction is thus a convenient technique (Table 4). Since no sample was withdrawn from the flask for analysis, bacterial contamination was rather unlikely to occur. The experiment was normally run for a month, a period sufficient for adaptation or mutation of the cells to be detected (Stockner and Antia, 1976). On the other hand, the experiment was run under a static condition with no renewal of the medium. The nutrients would be depleted while the catabolic wastes would be accumulated in such a closed system, resulting in the autoinhibition of the cells (Jorgensen, 1956). Furthermore, the optical density measurement was a relatively insensitive indicator and could not distinguish live and dead cells.

3.3.2.   Cell Count

This technique is essentially the same as the one just described except in this case the algal reproduction was followed by microscopic cell count instead of optical density measurement. As shown in Fig. 4, the addition of $1.0\times$ and $0.5\times$ metal mixture to the medium reduced both the rate and extent of cell reproduction. The pattern of growth inhibition was very similar to that in Fig. 3. The calculated growth rates (Table 3) were reduced from 0.74 division/day for the control to 0.55 and 0.22 division/day for the $0.5\times$ and $1.0\times$ metal-treated cells. The generation times for the control, $0.5\times$, and $1.0\times$ metal-treated cells were 32, 43, and 109 hr respectively. The cell count

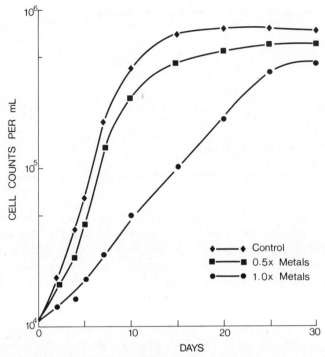

Figure 4.   Batch culture. Effect of a mixture of metals on the reproduction of *A. falcatus*. The algal reproduction rate was followed by cell counts.

technique is one of the most frequently used methods in algal assays because of its simplicity and low cost (Table 5). In addition, the morphological changes of the algae caused by the toxicant can also be discerned under the microscope. However, cell counting is tedious and can be subjective, especially when the cells are clumped together. Since an aliquot of the medium has to be withdrawn for daily counting, the volume in the culture flask would decrease with time. Furthermore, the frequent withdrawals of the medium

Table 5.   Reproduction (Cell Count)

Advantages	Disadvantages
1. Inexpensive	1. Microscopic count tedious and
2. Reproduction rate measured by	subjective
cell count	2. Cannot distinguish dead and live cells
3. Fairly large sample sizes can be	3. Volume changes with time
handled	4. Nutrients depleted and metabolic
4. Adaptation or mutation can be	wastes accumulated
determined	5. Easily contaminated
5. Morphological changes can be	
detected	

increase the possibility of bacterial contamination. Similar to the previous method, this static incubation technique also suffers by its inherent properties; nutrient depletion, waste accumulation, and autoinhibition. To avoid some of these difficulties associated with the use of batch culture, the continuous culture techniques were used to test the effects of the metal mixture on *A. falcatus*.

3.3. Continuous Culture

3.3.1. Turbidostat

In this experiment, *A. falcatus* with and without exposure to $0.5\times$ and $1.0\times$ metal mixture was allowed to grow until reaching the cell density of approximately 6×10^5 cells/ml. As shown in Fig. 5, the control cells reached this level after 7 days of incubation while the $0.5\times$ and $1.0\times$ metal-treated cells took 15 and 22 days respectively to arrive at the same level. When the cell density exceeded the predetermined value, fresh medium would flow in from the reservoir to maintain the cell level. Therefore the faster the cell growth rate, the larger the volume of the medium required to maintain the cell density. The average flow rates of the medium for control, $0.5\times$, and $1.0\times$ metal-treated cells were 240, 152, and 70 ml/day respectively. The calculated growth rates were 0.55, 0.36, and 0.16 division/day for the control, $0.5\times$, and $1.0\times$ metal-treated cells respectively (Table 3), which compared very favorably with the growth rates obtained from the other two techniques. The effect of mercuric acetate on several marine algae incubated in the batch and turbidostat culturing conditions was found to be not much different (Kayser, 1976). In contrast, a species of green alga, *Selenastrum,* was observed to be five times more sensitive to cadmium in a turbidostat than in a batch culture (Premazzi et al., 1978).

The major advantages and disadvantages of the turbidostat technique are outlined in Table 6. The ability of the turbidostat to maintain a constant cell number and a fixed ratio of cell number and toxicant in the course of the experiment makes this technique very suitable for ecological and toxicological studies. At the same time, very low nutrient levels can be used to obtain a dynamic equilibrium between nutrient input and growth, similar in principle to that existing in natural waters (Rhee, 1980). The various growth phases of the cells can be controlled in this technique and thereby the sensitivity of the growth phases to the toxicant can be tested. In spite of these advantages, the turbidostat technique has not been commonly used in algal studies. One of the reasons is that the commercially available turbidostats are quite expensive. Other technical problems of the turbidostat involve "wall growth" of the cells, insensitivity of the photoelectric sensor, and interference of the light transmission by foaming and bubbling (Watson, 1972). Of these problems, the fouling of the vessel walls by algae or bacterial contamination is the most serious. Various ingenious devices and techniques

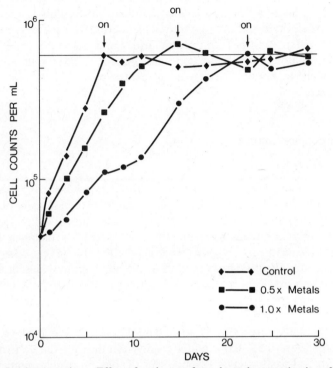

Figure 5. Continuous culture. Effect of a mixture of metals on the reproduction of *A. falcatus* grown in the turbidostat. The arrows indicate the days that the solenoid valves of the turbidostat were turned on to let in fresh medium from the reservoirs to dilute the cell density to a predetermined value.

have been suggested to solve this problem (Sorgeloos et al., 1976; Ricica, 1966). In our experiments, in spite of the thorough mixing of the medium by magnetic stirrer and air bubbling, the wall growth of the culture occurred after about 30 days. Therefore the experiments were run for less than one month. Similar problems were observed by Premazzi et al. (1978), who could not carry their experiments for more than 45 days.

Table 6.   Turbidostat

Advantages	Disadvantages
1. More related to natural environment	1. Time consuming in setting-up
2. Maintain constant cell number	2. Difficult to adjust the photodetectors to same degree
3. Obtain cell number and toxicant ratio	3. Insensitivity of the photodetectors and control panel
4. Adaptation and mutation measured	4. Wall growth
5. Synchronizing cells	5. Microbial contamination

3.3.2. Chemostat

Finally, the toxicity of the metal mixture on *A. falcatus* was tested with another continuous culture technique, the chemostat. The organism was grown as batch culture for 10 days or until the cells reached a steady state of growth. Then the continuous medium flow was switched on at a flow rate ranging from 100 to 700 ml/day. Simultaneously, the metal mixtures at $0.5\times$ and $1.0\times$ concentrations were added to the medium in the reservoirs as well as to the experimental flasks. The flow rates of the medium with and without the metal mixtures were controlled by means of a peristaltic pump. When the flow rate was faster than the cell growth rate, the cells were all washed

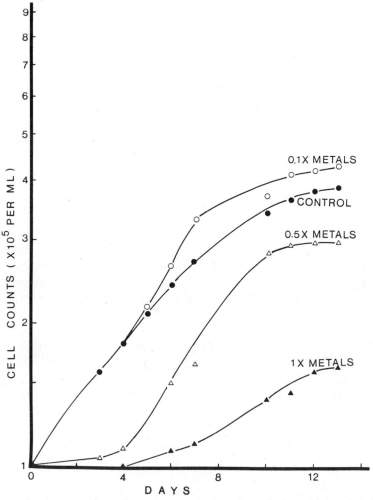

Figure 6. Continuous culture. Effect of a mixture of metals on the reproduction of *A. falcatus* grown in the chemostat. The flow rate of the medium in this experiment was 300 ml/day.

Table 7.   Chemostat

Advantages	Disadvantages
1. More related to natural environment	1. Time consuming in setting-up
2. Toxicant and nutrient in constant supply	2. Microscopic count tedious and subjective
3. Metabolic wastes removed	3. Difficult to adjust same flow-rate
4. Reproduction measured by cell count	4. Reproduction rate varied and hard to duplicate
5. Measure adaptation and mutation	5. Wall growth
	6. Microbial contamination

out from the flask. Therefore a series of flow rates was tested. For an average flow rate of 300 ml/day, a typical growth response of *A. falcatus* is shown in Fig. 6. The control alga grew rapidly and reached a steady state level 11 days after the introduction of continuous flow medium. In $0.5 \times$ metal mixture, there was an initial decrease in cell number during the first 2 days. After that, the cells recovered and grew rapidly. For $1.0 \times$ metal mixture, the recovery and growth of the cells were much slower. The calculated growth rates for control, $0.5 \times$, and $1.0 \times$ metal mixture cells were 0.76, 0.45, and 0.23 division/day, respectively (Table 3). Therefore, exposing the cells to $0.5 \times$ and $1.0 \times$ metal mixture resulted in 41 and 70% decreases in growth rate. These values were quite similar to those obtained by other techniques.

The chemostat and turbidostat techniques share many similar advantages and disadvantages in the toxicity bioassays since both involve a continuous supply of fresh medium to the cells (Tables 6 and 7). However, the chemostat is a more popular technique, possibly due to the low cost (no photodetector or optic-electronic system required) and availability of the components (commercial turbidostats were not readily available until recently). The chemostat has been used most extensively in the study of nutrient-limitation on algal growth (Droop, 1969; Rhee, 1980) and also in the study of interactions between bacteria and algae (Mayfield and Inniss, 1978); and the toxicity of PCB (Fisher et al., 1974), mercury (Kayser, 1976), and cadmium (DeNoyelles et al., 1980) on algae. Some of the difficulties in our chemostat experiments were cells growing on the walls of the culture flasks and the maintenance of the same flow rate of the medium to several culture flasks. In spite of these problems, the chemostat was our preferred technique over the turbidostat.

4. SUMMARY

Five techniques were used to study the effects of a mixture of 10 metals at the recommended Great Lakes Water Quality Objective levels on a freshwater green alga, *Ankistrodesmus falcatus*. The first three techniques involved batch culture and the other two were continuous culture techniques. The batch culture techniques included ^{14}C-NaHCO$_3$ uptake, cell count, and optical measurement of cell growth. The continuous culture techniques involved a turbidostat and a chemostat. There were advantages and disadvantages of each of these five techniques in algal bioassays. However, the results from these techniques all indicated that the metal mixture was toxic to the green alga.

REFERENCES

Chau, Y. K., Chawla, V. K., Nicholson, H. F., and Vollenweider, R. A. (1970). Distribution of trace elements and Chlorophyll *a* in Lake Ontario. *Proc. 13th Conf. Great Lakes Res.,* pp. 659–672.

DeFilippis, L. F. and Pallaghy, C. K. (1976). The effect of sublethal concentrations of mercury and zinc on *Chlorella*. III. Development and possible resistance to metals. *Zeitschrift Pflanzenphysiol.* **79**, 323–335.

DeNoyelles, F., Jr., Knoechel, R., Reinke, D., Treanor, D., and Altenhofen, C. (1980). Continuous culturing of natural phytoplankton communities in the Experimental Lakes Area: effects of enclosure, in situ incubation, light, phosphorus, and cadmium. *Can. J. Fish. Aquat. Sci.* **37**, 424–433.

Droop, M. R. (1969). Algae. In: R. Norris and D. W. Ribbons, Eds., *Methods in microbiology,* Vol. 3B. Academic Press, London, pp. 269–313.

Fay, P. and Kulasooriya, S. A. (1973). A simple apparatus for the continuous culture of photosynthetic microorganisms. *Br. Phycol. J.* **8**, 51–57.

Ferrara, R., Grassi, S., and Del Carratore, G. (1975). An automatic homocontinuous culture apparatus. *Biotechnol. Bioeng.* **17**, 985–995.

Fisher, N. S., Carpenter, E. J., Remsen, C. C., and Wurster, C. F. (1974). Effects of PCB on interspecific competition in natural and gnotobiotic phytoplankton communities in continuous and batch cultures. *Microb. Ecol.* **1**, 39–50.

Fogg, G. E. (1975). *Algal cultures and phytoplankton ecology.* The University of Wisconsin Press, Madison, Wisconsin, 175 pp.

Guillard, R. R. L. (1973). Division rates. In: J. R. Stein, Ed., *Handbook of phycological methods.* Culture methods and growth measurements. Cambridge University Press, Cambridge, pp. 289–311.

Hutchinson, T. C. and Stokes, P. (1975). Heavy metal toxicity and algal bioassays. In: *Water quality parameters.* American Society for Testing of Materials, Spec. Tech. Publ. 573, Philadelphia, pp. 320–343.

International Joint Commission. (1976). Report of the Water Quality Objectives Subcommittee. *Appendix A to the water quality board report to the IJC.* (Published by the regional office of the IJC, Windsor, Ontario).

Jorgensen, E. G. (1956). Growth inhibiting substances formed by algae. *Physiol. Plants* **9**, 712–726.

Kayser, H. (1976). Waste-water assay with continuous algal cultures: the effect of mercuric acetate on the growth of some marine dinoflagellates. *Mar. Biol.* **36**, 61–72.

Malek, I. and Fencl, Z. (1966). *Continuous culture of microorganisms.* Academic Press, New York.

Mayfield, C. I. and Inniss, W. E. (1978). Interactions between freshwater bacteria and *Ankistrodesmus braunii* in batch and continuous culture. *Microb. Ecol.* **4**, 331–344.

Monod, J. (1950). La technique de culture continue. Theorie et application. *Ann. Inst. Pasteur* **79**, 390–410.

Munson, R. J., (1970). Turbidostats. In: J. R. Norris and D. W. Ribbons, Eds., *Methods of microbiology,* Vol. 2. Academic Press, New York, pp. 349–376.

Myers, J. and Clark, L. B. (1944). Culture conditions and the development of the photosynthetic mechanism. An apparatus for the continuous culture of chlorella. *J. Gen. Physiol.* **28**, 103–112.

Premazzi, G., Ravera, O., and Lepers, A. (1978). A modified turbidostatic system for algal population studies. *Mitt. Intern. Verein. Limnol.* **21**, 42–49.

Rai, L. C., Gaur, J. P., and Kumar, H. D. (1981). Phycology and heavy-metal pollution. *Biol. Rev.* **56**, 99–151.

Rhee, G. Y. (1980). Continuous culture in phytoplankton ecology. *Adv. Aquat. Microbiol.* **2**, 151–204.

Ricica, J. (1966). Technique of continuous laboratory cultivations. In: I. Malek, Ed., *Theoretical and methodological basis of continuous culture of microorganisms.* Academic Press, London, pp. 157–313.

Silverberg, B. A., Wong, P. T. S., and Chau, Y. K. (1977). Effect of tetramethyl lead on freshwater green algae. *Arch. Environ. Contam. Toxicol.* **5**, 305–313.

Solomons, G. L. (1972). Improvements in the design and operation of the chemostat. *J. Appl. Chem. Biotechnol.* **22**, 217–228.

Sorentino, C. (1979). The effects of heavy metals on phytoplankton—a review. *Phykos.* **18**, 149–161.

Sorgeloos, P., Van Outryve, E., Persoone, G., and Cattoir-Reynaerts, A. (1976). New type of turbidostat with intermittent determination of cell density outside the culture vessel. *Appl. Environ. Microbiol.* **31**, 327–331.

Stockner, J. G. and Antia, N. J. (1976). Phytoplankton adaptation to environmental stresses from toxicants, nutrients and pollutions—a warning. *J. Fish. Res. Board Can.* **33**, 2089–2096.

Stokes, P. M., Hutchinson, T. C., and Krauter, K. (1973). Heavy-metal tolerance in algae isolated from polluted lake near the Sudbury, Ontario smeltors. *Water Pollut. Res. Can.* **8**, 178–201.

Stratton, G. W. and Corke, C. T. (1979). The effect of mercuric, cadmium and nickel ion combinations on a blue-green alga. *Chemosphere* **10**, 731–740.

Ukeles, R. (1973). Continuous culture—a method for the production of unicellular algal foods. In: J. R. Stein, Ed., *Handbook of phycological methods.* Culture methods and growth measurements. Cambridge University Press, Cambridge, pp. 233–254.

Watson, T. G. (1972). The present status and future prospects of the turbidostat. *J. Appl. Chem. Biotechnol.* **22**, 229–243.

Wong, P. T. S., Chau, Y. K., and Luxon, P. L. (1978a). Toxicity of a mixture of metals on freshwater algae. *J. Fish. Res. Board Can.* **35**, 479–481.

Wong, P. T. S., Silverberg, B. A., Chau, Y. K., and Hodson, P. V. (1978b). Lead and the aquatic biota. In: J. O. Nriagu, Ed., *Biogeochemistry of lead.* Elsevier, New York, pp. 279–342.

Wong, P. T. S., Chau, Y. K., and Patel, D. (1983). Physiological and biochemical responses of several freshwater algae to a mixture of metals. *Chemosphere* **11**, 367–376.

17

DETAILED METHOD FOR QUANTITATIVE TOXICITY MEASUREMENTS USING THE GREEN ALGAE *SELENASTRUM CAPRICORNUTUM*

Gérald Joubert

Environment Québec,
Gouvernement du Québec,
Sainte-Foy, Québec*

*Reprints are available from Environment Québec, Complexe Scientifique, 2700 rue Einstein, Sainte-Foy, Québec, Canada, GIP 3W8.

1. INTRODUCTION

Ever since man realized that, as the highest form of life, he must protect the environment, and in view of the fact that chemical and physical tests have not proved sufficient to demonstrate potential effects on the environment and living organisms, bioassays have become an indispensable tool for evaluating the effects of pollution on aquatic life. Ever since the first tests were carried out (Hart et al., 1945; Doudoroff et al., 1951; Sprague 1969, 1973), researchers have been working ceaselessly to prepare various tests using organisms from different levels of the food chain (APHA, 1980). In recent years, algae, and particularly the unicellular alga *Selenastrum capricornutum,* have become effective tools in various biological tests because of their versatility and sensitivity (EPA, 1971, 1978; Miller and Maloney, 1971; Maloney et al., 1973; Chiaudani and Vighi, 1974; Miller et al., 1974; Greene et al., 1975; Payne, 1975; INRS-Eau, 1976). *Selenastrum capricornutum* is favored because it is easy to grow and its response is easily reproduced; consequently it has been used increasingly to evaluate the toxicity of pollutants (Bartlett et al., 1974; Chiaudani and Vighi, 1978; Klotz et al., 1975; Maloney and Miller, 1975; INRS-Eau, 1977; Hendricks, 1978).

Factors such as the limited number of tests that can be carried out on fish, the high cost of such tests, the great number of samples required, and the need for increasingly sensitive and versatile instruments certainly call for a novel technique that makes it possible to carry out a large number of tests at a reasonable cost. A bioassay using the alga *Selenastrum capricornutum,* which is based on the inhibition of cell division mechanisms and which makes it possible to plot a straight toxicity line, provides the solution to current needs.

This test, developed in our laboratory, is based on the method worked out by Porcella et al. (1970). This method was followed by Toerien et al. (1971), put into practice by the EPA (1971, 1978), and published by Standard Methods (APHA, 1975, 1980). It can be applied to samples of industrial effluents as well as to samples of natural water from various sectors of human activity. It enables us to quantify toxicity from a straight line relating the different concentrations to their corresponding percentages of inhibition (Joubert, 1980); this in turn enables us to obtain a value for IC50 (the concentration which inhibits algal growth by 50%), and to express toxicity in toxic units as defined by Sprague and Ramsay (1965).

2. EQUIPMENT AND METHOD

2.1. Sampling

The use of a 1-liter polypropylene container which has been subjected to special washing procedures is recommended (see Section 2.4). Whenever possible, precondition it by rinsing on site with a presample. Then take the sample by filling the bottle to the top in order to eliminate as much air as possible. Store the bottle immediately in coolers containing ice or icepacks. The bottles should be delivered to the laboratory within 24 hr of being filled to ensure that the samples remain cool and to prevent any degradation which could influence the test results.

2.2. Storage

The samples should be stored in the dark at temperatures between 0 and 4°C. The tests should be begun as soon as possible since unsuspected changes could occur no matter what the storage conditions (APHA, 1980; EPA, 1978).

2.3. Adjusting the pH

In order to promote the growth of the alga *Selenastrum capricornutum* and eliminate the effect of pH, the pH of each sample must be brought to between 6.5 and 8.0 with dilute solutions of NaOH (5%) or HCl (5%). If the pH is below 6.5, it must be raised to 6.5; if it is above 8.0, it must be lowered to

8.0. Ideally, the pH should be adjusted the day before the tests are begun and a few hours before filtration to allow restabilization.

2.4. Preparing and Washing the Glassware

All the glassware used for the algae and the samples on which the tests will be carried out must be subjected to a special washing procedure, the various steps of which are as follows:

1. Soaking for 30 min in a boiling Decon® 75 solution.
2. Scrubbing.
3. Rinsing by hand under tap water.
4. Washing (without soap), automatic washer.
   (a) Prerinsing (tap water).
   (b) Washing (tap water).
   (c) Rinsing (tap water).
   (d) Rinsing (deionized water).
5. Rinsing with acid: HCl 10%.
   (a) Shaking.
   (b) Soaking for 30 min.
6. Rinsing with a saturated Na_2CO_3 solution.
7. Rinsing 7 times with deionized water.
8. Drying for at least 30 min at 100–105°C.

2.5. Filtration and Chemical Analyses

The sample is filtered to avoid excessive interference in the evaluation of the biomass during the cell count. Before beginning, measure the pH again to verify stability. If necessary the pH may be adjusted slightly at this point.

A 0.45-μm filter (Millipore®, type HA) is used. For better filtration, a fiberglass primary filter (Millipore®, type AP) may also be used, in which case a few drops of ultra pure water* are placed between the two filters to avoid creating air bubbles that could affect filtration. The pressure on the filter should not exceed 38 cm of Hg (15 in) or 0.5 atm (8 psi). The entire unit

*All the ultrapure water used in this test is treated municipal water which first passes through a deionized laboratory-grade water system comprising a cylinder of activated carbon and cylinders containing ion-exchange resins; it then goes through a Super-Q Millipore® purification system comprising a primary filter, activated carbon, an ion-exchange resin, a 0.45-μm filter, and a conductivity meter. A 1% CO_2 and 99% air mixture is then bubbled through the water. Minimum bubbling time is 2 min/liter. If it is not possible to use water treated in this way, use distilled autoclaved water.

is rinsed with 500 ml of ultrapure water to remove any possible contaminants.

To check the quality of the filters, take two samples during rinsing: 100 ml from the first 250 ml and 100 ml from the second 250 ml. This procedure is carried out once for each day of filtration. The samples are then analyzed for the amount of nitrogen and phosphorus (see following paragraph).

The original sample is then filtered and, if more than one filter is required, each one is rinsed with 500 ml of ultrapure water. After filtration, a large enough sample is taken to test it for nitrogen and phosphorus. The required analyses are: dissolved inorganic phosphorus, in the form of orthophosphates (PO_4 in mg/liter of P), and dissolved inorganic nitrogen, in the form of nitrites, nitrates, and ammonia nitrogen (NO_2, NO_3, and NH_3 in mg/liter of N). The measuring methods used are modified Standard Method techniques (APHA, 1975) applied to AutoAnalyzers®. These analyses are indispensable in making the calculations for the test, since we must know the quantity of nutrients present in the sample and be capable of producing a certain algal biomass, as well as the quantity of nutrients added for enrichment purposes (see Section 2.10).

2.6. Incubators

Incubators are needed to grow the algae. The chambers, which may be made of wood, are 129 cm wide, 61 cm deep, and 55 cm high on the inside.

The inner surfaces are painted a flat white. A fan (Torcan T-3-10) is installed at the top center of the back wall opposite the doors, to make the air penetrate the chamber and thus promote the exchange of air and CO_2. Small openings on each side near the bottom of the side walls facilitate evacuation of the air, which circulates from top to bottom. The lighting within each chamber must have an intensity of 4304 lux. It is provided by three 40-watt "Cool-white" fluorescent bulbs (122 cm) set in the top. It is preferable to control the intensity with a dimming ballast to maintain lighting at 4304 lux at the surface of the liquid. Room temperature should be maintained at 24 ± 2°C.

2.7. Stock Cultures

2.7.1. Composition of the Culture Medium

The culture medium used is the same as for the Algal Assay Procedure Bottle Test, developed by the EPA (1971, 1978). The composition of the Algal Assay Medium and the different steps are as follows:

To approximately 900 ml of ultrapure water, add 1 ml of each of the following stock solutions, from (a) to (g) in the order given, shaking lightly after each addition. Add sufficient water to obtain 1 liter. Adjust the pH of the final medium to 7.5 ± 0.1 using a 0.1 N NaOH or HCl solution.

Filter the pH-adjusted medium through a 0.45-μm membrane under a vacuum not exceeding 380 mm (15 in) of mercury or under pressure not exceeding 0.5 atm (8 psi).

(a)	Sodium nitrate, $NaNO_3$	25.500 g/liter
(b)	Magnesium chloride, $MgCl_2$	5.700 g/liter
	or $MgCl_2 \cdot 6 H_2O$	12.164 g/liter
(c)	Calcium chloride, $CaCl_2 \cdot 2 H_2O$	4.410 g/liter
(d)	Stock solution of micronutrients	(see following)
(e)	Magnesium sulphate, $MgSO_4 \cdot 7 H_2O$	14.700 g/liter
(f)	Potassium phosphate, K_2HPO_4	1.044 g/liter
(g)	Sodium bicarbonate, $NaHCO_3$	15.000 g/liter

The stock solution of micronutrients is prepared as follows. In 500 ml of ultrapure water, dissolve:

1.	H_3BO_3	92.760 mg
2.	$MnCl_2$	132.132 mg
	or $MnCl_2 \cdot 4 H_2O$	207.810 mg
3.	$ZnCl_2$	1.635 mg
4.	$FeCl_3$	48.000 mg
	or $FeCl_3 \cdot 6 H_2O$	80.000 mg
5.	$CoCl_2$	0.390 mg
	or $CoCl_2 \cdot 6 H_2O$	0.714 mg
6.	$Na_2MoO_4 \cdot 2 H_2O$	3.630 mg
7.	$CuCl_2$	0.0045 mg
	or $CuCl_2 \cdot 2 H_2O$	0.006 mg
8.	$Na_2EDTA \cdot 2 H_2O$	150.000 mg

[Disodium (Ethylenedinitrilo) tetraacetate]

2.7.2. Erlenmeyer Flasks for Cultures

Pour 200 ml and 400 ml of prepared medium into a 1-liter and a 2-liter Erlenmeyer flask, respectively, in order to preserve a 1 to 5 surface-volume ratio. Autoclave the flasks and store them in a dark refrigerator.

Examine the preceding week's culture under a microscope to determine its quality before using it for the weekly inoculation.

2.7.3. Weekly Stock Transfers

Inoculation is carried out under aseptic conditions in two volumes of culture medium for algae: a 1-liter and a 2-liter Erlenmeyer flask. The 1-liter flask is kept sterile and is used solely to inoculate the culture the following week, to avoid any contamination, while the 2-liter Erlenmeyer flask serves as stock for inoculating the samples.

Using a sterile pipet, put a 2-ml sample of the culture from the 1-liter Erlenmeyer into each of the 2 flasks to ensure growth.

Store the cultures in a special incubator with an automatic switch so that there is a photoperiod of 16 hrs of light per day. To optimize algae density and avoid sticking, the flasks should be shaken at least once a day. Polystyrene mini-beakers (Fisher nos. 2-544-37 and 2-593-504) or foam plugs are used on each Erlenmeyer flask to ensure that the gases circulate freely and to reduce evaporation.

The algae stock to be used for inoculation should be 1–2 weeks old. Older stock should be thrown away.

2.8. Preparing the Concentrated Nutrient Solution

Using ultrapure water, prepare a stock solution of concentrated nutrients from a modified culture medium with no EDTA (modified AAM). The solution should be 62.5 times more concentrated than the normal solution. The composition of this modified medium is the same as in Section 2.7.1, except for item (d), stock solution of micronutrients, which is made up differently (Chiaudani and Vighi, 1978).

This last solution is known as a modified stock solution of micronutrients and is prepared as follows. In 1 liter of ultrapure water, dissolve:

1. H_3BO_3 0.18552 g
2. $MnCl_2 \cdot 4\ H_2O$ 0.41561 g
3. $ZnCl_2$ (concentrated)   0.333 g/1000 ml: Use 1 ml in 1 liter
4. $CoCl_2 \cdot 6\ H_2O$ (conc.)   0.2824 g/1000 ml: Use 1 ml in 1 liter
5. $CuCl_2 \cdot 2\ H_2O$ (conc.)   0.12 g/1000 ml: Use 1 ml in 1 liter
6. $Na_2MoO_4 \cdot 2\ H_2O$ (conc.) 0.726 g/100 ml: Use 1 ml in 1 liter
7. $FeSO_4 \cdot 7\ H_2O$ 0.2738 g

The stock solution of concentrated nutrients is prepared in a 2-liter volumetric flask. Add 800–900 ml of ultrapure water. Using volumetric pipets, add 125 ml of each of the seven original solutions of nutrients, following the order established from (a) to (g). Shake lightly after each addition. Add sufficient water to obtain 2 liters.

This solution will serve both as a source of nutrients to enrich the sample and for preparing the dilution water so that the concentrations of nutrients are identical. It should be kept in the dark, in a refrigerator. It is important to shake the solution thoroughly before taking any samples, since the absence of EDTA results in the formation of a ferrous deposit. This precipitate will disappear when the solution is diluted.

2.9. Preparing the Dilution Water

Using a 2-liter volumetric flask, pour exactly 24 liters of ultrapure water into a 50-liter polypropylene carboy. Using a second volumetric flask, pour exactly 500 ml of the stock solution of concentrated nutrients (shake well before taking the sample) into the first 2-liter flask and add ultrapure water to fill up to 2 liters. Add this to the carboy, as well as 24 more liters of ultrapure water, for a final volume of exactly 50 liters. The concentration thus obtained is 62.5% v/v of the normal concentration, and makes algal growth of almost 50 mg/liter (see Section 2.12.2) possible, since a solution with a normal concentration (100% v/v) supports a biomass of almost 80 mg/liter, as established by Shiroyama et al. (1975). The carboy must be shaken thoroughly (just as it must be before samples are taken), and stored in the dark, in a refrigerator, at between 1 and 4°C.

A series of chemical analyses, such as the ones done on the sample and described in Section 2.5, must be carried out to determine the exact concentrations of nitrogen and phosphorus in the prepared dilution water, and, at the same time, the concentrations of the stock solution of concentrated nutrients. The averages obtained with these measurements are indispensable for later calculations.

2.10. Beginning the Test

2.10.1. Preparing the Dilutions and Standards

(a)   Thoroughly shake the sample and, depending on its origin, choose the most appropriate series of dilutions as per Table 1.

For 100–10% v/v dilutions, pour 250 ml of the sample into a 500-ml graduated cylinder, add 3 ml of the concentrated nutrients solution (shake well before pipetting) and make up to 300 ml with the sample. Add a magnet and, using a magnetic stirrer, agitate the contents thoroughly to obtain a homogeneous solution.

For dilutions of from 100 to 1% v/v, pour 150 ml of the sample into a 250-ml graduated cylinder, add 2 ml of the concentrated nutrient solution (shake the solution well before pipetting) and fill up to 200 ml with the sample. Add a magnet and, using a magnetic stirrer, agitate the contents thoroughly to obtain a homogeneous solution.

This preparation increases the growth potential of the sample by 50 mg/liter of algae, that is, by a potential equal to that of the dilution water.

(b)   Remove the magnet by sliding a larger magnet along the outer wall of the cylinder.

(c)   Using Table 2 and the required dilution scale, and beginning with the weakest concentration, pour the stated quantity of enriched sample into a

Table 1.   Suggested Logarithmic Dilution Scales[a]

Series of concentrations	
100% to 10% v/v	100% to 1% v/v
100	100
75	56
56	32
42	18
32	10
24	5,6
18	3,2
13,5	1,8
10	1,0

[a] See Doudoroff et al. (1951) and APHA (1975).

100-ml cylinder and fill up to 75 ml with dilution water. Place a small magnet in the cylinder and agitate the contents thoroughly with a magnetic stirrer to obtain a homogeneous solution. Using a second 25-ml cylinder, separate the volume into three equal 25-ml portions, and pour each one into one of the 125-ml Erlenmeyer flasks* to be used. Follow the same procedure for the other concentrations, proceeding in a progressive manner. Finish with the 100% v/v concentration taken directly (in triplicate), with a small 25-ml cylinder, from the 500- or 250-ml cylinder containing the enriched sample. Then take one additional 25-ml sample and put it in the Erlenmeyer flask to be used to count the background particles of the sample.

(d)   A standard is prepared by taking three 25-ml replicates of dilution water and putting them in 125-ml Erlenmeyer flasks.

At the end of the test, not only is a cell count of the standard taken, but the dry weight is determined in order to establish the Conversion Factor in Biomass (CFB).

(e)   All the Erlenmeyer flasks for a test are put in a metal (aluminum) dish with a flat white inner surface. The bottom is divided into squares, with each square holding three Erlenmeyer flasks containing triplicate solutions. Each dish can hold 36 flasks. The dishes are made in such a way that they can be piled one on top of the other. The inner dimensions are 6.0 cm deep, 59.8 cm long at the bottom, 62.3 cm long at the longest point, 27.0 cm wide at the bottom, and 29.1 cm wide at the widest point.

(f)   Before inoculating the flasks, make sure that the contents are the same temperature as the inoculum in order to avoid a thermal shock that could affect algae growth.

---

*All the Erlenmeyer flasks used should be of the same make and model so as to avoid variations in growth. We used Pyrex, no. 4980.

Table 2. Preparation of Various Concentrations

Series of concentrations			
100% to 10% v/v	Quantity of sample	100% to 1% v/v	Quantity of sample
100%	75 ml	100%	75 ml
75%	56 ml	56%	42 ml
56%	42 ml	32%	24 ml
42%	31,5 ml	18%	13,5 ml
32%	24 ml	10%	7,5 ml
24%	18 ml	5,6%	4,2 ml
18%	13,5 ml	3,2%	2,4 ml
13,5%	10 ml	1,8%	1,35 ml
10%	7,5 ml	1,0%	0,75 ml

2.10.2. Preparing the Inoculum

Pour 40 ml of stock culture one to two weeks old into a conical centrifuge tube (50 ml) and centrifuge the solution for 15 min. Discard the supernatant. Wash the cells with autoclaved ultrapure water and fill up to 40 ml with the same solution. Centrifuge again and discard the supernatant in order to resuspend the sediment in 20 ml of water. Shake thoroughly and make a cell count of the solution with a view to bringing the cell concentration back to 25,000 cells/ml (EPA, 1978).

To establish this concentration, count the cells in 1 ml of the algae solution obtained, diluted in 19 ml of isoton (Section 2.11.1), using the following formula:

$$\frac{A \times B \times C}{D} = Q$$

where A = final volume of inoculum (ml)
B = final concentration of inoculum in the Erlenmeyer flasks (cells/ml)
C = volume of solution in all the Erlenmeyer flasks (ml)
D = initial cell count in washed inoculum (cells/ml).

Example: (C) 180 Erlenmeyer flasks containing 25 ml of solution are required for the tests.

(B) Each flask must be inoculated with 1000 cells/ml for the final concentration.

(A) 200 ml of suspended algae must be prepared to ensure an adequate supply of inoculum.

The product of A, B, and C is divided by the initial cell count (D). The result (Q) gives the volume (ml) of the suspension (D) to be added to the volumetric flask (A) before making up the final volume of inoculum desired (200 ml).

2.10.3. Inoculation of the Erlenmeyer Flasks and Incubation

(a)   Add 1 ml of inoculum containing 25,000 cells/ml to each Erlenmeyer flask, except the one to be used for the background particle count. The initial cell concentration will thus be about 1000 cells/ml.

(b)   Put polystyrene mini-beakers (Fisher no. 2-544-30) or foam plugs in all the Erlenmeyer flasks in the dish. The mini-beakers have small notches that permit the exchange of gases while restricting evaporation.

(c)   Put the dishes containing the flasks in the incubators at 24°C. The incubation period lasts 8 days under continuous lighting at an intensity of 4304 lux.

(d)   During the incubation period, each dish is shaken twice a day until complete homogeneity is obtained. Continuous mechanical shaking at 100 oscillations per minute, as recommended by the EPA (1978), may also be used.

The pH must be maintained below 8.5 to ensure the availability of CO_2 during the incubation period. In critical cases, the incubator must be supplied with additional CO_2.

2.11. Evaluating the Biomasses Produced

2.11.1. Preparing the Isoton

Pour 200 g of NaCl and 20 g of NaN_3 (sodium azide) into 20 liters of ultrapure water. Mix thoroughly and measure the conductivity with a conductivity meter. The conductivity should measure 17 mmho. If it measures more than 17, dilute with ultrapure water until a reading of 17 is obtained. If it measures less than 17, add NaCl until a reading of 17 mmho is obtained. The solution should be filtered through a 0.22-μm (Millipore®, type GS) filter.

2.11.2. Cell Count

The algae are counted after exactly 8 days of incubation, during the same half-day that the inoculation was made in. To this end, prepare disposable cuvettes containing 19 ml of isoton solution each.

Shake the Erlenmeyer flask thoroughly using a rotary motion to obtain complete homogeneity. Take a 1-ml sample of the algae solution, place it in the corresponding cuvette and shake the cuvette by repeatedly turning it upside down and right side up. A Coulter Counter with a 70-μm cell is used to count the cells.*

Start by counting the isoton background particles. Repeat until no more than 100 particles can be counted. Next count the sample background parti-

---

*A correction factor, known as the coincidence factor, is applied to each count obtained. Refer to the manufacturer's instruction manual.

cles and the cells in the standards and the samples. When counting the concentrations, start with the strongest one and work progressively up to the weakest one to avoid any contamination. For the same reason, the counting cell should be rinsed thoroughly after each sample.

All counts are recorded to three significant digits, the third being rounded off. When the count is finished, keep the flasks containing the standards, as these will be used in determining the dry weight.

2.11.3. Dry Weights of Standards

Put aluminum weighting scoops in an oven at 70–72°C and leave them in for about 1 hr. Then place them in a desiccator to cool. Weigh each one in a precision scale and record the mass.

Take all the standards from the same incubator and place them in groups of three. Measure the volume of each group and pour the liquid into 50-ml graduated centrifuge tubes. Thoroughly rinse the bottom of the Erlenmeyer flasks and the graduated cylinder with autoclaved ultrapure water. Centrifuge for at least 15 min at 1000 g or more. Carefully remove the supernatant from each tube, using a syphon and a vacuum pump. Resuspend the cells with autoclaved ultrapure water and centrifuge once again. Repeat this step twice. Remove the supernatant and resuspend the algae in a smaller volume of autoclaved ultrapure water; pour the solution into an aluminum weighing scoop. Rinse the tube with a small amount of water. Place the weighing scoops in an oven at 70–72°C for at least 12 hr. Remove them and place them in a desiccator. When the temperature has stabilized, weigh the weighing scoops and record the masses obtained. Calculate the biomass in the following manner:

$$\text{Biomass of algae in mg/liter} = \frac{\text{Dry weight in mg}}{\substack{\text{Volume of group of} \\ \text{three Erlenmeyer flasks} \\ \text{in ml}}} \times 1000$$

2.12. Calculations

All the results obtained may be processed by computer.* The following information is fed into the computer: identification of samples, nitrogen and phosphorus concentrations (in mg/liter of N and in mg/liter of P) of the nutrients in the standards (dilution water) and in the sample, the value of the background particle count for the sample, the series of concentrations made, and the cell counts of the triplicates. The formula for the correction or coincidence factor applicable to the cell count is also included in the program.

*A Hewlett-Packard minicomputer, model 21 MX-E, was used. A copy of the program is available on request.

2.12.1.　Calculating the Biomasses Obtained

Take the average of the three cell counts for each triplicate. If each of the three values differs by less than 15% from the average, keep them. If there is a discrepancy of over 15%, compare the three values by groups of two and eliminate the value that differs most from the other two. Then establish the average using the two remaining values. This method is statistically more exacting than calculating the confidence limit to 95% but it allows a better resolution of the points on the straight line.

To calculate the values of the biomasses of the various concentrations of a given sample, the conversion factor in biomass (CFB) obtained from the dry weight and cell count of the standards is used. The conversion factor in biomass may be calculated as follows:

$$\text{CFB} = \frac{\text{Dry weight of standard in mg/liter}}{\substack{\text{Corresponding cell count} \\ \text{(in millions of cells)}}}$$

2.12.2.　Theoretical Biomasses

The theoretical biomasses are obtained by applying the multiplication factors established by Greene et al. (1975) and Shiroyama et al. (1975). The orthophosphate (PO_4 in mg/liter of P) result is multiplied by 430 if the concentration of phosphorus is ≥ 0.010 mg/liter; if $P < 0.010$ mg/liter, it is multiplied by 100. The theoretical algal biomass for nitrogen may be obtained by adding the nitrites-nitrates and ammonia nitrogen (in mg/liter of N) result and multiplying the sum by 38. The theoretical biomass to be used is the smaller of the results obtained for nitrogen and phosphorus. The total quantity of nutrients in the sample and the quantity present in the dilution water must be taken into account, as well as the ratio for each concentration. For example, in the 56% v/v concentration, 56% of the nutrients come from the sample and 44% from the dilution water. Before beginning the calculation, then, the concentrations of nutrients already in the sample must be added to the quantity obtained through enriching, which is determined by analyzing the dilution water.

2.12.3.　Calculating Percentages of Inhibition

The percentage of inhibition is obtained from the measured biomass and the theoretical biomass of each concentration, using the following formula:

$$\% \text{ of inhibition} = 100 - \left(\frac{\text{Measured biomass}}{\text{Theoretical biomass}} \times 100 \right)$$

2.12.4.　IC50 and Toxic Units

The IC50 is the concentration that inhibits the growth of 50% of the algal population. Refer to any valid method of calculating bioassays (Stephan, 1977) such as Probit, moving average, Litchfield and Wilcoxon (1949), and apply the steps given.

The toxic unit (TU) as defined by Sprague and Ramsay (1965) is the expression of toxicity as an absolute number. It is determined by dividing 100% v/v by the value obtained for IC50. At the same time, the toxic unit gives the dilution factor for bringing toxicity back to a IC50 of 100% v/v.

Given the sensitivity of this test, it may be stated that:

1–2 Toxic Units represents low toxicity.

2–5 TU represents average toxicity.

5–10 TU represents high toxicity.

10 and more TU represents very high toxicity.

2.13. Example

Table 3 gives a typical example of the results, obtained by computer, of a bioassay on a river water sample taken from a zone affected by toxic waste. The initial pH of the sample was 7.0. The theoretical biomass values, calculated on the basis of the multiplication factors mentioned previously, are the biomasses that would have been obtained had there been no toxic effect. The measured biomass is the cell count converted into dry weight using the CFB obtained with the standard, which is the dilution water multiplied by the mean $(\bar{X}_3)$ of the counts for the three Erlenmeyer flasks.

The percentages of inhibition are then calculated for each concentration on the basis of the ratio of the measured biomass to the theoretical biomass, according to the equation given in Section 2.12.3.

Figure 1 gives the straight toxicity line plotted on "probability × 2 log cycles" graph paper (Keuffel and Esser no. 46-8040) using the percentages of inhibition and the corresponding concentrations taken from Table 3. The value of IC50 is 17% v/v and the 95% confidence limits* calculated according to the Litchfield and Wilcoxon method (1949) are 5.4 to 54.0. The number of toxic units is

$$TU = \frac{100\% \text{ v/v}}{17\% \text{ v/v}} = 5.9.$$

3. DISCUSSION AND CONCLUSION

Tests carried out in our laboratory have shown that the natural growth potential of a sample, that is, the potential without added nutrients, when

---

*Since the test is based on the inhibition of algal cell division mechanisms, and since it is therefore impossible to use a fixed number of organisms per concentration and terminate the test with the same number of cells, the number of organisms used per concentration is in this case considered to be the number of replicates, since the contents of each Erlenmeyer flask in fact represent a unit and behave like a single complex organism.

Table 3. Results of Computer Calculations for a Bioassay of a River Water Sample Taken in a Zone Affected by Toxic Waste

	CONCENTRATION IN % v/v									Modified AAM 62,5% v/v
	100	56	32	18	10	5,6	3,2	1,8	1,0	
Number of cells in million in each triplicate	0,150 0,175 0,159	0,093 0,090 0,079	1,407 1,284 1,343	2,250 2,325 2,092	2,776 3,056 2,767	2,952 3,430 3,587	3,371 3,875 3,536	3,726 3,959 3,959	3,559 4,146 3,856	4,252 4,210 4,465
$\bar{X}_3$	0,161	0,087	1,345	2,222	2,866	3,323	3,594	3,881	3,854	4,309
2S	0,025	0,015	0,123	0,238	0,329	0,661	0,514	0,269	0,587	0,273
CV	7,75	8,01	4,58	5,35	5,72	9,95	7,15	3,46	7,62	3,18
Measured biomass Theoretical biomass	1,85 57,33	1,00 53,93	15,42 52,08	25,49 51,00	32,88 50,38	38,12 50,04	41,23 49,85	44,52 49,74	44,21 49,68	49,43 49,60
% Inhibition	97	98	70	50	35	24	17	10	11	–
CFB										11,47

AAM Algal Assay Medium
CFB Conversion factor in biomass
CV Coefficient of variation
2S 2 x the standard deviation
$\bar{X}_3$ Mean of the three cell counts

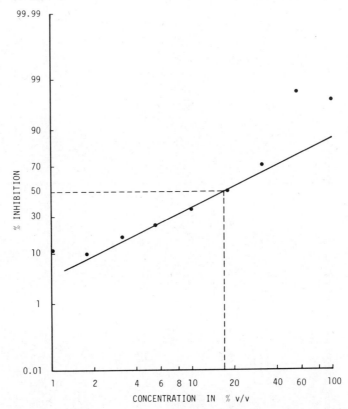

Figure 1.   Straight line of toxicity corresponding to the results in Table 3.

compared to the theoretical growth potential used by some authors to evaluate toxicity, frequently gives questionable results. When algal growth is limited by weak concentrations of nutrients, there is no resolution and a high percentage of errors, which makes the results invalid. In other cases, under certain conditions there is a false toxicity response due to a deficiency in an essential micronutrient. The procedure described in this chapter resolves these difficulties because it involves the addition of complete nutrients equivalent to an algal growth of 50 mg/liter.

In the present test, the growth potential of each concentration is identical at the outset, with the exception of a slight increase in the theoretical biomass as we go from the lowest concentration to the highest, due to the quantity of nutrients in the sample itself before enrichment. It is therefore obvious that the percentages of inhibition obtained and their gradual decrease as the concentrations diminish are the result of toxic effects caused by substances in the sample. This type of tendency may be compared to the model obtained in the various classic bioassays, in which higher organisms or fish are used. We may therefore calculate and interpret the results in much the same way.

The main effect of the toxic content of the sample is to inhibit cell division mechanisms and not to retard growth, since the incubation period for certain tests was extended from 8 to 14, 18, 21, and 25 days without any significant and proportional increase in the number of cells compared to the increase in the biomass. Most of the time, there was a slight increase in the biomass when the incubation period was extended beyond 8 days, but without a proportional increase in the number of cells. This phenomenon may be explained by the fact that, because cell division is reduced or blocked by the toxic effect, there is an excess of nutrients available for the cells present, which therefore accumulate a greater quantity of nutritional reserves. This was confirmed by Samson (1980), who observed an increase in glucids, lipids, and cell carbon during the stationary growth phase in nine species of endogenous algae. Moreover, the growth curves established by Shiroyama et al. (1975) show that the maximum standing crop is reached after a 7-day incubation period. However, following a number of tests made on various samples of industrial effluents, and using incubation periods of 7, 8, 10, and 14 days, it was shown that most of the tests with 7-day incubation periods resulted in a wider dispersal of points on the straight toxicity line than did the tests with 8-day incubation periods. An 8-day incubation period for the test is thus ideal, in view not only of the foregoing, but also of the fact that the overaccumulation of nutritional reserves that occurs after the 8-day limit is avoided.

A comparative study (Joubert, 1981) involving *Salmo gairdneri* trout, *Daphnia magna,* Microtox®, the alga *Chlamydomonas,* and the present test showed that this test is much more sensitive than the so-called classic bioassays, and therefore increases the radius of toxicity detection. The principle behind it places it among the so-called chronic sublethal bioassays.

Its main limitation is that it cannot be used to measure the toxic effects of ammonia nitrogen, nitrites, nitrates, and phosphorus, because these compounds constitute the nutrients for the algae. This drawback is alleviated, however, by the fact that these analyses are an integral part of the test and therefore necessary, as well as by our knowledge of the effects of these substances on the various living organisms in the environment (EPA, 1973).

This bioassay, then, which uses an organism already well known in standard biologic tests, when compared to various classic bioassays, constitutes a simple, sensitive, and inexpensive method of measuring the toxic effects of elements present in various types of liquid samples.

ACKNOWLEDGMENTS

The author would like to thank the ministère de l'Environnement du Québec which gave the go-ahead and provided the financial assistance for the research that made this test possible. Thanks are also due to Mr. R. Cardin who provided technical assistance for the laboratory work, to Miss C. Audet who prepared the typed copy, and to Gillian Baird and Robert Eatock of the Direction de la traduction, ministère des Communications du Québec, who prepared the English version.

REFERENCES

APHA-AWWA-WPCF (1975). *Standard methods for the examination of water and wastewater*, 14th ed. American Public Health Association, New York, 1193 pp.

APHA-AWWA-WPCF (1980). *Standard methods for the examination of water and wastewater*, 15th ed. American Public Health Association, New York, 1134 pp.

Bartlett, L., Rabe, F. W. and Funk, W. H. (1974). Effects of copper, zinc and cadmium on *Selenastrum capricornutum*. *Water Res.* **8**, 179–185.

Chiaudani, G. and Vighi, M. (1974). The N:P ratio and test with *Selenastrum* to predict eutrophisation in lakes. *Water Res.* **8**, 1063–1069.

Chiaudani, G. and Vighi, M. (1978). The use of *Selenastrum capricornutum* batch culture in toxicity studies. *Verh. Int. Ver. Theor. Angew. Limnol.* **21**, 316–329.

Doudoroff, P., Anderson, B. G., Burdick, G. E., Galtsoff, P. S., Hart, W. B., Patrick, R., Strong, E. R., Surber, E. W., and Van Horn, W. M. (1951). Bioassay methods for the evaluation of acute toxicity of industrial wastes to fish. *Sewage Ind. Wastes* **23**, 1380–1397.

Environmental Protection Agency. (1971). *Algal assay procedures: bottle test*. National Eutrophication Research Program, Pacific Northwest Environmental Research Lab., Corvallis, Oregon, 82 pp.

Environmental Protection Agency. (1973). *Water quality criteria 1972*. Ecological Research Series. National Academy of Sciences and Engineering, EPA-R3-73-033. Washington, D.C., 594 pp.

Environmental Protection Agency. (1978). *The Selenastrum capricornutum Printz algal assay bottle test*. Experimental Design, Application, and Data Interpretation Protocol, EPA-600-/9-78-018. Corvallis Environmental Research Laboratory, Office of Research and Development, Corvallis, Oregon, 126 pp.

Greene, J. C., Miller, W. E., Shiroyama, T., and Maloney, T. E. (1975). Utilization of algal assays to assess the effect of municipal, industrial and agricultural wastewater effluents upon phytoplankton production in the Snake River system. *Water Air Soil Pollut.* **4**, 415–434.

Hart, W. B., Doudoroff, P., and Greenbank, J. (1945). *The evaluation of the toxicity of industrial wastes, chemicals, and other substances to freshwater fishes*. Atlantic Refining Co., Philadelphia, Pennsylvania, 317 pp.

Hendricks, A. C. (1978). Response of *Selenastrum capricornutum* to zinc sulfides. *J. Water Pollut. Control Fed.* **50**, 163–168.

INRS-Eau (1976). Etude intégrée de la qualité des eaux des bassins versants des rivières Saint-François et Yamaska. Vol. 2, Secteur des substances nutritives. Rapport scient. no. 52, 127 pp.

INRS-Eau (1977). Impact de flottage du bois sur les eaux du lac Talbot; évaluation à l'aide de tests biologiques. Rapport scient. no. 77, 37 pp.

Joubert, G. (1980). A bioassay application for quantitative toxicity measurements, using the green algae *Selenastrum capricornutum*. *Water Res.* **14**, 1759–1763.

Joubert, G. (1981). Etude comparative des réactions à la toxicité entre la truite *Salmo gairdneri* et quatre autres intégrateurs biologiques sur 36 cas de bioessais statiques. (Comparative study of reactions to toxicity between the *Salmo gairdneri* trout and four other biological integrators in 36 cases of static bioassays.) In: N. Bermingham, C. Blaise, P. Couture, B. Hummel, G. Joubert, and M. Speyer, Eds., *Proceedings of the Seventh Annual Aquatic Toxicity Workshop:* November 5–7, 1980, Montreal, Quebec. Can. Tech. Rep. Fish. Aquat. Sci. 990, 519 pp.

Klotz, R. L., Cain, J. R. and Trainor, F. R. (1975). A sensitive algal assay: an improved method for analysis of freshwaters. *J. Phycol.* **11**, 411–414.

Litchfield, J. T., Jr. and Wilcoxon, F. (1949). A simplified method of evaluating dose-effect experiments. *J. Pharmacol. Exp. Ther.* **96**, 99–113.

Maloney, T. E. and Miller, W. E. (1975). Algal assays: development and application. *Water quality parameters, ASTM STP 573*. American Society for Testing and Materials, Washington, D.C., pp. 344–355.

Maloney, T. E., Miller, W. E., and Blind, N. L. (1973). Use of algal assays in studying eutrophication problems. In *Advances in water pollution research*. Proc. Sixth Int. Conf., 8–23 June 1972. Pergamon Press, Oxford, pp. 205–214.

Miller, W. E. and Maloney, T. E. (1971). Effects of secondary and tertiary wastewater effluents on algal growth in a lake–river system. *J. Water Pollut. Control Fed.* **43**, 2361–2365.

Miller, W. E., Maloney, T. E. and Greene, J. C. (1974). Algal productivity in 49 lake waters as determined by algal assays. *Water Res.* **8**, 667–679.

Payne, A. G. (1975). Responses of the three test algae of algal assay procedure: bottle test. *Water Res.* **9**, 937–955.

Porcella, D. B., Grau, P., Huang, C. H., Radimsky, J., Toerien, D. F., and Pearson, E. A. (1970). *Provisional algal assay procedures*. First Annual Report. Sanitary Engineering Research Laboratory College of Engineering and School of Public Health, Berkeley, 180 pp.

Samson, R. (1980). Caractéristiques physiologiques de la croissance et de la production de polysaccharides chez neuf espèces d'algues endogènes isolées des effluents du traitement secondaire de l'usine d'épuration de Valcartier. Université Laval, Québec, Faculté d'Agriculture et d'Alimentation. Thèse pour l'obtention du grade de Maître es science (M.Sc.), 99 pp.

Shiroyama, T., Miller, W. E., and Greene, J. C. (1975). Effect of nitrogen and phosphorus on the growth of *Selenastrum capricornutum*. In: *Proc. Biostim. Nutr. Assess. Workshop*. 16–17 October 1973, EPA-660/3-75-034, pp. 132–142.

Sprague, J. B. (1969). Measurement of pollutant toxicity to fish. I. Bioassay methods for acute toxicity. *Water Res.* **3**, 793–821.

Sprague, J. B. (1973). The ABC's of pollutant bioassay using fish. *Biological methods for the assessment of water quality, ASTM STP 528*. American Society for Testing and Materials, Washington, D.C., pp. 6–30.

Sprague, J. B. and Ramsay, B. A. (1965). Lethal levels of mixed copper-zinc solutions for juvenile salmon. *J. Fish. Res. Board Can.* **22**, 425–432.

Stephan, C. E. (1977). Methods for calculating an LC50. In: F. L. Mayer and J. L. Hamelink, Eds., *Aquatic toxicology and hazard evaluation, ASTM STP 634*. American Society for Testing and Materials, Washington, D.C., pp. 65–84.

Toerien, D. F., Huang, C. H., Radimsky, J., Pearson, E. A., and Scherfig, J. (1971). *Final report provisional algal assay procedures*. Sanitary Engineering Research Laboratory, College of Engineering and School of Public Health, University of California, Berkeley, 211 pp.

18

USE OF ALGAE IN
AQUATIC ECOTOXICOLOGY

R. Van Coillie

Éco-Recherches, Inc. (C.I.L.)
Pointe-Claire, Québec

P. Couture

Institut National de la Recherche Scientifique
Université du Québec
Sainte-Foy, Québec

S. A. Visser

Département des Sols
Université Laval
Cite Universitaire, Québec

1. INTRODUCTION

Rapid deterioration of aquatic environments as a result of the different ways of their utilization, has led to the development of methodologies that assess water quality. As the effects of pollutants on biological processes in the aquatic environment cannot be adequately assessed from only chemical or physical parameters, several of these methodologies are based on the use of biological indicators (Maciorowski et al., 1981). They have been accepted by such organizations as the American Public Health Association, the American Water Works Association and the Water Pollution Control Federation (APHA, 1980). Because any effect on the lowest level of the food chain will also have consequences on the other trophic levels, algae are very suitable organisms for the determination of the impact of toxic substances on the aquatic environment (Cabridenc, 1979; Joubert, 1980).

Allen and Nelson (1910) are considered to have been the first to use algae in a bioassay. Later, Schreiber (1927) described a procedure for assessing the chemical factors responsible for the phytoplankton production in seawater. Next, various researchers such as Skulberg (1964), Oswald and Gaonkar (1969), and Berland et al. (1972) introduced the following two types of bioassay procedures as defined by Berland et al. (1972): biological assays, and biological tests. By using pure algal cultures the former method is suitable for the determination of the impact of certain chemical elements in the environment. Thus by estimating the biomass of *Selenastrum capricornutum*, the concentration can be determined of, for instance, bioavailable nitrogen and phosphorus (EPA, 1978; Couture et al., 1981b). With biological tests, on the other hand, biostimulatory or inhibitory effects of substances can be evaluated (Miller et al., 1974; Greene et al., 1975). The Fertility and Toxicity Test, formerly known as the Algal Assay Procedure Bottle Test (EPA, 1971), using *S. capricornutum*, is presently widely used. Chiaudani and Vighi (1978) considered it the only algal growth test that has been properly evaluated and which is sufficiently refined to give reliable and reproducible results. This is also evident from a bibliographic review by the EPA (1979) in which the effects of various nutrients, toxicants, and industrial wastes are assessed on *Selenastrum*. The test makes it possible to determine in a water, besides the presence of bioavailable nutrients such as nitrogen and phosphorus, also other substances with a stimulatory or inhibitory effect (Greene et al., 1975; Couture et al., 1981a,b). Contrary to bioassays with fish, the method can be performed on small volumes and without costly installations. It is also less subject to variations due to functional or genetic diversities in the organisms than, for instance, tests with bacteria; and for wastewater samples it is normally more sensitive than other microbiological tests (Joubert, 1981; Van Coillie et al., 1981b). Its main disadvantage, which is the delay of about 10 days required to obtain a clear indication of cellular growth, can be overcome, as is indicated in the following section, by studying parameters such as ATP content, fluorescence, or radioactive carbon assimilation.

2. METHODOLOGY

2.1. Algal Species

Besides *Selenastrum capricornutum*, recommended by EPA (1979), several other species of green algae, such as *Chlamydomonas reinhardii*, *Chlamydomonas variabilis*, *Chlorella pyrenoidosa*, *Chlorella vulgaris*, and *Scenedesmus quadricauda*, have been used for tests in aquatic toxicology (Cabridenc, 1979; APHA, 1980).

2.2. Sample Preparation

Toxic effects can be determined either on single compounds or on mixtures, such as effluents (see Wong et al., this volume). Single compounds are normally analyzed without any preliminary treatment by dilution with mineral algal growth medium. Although the original substrate recommended by the EPA (1971) can be used, Chiaudani and Vighi (1978) suggested, for toxicity studies, several modifications to it, such as the omission of EDTA (Table 1). In the case of an effluent or other type of complex mixture, several

Table 1.   Composition of Mineral Medium for Algal Toxicity Studies[a]

Elements	Solution Concentration
Major Elements (mg/liter)	
N 4.20	($NaNO_3$: 25.50 mg/liter)
P 0.19	(K_2HPO_4: 1.04 mg/liter)
K 0.47	—
Na 11.00	($NaHCO_3$: 15.00 mg/liter)
Mg 2.90	($MgCl_2$: 5.70 mg/liter)
Ca 1.20	($CaCl_2 \cdot 2H_2O$: 4.41 mg/liter)
Cl 6.26	—
S 1.91	($MgSO_4 \cdot 7H_2O$: 1.91 mg/liter)
Trace Elements (µg/liter)	
B 32.46	(H_3BO_3: 186 µg/liter)
Mn 115.37	($MnCl_2$: 264 µg/liter)
Zn 1.57	($ZnCl_2$: 3.34 µg/liter
Co 0.07	($CoCl_2$: 0.154 µg/liter)
Cu 0.004	($CuCl_2$: 0.009 µg/liter)
Mo 2.88	($Na_2MoO_4 \cdot 2H_2O$: 7.26 µg/liter
Fe 55.00	($FeSO_4$: 149.60 µg/liter)

[a] EPA (1971) medium with modifications by Chiaudani and Vighi (1978).

initial treatments can be applied to the sample (APHA, 1980) such as filtration (0.45 µm), heat sterilization, or both heat sterilization and filtration. Subsequently the procedure indicated for single compounds is normally followed.

2.3.   Incubation

The product that is being tested at different concentrations is inoculated with the selected algae (1000–2000 cells/ml) from an exponentially growing culture, and is incubated for several days under conditions indicated in Table 2.

Table 2.   Conditions of Incubation for Algal Toxicity Test Procedure

Initial pH	7.5
Temperature	24°C ($\pm$ 2°C)
Illumination	5400 lux ($\pm$ 10%)
Photoperiod	16-hr illumination per 24 hr
Agitation	100–150 oscillations per minute

2.4. Physiological Parameters

2.4.1. Cell Growth

To determine the amount of growth that has taken place during the incubation period, the number of algae per ml is determined after an 8–21-day period and compared to the initial amount immediately present after inoculation. For filtered samples the number may be determined using an electronic particle counter (EPA, 1978). As in unfiltered material the algal cells have to be distinguished from other particles; the number in this case is normally obtained microscopically by means of a hemacytometer.

The usual delay of 8–21 days in growth experiments is generally unacceptable to government services, but it is often possible to shorten the time period to 1–7 days by measuring other parameters.

2.4.2. Fluorescence

The herbicide DCMU (3,4-dichlorophenyl-1,1-dimethylurea) which blocks the transfer of electrons from chlorophyll to cytochrome B-559, and therefore inhibits oxidative phosphorylation, is known to increase chlorophyll fluorescence (Cramer, 1977; Roy and Legendre, 1980). Because this increase ($F_{DCMU} - F$) depends on the physiological state of the chlorophyll complex, external conditions affecting it also influence chlorophyll fluorescence intensity (Samuelsson et al., 1978). Such meaurements are made with a spectrofluorimeter before and after addition of $10^{-5}M$ DCMU.

2.4.3. Carbon Assimilation

To evaluate the photosynthetic activity of algae, the organisms are brought into contact with $NaH^{14}CO_3$. When, after a fixed period, assimilation is stopped and the excess $^{14}CO_2$ removed, the chlorophyll is photodegraded and the radioactivity of the degradation products determined by means of a liquid scintillation counter (Schindler et al., 1972; Campbell et al., 1976b).

2.4.4. Adenosine-tri-phosphate

The ATP content of a cell depends on its physiological state and can serve as an indicator of its active biomass (Berland et al., 1972; Brezonik et al., 1975; Falkowski, 1977). Different methods have been used for extraction of ATP from algae (Larsson and Olsson, 1979). A new method, based on extraction with DMSO (dimethylsulfoxyde) has recently been developed for bacteria (Jakubczak and Leclerc, 1980). It can easily be adapted for algae; after filtration (0.45 μm) the residue from algal suspensions is dissolved in DMSO, and a buffer (pH 7.4) is added. The amount of ATP is determined by measuring luminescence using the luciferine-luciferase complex.

Table 3.   Inhibition (%) of *Selenastrum capricornutum* by Copper as Determined by Four Parameters

Copper Concentration (μg/liter)	Incubation Period (days)	Cellular Growth	ATP	Fluorescence	C-14 Assimilation
2	1	9	24	25	31
	7	0	10	26	0
4	1	21	39	42	38
	7	0	—	50	12
8	1	57	74	65	76
	7	24	10	51	21
16	1	62	75	80	92
	7	90	96	96	98
32	1	64	96	95	98
	7	100	100	100	100

2.4.5.   Comparison between Parameters

The sensitivity of the parameters just mentioned has been compared in the presence of the algal toxicant $CuSO_4$ (Chiaudani and Vighi, 1978). As Table 3 indicates, copper toxicity is already noticeable after an incubation period of just one day. During a period of 7 days, two tendencies are observed: first an initial loss in toxicity which, according to Rai et al. (1981), would be the result of the excretion by the algae of polypeptides capable of complexing inorganic material and rendering it non-bioavailable. The remaining toxicity is found to increase with time (see concentrations of 16 and 32 μg/liter for a 7-day incubation). Toxicity can be detected by means of the fluorescence method after an incubation period of 1–4 days.

2.5.   Anabolic Parameters

Anabolic parameters, such as those based on protein, RNA and DNA synthesis, are generally more sensitive to toxic products than is algal growth by itself. To evaluate the anabolic rates involving these three processes, specific ^{14}C- or ^3H-labelled radioactive precursors can be used, in the form of L-leucine for proteins, uridine for RNA, and thymidine in the case of DNA. The incorporation of these precursors in the algae normally takes place in less than 60 min and generally no signs of radiotoxicity are shown at levels of 0.5–5.0 μCi/ml. Incorporation can be stimulated by the addition of non-radioactive leucine, uridine, or thymidine (Van Coillie et al., 1981a). After centrifugation, the algae are rapidly homogenized in TRIS buffer (pH 7.2 at 0°C) and the macromolecular fraction is obtained by means of one of the following methods: precipitation by trichloroacetic acid for proteins (Mans and Novelli, 1971), separation with phenol for RNA (Parish, 1972), and extraction by ethanol for DNA (Clark, 1964). Whereas the concentration of the macromolecules can be determined spectrophotometrically by using Folin-Ciocaltau reagent, orcinol, or diphenylamine (Clark, 1964), their radioactivity can be obtained by measurement in a scintillation counter.

3.   APPLICATIONS

3.1.   Sublethal Toxicity

There is a growing demand in environmental research for tests measuring sublethal toxicity levels. Therefore the IC50*, as distinct from the LC50†, is becoming a popular parameter. In the case of *Selenastrum capricornutum* and *Chlamydomonas variabilis*, the determination of IC50 normally takes between 1 and 7 days for biochemical parameters and between 8 and 21 days in the case of cellular growth tests. For *Chlorella variabilis*, the IC50 readings based on a gradual loss of mobility, are normally already taken after only 24 hr contact with the toxicant (Cabridenc, 1979). For a toxicity test this delay is rather short and the test's sensitivity is consequently relatively low (Joubert, 1981). However, because the method allows the rapid estimation of the order of sublethal toxicity, it can provide useful preliminary information. As is illustrated in Table 4, in which the LC50 96-hr values obtained with *Salmo gairdneri* are compared with the LC50 14-day values for *Chlamydomonas variabilis* at three time intervals after sampling, tests using algae often provide IC50 values that are lower than the values of LC50 obtained with other types of organisms (Joubert, 1980).

3.2.   Change in Toxicity Values with Sample Treatment

As Table 4 indicates, the toxicity of a sample can diminish with length of storage and temperature. This effect may be due partly to microbial activity. The toxicity was also found to be substantially reduced by such treatments as sterilization and filtration (increase in IC50 and, to a lesser degree, in LC50).

   Environmental services are obviously interested in the initial toxicity of a sample, but in the case of fish bioassays the transport of large volumes of effluent often causes a delay of several days. In algal bioassays this incon-

---

*Inhibiting concentration of a toxic product resulting in the 50% reduction of a physiological parameter.

†Concentration of a product lethal to 50% of the population.

Table 4. Comparison of Toxic Effect of an Industrial Effluent on *Salmo gairdneri* (LC50–96 hr) and on *Chlamydomonas variabilis* (IC50–14 day)

Conditions of Storage		LC50–96 hr (juvenile *Salmo gairdneri*) (%)	IC50–14 day (*Chlamydomonas variabilis*) (%)
Duration (hr)	Temperature (°C)		
0–2	0–4	27	12
24	0–4	25	19
24	20–24	32	35
96	0–4	35	23
After immediate sterilization		38	38
After immediate filtration		42	55

venience can easily be avoided because the effluent can be inoculated with the organisms at the sampling site. Of course, a similar methodology can also be applied to daphnia or bacteria (e.g., Microtox test), but as Joubert (1981) has shown, these tests are normally less sensitive than those based on algal cellular growth.

3.3.   Ecotoxicological Impact Studies

There is increasing demand in environmental research for ecotoxicological data. As these can normally not be obtained by conventional bioassay techniques, algal bioassay techniques, because of their previously mentioned benefits, can be used to a distinct advantage. To illustrate this point, a comparison will be made between results obtained from bioassays with algae and with fish, designed to predict the ecological impact of a new reservoir on the Bulstrode river near Victoriaville, Quebec (Campbell et al., 1975, 1976a). To evaluate the effects on water quality of the inundation of intact or stripped soils, 14 experimental tanks (1.2 m height x 5 m diameter) were filled with 17,500 liters of water from the Bulstrode river. To simulate the conditions in the future reservoir, the water was continuously replaced at a rate of 0.36 m^3/24 hr. In each tank were placed 40 two-year-old specimens of the most abundant fish species in the Bulstrode river (*Notropis cornutus*). Water samples collected after 64 days were sterilized, filtered (0.45 μm), and inoculated with either *Selenastrum capricornutum* or *Chlorella vulgaris* (5000 cells/ml). Table 5 shows the results of the cell count after 21 days as well as the results from an inoculation of the algae system with ^{14}C L-leucine on the fifth day. The data indicate that stripped soils favor algal growth less than do intact soils. Study of the photosynthesis appeared to give more consistent and more rapid results than assays based on cellular growth.

Table 5. Algal Growth and Photosynthesis in Water for the River Bulstrode in Contact with Intact or Stripped Soils[a] from Victoriaville, Quebec

	Algal Species		
Type of soil	S. capricornutum (growth)[b]	C. vulgaris (growth)[b]	C. vulgaris (photosynthesis)[c]
None (blank)	91	183	339
Clay loam			
intact	381	628	1186
stripped	144	330	550
Sandy loam			
intact	258	541	1048
stripped	129	276	410
Loamy sand			
intact	150	347	701
stripped	49	89	126

[a] After removal of top 30 cm.

[b] Average number of algae per μl after 21 days of incubation (confidence interval < 10–15%, $p = 0.95$, $n = 6$).

[c] Average number of dpm per μCi of ^{14}C-L-leucine per hour per mg of protein per g of dry weight (confidence interval $< 17\%$, $p = 0.95$, $n = 8$).

Table 6. Weight Increases in *Notropis cornutus* in Water from the River Bulstrode in Contact with Intact or Stripped Soils from Victoriaville, Quebec[a]

Type of Soil	Period of Contact (days)	W^b	L^c	$\dfrac{100\ W^d}{L^3}$
None (blank)	0	2.3	5.5	1.38
	64	2.7	5.9	1.32
Clay loam				
intact	64	4.9	6.7	1.63
stripped	64	3.9	6.3	1.56
Sandy loam				
intact	64	2.6	5.7	1.41
stripped	64	4.8	6.6	1.67
Loamy sand				
intact	64	3.9	6.2	1.64
stripped	64	4.2	6.3	1.68

[a] Confidence interval $< 12\%$, $p = 0.95$, $n = 32$–72.

[b] Average dry weight (g).

[c] Average fork length (cm).

[d] Condition coefficient.

Results obtained with the fish bioassays are listed in Table 6 and show that during the 64-day period, stripped and intact soils both had a favorable effect on the growth of the fish. It followed from this work that in ecotoxicological impact studies algae, as they are easily handled and give fast, differentiated and accurate results, are more useful bioindicators than fish.

Another interesting application of the use of algae for ecotoxicological impact studies has been described by Visser and Couture (1981). They showed that during the flooding of a hydroelectric reservoir in the semiarctic region of the James Bay (Quebec), allochthonous organic matter had an unfavorable effect on the indigenous algal flora.

3.4. Delayed Toxicity

To study the phenomenon of delayed toxicity, the concept displayed in Table 7, the following procedure was adopted (Van Coillie et al., 1981a):

1. Synchronization of an algal culture (in particular *Chlorella pyrenoidosa*) in AAP medium by the use of 12 hr light and 12 hr darkness cycles at

Table 7.   Effects of Delayed Toxicity

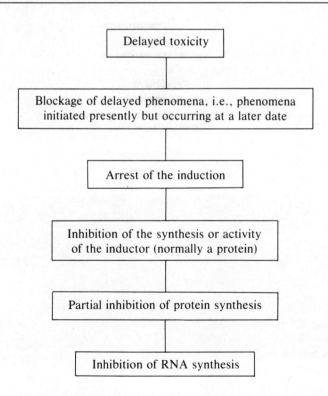

20°C. The cellular cycle then becomes progressively synchronized (4.5 hr for the mitosis and 7.5 hr for the interphase) and is able to maintain itself at a 90% level during more than five divisions (Cameron, 1966).

2. Contact with the toxic compound for 2–4 hr immediately after the end of a mitosis.

3. Centrifugation.

4. Transfer of the alga to a standard substrate.

5. Determination, with radioactive uridine, of the rate of synthesis of the RNA (Section 2.5).

6. Determination of the rate of cellular growth during four cycles.

The results (Table 8) obtained by applying the foregoing method on cadmium show that a 2-hr treatment with 2–8 μg/liter of Cd at the start of the interphase of a synchronous culture of *Chlorella pyrenoidosa* results in a sublethal toxicity which increases with metal concentration. At the end of the treatment, RNA synthesis was reduced by 16, 48, and 78% in the presence of 2, 4, and 8 μg/liter respectively, of Cd. Twenty-nine hours after treatment (i.e., after two cellular cycles) a lowering in cellular growth by 90% could be detected. To explain this delayed toxicity it has to be remembered that the RNA precursors necessary for mitosis are formed two or three cycles before the start of the interphase (Cameron, 1966; Perry et al., 1976). It is, therefore, not surprising that under conditions where 4 μg/liter Cd inhibited approximately 50% of the RNA synthesis at the beginning of the interphase, more than 50% reduction in the algal growth was observed in two to three cycles. Such a mechanism of delayed toxicity has also been observed for other compounds such as dimethylarsenate and petroleum distillates (Van Coillie et al., 1981a). By using the foregoing procedure the concentrations at which a product causes a delayed toxicity could be rapidly assessed by means of synchronous algal cultures.

3.5. Other Applications

In aquatic ecotoxicology certain other applications with algae are also possible, but the methods are either relatively complex or still in a very preliminary stage of development. We nevertheless attempt to describe them briefly in the following sections.

3.5.1. Mutagenicity Tests

To determine whether a compound has mutagenic effects, the Ames test on bacteria is normally applied. Nevertheless, it would not be impossible that the alga *Selenastrum capricornutum* could be used equally well. As a matter of fact, persistent morphological changes were observed in the organism after application of 1 mg/liter of the mutagenic agent 5-fluoro-uracil or of 56

Table 8.   Delayed Toxicity of Cadmium on a Synchronous Culture of *Chlorella vulgaris*

Parameter	Cadmium Concentration (µg/liter)			
	0	2	4	8
Growth (number of algae/ml × 10⁴)				
At start of synchronous cycle	1	1	1	1
During period elapsed since addition of CdSO₄ at end of mitosis:				
5 hr	7.6	7.6(= 0%)	7.4(= −3%)	3.4(= −55%)
17 hr	59	53(= −10%)	52(= −12%)	10(= −83%)
29 hr	456	392(= −14%)	97(= −79%)	46(= −90%)
41 hr	3494	3040(= −13%)	662(= −81%)	249(= −93%)
RNA Synthesis[a]				
During 60-min period after addition of CdSO₄	102	86(= −16%)	53(= −48%)	23(= −78%)

[a] dpm/µCi of ¹⁴C uridine · hr · mg RNA · g of dry weight.

mg/liter of potassium phthalate. It is, however, too early to make a proposal for the alga as a definite test organism in mutagenic research.

3.5.2.   Sublethal Toxicity of Mixtures

To understand the toxicity of a mixture it is often necessary to determine the toxicity of its constituents. However, for the investigation of antagonistic or synergistic effects, reconstituted samples should be used (see Wong et al., this volume). A sublethal toxicity test of 3 days or less, using algae, has been adopted for *Selenastrum capricornutum* on an effluent from a plating industry. It was found that 82% of algal fluorescence was inhibited by 0.3% of the effluent. Toxicity was due mainly to the presence of Cu (23 µg/liter), Ni (204 µg/liter), Cr (64 µg/liter), and Zn (6 µg/liter). The sum of the toxicities of the separate metals greatly exceeded that of the original effluent, which was explained by a competition in toxicity between various metals such as Cu versus Ni, Cu versus Cr, and Ni versus Cr. By chelating various inorganic compounds with EDTA, Couture et al. (1981a), in a study on sewage from Montreal, were able to compare the total toxicity of the effluents with the toxicity due to the major organic and/or inorganic components.

3.5.3.   Effect of Toxicants on Species Diversity

It is sometimes desirable to determine the effect of a toxic substance on the diversity of phytoplanktonic species. One possible approach to studying this effect is by investigating *in situ* the changes in the composition of the phytoplankton induced by toxicant concentration and environmental factors (nutrients, pH, temperature). This procedure normally leads to very complex correlations (Rai et al., 1981). On the other hand, the effect can be studied under well-controlled optimal conditions in systems such as used in CEEs (Controlled Ecosystem Enclosures), CEPEX (Controlled Ecosystem Pollution Experiment), and MAAP (Microcosm Algal Assay Procedure). The results, although less representative of the natural environment than in the *in situ* experiments, are obtained more readily and with simpler equipment. Thomas and Seibert (1977), by using a CEPEX, showed that Cu at concentrations of 5–10 µg/liter had an unfavorable effect on the majority of green algae with the exception of certain microflagellates.

3.5.4. *Transfer of Toxic Compounds between Trophic Levels*

Several persistent toxic chemicals (heavy metals, nonbiodegradable pesticides, PCBs, etc.) can be bioaccumulated in the various trophic levels of an aquatic ecosystem. This bioaccumulation can take place in two ways: either by direct absorption of the toxic compound or by its transfer from a lower to a higher trophic level (see Boudou et al., this volume). To differentiate between these two types of bioaccumulation and to quantify the rate of transfer of the product between the levels, several experimental systems with ecological food chains have been developed (Aubert et al., 1972). Algae play a major role in these studies. It has been demonstrated that they can accumulate larger quantities of heavy metals per unit weight than is the case of organisms in higher trophic levels. Moreover, the metals are accumulated in different amounts in the algae than they are, after trophic transfer, for instance, in fish (Aubert et al., 1972).

3.5.5. *Biological Changes in Toxicity Levels*

Changes in the level of toxicity can occur by transformation of toxic compounds by means of biological mechanisms. The methylation of mercury is a well-known case. This phenomenon is often ascribed to bacterial action, although it can occur equally well under the influence of algae (Rai et al., 1981). Nevertheless, because the rate of methylation depends on the metabolic activity of the organism, and because in bacteria, metabolism per unit weight is faster than in algae, the latter are the less efficient organisms in the methylation process. On the other hand, algae are able to methylate more mercury per unit weight than fish. This is evident from the inactivation by methylation of RNA precursors, which process is known to be inhibited by mercury: after 60-min treatment using 25 µg/liter Hg, the methylation of RNA per unit weight was found to be inhibited by 43% in *Selenastrum capricornutum* and by only 29% in the trout *Salmo gairdneri* (Thellen et al., 1980).

ACKNOWLEDGMENTS

Several results discussed in the article were cited from work made possible by grants or research contracts from the following sources: Ministry of Education (Quebec), Environment Canada and Quebec Ministry of Environment. The authors also wish to express their gratitude to Ms. V. Heath for her assistance in correction of the manuscript.

REFERENCES

Allen, E. J. and Nelson, E. W. (1910). On the artificial culture of marine plankton organisms. *J. Mar. Biol. Assoc.* **8,** 421–474.

APHA-AWWA-WPCF. (1980). Bioassay methods for aquatic organisms. In: A. E. Greenberg, J. J. Connors, and D. Jenkins, Eds., American Public Health Association, American Water Works Association and Water Pollution Control Federation, Washington, D. C., pp. 615–743.

Aubert, M., Bittel, R., Laumond, F., Romeo, M., Donnier, B., and Barelli, M. (1972). Utilisation d'une chaîne trophique de type pélagique pour l'étude des transferts des pollutions métalliques. *Rev. Intern. Oceanogr. Med.* **28,** 27–52.

Berland, B. R., Bonin, D. J., Maestrini, S. Y., and Pointer, J. P. (1972). Étude de la fertilité des eaux marines au moyen de tests biologiques effectués avec des cultures d'algues. I. Comparaison des méthodes d'estimation. *Int. Rev. Ges. Hydrobiol.* **57,** 933–944.

Brezonik, P. L., Brown, F. X., and Fox, J. L. (1975). Application of ATP to plankton biomass and bioassay studies. *Water Res.* **9,** 155–162.

Cabridenc, R. (1979). *Les bioessais en écotoxicologie.* Institut national de recherche chimique appliquée, Vert-le-Petit, pp. 162.

Cameron, I. (1966). *Cell synchrony.* Academic Press, New York, pp. 189.

Campbell, P. G., Bobée, B., Caillé, A., Demalsy, M. J., Demalsy, P., Sasseville, J. L., and Visser, S. A. (1975). Pre-impoundment site preparation: A study of the effects of topsoil stripping on reservoir water quality. *Verh. Intern. Verein. Limnol.* **19,** 1768–1777.

Campbell, P. G., Bobée, B., Caillé, A., Demalsy, M. J., Demalsy, P., Sasseville, J. L., Visser, S. A., Couture, P., Lachance, M., Lapointe, R., and Talbot, L. (1976a). *Effet du décapage de la cuvette d'un réservoir sur la qualité de l'eau emmagasinée: élaboration d'une méthode d'étude et application au réservoir de Victoriaville (rivière Bulstrode, Québec).* Institut national de la recherche scientifique (INRS-Eau), Québec, Rapport scientifique no. 37, pp. 238 + 49.

Campbell, P. G. C., Couture, P., Talbot, L., and Caillé, A. (1976b). Nutrient dynamics in running waters: production assimilation and mineralization of organic matter. In: J. O. Nriagu, Ed., *Environmental biochemistry.* Vol. 2. Ann Arbor Science, Ann Arbor, Michigan, pp. 681–704.

Chiaudani, G. and Vighi, M. (1978). The use of *Selenastrum capricornutum* batch cultures in toxicity studies. *Mitt. Internat. Verein. Limnol.* **21,** 316–329.

Clark, J. M. (1964). *Experimental biochemistry.* Freeman, San Francisco, pp. 228.

Couture, P., Couillard, D., and Croteau, G. (1981a). Un test biologique pour caractériser la toxicité des eaux usées. *Environ. Pollut.* Ser. B. **2,** 217–222.

Couture, P., Sylvestre, A., and Visser, S. A., (1981b). Étude à l'aide d'un bioessai des variations dans les caractéristiques nutrionnelles d'une rivière suite à l'implantation d'un barrage. *Water Pollut. Res. J. Can.* **15,** 233–254.

Cramer, W. A. (1977). Cytochromes. In: Photosynthesis. I. Photosynthetic electron transport and photophosphorylation. *Encycl. Pl. Physiol. New Ser.* **5**, 231–235.

Environmental Protection Agency (1971). *Provisional algal assay procedures*. Final report. Sanitary Engineering Research Laboratory, College of Engineering and School of Public Health, University of California, Berkeley, pp. 211.

Environmental Protection Agency (1978). The *Selenastrum capricornutum* Printz algal assay bottle test. U.S. EPA, Corvallis, pp. 126.

Environmental Protection Agency (1979). Bibliography of literature pertaining to the genus *Selenastrum*. U.S. EPA, Corvallis, Oregon, pp. 192.

Falkowski, P. G. (1977). The adenylate energy charge in marine phytoplankton: the effect of temperature on the physiological state of *Skeletonema costatum*. *J. Exp. Mar. Biol. Ecol.* **27**, 37–45.

Greene, J. C., Miller, W. E., Shiroyama, T., and Maloney, T. E. (1975). Utilization of algal assays to assess the effects of municipal, industrial and agricultural wastewater effluents upon phytoplankton production of the Snake River system. *Water Air Soil Pollut.* **4**, 415–434.

Jakubczak, E. and Leclerc, H. (1980). Mesure de l'ATP bactérien par bioluminescence: étude critique des méthodes d'extraction. *Ann. Biol. Clin.* **38**, 297–304.

Joubert, G. (1980). A bioassay application for quantitative toxicity measurements using the green alga *Selenastrum capricornutum*. *Water Res.* **14**, 1759–1763.

Joubert, G. (1981). Étude comparative des réactions à la toxicité entre la truite *Salmo gairdneri* et quatre autres intégrateurs biologiques sur 36 cas de bioessais statiques. *Can. Tech. Rep. Fish. Aquat. Sci.* **990**, 251–264.

Larsson, C. M. and Olsson, T. (1979). Firefly assay of adenine nucleotides from algae: comparison of extraction methods. *Plant Cell. Physiol.* **20**, 145–155.

Maciorowski, A. F., Sims, J. L., Little, L. W., and Gerrard, F. O. (1981). Bioassays, procedures and results. *J. Water Pollut. Control Fed.* **53**, 974–993.

Mans, R. J. and Novelli, D. E. (1971). Measurement for the incorporation of amino acids into protein by a filter paper disk method. *Arch. Biochem. Biophys.* **94**, 48–59.

Miller, W. E., Maloney, T. E., and Greene, J. C. (1974). Algal productivity in 49 lake waters as determined by algal assays. *Water Res.* **8**, 667–679.

Oswald, W. J. and Gaonknar, S. A. (1969). Batch assays for determination of algal growth potential. In: E. J. Middlebrooks, T. E. Maloney, C. F. Powers, and L. M. Kaak, Ed., *Proceedings of the eutrophication–biostimulation assessment workshop, California*, pp. 23–38.

Parish, J. H. (1972). Isolation and fractionation of RNA. In: G. D. Birnie, Ed., *Subcellular components: preparation and fractionation*. Butterworth, London, pp. 251–278.

Perry, R. P., Bard, E., Hames, B. D., Kelly, D. E., and Schibber, V. (1976). The relationship between Hn RNA and m RNA. In: N. E. Cohn and E. Valkin, Ed.,, *Progress in nucleic acid research and molecular biology*. Vol. 12. Academic Press, New York, pp. 275–292.

Rai, L. C., Ear, J. P., and Kumar, H. D. (1981). Phycology and heavy metal pollution. *Biol. Rev.* **56**, 99–151.

Roy, S. and Legendre, L. (1980). Field studies of DCMU-enhanced fluorescence as an index of *in situ* phytoplankton photosynthetic activity. *Can. J. Fish Aquat. Sci.* **37**, 1028–1031.

Samuelsson, G., Oquist, G., and Halldal, P. (1978). The variable chlorophyll *a* fluorescence as a measure of photosynthetic capacity in algae. *Mitt. Internat. Verein. Limnol.* **21**, 207–215.

Schindler, D. W., Schmidt, R. V., and Reid, R. A. (1972). Acidification and bubbling as an alternative to filtration in determining phytoplankton production by the ^{14}C method. *J. Fish. Res. Board Can.* **29**, 1627–1631.

Schreiber, R. (1927). Die Reinkultur von marinem Phytoplankton und deren Bedeutung für die Erforschung der Produktionsfähigkeit des Meerwassers. *Wiss. Meeresunters. Abt. Helgoland* **16**, 1–34.

Skulberg, O. M. (1964). Algal problems related to the eutrophication of European water supplies, and a bio-assay method to assess fertilizing influences of pollution on inland waters. In: D. F. Jackson, Ed., *Algae and man*. Plenum Press, New York, pp. 262–299.

Thellen, C., Joubert, G., Legault, R., and Van Coillie, R. (1980). Relation entre la méthylation du mercure et sa répartition interne chez la truite. Proc. 7th Annu. Aquat. Tox. Workshop, Montréal, 5–7 Nov. 1980, p. 14.

Thomas, W. H. and Seibert, D. L. R. (1977). Effect of copper on the dominance and diversity of algae: controlled ecosystem pollution experiment. *Bull. Mar. Sci.* **27**, 23–33.

Van Coillie, R., Thellen, C., and Dol, J. C. (1981a). Détection des toxicités retardées en pollution aquatique. *Waer Pollut. Res. J. Can.* **15**, 203–216.

Van Coillie, R., Visser, S. A., and Couture, P. (1981b). Utilisation de bioessais avec des algues pour l'étude des répercussions liées à la mise en eau des réservoirs. *Ann. Limnol.* **17**, 79–91.

Visser, S. A. and Couture, P. (1981). Les effets de la matière organique dissoute d'une eau douce sur la croissance de l'algue *Selenastrum capricornutum*. *Water Res.* **15**, 1355–1361.

19

ALGAL FLUOROMETRIC DETERMINATION OF THE POTENTIAL PHYTOTOXICITY OF ENVIRONMENTAL POLLUTANTS*

R. P. Moody and P. Weinberger

*Department of Biology
University of Ottawa
Ottawa, Ontario*

R. Greenhalgh

*Chemistry and Biology Research Institute
Canada Agriculture
Ottawa, Ontario*

*Supported in part by NSERC Grant A1737 and the USDA Dept. Forestry CANUSA grant 23–245.

1. INTRODUCTION

A rapid method for determining the algicidal activity of environmental pollutants was developed. The method relied on the fluorometric determination
of algal photosynthetic activity with a miniaturized Kautsky apparatus. Several pesticides and formulation adjuvants used in spruce budworm control
spray programs were tested for their ability to inhibit photosynthesis in the
green alga, *Chlamydomonas reinhardii*. Concentrations of test chemicals
causing 100% inhibition of the fluorescence response (P-T transient) are
reported as ICF_{100} values. The most toxic constituents of the Fenitrothion
and Matacil formulations were Aerotex 3470 (ICF_{100} of 1–5 ppm) and Nonylphenol (ICF_{100} of 0.5–0.75 ppm), respectively. The potential use of algal
fluorometry as a rapid screening procedure is discussed.

Fluorescence induction determinations are sensitive indicators of photosynthetic activity (for review see Papageorgiou, 1975) and have been used to
determine the effects of environmental conditions (temperature, CO_2, O_2,
light, etc.) on algal photosynthesis (Krause, 1973; Schreiber and Vidaver,
1974) and ozone on photosynthesis in higher plants (Schreiber et al., 1978).
The present study describes a rapid fluorometric screening procedure designed to determine the relative algicidal activity of pollutants (pesticides,
petroleum hydrocarbons, industrial effluents, etc.) that contaminate aquatic
habitats. The effects of pesticides and petroleum hydrocarbons on algae
have been reviewed by Butler (1977), and O'Brien and Dixon (1978), respectively.

Since reporting that Fenitrothion accumulated in aquatic plants following
spruce budworm spray programs (Moody et al., 1978), concern was expressed that the insecticide or its formulation adjuvants (Aerotex 3470 and
Atlox 3409F) might be phytotoxic to unicellular phytoplankton. Subsequent
studies have demonstrated several toxic effects of the petroleum distillate
Aerotex 3470 on the green alga *Chlamydomonas reinhardii* (Moody et al.,
1981). The present study reports the use of a miniaturized Kautsky apparatus (Schrieber et al., 1975) for determining the percentage inhibition of
photosynthesis of *C. reinhardii* treated with two insecticides (an organophosphate, Fenitrothion, and a carbamate, Matacil) and several formulation adjuvants (Aerotex 3470, Atlox 3409F, Dowanol, Diluent-585, and

Nonylphenol) that have been used extensively in budworm spray programs (Symons, 1977; Varty, 1980).

2. MATERIALS AND METHODS

2.1. Algal Culture

Chlamydomonas reinhardii (+ strain) was obtained from the Culture Collection at Indiana University and was cultured in autoclaved Bold's Basal Medium (BBM), pH 6.7 (Bold, 1949). Algal cultures (1 liter) were held in 2800-ml Fernbach-type flasks (Pyrex #4420) on an Eberach shaker (78 oscillations per minute). Cultures were maintained in a Hotpack growth chamber (5 klux; 16 hr light, 8 hr dark photoperiod; 23°C). Cell counts were made with an improved Neubauer hemacytometer.

2.2. Algal Treatment

The pesticides and adjuvants selected for screening, and their source of origin are listed in Table 1. Stock preparations of each test compound (100 mg/100 ml) were made immediately prior to use by one of two methods:

1. Stock solutions of nonvolatile, acetone-soluble compounds were prepared with acetone. Suitable aliquots of stock solution were dispensed into 50-ml screw-cap Erlenmeyer flasks. The acetone was blown-off under an air stream, and 45 ml of BBM containing sufficient $NaHCO_3$ (CO_2 source) to provide a 1-mM concentration in 50 ml were immediately added to each flask. An identical aliquot (5.0 ml) of a 9–12-day-old culture of *Chlamydomonas* in late log phase was then added to each flask to provide a final cell concentration of 2.6×10^4 cells/ml. The flasks were capped tightly, shaken, and placed on a shaker in the dark at 23°C. Dark conditions were used to negate the possibility of photodegradation of the toxicant.

2. Water soluble or volatile test compounds were suspended in BBM by mixing in a Polytron sonicator (No. 4369) at setting No. 5. Subsequent treatment followed the procedures just outlined for the acetone stock solutions, except that the total volume was corrected for the addition of algal medium.

A wide range of treatment concentrations (0.1, 1, 10, and 100 ppm) was initially tested to determine the proper range for subsequent studies. Triplicate flasks were used for each treatment concentration.

Table 1. Test Chemical, Description, and Source

Chemical	Description	Source
Fenitrothion	*O,O*-dimethyl-*O*-(3-methyl-4-nitrophenyl) phosphorothioate	Sumitomo Chemical Co.
Aerotex 3470	Petroleum distillate	Texaco Canada Ltd.
Atlox 3409F	Detergent mixture	Atlas Chemical Co.
Dowanol	Dipropylene glycol methyl ether	Dow Chemical Co.
Matacil	4-dimethylamino-*m*-tolyl methyl carbamate	Chemagro Ltd.
Matacil 1.8-D[a]	Commercially prepared field formulation containing Matacil, Nonylphenol and Diluent-585 [1.00:2.54:1.52(v/v)]	Chemagro Ltd.
Nonylphenol	Mixture of monoalkyl phenols (predominantly para-substituted)	Chemagro Ltd.
Diluent-585	Petroleum distillate	Chemagro Ltd.

[a] Final treatment preparation followed the field dilution recipe (6) provided by Chemagro Ltd. [Matacil 1.8-D:Diluent-585 (1:1.88)].

2.3. Fluorometric Analysis

A Plant Productivity Fluorometer (model SF-10) was obtained from Richard Brancker Research Ltd., Ottawa, Canada. The fluorometer was used in conjunction with a Fisher Recordall® Series 5000 chart recorder (signal input 10 vdc, chart speed 13 cm/min). The fluorometer was set at a light (670 nm) exposure of 10 sec and at maximum intensity (10^4 ergs/cm^2 · sec).

After a 1-hr treatment, each 50 ml algal sample was filtered under vacuum through a Whatman GF/C glass fiber filter. The glass filter was then placed on top of two Whatman No. 1 filter papers premoistened with BBM, and the fluorometer probe was centered on top. During the filtration step and positioning of the probe, the algae were inevitably exposed to light. This reduced the sensitivity of the fluorometer response and it was necessary to readapt the cells to the dark. This was accomplished by leaving the probe on top of the algae for 30 sec. An exact time period was required to obtain reproducible results. In this connection, previous studies have shown that the size of the initial fluorescence peak is directly proportional to the length of the preceding dark period (Krause, 1972). A period of 30 sec dark adaptation was found to give sufficient sensitivity of response to permit accurate quantitation of the fluorescence transients in the present study. Duplicate analyses were made for each sample by repositioning the probe on the glass filter. Finally, the glass filter was washed under vacuum with 25 ml of BBM and reanalyzed to determine the reversibility of the treatment effect.

Following this procedure, duplicate analyses of triplicate samples could be performed in less than 10 min. A maximum of 2 hr was required to determine the minimum concentration required for any compound to totally suppress the fluorescence response.

3. RESULTS

Figure 1 shows a typical fluorescence transient obtained for untreated (control) cultures of *Chlamydomonas* showing the peak (P) characteristic of photosynthetically active cells which was absent for treated cultures. O, P, M, and S divide the fluorescence transient into segments that are indicative of several photosynthetic partial reactions (Papageorgiou, 1975). The letter T on Fig. 1 designates the termination of peak P. The length of the P–T transient was used to quantitate photosynthetic activity.

A progressive decrease in the length of the P–T transient was observed as the treatment concentration of a test compound neared the level at which the fluorescence transient became flat as in Fig. 1. A flat fluorescence transient was also obtained for heat-treated (80°C), frozen (− 60°C), or dessicated algae in the present study, and is generally held to be indicative of the absence of photosynthetic activity (Papageorgiou, 1975). The results obtained were quantitated by measuring the length of the P–T transient and expressing this as a percentage reduction (% inhibition, Table 2) of the control value. An analysis of variance was performed initially on the six replicate P–T values (3 replicate flasks × 2 sample analyses) obtained for

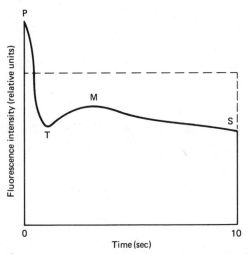

Figure 1.   The fluorescence transient in *Chlamydomonas reinhardii*: 670 nm; incident intensity 10^4 ergs/cm^2·sec. The solid line depicts a typical transient for untreated cells showing the points O, P, T, M, and S. The dashed line depicts a typical transient for cultures inhibited by chemical treatment.

Table 2. Inhibition (%) of Photosynthesis as Determined by Fluorometric Analysis of *C. reinhardii* Treated for 1 hr

Chemical	Treatment Procedure[a]	Treatment Concentration (ppm)											
		0	0.1	0.2	0.5	0.75	1.0	5.0	10	20	30	40	100
Fenitrothion	D	0 (13.6)					−11.4[b] (31.1)	40.9 (19.7)	68.2 (7.6)	100 (0)			
Dowanol	W	0 (5.1)					−3.2 (10.2)	−1.9 (7.0)	6.4 (12.7)				2.5 (21.7)
Atlox	W	0 (13.6)					−11.7 (17.4)	−1.9 (13.2)	5.2 (11.7)	60.1 (19.3)	100 (0)	100 (0)	
Aerotex	W	0 (6.1)					52.8 (9.8)	100 (0)	100 (0)	100 (0)			
Fenitrothion: Aerotex: Atlox[c] (10:1:1)	W	0 (4.8)			−16.8 (11.1)		−9.6 (10.6)	25.5 (13.9)	41.3 (9.1)	100 (0)			
Matacil	D	0 (14.9)					6.9 (4.6)	10.3 (9.1)	10.3 (5.7)	15.4 (4.6)			51.4 (8.0)
Diluent-585	W	0 (14.7)					−8.0 (10.7)	8.0 (8.0)	3.3 (4.0)	71.3 (5.3)			
Nonylphenol	D	0 (7.8)	−17.2 (14.1)	0 (11.7)	54.7 (16.4)	100 (0)	100 (0)				100 (0)	100 (0)	
Matacil 1.8-D[d]	D	0 (16.8)	−3.2 (16.1)		80.6 (12.3)	100 (0)	100 (0)						

[a] D = dry treatment (in acetone blown off); W = wet treatment (in BBM).
[b] A negative value was obtained when the P–T transient was greater than the control.
[c] Results are reported for the Fenitrothion concentration (ppm) of the formulation.
[d] Results are reported for the Nonylphenol concentration (ppm) of formulation.

each treatment concentration. In all cases, $F_{2,3}$ was less than 9.55 ($p < 0.95$), permitting reporting data as a pooled mean standard deviation (Table 2).

The data obtained for the constituents of the Fenitrothion and Matacil formulations are given in Table 2. When a pesticide formulation was used, the fluorometer results were reported for the concentration present for one of the formulation constituents. For example, the fluorometer data recorded for Matacil 1.8D [Matacil:Nonylphenol:Diluent-585, 1.00:2.54:1.52(v/v)] was reported for the concentration of Nonylphenol present during treatment (Table 2, footnote *d*).

The second column in Table 2 indicates the treatment procedure used. As discussed previously, the test compound was applied either in acetone which was then volatilized, or solubilized directly in BBM. It is imperative to note the importance of adopting a correct treatment procedure. For example, Aerotex at 10 ppm did not inhibit the fluorometer response for *Chlamydomonas* if Aerotex was dissolved in acetone and then exposed to an air stream for 5 min prior to treatment. If applied in aqueous emulsion, however, Aerotex at 5 ppm was sufficient to totally suppress the fluorometer (P–T transient) response (Table 2). In this connection, gas chromatographic (GC) analysis (Moody et al., 1981) of Aerotex standards prepared in acetone demonstrated that $\geqslant 50\%$ of each of the hydrocarbon constituents of Aerotex had volatilized after 10 min exposure to an air stream. Similar GC analyses of Fenitrothion and Matacil standards did not demonstrate significant volatilization after 10 min exposure to an air stream. A maximum of only 15–20 sec exposure to the air stream was sufficient to volatilize the acetone in the toxicity studies.

Generally, the results (Table 2) demonstrated a slight increase in the length of the P–T transient at low concentrations of the test compounds. Higher treatment concentrations were associated with a decrease in the length of the P–T transient which was reported as an increase in the percentage inhibition of photosynthesis. The length of the P–T transients before and after washing with BBM did not differ significantly, except for Matacil at 100 ppm, which, before washing, gave $51.4 \pm 8.0\%$ inhibition compared to $21.7 \pm 6.6\%$ after washing.

The lowest concentration of a test compound required to totally suppress the fluorometer response (P–T = 0) is designated here as the ICF_{100} value. This value is reported as a concentration range for each test compound in Table 3. For example, 1 ppm of Aerotex was shown to cause 52.8% inhibition of photosynthesis while 100% inhibition was recorded for 5 ppm (Table 2). Hence, the ICF_{100} value for Aerotex is reported as 1–5 ppm (Table 3). The ICF_{100} value for Fenitrothion (10–20 ppm) was the same for the pesticide either alone, or in formulation with Aerotex and Atlox, or Dowanol and Atlox. Similarly, the ICF_{100} value for Nonylphenol was 0.5–0.75 ppm, either alone or when present in the Matacil 1.8-D formulation. The ICF_{100} values reported in Table 3 were obtained for a 1-hr treatment duration. Figure 2 plots the percentage inhibition of photosynthesis (decrease of P–T transient)

Table 3. ICF$_{100}$ values: Concentration (mg/liter) Required to Totally Inhibit Photosynthesis in *Chlamydomonas reinhardii* within 1 hr of Treatment

Chemical	ICF$_{100}$ (ppm)
Fenitrothion	10–20
Aerotex 3470	1–5
Atlox 3409F	20–30
Dowanol	> 100
Fenitrothion : Aerotex : Atlox (10 : 1 : 1)	10–20 (Fenitrothion)
Fenitrothion : Dowanol : Atlox (10 : 1 : 1)	10–20 (Fenitrothion)
Matacil	> 100
Matacil 1.8-D	0.5–0.75 (Nonylphenol)
Nonylphenol	0.5–0.75
Diluent-585	20–30

versus duration of treatment with 5 ppm (upper limit of ICF$_{100}$, Table 3) of Aerotex. The time required to cause 50% inhibition was less than 10 min, while flat transients were obtained 30 min post-treatment. Flat transients were also obtained after 24-hr treatment for all test chemicals when treatments were conducted at the upper range of the respective ICF$_{100}$ value. The 24-hr control algae still exhibited the P–T transient.

4. DISCUSSION

The present study was undertaken to establish a rapid, reproducible means for assessing the relative algicidal activity of a wide array of environmental pollutants. The results indicate that algal fluorometry could provide a suit-

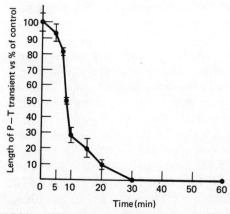

Figure 2. Percent inhibition of fluorometer (P-T) transient vs. duration of treatment with Aerotex (5 ppm). Mean values of triplicate samples are shown together with standard deviation bars.

able screening procedure for further laboratory and field studies. The method is extremely rapid (maximum of 2 hr required to determine ICF_{100} for any compound), the apparatus is portable for field use, and sensitivity would depend only on the algal species selected for screening. A wide variety of species could be employed in future studies to establish an order of species tolerance that could be used to relate the species composition of endemic algal populations to the water quality of a particular habitat. Such a table has been composed previously (Palmer, 1969) by arbitrarily conferring extra tolerance to those algal species reported most frequently inhabiting polluted water. It is notable that *C. reinhardii* was among the most tolerant species listed.

The observation that 1–5 ppm of Aerotex was sufficient to totally suppress the fluorometer response (ICF_{100} = 1–5 ppm) in *C. reinhardii* was consistent with our previous report that Aerotex (1–10 ppm) inhibited cell motility, population growth, and ATP synthesis, and induced ultrastructural changes in membrane configuration (Moody et al., 1981). The enhanced photosynthesis suggested by the fluorometer results (Table 2) for low concentrations of several test chemicals was consistent with enhanced algal $^{14}CO_2$ fixation demonstrated in our laboratory for low Aerotex concentrations. Further, the reported ICF_{100} values were consistent with the results of extensive tests conducted in our laboratory with standard bioassay procedures (population growth, $^{14}CO_2$ fixation, cell leakage studies, etc.) (Moody, 1982).

The relevance of the present results concerning the *in situ* algicidal potential of Aerotex has been discussed previously (Moody et al., 1981). Of even greater consequence was the observation that the ICF_{100} of Nonylphenol for *C. reinhardii* was between 0.5 and 0.75 ppm either alone, or when present in the Matacil 1.8-D field formulation recently sprayed in New Brunswick, where levels as high as 0.1 ppm of Nonylphenol have been reported in standing water following experimental applications (albeit under "worst case" conditions) (Caldwell, *in* Varty, 1980). Holmes and Kingsbury (1980), however, reported levels of Nonylphenol up to 1.1 ppm in stagnant water following an operational spray program in Ontario. When assessing field reports of pesticide concentrations in water, it is essential to consider the effect of dilution within the water column. Initial concentrations in the surface layer would be relatively high, and the present results indicate that even a brief (1 hr) exposure of algae inhabiting this layer (e.g., neuston) would suffice to inhibit *in situ* photosynthesis.

REFERENCES

Bold, H. C. (1949). The morphology of *Chlamydomonas chlamydogoma* sp. nov. *Bull. Torrey Bot. Club* **76**, 101.

Butler, G. L. (1977). Algae and pesticides. *Pesticide Rev.* **67**, 19–58.

Holmes, S. and Kingsbury, P. D. (1980). The environmental impact of Nonylphenol and Matacil formulation. Part 1: Aquatic ecosystems. *For. Pest. Manage. Rep.* FPM-X 35, 52 pp.

Krause, G. H. (1973). The high energy state of the thylakoid system as indicated by chlorophyll fluorescence and chloroplast shrinkage. *Biochem. Biophys. Acta* **292**, 715–728.

Moody, R. P. (1982). Algicidal activity of formulated Fenitrothion. The effect of the cosolvent Aerotex 3470 in unicellular freshwater algae. Ph.D. thesis, University of Ottawa.

Moody, R. P., Greenhalgh, R., Lockhart, L., and Weinberger, P. (1978). The Fate of Fenitrothion in an aquatic ecosystem. *Bull. Environ. Contam. Toxicol.* **19**, 8–14.

Moody, R. P., Weinberger, P., Greenhalgh, R., and Massalski, A. (1981). Algicidal properties of the pesticide cosolvent Aerotex 3470: Growth ATP synthesis and ultrastructure. *Can. J. Bot.* **59**, 1003-1013.

O'Brien, P. Y. and Dixon, P. S. (1976). The effects of oils and oil components on algae: A review. *Br. Phycol. J.* **11**, 115–142.

Papageorgiou, G. (1975). Chlorophyll fluorescence: an intrinsic probe of photosynthesis. In: Govindjee, Ed., *Bioenergetics of photosynthesis.* Academic Press, New York, pp. 319–371.

Schreiber, U. and Vidaver, W. (1974). Chlorophyll fluorescence induction in anaerobic *Scenedesmus obliquus. Biochim. Biophys. Acta* **368**, 97–112.

Schreiber, U. and Vidaver, W. (1978). Chlorophyll fluorescence assay for ozone injury in intact plants. *Plant Physiol.* **61**, 80–84.

Schreiber, U., Groberman, L., and Vidaver, W. (1975). Portable solid-state fluorometer for the measurement of chlorophyll fluorescence induction in plants. *Rev. Sci. Instrum.* **46**, 538–542.

Symons, P. E. K. (1977). Dispersal and toxicology of the insecticide fenitrothion; predicting hazards of forest spraying. *Residue Rev.* **68**, 1–36.

Varty, I. W., Ed. (1980). *Environmental surveillance in New Brunswick 1978–1979: Effects of spray operations for forest protection.* University of New Brunswick Report, Fredericton, N.B., Canada, 76 pp.

INDEX

Aberrant anaphase figures in rainbow trout, 347-348

Accidental contamination of surface waters with pesticides, 366-367

Accumulation capacity, mercury in fish organs, 104-111

Achyla sp., influence of pH on metal toxicity to, 9

Acidofilic fungus, effect of pH on metal toxicity to, 8

Acridine, effect on *tetrahymena,* 406

Adaptation of aquatic biota to metal pollution, 196-201

Adenine nucleotide levels in lobster, 319

Adenosine triphosphate (ATP):
  activation of, by sodium and potassium, 321-322
  determination of, 310-311
  indication of sublethal effects of xenobiotics by, 326-327
  inhibition of, by vanadium, 174
  inhibitory effects of organic xenobiotics, 322-323
  osmoregulation by, 321-322
  production of, in algal cultures, 491-492

Adenylase energy charge:
  determination of, 309-310
  effects on:
    anaerobic metabolism, 313-316
    metal toxicity, 318-320
    organic xenobiotics, 316-317
    salinity, 312-313
    temperature, 313
  indication of sublethal effects of xenobiotics by analysis of, 326-327
  levels in lobster, 319
  redox effects on, 313-317

Aerial transport of pesticides, 367-368

Aerotex, phytotoxicity to algae, 506-511

Aldrin:
  inhibitory effect on ATP, 323

  insecticidal use of, 364

Algae:
  accumulation of mercury by, 124
  assessment of sublethal toxicity of pollutants to, 493
  batch culture study of metal toxicity to, 457-461
  bioassays using, 451-455, 467-480, 489-493, 505-507
  biodegradation of metacil by, 445
  cell counts for, 477-478
  continuous culture study of metal toxicity to, 461-464
  copper toxicity to, 31, 63-64, 455-464
  culture media for, 451, 471-472, 489-490, 505
  culturing techniques for, 451-455, 467-480, 489-493, 505-507
  delayed toxicity of pollutants to, 496-497
  dry weight standards for, 478
  effects of metals on biochemistry of, 3-6
  filtration techniques for cultures of, 470-471
  fluorometric determination of phytotoxicity of pollutants to, 503-511
  incubation of, 453-455, 471, 477, 490-491
  influence of pH on metal toxicity to, 6-12, 56-66
  measurements of cell growth, 452-455, 477-478, 491-493
  mutagenicity tests using, 497-498
  occurrence and effects of vanadium in, 165-171
  phytotoxicity of metacil to, 444-446
  role of organics in toxicity of metals to, 49-53
  species diversity, effects of pollutants on, 498-499

Algicidal activities of pollutants, 503-511

Alkyl benzene sulfonate, response of aquatic organisms to, 261-262

Aminoacids, role in chemoreception in aquatic organisms, 291-296

Aminocarb, *see* Metacil

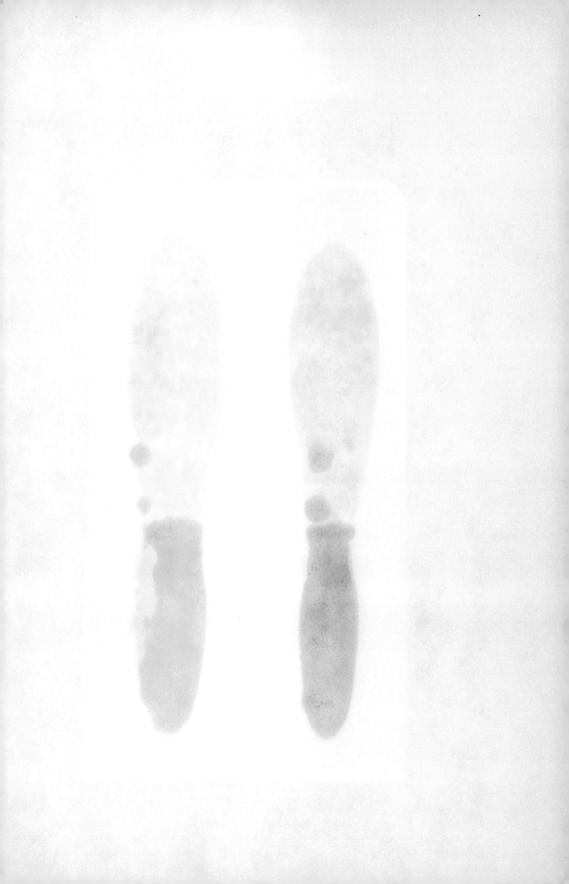